ALTERNATIVE REALITIES

---

*The Paranormal, the
Mystic and the Transcendent
in Human Experience*

Leonard George, Ph.D.

Facts On File®

AN INFOBASE HOLDINGS COMPANY

In Memory of my Mother, Helen George
(1921–1993)

ALTERNATIVE REALITIES
The Paranormal, the Mystic and the Transcendent in Human Experience

Facts On File, Inc.
460 Park Avenue South
New York NY 10016

Library of Congress Cataloging-in-Publication Data

George, Leonard.
 Alternative Realities:the paranormal, the mystic and the transcendent in human experience / Leonard George.
   p. cm.
 Includes bibliographical references and index.
 ISBN 0-8160-2828-1 (hardcover)
 ISBN 0-8160-3213-0 (paperback)
 1. Parapsychology. I. Title.
BF1031.G36 1995
133.8—dc20   94–7630

Facts On File books are available at special discounts when purchased in bulk quantities for businesses, associations, institutions or sales promotions. Please call our Special Sales Department in New York at 212/683-2244 or 800/322-8755.

Text design by Carla Wiese/Layout by Robert Yaffe
Jacket design by Paul Agresti
Printed in the United States of America

RRD FOF 10 9 8 7 6 5 4 3 2 1

This book is printed on acid-free paper.

"*Jupiter's moons are invisible to the naked eye and therefore can have no influence on the earth, and therefore would be useless, and therefore do not exist.*"

—FRANCISCO SIZZI (PROFESSOR OF
ASTRONOMY, CONTEMPORARY OF GALILEO)

"*Let the mind be enlarged, according to its capacity, to the grandeur of the mysteries, and not the mysteries contracted to the narrowness of the mind.*"
—SIR FRANCIS BACON

"*All of us must remember science can tell us what is empirically unlikely but not what is empirically impossible. Evidence in science is always a matter of degree and is seldom if ever absolutely conclusive.*"
—MARCELLO TRUZZI

"*The irrational fullness of life taught me never to discard anything, even when it goes against all our theories . . . It is of course disquieting, and one is not certain whether the compass is pointing true or not; but security, certitude, and peace do not lead to discoveries.*"
—C. G. JUNG

CONTENTS

ACKNOWLEDGMENTS

In my work on this book, I have been educated and inspired by the writings of far too many scholars to thank in a limited space. Of these, I must single out Dr. Carol Zaleski, whose investigation of near-death experiences is a marvel of rigor, depth and clarity.

The lion's share of my gratitude goes to Dr. Richard Noll of Harvard University, who for many years has provided me with invaluable help of all sorts, and is a cherished friend. He also introduced me to Dixie Blackened Voodoo beer—I think. Thank you, Sol Invictus, Frater Pneumatikos.

This book would not have been written without the aid of my two heart-women: Vivian Alie, who inspired me with her magnificence, her earrings and her choice in wine; and my mother, Helen George. I wouldn't even be here without the latter woman, so to her I dedicate the book.

I wish to thank those scholars who generously shared their knowledge with me during the book's preparation, including Dr. Carlos Alvarado, Dr. Barry Beyerstein, George Hansen, Dr. Harvey Irwin, Dr. Krishna Kumar and Dr. Michael Thalbourne. Any errors in this book are, of course, my own.

Many thanks also to my agent, Bert Holtje of James Peter Associates, a most kind, gracious and effective gentleman; and to my editors at Facts On File, Kathy Ishizuka and Drew Silver, who offered vital help at various stages of this project.

I greatly appreciate the various kinds of encouragement, support, teaching, entertainment, sustenance and distraction offered by the following people as I labored on *Alternative Realities:* Jill Jacobson, Gaetan LaBelle, the Harcos, the Parliaments, Dr. Malcolm Kennard, Dr. Robin Gunn, Alex Novak, Susan Naylor, Marian Buchanan, Doug Tuck, Vicki Gabereau, Bill Richardson, Patrick Dubois, the Columbia Centroids and the wondrous staff of Caffe Barney and the Big News Cafe in Vancouver. A special thanks to Drs. Con Rae, Tony LePage and Merv Gilbert for their support, written and conversational.

The soundtrack for the writing of this book—indeed, for much of my life—was by Leonard Cohen: "O bless the continuous stutter of the Word being made into Flesh."

And, last but never least, thanks be to Father Trismegistus of St. Raven's Cathedral, Mount Seymour, British Columbia, for his wordless advice.

INTRODUCTION

The Beckoning Darkness

The Cave of the Senses

This is a book about shadows and light.

In his famous "Parable of the Cave," Plato suggested that our awareness of everyday life is based on a mistake. We live as if chained facing the wall within a torchlit cavern. As real objects pass by behind us, we perceive only their shadows and believe these to be the things themselves. Light is mistaken for shadow, and shadow for light. Plato notes that anyone who glimpses the nature of the error—who comprehends that the world of ordinary appearance is delusory—is apt to be ridiculed, muzzled or even executed, if that person tries to awaken others to this upsetting realization.

And yet, throughout history and across cultures, people have continued to report experiences hinting that the world of everyday consciousness is not what it seems to be. Some of these individuals have brought religious inspiration, solutions to technical and scientific problems, works of art and healing to their societies. Others have paid for their strange encounters with their reputations, their freedom and even, as Plato predicted, their lives.

Today, as ever before, we dwell in the cave of the senses. But rumors of strange happenings persist. Indeed, they are common. Recent surveys indicate that in many western countries, roughly one in five people has experienced a vision; one in five have had out-of-body experiences; almost half believe they have felt the presence of supernatural beings; and the majority claim to have experienced clairvoyance or telepathy.

As Western culture nears the end of the second millennium, more and more people are questioning appearances. The old answers no longer convince. Many are now willing to admit that they too have had experiences which could have brought them to a fiery death at the stake not so long ago. For the thoughtful, the questions raised by these events are not put to rest either by the dismissals of cynics or the revelations of New Age celebrities. Those who have been touched by these questions sense an importance, as well as a danger, in their puzzling encounters, and yearn to understand. From beyond the cave of the senses, something seems to be beckoning. But is it shadow, or light?

Mysteries of the Ordinary

Before we can properly approach the extraordinary, we must first take a closer look at the ordinary. Is everyday reality what it seems to be?

We can divide normal daily experience into four domains: the *external world,* including the society and the cosmos within which we live; the *body* that interfaces us with the outer world, and within which is a world of sensation unto itself; the realm of the *past,* which we relive through our memories; and the *inner world,* populated by our thoughts, emotions and fantasies. We take much of what ordinarily happens in these four domains for granted. We rarely think to question the "obvious," "common sense," what "everybody knows." But let us do so now.

The External World

We are connected to the events around us through our senses and our actions. The surface of the body is covered by specialized organs that convert physical energies of various kinds—light, air pressure changes, mechanical forces impinging on the skin—into nerve signals. The nerve cells, or neurons, use a system of electrical and chemical communication to send messages from the sense receptors to the brain. Our awareness of the external world is based on these messages. And what do they tell us? That's "obvious": the world is made of solid, separate things with fixed identities and meanings—tables, chairs, books, buses, bodies. Furthermore, the objects that compose the world do not depend on us for the characteristics we perceive them to have—the softness of the chair, the rhythm of the music, the redness of the apple, seem to be *out there,* completely disconnected from our own state. We do not experience the world as a place that we *construct,* but as a collection of sovereign things that we *discover.* When we open our eyes each morning, we do not have to plan how to organize the contours and colors in front of us into a perception of the bedroom; we simply see the bedroom.

These givens of everyday life—the coherence and fixed, independent existence of things—seem beyond doubt—until we begin to look more closely. William James, the great American psychologist and philosopher, observed that "Whilst part of what we perceive comes from the object before us, another part (and it may be the larger part) always comes out of our mind." Research into the nature of perception has indicated that, contrary to appearance, the coherence and fixed identities of things are not "from the object before us," but rather arise "out of our mind."

Although we seem to experience the world directly, as it actually is, in fact our awareness is the end product of an immensely complicated and imperfectly understood process taking place in the central nervous system. What reaches our brain via the nervous system is not a meaningful picture of free-standing objects, but a deluge of nerve impulses. To an observer positioned within the brain, the effect would be similar to receiving millions of Morse Code messages simultaneously. These signals are but the raw materials for a mental act of world construction. And what is the skeleton that gives shape to this world?

The framework of ordinary reality is made of our assumptions and expectations, our desires and fears. The angry dwell in a world of enemies; the ambitious, in a world of opportunities; the consumer, in a world of commodities. These are not just "attitudes"—they actually determine, to a large extent, our very perceptions. Research has demonstrated that the poor perceive coins to be larger than do the rich. A botanist and a hunter, walking together through the woods, will notice vastly different aspects of the possibilities of that situation. As you read this, you are aware of only a tiny sample of what is happening around you. I wonder what looms behind you, unnoticed, right now?

The crafting of the brain's neural bombardment into a meaningful world is accomplished within a fraction of a second—edges and similarities are detected and knitted together into objects, depth is added, comparisons with memory traces are undertaken, uninteresting or unidentifiable material is discarded, threats and opportunities are labeled and highlighted, and much else. The construction of experience happens miraculously quickly, but it does take time—perhaps 60 to 80 milliseconds. So, the "present," with its veneer of solidity and meaningfulness, is actually an experience of the past. And the past, as we ordinarily think of it, does not exist in a substantial way.

The Body

Perhaps our experience of the outside world is constructed in this way, but what about our awareness of our own bodies? Bodily sensations are the hub around which the physical world of each person is arranged. Like external objects, our embodiment *feels* unquestionably to be a directly experienced, solid and independent entity. And yet, body awareness too is a construction, not a simple discovery. The shape, actions and boundaries of the body that we experience are those of a mental image synthesized by the brain and projected onto the screen of consciousness. This image may or may not match the functions of the body as measured by physiologists. In extreme cases, such as phantom limb syndrome, a person can feel a body part that is not there at all.

The Past

What about memories? Perceptions of the "present moment" may be constructions, but surely our recollections of past events are, in some sense, beyond doubt. When I recall my 10th birthday, the vision of cake and candles that appears before my mind's eye has a compelling aura of reality. This image feels like certain *knowledge,* a photograph preserved in my mental archives, not a mere fabrication. Yet memory is not the passive record that it seems to be. In fact, remembering is literally that, a "remembering," or active reconstruction, of a picture of the past. The image we summon from the vault of memory is more like an oil painting of the bygone event than like a photograph. The artist is our own mind, which draws inspiration not only from the actual past event, but also from our current feelings and needs. At times, the past we compose on our mental canvas can be quite realistic; but at other times, fantasy elements dominate. A typical remembrance is likely to be a blend of accurate information about the recalled event and invented material. And the experience of recollection itself contains no sure clues that can tell us which is which. Most people resist the idea that memory is an invention; the implications are profoundly disturbing. But psychological research has established that it is so.

The Inner World

Nothing could seem more direct and unmediated than our experience of our thoughts, emotions and mental images, the very stuff of the self. Even Descartes, the French philosopher who attempted to strip every uncertainty from his experience, stopped here. "Cogito, ergo sum," he declared—"I think, therefore I am." He could not bring himself to doubt the immediate reality of his own thoughts, which he took to be the essence of his identity. There would seem to be no room for constructive processes here. "I," as crystallized in the contents of my mind, exists as the solid core of my experiential universe. The boundaries are clear and distinct; I do not confuse myself with other objects. But look again. When we dream, we encounter all sorts of things that seem, at the time, to lie outside of ourselves; yet, upon awakening, we conclude that they were facets of our dreaming self. This conclusion is not shared by all sane, awake people—in many cultures, dream beings have traditionally been thought to be spirits. As young children, we might have an "imaginary companion" who seems quite real and external to us. As we mature, we shift the boundary of the self to encompass our friend, converting him or her into a "childish fantasy." Viewed over the course of a day, and even more so over a lifetime, the perimeter of the self does not remain fixed, but expands and contracts—again, like all of the other domains of experience, in dependence on the prevailing biological and psychological states of the individual.

Where, in all this flux, is that solid self that seemed to be beyond doubt? Careful observation of the stream of consciousness reveals an ever-changing procession of sensations and images. But my itchy foot is not my self; neither is the moon I see outside my window, or my memory of breakfast, or my fantasy about my girlfriend. The more closely I search for a substantial self, the less substantial it becomes.

To summarize: In everyday life it is almost impossible to doubt the evidence of our senses, our thoughts and our memories. These faculties present to us a world filled with (mostly) identifiable, free-standing objects, an accurate record of past experiences, a familiar body within which we live. It appears that we experience these things directly, as they are, separate from the self that senses them. But, as we probe each of these kinds of experience, we find signs that matters are not as they seem. The contents of our awareness are the products of elaborate mental processes, steered by a complex of beliefs and motives. In short, consciousness is a construction, not a direct encounter with naked reality. The solid appearance of our mentally synthesized worlds of experience is an illusion.

Just as Plato suspected.

The Birth of Meaning

As noted above, the organizing of brain inputs into a meaningful experiential world is controlled by our beliefs and motivations. Our beliefs are not random, of course. They form a map of reality that informs us of what is possible and impossible, both for ourselves and the world we live in. This web of assumptions has various names in the human sciences. Let us use one of the most common—world view.

Humans are the tool-using species. And our most valuable tool is our world view. Nothing else can be accomplished without it. It is the most significant gift presented to a newborn person by the parental culture. Researchers no longer view babies as "blank slates" upon which social influences inscribe their every characteristic. Some basic features of personality appear to be genetically determined; and infants may be "programmed" to be receptive to human language sounds. However, neonates are still ill-equipped to make sense out of the buzz of novelty they constantly encounter. Without a world view to inform the experience-building machinery which stimuli to weave into the picture and which to ignore, they cannot organize their own actions. And, when the brain senses that they are disoriented and helpless, it pulls the alarm. The result: fear.

The infant is therefore driven to acquire a world view, to quell the craving for meaning and control and to reduce anxiety. The basic assumptions of this world view are usually absorbed from the parents. These beliefs are reinforced throughout childhood by the society's formal education. It is important to note that we take in the basic features of the world view early in life, "along with our mother's milk," as it has been put. The foundations of belief about cosmos, society, body and self are laid even before we fully learn to speak. Throughout life, these primordial convictions will remain impossible to express—and therefore impossible to question.

Furthermore, in the child's experience, there are two options: embracing the world view of the culture; or the anxious chaos of refusing to do so. Some choice. The only world view known to the child will quickly take on an aura of absolute reality, if the only known alternative is meaninglessness. A child cannot know that the ideas comprising the parental world view are the result of social and historical forces, that world views are constantly changing and that cultures have produced an immense panorama of mutually inconsistent world views, all of which effectively govern the mechanisms of experience-making for those who believe in them. Instead, the parental world view acquires the mantle of unquestionable truth. The tool with which we filter our sensory inputs—one of many options in the collective toolbox of world culture—is mistaken for reality itself. Later in life, a person might challenge some of the surface details of the world view, trading them in for other beliefs; but the most fundamental, deeply buried assumptions continue, unnoticed, to sculpt awareness in their own image.

World View Maintenance

A world view, like a body, requires some flexibility to adapt to changing circumstances. Also like a body, a world view must have methods of preserving itself from disintegration in the face of challenges. Swiss psychologist Jean Piaget discussed two main mechanisms by which a world view deals with new information. He called these processes *assimilation* and *accommodation*. When, say, a new species of warbler is encountered, a birdwatcher will be able to fit this experience into an already existing category within his or her understanding of birds—the class of warblers. The world view is enriched without altering its main features (spotting a new warbler may be interesting, but it is hardly revolutionary). If a singing, feathered thing with three wings flutters by, however, the observer could react in one of two ways: the perception of the third wing could be ignored or dismissed, and the bird slotted in one of the previously defined pigeonholes for types of birds; or, a new category could be created for three-winged avians. The first response is an assimilation—the world view remains unchanged. In the second response, the observer accommodates the new knowledge that there are three-winged birds by making a significant change in the compartment of his or her world view dealing with birds. Via these twin processes, we navigate our daily lives, either conforming our experience to our assumptions (assimilation), or changing our beliefs to absorb new facts (accommodation).

Our reaction to novelty—whether we assimilate, accommodate or simply ignore—is affected by the responses of those around us. One of the most powerful clues available to us about the reality we share with others is what those others tell us about it. Thus, if everyone else in a group of bird watchers agrees that the creature that just went by had the normal complement of wings, the one observer who glimpsed the third wing will usually convince himself or herself that he or she did not see it. The conventions of culture stabilize an individual's awareness from two directions: from within, via the world view; and from without, via social influences.

Supranormal Experiences, Invading and Invited

Most of the time, this arrangement works rather well. As adults with a richly developed world view, we can categorize most of the things we meet in our daily lives. We are rarely called upon to question appearances. "Common sense" (also defined by our world view) is an adequate guide. But not always.

The conventional world view of the modern West is primarily defined by science. And modern science, on the surface of it, does not have a place for encounters with spirits, for souls that leave the body or reincarnate or for mental powers that are not subject to the limitations of the body's muscles and senses. The mainstream world view *could* accommodate visitors from other planets, provided they got here via technology rather than magic; and even strange creatures living in lakes or forests would be acceptable, if they turned out to be biological entities of some sort. But even these possibilities are not currently accepted, for lack of convincing evidence. Experiences implying that any of these things might be true do not fit the picture of reality, as currently presented by the spokespersons of science.

Such experiences are the subject matter of this book. They are "unusual" only in that they appear, to the observer, to violate basic assumptions of the prevailing world view; as noted earlier, many of them are not unusual at all in the sense of statistical rarity.

If, as James stated, experiences come in part from the object and in part from the mind, we can infer that unusual experiences can occur for two reasons: the presence of unusual conditions in the observer's environment; or, unusual functioning in the mental machinery of experience-construction. These factors can also occur together.

External Influences

There are a number of environmental factors that predispose people toward having supranormal experiences. One of the most important of these is contact with other people who have had, or are having, the same experience. Generally speaking, it is more likely that we will see a ghost, or a UFO or a vision of the Virgin Mary if we are in the company of people who tell us that *they* are having these experiences. Just as social cues help to anchor our ordinary perceptions, they can stimulate our extraordinary ones.

Unusual experiences are also more likely if the standard operation of the senses is impaired. For example, dimly lit settings, like seance rooms and cemeteries at midnight, reduce the clarity of the familiar sights that stabilize our normal experiences. Rhythmic sensory input—drumming, dancing, flashing lights—also perturbs the normal sensory functions.

In addition to social and sensory conditions, some researchers believe that electromag- netic influences might play a part in inducing supranormal experiences. Naturally occurring electromagnetic fluctuations generated by thunderstorms or quartz deposits in the ground could be capable of altering nervous system activities. This influence could wreak temporary havoc on the processes of experience-construction, opening the door to strange perceptions.

Singular experiences can arise from encountering truly unusual objects. Some of these objects may be known to, and at least partially understood by, contemporary science. For example, witnesses have interpreted uncommon natural events such as ball lightning, or hordes of parachute spiders riding clouds of gossamer thread, in exotic ways (luminous ghosts, UFOs). And, of course, meeting an actual discarnate spirit or Sasquatch or UFO occupant, if indeed there are such things, would likely do the trick.

Internal Influences

Anything that affects the mental processes by which we manufacture awareness can give rise to strange experiences. Severe stress reactions, developmental problems and perhaps biological malfunctions can contribute to the unpleasant conditions we call mental disorders. Many kinds of psychological problems are accompanied by supranormal experiences. In some cases, not only are the person's emotions or thoughts altered, but his or her perceptions.

Disturbances in brain function can also shake the underpinnings of consciousness. Various neurological disorders are associated with abnormal experiences, both discomfiting and blissful. Ingesting psychedelic substances that amplify or inhibit signal transmission between neurons can produce similar effects.

Most supranormal phenomena are experienced by people who are neither mentally nor neurologically disordered in any obvious way. This fact is camouflaged in modern culture by the ridicule that attaches to reports of anything apparently supernatural or outside the bounds of ordinary reality. Those who report seeing "impossible" things run the risk of having their honesty or sanity questioned; so many stay silent.

Some people are more likely than others to have unusual experiences. Although research on this important finding is just beginning, a pattern is starting to emerge. Perhaps the most frequently noted characteristic of "encounter prone" persons, as they have been called, is a flexibility of attention. Controlling attention is one of the main ways in which a world view molds experience. We focus on what we believe to be real, valuable or threatening, and ignore that which we consider meaningless or trivial. As a result, we miss most of what is going on around us and within us. It follows that people whose attentional focus is less tightly controlled by expectations will occasionally notice features of the world that are undetected by others and imbue these observations with special meaning.

Another factor that opens people toward having unusual experiences is the holding of unusual beliefs. If our world view includes belief in reincarnation, for instance, we are more likely to interpret dreams of Egyptian temples as a memory of a past life; nonbelievers would interpret them in a way consistent with their perceptions of psychological reality, if they noticed them at all.

The Social Impact of Supranormal Experiences

Reports of a dimension of life beyond the cave of the senses can elicit a variety of responses from the society to which the witnesses belong. If only one person has the experience, it might be viewed as either a special revelation or a personal pathology. Sometimes, the experience spreads to others. Perceptions can be contagious. Many forms of supranormal experience, from Marian apparitions to demonic possession to encounters with Bigfoot, happen in waves, rippling through the social fabric like rings radiating from a pebble tossed into a pond. Whether the "pebble"—the initial report that sets the social process in motion—turns out to be a hoax, a misinterpretation of an ordinary event, or something else, the agreement of others that "we saw it too" strengthens the phenomenon's reality status in the culture, and can even grow to pose a challenge to the conventional world view.

Most societies have a place for unusual experiences and for those who are susceptible to them. In many cultures at least some "encounter prone" persons are valued as blessed with special talents. These individuals are trained to peer through the holes in the map of everyday reality rather than to patch them. In hunting-and-gathering cultures, shamans deliberately subject themselves to conditions that disrupt ordinary awareness, trying to propel themselves (personally or communally) into enriching experiences of alternative realities.

Within more complex societies, special groups practice meditation, intensive prayer or magical rituals to leave the world of ordinary reality and gain access to the resources thought to lie beyond. Such practices have been part of Western culture since the most ancient times. Mainstream Christianity in the West developed early on a distaste for the pursuit of the supranormal associating such things with its heretical and pagan competitors. Centuries of suppression followed. Despite the efforts of orthodoxy's thought police, non-Christian techniques for inducing mystical or supranormal states were preserved and developed in the margins of Western culture in traditions like alchemy, ritual magic and kabbalah.

What is the place of the supranormal in the culture of the modern West? Nonrational thinking forms the backbone of innovation in our creative institutions. This is widely recognized with respect to the arts. It is equally so concerning the sciences. Scientists rely on reason and experiment to verify their hunches. The hunches themselves, however, emerge from the shadows (or is it light?) of awareness, garbed as dreams, visions, reveries.

With the diminishing authority of the traditional religious bodies, many have turned to less orthodox groups built around supranormal experience of various sorts. A number of these groups teach methods to induce mystical and other kinds of special awareness. Some seekers may well have found satisfying alternatives to the conventional beliefs they no longer find credible. Although the "New Age" and similar movements might appear to bear the seeds of a revolution—certainly their adherents talk excitedly about "Aquarian conspiracies" and "new paradigms" waiting just around the corner—these groups generally act to preserve, rather than overturn, the status quo. A danger of chasing after revelations is that it can inflate our sense of superior insight while removing us from the field of action. Channeling the energies of alienated souls only into marginal spiritual activities can act as a cultural safety valve, leaving social institutions without serious challenge. So, in modern times, supranormal experiences have both changed the conventional world view (through scientific insights) and been harnessed to preserve it (through the venting of harmless unorthodoxies).

Explanations

Human nature abhors an explanatory vacuum. The unknown might contain dangers; so we are driven to clarify, to assimilate or accommodate all the pieces of experience that seem not to harmonize with our world view. In the modern setting, there are two main explanatory systems available with which to make sense of the supranormal. Parapsychologist John Palmer refers to these as "conventionalist" and "extensionist"; they roughly correspond to the strategies of assimilation and accommodation.

The *conventionalist* approach is to explain extraordinary experiences in ordinary terms. This perspective has proven quite valuable. Many supranormal experiences involve misinterpretations of events that can be understood in conventional terms. Taking a conventionalist standpoint, we can explain a great many seeming violations of conventional reality as illusions, hallucinations and hoaxes. In such cases the challenge to the orthodox world view is only apparent. In many cases, of course, there is no way of knowing exactly what caused an experience; but often a plausible conventional explanation can be surmised.

Another approach is to argue that conventional explanations do not suffice. *Extensions* of, or alternatives to, the mainstream world view are then offered. For example, the occult traditions provide explanations for all manner of strange events within the framework of a magical world view: an animated universe, populated with powerful, normally hidden intelligences called spirits. Many parapsychologists have endorsed the idea that the human mind possesses faculties which transcend the ordinary limits of space and time. Some have devised theories as to how these faculties operate, stretching ideas borrowed from quantum mechanics. Religious individuals sometimes use concepts derived from their faith to explain unusual experiences as miracles or demonic pranks. All of these approaches require major add-ons to the reality endorsed by mainstream science.

We should not lose sight of the immense variety of extensionist opinions. Occultists eschew the scientific method for other means of seeking knowledge; parapsychologists (not all of whom are extensionists) rely on experiment and critical investigation to explore the mind's more arcane possibilities. And some religious traditionalists damn both the occultists and the scientist, because only *they* are privy to God's design.

The conventionalist and extensionist camps tend not to get along very well. Conventionalists often accuse extensionists of rejecting ordinary explanations because of emotion rather than reason; extensionists frequently charge conventionalists of clinging to inadequate conventional explanations out of fear of the unknown. And both charges, at times, are likely correct. It is a basic feature of being human that we defend our world view from contradiction. Taken together, both sides have something valuable to say. Conventionalists remind us of the dangers of credulity and of the immense explanatory power of conventional concepts. Extensionists remind us not to assume that the orthodox world view of the late 20th century will always be immune from the need for substantial revisions.

A third position—championed by Palmer with respect to psi (ESP and psychokinesis)— may be dubbed the "anomalistic." This perspective concurs with the extensionists that some unusual experiences have not been fully explained in conventional terms, and agrees with the conventionalists that the various paranormal theories are inadequate too. This is not to say that claims of ESP, for instance, may not turn out someday to be explicable in ordinary terms; but, as of now, we simply do not know for sure. Similarly, there are puzzling features in every kind of supranormal phenomenon, from cryptic animals to near death visions. Perhaps these puzzles can all be explained conventionally; or perhaps they will eventually require a major change in the prevailing world view. But for now, they remain, to some degree, mysteries.

The following observation of William James concerning the supranormal made at the turn of the 20th century, still stands at the turn of the 21st:

> *I confess that at times I have been tempted to believe that the Creator has eternally intended this department of nature to remain* baffling, *to prompt our curiosities and hopes and suspicions all in equal measure, so that, although ghosts and clairvoyances, and rays and messages from spirits, are always seeming to exist and can never be fully explained away, they also can never be susceptible of full corroboration.*

Resisting the leap to a conclusion, one way or another, goes against the human urge for closure. But it is more intellectually honest to resist premature closure than simply to nestle unquestioningly in the cave of the senses for comfort's sake.

The anomalist position was held by Plato's mentor, Socrates. In ancient Greece the Delphic oracle recognized Socrates as the wisest man. What was his wisdom? He is said to have summarized it thus: "I know that I know nothing." This suspension of certainty, if balanced by a grounding in disciplined curiosity, can open us to discovery.

The Lessons of Darkness

> *Science is a match that man has just got alight. He thought he was in a room—in moments of devotion a temple—and that his light would be reflected in pillars carved with philosophical systems and wrought into harmony. It is a curious sensation, now that the preliminary sputter is over and the flame burns up clear, to see his hands lit and just a glimpse of himself and the patch he stands on visible, and around him, in place of all that human comfort and beauty he anticipated—darkness still.*

So observed H.G. Wells in a *Fortnightly Review* article in 1891. A century later, the flame of science burns brighter—and the darkness is as dark as ever. Science has not eliminated violence, poverty or the enslavement of every heart by hatred and desire. We still have everything to learn about the sources of our self-inflicted suffering, its roots trailing off into the shadows. The darkness beckons. What might we learn from it?

First, we should learn not to pathologize every report of an unusual experience. This is merely a bad habit of our society and it creates unnecessary fear and ridicule.

Second, we should learn to ask more questions. We should respectfully probe accounts of unusual experiences offered by others; we should critically examine our own unusual experiences, rather than leaping to the security of premature conclusions. Then, we should turn the laser of doubt onto *ordinary* experience. If we can learn to notice the ephemerality of the daily shadow show projected onto the cavern wall, perhaps those shadows that dominate our actions will seem less compelling. Would the mass awareness that our world view—*any* world view—is a tool, not the truth, help our species toward greater compassion and wisdom? I do not know. It has never been attempted on a broad scale. But it might be worth a try.

This book introduces you to the range of the supranormal, to the experience of alternative realities. The directory that follows provides an overview of the topics covered. I have included general material on the dominant approaches and ideas within the main research disciplines. Each of these disciplines has its own specialized literature, much of which requires advanced training in statistics and experimental design to understand fully; perusal of *Alternative Realities* can be a first step toward approaching the more complex levels of study. More informed students will hopefully find material of interest as well.

Understanding the factors associated with supranormal phenomena is a key to appreciating their origins and functions. This burgeoning research area is explored in the Appendix, as well as in the entries concerning each factor and type of experience.

Any and all facets of daily experience—the outer world, the body, the past, the inner world—can be invaded by supranormal phenomena. I have included entries on many types of such phenomena for each of these aspects.

I have also provided entries on methods of inducing unusual states of awareness, and the experiences reported by their practitioners. Asian traditions, especially Buddhism and Hinduism, are the most highly developed in this regard and are only superficially familiar to most Westerners, so I have explored these approaches in some depth. Islamic, Western and other traditions are also addressed; for every culture has groups and individuals experimenting with altered states, even if the mainstream society is unsupportive.

Through following the cross-references and suggested readings noted in the major entries, your introduction to this fascinating dimension of human life will be thorough. As advice for getting the most out of *Alternative Realities,* I could not improve on that given in the *Mutus Liber,* a 17th century alchemy text of unknown authorship: "Ora, Lege, Lege, Lege, Relege, Labora et Invenies" (Pray, Read, Read, Read, Reread, Labor, and Discover).

—LEONARD GEORGE
VANCOUVER, BRITISH COLUMBIA

DIRECTORY OF ENTRIES

A. General Topics

Approaches, Attitudes and Interpretations

These entries consider some basic terms commonly used in discussions of unusual or supranormal phenomena, note the range of attitudes toward them and identify the main disciplines that specialize in their study.

> *abnormal psychology*
> *altered state of consciousness*
> *anomalistic psychology*
> *anomaly*
> *anomalous belief*
> *cryptozoology*
> *paranormal*
> *parapsychology*
> *preternatural*
> *psychical research*
> *scientism*
> *skepticism*
> *supernatural*
> *supernormal*
> *transpersonal psychology*
> *zeteticism*

Correlates

Supranormal phenomena are more likely to be experienced by certain people, under certain conditions. Research has identified a number of factors linked to them. These correlates are discussed in the following entries (see also the Appendix).

> *absorption*
> *age*
> *ambiguity*
> *belief, anomalous*
> *childhood alternate reality*
> *childhood trauma*
> *conformity*
> *control needs*

> *creativity*
> *death concerns*
> *dogmatism*
> *education*
> *emotional arousal*
> *encounter prone personality*
> *experience, unusual*
> *fantasy proneness*
> *gender*
> *geophysical influences*
> *group dynamics of unusual experiences*
> *head injury*
> *hypnotizability*
> *intelligence*
> *locus of control*
> *magical thinking*
> *narcissism*
> *psychological adjustment*
> *reasoning skills*
> *religiosity*
> *sensation seeking*
> *sensory deprivation*
> *social interest*
> *temporal lobe abnormality*
> *unlikely virtue*

Mental Disorders

Most people who experience supranormal phenomena are not suffering from a mental disorder. Many of these occurrences seem to be part of the spectrum of normal experience, albeit one that is not always discussed openly. Undoubtedly, however, mental disorders can cause unusual experiences. A selection of phenomena associated with psychological problems is considered in these entries. (This is not an exhaustive list. I have focused mainly on disorders characterized by disturbances in perception, thought or memory; most mood disorders, personality disorders and some other classes are not included).

delusion
dissociative disorder
folie à deux
fugue
hysteria
idea of reference
induced psychotic disorder
multiple personality disorder
panic
paranoia
pseudologia phantastica
psychosis
schizophrenia
somatoform disorder

Organic Disorders

Anything that interferes with the ordinary functioning of the nervous system can produce extraordinary experiences. The following entries cover the most common sorts of organically based unusual experiences. Many others are discussed in the medical literature. (See also entries on drugs.)

alcohol hallucinosis
blindsight
delirium
delirium tremens
epilepsy
migraine
neurological disorder
organic mental disorder
palinacousis
palinopsia
tinnitus
Tourette's Syndrome

History

Supranormal phenomena occasionally erupt onto the stage of history, sometimes with profound consequences. These entries explore selected historical incidents that highlight important aspects of our topic, particularly with respect to the experiences of groups.

airship sightings

Aix-en-Provence nuns, possession of
Auxonne nuns, possession of
bowmen of Mons
charismatists
Constantine, vision of
Convulsionaries
dancing mania
Fatima apparitions
foo fighters
ghost rockets
Hildegard of Bingen, visions of
Loudun nuns, possession of
Louviers nuns, possession of
Medjugorje apparitions
Mothman
myroblutai
New Jersey Vegetable Monster
preaching sickness
Ramanujan, Srinivasa
St. Anthony, visions of
St. John's Dance
St. Vitus' Dance
Springheel Jack
tarantism
Vision of Paul
windshield pitting epidemic
Zeitoun apparitions

B. Varieties of Unusual (Supranormal) Experience

Body and Self

These entries discuss experiences featuring an unusual awareness of the body, the self or the relation between the two.

astral projection
aura
auto-oxidation
autoscopy
bilocation
body image distortion
burial alive
deathbed vision

Mystical and Related Experiences

The experiences discussed in these entries involve various degrees of transcendence of the boundaries of self, world and spirit as they are ordinarily sensed. Experiences in which God is "felt within" could be classed either as a type of mystical experience, or as a form of possession (considered below under "Automatized Experiences").

Automatized Experiences

Normally, many of our thoughts and behaviors seem to be under our conscious control. The following entries explore cases in which ordinarily voluntary functions fall under the influence of forces outside of normal awareness. Frequently, these forces are believed to be external beings, such as spirits or gods. In the extreme, voluntary consciousness may be lost completely, as the person is "possessed" by the alien power.

Memory Phenomena

Memory is the foundation in which our identity is anchored. But feelings of familiarity, recognition and recollection can behave in unsettling ways. The following entries discuss various unusual memory experiences.

fugue
hypermnesia
illusion des sosies
jamais vu
missing time
paramnesia
past life recall
presque vu
pseudo-presentiment
reincarnation memory
time gap phenomenon
xenoglossy
xenography
xenolalia

Sleep-Related Experiences

Many supranormal experiences are associated with the states of waking and sleeping, and the transitions between them. Various kinds of unusual dreams are considered here, as are conditions in which the dream world invades waking consciousness. We do not always know whether we are awake or asleep; so sleep-related experiences might be relevant to many other types of unusual experience in which the witnesses think they were awake.

false awakening
high dream
hypnagogic state
hypnopompic state
incubus nightmare
lucid dream
metachoric experience
myoclonic jerk
nightmare
night terror
Old Hag experience
pavor nocturnus
sleep drunkenness
sleepwalking
waking dream

Sensory and Perceptual Anomalies

These entries discuss unusual sensations and their interpretation. Included under this heading are: sensations that are produced by disturbed sensory processes (such as entoptic phenomena); mental images that are mistaken for perceptions (hallucinations); and false perceptions (illusions).

autokinetic effect
autostatic effect
cryptaesthesia
cryptopsychism
derealization
eidetic imagery
electronic visual phenomenon
electronic voice phenomenon
entoptic phenomenon
entotic phenomenon
eyewitness accounts of unusual experiences
floaters
form constant
hallucination (see also separate entries for subtypes of hallucination: auditory, cenesthetic, formication, gustatory, kinesthetic, lilliputian, negative, olfactory, paranormal, retrospective, tactile, verbigeration, visual)
hallucinosis
ideophany
ideoretinal light
illusion
Isakower phenomenon
jet lag syndrome
macropsia
micropsia
pareidolia
phosphene
pseudohallucination
Scheerer's Phenomenon
synesthesia

Psi

Many paranormal experiences suggest that the mind can acquire knowledge of objects or events without sensory contact (often called "extrasensory perception"); others seem to indicate that the mind can influence the external world directly, without the use of muscles or other physical means ("psychokinesis"). Together, these possibilities are dubbed "psi." The reality of psi is by no means universally accepted among researchers in this field. If it does exist, it probably plays an important role in many kinds of supranormal experience. The following entries introduce this vast and controversial topic.

Barnum effect
clairaudience
clairvoyance
Clever Hans effect
extrasensory perception
fallacy of personal validation
GESP
metagnomy
metakinesis
parapsychology
parascopy
precognition
premonition
psi
psychic
psychical research
psychokinesis
retrocognition
RSPK
telekinesis
telepathy
teleportation
telepsychosis

Encounters with Otherworldly Beings

Entities that have no place in the currently prevailing world view appear in a range of forms: feelings of an "invisible presence"; glimpses of cryptics or "impossible animals" like Sasquatch or the Loch Ness Monster; apparitions and poltergeists, often attributed to discarnate spirits or demons; and UFOs and their occupants.

apparition

Bigfoot
cryptic
diabolical experience
doppelganger
ghost
haunting
humanoids, anomalous
imaginary companion
invisible presence
Loch Ness Monster
mokele-mbembe
poltergeist
Sasquatch
thorybism
UFO abduction experience
UFObia
UFO encounter
UFOmania
UFOria
wraith
Yeti

Unusual Natural Phenomena

Little-known and poorly understood processes constantly affect our natural environment. Occasionally, these forces give rise to puzzling effects, often interpreted by observers as supernatural phenomena or UFO visits.

aerial blob
airquake
alpenglow
angel hair
aurora
ball lightning
birds
Brocken spectres
cemetery light
clouds
corpse light
cosmic dust bunnies
countersun
dark day
devil's jelly
earth sound

fafrotskies
Fata Morgana
fox fire
gelatinous meteorite
ghost light
heiligenschein
ignis fatuus
infrasound
insects
kaleidoscopic sun
lightning
manna from heaven
meteor
mirage
mock moon
mock sun
mountaintop glow
ocean light
paraselenae
parhelia
planets
plasma
St. Elmo's fire
sleeks
subsun
swamp gas
te lapa
temperature inversion
thunderstone
water gun
will-o'-the-wisp

C. Deliberate Inducement of Unusual Experiences

Induced Unusual Experiences—General

These entries sample the many ways in which people have interfered with the stabilizing mechanisms of ordinary awareness in order to experience other types of perception.

auditory driving
dancing
deautomatization

drumming
flagellation
hypnosis
meditation
mediumship
photic driving
rhythmic sensory stimulation
shamanism
somnambulism
vision quest

Drugs

The "royal road" to transcendence has always been the ingestion of drugs. The effects of the consumed substances arise only in part from their pharmacological properties; drug experiences are largely determined by the mental and social contexts within which the drug is taken. These entries explore drug experiences in various cultural settings. I have excluded from discussion the most commonly used psychoactive substances in modern Western culture; the effects of alcohol, tobacco, caffeine, marijuana and the host of synthetic prescription and nonprescription drugs are hardly unusual and are covered in depth in many other easily accessible sources.

bad trip
datura
drugs
entheogen
ergot
flashback
fly agaric
iboga
peyote
posthallucinogen perception disorder
St. Anthony's fire
teonanacatl
Vinum Nostrum
witches' ointment
yaje

Methods and Experiences Associated with Specific Traditions

1. Buddhism, Indo-Tibetan

Buddhists in India and Tibet have systematically explored the range of human experience for 2,500 years. Their methodical approach, based primarily on meditation, has produced a large literature of transcendence and how to achieve it. Many of these practices claim to yield insights and abilities unavailable to ordinary awareness.

abhidharma
abhijna
bardo
bhavana
bodhi
Buddhahood
chakras
dhyana
emptiness
enlightenment
jhana
kundalini
lung-gom
mandala
mantra
mindfulness
Naropa, Six Yogas of
nimitta
nirodha
nirvana
prajna
pseudo-nirvana
riddhi
sadhana
samadhi
samapatti
shamatha
siddhi
Tantra, Buddhist
terma
vipassana
yidam
yoga

2. Buddhism, Zen

Meditators in the Japanese Buddhist tradition called Zen (from the Chinese *Ch'an;* known in Korea as *Son*) built on the earlier Indian teachings, but developed their own rich literature of transcendence. While the aim of Zen meditation is not merely to chase after strange sensations and perceptions, such things arise during various stages of progress on the path of spiritual attainment, according to the tradition.

aku-byodo
byodo-kan
daishi
goseki
hakushi
jobutsu
joshin
kensho
koan
kokushittsu
makyo
satori
shikan-taza
tongo
zazen
zembyo
zengo

3. Christianity

Since its birth, the Christian tradition has discussed the meaning of unusual or miraculous experiences. Many strange occurrences were attributed to the Devil; but some were thought to be signs of God's presence and favor. The charisms were associated with saintliness. Christianity developed its own methods of classifying and inducing transcendent experiences on the spiritual path.

Biblical prophecy
charisms
contemplation
exchange of hearts
glossolalia

hesychasm
holy blood miracles
incendium amoris
locution
Marian apparition
metanoia
odors of sanctity
prayer
reading of hearts
stigmata
theoptia
theophany
theosis
tongues, speaking in
unio mystica
vision

Nirvikalpa Samadhi
nirvitarka-samapatti
Raja Yoga
sahaj samadhi
samadhi
samprajnata samadhi
samyama
savicara-samapatti
savikalpa samadhi
savitarka-samapatti
siddhi
Tantra, Hindu
Turiya
videha-mukti
viveka-khyati
yoga

4. Hinduism

Ancient Hindu writings contain the earliest known classification system of states of consciousness. The Hindu tradition was heir to meditation practices of prehistoric antiquity. Almost three millennia of Hindu writings have documented the types of awareness associated with these methods.

anandamaya
ananda-samapatti
asamprajnata samadhi
asmita-samapatti
bhava-pratyaya samadhi
cathurta
chakras
dharma-megha samadhi
jivan-mukti
kaivalya
kundalini
mandala
mantra
moksha
mukti
nirananda-samapatti
nirasmati-samapatti
nirvicara-samapatti
nirvicara-vaisharadhya

5. Islam

The aspect of the Muslim faith that aims at a direct experience of God is called Sufism. Since the seventh century, Sufis have charted a number of experiences associated with their quest.

baqa
fana
mahabba
makhafah
ma'rifah
qurb
ruya'ha

6. Judaism

While the biblical Hebrew prophets were revered as God's messengers, the deliberate inducement of mystical states formed no part of mainstream Judaism. The (post-biblical) Jewish tradition called Kabbalah did develop meditation practices, probably with some influence from the Sufis. Kabbalah has been viewed with suspicion by mainstream Judaism for much of its history.

Biblical prophecy
devekut
kabbalah

7. Taoism

The ancient Chinese faith called Taoism developed from primordial forms of nature mysticism. In ancient times, the Taoist tradition was strongly affected by the ideas of alchemy, and later by Buddhism; but it mingled these influences in unique ways. Some Taoist literature discusses unusual experiences associated with spiritual practices.

> *fang-chung shu*
> *nei-tan*

8. Western Esoteric Traditions

Official Christianity discouraged the exploration of most types of supranormal experience, suspecting their infernal origin. In response, there arose an enduring counterculture that practiced a host of inducement techniques. The most important strands of the Western esoteric tradition include: alchemy, which aimed at personal transformation through meditation on physical processes, and, perhaps, drug taking; ritual magic, which taught methods for triggering encounter experiences; and the Jewish mystical school of Kabbalah, which contributed techniques and ideas to both alchemy and magic. Other underground traditions involving "forbidden" practices might have been uncovered during the witch hunts of the Renaissance and Reformation.

> *alchemy*
> *kabbalah*
> *ritual magic*
> *witches' sabbath*

A–Z Entries

◆

Cross-references appear in small capital letters within an entry and after the words "See also" following an entry. Every entry in the book is listed in the index. Suggested further readings on a topic are listed after the words "For further reading"; the complete bibliographic citations can be found in the Bibliography at the back of this book.

Abhidharma A Sanskrit term, composed of two roots: *dharma,* which in this context means "teaching," and the prefix *abhi,* or "special." This "special teaching" was the earliest attempt in Buddhism to develop a systematic psychology based on the doctrines of the founder, Gautama Buddha. Like most religious founders, Gautama left no written record of his teachings, and the ideas he shared during his lifetime were adapted to the particular situations in which he taught them. Following his death, the Buddhist community tried to devise an ordered presentation of the Buddha's insights. The result—the Abhidharma—took form between the Buddha's death in the fifth century B.C. and its mature expression in Buddhaghosa's text, *Visuddhimagga* ("Path of purification"), which appeared in the fifth century A.D.

There are several versions of the Abhidharma teaching. They differ in various details, but they all offer a comprehensive mapping of the states of consciousness available to humans and thus address a huge range of unusual experiences, as well as ordinary ones. According to the Abhidharma, human awareness generally seems to be a continuous stream of consciousness consisting of thoughts, images and feelings. The origin of many of these mental phenomena is not obvious to the untrained mind—moods and ideas arise and pass as if they have a life of their own. Meditators, however, can discover that the "stream" is actually a succession of thought-moments that appear and vanish at a very rapid rate. These "flashes" create the illusion of continuity, rather like a movie picture, which is actually a quickly presented series of still images. The characteristics of each thought-moment are caused by *cetasiksas,* or "factors of consciousness." In one typical list from the Abhidharma literature, 52 factors are identified. The tradition claims that the lists represent the findings of the extremely close observation of mental activities by skilled meditators.

The Abhidharma also classifies types of consciousness according to the type of object they are observing. Three worlds of objects are reported. The first, called the realm of sensuous form, includes the objects of the ordinary states of consciousness—all of the things to which people habitually cling for pleasure or security, as well as those that are pushed away because of fear or hatred.

The second realm is that of pure form. Like the world of sensuous form, the domain of pure form consists of finite objects; but, unlike sensuous forms, people are not pulled into habitual accepting or rejecting of pure forms. Usually, these objects are perceived only by those who have mastered the meditative states of intense concentration called JHANAs. Occasionally, an untrained consciousness might catch a glimpse of the realm of pure form. For instance, if one suddenly views a magnificent sunset, one might notice the pure form of the sun in the first moments, before the mind's habitual grasping at beauty encrusts the object. Because the mind had not been prepared by meditation, this encounter might be an overwhelming MYSTICAL EXPERIENCE or an EPIPHANY. Or, if the mind was deeply mired in the realm of sensuous form, a brief experience of something beyond its familiar horizons might be quickly suppressed and forgotten.

The third domain of objects is the realm of non-form. Like the objects of the previous realm, those of non-form are purified of habitual clinging and rejecting. However, as the name suggests, these objects have no boundaries. For instance, space and consciousness are regarded as formless objects. Although a "formless object" sounds like a mere abstraction, the Buddhist masters assert that these things can be directly experienced—but only by one who has mastered the more advanced jhana meditations.

The Abhidharma map of awareness depicts 121 possible states of consciousness, each of which is composed of various combinations of the 52 mental factors. Fifty-four states have sensuous forms as their object; 27 states attend to the realm of pure form; and 40 are focused on formless objects. Given that Buddhism is often misrepresented as a gloomy world view which highlights the pervasiveness of suffering, it is noteworthy that, of the 121 states of awareness discussed by the Abhidharma, only three are said to include the feeling of misery or suffering—the rest are either neutral or joyous. Many people spend a lot of time in these three states. Buddhists say, however, that all the other states are open to people, if they would choose to develop spiritually.

Since the 1960s, the Abhidharma has attracted considerable attention from transpersonal psychologists (see TRANSPERSONAL PSYCHOLOGY). Some of these researchers believe that the extensive range and analytical precision of the Abhidharma could greatly enrich modern psychology's understanding of the mind. Very few of the 121 states of consciousness have even been mentioned in the scientific literature of the West.

See also MINDFULNESS.

For further reading: Buddhaghosa; Govinda (1974).

abhijna This Sanskrit term is used by Buddhists to refer to the supernormal abilities and knowledge attained through the practice of meditation. There are many lists of abhijnas in Buddhist literature, showing only minor variations in content. The descriptions of abhijnas closely resemble those of supernormal powers in Hindu meditational writings; there is no doubt that belief in the abhijnas derived from sources predating the founding of Buddhism in the sixth century B.C.

A requirement for the attainment of any abhijna is mastery of the meditative states called the JHANAs. In addition, the various kinds of abhijna require specific meditation practices, generally involving focusing on a kasina, or patch of color, and reciting a magical phrase. After describing a series of meditation exercises, the fifth century text called the *Visuddhimagga* by Buddhaghosa notes:

> So just as when a goldsmith wants to make some kind of ornament, he does so only after making the gold malleable and wieldy by smelting it, etc., and just as when a potter wants the clay well kneaded and malleable, a beginner too must likewise prepare for the kinds of supernormal powers by controlling his mind in these fourteen ways; and he must do so also by making his mind malleable and wieldy.

A standard list of abhijnas, found in the *Visuddhimagga,* includes the following: magical transformations and movements of the body, known as RIDDHI; awakening the Divine Ear Element, or CLAIRAUDIENCE; penetrating the minds of others, or telepathy; PAST LIFE RECALL; and awakening the Divine Eye Element, which can perceive the cycles of birth, death and rebirth of all beings.

Practicing the abhijnas usually involves a progression from the coarse features of ordinary experience to the subtle levels available only to advanced meditators. For instance, in developing the Divine Ear, one first concentrates on easily perceptible sounds, such as nearby voices; then on fainter stimuli, such as those made by lions prowling in the forest, and ants moving underground; eventually, one can detect sounds coming from other realms of being, such as the conversations of deities. In cultivating past life recollection, one first focuses on remembering the immediately preceding moment, and systematically extends the memory back before one's birth. This procedure seems to resemble the standard method used in modern hypnotic past life regression. Buddhists, however, strongly reject the identification of their meditative practices with HYPNOSIS.

The attainment of such powers is not the aim of Buddhism. The Buddha taught that magical feats are trivial compared to the goal of enlightenment, or liberation from cyclic existence. Early Buddhists admitted that the abhijnas could be attained even by non-Buddhists, if they mastered the appropriate meditations. Buddhist masters could use the abhijnas to engage in compassionate activities—for example, it was said that the Buddha's telepathic ability to discern the mental sufferings of his students enabled him to recommend the best meditation practices for them. There were grave dangers, however; the practitioner might become proud, or might be tempted to use the powers for mundane ends, and thus create obstacles to enlightenment. For this reason, anyone who demonstrated the abhijnas in public was ejected from the Buddhist order.

See also SIX YOGAS OF NAROPA; SIDDHI.

For further reading: Buddhaghosa; Eliade (1969).

abnormal psychology   The scientific study of the causes and treatments of mental illness. Sufferers of many types of psychological disorders have unusual experiences; but a great number of people without mental illnesses also have such experiences. A related discipline, ANOMALISTIC PSYCHOLOGY, studies the mental and social processes involved in the seemingly PARANORMAL events experienced by normal people.

Abominable Snowman   A hairy humanoid (see HUMANOID, ANOMALOUS), featured in Himalayan folklore and occasionally sighted in remote parts of that region.

See also CRYPTICS.

absorption   An experience in which one's attention is totally focused on an object. For example, when a person is so engrossed in a novel that he or she does not notice someone else's entrance into the room, or when a horror movie audience temporarily "forgets" the unreality of the monster and screams when it leaps from a closet, attentional absorption has occurred. The first psychologists to study absorption were Tellegen and Atkinson. They noted that in absorbed experiences, every thought, image, perception and action is trained on the object. The focus of absorption can be an external object or a mental one. During the absorbed state, the object seems to become absolutely real, while other objects disappear; the ordinary sense of self and reality may be altered, and time may seem to accelerate, slow or stop. Absorption seems to be a key factor in the occurrence of many types of unusual experience.

Irwin noted that absorption can be considered from three angles: opportunity, capacity and need. Certain conditions seem to provide a greater opportunity for absorption to happen. States of great calm and excitement are conducive for absorption. Many of the techniques used to evoke unusual experiences, from HYPNOSIS and MEDITATION through DRUGS and RHYTHMIC SENSORY STIMULATION, aim to produce extreme arousal states. In these methods, a simple object is often presented on which one is instructed to focus attention, inducing an absorbed condition.

Individuals differ in their capacity for absorption. A background of childhood trauma is one of the factors that predisposes a person to become easily absorbed. Many studies have reported that the capacity for absorption is linked to the tendency to have spontaneous unusual experiences. Types of anomalous experience that have been found to correlate with absorption capacity include: general paranormal experience; ESP; MYSTICAL and DIABOLICAL EXPERIENCE; NEAR DEATH EXPERIENCE; EIDETIC IMAGERY; SYNESTHESIA; and OUT OF BODY EXPERIENCE. Nelson (1989), who examined several psychological traits in relation to unusual experience reports, concluded that absorption capacity is the single best predictor of whether or not a person is prone to have anomalous experiences. This trait is closely associated with other correlates of unusual experiences, including HYPNOTIZABILITY and FANTASY PRONENESS (many researchers view absorption capacity and fantasy proneness as identical).

A person could be in an absorption-conducive situation, and possess a high absorption capacity, and yet not become absorbed because she feels no desire or need to do so. Irwin discovered that some people have a recurrent urge or need for absorption, and may seek out such opportunities. He reported that individuals with high absorption needs are more likely to report ESP experiences and encounters with APPARITIONs, but not PK experiences, than those who are not attracted to absorption.

Absorption could contribute to the occurrence of unusual experiences in various ways. Tellegen and Atkinson noted that "objects of absorbed attention acquire an importance and intimacy that are normally reserved for the self and may, therefore, acquire a temporary self-like quality." The observer's own consciousness and knowledge could seem to belong to the object, which would be transformed from an ordinary thing into a strange being. Absorption may temporarily disrupt habitual perceptions, allowing an observer to detect aspects of the world that normally remain unnoticed. Absorption can also blur the boundaries between perceptions, memories and fantasies.

See also Appendix; EMOTIONAL AROUSAL; EXPERIENCE, UNUSUAL; JHANA.

For further reading: Irwin (1985b); P. Nelson; Tellegen and Atkinson.

aerial blob   In the turbulent soup of the atmosphere, air pockets are often created which possess different densities, temperatures or moisture contents than the surrounding air. Ordinarily, aerial blobs (also called sky dimples) are invisible, but their effects can easily be observed—the twinkling of the stars is largely due to the invervening passage of these atmospheric structures. Astronomers sometimes notice that photographed images of stars are distorted by the blobs. Observers occasionally see the sudden dimming of a star in a cloudless sky, as an unseen volume absorbs some of its light.

By studying these light scattering effects, researchers have determined that aerial blobs occur in a variety of shapes, including spheres, lenticular forms and cylinders. Despite the dispersing influence of air turbulence, these forms can endure for hours. The blobs range from millimeters to several meters in diameter. Packs consisting of hundreds of aerial blobs have been detected, drifting with the wind at various heights.

Aerial blobs might be responsible for a variety of unusual atmospheric displays. KALEIDOSCOPIC SUNs, in which the solar disc "dances" in the sky while radiating multicolored beams, might be caused by sunlight cascading through layers of aerial blobs with different refractive properties.

The blobs might themselves become visible under certain conditions—if they carried highly reflective or absorptive dust or gas, for instance. The spectacle reported in 1808 (cited by Corliss) in cloudless skies over Sweden is suggestive:

there appeared at the western horizon, from where the wind blew, to arise gradually, and in quick succession, a great number of balls, or spherical bodies, to the naked eye of a size of the crown of a hat, and of a dark brown colour. The nearer these bodies . . . approached towards the sun, the darker they appeared, and in the vicinity of the sun, became entirely black. At this elevation their course seemed to lessen, and a great many of them remained, as it were, stationary; but they soon resumed their former [course], and an accelerated motion, and passed in the same direction with great velocity and almost horizontally. . . . The phenomenon lasted uninterruptedly upwards of two hours, during which time millions of similar bodies continually rose in the west, one after the other irregularly, and continued their career exactly in the same manner.

Some of these spheres were observed to fall to the ground where they dispersed, leaving an iridescent scum. Corliss suggested that such blobs might account for the appearance of the mysterious gelatinous deposits known as DEVIL'S JELLY.

Even more intriguing than the possibility of opaque aerial blobs is the suggestion that there might be a luminous variety. There have been rare accounts of thousands of softly glowing spheres in the vicinity of natural electrical activity, such as thunderstorms. Unlike BALL LIGHTNING, these luminous globes do not tend to burn and explode. Perhaps they are pockets of phosphorescent gases, an explanation for the WILL-O'-THE-WISPs seen in swamps. But if so, their distance from known sources of such gas, and their proximity to storms, is hard to explain.

For further reading: Corliss (1984).

age Surveys have found that age is one of the strongest correlates of anomalous belief. Research conducted in several countries, including England, New Zealand and the United States, has indicated that older people tend to have lower levels of general belief in anomalous phenomena than younger people.

One interpretation of the negative correlation of age and belief is that people tend to discard anomalous beliefs as they grow older. Another explanation is that the correlation is caused by cultural changes, rather than aging—perhaps older generations grew up in a more disbelieving cultural atmosphere, whereas younger generations have adopted a more sympathetic attitude toward paranormal claims. In order to decide which interpretation is correct, a study would have to track changes of belief in a group of subjects as they aged; this research has not yet been done.

Few studies have examined the relationship between age and unusual experiences. It is generally believed that children are more prone to HALLUCINATIONs than adults, because they have not yet learned how to draw the culturally dictated line between reality and unreality. Bereaved individuals, who are often older people, are susceptible to hallucinations and PSEUDOHALLUCINATIONs of their dear departed.

See also Appendix; BELIEF, ANOMALOUS; IMAGINARY COMPANION.

For further reading: Emmons and Sobal; Irwin (1993).

agnosia In some cases of head injury, parts of the cerebral cortex that comprehend the meaning of sensations are damaged. The result may be agnosia—the inability to recognize a previously familiar stimulus. Usually, agnosia occurs in only one sensory mode, corresponding to the area of brain damage. Someone with an injury of the visual processing region may be unable to recognize common objects or the faces of loved ones, although they can still see them; if the brain area that handles the skin senses is damaged, one may not be able to identify objects that were formerly familiar by touch. Agnosia is different from JAMAIS VU. In jamais vu, one can identify familiar objects and know that one should be familiar with them, but temporarily feels they are novel or alien; in agnosia, one can perceive familiar objects, but cannot identify what they are. Agnosia sometimes fades gradually following the head injury, but often it is a permanent condition.

See also AMNESIA.

airquake The atmosphere is full of well-known sources of sound. Familiar are the noises of thunder, wind, birds and planes. Less familiar to many, but unmysterious in origin, are the hissing sounds and occasional explosions caused by meteors disintegrating as they fall toward the earth. But people are puzzled when sounds come from the sky far from storm fronts, without the tell-tale streaks and flashes of meteor break-ups; these noises are called airquakes.

When a stable boundary forms between air masses of different temperatures high in the atmosphere, it can function as a sounding board, deflecting noises over great distances. Thunderclaps from storms beyond the horizon can sometimes be heard in areas experiencing clear weather. There are also many reports of earthquake noises coming from above, probably due to the same mechanism.

The best known recent airquake was the series of aerial detonations heard along the eastern coast of North America in 1977 and 1978. From Nova Scotia to South Carolina, thousands were startled by loud offshore explosions that were sometimes accompanied by brilliant yellow flashes. In some cases, the vibrations were powerful enough to shatter windows and dishes. Researchers pinpointed the origin of the quakes over the ocean, about 50 miles from the coast. Most of those studying the case concluded that weather conditions had likely formed an unusually stable atmospheric sounding board, which echoed normally inaudible sonic booms produced by military planes and the supersonic Concorde jet. Some researchers remain convinced, however, that at least some of these airquakes were not caused by planes (as planes could not have created the luminous effects), suggesting the possibility of UFO activity.

See also EARTH SOUND; UFO ENCOUNTER.

For further reading: Claflin-Chalton and MacDonald; Corliss (1983a).

airship sightings At the end of the 19th century, thousands of Americans believed they had witnessed a strange craft floating through the sky. The airship sightings comprise the most striking episode of apparent contact with otherworldly beings in the period, bridging the reports of meetings with fairies in premodern literature and the UFO ENCOUNTERs of the 20th century. Many themes that appear in the airship stories recur in UFO accounts several decades later.

The first airship sighting occurred in November 1896. Passengers on a streetcar in Oakland, California, reported viewing a cigar-shaped object with fixed wings glide overhead, shining a brilliant spotlight onto the ground. Other accounts from the San Francisco Bay area followed. Nothing further was heard about the airship until mid-March of 1897, when sightings were made across the American midwest. The craft was not shy of urban areas—it was witnessed by crowds in Chicago, Milwaukee and Iowa City. Reports tapered off in May, and few further sightings were noted by the press after that time.

Descriptions of the airship were inconsistent. It was frequently said to be shaped like a cigar or egg. Propellers, fanlike wheels or flapping wings were sometimes noted. Estimates of its length ranged from 12 to 70 feet. Beams of colored light were commonly observed. Sometimes orchestral music was heard as the object drifted past. Witnesses who got close enough to make detailed observations mentioned features that seemed to represent advanced versions of contemporary human technology. Railroad conductor James Hooton of Arkansas (quoted in Vallee, 1988) came upon a landed airship:

> A close examination showed that the keel was divided into two parts, terminating in front like the sharp edge of a knife-like edge, while the side of the ship bulged gradually toward the middle, and then receded. There were three large wheels upon each side made of some bending metal and arranged so that they became concave as they moved forward. . . . just in front of each wheel a two-inch tube began to spurt air on the wheels and they commenced revolving. The ship gradually arose with a hissing sound. The aeroplanes suddenly sprang forward, turning their sharp end skyward, then the rudders at the end of the ship began to veer to one side and the wheel revolved so fast that one could scarcely see the blades. In less time than it takes to tell you, the ship had gone out of sight.

Hooton's encounter, like many others of the time, included contact with the airship's occupants. Most reports described friendly and polite humans of normal appearance, speaking English with American accents. On one occasion, the visitors invited witnesses for a ride; the witnesses declined, being unsure where they would end up. On another, an airship pilot requested some lubricating oil and a couple of chisels, for which he presented a $10 bill. For some reason, many reports note that one of the airship pilots mentioned that his name was Wilson.

Not all of the reported contacts were as friendly. In Kansas, witnesses saw the airship carting off a farmer's cow; the following day, the legs, hide and head of the animal were discovered in a neighbor's field. This case foreshadowed the wave of animal mutilations in the West during the 1960s and 1970s, which many people blamed on UFOs.

In April 1897 the *Dallas Morning News* reported that the airship had collided with a windmill and crashed in Aurora, Texas. A military official identified the deceased pilot as a Martian; the townspeople gave him a Christian burial in the local cemetery. Many years later, Hynek investigated this case. He found that there had never been a windmill in Aurora. Cemetery records indicated that every grave was occupied by a known human. Apparently, the story had been a hoax. Its importance lies in being the forerunner of a host of rumors about crashed UFOs that have circulated in the United States since the late 1940s.

Nor was the Aurora story the only fraud in the airship episode. As excitement about the reports spread across the country, pranksters began to launch small hot-air balloons with candles suspended underneath them, prompting further sighting reports. A photograph of the airship, published by newspapers in New York and Chicago, proved to be a hoax—likely the first of thousands of alleged UFO photographs. The airship excitement was fanned—and some say originated—by newspaper publishers, who were not averse to printing grossly sensationalized tales to stimulate sales.

During the period of the airship sightings, the fantasy of human flight was prominent in public awareness. Many inventors were trying to build flying machines; two years after the airships were seen, the Wright brothers began their work in this field. Perhaps some unusual aerial phenomenon was present in the American skies in 1896–1897; observers' perceptions could have been structured by their expectations of an imminent technological breakthrough. This idea cannot account for the stories involving chats with airship pilots, of course. The nature of the stimuli that could have provoked so many reports from such a wide area remains unclear—PLASMA, METEORs and PLANETS, as well as a massive hoax, have all been advanced as candidates. Some prefer the idea that the airship was a craft from another world or dimension, thoughtfully made to appear in a form comprehensible to turn-of-the-century Americans.

For further reading: Bartholomew (1990); Jacobs (1975); Vallee.

Aix-en-Provence nuns, possession of In the early 17th century in the south of France one of the most important cases of mass POSSESSION occurred. The first person to show signs of demonic assault was Madeleine de la Demandolx de la Palud, a 16-year-old girl with a history of emotional disturbance. Four years previously, she had been sent to live at the small Ursuline convent at Aix-en-Provence. But Madeleine fell into a depression and was returned to her parents. She was placed under the religious supervision of a parish priest, Louis Gaufridi, and the two became close. Madeleine was infatuated with Gaufridi and they might have been lovers.

When rumors began to circulate about the relationship between the priest and his young charge, Madeleine was sent to the convent at Marseille, and then back to the convent at Aix. In 1609, following her return to this site of her pubescent misery, she began to display characteristic signs of demonic possession. She had convulsions, reported visions of tormenting devils and reacted violently to Christian symbols, on one occasion smashing a crucifix.

In the following months, eight other nuns in the convent became possessed. Repeated attempts at exorcism only seemed to amplify the behavior, as if the attention being paid to these cloistered, sexually restricted young women was rewarding. Madeleine began to accuse Father Gaufridi not only of being her sex partner but of being a Satanist.

Gaufridi was questioned, and he denied the charges. He was compelled to attempt to exorcise the nuns himself, but this only excited them more, and from their lips came lurid details of his evil deeds—"Louis Gaufridi outside makes believe that he is a saint; however, inside he is full of iniquity. He feigns to abstain from flesh; nevertheless he makes himself drunk with the flesh of little children . . . whom he has eaten, the others whom he has suffocated and afterwards dug up all cry before God for vengeance." The priest was imprisoned, but his friends in high places obtained his release. However, he also had powerful opponents, who decided to use the nuns' accusations to eliminate him. Gaufridi was taken to trial, confessed under torture to witchcraft, and was burned at the stake.

One of the pieces of evidence used to verify the demonic source of Madeleine's complaints was the discovery of "devil's marks," regions of numbness on her body. Her dramatic performances included violent contortions of the limbs, pelvic thrusting in imitation of the sex act, abnormal cracking of the joints, vomiting of repulsive substances and vocalizations, ranging from animal sounds to ravings about attendance at the WITCHES' SABBATH. Another possessed nun, Louise Capeau, reported that Madeleine was occupied by 6,666 demons; she herself was possessed by three, who would seemingly speak from her abdomen.

After Gaufridi's execution, Madeleine's symptoms abated. Louise Capeau remained possessed, causing a blind girl to be burned to death

for bewitching her. Another nun, Marie de Sains, visited the convent at Aix during this time. Upon return to her convent at Lille, she and three other nuns became possessed. Marie's behavior was obviously modeled on that of Madeleine of Aix; Marie also described the abandoned sexuality of the sabbath, including detailed accounts of sodomy, homosexuality and bestiality. The mass possession at Aix was widely discussed, and probably served as the inspiration for repeated waves of demonic disturbances in French convents in the 17th century.

See also Possessions of AUXONNE NUNS; LOUDUN NUNS; LOUVIERS NUNS.

For further reading: Maple; Robbins.

aku-byodo A Japanese term literally meaning "bad sameness," it refers to a pitfall into which one can stumble on the path to ENLIGHTENMENT, according to Zen Buddhism. Zen teaches that all things share the same Buddha-nature. Becoming aware of this nondistinction of nature is a transformative experience arising from meditation practice. This sameness can be misunderstood, however, as denying that individual things exist in *any* sense. The enlightened mind does not negate individuality, but rather is aware both of the sameness of Buddha-nature *and* of the diverse characteristics of objects. Becoming stuck in the erroneous understanding of sameness is aku-byodo.

See also BYODO-KAN.

alchemy The Hermetic Art, or alchemy, has been practiced since the time of ancient Egypt. Most people today think that alchemy was merely a misguided attempt to change lead into gold based on a poor understanding of the nature of matter. Many alchemists did indeed try to transmute metals. However, in the premodern world view, both alchemists and metals were seen as parts of an interconnected, living cosmos—in order for alchemists to change a base substance into a precious one, they also needed to transmute the crude and habitual aspects of their own being into a refined and "golden" state. In short, classical alchemy was a holistic tradition of spiritual development as well as physical transmutation. As noted by Salomon Trismosin, a 16th century alchemist, "All that is without thee, Also is within." The alchemical goal was not ordinary gold, but "rich gold" or "our gold"—spiritual as well as material wealth. Unusual experiences, both spontaneous and induced, played a significant role in the "Opus Magnum," or Great Work, as the activities of the alchemists were known.

From its origins in Egypt to the present day, emphases within alchemy have shifted. In certain periods, the external work in the laboratory was highlighted. Substances were subjected to heating, crushing, dissolving and other operations, and the resultant changes closely studied. At other times, soul alchemy—studying the processes of growth and change within the alchemist—was emphasized. The complete alchemical path has always involved both domains, however.

The methods and aims of alchemy have been difficult to understand, because the books of the alchemists rarely give precise, literal instructions. Instead, these texts are filled with strange symbols and obscure prose, which often sound more like records of dreams than of chemical processes. There were several reasons for this vagueness of communication. First, as noted above, the work of alchemy took place on several levels—in the external world, as well as in the alchemist's body, soul and spirit. Dry, precise language is less adequate to describe such multidimensional processes than is poetic and symbolic expression. However, to comprehend the latter, personal instruction from an alchemist was required. Second, the alchemists formed a marginal subculture; they were always suspected (perhaps with good reason) of cultivating experiences and beliefs that were unorthodox, even heretical. Alchemists tended to shroud the nature of their operations in secrecy to protect themselves from persecution. Third, in alchemy, as in every endeavor, there were frauds; some impenetrable alchemical writings were likely just camouflaged incompetence.

The path of the Great Work has usually been depicted in three, or sometimes four, stages. These stages correspond to the typical sequence found in INITIATORY EXPERIENCES. First, the *nigredo,* or black phase, requires the alchemist to pass beyond the familiar appearances of matter and mind and plummet into the darkness. Neglected, painful truths about oneself are confronted; dangerous accidents in the laboratory are likely as the alchemist attempts to break substances down into their primordial forms. Next is the *albedo,* or white phase. The alchemist undergoes purification and makes contact with inner values; the primordial matter begins to reform into something precious. The *citrinitas,* or yellow phase, is sometimes noted as a transition to the final phase—the *rubedo,* or redness. This is the color of the dawn, signifying the emergence of the enlightened consciousness, as well as the birth in the laboratory of the Philosopher's Stone—the material that can transmute lead into gold.

In addition to the alembics, cucurbites and other contraptions of the alchemical laboratory, the Great Work required certain psychological tools. Many alchemists stressed the necessity of developing the faculty of "imaginatio vera," or "true imagination." Ordinary imagination, taught the alchemists, was of little help in achieving the alchemical goal. But meditation on the processes of the laboratory, as well as on the mysterious images in the texts, could produce dreams and visions. Some books depict the alchemist being visited by a winged figure who emerges from a cloud; Martin Ruland (quoted in Fabricius), a 17th century alchemist, defined meditation as "internal talk of one person with another who is invisible, as in the invocation of the deity, or communion with one's self, or with one's good angel." These manifestations of *imaginatio vera* were revelations concerning the appropriate way to proceed. Simply following recipes written by another could not produce the goal of the Opus, the Philosopher's Stone.

Some modern writers on alchemy have suggested that the visions of the alchemists might have been based in part on the ingestion of psychoactive substances. The laboratory work of alchemy involved the repeated heating of a great variety of materials. Some of these items gave off vapors which could well have triggered HALLUCINATIONs if the fumes were concentrated in a poorly ventilated space.

In addition, Fabricius has speculated that some practitioners of the Hermetic Art were deliberately consuming psychedelic drugs. There seems to have been knowledge concerning plant hallucinogens in medieval and Renaissance Europe, as suggested by the recipes for the WITCHES' OINTMENT. Alchemists would almost certainly have known about such substances, as they used many botanical materials in their experiments. In the *Rosarium Philosophorum,* one of the most important alchemical texts, the seeker is instructed to concoct a drink—vinum nostrum, or "our wine"—from three mysterious substances: virgin's milk, fountain's vinegar and water of life. The text says of the wine, "The chosen one who drinks of this water will soon experience his rebirth."

See also NEI-TAN; TANTRA, BUDDHIST.

For further reading: Fabricius; Haeffner.

alcohol hallucinosis Middle-aged alcoholics, especially men, are prone to developing this disorder. Within 48 hours of their last drink, some alcoholics begin to experience AUDITORY HALLUCINATIONs. Indistinct sounds resembling buzzing, mumbling or crackling mark the onset; these evolve into voices that are usually hostile and threatening. The voices can predict harm to the alcoholic or his or her family; they may even command the person to inflict harm. Alcohol hallucinosis can be a dangerous condition—hallucinators may be tempted to obey the voices, or hurt themselves attempting to flee them.

In most cases, alcohol hallucinosis only lasts for up to three days; sometimes the voices continue their torment for weeks or months. Rarely, the condition will become chronic, and sufferers must deal with the hallucinations for the rest of their lives.

Alcohol hallucinosis is distinct from DELIRIUM TREMENS, another experience related to alcohol withdrawal. The delirious person is subject to disturbed thinking and disorientation, and has primarily visual hallucinations. Alcohol hallucinosis is not normally associated with confused thought and consists of voices rather than visions.

See also ORGANIC MENTAL DISORDER; TINNITUS.

alpenglow The spectacle of mountains that begin to shine after darkness has fallen was first described in the Alps; hence the generic term for this sight, alpenglow. The phenomenon is not uncommon in the Rockies and other high mountain ranges. At sunset on clear evenings, mountain peaks catch the last rays of light as the lower slopes settle into darkness. A wave of deep red color sometimes appears at this moment near the base of the mountain and sweeps upward toward the peaks; in France this flush is called *teinte cadavereuse,* or "corpse color." After this light fades, the mountain may gradually brighten again; this time, a rosy luminosity colors the entire mountain, from base to peak. Rarely, another cycle of darkening and illumination follows. Mountains can shine in this fashion for up to an hour after the sun sets. Alpenglow is thought to be produced by the refraction of sunlight onto the mountains by dust high in the atmosphere. It should not be confused with MOUNTAINTOP GLOWs, which are caused by electrical discharges from the mountains into the air.

For further reading: Corliss (1984).

altered state of consciousness A state of consciousness is a pattern of mental functioning that underlies and determines thought, imagery, feeling and action. The ordinary waking state is defined by the world view taught to us in our earliest years by the representatives of our culture—in most cases, our parents. In this state, we tend to have roughly similar experiences to other members of our society. In part, this similarity arises from the fact that we live in the same environment; but in part it is due to the influences of our shared world view, which guides us in choosing what to notice, what to value and what to disregard. This common experiential world has been called the consensus reality. Conditions in which awareness is patterned differently are called altered states of consciousness.

The ordinary waking state is not completely stable; we experience almost continuous fluctuations in mood, arousal and interest. The difference between the ordinary condition and an altered state consists of changes in some basic features of consciousness. Tart (1969) stated that:

> An altered state of consciousness for a given individual is one in which he clearly feels a *qualitative* shift in his pattern of mental functioning, that is, he feels not just a quantitative shift (more or less alert, more or less visual imagery, sharper or duller, etc.), but also that some quality or qualities of his mental processes are different. Mental functions operate that do not operate at all ordinarily, perceptual qualities appear that have no normal counterparts, and so forth.

For most people, the most familiar altered state is the dream state. Between sleep and waking are the HYPNAGOGIC and HYPNOPOMPIC STATEs, which are often barely noticed. Many are also acquainted with drug-induced states. A host of other states are also possible, each with its own potentials, limitations and definitions of time, space, world and self. Unusual experiences often occur when we enter altered states, or when aspects of altered functioning intrude into the ordinary waking state.

Ludwig outlined ten common features of altered states of consciousness: (1) changes in thinking, including extraordinary ideas about cause and effect; (2) disturbed sense of the passage of time; (3) a loss of control over some normally voluntary functions; (4) extreme emotions, ranging from extreme fear to bliss; (5) BODY IMAGE DISTORTIONs, and shifts in the boundary between self and not-self; (6) perceptual alterations, including HALLUCINATIONs, ILLUSIONs and SYNESTHESIA; (7) changes in the meaning of things, including feelings of profound insight and revelation; (8) a sense that the experience cannot be described in words, or even remembered; (9) feelings of rejuvenation or rebirth; and (10) enhanced suggestibility.

The ordinary pattern of functioning is prevented from breaking down by psychological processes that act to stabilize it. Tart described four consciousness-stabilizing processes. Paying attention to familiar sensations and thoughts helps us not to notice anything that could disturb the ordinary state. Many people reward themselves with feelings of comfort or pleasure for remaining within the bounds of conventional experience; we crave security, and the ordinary state of consciousness is where we tend to find it. Conversely, drifting into altered states may be discouraged by feelings of fear or discomfort. Finally, we may guard our ordinary awareness by preventing potentially disrupting processes from exceeding certain limits—for instance, we may take tranquilizers to dampen our excitement, lest the extreme arousal jolt us into the unpleasant altered state called a panic attack.

Moving from the ordinary state into an altered state thus requires that these stabilizing functions be weakened. Humanity has developed an immense technology of induction methods. Ludwig described five kinds of factors that are widely used to undermine normal awareness: reducing stimulation, as in SENSORY DEPRIVATION or VISION QUESTs in isolated places; increasing stimulation, including dancing, drumming and various forms of RHYTHMIC SENSORY STIMULATION; focused attention and hyperalertness, as in concentrative MEDITATION; lowered alertness, as in the states bordering sleep and some forms of HYPNOSIS; and psychophysical factors such as stress and drugs.

Once the stabilizing forces of ordinary awareness are disrupted, consciousness remains in flux until it is anchored again, either via a return to the normal state or in an altered state. Often, this patterning involves the person's expectations and beliefs regarding the nature of the altered state. If the nonconsensual reality experienced following an ecstatic dance is thought to be the abode of devils, then the person may well feel as if he or she has encountered some. Or, if the dancer expects a divine visitation after the dance, a very different altered state will likely happen.

Modern Western culture holds that the ordinary state is superior to all others for most purposes. Our society does not formally utilize altered states to acquire knowledge or powers that are not available to normal consciousness. This devaluation of altered states is not typical among human societies. In most cultures altered states are routinely harnessed, either by specialists or by others, for the benefit of the community. Tart has argued that the modern habit of judging altered states against the standards of the ordinary state may blind us to the potential value of altered states. Contemporary science has mostly been conducted by individuals in the ordinary waking state. The result has been a vast accumulation of knowledge about the universe as it is experienced in the ordinary state. Perhaps there are features of reality that are not detectable by scientists in the normal state. Tart has called for the development of state specific sciences; in order to determine the possibilities available in a particular state, researchers should enter the state to conduct observations and experiments. To date, there has been little response to Tart's idea.

See also ECSTASY; ENSTASY; TRANCE.

For further reading: Bourguinon; Ludwig; Tart (1969, 1975).

ambiguity We do not perceive the objects around us directly; rather, we create perceptions from the information that reaches our sense organs. When inadequate information reaches the senses to identify the object with certainty, it is known as an ambiguous stimulus. The human mind is driven to extract as much meaning as possible from incoming sensory information. When the nature of the stimulus is vague, we are likely to mistake our expectations about the object for the object itself.

Thus, ambiguity is a prime condition for the occurrence of ILLUSIONs—the perceiving of something as other than what it is. A muffled sound may be heard as a voice; a flash of light in the sky may be seen as a spacecraft. The shapes of water stains, ink blots and clouds are ambiguous because they are meaningless; in these cases, the mind's "drive to meaning" can create illusory objects, called PAREIDOLIA, where none exist.

Individuals differ in their reactions to ambiguity. Some people are uncomfortable with ambiguous stimuli and tend either to ignore them or to jump to a conclusion about their identity. Others are more tolerant of ambiguity and may be more willing to explore the nature of the stimulus, or to wait for the stimulus to present itself more clearly. Some studies have found that people who report MYSTICAL EXPERIENCEs tend to have higher tolerance for ambiguity than nonmystical experients.

See also Appendix; EXPERIENCE, UNUSUAL.

For further reading: Hood, Hall, Watson, and Biderman.

amnesia Amnesia is the inability to retrieve information from memory. There are several varieties. *Localized* amnesia involves forgetting everything from a particular time period; in *selective* amnesia, only certain details from the period cannot be recalled. The inability to remember events immediately prior to *a point in time* is *retrograde* amnesia; forgetfulness concerning what happened after a specific moment is the *anterograde* variant. In some instances, anterograde memory failure persists from its onset to the present time, in which case it is called *continuous* amnesia. In *source* amnesia, one can remember something, but cannot recall how the information was learned. Everyone has *infantile* amnesia—the inability to remember one's experiences during the first three years of life. *Psychogenic* amnesia is forgetfulness for psychological reasons. Complete failure to remember anything is known as *generalized* amnesia.

Amnesia can be caused by the disruption or immaturity of the brain mechanisms that store and retrieve memories. We cannot remember our infancy because the young nervous system had not yet developed enough connections for adequate memory processing. Brain diseases, head injuries or alcoholism can interfere with the physical basis of memory. Most people who become permanently amnesic following head injury have been damaged in the hippocampus, a central brain structure that transfers newly learned information into long term memory storage. They can recall their lives prior to the injury, but have continuous amnesia for subsequent events. Damage to the hippocampus does not usually affect an amnesiac's ability to acquire new skills; he will not remember that he has the skill, however. Hippocampally damaged people wake up each morning believing that their injuries occurred the previous day.

People suffering from severe depression are sometimes treated with electroconvulsive therapy (ECT or "shock" treatment). The electric current that passes through the brain leaves the patient with retrograde amnesia for the three hours prior to treatment. Incidents of more serious memory loss following therapy sessions were more common in the past when the technology was cruder; today, such reports are rare.

Motivations affect what people retrieve from memory. Psychogenic amnesia is the extreme case in which one is motivated not to recall the memory at all. Highly hypnotizable subjects can have amnesia for hypnotic experiences; the motivation in such cases is to please the hypnotist, or to display their responsiveness to HYPNOSIS.

Recall can also be blocked if the memory poses a threat to a person's self esteem or beliefs about reality. In cases of post-traumatic stress disorder, people who have endured a horrifying experience might be overwhelmed by a vivid memory of the event; they may protect themselves with localized or selective amnesia. Amnesia can also figure in MULTIPLE PERSONALITY DISORDER. The sufferer normally cannot remember his or her actions when they are behaving as alternate personalities.

When confronted by a gap in memory, the mind tends to fill in the space with fantasies masquerading as recollections, called false memories. This confusion of memory and nonmemory happens in both biologically based and psychogenic amnesias. Severe alcoholics can sink into a brain damaged condition known as Korsakoff's psychosis, characterized by memory deficits. Korsakoff's sufferers are notorious for confabulating a life story to replace the one they have forgotten. People with FUGUE, a psychogenic condition, forget their identities, but quickly replace them with invented ones.

See also CRYPTOMNESIA.

For further reading: American Psychiatric Association; Ashcroft; Baddeley.

anandamaya This term refers to a state of consciousness characterized by intense feelings of bliss (Sanskrit *ananda*). Anandamaya is first mentioned in the Upanishads, the ancient Hindu mystical writings. The condition occurs during wakefulness, but differs from other waking states in two ways: In anandamaya, awareness is very clear, and the feeling is consistently blissful; in normal wakefulness, the clarity of awareness is middling, and the feeling tone is highly variable, ranging from joy to the depths of despair.

Anandamaya can occur spontaneously. These sudden eruptions of inexplicable bliss are usually brief. They provide the ordinary suffering mind with a taste of other conscious states, attainable through meditation, in which bliss can be more consistently established.

In some Hindu schools the anandamaya experience is regarded as awareness of one of the bodies that clothe the self. Five such bodies are noted, corresponding to five types of bodily awareness. The "body of food" is the coarse structure experienced by everyone. Interwoven with it are bodies of life force, mind and awareness. The *anandamayakosha* ("sheath composed of bliss") is the most spiritual form housing the self, and it interpenetrates the other four, less refined, envelopes.

See also TURIYA.

For further reading: Feuerstein (1989, 1990); Friedrichs.

ananda-samapatti "Merging with bliss," a state of concentrated awareness discussed in the literature of RAJA YOGA. It is a type of SAMPRAJNATA SAMADHI.

angel hair Mysterious material that falls from the sky has traditionally been ascribed a divine origin. Not surprisingly, then, when that material consists of threads and tangles of white filament it has most commonly been dubbed "angel hair." The supernatural aura surrounding these substances is increased by one of their most commonly reported properties—angel hair tends to disappear when handled and vanishes even after being scooped into containers. Falls of angel hair have been sighted around the world; the greatest number of reports have come from the U.S.A., western Europe, eastern Australia and New Zealand. Frequently, falls of angel hair have occurred in conjunction with UFO ENCOUNTERs.

Stories of angel hair most likely originate in the activities of spiders. Charles Darwin observed a shower of gossamer threads on the deck of the *Beagle,* while that ship was traveling off the coast of South America. He noticed that the threads were occupied by spiders so tiny that they were scarcely visible to the eye. As he watched, the small travelers spun new webs with which to catch the breeze. Since Darwin's report, biologists have confirmed that certain types of spiders migrate through the air, sometimes in vast numbers, on cobweb gliders. The threads are so delicate that they tend to dissolve upon handling or shaking, leaving no easily detectable trace.

Many of the UFOs spotted in conjunction with angel hair were probably cobweb balls. An eyewitness report from Ontario in 1948 (quoted in Corliss, 1983b) describes the spectacle presented by windblown tangles of cobweb reflecting bright sunlight:

> This day was warm and the sky cloudless. We had had dinner in the garden and I was lying on my back on the lawn . . . when I was startled to see an object resembling a star moving rapidly across the sky . . . At first it was easy to imagine that recent reports of 'flying saucers' had not been exaggerated. More of these objects came sailing into view over the ridge of the house, only to disappear when nearly overhead. With field glasses I was able to see that each was approximately spherical, the centre being rather brighter than the edges. . . . Also visible every now and then were long threads . . . Some of these were seen to reflect the light over a length of three or four yards, but any one piece may of course have been longer. . . . In one case an elongated tangled mass of these gave the appearance of a frayed silken cord.

Not all instances of angel hair are produced by spiders. In several cases, a more enduring type of filamentous substance has apparently tumbled from the sky, and has been subjected to laboratory analysis. Sachs reported that "angels' hair contains boron, silicon, calcium and magnesium. It is similar in composition to borosilicate glass." The aerial source of such material remains uncertain.

See also FAFROTSKIES.

For further reading: Corliss (1977, 1983b); M. Sachs.

anomalistic psychology　This term was coined by Zusne and Jones: "Anomalistic psychology . . . deals with phenomena of behavior and experience that have been explained in paranormal, supernatural, occult, in short, magical terms." This branch of psychology does not itself use such explanations; rather, it studies phenomena that have received such interpretations by others. All experiences, whether ordinary or unusual, involve basic psychological processes like perception, thinking, believing, arousal and memory. Anomalistic psychologists examine the roles played by these processes in events that are often labeled paranormal—that is, pointing to a reality beyond the mainstream world view.

For instance, apparitions have traditionally been understood as manifestations of the spirit world, a concept that is no longer part of the conventional Western reality. Anomalistic psychologists examine how factors such as ENTOPTIC PHENOMENON, HALLUCINATION and ILLUSION might be mistaken for a ghost.

Anomalistic psychology must be distinguished from another division of psychology, abnormal psychology. The latter field studies the causes and treatment of mental disorders. While paranormal experiences may sometimes be caused by mental illness, they are also had by many people who are not mentally disturbed.

Anomalistic psychology does not in principle rule out the possibility that some unusual experiences may be caused by a paranormal factor; but many anomalistic psychologists seem to be convinced nonbelievers in the paranormal.

For further reading: Neher (1990); Reed (1988); Zusne and Jones.

anomalous belief　Belief in concepts or phenomena that are not accepted by the cultural mainstream is known as anomalous or unconventional belief. In modern Western society, belief in phenomena like ESP, ghosts, alien spacecraft, past lives, and extraordinary life forms such as Bigfoot are classed as unconventional, though not uncommon. Where these ideas originate, how people maintain them in the face of social pressures to replace them with more broadly acceptable views and why they are sometimes discarded have been the subjects of debate for many years. There is also a small body of research addressing the correlates of anomalous belief.

Any belief, conventional or anomalous, is acquired because it fulfills a need of the believer. One of people's deepest needs is to be able to comprehend the world; without the ability to make sense of our experiences, humans are disoriented and helpless. Newborns are thus powerfully motivated to embrace the model of reality taught to them by their first teachers, usually their parents. Adopting the beliefs of one's parents is usually rewarded by their approval and by an increased ability to communicate with them. Anomalous beliefs are prevalent in every culture, so the family must be a major site for the transmission of these beliefs to new generations.

Schumaker suggested that the need served by paranormal beliefs is so basic that our species is genetically predisposed to have these beliefs. The human brain gives us an awareness of the world that has led to great success for our species, at least for now. But this awareness comes with a price—the knowledge of unavoidable human mortality. The prospect of death is so terrifying that, without protection from the knowledge of its certainty, people would be unable to function. The brain has therefore been programmed to adopt beliefs that camouflage the ugly fact. Any concepts that involve spiritual dimensions of the self, or the presence of nonphysical powers in the world, are acceptable because they imply that people may be more than animals destined shortly to become worm fodder. The nervous system rewards us for embracing such ideas by secreting a pleasure-inducing dose of endorphins every time a person thinks positively about the paranormal, Schumaker speculates. He rejects the possibility that paranormal beliefs could be true, but regards them as essential for mental health: "Without 'crazy' belief systems we would have become insane and, in all probability, extinct."

Many writers have suggested that paranormal beliefs, especially those involving unusual personal powers or helpful supernatural entities, would hold special appeal for the sectors of society that have little real power. Some evidence supports the view that religion, astrology and superstition are more strongly endorsed by members of lower social classes, but paranormal beliefs in general do not appear to cluster in any segment of society.

Another reason for adopting a paranormal belief is an experience that seems to be best explained by an anomalous concept. A dream that later comes true in every detail does not seem to be a coincidence, but an act of foretelling the future; if one believes in life after death, it is easy to interpret an apparition of a recently departed relative as a visit from their spirit. Individuals who have anomalous experiences are more likely to hold anomalous beliefs. Many of the factors associated with a tendency to have unusual experiences, such as FANTASY PRONENESS and SENSATION SEEKING, are also correlates of unconventional beliefs.

Many disbelievers in the paranormal feel that something must be wrong with those who disagree with them—that anomalous believers must have some kind of deficiency to believe in the "impossible." Some skeptics have viewed the alleged problem as simply one of ignorance: Believers suffer from a lack of good education and simply do not know any better. Research into the relationship between anomalous belief and factors like academic achievement, attainment and level of science education have not clearly supported this contention. Other disbelievers have suggested that believers have low intelligence or lack reasoning skills; again, research has not provided much support for this view.

It has also been suggested that anomalous belief is a sign of mental illness. In some cases, this is certainly so—sufferers of SCHIZOPHRENIA,

for instance, often have DELUSIONS. Studies of the normal population have often found that people suffering from problems of PSYCHOLOGICAL ADJUSTMENT report higher levels of anomalous belief. Paranormal beliefs may serve a special need for some people who are struggling to meet the challenges of living. It is not the case, however, that anomalous beliefs are usually connected with psychological disorders.

Irwin's model for the acquisition of paranormal belief integrates many of the research findings on this topic. He notes that paranormal beliefs can help to create a sense of control over one's life. People who have experienced CHILDHOOD TRAUMA are likely to have high CONTROL NEEDS; they also tend to have fantasy-prone personalities, developed as a means to escape the unpleasantness of their early environment. The greater attunement of fantasy-prone people to their inner lives makes them more likely to have unusual experiences, and to interpret them in anomalous terms. The ideas already available in one's social and cultural environment determine the specific form of the paranormal beliefs, according to Irwin's model.

Beliefs do not exist in isolation, but tend to be part of a consistent view of the world. This world view guides perception and memory, and we usually notice and remember things in accordance with our expectations. If a person's world view contains anomalous beliefs, they will be biased to have experiences that confirm the validity of those beliefs. Belonging to a group or community that espouses anomalous views will strengthen this bias. And, if the belief works—that is, if it successfully meets a person's need for feelings of meaningfulness and control—his or her conviction that the belief is a true one will deepen.

Once a belief is established it resists change, even when challenged by the evidence. Anomalous beliefs are no exception. When a magic trick is performed in front of an audience, it is usual that some audience members will continue to believe that they witnessed a paranormal event, even after the trick has been revealed. Even Houdini, an inveterate debunker of paranormal claims, was suspected by some of secretly using psychic powers in his awesome performances. Zusne and Jones reported that many students who saw a simulated ESP demonstration in the classroom later refused to accept their professor's explanation of the hoax; one student suggested, "Maybe you have ESP but don't know it!" Whether paranormal beliefs are more resistant to change than other sorts of deeply held convictions is unknown.

Even though ingrained beliefs can persist when they have outlived their usefulness, they are not completely fixed. Sometimes beliefs change gradually, in the face of accumulating evidence to the contrary or shifting needs. Believers in anomalous concepts have been known to grow more skeptical over time, and skeptics less so. Under conditions when ordinary mental processes are disrupted, such as extreme stress, rapid alterations in belief can occur. This is the basis of religious conversion, as well as attempts at indoctrination or brainwashing. Dramatic anomalous occurences like OUT OF BODY EXPERIENCEs and especially NEAR DEATH EXPERIENCEs can cause a deep restructuring of world view.

See also Appendix; AGE; CREATIVITY; DEATH CONCERNS; DOGMATISM; DRUGS; GENDER; HYPNOTIZABILITY; LOCUS OF CONTROL; MAGICAL THINKING; NARCISSISM; RELIGIOSITY; SOCIAL INTEREST; TEMPORAL LOBE ABNORMALITY.

For further reading: Irwin (1993); Schumaker (1990); Zusne and Jones.

anomaly This word, and its adjectival forms "anomalous" and "anomalistic," is frequently used to describe the content of an unusual experience, yet it does not have a generally accepted definition. For some, an anomaly is merely an event or experience that lies outside the normal range. In this sense any departure from routine experience is an anomaly, including seeing comets and purple Volkswagens, as well as ghosts and UFOs.

Others take "anomaly" to be a synonym for paranormal—that is, referring to events that cannot be explained in terms of the prevailing model of reality. Statistically uncommon but explainable occurrences, like viewing a rare bird or being caught in a flood, are excluded from this definition, and phenomena such as communication with the dead and TELEPATHY are included.

According to a third definition, an anomaly is an event that is not yet explained in conventional terms. This type of anomaly may someday turn out to be caused by ordinary means, or it may not. At present, however, such anomalies are unsolved mysteries. Debate rages concerning which phenomena fall under this heading. Some believe that apparent instances of ESP are all explainable in terms of errors in perception, FALSE MEMORY, mental illness, flaws in experimental procedures and fraud; whereas others suggest that there remain a number of experimental findings that resist explanation in these terms.

See also PRETERNATURAL; SUPERNATURAL; SUPERNORMAL.

For further reading: Palmer (1986, 1992); Zusne and Jones.

apparition An apparition is a perception-like experience of a person (or sometimes an animal) that is not physically present. People in almost every culture and historical period have reported them. Perhaps the earliest mention of an apparition is found in the Babylonian tale, *Epic of Gilgamesh,* which is over 4,000 years old. The hero, Gilgamesh, encounters the phantom form of a departed friend. The Egyptians wrote of recurrent apparitions, or GHOSTs. The Greeks and Romans believed in two classes of apparitions, *lares* and *lemures*—good and bad souls, respectively.

The Bible contains references to apparitions. In the Old Testament, King Saul incites the Witch of Endor to evoke the spirit of Samuel;

and she observes that "An old man comes up; and he is covered with a mantle" (I Samuel 28:14). And, in the New Testament, the disciples mistake Jesus for an apparition both before (Matthew 14:26) and after (Luke 24:37) his resurrection. The fifth century Catholic leader St. Augustine wrote of apparitions. Thus, expectations concerning this type of experience were built into the foundations of Western culture.

Records of apparitions were scarce during the Dark Ages, but accounts reappeared in abundance in the later Middle Ages and have featured prominently in chronicles and folklore ever since. The possibility of fraud in apparition reports was demonstrated in a 16th century case noted by Erasmus (cited in Haining). An apparition appeared to a "rich woman, well monied and withall very covetous"; she responded by beating it with a stick until it cried for mercy. As it turns out, the "apparition" was an acquaintance who was rather "covetous" himself—he had donned a white sheet and made "certaine rumblings and noyses in the ayre," in an attempt to frighten the woman to death and steal her wealth.

Investigative research on apparition reports has been a central feature of PSYCHICAL RESEARCH since its inception with the work of Joseph Glanville in the 17th century. The first major project undertaken by the Society for Psychical Research after its founding in 1882 was the *Census of Hallucinations,* a collection and analysis of apparition accounts.

Over the past 20 years, surveys have shown that people continue to believe in, and to experience, apparitional phenomena. The highest rate of apparitional experiences was reported in Canada; a survey of Canadians by Persinger found that 32% of respondents admitted to having seen an apparition. The 1990 Gallup poll on paranormal phenomena estimated that one quarter of Americans believe in ghosts and 9% have seen them.

Tyrrell suggested four main categories of apparitions. *Crisis* apparitions are those that appear around the time of a crisis in a person's life—typically, the crisis is death. For research purposes, an apparition is placed in this class if it occurs within 12 hours prior to or following a death. Traditionally, an apparition at the moment of death is called a wraith. The *post-mortem* apparition is one that appears later than 12 hours following a death. This is probably the most commonly reported type. A recurrent apparition is a ghost; a series of ghostly appearances is known as a HAUNTING. The least common type are the *experimental* apparitions, in which people deliberately try to make apparitions of themselves appear to others. Other kinds of apparitions include depictions of animals, objects (such as "phantom ships"), the witnesses themselves (the DOPPELGANGER) and visions of religious figures. Historically, the most important phenomena in this residual category are the MARIAN APPARITIONs.

Since the *Census of Hallucinations,* several other case collections and surveys of apparitions have been compiled. The common characteristics of apparitional experiences were summarized by Irwin. Most apparitions first appear as complete forms, usually indoors. Contrary to most fictional portrayals, the average apparition is described as appearing real and solid. Some cast shadows and are reflected in mirrors; they tend to display different surfaces when viewed from various angles, just like a three-dimensional object. Most apparitions seem to be aware of their surroundings, with the exception of ghosts; the typical ghost acts out the same behavior each time it is seen, like a character in a repeating film loop. Apparitional experiences end in a variety of ways: The form may vanish suddenly; it may disappear one part at a time; or, it may leave the setting, usually via a door rather than through a wall.

About 80% of reported apparitions last less than five minutes; half endure less than 60 seconds. Most are strictly visual experiences, although about a third also have an auditory feature, such as the rustling of phantom clothing or, rarely, a voice. About 12% of apparition cases involve more than one witness. Up to eight simultaneous observers have been reported; if religious visions are included, some of these spectacles have been attested by tens of thousands at a time. In multiple witness cases, it is common that not everyone present perceives the apparition.

Apparitions do not seem to affect their physical environment. When they are seen to move an object or open a door, these actions are later found to have been part of the apparitional experience—the object or door remains as it was prior to the apparition. There are no authenticated cases of apparitions leaving footprints or being photographed. Witnesses who try to touch an apparition normally report that their hand passes through the image, although sensations of cold are sometimes noted.

Several studies have examined the characteristics of people who experience apparitions. Most are healthy at the time of the experience and are apparently in relatively low states of EMOTIONAL AROUSAL. They are more likely to be female. Two closely related personality features have been found to correlate positively with reporting apparitions: the need for ABSORPTION and FANTASY PRONENESS.

Several theories have been offered to explain apparitions, none of which are fully satisfactory. The most popular explanation is that apparitions are the spirits of the represented beings. This notion may at least be conceivable to people who believe in survival after death, with respect to many crisis and post-mortem apparitions. But what about the clothing worn by apparitions? Do garments have souls? And what about phantom animals, objects and apparitions of the living?

Many scientists dismiss apparitions as merely a type of hallucination, a mental image mistakenly thought to be a perception of an external object. At least some apparitions are hallucinations. But apparitions have features that are very uncommon in hallucinations: Apparitions sometimes convey information that was apparently unknown to the witness. For instance, crisis apparitions have been said to signify the unexpected deaths of the people represented; unlike most hallucinations, apparitions often depict people who are known to the witness; and multiple witness apparitions seem to be more common than mass hallucinations.

If apparitions are falsely interpreted mental images, one might predict that people who witness apparitions would have some differences in their mental imagery compared to non-experients. Campbell (cited in Irwin) queried apparition experients and nonexperients with respect to the vividness of their everyday mental imagery and found that the experients rated their imagery as significantly *less* vivid. Irwin speculated that the experients were sensitive to the possibility that their apparitions could be dismissed as mental images, and so deliberately reported less vivid daily imagery. Another explanation for Campbell's findings could be that the experients and nonexperients differed in their ability to recognize mental imagery. The nonexperients might have identified all imaginings, whether dull or vivid, as mental images. Perhaps the experients only recognized less vivid images as mental phenomena; they might have placed more vivid imaginings in a different category—that of apparitions.

Cases in which apparitions convey information (known as veridical hallucinations) are challenging to the hallucination theory, although in some cases the correspondence between an apparition and a distant event (such as a death) could be coincidental. In others, the apparition witness might have noticed some clues to an impending crisis (for instance, observing a bout of clumsiness in someone about to embark on a long drive), unconsciously drew inferences from these clues (the driver may be at risk because of her clumsiness) and then later presented the results of this unconscious reasoning to their conscious mind via a hallucination (a vivid image of the driver having an accident).

Researchers who are not satisfied with such prosaic explanations, but who do not endorse the spirit explanations either, have advanced the idea that some apparitions may be manifestations of ESP. In this view, the source of the apparition may not be the person depicted, but the psychic abilities of the witness. The information that is conveyed in an apparition is acquired unconsciously by a witness, using ESP. If there are multiple witnesses, the knowledge is shared via telepathy. Then the unconscious minds of the witnesses, acting collectively, compose a hallucinatory drama that is presented to the group. Some psychical research organizations have tried deliberately to create such "telepathic collective hallucinations," without success.

See also Appendix; METACHORIC EXPERIENCE; SENSORY DEPRIVATION.

For further reading: Gallup and Newport; C. Green; Haining; Irwin (1989); Owen and Sparrow; Persinger (1974); Tyrrell.

asamprajnata samadhi   This Sanskrit term refers to states of consciousness in which the awareness of objects is transcended. In Raja Yoga meditators attempt to ascend the scale of concentrative states. In the lower states, the SAMPRAJNATA SAMADHIS, meditators train their attention upon specific objects. When concentration has attained sufficient strength, this practice triggers the experience of VIVEKA-KHYATI, a vision in which the true nature of the Self is clearly distinguished from everything else. Practitioners can then enter the asamprajnata states, where the focus of concentration rests on this Self. The result is said to be the achievement of KAIVALYA, the supreme realization according to Raja Yoga.

While rising through the lower samadhis, various mental functions are eliminated, and their energy harnessed to sharpen concentration. In the asamprajnata states, all mental functioning has been pacified, all sense of a distinction between objects and Self is erased. However, the "seeds" of activity—habits and reflexes established in the past—remain. These old tendencies constantly stir the quiet mind back into action; thus, at first asamprajnata samadhi is unstable and can be maintained only momentarily.

With practice, the meditator learns to hold this highly refined state for longer periods. During these times, the old mental habits are deprived of energy and gradually die out, like plant seeds that receive no water. The mind now enters an utterly undisturbed state, the DHARMA-MEGHA SAMADHI or concentrated state of the "virtue cloud." Awareness is showered with virtue as it approaches its complete freedom from the vicissitudes of the mind—the state of kaivalya.

For further reading: Feuerstein (1989, 1990); Friedrichs.

asmita-samapatti   "Merging with the feeling of 'I am,'" a concentrative state identified by the RAJA YOGA school as a type of SAMPRAJNATA SAMADHI.

astral projection   An occult term referring to the OUT OF BODY EXPERIENCE. Believing that these experiences are caused by the soul or spirit departing from the body, occultists have developed many exercises to induce them. Astral projection practices differ in the details, but most of them consist basically of three elements: developing the confidence that one can do it; deeply relaxing the muscles, or otherwise focussing the attention away from ordinary bodily sensations; and visualizing the launching of consciousness out of the body, typically into an "astral body."

auditory driving   For many thousands of years, humans have employed rhythmic sounds, such as drum beats, in ceremonies designed to elicit unusual experiences. The writer Aldous Huxley, in quaint but vivid language, observed:

No man, however highly civilized, can listen for very long to African drumming, or Indian chanting, or Welsh hymn-singing, and retain intact his critical and self conscious personality . . . if exposed long enough to the tom-toms and the singing, every one of our philosophers would end by capering and howling with the savages.

The power of sound in banishing our ordinary sense of reality is based on a direct impact of auditory stimulation on the human nervous system. This effect is known as auditory driving.

The electrical activity of the neurons in the brain tends to be rhythmic, as revealed by the wavelike patterns of EEG tracings. This natural pattern of activity is susceptible to influence by rhythmic sensory input; brain cells tend to fire in synchrony with repetitive sounds.

Walter and Walter, in their early work on the related phenomenon of PHOTIC DRIVING, speculated that brain activity could also be driven by the rhythmic "sound such as that produced by an untuned percussion instrument or an explosion." Neher exposed subjects to rhythmic drumming sounds, while monitoring their EEG activity. He found that the neural firing of every subject conformed itself to the frequency of the drumming. Also, the subjects reported shifts in awareness, characterized by "fear, astonishment, amusement, back pulsing, muscle tightening, stiffness in chest, tone in background, humming, rattling, visual and auditory imagery." The visual imagery often took the form of the luminous geometric structures called FORM CONSTANTS. Evidently, the rhythmic sensory stimulation was disrupting the normal functioning of the brain, causing unusual experiences. Neher stated that the effect was heightened by simultaneous rhythmic input from other senses, such as touch, as well as increased stress and hyperventilation.

Interpretation of the strange sensations caused by auditory driving is shaped by one's beliefs and expectations. If the effects are produced in a religious setting, such as a drumming ceremony, they will probably be regarded as signs of contact with a spiritual reality. With the ordinary sense of self unanchored, a person would be more subject to the influence of the context within which the experience occurs; at the extreme, POSSESSION could result. Such was the case with the filmmaker Maya Deren. While making a documentary on the Haitian religion of voodoo, she was exposed for hours to the rhythmic sounds of a Voodoo ceremony and succumbed to the power of the drums:

> Resting . . . I felt a strange numbness . . . I say numbness, but that is inaccurate . . . To be precise I must call it a white darkness, its whiteness a glory and its darkness terror. It is the terror which has the greater force . . . The white darkness starts to shoot up . . . My skull is a drum . . . This sound will drown me . . . the white darkness moves up the veins of my leg like a swift tide rising, rising; is a great force which I cannot sustain or contain, which, surely, will burst my skin. It is too much, too bright, too white for me; this is its darkness. "Mercy!" I scream within me. I hear it echoed by the voices, shrill and unearthly: "Erzulie". The bright darkness floods up through my body, reaches my head, engulfs me. I am sucked down and exploded upward at once. That is all.

Deren behaved as if she were possessed by the voodoo goddess Erzulie. Later, she had no recollection of her possessed behavior.

For further reading: Deren; Huxley; Neher (1961, 1962); Walter and Walter.

auditory hallucination Ordinary hearing begins with waves of air pressure shaking delicate bones within the ear; the vibrations of these bones, in turn, trigger impulses which are transmitted via the auditory nerve to the brain regions that create the experience of sound. When people hear sounds in the absence of this process, they are said to have auditory hallucinations; or, in common parlance, they are "hearing things."

Contrary to widespread belief, auditory hallucinations are not experienced only by the mentally disturbed. Hearing the voice or footsteps of a deceased loved one is a quite common part of the grief reaction of bereaved persons. (Most people do not mistake these sensations for actual sounds; thus, the experiences are technically pseudohallucinations). Posey and Losch reported that 71% of surveyed college students admitted to occasional auditory hallucinations, primarily voices. Five percent had carried on conversations with the voices. False sounds are commonly heard by consumers of hallucinogenic drugs, as well as those undergoing withdrawal from addictive substances.

Auditory hallucinations can originate inside or outside of the head. The distinction between hallucinations, INNER VOICEs and merely thinking in words cannot always be drawn precisely; hallucinations can be said to have a more soundlike quality than inner voices, and are more soundlike and less voluntary than deliberate thoughts. Inner voices may be somewhat more soundlike, and are less under voluntary control, than deliberately generated verbal thoughts.

A sizable portion of the population can experience vivid auditory images of nearly hallucinatory intensity in response to suggestion. Barber and Calverly asked their experimental subjects (secretarial students) to imagine a phonograph playing a recording of the song "White Christmas"; 49% reported that they clearly heard the music; 5% said they believed the record was actually being played. These findings have been successfully replicated several times, with different groups of normal subjects.

In the beliefs of laypersons and many mental health professionals, auditory hallucinations are closely identified with SCHIZOPHRENIA. Most studies of schizophrenic symptoms have reported that "hearing voices" is the most common hallucinatory experience of schizophrenics. But a study by Goodwin, Alderson and Rosenthal found that auditory hallucinations are no more frequent among schizophrenics than they are among alcoholics or sufferers of emotional disturbances such as depression and anxiety disorder. Both schizophrenics and alcoholics—especially sufferers of ALCOHOLIC HALLUCINOSIS—are prone to "command hallu-

cinations," voices ordering them to commit hostile or bizarre actions.

In at least some cases, hallucinated voices seem to originate in the larynx. Several studies have found that schizophrenic hallucinations are often accompanied by "subvocal speech": the activation of the hallucinator's vocal apparatus. Electrical monitoring revealed that the words heard by the hallucinators were actually being resonated inaudibly in the larynx. Seemingly, the hallucinators were hearing their own subvocalizations and mistaking them for independent voices. Attempts to combat auditory hallucinations by disrupting subvocal speech—through humming, singing, gargling or opening the mouth wide—have shown some success.

The seriousness with which psychiatrists take reports of auditory hallucinations was highlighted in a classic study by Rosenhan. He instructed his assistants (none of whom were suffering from a mental disorder) to present themselves at the admitting units of local psychiatric hospitals, complaining of a single symptom: hearing voices saying words like "empty" or "hollow." Most were admitted as patients; they were diagnosed as schizophrenic. From then on, they denied any symptoms and acted normally. Based solely on their report at intake, these "pseudopatients" were held in psychiatric wards an average of 19 days before they were discharged; one was confined for 52 days. The supervising psychiatrists released their patients not because they were felt to be cured; they were, it was thought, temporarily "in remission." In the face of such strong professional reaction to reports of auditory hallucinations, it is no wonder that very few nondisturbed people ever admit publicly to "hearing things."

See also ALCOHOL HALLUCINOSIS; CLAIRAUDIENCE; IMAGINARY COMPANION.

For further reading: Barber and Calverly; Goodwin, Alderson and Rosenthal; Posey and Losch; Rosenhan.

aura   Perceiving luminous envelopes surrounding objects, creatures or especially human beings seems to be a primordial and universal experience. In the rocky massifs of the Sahara Desert, paintings dating to the ninth millennium B.C. depict human forms apparently ringed with light. Throughout the ancient world, halos were included in portrayals of gods and sanctified people. While these renderings were likely artistic conventions, they probably arose from experiences of seeing auras, which continue to be reported today.

The annals of the Catholic church contain many eyewitness descriptions of strange luminosities, generally associated with great piety. Pope Benedict XIV, in his discussion of CHARISMS or phenomena that may be indicative of sanctity (quoted in Murphy), described these reports as follows:

> It seems to be a fact that there are natural flames which at times visibly encircle the human head, and also that from a man's whole person fire may on occasion radiate naturally, not, however, like a flame which streams upwards, but rather in the form of sparks which are given off all round; further, that some people become resplendent with a blaze of light, though this is not inherent in themselves, but attaches rather to their clothes, or the staff or to the spear which they are carrying.

Thurston collected accounts of auras from the Catholic literature:

> we read of the fourteenth-century Carthusian, John Tornerius, then at the Grande Chartreuse near Grenoble, that when he did not arrive in time to celebrate his first Mass, the sacristan went to this cell to fetch him, and found that the little room was radiant with light which seemed to be diffused all round the good Father. Similarly, in the process of beatification of the Franciscan Observant, Blessed Thomas da Cori, witnesses stated that the whole church on a dark morning was lit up by the radiance which glowed in the Father's countenance. Further, we learn from what is seemingly the earliest

account preserved to us of Blessed Giles of Assisi, that in the night time on one occasion 'so great a light shone round him that the light of the moon was wholly eclipsed thereby.' So again, that the house of Blessed Aleidis of Scarbeke seemed to be on fire when she, with a radiant countenance, was praying within.

This excerpt comprises a very small sample of the aura reports from orthodox Christian sources. Allowing for the exaggerating effects of memory and political utility, the sheer bulk of such accounts suggests an experiential core involving the perception of luminosity around revered people.

Auras have not historically been restricted to holy people, however; the occult tradition also mentions the phenomenon. The 16th century occultist Paracelsus stated that each person has an aura, which he described as a "fiery globe." And Emanuel Swedenborg, a visionary of the 18th century, similarly observed a "spiritual sphere" encompassing every individual. By the late 19th century, aura viewing had become a standard exercise of western occultists.

The modern literature on auras is immense. The aura is usually interpreted in occult terms, as the perception of a nonmaterial or subtle material body that displays the subjective states of a person more clearly than does the coarse body. Reviews of descriptions of the aura's characteristics and meanings have found little consistency. Auras can range from pale shimmerings floating just above the skin to multicolored coronas extending for several feet. There seem to be as many systems claiming to match aura colors with states of mind or health as there are interpreters of auras.

Exercises for the development of aura viewing ability have also been published. For the most part, these practices suggest one of the two approaches: observing a person under conditions of high contrast, such as a silhouette against a bright background; or, conversely, under circumstances of low contrast, such as a dimly lit room, in which perception of a person's boundaries may be ambiguous.

Many attempts have been made to understand the aura in terms of physical science. Baron Karl von Reichenbach, in the mid-19th century, observed colored light emissions from animals, plants and inanimate objects when he viewed them in darkened rooms. He proposed a previously unknown form of physical energy, the Odic Force, as the explanation. Similarly, Blondlot reported in 1903 that a variety of metals glowed faintly in the dark, and concluded that they were emitting "N rays," analogous to the recently discovered X rays. Almost 100 scientific papers were published confirming Blondlot's initial observations. In the case of both Odic Force and N rays, however, there proved to be no detectable external phenomenon producing the experiences. Most researchers eventually concluded that von Reichenbach and Blondlot had misinterpreted their own mental images to be physical luminosity.

In 1911, Kilner reported that a person's "etheric body" could be rendered visible by looking at the individual through a filter of coal tar dye. A faint cloud does seem to surround a body when viewed in this fashion. However, most researchers regard the cloud as a simple optical effect produced by the filter, rather than a revelation of an unknown energy.

Rochas d'Aiglun reported in 1899 that when a high voltage, high frequency electric current is passed through an object, photographic paper placed adjacent to the object will depict a spectacular pattern of discharge surrounding it. This photographic effect was rediscovered by Kirlian in 1939; hence the currently popular name for it, "Kirlian photography." Any object, when placed in the Kirlian apparatus, will display the characteristic luminous rim—coins, leaves or hands. Since the 1970s, many writers have claimed that the Kirlian pictures make visible to everyone the auras perceived by clairvoyants and others. However, there is no evidence to link the Kirlian phenomenon with the experience of aura

viewing. The Kirlian effect is produced by the ionization of the gases surrounding the object through which the current is passing, and such conditions are very rarely found in the world of human life. Contrary to early reports, the size and colors of the Kirlian image do not correspond to emotional states, health conditions or acts of "psychic healing"; rather, the most important variable determining the image is the amount of moisture on the object's surface.

If there is a visible radiation surrounding the human body, then it should still be visible when the body itself is obscured by a barrier, in the same manner that the solar corona is visible when the sun's body is eclipsed by the moon. Thus reasoned Charles Tart, who in 1972 proposed a "doorway test" for the physical reality of auras. Someone with the ability to see auras should be able to detect whether or not a person is standing concealed next to an opening such as a doorway; the aura should protrude into the viewer's line of sight. Obviously, all sensory cues otherwise revealing the person's presence must be eliminated in order to attribute successful detection to perception of the aura. To date, there have been no reports that an aura viewer has consistently been able to pass Tart's doorway test.

Psychologists have suggested that many aura viewing experiences are caused by properties of the human visual system itself. The appearance of "thin" auras—those seen close to a person's surface—could be produced by afterimages. If a light source is removed after stimulating the retina for a period of time, the observer sees an afterimage, or trace, which briefly persists. The afterimage appears in the complementary color to the color of the stimulus (e.g., a green stimulus leaves a red afterimage, and vice versa). Because the eyes are constantly moving slightly, when we try to fix our gaze on something we can soon notice a shimmering smudge of afterimages surrounding the object. If we believe in the existence of an etheric body, we could interpret this effect as a glimpse of it.

Aura vision could also result from contrast effects. Cells in the retina, called bipolar cells, act to sharpen the boundaries of the objects we see. When light from a visual edge enters the eye, these cells cause the bright region adjacent to the boundary to appear slightly brighter, and the dark region next to the boundary to appear slightly darker than the surrounding areas. These bands of enhanced brightness and darkness that highlight contours are sometimes called Mach bands (after Ernst Mach, who described them). They are especially visible under conditions of high contrast, such as those sometimes recommended in aura viewing exercises. As in the case of afterimages, belief in the physical reality of auras could lead the viewer to interpret Mach bands as a glowing emanation from the observed object itself.

Neither afterimages nor contrast effects can explain reports of "thick" auras—those that seem to extend more than an inch or so from the surface of the body. In such cases, it could be that a confusion of mental imagery with perception—in other words, HALLUCINATION—could account for some instances. Little research into the psychological characteristics of people who see auras has been undertaken. Some studies have suggested that individuals who have a high capacity for HYPNOTIZABILITY are more likely to report seeing auras.

See also Appendix; EPILEPSY; MIGRAINE.

For further reading: Murphy; Tart (1972); Thurston; Watkins and Bickel.

aurora The aurora borealis and aurora australis, commonly known as the northern lights and southern lights, are thought to be produced by the collision of electrically charged particles moving through space with the upper atmosphere. The particles are jets of plasma ejected by the sun, particularly during periods of intense sunspot activity. The clustering of aurora activity around the polar regions is an effect of the earth's magnetic field.

Many people are familiar with the multicolored auroral displays—glowing arcs, rays, curtains, pillars, flames and coronas are commonly seen at night in the higher latitudes and, more rarely, closer to the equator. Less common variants of the aurora can easily be misinterpreted. On November 17, 1882, thousands witnessed a UFO over northern Europe. The object was described as shaped like a spindle, cigar or disc; some reported viewing an internal structure, while others saw only a glow. Astronomers confirmed that the spectacle was the northern lights.

Another auroral effect—the so-called auroral meteor—has likely produced other reports of UFO ENCOUNTERs. Probably caused by a gust of plasma grazing the outer surface of the atmosphere, these whitish ovals of light can take two minutes to transit the sky—far too quickly for a comet, and much too slowly for even the tardiest meteor.

Auroras occur high in the atmosphere; they are generally thought to be restricted to the layer between 60 and 600 miles above the planetary surface. Some reports suggest that auroral effects can, on occasion, reach down to the ground. Rarely, auroras have been seen to pass in front of distant geographic features, such as mountain ranges. Chapman (quoted in Corliss, 1982) described an apparent extension of an aurora overhead that engulfed observers at an Arctic radio station in 1917:

> [they] were enveloped in a light mist or fog-like substance in the aurora; a hand extended could be seen as if in a coloured fog and a kaleidoscope of colors was visible between the hand and the body. It was impossible to feel this visible fog or mist, and there was no dampness. By stooping close to the ground it was possible to see under this light which did not go below four feet from the ground.

Massive electromagnetic disturbances at high altitudes might be able to ionize air particles beneath them. Corliss suggested that aurora-like processes extending to the surface of the sea might explain some features of OCEAN LIGHTs.

For further reading: Corliss (1977, 1982); Menzel and Taves.

autokinetic effect   A kind of optical ILLUSION in which movement is falsely perceived in a stationary object or source of light.

When light enters the eye, the lens of the eye focuses the light into an image of the light source, projected onto the retina at the back of the eyeball. This image changes its position on the retina if either the object or the eyeball moves. Under ordinary viewing conditions, the brain has no trouble discerning which kind of movement has occurred: When the eyeball shifts position, all of the images on the retina move; but when an object moves, its retinal image changes location relative to those of adjacent objects. When there are no visible nearby features, however, the brain can make mistakes. If a point of light is observed in a completely darkened room, or in the night sky, for instance, the movements of the image across the retina produced by the eye's constant scanning motions can be misperceived as movements of the light source. This illusion is called the autokinetic effect.

Autokinesis is likely responsible for many reports of paranormal events. Bright stars or planets have been seen to dart about in the sky; observers have described aerial lights (which later proved to be airplane lights) that suddenly zigzagged or executed other maneuvers beyond the capacity of human technology. Such events have often been reported as UFO ENCOUNTERs.

Seances are traditionally conducted in total darkness. The spirits, it is said, are shy of light. These conditions are also conducive to the autokinetic effect. Various implements for ghostly use, such as fans or trumpets, are often placed on the table around which the participants sit. The objects may be tagged with luminous material so the sitters can detect whether the spirits move them in the dark. Frequently the tags are seen to move. Barring fraud or actual paranor-mal effects, autokinesis is probably responsible for such perceptions.

In 1985, reports out of Ballinspittle, Ireland, described a statue of the Virgin Mary that was seen to sway gently. Crowds of devotees and journalists witnessed the miracle. Even a team of scientists from University College, Cork, saw the statue move—but a videotape they made of the event showed only a motionless statue. Further investigation determined that the autokinetic effect was at play. The viewers themselves had been unconsciously swaying; as they gazed expectantly at the statue, they mistakenly attributed their own movement to it.

Psychologists have found that individuals differ in their propensity for the autokinetic effect. When experimental subjects are asked to view a point source of light in a darkened setting, some see only small movements, while others report motions of up to eight inches. Sherif, in a classic study, established that autokinesis is subject to group suggestion influences; when several subjects observed the light together, their estimates of the degree of movement tended to converge toward a single value. Later, when these subjects viewed the light individually, they continued to perceive the same amount of movement seen by the group. Sherif's research powerfully demonstrates that consensus cannot be relied upon to determine the objective reality of a witnessed phenomenon; multiple observers of an ambiguous stimulus are quite capable of erring together.

See also AUTOSTATIC EFFECT; GROUP DYNAMICS OF UNUSUAL EXPERIENCES.

For further reading: Neher (1990); Nickell; Sherif.

automatism   An automatism is a behavior that occurs without a feeling of having deliberately willed the act. The most common and mundane example of automatism is doodling while chatting on the telephone; the drawings seem to flow effortlessly from the pen, with minimal conscious involvement, and may contain elements that surprise the author. More dramatic are instances of so-called "automatic" writing. In these cases, the writing arm seems to have a will of its own as it writes and may express ideas and idioms that seem alien to the writer. Drawing and painting can also be executed "automatically." Automatic speaking is called GLOSSOLA-LIA, a common occurrence in certain religious and mediumistic settings.

The degree of conscious involvement in automatic behavior varies. Some automatists are unaware of their automatic acts; others sense that an automatism is happening, but do not know its content; and automatisms also occur in which the actor is aware of the content, but cannot predict what will emerge next. Automatisms can commence spontaneously, as in cases of POSSESSION, or they may be learned. The ability to relinquish control over limb or larynx, thus permitting the emergence of automatisms, is a cultivable skill.

Anyone who can write can also produce automatic writing, if they are able to enter the appropriate frame of mind. Some automatic writers, after picking up a pen, distract themselves by reading or watching television while the unattended hand writes by itself; others enter a light trance state, and imagine that their writing arm is no longer part of their body. Automatisms can often be produced using HYPNOSIS. First attempts at automatic writing often produce nothing or meaningless lines and repeated letters. With practice more elaborate expressions often develop. In some cases, automatic writing can be of greater literary merit than anything the writer could produce deliberately. (This technique was frequently employed by the French surrealists of the 1920s and 1930s.)

A popular extension of automatic writing is the use of the Ouija board. This device consists of a polished wooden board, displaying letters and numbers on its surface. A heart-shaped platform, mounted on three felt-tipped legs, is placed on the board. The platform, known as a planchette, bears a pointer. The Ouija board is normally operated by more than one person who rest their fingers lightly on the planchette. After a short period, the planchette usually begins to slide around on the board spelling out messages and answers to questions. The Ouija board (named for *oui* and *ja,* the French and German words for yes) was invented and patented in 1892 by an American inventor, Isaac Fuld. A variant of the Ouija board method employs a planchette mounted with a pen or pencil. Operators touch this device as it rests on paper, allowing it to trace out messages.

Given the alien quality of automatic writing, it is unsurprising that supernatural beings have been identified as the true authors, who have temporarily gained control of writers' arms.

The role of automatic writing in cultural history may be considerable. Many works that are traditionally held to have originated from spirits might have been produced by automatism. The original *Prajnaparamita,* or "Perfection of Wisdom" text, was one of the earliest works of the Mahayana branch of Buddhism. Its first century B.C. author, Nagarjuna, claimed that he retrieved the document from the land of the Nagas, or water spirits, where it had been stored since its original dictation by the Buddha centuries earlier. The Koran, Islam's sacred text, was conveyed to Mohammed by the angel Gabriel. It is plausible that these works could be mythologically clothed episodes of automatic writing.

In the 20th century, whole books have been produced automatically. These books tend to fall into two categories: historical novels, supposedly composed by the spirits of individuals who possess first-hand knowledge of the periods used as the novels' settings; and discourses on the nature of reality, usually referring to the existence of spiritual dimensions. The best known works of the first category were those of Pearl Curran, a Missouri homemaker who began to experiment with a Ouija board in 1913. The planchette spelled out messages from Patience Worth, allegedly a 17th century Englishwoman. Curran progressed from using the board to hearing Patience Worth in her head as an INNER

VOICE. Over the next 20 years, Curran received Worth's dictation of poems, novels and plays. Her first novel, *The Sorry Tale,* was 325,000 words long; its authorship was attributed to Patience Worth. The book received favorable reviews in the press, as did Curran's later publications of Worth's writings.

A well-known example of automatic composition of the second category—metaphysical works—is the work of Jane Roberts. She was playing with a Ouija board in 1963 when it began to spell out messages from an entity that called itself Seth. Soon, Seth began to manifest through automatic speaking and then through full mediumistic possession of Roberts. Roberts, as Seth, dictated several books that became best sellers. These works teach that the human self as ordinarily known is only a tiny portion of a much grander being that exists beyond space and time. They encourage people to develop special senses, including ESP and "inner vibrational touch." Although Roberts died in 1984, the Seth books continue to attract students. Her work laid an important foundation for the rise of interest in CHANNELING during the 1980s.

Another phenomenon regarded by most researchers as a type of automatism is called table-tipping or table-turning. A group gathers around a table, with hands resting on top. The table may begin to move, seemingly on its own, starting with a trembling or rocking and sometimes progressing to sliding rapidly around the room. The participants are usually convinced that they are following the movements of the table, rather than causing them, even though the table never moves when no one is touching it. Generally, spirits are held responsible. Table-tipping became very popular in the 19th century as part of the widespread interest in Spiritualism. In 1853, the renowned physicist and inventor Michael Faraday published an experimental report on table-tipping. He equipped a table with levers and other devices that enabled him to determine that the force propelling the movements was the participants' own unconscious muscular action:

They were pushing the table without being aware of it.

In the early 1970s, members of the Toronto Society for Psychical Research demonstrated that "spirits" are not the only sources of table movement phenomena. They were able to produce table movements of such vigor that sessions often ended with the table broken apart from crashing against the walls. The entities allegedly responsible for the movements communicated to the group via rappings from the table. The group generated these effects by playfully "conjuring up" Philip, a fictional character from a short story. They also communicated with a dolphin named Silk, and even Santa Claus. The origin of the rappings—a common feature of Spiritualist seances—is uncertain, but at least some of them could have been creaks produced unconsciously by coordinated pressure on the table by the participants.

Many systems of divination employ automatisms. In pendulum divination, a small object such as a crystal or button is held suspended by a thread. In response to questions, the object swings, seemingly without the aid of the diviner, and the patterns it traces are interpreted as answers. As the pendulum moves only when held by someone, a muscular origin of the movements cannot be disregarded. The practice of dowsing or water witching is also popular. A dowser holds a forked twig or a pair of rods and walks across the landscape. It is said that mysterious forces cause the twig to bend or shake, or the rods to cross, when the dowser passes over buried water, oil or treasure. As with the pendulum, dowsing rods only move when they are held. Many claims have been made for the usefulness of dowsing in detecting hidden substances. Whenever dowsers have plied their trade in controlled experiments, however, their accuracy has not exceeded the level of chance.

Automatisms demonstrate that complex mental processes, including literary composition and highly coordinated muscular actions, can occur outside of awareness. Various theories have been suggested to account for this phenomenon. Muhl, a psychoanalyst, believed that automatisms originate from an unconscious domain consisting of desires that we cannot accept consciously. Hilgard argued that automatisms are not *un*conscious in this sense; part of us *is* aware of our automatisms, but that part is split off or dissociated from ordinary consciousness. Honnegger proposed that most people possess independent verbal systems in each hemisphere of the brain. Many automatisms could originate from a region in the right hemisphere called the inferior temporal nodule, she suggested.

Whatever their origin, most people who have experienced automatisms have simply found them puzzling and perhaps delightful. Occasionally, however, automatic behavior can evolve into psychological problems. Some automatic writers have found it difficult to stop writing. In most cases, this problem ceases when the practitioner stops attempting to produce automatisms. Rarely, the compulsions resist efforts to remove them. The best known such case is that of Ludwig Staudenmaier. Although he enjoyed his automatic writing at first, his writing behavior became increasingly independent to the point of being troublesome. Staudenmaier then began automatic hearing—in effect, uncontrollable AUDITORY HALLUCINATIONs. He struggled unsuccessfully until his death to suppress his automatisms. It should be noted that any feelings of fear or uneasiness connected with automatisms are signs that one should not practice them.

For further reading: M. Faraday; Hilgard; Honnegger; Lynn, Rhue and Weekes; Muhl; Owen and Sparrow.

auto-oxidation Variant term for SPONTANEOUS HUMAN COMBUSTION.

autoscopy Literally, "self-seeing"; a VISUAL HALLUCINATION of one's own body. Autoscopy can feature in a broad range of disorders, including SCHIZOPHRENIA, EPILEPSY, DELIRIUM and various brain disorders. This experience sometimes occurs to normal, healthy persons, as in encounters with a DOPPELGANGER. Viewing one's own body from a location outside the skin—commonly reported in NEAR DEATH EXPERIENCEs and OUT OF BODY EXPERIENCEs—is often classified as autoscopy. The experience of failing to perceive oneself in a mirror is known as negative autoscopy, a form of NEGATIVE HALLUCINATION.

See also BODY IMAGE DISTORTION.

autostatic effect A kind of optical illusion in which interruptions or sudden stops and starts are falsely perceived in the movement of an object or source of light.

The movement of an observer's eye as it tracks an object is not smooth; rather, eye movements occur in short segments called saccades, interspersed with very brief periods when the eye is still. If there are no other features in the field of vision, the brain can mistake these stop-and-start motions of the eyeball for interruptions in the movement of the object itself. This illusion is known as the autostatic effect. It can cause objects moving in ordinary ways to appear otherwise. Light from a satellite or plane passing overhead at night can seem to hover momentarily at points along its flight path. Convinced that no known object could behave in such a manner, observers may conclude that they have had a UFO ENCOUNTER, when they have merely experienced the movement pattern of their own eyes.

See also AUTOKINETIC EFFECT.

Auxonne nuns, possession of In the French town of Auxonne, members of the convent reported demonic mass POSSESSION from 1658 to 1663. The incident began when several nuns complained of obsessive sexual fantasies concerning one of the convent's confessors, Father Nouvelet. Witchcraft was suspected. Father Nouvelet, perhaps remembering the fate of priests in the past who had been burned at the stake following the accusations of nuns, quickly suggested that he too was bewitched. Two local peasants were charged with witchcraft; released for absence of evidence, the accused persons were murdered by a mob outside the courthouse.

Father Nouvelet attempted to exorcise the tormented nuns, but his effort produced increasingly strange behaviors in the afflicted women. One reportedly developed superhuman strength, lifting a massive vase into the air with two fingers. Others displayed contortions, lying on their bellies and grabbing their feet behind their backs when presented with the eucharistic host.

The mother superior, Barbara Buvée, objected to the priest's exorcistic techniques, which had progressed from the conventional gestures to lying in bed with the possessed women. In reaction, Buvée was accused by the demoniacs of having sexually assaulted them, as well as sending the devils which tormented them. She was arrested, but the charges were later dismissed.

Medical investigators failed to find clear signs of true demonic possession among the nuns. Unusual behaviors were present, but supernatural manifestations such as GLOSSOLALIA or LEVITATION had not been seen. Buvée was transferred to another convent, the authorities lost interest, and the nuns, now removed from the limelight, gradually returned to their ordinary state.

See also Possessions of AIX-EN-PROVENCE NUNS, LOUDUN NUNS, LOUVIERS NUNS; GROUP DYNAMICS OF UNUSUAL EXPERIENCES.

For further reading: Robbins.

bad trip   An unpleasant experience following the ingestion of a psychedelic drug. Reports of bad trips have caused widespread fear of hallucinogens in contemporary society and have helped lawmakers in many countries justify forbidding their use.

Negative experiences are only part of the spectrum of emotional responses to the effects of drugs. Naranjo describes potential drug reactions as spanning the entire range of human experiences, including those we ordinarily avoid:

> To the aesthetic level and the perception of beauty, on the positive end of the feeling range, there corresponds an intensified perception of ugliness, where any particular object or the world as a whole becomes something flat, caricature-like, grotesque, in bad taste, artificial, hideous, and so forth. To love there corresponds, on the negative end, a lovelessness that can be the background of a state of forlornness and depression or of a paranoid state, in which the world or others are perceived as hateful, malevolent, demonic. . . . To the highest level of value—the sense of the holy—there corresponds, as a counterpart, a complete desacralization of life, an absence of being, a sense of unreality, insubstantiality, or emptiness of self and of the world.

Aversive experiences such as these arise occasionally in ordinary as well as ALTERED STATES OF CONSCIOUSNESS. One does not always react to them with the anxiety and confusion so prominent in bad trips. In order to have a bad trip, one must not only experience unpleasant sensations or thoughts, but feel—and fear—the inability to control the experience. Individuals who can simply allow aversive feelings to appear and pass away on their own are less likely to suffer from full-fledged bad trips.

Generally, the best way to help a person through a bad trip is to provide a stable, calming environment. The "tripper" may be soothed by reassurances that the negative aspects of the experience are temporary and by focusing his or her attention on pleasant stimulation, such as music. The psychedelic guide must be a credible advisor in the eyes of the sufferer; someone who has extensive personal experience with the drug is often best suited for this task.

Panton and Fischer studied the effects of the hallucinogen psilocybin (derived from the Psilocybe mushroom) on volunteers. They divided their subjects into two groups: those who tended to seek out sensory stimulation (sensory maximizers) and those who wished to avoid high levels of stimulation (sensory minimizers). The researchers found that maximizers did not experience psychedelic effects from the drug when they were in an unstimulating environment, such as a dimly lit, quiet room. In order to end a maximizer's bad trip, they stated, one need only place the sufferer in a condition of sensory deprivation. If the bad trip persists, or if the drug is affecting the body's life support functions, medical intervention may be required.

Even after the effects of the drug wear off, elements of a bad trip can return as FLASHBACKS. In 1935, French writer Jean-Paul Sartre took mescaline, which plummeted him into a hallucinatory realm of hostile creatures like octopuses, apes and giant flies. For a year following his bad trip, Sartre had flashbacks in which he was pursued by enormous lobsters. Flashbacks usually fade in intensity and frequency over time.

For further reading: Fischer; Naranjo; Panton and Fischer; Stafford; Tart (1977).

ball lightning   A common term for luminous pockets of PLASMA, most frequently seen in the vicinity of thunderstorms. Although its disappearance is often marked by a clap of thunder, it is not true LIGHTNING. In the case of lightning, the electrical discharge is concentrated and rapid; ball lightning can persist for many minutes, and discharge electricity in a more diffuse manner.

baqa   Arabic term, literally meaning "residue." Baqa refers to the state of being that is the goal of Sufism, the mystical branch of Islam. Each human, according to the Sufis, consists partially of mortal and unwholesome aspects, which are ultimately unreal. In addition, we all have a divine aspect that transcends death. In the experience of spiritual purgation, known as FANA, the former elements are stripped away, leaving the residue. This condition is essentially unification with God and is beyond all literal description. The Sufi writer Al-Ghazali (quoted in Bakhtiar) described the nature of baqa thus:

> Each thing has two faces, a face of its own, and a face of its Lord; in respect of its own face it is nothingness, and in respect of the Face of God it is Being. Thus there is nothing in existence save only God and His Face, for everything perishes but His Face.

See also RUYA'HA.

For further reading: Bakhtiar, Schimmel.

bardo   In Tibetan, *bar* means "between," and *do* means "two"; thus, *bardo* is "the state of being in between." Bardo usually refers to the states of consciousness that supposedly exist between the end of one lifetime and rebirth into the next. More generally, however, in Tibetan Buddhism every state of awareness is a type of bardo; at all times, consciousness stands between the previous moment, which no longer exists, and the following moment, in which it does not yet exist. And yet, the meaning and qualities of our present consciousness depend on these two nonexistent points. Therefore, none of the contents of awareness can exist as solid, independent things that endure over time, despite appearances to the contrary; ultimately, the foundation of everything is EMPTINESS, the central insight of Mahayana Buddhism.

Some Tibetan texts divide the range of human awareness into six types of bardo. First is the Bardo of the Realm of Life. This bardo is the ordinary waking state between birth and death, the normal condition of consciousness. If we can train ourselves to resist the appearance that the contents of awareness possess some sort of solid reality of their own, independent of our minds, we can attain liberation from the world of suffering.

The second bardo is that of the Dream State. When we are dreaming, awareness is dominated by mental images which we usually believe to be real, until we awaken. Buddhist TANTRA teaches methods of recognizing the lack of independent existence of dream images while still in the dream state—in effect, a kind of lucid dreaming. The contents of both dreaming and waking consciousness share the feature that they do not exist as they seem.

The Bardo of Meditation arises as a result of practices to induce altered states of awareness. The concentrated mental conditions called JHANAS and SAMADHIS lead to this bardo. Those who have completely mastered Buddhist meditations are said to have a direct experience of the emptiness of all things. If this wisdom is united with a compassionate awareness, the meditator has achieved the supreme goal of Buddhahood.

The next three bardos are experienced by those who are dying or dead. According to the Tibetan tradition, 49 days normally elapse between the time of death and the moment of entry into the womb of one's next mother. During this period, there are many opportunities to free oneself from the endless cycle of birth and death.

One can choose to enter NIRVANA permanently; or, out of kindness, one can opt to reincarnate. Most of us are too deluded by the after-death events to make any deliberate choices—we are compelled to be reborn. A compassionate being who chooses to return to life is no longer controlled by fear and desire and can act effectively to help others attain liberation from the tyranny of these emotions.

The famous text known as the *Tibetan Book of the Dead* describes in detail the bardo states between lives. The book was intended to be read aloud by a lama during the 49 days following someone's death, in order to remind the deceased person of the chances for liberation occurring at that time. Hence, the actual name of the text in Tibetan—*Bardo thodol,* or "Liberation through hearing in the bardo."

The first of the after-death bardos occurs briefly at the moment of death. As external reality falls away, a radiant, pure white light fills the newly deceased consciousness. This is the glow of ultimate reality, the emptiness which is the essence of everything. The Bardo of the Moment of Death is the ideal opportunity to attain ENLIGHTENMENT. If a person is able to recognize the light as his or her *own* true nature, liberation follows immediately.

Most people are overwhelmed by the brilliance and confused by the death process, and fail to identify the light. They then become unconscious for a period. During this time, a psychic body is formed, in which they will journey through the after-death realms to follow.

Upon reawakening, they move into the second post-mortem state, the Bardo of the Experience of Reality. In this bardo one has a series of powerful visions; each encounter represents another chance for liberation and another opportunity to fall into confusion. In all cases the key to freedom is the recognition that all of the visions are mere phantoms, without substantial existence—in effect, projections of one's own mind. Due to their stirring nature, however, very few are able to muster the concentration re-

quired to detect the true nature of the manifestations.

In the Bardo of the Experience of Reality, one is first visited by a succession of giant Buddha images. Each one represents a quality of the enlightened mind, and if one can view them as one's own mind, one becomes enlightened. These images are very bright, however, and might cause the person to flee, in which case they will plummet into reincarnation. First, the blue Buddha, Vairocana, arises; escaping from him, one is born into the realm of the gods. (This fate might sound desirable, but from the Buddhist viewpoint, it is not; eventually, even the gods die, and experience terrible suffering as they are deprived of their pleasures). Then Vajrasattva appears, sparkling like a diamond; avoiding him sends one straight to hell. Next comes Ratnasambhava, with a yellow light; one falls into a human rebirth by recoiling from him. Then arises red Amitabha; if one flees, one becomes a hungry ghost, a frustrating condition in which one has a vast, unfillable belly and a mouth the size of a pinhole. One then meets the green Buddha, Amoghasiddhi; the person who is chased away ends up in the realm of the angry demons. These five visions represent the five main classes of deity visualized in Tantric sadhana practice. One who has performed these meditations during life has a better chance of recognizing their nature in this bardo.

The procession of visions continue. Now, a mind-boggling array of 42 peaceful deities surround the person. Attempts to escape this sight could propel one into rebirth as a god—or an animal! If the deceased mind still has not recognized the illusory nature of the show, a nightmarish quality takes hold. One is now visited by 58 wrathful deities (actually, one's own mind) which take grotesque forms:

> With teeth biting the lower lip, glassy-eyed, their hair tied on top of their heads, with huge bellies and thin necks, holding the records of karma in their hands, shouting 'Strike!' and 'Kill!', licking up brains, tearing heads from

bodies, pulling out internal organs: in this way they will come, filling the whole universe.

Recognizing this unnerving spectacle as one's own mind is said to be extremely difficult.

The dead person, having endured these sights, moves into the last after-death state, the Bardo of Rebirth. Cold winds, hailstorms, darkness and menacing crowds appear, driving the person toward the safety of an empty womb. Visions of couples having sex present themselves to the consciousness. If one is attracted to a male figure in these couples, one will be reborn as his daughter; attraction to a female will result in rebirth as her son. Even at this point, if the fundamental emptiness of all these things is recognized, the person can "close the womb door" and attain liberation.

Each of the bardos of life is linked to one of the bardos of death. The Bardos of the Realm of Life and Rebirth contain material bodies. The visions that populate the Bardos of the Dream State and the Experience of Reality are insubstantial images. And the clear light of emptiness appears in both the Bardo of Meditation and that of the Moment of Death. Meditative training undertaken while in the bardos of life assist one in successfully awakening during the bardos of death.

See also NAROPA, SIX YOGAS OF; NEAR DEATH EXPERIENCE.

For further reading: Ehrhard; Evans-Wentz; Govinda (1969).

Barnum effect Since the days of the Delphic oracle in ancient Greece, diviners have been notorious for giving ambiguous responses to questions. For instance, when Croesus of Lydia asked the oracle whether he should launch an attack on the Persian Empire, he was told that if he did so, "a mighty empire will fall." Thus emboldened, he declared war and lost. A mighty empire did fall, but it was his own. And everyone was impressed with the oracle's prescience. Such slipperiness has not interfered with the continu-

ing popularity of divination, or with the widely held conviction that newspaper horoscope columns provide useful tips about oneself and the future. The enduring popular interest in divination derives in part from the Barnum effect. This psychological principle is named after the famous fleecer of the gullible, P.T. Barnum. The Barnum effect is the tendency for people to perceive vague, highly generalized information as referring specifically to them.

The first research on the Barnum effect was conducted by Forer in 1949. He administered a personality questionnaire to students in a psychology course. In the following class he presented each student with a personality description, allegedly based on the questionnaire, and asked them to rate how well the description fit their personality. In fact, the questionnaire data were not used—every student received the same description. This "stock spiel," as Forer called it, went as follows:

> Some of your aspirations tend to be pretty unrealistic. At times you are extroverted, affable, sociable, while at other times you are introverted, wary and reserved. You have found it unwise to be too frank in revealing yourself to others. You pride yourself on being an independent thinker and do not accept others' opinions without satisfactory proof. You prefer a certain amount of change and variety, and become dissatisfied when hemmed in by restrictions and limitations. At times you have serious doubts as to whether you have made the right decision or done the right thing. Disciplined and controlled on the outside, you tend to be worrisome and insecure on the inside.
>
> Your sexual adjustment has presented some problems for you. While you have some personality weaknesses, you are generally able to compensate for them. You have a great deal of unused capacity which you have not turned to your advantage. You have a tendency to be critical of yourself. You have a strong need for other people to like you and for them to admire you.

Presented with this cobble of unremarkable statements, almost half of Forer's subjects rated it an absolutely precise description of themselves; the average accuracy rating was 4.26 out of a possible 5. Forer named this phenomenon the "fallacy of personal validation." It is more commonly called the Barnum effect.

Subsequent research has refined the understanding of the Barnum effect. The "stock spiel" is most effective if subjects believe it comes from a credible source; devotees of astrology are most impressed if led to think that the description is based on their birth chart, whereas believers in psychology respond most strongly to a supposed analysis of psychological test data. Subjects who are told that the spiel is prepared for them personally tend to perceive it as describing features that are unique to themselves. Hyman developed a recipe for designing the most impressive stock spiel: 75% of the items should describe personality features that most people view as desirable and uncommon, and 25% should present features considered undesirable and very common. The presence of the undesirable items makes the spiel more plausible, and the sense that they are true of most people makes them palatable.

The Barnum effect is produced by a basic human drive: the need to make sense of the world. In the primordial setting within which our species evolved, a faint sound or slight movement could signal the presence of a predator. Only those organisms that could quickly resolve AMBIGUITY were able to survive. This tendency became a human characteristic. Today, people often perceive meaningful forms where none exist (PAREIDOLIA); and, when led to believe that presented stimuli refer to us, we tend to perceive personal meaning.

See also PSYCHIC.

For further reading: Forer; Hyman (1977); Snyder and Shenkel.

belief, anomalous   See ANOMALOUS BELIEFS.

berserk   In modern parlance, to go berserk means to be seized by an uncontrollable rage. The word derives from an Old Norse term, *berserkr,* referring to a common type of mercenary warrior among the Vikings. The berserkrs did have a reputation for ferocious violence. But their berserk acts were not simply losses of control, they deliberately cultivated altered states in which they became the incarnations of merciless, destructive force.

The berserkrs were devotees of Odin, the deity of battle, animals, magic and death. They lived apart from society, with few possessions; wherever they were, they were so feared that they could help themselves to whatever—or whomever—they desired. In the *Ynglinga Saga,* Snorri describes them on the battlefield (quoted in Davidson):

> His men went without their mailcoats and were as mad as hounds or wolves. They bit their shields, and were as strong as bears or bulls. They slew men, but neither fire nor iron had effect on them. This is called 'to run berserk'.

Contemporary accounts, confirmed by the condition of skeletons found in Scandinavian cemeteries from the Viking period, indicate that these warriors could strike off an opponent's limb or head with a single sword stroke.

The comparison of berserkrs with various beasts in the *Saga* was not intended as mere simile. Odin could transform his followers into animals, and it is likely that the berserkrs tried to induce such transformations in themselves. The word berserkr literally means "bearskin shirt" in Norse; in some accounts, they are also called wolf-coats. These phrases may point to the donning of skins in order to identify with the animals' fierce souls. Prior to battles, the berserkrs would howl and bay while leaping about in an agitated manner, apparently aiming at a state of inhuman POSSESSION.

Many authorities have suspected that the berserkrs may also have eaten the hallucinogenic FLY AGARIC mushroom to promote their frenzy.

This mushroom was widely used by shamans across northernmost Europe, and, unlike most plant hallucinogens, reportedly it could produce states of restless movement rather than somnolence. There are, however, no references to the mushroom in Old Norse literature. Quaffing mead (an alcoholic liquor) may also have played a role in evoking the fighters' renowned ferocity and insensitivity to pain; Odin was also the patron of brewers. But "in any case," as Davidson observed, "it would not be difficult to stir up a band of tough and highly-trained youths into a state of murderous rage and fearless confidence."

See also LYCANTHROPY

For further reading: Davidson; Schultes and Hofmann.

bhavana　In the Sanskrit and Pali languages this term refers to all forms of meditation employed in Buddhism. The aim of bhavana is the cultivation of two mental capacities: calm abiding (SHAMATHA) and insight (VIPASSANA).

bhava-pratyaya samadhi　A type of samadhi, or state of consciousness in which attention is greatly concentrated. Bhava-pratyaya is discussed in the classic text of RAJA YOGA, Patanjali's *Yoga Sutras*. In this condition awareness has become so thoroughly absorbed in an object that one has no consciousness of oneself, or of the object as such. An example would be an intense orgasm, in which awareness of oneself and one's partner momentarily vanishes. Bhava-pratyaya samadhi resembles the spiritual state called ASAMPRAJNATA SAMADHI, in that both conditions transcend the awareness of objects. In bhava-pratyaya, however, the destruction of the seeds of karma achieved in asamprajnata does not take place. Bhava-pratyaya may have some motivational value as a hint of the bliss that can be reached in higher states of consciousness; but the yogis warn against confusing the two.

Biblical prophecy　Probably the most important and influential cultural production in Western history, the Bible presents a range of unusual experience accounts under the rubric of prophecy. As documentary evidence regarding specific unusual experiences, the Biblical books cannot be viewed as reliable sources. In many cases the stories were not written down until generations of oral transmission had passed, introducing unknown amounts of editing, deliberate and otherwise. In some instances prophecies were composed *after* the events had occurred, and the accounts were then disguised to appear as if they had been recorded prior to the predicted occurrences. Most scholars believe that the book of Daniel, which contains predictions regarding events in the sixth century B.C., was written about 400 years later. The Bible stories are still valuable for the student of the paranormal, however. They reflect the beliefs of the time—whether or not the experiences actually happened as they are described, they were certainly viewed as possible. And these beliefs have continued to influence expectations concerning unusual experiences throughout the history of the Judeo-Christian tradition.

In common usage, the word prophecy is usually synonymous with precognition, or foretelling the future. In the Biblical context, precognitive activities are only part of the prophet's functions. Some historians emphasize that the Old Testament prophets were not merely "foretellers," but "forthtellers"—they expressed God's opinions concerning the moral qualities of the contemporary society. These judgments did not always contain predictions about future events.

In Bible stories where prophets do utter predictions, there are many instances in which these foretellings turn out to be wrong. In the eighth century B.C., Isaiah predicted that Jerusalem would shortly be destroyed (Isaiah 3:1). A few years later, the Assyrians invaded, but did not wreck the city. The prophetess Hulda informed King Josiah that he would die a peaceful death

(II Kings 22:19–20), but he was killed in battle against the Egyptians. The great prophet Ezekiel predicted that the city of Tyre and the land of Egypt would fall to the armies of Nebuchadrezzar (Ezekiel 26–28; 29:19); neither event occurred. Of course, far more typical are the accounts in which prophets have accurate premonitions—Amos, Hosea, Isaiah and Micah were all said to have predicted the collapse of the kingdom of Israel, which happened in the eighth century B.C.

Clairvoyance, or paranormal access to information about distantly occurring events, is also featured in some prophetic tales. Ezekiel, for example, was told by God that at that moment, the Babylonian army was besieging Jerusalem (Ezekiel 24:1).

Biblical prophecies took a variety of forms. Both visions and voices were frequently reported; whether these experiences were dreams, HALLUCINATIONS or HYPNAGOGIC imagery is often difficult to determine. Some evidently occurred in the dream state; following a revelation, Jeremiah noted that "Thereupon I awoke and looked, and my sleep was pleasant to me" (Jeremiah 31:25), implying that the revelation occurred during sleep.

Other prophetic instances happened while the experient was in some sort of altered state. Ezekiel repeatedly mentioned that "the hand of the Lord" was upon him during his experiences, and the famous encounter of Saul with Christ on the road to Damascus apparently began while he was awake. The reported nature of Saul's experience (he fell to the earth with eyes closed, and trembled), and its aftermath (inability to eat, drink or see for three days) have suggested to some researchers that the voice of Christ was a hallucination associated with an episode of EPILEPSY.

Bennett has observed that many visions described in the Bible occur as brief flashes of simple images, such as a basket of fruit (Amos 8:1–3) or the branch of an almond tree (Jeremiah 1:11–12). He noted that these experiences sound like instances of the hypnagogic imagery that often occur during the transition between wakefulness and sleep. The culture of the Biblical prophets would not have been the only one to interpret such images as divine revelations.

Some of the unusual experiences mentioned in the Bible may well be examples of OUT OF BODY EXPERIENCEs. Ezekiel reported that God carried him, by a lock of his hair, to faraway Jerusalem where he viewed the proceedings (Ezekiel 8–11). And Paul flew up to the third heaven, "whether in the body or out of the body I know not, God knows" (II Corinthians 12:1–5).

In addition to their familiarity with spontaneous unusual experiences, the ancient Hebrews were aware of methods to induce them. King Solomon, famous in legend for his magical skills, performed sacrificial rituals in order to meet God in a dream (I Kings 3:4–15). According to the New Testament, certain members of the earliest orthodox Christian communities could induce prophetic states (I Corinthians 12:10, 28). Known as prophets or charismatists, these individuals spoke under the inspiration of the Holy Spirit. Afterwards, they might not remember what they said, suggesting that the prophetic condition was an altered state of consciousness. These Christian prophets are clearly distinguished from those possessing another spiritual gift—GLOSSOLALIA, or speaking in tongues. Prophetic statements were made in an intelligible language, whereas glossolalic utterances were not understood even by those who made them.

Because of the Bible's authority in Christian culture, the unusual experiences described therein established the range of acceptable spiritual events for Christians in succeeding ages. Anything falling outside of this range could be assumed to be demonic in origin.

The modes of prophecy that were clearly accepted by the first century orthodox Christian community were later suppressed. The New Testament itself foreshadows the problems of prophecy within an institutionalized religion, warning about the rise of false prophets. As the church developed into an organization with established dogmas and chains of authority, prophets proclaiming new revelations came to be viewed as dangerous. The freelance spiritual adventures described by the Biblical prophets were potentially subversive to the Catholic hierarchy; it became necessary to discourage such manifestations among the faithful. A text of the early second century, the *Ascension of Isaiah* (probably composed before the New Testament itself had been completed) predicts: "And the Holy Spirit will withdraw from many. Nor will there be in those days many prophets or those who speak things confirmed, except a few in a few places."

From then on, most of the prophetic experiences reported by orthodox sources occurred to members of especially devout populations controlled by the church, such as monks; the contents of these revelations usually supported official doctrines. Experiences reported by laypersons were either rejected as demonic, or interpreted to conform to orthodox dogma. Heretical groups like the Gnostics and the Montanists continued to prophesy; indeed, they argued that the waning of prophetic activity within the Catholic church proved that the church had lost touch with God. In response, the church ruthlessly suppressed these dissenters.

For further reading: Bennett; Berman; Guillaume; Kapelrud.

Bigfoot The popular American name for a hairy humanoid occasionally sighted in wooded areas, mostly in the northwest coast region.

See also CRYPTIC; HUMANOIDS, ANOMALOUS.

bilocation The presence of a person or object in two places at once is a widely reported paranormal experience. Bilocation is recognized as an ability possessed by religious adepts in both Eastern and Western traditions; and, in addition, reports abound of spontaneous occurrences.

Among the Taoists of China, it is believed that sages can appear simultaneously in different locations because of the magical forces residing in their "diamond bodies," produced by meditative alchemy (NEI-TAN). Practitioners of both Buddhist and Hindu tantra include bilocation in their lists of SIDDHIS, or extraordinary powers, allegedly accessible to masters of meditation.

In the Christian tradition, a host of renowned holy men have been observed in two places at once, including St. Ambrose (fourth century), St. Anthony of Padua (13th century) and, in the present century, Padre Pio Forgione. In 1774, St. Alphonsus Maria de'Ligouri was observed at the deathbed of Pope Clement XIV; at the time, the saint was confined to a distant meditation cell. Bilocation is accepted as a CHARISM, or manifestation of holiness, by the Roman Catholic church.

Most modern students of such occurrences believe that the duplication of material substance in bilocation reports only is apparent. Cases in which persons experience *themselves* in two places simultaneously may be instances of OUT OF BODY EXPERIENCE; ordinarily, the OBE is understood by the experient to be a separation of soul from body, but some might interpret the sensations as a doubling of the material body. When *others* observe an apparently bilocated person, it is likely an apparition—that is, a perception without material basis. Such apparitions of the living are commonly known as DOPPEL-GANGERS.

For further reading: Murphy; Tyrrell.

birds In most parts of the globe, viewing a bird is hardly a mystical experience. However, under certain conditions, birds have presented startling spectacles; they have been reported as UFOs as well as APPARITIONS.

Owls are fond of roosting in dead tree trunks during the day. Decaying trees are also the favored environment of a luminescent fungus, *Armillaria mellea*. On occasion, the fungus has adhered to the feathers of an owl, which then glows in the dark. In one recorded instance, a mysterious forest light was identified by its hooting cry; in another case, a gamekeeper shot a gleaming nocturnal spectre and retrieved a dead owl, which continued to luminesce for several hours.

Unusual light reflection can also enhance a bird's mysterious quality. In 1951, the residents of Lubbock, Texas, were frequently amazed by formations of UFOs that overflew the town at night. It was eventually determined that the objects were plover, reflecting Lubbock's newly installed street lamps from their white breasts. UFOs detected by radar have sometimes proven to be birds; a large bird nearby can produce a radar image similar to that of a much larger object at a greater distance.

See also GHOST LIGHT.

For further reading: Corliss (1981); Menzel and Boyd.

blindsight Individuals who sustain damage to the brain region involved in the visual sense often lose the ability to see certain features or areas in their field of vision. In some cases, although unaware of sensing anything in the blinded part of the field, they are able to respond to information visible in that area. For instance, a person may deny being able to see an array of dots on paper presented to him or her; but when asked to guess how many dots there are, the person will repeatedly guess the correct number. This phenomenon is called blindsight. The opposite of blindsight is PHANTOM VISION, in which a person with damaged eyes has visual experiences without actually seeing anything.

bodhi This Sanskrit word literally means "awakening" and refers to the state of consciousness of one who has experienced EN-LIGHTENMENT in Buddhism. The complete enlightenment of BUDDHAHOOD is called *mahabodhi,* or unsurpassable awakening, compared to which ordinary consciousness is like a condition of deep sleep. In the Mahayana tradi-

tion of Buddhism, the heroic ideal is the *bodhisattva,* the being who is dedicated to awakening for the benefit of all sentient creatures. *Bodhicitta,* or "awakening consciousness," is characterized by profound wisdom combined with infinite compassion; its cultivation is the aim of many Buddhist meditation practices.

body image distortions We do not experience our bodies directly; rather, our bodily awareness is constructed by the mind from sensations, memory, belief, need and expectation. The result of this creative activity is the *body image,* or body self. The body image has several components: the sense that the self is located inside the body; the feeling of "body ownership," that this is *my* body; and the awareness of the proportions and boundaries of body parts. Under ordinary circumstances, the body image matches the actual body well enough for us to function effectively. All of the body image components are subject to distortion, both short-term and chronic.

The basis of the body image is thought to be a network of regions in the brain, called the neuromatrix by Melzack. Although the main features of this neural image are probably genetically determined, they are sculpted by experiences throughout life. A newborn baby discovers where its body stops and the outside world begins. As children, we learn about the basic features and abilities of our body, and develop our attitudes toward it. This learned information is encoded in the neuromatrix, becoming part of our fundamental body experience. Severe or lasting disturbances in this developmental process put one at risk for later mental illness. Temporary disturbances, such as are caused by psychoactive drugs or unusual sensory stimulation, can destabilize the body image for short periods.

The sense of being located within the body is so deeply established that it is rarely disrupted for long. Under conditions when ordinary body sensations are reduced, one may feel that the self is no longer bound within the skin. This is called the OUT OF BODY EXPERIENCE. Having a vision of one's own body, or autoscopy, while still feeling that one is embodied is a less extreme self-location distortion.

Disturbances of body ownership take a variety of forms. Many mental disorders involve depersonalization, a feeling of alienation from oneself. Depersonalization often includes a sense that the body is an automaton. Damage to the parietal lobe of the brain can produce the sensation that a body part does not belong to oneself; parietal lobe patients have been known to push one of their own legs out of their hospital bed, convinced that it belonged to a stranger. Altered body ownership may be deliberately sought. Practitioners of AUTOMATISMs, such as automatic writing, cultivate the feeling that a limb is not part of themselves, in order to allow it to act without conscious control.

Distortions of body proportion and boundary are widespread. Thompson found that American women tend to view their cheeks, waist and hips as being larger than they actually are. Mainstream American culture's high valuation of extremely thin female models is the likely cause of this misperception. Such cultural pressures also play a role in eating disorders such as anorexia nervosa and bulimia. People with eating disorders usually have disturbances in body image; emaciated anorexics on the verge of starvation can perceive themselves as fat.

Temporary changes in sensed body proportions are frequent whenever ordinary physical sensations are disrupted. HYPNOSIS normally involves deep relaxation, which changes the signals sent from the muscles to the brain. Feeling that one's limbs have become larger or smaller is a common sign of deepening hypnotic experience.

PHANTOM LIMB SENSATIONS are an instance of extreme body proportion distortion. In such cases people sense body parts that are actually severed from the body; they are, of course, not sensing the actual limb, but activity within the neuromatrix. Profound alterations of body image can arise from severe mental illnesses like SCHIZOPHRENIA. Noll reported:

> A former patient of the author's was fully experiencing the feeling that his face had turned into that of a dog's, and that this was how people were actually perceiving him. Others may believe that they have huge, gaping holes in the middle of their torsos through which they experience the wind passing, or feel much thinner or fatter than they really are.

For further reading: Cash and Pruzinsky; Melzack; Thompson; Noll (1992a).

bowmen of Mons   An unintentional experiment in the GROUP DYNAMICS OF UNUSUAL EXPERIENCES occurred in 1914. In August of that year, soldiers of the British Expeditionary Force were forced to retreat from the Belgian town of Mons by German troops. English novelist Arthur Machen wrote a short piece of fiction based on the event, which was published by the *London Evening News* in September to boost public morale. In Machen's story "The Bowmen," the ghosts of medieval archers materialize on the battlefield to aid the retreating Britons, scattering the German soldiers with their phantom arrows.

Soon, Machen's little tale was circulating as a rumor, and, before long, its origin as a fictional work was forgotten. Many British soldiers who had been present at Mons later confirmed that they had indeed witnessed the appearance of the bowmen. Interviews with the German troops also uncovered witnesses willing to swear that the rumors about the apparitions were true.

Apparently, the imagery of the bowmen, concocted and introduced into popular consciousness by Machen, had found its way into the memories of the participants. There, accurate recollections mingled with the fantasy material until they were indistinguishable. In this instance, an unusual event sincerely attested by witnesses across Europe can be demonstrated never to have occurred. The bowmen of Mons serves as a cautionary tale about the reliability of EYEWITNESS ACCOUNTS.

For further reading: Haining; Sachs.

Brocken spectre   The Brocken is a mountain in Germany with a haunted reputation—it is said to be a site of the WITCHES' SABBATH during the Great Witch Hunt. This peak has lent its name to a striking type of shadow. When a person's shadow is cast onto a bank of fog or mist, as can happen when one is standing on a mountain top or at a cliff edge, the silhouette can assume immense proportions. If the mist is billowing, the distance from the observer of the surface upon which the shadow is projected continuously changes; this can create the appearance of the shadow rushing toward the observer, then falling back. A story often told, although historically unverified, claims that a man who climbed the Brocken was so startled by the huge shadow looming up at him that he slipped and fell to his death.

While the shadow itself is easy to explain, other features of the Brocken spectre are more puzzling. Frequently, the head of the shadow is seen to be encircled by up to five concentric rainbows. If more than one person casts a Brocken spectre at the same time, each person sees the rainbows centered on the shadow of his or her own head. It is believed that these halos are somehow produced as light is reflected and refracted by water droplets in the mist, although the exact nature of the process is unclear.

Even more mysterious are the "grey rays" sometimes seen radiating from the head and other projecting features of the shadow. No physical mechanism to account for this effect has been suggested.

The Brocken spectre phenomenon is not restricted to the Brocken. It can happen anywhere an observer's silhouette can be projected onto a layer of mist. Perhaps the best known Brocken spectre is routinely observed from Adams Peak in Sri Lanka. The Grand Canyon in Arizona is another favorite viewing spot.

See also HEILIGENSCHEIN.
For further reading: Corliss (1984).

Buddhahood   A Buddha is literally "one who has awakened." The attainment of Buddha consciousness, in comparison to which our ordinary awareness is like a deep sleep, is the highest goal of Buddhism. Buddhas are distinguished from all other beings by their successful conquest of two obstacles: the barriers to liberation from suffering, and the barriers to omniscience. A less complete form of ENLIGHTENMENT is also recognized by Buddhist tradition in which only the barriers to liberation are conquered. One who accomplishes this lesser attainment is known as an *arhat* ("foe destroyer"), not a Buddha.

The two major surviving divisions of Buddhism, Theravada and Mahayana, differ somewhat on their views concerning Buddhahood. The Theravada denies that omniscience means total knowledge of everything in the universe; instead, the Buddha's omniscience entails complete knowledge of the means of liberation from suffering. In addition, a Buddha is thought to possess the "ten powers" (Sanskrit *dashabala*). These powers arise from profound knowledge concerning the workings of the mind and causality and enable a Buddha to act in extremely effective ways in order to help others attain enlightenment. The achievement of Buddhahood is so difficult that only one person in each eon can attain it; the rest of us can only aspire to become foe destroyers (in itself a very challenging task that is said to take many lifetimes of effort).

The name for the other division of Buddhism, Mahayana, means "great vehicle" in Sanskrit, because it claims to provide the tools necessary to carry everyone to Buddhahood. The foe destroyer in this tradition is viewed as a rather uncompassionate being, who chooses to escape from the world of suffering without trying to help free the rest of us. In the Mahayana the ideal is not the arhat, but the *bodhisattva*—one who postpones his or her own escape in order to acquire the salvational skills of a Buddha.

Within the Mahayana, two paths to Buddhahood are available—sutra and tantra. Both approaches share the basic notion that ultimate reality is EMPTINESS, that is, the absence of independent or inherent existence. The direct experience of emptiness is required in order to surmount the obstacles to liberation, as well as those to omniscience. In the sutra path, bodhisattvas develop meditative skills until they can experience the empty nature of things directly. However, when they are having this profound experience, the conventional world of objects disappears from their awareness. During these times, bodhisattvas cannot function to help others in the world. By alternating the awareness of emptiness with compassionate awareness of the world of objects, the two kinds of awareness eventually blend, until they both occur simultaneously. This is the achievement of omniscience and of Buddhahood—things are seen perfectly as they are, possessing form, yet lacking inherent existence. With this perfect perception, Buddhas can see perfectly how best to help unenlightened beings dispel the ignorance which gives rise to suffering.

The sutra path of the bodhisattva is said to be effective, but slow—it takes three great eons of reincarnations, according to tradition, between setting out on the bodhisattva's path and attaining Buddhahood in this manner. Tantric Buddhism claims that its methods can bring supreme enlightenment within the span of a single lifetime. In tantra, the meditations called SADHANAs are employed. In sadhana practice, meditators imagine that they are already enlightened beings and that the universe is already being emptied of suffering. By mimicking the consciousness of a Buddha, actual Buddhahood can be speedily achieved. The tantric methods are also said to be full of pitfalls, and the tradition requires that practitioners are closely supervised by an authoritative teacher.

What does the world look like from the lofty vantage point of a Buddha? To the extent that Buddhahood is an experiential possibility and not an abstract ideal, the *Avatamsaka Sutra*, a text revered by the Hua Yen school of Chinese Buddhism, is said to provide the most vivid description of a Buddha's awareness. Without any obstacles to knowledge, the Buddha's perception reveals that everything in the universe can be found within everything else. In this grand interpenetration, however, each thing maintains its individual form without disturbance. Such a dizzying vision cannot be conveyed literally; Buddhists hold that the ordinary, undeveloped mind would be shattered by such an experience. The Sutra, therefore, employs metaphors, such as the "net of Indra," a network of pearls so positioned that each one reflects the image of all the others. In another compelling passage, a meditator named Sudhana attains Buddha consciousness, represented by a vision of the universe as an immense tower. (It is interesting that the vision seems to contain hints of such modern perceptions as holography and fractal geometry). The following is a paraphrase by Suzuki:

> The Tower is as wide and spacious as the sky itself. The ground is paved with (innumerable) precious stones of all kinds, and there are within the Tower (innumerable) palaces, porches, windows, staircases, railings, and passages, all of which are made of the seven kinds of precious gems . . . And within this Tower, spacious and exquisitely ornamented, there are also hundreds of thousands . . . of towers, each one of which is as exquisitely ornamented as the main Tower itself and as spacious as the sky. And all these towers, beyond calculation in number, stand not at all in one another's way; each preserves its individual existence in perfect harmony with all the rest; there is nothing here that bars one tower being fused with all the others individually and collectively; there is a state of perfect intermingling and yet of perfect orderliness. Sudhana . . . sees himself in all the towers as well as in each single tower, where all is contained in one and each contains all.

For further reading: G.C.C. Chang (1971); Hopkins (1984); Suzuki.

burial alive Awakening to the silence, darkness and confinement of a buried coffin is many people's idea of the worst imaginable nightmare. Burial alive is not merely a feature of horror novels; it has happened throughout history, and continues to occur today. A person can end up buried alive in one of three ways: by accident, voluntarily and by coercion.

The accidental interment of a living person results from a misdiagnosis of death. The typical signs of death have long been recognized, including absence of respiration and heartbeat; decreased body temperature; pallor of the skin; tractability of the eyelid; rigor mortis; relaxation of the sphincter; and, eventually, decomposition of the body. Recent technological advances have added absence of electrical activity in the brain and heart to the list. With the exception of putrefaction, all of these indications can be misleading under certain circumstances. The effects of disease, drugs and individual differences in biology, combined with error on the part of the person charged with pronouncing death, have led to the misdiagnosis and burial of an unknown number of people.

In ancient literature Plato, Plutarch and Pliny the Elder all mention individuals who awoke on their own funeral pyres; some were burned to death while others were rescued. The famous Italian Renaissance poet Petrarch revived moments before he was to be buried. Vesalius, the greatest physician of his day, actually killed someone by performing an autopsy on him. It is logical to assume that similar diagnostic mistakes were occurring, undetected, to people whose bodies were buried.

Perhaps the most bizarre incident of misdiagnosis was reported in France. A young woman, pronounced dead, was to be buried the following day. A traveling monk offered to oversee the body during the night, presumably for religious reasons. Instead, he stripped the body and had sex with it; by the morning, he had left. Shortly before burial, the woman revived. Nine months later the "corpse," now restored to health, gave birth to a child.

In the 18th and 19th centuries, interest in the possibility of premature burial led to research programs in which bodies were disinterred to look for signs of revival in the grave. Cases were reported in which the body had evidently been moving in the coffin; damage to the interiors of coffins, caused by frantic escape attempts, were also noted. In 1742 Bruhier reported 52 apparent cases of premature burial in France; Hadwen in 1905 described 149 cases in England. The likelihood of meeting this dire fate was debated by medical authorities. Estimates of premature burial rates varied from one per thirty thousand to the shocking result of an American study—one hundred graves had been examined, and evidence of burial alive was found in two, yielding an estimate that one person in fifty awakens in the grave!

The 19th century saw many people's attempts to avoid being buried alive. People left instructions that their heads be severed, their hearts stabbed or their blood drained following the pronouncement of death. Some even arranged for the installation of alarm systems that would call attention if their bodies reanimated in the grave. One such apparatus involved placing a glass sphere on the chest of the corpse. If the body began to breathe in the coffin, the sphere would be dislodged, causing an air channel to open, a flag to unfurl above the grave and a bell to ring for 30 minutes. In a morgue in Munich, cords tied to the corpses were attached to bells in the central office, alerting the staff to any movements.

In the late 20th century, modern medical procedure and the practice of embalming have certainly reduced the odds of premature burial. In much of the world, however, neither of these practices is routine. Conditions in tropical countries favor the rapid disposal of the body before putrefaction (the only certain indicator of death) appears.

In Japan, the practice of eating the poisonous puffer fish often leads to fugu poisoning, a condition easily mistaken for death, in which the victim remains conscious but is completely paralyzed. Cases have been reported in which fugu victims have revived shortly before cremation or burial. In 1983 one such case involved a man who awoke after his coffin lid had been nailed shut. By law, those who have died from consuming the puffer fish must be left unburied for three days—just in case.

Some people have volunteered to be buried alive. In Russia during the late 19th century, there was an outbreak of mass voluntary interment. The Tsarist government declared a census, which a sectarian leader called Kovalev announced was a ploy by Satan to add names to his list of damned souls. In response to this sign, dozens of Kovalev's followers insisted on being buried in coffins to await Christ's second coming, which they were convinced was imminent. Their wait continues today.

In India, individuals who survive burial for extended periods are viewed as spiritually advanced and they have often been materially rewarded by admirers for their feat. The most famous case of voluntary burial was that witnessed by Sir Claude Wade, British Resident at the court of the Maharaja of Lahore, in 1837. A fakir named Haridas claimed that he could survive burial in a box for six weeks. The site of interment was reportedly guarded around the clock. (The opportunity for fraud in such circumstances is great; the use of tunnels by which the fakir could leave his tomb undetected is one possibility.) When the fakir was uncovered, he was revived through massage and hot baths. The maharaja, impressed, presented Haridas with silk, pearls and gold.

Kothari, Bordia and Gupta studied the abilities of fakirs to modify their metabolic functioning and reported their findings in the *Indian Journal of Medical Research*. Under controlled conditions Shri Ramanand Yogi was able to decrease his oxygen consumption to levels that would be lethal to most people. He was placed in an airtight box for ten hours and showed no ill effects.

A variant of voluntary interment has tradiionally been practiced by meditators in Tibet. In order to perfect one's meditation skills, it was customary to be immured in a cave, leaving only a small, S-shaped passageway so that food could be passed in. Many meditators remained in such caves for a period of three years, three months and three days; some (such as the well-known lama Kalu Rinpoche) chose to remain isolated in the caves for 20 years. Tibetan tradition holds that, in the past, some practitioners requested that even the small remaining aperture to the outside world be sealed; they believed that their spiritual advancement had relieved them of the need for food.

The deliberate burial of the living against their will is quite uncommon. As a mode of punishment, this practice has been occasionally reported. The most refined version of coerced interment is the Haitian practice of ZOMBIFICATION, in which a person is poisoned, buried for up to several hours, and revived.

For further reading: Davis (1986, 1988); Kothari, Bordia and Gupta; Murphy.

byodo-kan A Zen Buddhist term, literally meaning "view of sameness" in Japanese. Byodo-kan is a state of awareness, attained through the practice of ZAZEN, in which all things are perceived as having an identical essence or basic nature—specifically, the Buddha-nature. The universe is already enlightened; all we need to do is to awaken to this fact. The byodo-kan experience is an important stage on the path to BUDDHAHOOD. A Buddha, in addition to perceiving the essential sameness of all things, is also keenly aware of their individual characteristics. Byodo-kan can lead the meditator astray in two ways: One can conclude that, if everything is already Buddha, there is no need for anyone to practice meditation (this error fails to take into account the fact that very few are truly *aware* of their enlightened nature); and one can focus exclusively on the sameness and lose sight of the individual aspects of reality (AKU-BYODO).

C

cacodemonomania The ancient Greeks referred to a hostile spirit as a *cacodaimon*. Cacodemonomania is a psychiatric term for the belief that one is possessed by a devil. It is a subtype of demonomania, the conviction that one is a victim of POSSESSION.

Capgras Syndrome Variant term for ILLUSION DES SOSIES. J.M. Capgras, a French psychiatrist, first described this condition in 1923.

cathurta In the Hindu belief system called Vedanta, this word is a variant term for TURIYA, the mystical "fourth state" of consciousness.

cemetery light Mysterious lights seen moving about burial grounds at night are the stuff of horror tales. But sincere witnesses have reported such sights in cemeteries around the world. Cemetery lights are often described as bluish in color, ranging in size from a spark to a basketball. These forms may be stationary or mobile; they always elude capture and disappear.

Graveyards after dark are wonderfully suggestive places, and no doubt the mental state of a nervous individual who sees a glint of moonlight from a tombstone could easily perceive it as a wandering light. Bunch and White investigated recurrent nocturnal lights reported in a Colorado cemetery and concluded that observers had been viewing starlight reflected from highly polished marble headstones.

It is also noteworthy that some of the gases of decay, such as phorphoretted hydrogen, can be luminescent; clouds wafting from the cemetery's long-term residents might be capable of producing brief light effects before dissipating. Other vapors of the dead are flammable and could cause displays similar to WILL-O'-THE WISPs.

See also CORPSE LIGHT.

For further reading: Bunch and White; Corliss (1982); Gaddis.

cenesthetic hallucination False perceptions of organs and other structures within the body. Sufferers of SCHIZOPHRENIA sometimes report burning sensations in the brain or feeling the blood flow within the blood vessels. Most internal body structures possess no sensory receptors and cannot be directly experienced.

See also BODY IMAGE DISTORTION; KINESTHETIC HALLUCINATION.

chakras This Sanskrit term meaning "wheel" originally designated special types of bodily experiences in the meditative traditions of Hindu and Buddhist TANTRA. Recently, the word has been applied to a range of unusual bodily sensations by mystically inclined Westerners.

In the tantric traditions the psychic and spiritual aspects of the human being are not located in the brain but are spread throughout, and beyond, the physical body. The chakras are points of intersection between the physical and psycho-spiritual realms. They are also sites where the hidden energies of life converge. The chakras are not merely physical, so attempts to equate them with physiological structures are misguided. Neither are they purely imaginary in the Western sense of something arbitrary and without effect. Tantric practitioners hold that through manipulation of the chakras, significant physical, mental and spiritual changes can be produced.

Various systems of chakras can be found in meditation manuals. The number of chakras said to exist in the psycho-spiritual body ranges from three to billions. The best known model identifies seven main chakras, arranged vertically in the center of the body. Each one is visualized as a lotus flower. Visualization of the chakra in the specified bodily location is said to activate it. This activation may manifest as unusual sensations at the spot, an image of the flower as spinning and radiating light and stimulation of the corresponding psychological condition.

At the base of the spine is the *muladhara chakra,* or Wheel of Foundation, with four red petals. At this site the life force called KUNDALINI sleeps, awaiting an accidental or deliberate call to spiritual awakening. This chakra is associated with basic survival instincts.

The *swadisthana chakra,* or Wheel at the Base of the Self, is situated in the genitals. This lotus with six vermilion petals governs sexuality and other sensual pleasures. Buddhist models of the chakras do not distinguish this chakra from the preceding one.

Next is the *manipura chakra,* Wheel of the Jeweled City, a flower with ten blue petals hovering at the level of the navel. This center pertains to egotistical drives, such as a craving to dominate others and amass symbols of personal achievement.

The *anahata chakra,* Wheel of the Soundless Sound, is found in the heart. It has 12 scarlet petals. From this center arises compassionate feelings and generous activities; it is rarely activated in most people.

The three highest chakras are associated with refined spiritual states. Their activation is associated with the acquisition of profound insights and supernormal powers, or siddhis. If the higher chakras are aroused in one who is spiritually immature, the experience may be overwhelming.

The throat is the site of the *vishudda chakra,* Wheel of Purity. It takes the form of a lotus with sixteen dark crimson petals.

The *ajna chakra,* Wheel of Command, is situated in the center of the head, behind the forehead. Its flower has two white petals. Tibetan Buddhists do not recognize this center as a separate chakra.

Perched at the crown of the head is the *sahasrara chakra,* the Wheel of Shiva's Seat. It is so called because in Hindu Tantra the highest spiritual consciousness, represented by the god Shiva, resides here. A thousand-petalled lotus of radiant white light is the image of this chakra.

In the 19th century, some Western students of esoteric philosophy learned about the doctrine of the chakras. Through the Theosophical Society, an immensely popular attempt to combine occult ideas from Eastern and Western sources, the chakras were introduced to Europeans and North Americans. Today, the chakras have become a mainstay of occult teaching. The astral body or auric body, corresponding to the subtle "sheathes" of Eastern teaching, is studded with chakras, according to clairvoyants.

Some modern visionaries claim that sluggish and irregular movements in the chakras indicate illnesses and psychological troubles. Treatment is often offered to balance the chakras, in the form of bodily massage—or perhaps by massaging the auric body through hand passes just above the skin. Of course, such procedures will produce all manner of interesting sensations in suggestible individuals. A Japanese researcher, Hiroshi Motoyama, has reported that he has built a machine that can detect chakra energies. No independent verification of his claim has been noted.

See also ANANDAMAYA.

For further reading: Govinda (1969); Karagulla and Van Gelder Kunz; Motoyama.

channeling   The phenomenon of channeling rose to prominence in the United States during the 1980s. A definition of channeling was offered by Klimo:

> Channeling is the communication of information to or through a . . . human being from a source that is said to exist on some other level or dimension of reality than the physical as we

know it, and that is not from the normal mind (or self) of the channel.

Channeling, thus broadly defined, would include the activities of traditional shamans, the voluntary POSSESSION trances found in most of the world's cultures and MEDIUMSHIP as practiced by Spiritualists. Rogo (cited in Klimo) distinguished mediumship and channeling:

Mediumship is the art of bringing through spirits of the dead specifically to communicate with their relatives. Channeling I define as bringing through some sort of intelligence, the nature undefined, whose purpose is to promote spiritual teachings and philosophical discussion.

The contemporary channeling movement generally accords with Rogo's definition. Although departed spirits still put in occasional appearances, channelers nowadays are more likely to contact extraterrestrials or beings from other dimensions.

Channeling is a central activity of the New Age movement. A 1990 Gallup poll estimated that 11% of adult Americans believe in the validity of channeling, and 2% have done channeling themselves.

Typically, channeling is done while in a trance. The behavior of the channeler is apparently taken over by the alien intelligence, which acts or speaks through him or her. Afterward, the channeler usually claims to have no memory of the episode. The following account, by Grunwald, typifies the onset of the channeling experience:

While John David set up the tape recorder, Steve leaned back in his chair and tried to relax. After some five minutes of quiet, it was obvious he was having trouble, and John David, thinking perhaps it might calm him, asked Steve to look into his eyes and told him to relax. Steve closed his eyes again, breathed easily for a moment or two, and then began to speak in a voice which was of the same tenor as his normal voice, but strikingly more intense. The first thing he said in a state of trance was, 'You haven't permitted me to be in touch with you for a while . . . I have come to you to explain the systematization of the universe . . . I am called Sepotempuat.'

The nature of the channelers' entranced state has barely been explored. Hughes and Melville monitored the electrical activity of channelers' brains before, during and after trances. They reported that the channeling brain appears to shift into a unique state of activation, marked by increases in the rhythms of electrical excitation called alpha and beta waves. This state differed from the channelers' ordinary waking brain patterns; it also differs from the brain activity patterns that are normally found in hypnotized or meditating subjects.

Although the dramatic behavioral shifts channelers undergo may seem unusual, there is no evidence that channeling is linked to mental disorders. Hughes assessed the psychological functioning of ten channelers and concluded that they were not afflicted with MULTIPLE PERSONALITY DISORDER, SCHIZOPHRENIA, FUGUE or psychogenic AMNESIA. Nor were they prone to report histories of substance or physical abuse. The channelers did claim to have had a large number of paranormal experiences aside from their channeling activities.

On the basis of extensive interviews with 13 channelers, Chandley (cited in Hastings) reported a typical pattern of development. The future channeler avoids uncontrolled anomalous experiences that are not fully comprehended, but these experiences later come to be interpreted as contact with a nonphysical reality. Gradually, the nature of the relationship between nonphysical reality and the channeler is worked out. At some point, the channeler makes a conscious decision to channel; the channeling experience tends to become more comfortable and trusted after this commitment. In the final phase the implications of channeling as a method of personal or spiritual growth are recognized. Not all channelers reach this mature level, noted Chandley.

While some take channeling at face value, accepting that external beings are communicating through human bodies, others suspect that the "alien intelligences" are nothing more than roles enacted by the channelers. Such role performances need not be fraudulent; they may be accompanied by DISSOCIATION, so that the channeler's ordinary personality is temporarily set aside. In this view, channeling is simply an extreme version of AUTOMATISMs like the Ouija board or automatic writing.

If the statements of the channeled entities contain information or wisdom that was beyond the capability of the channeler, the case for external influence is strengthened. As Reed observed, much channeled material "consist[s] solely of strings of loosely associated gobbets of naive ideas and verbal formulae." Some channelers do present coherent philosophies and descriptions of the universe; but none of their proclamations have contained details that could be verified by scientific means. Channeling devotees have received solace and meaningful personal advice from channeled entities; but again, ordinary human counselors can sometimes be as effective.

Many entranced channelers speak in an accent; they may also employ idioms from particular historical periods. Thomason—a linguist who studied audiotapes of channelers—reported that, unlike normal accents, the accents of the entities were unstable, tending to deteriorate back into the channeler's ordinary speech inflections over the course of the trance session. In cases studied by Thomason in which the channeled entity claimed to be from a known historical period, the entity's accent was inaccurate, as was information about the period supplied by the entity. These findings are more consistent with the idea that channeling involves the performance of entity roles, rather than visitations of superior beings.

For further reading: Grunwald; Hastings; Hughes; Hughes and Melville; Klimo; Reed (1989); Thomason (1989).

charisms This term (from the Greek *charismata*, "gifts of grace") in the Roman Catholic tradition refers to apparently supernatural manifestations associated with holy people, especially saints. The high honor of canonization has never been bestowed lightly, but only after extensive investigation by church authorities. As a result, over the centuries a vast body of documentation regarding the occurrence of charisms has accumulated.

During the early Middle Ages, the responsibility of canonization lay with regional bishops. They would investigate stories of remarkable phenomena connected to holy persons, applying their own tests for assessing the validity of the reports. There was no standard method of investigation used throughout the church; as a result, the early accounts of charisms are little more than legends. In later medieval times, the papacy moved to gain control of canonization procedures and to establish uniform methods of evaluating charismatic occurrences. In 1588, Pope Sixtus V empowered a central body, the Congregation of Rites, with the task of authenticating charisms.

Prior to his ascension to the papacy, Benedict XIV had extensive personal experience in researching charisms—he had served as Devil's Advocate, whose role was to challenge evidence in canonization proceedings. Benedict codified the investigatory procedures and process of canonization in the 1730s. The approach he outlined is still followed today. The occurrence of well-documented charisms is not sufficient for sainthood; and belief in their supernatural origin is not required of the Catholic faithful. Indeed, Father Robert Smith takes a very skeptical position in his book, *Comparative Miracles* (cited in Rogo). However, a review of the historical literature on the saints suggests that charisms feature in the accounts of many a holy life.

Charisms recognized by the Roman Catholic church today include: AURAs; BILOCATION; EXCHANGE OF HEARTS; INCENDIUM AMORIS; LEVI-

TATION; LOCUTIONs; ODORS OF SANCTITY; READ-
ING OF HEARTS; STIGMATA; and VISIONs.

For further reading: Murphy; Nickell;
Rogo; Thurston.

charismatists A variant term for the early
Christian prophets, mentioned in the New Testament and other ancient sources. Charismatists
would enter an altered state inspired by the Holy
Spirit and utter intelligible prophecies, or GLOS-
SOLALIA. Afterwards, they might remember
nothing of the experience.

See also BIBLICAL PROPHECY.

childhood alternate reality People who perceive nonphysical realities during childhood are
more likely to report NEAR DEATH EXPERIENCEs
and UFO ENCOUNTERs later in life, according to
Ring. Relevant items on his questionnaire of
childhood experiences included: "As a child, I
was aware of nonphysical beings while I was
awake"; and "As a child, I was able to see into
'other realities' that others didn't seem to be
aware of." Most researchers take such stories as
evidence of FANTASY PRONENESS, or as instances
of IMAGINARY COMPANIONs. Ring, however, resisted the implication that these experiences are
mere confusions of reality and imagination. Subjects who reported the childhood alternate realities said their experiences were not fantasy-like
but "subjectively real," he noted, leaving open
the possibility that they were valid perceptions
of a nonphysical kind.

See also Appendix; CHILDHOOD TRAUMA.

For further reading: Ring.

childhood trauma Some skeptics have argued
that paranormal beliefs are comforting delusions
which create an illusion of control in the face of
a chaotic and disturbing world. If this is so, one
would expect higher levels of anomalous belief
among those who faced great uncertainty during
their formative years. Irwin surveyed Australian
university students on their paranormal beliefs
and childhood experiences. He found that individuals who reported being traumatized as children—including sexual or physical abuse, loss of
loved ones, major illness or accident, isolation or
other sorts of family disruptions—were more
likely to believe in anomalous phenomena. Irwin
noted that childhood trauma has been linked to
the development of FANTASY PRONENESS, which
has often been shown to correlate positively with
paranormal beliefs.

Ring examined the relationship between reported childhood trauma and two categories of
unusual experience among American subjects:
UFO ENCOUNTERs, including UFO abductions;
and NEAR DEATH EXPERIENCEs. He confirmed
that a positive correlation exists between childhood trauma reports and both types of anomaly.
Ring suggested that some children learn to escape from unpleasant circumstances by developing the ability to focus their attention in unusual
ways. They can then tune out unwanted perceptions, and may be more able to notice strange or
unexpected phenomena than those with ordinary attentional habits. Ring speculated that
some people who faced early traumas:

> are actually the unwitting beneficiaries of a kind
> of compensatory gift in return for the wounds
> they have incurred in growing up. That is,
> through the exigencies of their difficult and in
> some cases even tormented childhoods, they
> also come to develop *an extended range of
> human perception beyond normally recognized
> limits.* Thus, they may experience directly what
> the rest of us with unexceptional childhoods
> may only wonder at.

From this viewpoint, the link between childhood
trauma and paranormal belief may not simply
reflect a need for comforting delusions, but an
effort to make sense out of a greater than normal
amount of unusual experiences.

Another possible explanation for the link between childhood trauma reports and accounts of
anomalous experience as adults is that both
types of report are based on memory. Some
people may tend to produce dramatic FALSE
MEMORIES; they might misremember their child-

hoods as being worse than they actually were and misremember strange occurrences as being more anomalous than they actually were.

See also Appendix; CHILDHOOD ALTERNATE REALITY; IMAGINARY COMPANION.

For further reading: Irwin (1992); Ring.

clairaudience The alleged ability to hear distant events or inaudible sounds without using the ordinary hearing sense. Hearing the cry of a friend in trouble who is on another continent would be an instance of clairaudience. Some mediums report that they hear the voices of the dead during seances. Clairaudience is included as a subtype of EXTRASENSORY PERCEPTION; it is also often subsumed within the category of CLAIRVOYANCE.

See also AUDITORY HALLUCINATION; INNER VOICE.

clairvoyance The alleged ability to obtain information about events or objects without the use of any known senses. Clairvoyance is traditionally distinguished from two other major types of psychic phenomena, precognition and telepathy. Unlike precognition, or foretelling the future, clairvoyance refers to paranormal knowledge about occurrences in the present. Telepathy is the ability to read minds, whereas clairvoyance refers to psychic knowledge of external events. In fact, it would be almost impossible to distinguish telepathy and clairvoyance, for reading a mind might simply be clairvoyant knowledge of another person's brain activities. Clairvoyance and these other types of psychic phenomena are subsumed under the heading of EXTRASENSORY PERCEPTION. A 1990 Gallup poll estimated that about 26% of adult Americans believe in clairvoyance.

See also GESP.

For further reading: Gallup and Newport.

Clever Hans effect Clever Hans was a horse with seemingly amazing powers. When asked to perform mathematical calculations, or to tell the time, Hans was able to tap out the correct answer with his hoof. Many observers thought that the horse was either a genius or had ESP. Careful study revealed that Hans' "cleverness" lay in his ability to notice the body movements of the person questioning him. With each tap of the hoof, the questioner tended to nod slightly; when the correct answer had been reached, the questioner unconsciously altered his or her posture, which Hans took as a signal to cease tapping. The questioner possessed the knowledge, not Hans; the animal simply acted as a mirror. The name of the famous horse has become affixed to a similar phenomenon that takes place between humans.

People are constantly conveying information about themselves through their utterances, behaviors, posture, clothing and smell. When a person gleans information by observation and presents these cues to the scrutinized individual, this interaction is called the Clever Hans effect. We may engage in such feedback without fully understanding the source of our impressions. For instance, one may sense a friend's sadness, and say, "You seem sad today." The basis for our intuition may be the friend's cramped posture, tear-stained shirt and low voice—but neither we nor they may realize this. Instead, we might conclude that we are telepathically linked.

The Clever Hans effect can also be deliberately utilized to create the impression that one has ESP. Magicians and fake psychics pay close attention to the information that clients unwittingly impart. When they feed back what they have learned through observation, mixed with some judicious inferences, the clients may be convinced that only supernatural powers could have provided such knowledge. In their excitement the clients may then let slip more information, which can again be fed back. Hyman recounted a story told by the famous magician John Mulholland that illustrates this use of the Clever Hans effect:

A young lady in her late twenties or early thirties visited a character reader. She was wearing expensive jewelry, a wedding band, and a black dress of cheap material. The observant reader noted that she was wearing shoes that were currently being advertised for people with foot trouble. . . . By means of just these observations the reader proceeded to amaze his client with his insights. He assumed that this client came to see him, as did most of his female customers, because of a love or financial problem. The black dress and the wedding band led him to reason that her husband had died recently. The expensive jewelry suggested that she had been financially comfortable during marriage, but the cheap dress indicated that her husband's death had left her penniless. The therapeutic shoes signified that she was working to support herself since her husband's death. The reader's shrewdness led him to the following conclusion—which turned out to be correct: The lady had met a man who had proposed to her. She wanted to marry the man to end her economic hardship. But she felt guilty about marrying so soon after her husband's death. The reader told her what she had come to hear—that it was all right to marry without further delay.

Most people who visit psychics insist that they do not disclose anything to the diviner; indeed, some clients take pride in their ability to eliminate cues, even donning disguises and faking accents. But try as they might, people are always broadcasting information. And, in the excitement of a psychic consultation people may not be the most reliable observers of their own acts. Hyman described how, on one occasion, he witnessed a tea-leaf reader with a client. Afterward, the client, who had been impressed by the psychic's accuracy, swore that she had not said a word during the reading; but in fact, she had taken up three-quarters of the session talking. As Hyman stated, "The client praised the reader for having so astutely told her what in fact she herself had spoken."

See also CRYPTAESTHESIA.

For further reading: Hyman (1981); Sebeok and Rosenthal.

clouds Although physically clouds are not very mysterious—they are composed of water droplets or ice crystals—they have featured in a range of seemingly paranormal manifestations. In many traditions the cloud-shrouded summits of mountains have been places where visionaries have sought communion with gods and spirits. The Old Testament reported that Moses had such an encounter: "And the Lord said unto Moses, Lo I come unto thee in a thick cloud" (Exodus 19:9). Strangely shaped clouds have often been viewed as signs of a supernatural presence. Again, Exodus recounts that "the Lord went before them by day in a pillar of a cloud, to lead them the way" (14:21).

The continuous churning of the atmosphere can produce almost any imaginable cloud shapes. The less common of these forms can still evoke wonder and be interpreted as otherworldly manifestations. In mountainous regions, great discs of vapor known as lenticular clouds can form as air passes over the elevations. These impressive forms can hover for hours before dissipating. Lenticular clouds account for some reports of UFO ENCOUNTERs.

Parallel bands of high clouds, filling the sky, have sometimes been observed. This phenomenon is likely produced by the aerial droplets aligning with the earth's magnetic field, although how water vapor can become magnetically sensitive is unclear. Other strange-looking cloud displays include the formation of long, vaporous cords arching between widely separated clouds, and perfectly circular holes being punched into cloud decks by invisible movements of air.

For further reading: Corliss (1983b); Sachs.

confabulation Variant term for FALSE MEMORY.

conformity Individuals differ in their need to have similar perceptions and beliefs to those around them. Given that a person's beliefs and expectations affect what they experience, it might be predicted that people with conformist tendencies would be unlikely to report experiences that do not fit the conventional world view. Several studies have found instead that people who have low *or* high conformity needs are most prone to experiencing strange phenomena.

Researchers have wondered about the relationship between conformity and MYSTICAL EXPERIENCE. Mainstream Christian denominations do not tend to encourage intense religious experiences among their members, so it might be thought that conformity to the beliefs of a conventional denomination would be negatively related to mystical occurrences. Or, it could be that people who are strongly committed to a religion would be more likely to interpret unusual feelings in spiritual terms; this viewpoint would predict that mystical experiences would be *more* probable among people who conform to an orthodox doctrine. Studies have partially supported both predictions, assuming that frequency of church attendance reflects the degree of conformity with the church's teachings; people who attend church a moderate amount report fewer mystical experiences than either rare or frequent attenders. Whether a similar relation holds between unusual experiences and participation in more mystically oriented orthodoxies, such as Buddhism, is unknown.

See also Appendix; AUTOKINETIC EFFECT.

For further reading: Hood, Hall, Watson and Biderman; P. Nelson.

Constantine, vision of The visionary experience of the fourth century Roman Emperor Constantine fundamentally changed the course of Western history. In 312 A.D. the rulership of the Empire had become fragmented. The eastern portion was controlled by Licinius; in the west, Constantine and Maxentius struggled for power. The armies of the two western contenders assembled at the Milvian Bridge outside Rome in preparation for the battle that would decide the fate of the West.

At this time Christianity was still a banned religion. Despite periodic waves of official persecution, the number of Christians had grown steadily. Maxentius was hostile toward the new faith. Constantine's own mother had been a Christian, but he himself worshipped Sol Invictus, the pagan deity of the Unconquered Sun. As Constantine later confided to his biographer, Eusebius, his beliefs were altered forever by the vision he had shortly before the battle.

Constantine did not describe in detail his state of mind at the time, but it seems reasonable to assume that, facing the prospect of a possible defeat at the hands of Maxentius' troops, he must have been under considerable stress and uncertainty—conditions known to predispose people to unusual experiences. Looking into the sky, Constantine saw a shining cross superimposed on the face of the sun. Gleaming on the cross were the Latin words *"In hoc signo vinces"* ("In this sign, you will conquer").

Constantine understood the vision to indicate that his god of the Unconquered Sun was actually the God of the Christians. He ordered his soldiers to paint Christian symbols on their shields and to carry into battle a standard bearing the words from his vision. And, indeed, they conquered; Maxentius was killed and his forces were routed. Constantine, now the champion of Christianity, became the undisputed Emperor of the West.

In the following year Constantine and Licinius issued a proclamation legalizing the Christian faith and returning confiscated property to Christians. Under a Christian emperor, the social and political rewards of becoming a Christian increased, and the church saw tremendous growth. After several decades during which Christian factions fought for dominance, Catholic Christianity was adopted as the state religion of the Roman Empire in 391. If the mysterious sign had not appeared to Constantine, Christianity might never have achieved the state support it needed to establish itself as a world religion. In recognition of its significance, the words and symbols from the vision of Constantine can be found on display in many churches to this day.

See also VISION.

For further reading: Campbell (1976); Latourette.

contemplation   In Latin, *contemplari* referred to the act of looking for God's will, as practiced by Roman diviners. Contemplation, the derived English word, retained the connotation of spiritual seeking. In Christianity, contemplation traditionally refers to non-discursive prayer, that is, focusing the attention on a simple image, idea or feeling of God's presence. By so doing, devotees can actually contact the Divine and contemplate God themselves. This practice can lead to MYSTICAL and NUMINOUS experiences.

Roman Catholic contemplation is often divided into two types. *Acquired contemplation* is non-discursive prayer developed through practice; *infused contemplation* is a state thought to be caused by the action of God on a person's soul. Mystical writers like St. Teresa of Avila have presented more elaborate classification systems, dividing contemplation into several subtypes.

Thomas Aquinas emphasized that contemplation should be playful, rather than solemn and forced; casting one's mind toward God is not a means to an end, but an end in itself, he argued. Whether God responds to the mind's invitation is beyond human control.

Outside of the Catholic tradition, contemplation has referred to a variety of spiritual practices. Some writers have equated it with the Sanskrit SAMADHI, indicating a state of intensely focused concentration; others have used it as a synonym for meditation in general.

For further reading: Slade.

control needs   Under most circumstances, people prefer to feel in control of a situation, but individuals differ in the intensity of their need to feel in control. People who have stronger control needs tend to be socially dominant and to experience an "illusion of control"—that is, to believe that they are controlling the outcomes of events that, in fact, they cannot influence. Blackmore and Troscianko found that believers in ESP had a greater illusion of control concerning a computerized task than nonbelievers. Irwin found that people who were perceived by friends as needing to control social situations also tended to believe in ESP. These findings suggest that, for some, belief in ESP serves to meet a need to feel in control.

See also Appendix; BELIEF, ANOMALOUS; LOCUS OF CONTROL.

For further reading: Blackmore and Troscianko; Irwin (1992).

Convulsionaries   This group, which arose in France during the 18th century, is a classic case of mass compulsion. The focal point of the phenomenon was the tomb of Francois de Paris, a saintly man who had died in 1727 and was buried in the cemetery of St. Medard in Paris. At his funeral, a person experienced a miraculous cure; several more cures apparently occurred in the vicinity of his tomb over the next few years. But the unusual events commenced in earnest in 1731. Groups of visitors to the tomb were gripped by uncontrollable urges to dance or fall into seizures.

In these states the "convulsionnaires", as they came to be called, seemed to lose contact with the external world, even to the point of becoming insensitive to pain. They had religious visions and reported miraculous healings. On one occasion, a skeptic who came to the tomb to mock the proceedings found herself struck with paralysis.

At the time of the outbreak, tensions were running high within the French Catholic church. A substantial number of clerics had joined a movement called Jansenism. According to the Jansenists, the human will is too weak to perform any good deeds without God's grace. This negation of human will was regarded as extreme by Christian orthodoxy; in 1713, the pope declared Jansenism a heresy. The Jansenist position was sympathetic to the idea that one could be seized by God's will—indeed, the prevalence of Jansenist attitudes likely contributed to the occurrence of the Convulsionary phenomena. The orthodox view tended to perceive dramatic involuntary behaviors as instances of demonic POSSESSION. Within a short time, the Convulsionaries became aligned with the Jansenists.

In 1732, French authorities closed the cemetery of St. Medard as part of a campaign against the Jansenists. However, the Convulsionary movement continued underground and became more bizarre; adherents demonstrated God's miraculous protection by submitting to various tortures while in trance states. These treatments ranged from beatings and weights dropped on the abdomen to suspension over fire, mutilation and even crucifixion. Eventually, the movement dissolved under the pressure of persecution.

See also DANCING MANIA; FLAGELLATION.

For further reading: Cavendish.

corpse light   World folklore is full of stories of luminous forms seen around dead bodies. Considering the circumstances, a spiritual explanation of the lights would be hard to resist: the soul of the deceased must still be in the area. More prosaic, if much less pleasant, explanations have also been considered.

Carrington noted that, before the availability of refrigeration in morgues, corpses were sometimes seen to glow during warm weather. This effect was attributed to the presence of phosphoretted hydrogen, exuded by the body during the process of decay. The phosphorus in this substance absorbs radiation and re-emits it as light.

If an open flame is brought near a corpse, some of the body's invisible emissions could be inadvertently ignited, perhaps creating corpse lights. Gaddis reported a macabre experiment:

> gas formed in human bodies exposed to the air during early stages of putrefaction is flammable. Minute orifices can be pricked in bloated bodies and the gas ignited. The long, bluish flames may burn like tiny blow-pipes for several days before the combustibility of the gas ceases.

More spectacular reports of corpse lights, which include luminous spheres, require a different explanation—unless one dismisses them as the wishful thinking of the bereaved. The French physician Hippolyte Baraduc made use of his personal tragedies to explore the issue. He took a series of photographs of his wife's body, starting at the moment of death. The picture taken 15 minutes post mortem appears to depict three glowing balls, each larger than the corpse's head, hovering over the thorax and legs. One hour post mortem, the photograph reveals a single sphere of light, extending from the head to the waist. Upon the death of his son, Baraduc took photographs of the body reposing in the coffin. A picture taken nine hours after death shows a luminous cloud above the corpse. No one has yet attempted to replicate Baraduc's odd findings, or explain them.

See also: CEMETERY LIGHT; WILL-O'-THE-WISP.

For further reading: Carrington; Gaddis.

cosmic consciousness   One of the first modern writers on MYSTICAL EXPERIENCEs was the Canadian psychiatrist R.M. Bucke. In 1901, he published an influential book entitled *Cosmic Consciousness: A Study in the Evolution of the Human Mind*. According to Bucke, cosmic consciousness is a type of experience that occurs only to the most highly developed members of the human race. In it, feelings of bliss are accompanied by a sense of profound insight. To the cosmically conscious mind, the world appears as a living, harmoniously ordered whole, and the immortality of the self is obvious.

Bucke provided a vivid account of his own episode of cosmic consciousness. During a lengthy carriage ride:

> I was in a state of quiet, almost passive enjoyment, not actually thinking, but letting ideas, images, and emotions flow of themselves, as it were, through my mind. All at once, without warning of any kind, I found myself wrapped in a flame-colored cloud. For an instant I thought of fire, an immense conflagration somewhere close by . . . the next, I knew that the fire was within myself. Directly afterward there came upon me a sense of exultation, of immense joyousness accompanied or immediately followed by an intellectual illumination impossible to describe. . . . I did not merely come to believe, but I saw that the universe is not composed of dead matter, but is, on the contrary, a living Presence; I became conscious in myself of eternal life. It was not a conviction that I would have eternal life, but a consciousness that I possessed eternal life then; I saw that all men are immortal; that the cosmic order is such that without any peradventure all things work together for the good of each and all; that the foundation principle of the world, of all the worlds, is what we call love, and that the happiness of each and all is in the long run absolutely certain. The vision lasted a few seconds and was gone; but the memory of it and the sense of the reality of what it taught has remained during the quarter of a century which has since elapsed.

Cosmic consciousness is the mode of awareness toward which our species is evolving, thought Bucke; the difference between our ordinary awareness and cosmic consciousness is as great as that between our consciousness and the minds of other animals. Bucke's positive and naturalistic interpretation of mystical experiences contrasted with the major approaches of his day, which tended to view such experiences either as signs of mental illness or in terms of specific religious dogmas.

See also PEAK EXPERIENCE; TRANSPERSONAL PSYCHOLOGY.

For further reading: Bucke; James (1958).

cosmic dust bunnies Diffuse patches of light sometimes streak through the heavens at night, according to sky watchers. In appearance they can resemble a comet, but their movement through the sky is much faster, similar to that of typical METEORs. It is believed that the displays are probably meteoritic. Perhaps they are the fragmentary remains of very fragile meteoroids which shatter into clouds of small rocks as they enter the atmosphere. Gallagher called these delicate visitors from space "cosmic dust bunnies."
For further reading: Gallagher.

countersun Ice crystals in the atmosphere can act as tiny mirrors, reflecting incident light. If a layer of ice crystals is in the sky opposite the position of the solar disc, it can reflect an image of the sun. The image is called a countersun. Some reports of UFO ENCOUNTERs may have arisen from sightings of countersuns.
See also SUBSUN.

creativity Highly creative people are stereotypically believed to hold unusual beliefs about the world. The biographies of artists lend some credence to this idea. Social scientific research has also provided evidence for a link between anomalous belief and creativity. A survey by Moon discovered that artists are more likely to believe in ESP than non-artists. Other researchers have devised measures of creativity—for example, the number of answers given to a question like "How many uses can you think of for a brick?" These studies have confirmed that high levels of creativity are correlated with belief in ESP.
See also Appendix.
For further reading: Davis, Peterson and Farley; Moon; Raphael-Staude.

cryptaesthesia Literally "hidden sensation," this term refers to information gathered by the senses that enters awareness in another form, camouflaging its sensory origin. Flournoy, who coined the term, reported a case in which a woman suffering from HYSTERIA could not feel any sensation in a finger. When the finger was touched, however, she saw a mental image of it.

In another of Flournoy's reports, a man who had entered a forest encampment heard a voice commanding him to leave at once. Immediately after he did so, a tree fell and crushed the campsite. This individual later realized that he had noticed some termites on the tree when he passed it entering the site; unconsciously, he must have realized the danger posed by the termite-weakened tree and presented the information to himself as an auditory hallucination. If he had not recalled viewing the termites, this incident would have seemed a powerful example of precognition.

The unconscious utilization of sensory cues has proven a bane of research in PARAPSYCHOLOGY. Some early ESP experiments involved asking people to guess symbols printed on cards. Although the subjects could see only the backs of the cards, they reported images and intuitions of the symbols and, indeed, were correct much more often than would be expected by chance. It was later determined that the outlines of the symbols were faintly visible on the backs of the cards. The above chance accuracy of the guessers might not have been ESP, but cryptaesthesia—the subjects could have seen the symbol on the card and experienced this knowledge as a hunch or mental image. In order to argue that *extra*sensory perception is responsible for an experimental result, researchers must eliminate all *sensory* perception disguised by cryptaesthetic processes.

See also CRYPTOPSYCHISM; EXTRASENSORY PERCEPTION; SYNESTHESIA.

For further reading: Baker (1992); Flournoy (1911).

cryptic Cryptic as an adjective means "hidden"; and, as a noun, has come to refer to extraordinary animals, such as the SASQUATCH and LOCH NESS MONSTER, that have not been proven to exist. The scientific study of cryptic animal reports is known as CRYPTOZOOLOGY. Folklore and mythology are filled with tales of fabulous beasts. The continuing reports of encounters with fantastic animals today suggests that the old legends may have been based, in part, on actual experiences.

Strange creatures are often reported on the open sea and also in lakes. While it is extremely likely that the ocean contains yet unidentified species, it seems much less plausible that such could be the case for well-explored inland bodies of water, especially if the cryptics are said to be large. Nonetheless, hundreds of lakes around the world have been the sites of water monster sightings. Sightings of large water creatures with long necks are concentrated in lakes along the isotherm (a line connecting regions of equal temperature) of 10° Celsius in both the northern and southern hemispheres. Heuvelmans (1968) argued that the uneven distribution of sightings is circumstantial evidence that the creatures are real; but other factors, including the concentration of human observers, the distribution of lakes on the earth's surface and coincidence, may be involved. The most interesting reports of water monsters have come from Loch Ness, and from west Africa, where the MOKELE- MBEMBE is said to reside.

The best known land cryptics are the hairy HUMANOIDS glimpsed in wooded areas. North America has its Sasquatch or Bigfoot; Himalayan Asia has its Yeti; and many other parts of the world have had waves of sightings. Air cryptics have also been reported. Flying animals said to resemble the dinosaurs pterodactyl and pteranodon have been reported in Texas and west Africa. The MOTHMAN seen by many witnesses in West Virginia may also fit into this category.

The world's most active region for reports of cryptics is the Canadian province of British Columbia. Water monsters have been repeatedly sighted in 24 lakes in the area, as well as in the open sea off the mainland. The most famous of the province's water monsters is Ogopogo, the alleged denizen of Lake Okanagan. This water monster zone overlaps the heartland of Sasquatch sightings that extends along the west coast—indeed, the term "sasquatch" is borrowed from a Native language of southern British Columbia.

It is almost certain that species of life not yet cataloged by science exist on this planet, and some of the reported encounters with cryptics may eventually turn out to be true. But biology cannot accept the existence of an animal unless a body is available for study; and no one has ever managed to catch a hairy humanoid or a lake monster. Other forms of physical evidence for the reality of cryptics, such as photographs, footprints, feces, hair and audio recordings of alleged vocalizations, have not proven conclusive.

Factors other than undiscovered animals probably play a major role in most reports of cryptics. Many witnesses have been duped by hoaxes, as more than one trickster has been caught running around the woods in an ape costume, or launching an inflatable lake monster. Shadowed forests and the murky depths of lakes offer many vaguely glimpsed stimuli that can easily be misidentified as cryptics, especially if the witness has been primed by stories of other mysterious encounters at the site.

Little research has been done on the characteristics of people who report seeing cryptics. Several survey studies have examined belief in the existence of cryptics. People who include cryptics in their world view are most often young males. Cryptic belief tends to be negatively correlated with the level of EDUCATION. Psychological features that have been associated with belief in cryptics include FANTASY-PRONENESS, magical ideation, external LOCUS OF CONTROL, low SOCIAL INTEREST and DEATH CONCERNS.

See also Appendix.

For further reading: Corliss (1981); Heuvelmans (1958, 1968, 1986); Eberhart.

cryptomnesia   This term, which literally means "hidden memory," refers to memories that are not recognized as such. Instead of being identified as an ordinary memory, the retrieved material might seem to be an original idea; or, if it contains information that the person is unaware of having learned, it might be taken as evidence for an anomalous process such as ESP or past lives.

Cryptomnesia is a professional hazard of the artist. Musician George Harrison was sued for plagiarizing his song "My Sweet Lord" from the Chiffons; Harrison had not engaged in any dishonesty, but had mistaken his memory of the Chiffons' tune for a product of his own creative mind. The history of literature is filled with examples of cryptomnesia. Samuel Rosenberg (cited in Harris), a literary consultant on plagiarism suits, stated:

> Don't be fooled by the sometimes astonishing resemblances you will find when you compare *any two* films, plays, stories, books, or film scripts. During the past twenty-five years we have made hundreds of such comparisons in preparation for court trials, and in a great many cases we have found that *both* of the quarreling authors—each convinced that *he* was honest and the other writer was an idea-thief—had copied their plots, ideas, sequences from an *earlier* literary classic or from the bible or some "forgotten" childhood story.

In HYPNOSIS, MEDIUMSHIP and states in which AUTOMATISMs are produced, the tendency to mistake a fantasy for a memory is often increased. These conditions also favor mistaking a memory for a nonmemory, or cryptomnesia. Information learned long ago and apparently forgotten can resurface, in forms that support one's hopes and expectations. If a person is hypnotized in order to uncover REINCARNATION MEMORIES, for instance, a fantasy narrative can emerge into awareness that contains facts derived from forgotten sources. If the manner in which the person learned these facts is never discovered, it may seem as if they must have been learned during a previous existence. Kampman noted a case in which a hypnotized girl was able to sing a song in medieval English, a language to which she apparently had never been exposed. Kampman was able to determine that the girl had once glanced at the song in a library book. The girl's knowledge of medieval English was an ordinary memory, camouflaged as something more exotic.

In other contexts disguised memories might be taken as evidence for the POSSESSION of a person by a knowledgeable spirit. James described a case in which an illiterate woman in Germany, beset by a fever, began to babble in Latin, Greek and Hebrew. The local priest concluded that her sudden erudition could only be explained by demonic possession. It was later learned that she had boarded with a scholar as a child. The professor had been in the habit of pacing the halls while reading aloud. In his books were discovered the phrases uttered by the woman. Her fever had triggered their recall, without revealing their source.

See also FALSE MEMORY; XENOGLOSSY.

For further reading: Baker (1992); Harris; James (1950); Kampman; Zusne and Jones.

cryptopsychism Coined by Flournoy, this term refers to psychological processes that occur in disguised forms. One form of cryptopsychism, CRYPTOMNESIA, involves memories that are mis-taken for original ideas or impressions. In CRYPTAESTHESIA, sensory information is disguised as mental images or intuitions.

For further reading: Flournoy (1911).

cryptozoology The Belgian biologist Bernard Heuvelmans coined this term and defined it as "the science of hidden animals." cryptozoologists study reports of encounters with CRYPTICS, animals that do not fit the descriptions of any known species. Cryptozoological research involves compiling and studying witness reports to look for patterns, examining alleged physical traces left by the creatures such as footprints or sonar images and mounting expeditions to the supposed habitats of the cryptics. The main forum for serious research in this field is the journal *Cryptozoology*.

While most sightings of cryptics are probably explainable in conventional terms (hoaxes and misidentifications of known species, for instance), cryptozoologists derive hope from the story of the coelacanth. This large prehistoric fish was long thought to have become extinct 65 million years ago until a living specimen was netted near the Comoro Islands in 1938.

For further reading: Corliss (1981); Heuvelmans (1958, 1986).

daishi A Zen Buddhist word, daishi literally means "great death." In order to become fully enlightened, one must let go of all attachments, especially the clinging to one's ordinary self-definition. According to Zen, our true nature is Buddha-nature. However, most of us do not know ourselves as Buddhas, but as limited, ordinary beings. It is said that in Zen practice "at some point you must die on the meditation cushion"—that is, you must release your narrow self-concept and experience your BUDDHAHOOD.

dancing From the caverns of the Old Stone Age to contemporary music concerts, dancing has been a popular method to induce an ALTERED STATE OF CONSCIOUSNESS. Two components of vigorous, repetitive movements—EMOTIONAL AROUSAL and RHYTHMIC SENSORY STIMULATION—can overload and disrupt normal patterns of brain functioning.

dancing mania Involuntary dancing was a type of mass compulsion that broke out in Europe during the later Middle Ages. The age was rife with uncertainty, and the social structure of the time provided no legitimate channels for the lower classes to express their anxieties. Under such conditions, unusual behaviors which embody loss of control are likely to prove contagious, especially when these behaviors are rewarded.

The earliest recorded occurrence of the dancing mania began in the German town of Erfurt in 1237. More than 100 children were seized with an urge to dance and leap. They danced to Arnstadt, almost 12 miles away, where they collapsed.

In the late 14th century, western Europe was a disaster area. The Black Plague had killed nearly one-third of the population; the banks of the Rhine River had overflowed, devastating surrounding areas. Prayer proved powerless against the onslaught of nature. In 1374, in the German town of Aachen, the dancing mania occurred. Groups of poor men and women began to dance uncontrollably in the streets. They also experienced terrifying visions of demons, rivers of blood and religious figures such as Christ and the Virgin Mary. Many viewed the dancers as suffering from demonic POSSESSION; some took the phenomenon as a sign that the world was about to end.

The dancing mania was contagious. In the ensuing months, it spread into Belgium and the Netherlands to the west, and appeared also in nearby major urban centers in Germany, Cologne and Metz. In the cities the mania threatened to turn into a mass movement. Five hundred dancers were reported in Cologne; over 1,100 were cavorting on the streets of Metz at one time (see ST. JOHN'S DANCE).

The dancers received much sympathetic attention, being perceived as victims as well as harbingers. Religious processions were held, masses sung and exorcisms performed in order to heal them. The effectiveness of these rites proved temporary; indeed, the concern shown toward these hitherto marginalized people likely reinforced their strange behavior. In addition, the dancers were not held responsible for their actions while in the grip of the possessing forces. They could thus violate social norms, engaging in illicit sex acts and theft without reaping the ordinary consequences. Indeed, because of their seeming proximity to supernatural forces, they acquired a certain authority. In the city of Liege, for instance, the manufacture of shoes with pointed toes was banned, on the whim of the dancers.

After several months, the mania gradually subsided. The truly spontaneous performances had become diluted by crowds of young men and women who merely simulated the possession in order to enjoy a holiday from conventional morality, and the dancers' movement lost the sympathy of the public.

A massive resurgence occurred in 1418 in Strasbourg, on the French-German border, radiating through the Rhineland and Belgium. Performers called the ST. VITUS' DANCErs assembled at all hours of the day or night and moved through the streets, accompanied by musicians playing the bag-pipes. The authorities sought to stem the phenomenon by bringing groups of dancers to chapels where exorcisms and masses were performed. Again, obvious simulators mixed with the authentic dancers. The St. Vitus movement eventually dissolved.

Italy was subject to a dancing mania which recurred periodically between the 14th and 18th centuries. Known as TARANTISM, because it was said to be caused by the bite of the tarantula spider, its victims fell into depressed lethargies and could only be aroused by the sound of music. The CONVULSIONARIES' movement is an instance of dancing mania in early modern times; in the 18th century, groups of people in the vicinity of a tomb in the Parisian cemetery of St. Medard found themselves dancing and convulsing uncontrollably.

Modern psychiatric parlance might label such behaviors contagious instances of SOMATOFORM DISORDER. Direct physical causes are highly unlikely, although it is possible that the presence of psychoactive contaminants such as ergot in bread might have played a part.

See also GROUP DYNAMICS OF UNUSUAL EXPERIENCES.

For further reading: Cavendish; Merskey.

Dark Day   The historical record is dotted with accounts of mysterious darkness falling upon the land. These Dark Days are not merely episodes when the sun is obscured by ordinary clouds. Rather, on a Dark Day the light fades suddenly, replaced by the blackness of midnight. Not surprisingly, such occurrences have often evoked the conviction that the world was about to end.

One of the most famous Dark Days happened on May 19, 1780, in New England. Diarists recorded that "An uncommon degree of darkness commenced" at about 10:30 A.M. Over the next two hours, the light continued to fade, until it became impossible to read even the largest print on a page without the aid of a candle. Chickens had gone to roost, evening birds were singing and frogs piping. By now, many people were praying. Members of the Connecticut legislature, which was sitting in Hartford as the darkness gathered, moved for adjournment. They were rebuffed by the famous utterance of Col. Abraham Davenport: "Either the day of judgment is at hand or it is not. If it is not, there is no cause for adjournment. If it is, I wish to be found in the line of my duty. I wish candles to be brought." In the early afternoon the sky brightened, until by 3:15 the light level was that of a heavily clouded day.

New England's Dark Day was blamed on smoke from forest fires burning to the north in New Hampshire. This explanation was often used to account for Dark Days in early modern America, because the western territories were unknown by most settlers, and it was easy to imagine huge blazes just beyond the horizon. In the occasional instance where the darkness was accompanied by rains of ashes and soot, the forest fire theory was very probably correct. Volcanic eruptions have also created intense darkness under the umbrellas of their atmospheric discharge. "Volcanic nights" have been known to last for several days and extend for over 1,000 miles from the eruption. Many Dark Days in the present century have been caused by surges in air pollution.

In certain instances, however, aerial debris may not be a sufficient explanation. Fires or volcanoes are unlikely to produce anything that could cause a wave of darkness lasting eight to ten minutes to move across the landscape, unaccompanied by any obvious clouds. And yet, several such reports have been filed. In other cases the stars became visible during the daytime darkness, suggesting that the air was clear. In these instances, perhaps an object in space was positioned between the sun and the earth, casting a shadow in the manner of a miniature eclipse.

For further reading: Corliss (1977; 1983b).

dark night of the soul This phrase was coined by the 16th century Catholic mystic, St. John of the Cross. It refers to periods of discomfort and despair on the Christian path of spiritual development. The dark night generally follows a time when one has felt progress toward God, often marked by MYSTICAL EXPERIENCEs. The confidence and pride in one's spiritual attainments that can arise from experiencing God's presence are obstacles to further spiritual development, the mystics teach; the withdrawal of that presence, which plunges one into the dark night phase, is a reminder to abandon these obstacles.

St. John described the dark night of the soul:

That which this anguished soul feels most deeply is the conviction that God has abandoned it, *of which it has no doubt*; that He has cast it away into darkness as an abominable thing . . . the shadow of death and the pains and torments of hell are most acutely felt, and this comes from the sense of being abandoned by God, being chastised and cast out by His wrath and heavy displeasure. All this and even more the soul feels now, for a terrible apprehension has come upon it that thus it will be with it for ever. It has also the same sense of abandonment with respect to all creatures, and that it is an object of contempt to all, especially to its friends.

The onset of the dark night is usually gradual. The mystic begins to doubt whether God is present in his or her life, and the visions, blissful moments and other signs of the divine stop happening. No matter what the mystic does—praying, contemplating, meditating—the sense of God's presence cannot be regained.

This loss of spiritual contact can last for many years. During this time, the mystic must deal with an enhanced sense of his or her own personal flaws. There may be a crushing feeling of depression, and a paralysis of the will and intelligence. Strong temptations to violate one's moral precepts may arise. For some mystics, the torment reaches a crescendo called by Underhill the "dark ecstasy." St. John's teacher, St. Teresa of Avila, endured this phenomenon:

As long as this pain lasts, we cannot even remember our own existence; for in an instant all the faculties of the soul are so fettered as to be incapable of any action save that of increasing our torture. . . . This is a trance of the senses and the faculties, save as regards all which helps to make the agony more intense. . . . The pain thus grows to such a degree that in spite of herself the sufferer gives vent to loud cries, which she cannot stifle, however patient and accustomed to pain she may be, because this is not a pain which is felt in the body, but in the depths of the soul. . . . Although this state lasts but a short time, the limbs seem to be disjointed by it. The pulse is as feeble as if one were at the point of death; . . . She burns with a consuming thirst, and cannot reach the water. And this is a thirst which cannot be borne, but which nothing will quench.

According to the Christian mystical tradition, the dark night of the soul is a test of faith. If the mystic is able to keep belief alive in the absence of any spiritually comforting experiences, the soul's night will eventually end. The devotee, now purified, experiences the dawn of the final phase on the Christian Mystic Way—union with God.

The dark night of the soul, as described by Christian mystics, has parallels in other traditions. The general theme—that one must relinquish one's personal pride and attachments in order to experience fully the divine reality—is central to faiths like Judaism, Hinduism, Buddhism and Islam (which literally means "submission to God's will"). Zen practitioners speak of *daigidan,* or "great doubt," an uncomfortable awareness of the difference between the world as it appears to be and the fundamental nature of reality as taught by the Buddha. This doubt acts as a spur to vigorous spiritual practice. The idea that periods of emotional disturbance can be seen as painful stages of growth, rather than mere illnesses, is endorsed by many psychotherapists today.

See also UNIO MYSTICA.

For further reading: Kavanaugh; Peers; Underhill.

Datura Several species of plants belong to the genus Datura. They are attractive in appearance, characterized by bell- or trumpet-shaped flowers of various hues. Less obvious is the feature that has caused datura to be revered, as well as feared, around the world for centuries. The plant contains concentrations of the tropane alkaloids hyoscyamine, scopolamine and atropine. Ingesting datura can produce a variety of powerful psychological effects. But even a small overdose can lead quickly to coma and death.

Datura is found throughout southern Asia, Africa, southern Europe and temperate North America. While some of the traditional names of the plant sound innocuous—Thorn Apple, for instance—others hint at its dangerous powers: Devil's Weed, Torna Loco ("Weed of Madness"), Tuft of Shiva (the Hindu god of destruction).

The effects of ingesting Datura depend on the species (which vary somewhat in potency), the dosage and the psychophysiological condition of the person. Analgesic and medicinal effects for a range of disorders have been reported. As the tropane alkaloids interfere with central nervous system functioning, FORM CONSTANTs and HALLUCINATIONs of both auditory and visual nature can occur, as well as confusion, stupor and memory loss.

There are many cases of people accidentally unleashing the forces of the datura upon themselves. Even animals, including moths, birds and cattle, have been observed behaving strangely following a taste of the plant. In one noteworthy incident, a whole troop of British soldiers succumbed. They had been sent to Virginia in 1676 to put down a rebellion among the colonists. At Jamestown, the troop's creative cooks made thorn apple soup for the soldiers. Contemporary accounts describe how the partakers wandered about behaving crazily for up to 11 days. The plant involved, Datura stramonium, was dubbed "Jamestown weed," which has been corrupted to jimson weed.

Accidents with the devil's weed continue to occur today. Siegel noted:

> Many children have inhaled the pollen, swallowed the seeds, or chewed on the leaves; a few have even survived. The intoxications have been dramatic. One five-year-old boy, after playing with the flower and trying to blow it like a trumpet, crushed it against his forehead, chewed on the petals, then began masturbating while barking like a dog.

Across time and culture, people have employed this dangerous chemical tool toward a myriad of ends. In China, Datura was believed to have originated from the sky; it was known as the "Holy Flower of the North Star." Medicinal uses were noted in Chinese herbal texts. One writer, Li Shih-chen, experimented by taking datura himself, and discovered that one of its effects was enhanced suggestibility: he had the urge to imitate the behaviors of others, such as dancing or laughing, while intoxicated.

Hindus linked datura with Shiva, the lord of destruction. In sculptures depicting Shiva performing the dance of cosmic dissolution, bringing all things to their end, his whirling hair is plaited with datura flowers. The Thugs, from whose name comes the English term thug, were devotees of the goddess Kali. They offered her human sacrifices, using datura to incapacitate their victims. Some Indians infused datura seeds in alcoholic drinks to magnify their potency, but the employment of the plant as a sacred hallucinogen is not well attested in Asia.

In Europe, however, datura's psychedelic effects were well-known. It is found in recipes for the WITCHES' OINTMENT, which may have been used by peasants to induce hallucinatory experiences.

Some traditional African societies harnessed datura intoxication for their cultural needs. Mozambican groups fed datura to pubescent girls as part of the liminal phase in the INITIATORY EXPERIENCE. In northeast Africa among the Kunama people, women consumed the plant and then danced to bring on states of POSSESSION, during which the ancestors were thought to speak through them.

Interest in using datura to induce unusual experience seems to have been greatest in the New World. Cabieses (cited in Dobkin de Rios) believed that decorations on pottery of the Peruvian Nazcas, who thrived between the second and ninth centuries A.D., are depictions of datura. The Incas are known to have administered the plant to misbehaving children as a punishment. The Aztecs consumed datura in order to produce visions of the gods. It was administered to victims awaiting sacrifice atop Aztec temple-pyramids, either to stupefy them or to reassure them concerning the reality of the divine realm to which they would shortly be dispatched. Datura is still widely used in Mexico to this day, primarily as a medicine but also as a hallucinogen used by sorcerers.

Until recently, boys among tribes in the western Amazon would be made to drink datura tea, or receive datura infusions via a hollow bone inserted into the rectum. The children would continue to be drugged until they fell into coma; if they recovered, their NEAR DEATH EXPERIENCEs would be eagerly interpreted by elders for hints of the spirits' will. Some Amazonian groups took datura in conjunction with another hallucinogen, YAJE, the "vine of the soul."

The Algonquin, who resided in Virginia, also employed datura as part of initiation rites. On reaching puberty, boys were placed in wooden cages and compelled to take quantities of datura. A witness described the effect: "they became stark, staring mad, in which raving condition they were kept eighteen or twenty days." The aim was to erase all memory of the boys' childhoods, so they could be reborn as men who possessed no childish traits.

Plains Indians took datura for curative purposes, and also, in higher doses, to induce divinatory trances. If someone had been the victim of theft, it was believed the visions caused by the flower would reveal to them the identity of the thief or the hiding place of the stolen property. In the American southwest, priests of the Zuni used datura as their major avenue to the spirit world. They would rub powdered datura into their eyes to see occult beings and chew the roots to hear the voices of the ancestors.

For further reading: Dobkin de Rios; Schultes and Hoffman; Siegel (1989).

deathbed vision No one can say what the moment of death is like—by definition, witnesses do not live to tell the tale. The period immediately preceding death is another matter. In many cases, if the dying person is not incapacitated by medication or nervous system failure, they describe striking visual displays. The deathbed vision is distinguished from the near death experience; in the latter phenomenon, the witness does not describe the experience as it is occurring, but after being resuscitated.

Several surveys of deathbed attendants have been conducted to study the utterances of the dying. For the most part, deathbed visions are apparently positive, uplifting experiences. Most often described are luminous beings—images of departed friends and relatives, and supernatural beings. These forms are called "take-away apparitions," because they invite the dying person to leave with them for another world. Ninety percent of the deathbed visions in Osis and Haraldsson's major survey (conducted in India and the U.S.A.) included such visitations. In about one-third of the reports, the witness describes a vision of the otherworld, or even, visits it through an out of body experience. The visualized domain is typically said to consist of resplendent gardens or buildings, populated by spirits.

According to Osis and Haraldsson, about half of the deathbed visions lasted five minutes or less; 17% continued for over one hour. Three-quarters of the visionaries died within 10 minutes of their welcome into the unknown.

These accounts are taken by many to be glimpses of what awaits us following death. There is no way to know whether they are instead comforting HALLUCINATIONs. It is noteworthy, however, that deathbed visions have been reported by people who were not on any drugs and who had no signs of brain damage; so mechanisms other than these are required to explain the experience.

It is not uncommon for people caring for the dying to report unusual sights. A radiance in the vicinity of the patient's body is the most frequently reported event. Rarely, this luminosity is said to take the form of the dying person. Witnesses have sometimes reported that they could see the take-away apparitions, but whether their experiences corresponded to those of the dying person cannot be verified. The stress of witnessing a death may trigger hallucinations, according to some researchers.

See also CORPSE LIGHT.

For further reading: Barrett; Osis and Haraldsson; Zaleski.

death concerns According to some studies, people who find the topic of death to be unusually disturbing are more likely to hold paranor-

mal beliefs in general and belief in ESP and CRYPTIC animals in particular. Irwin suggested that the loss of control entailed by dying might be the link between death concerns and paranormal belief, as other research indicates that paranormal believers tend to have higher CONTROL NEEDS. Belief in life after death is also positively correlated with general paranormal beliefs and ESP beliefs. Perhaps belief in an afterlife is another strategy used to lessen death concerns by individuals who especially fear loss of control. People who have had OUT OF BODY EXPERIENCEs, and especially NEAR DEATH EXPERIENCEs, have frequently reported that these unusual events diminished their fear of death.

See also Appendix.

For further reading: Irwin (1993); Tobacyk (1983c).

deautomatization A general rule of the human mind is that any thought, sensation or behavior that happens repeatedly or constantly becomes habitual; it takes less and less conscious effort to produce and it eventually occurs automatically, without awareness. Experienced drivers can perform complex acts of steering and change gears without noticing; people with low self-esteem find their minds filled with recurring self-demeaning thoughts. The retrieval of habitual mental processes into the conscious sphere is called deautomatization.

The term was coined by Deikman as an explanation for experiences reported by subjects in a meditation experiment. The subjects were instructed to concentrate on a blue vase, allowing it to fill their field of awareness. Many participants reported that they experienced sensory distortions, such as changes in the apparent size of the vase, a flattening of depth perception and an increase in the brightness of colors. Afterward, they noted that their perceptions of the world retained a quality of freshness, aliveness or novelty. Deikman suggested that the unusual deployment of attention by the subjects in his experiment disrupted the habit patterns learned by the brain to organize sensations into a meaningful perception of the world.

This deautomatization did not lead to confusion or distress. Rather, it allowed the subjects to organize their experiences in more interesting and fulfilling ways. Consequently, they felt an enhanced sense of enjoyment and freedom. Deautomatization could explain many of the unusual experiences reported by meditators and practitioners of other consciousness-altering methods. It may also account in part for the great value attributed to meditation in many spiritual traditions.

For further reading: Deikman; Tart (1975).

déjà vu This French term literally means "already seen." It refers to a strong sense of familiarity coupled with an experience that one believes one has never had before. Déjà vu can range from a vague feeling that "I have been here before" to a belief that one can almost "remember" what will happen next. The déjà vu feeling can arise in connection with locations, people or events. It is one of the most common types of unusual experience; surveys suggest that 60 to 70% of the general population has occasionally had déjà vu. Reed described a typical instance of déjà vu:

> I was about fifteen at the time. We'd gone on a school excursion to York . . . I came around a corner from the High Street into one of those little eighteenth-century side streets. And suddenly *I knew I'd been there before*—I recognized the butcher's shop and the old inn sign—everything. The joke is that there's no doubt whatsoever that I'd never been near the place before in my life . . .

Such experiences are so compelling because we rely on the sense of familiarity to signal whether or not a perception matches a memory; if we are convinced that this memory could not have been formed in the ordinary manner, as a record of previous experience, the origin of the memory trace seems to require a paranormal explanation. Some people believe that déjà vu hints at the existence of REINCARNATION MEMORIES; if one has never had the familiar experience before in *this* life, the memory may date from a previous incarnation. Other déjà viewers suspect that they have visited the strangely familiar setting before during an OUT OF BODY EXPERIENCE, or perhaps psychically learned about it through ESP.

The mysterious aura of déjà vu experiences hinges on two questions. How reliable is the conviction that one has never before had this perception? And how reliable is familiarity as a sign that a memory trace exists to match the perception?

Research has demonstrated that people may not always know that something has been seen before. Bannister and Zangwill showed experimental subjects a set of pictures while under HYPNOSIS and suggested that they would forget having seen the pictures. Days later, the subjects were again shown the pictures. Most did not remember having viewed the stimuli before, but were struck by a mysterious feeling of familiarity with them. Some instances of déjà vu probably arise from similarly forgotten previous encounters. In cases where such earlier experiences are impossible—a déjà vu during a first visit to a distant country, for instance—the possibility that one has seen depictions of the place is difficult to rule out. Or, one may be mistaking a memory of a *similar* previous experience for that of an *identical* one; the vaguely remembered dream of a castle might resemble a castle one is now visiting sufficiently to trigger familiarity.

Although the sense of familiarity often points to the existence of a matching memory, this is not always the case. Electrical disturbances in the brain's cortex can cause whatever a person is perceiving at the moment to seem familiar:— Some sufferers of EPILEPSY have this experience immediately before a seizure, as do individuals whose cortical surface is being electrically stimulated prior to brain surgery. Some déjà vu may be caused by a momentary disruption in cortical functioning.

The left and right hemispheres of the cortex each have a region that receives sensory information from the eyes. If the visual input received by one of these regions was slightly delayed by a neural malfunction, then one hemisphere might generate a perceptual image before the other one. By the time the tardy hemisphere had constructed its image, it would already be receiving the same information from the hemisphere that received a head start on forming the image. Some researchers have speculated that such a process could create a feeling of "having seen this before"; one may not sense that "before" was a matter of milliseconds.

In some accounts, people who were struck by déjà vu were actually able to predict what happened next, as if the event was a movie they had viewed before, or they recalled a feature of a location that was not evident at the time, but was later verified. Chari, cited in Christie-Murray, recounted the tale of a French nurse who felt familiar with the castle of St. Germaine en Laye prior to entering it. She said that there was a small, sealed room at the top of a staircase. The existence of the hidden room was later established by consulting old documents. Barring coincidence, such reports suggest that some déjà vu cannot easily be explained in conventional terms. Unfortunately, as with most anecdotes, there is no way to be sure that these incidents happened exactly as they were later reported.

Déjà vu may be related to some other types of unusual experience. Isakower noted that the sensations accompanying a déjà vu are similar to those of the ISAKOWER PHENOMENON. Several studies have found that déjà vu reports are more common among people who experience mental imagery during the HYPNAGOGIC STATE.

See also CRYPTOMNESIA.

For further reading: Bannister and Zangwill; Christie-Murray; Reed (1988); Sno, Schalken, De Jonge and Koeter; Zusne and Jones.

delirium   Many psychological processes are altered in the delirious state, including thinking, perception and emotion. In delirium, thoughts become disorganized and delusional; ILLUSIONs and HALLUCINATIONs occur; and feelings of fear, sadness, anger or euphoria can arise. The behavior of a delirious person is unpredictable; he or she may speak incoherently, weep unconsolably or attempt to flee from menacing visions. Delirious sufferers have been known to harm themselves or others in their confusion. States of delirium can persist for up to a week.

Delirious hallucinations are usually simple and unformed, and they tend to be visual—an amorphous monster crouching at the bedside or little planes flying around the room. Any of the senses can be affected, however, and sometimes complex, dreamlike hallucinations unfold.

The immature brains of children and the deteriorating cortical blood circulation of the elderly render them most vulnerable to a delirious attack. Among children, diseases that cause high fevers are the most common cause; some children also have delirious reactions to medications. HEAD INJURIES, EPILEPSY, and various illnesses can disrupt brain functioning in adults to produce delirium.

Delirium can also happen during withdrawal from drugs such as narcotics, barbiturates and antidepressants. These substances have in common the suppression of the REM stage of sleep, in which most dreams occur. Individuals deprived of REM sleep display a phenomenon called "REM rebound"—when they are allowed to sleep, they enter the REM stage and dream almost continuously for hours, as if to make up for the missed dream activity. Lipowski suggested that the delirious states of drug withdrawal are caused by dreams spilling into wakefulness, as a wave of REM rebound activity overwhelms waking consciousness.

See also DELIRIUM TREMENS.

For further reading: American Psychiatric Association; Asaad.

delirium tremens   This type of DELIRIUM afflicts alcoholics during withdrawal from their addiction; hence the variant term, *alcohol withdrawal delirium*. The "DTs" usually begin within three days after the alcoholic's last drink, although they can begin up to one week into abstinence.

Delirium tremens usually begins at night. Sufferers become extremely restless as an uncontrollable physical excitement sets in; vivid nightmares may shock them out of sleep. As their agitation increases, a succession of weird perceptions arise. Illusions are common; many people have reported that spots on the wall or cracks on the ceiling have transformed into spiders and snakes. Micropsia—the perception of objects and persons as extremely small—may occur. And HALLUCINATIONs, primarily in the visual modality, often follow. Visions of small animals, such as rats and snakes, are typical. Hallucinations of elephants, pink or otherwise, have been reported. These images may fascinate the hallucinator for long periods. Lishman described a patient "who followed intently, and with excited comments, a game of football performed for half an hour on end by two teams of normal-colored miniature elephants in a corner of his room." Many people in the throes of DTs endure the sensation of insects or rodents crawling over their skin.

Bouts of delirum tremens normally last less than three days. People going through severe alcohol withdrawal should do so under professional supervision. Delirious alcoholics have been known to harm themselves in their confusion, and the physical stress of withdrawal has sometimes proven fatal. About 15% of those who enter the state of delirium tremens do not recover; they slip into a brain damaged condition known as Korsakoff's syndrome, in which they suffer permanent disorientation and memory impairment.

Alcohol is one of many addictive drugs that suppress the stage of sleep in which most dreams occur, known as REM sleep. When these dream-inhibiting substances are withdrawn, the brain produces a flood of REM activity to compensate for the lost REM periods. The hallucinations of delirium tremens likely represent the leakage of intense dreaming into the waking state, produced by this REM rebound.

See also ALCOHOL HALLUCINOSIS.
For further reading: Asaad; Lishman.

delusion   A fixed belief that is regarded as false by the consensus of one's society is called a delusion. Occasionally, a minority belief that has been labeled delusory is later accepted—for instance, in the Middle Ages, the idea that the earth orbits the sun, or that people would some day be able to build mechanical hearts. Conversely, a delusion can be a belief that used to be acceptable, but is now outmoded—such as the conviction that one is under attack by demons, or that the earth is shaped like a pancake, for example.

In modern terms a delusion is generally viewed as a kind of thought disorder, symptomatic of mental illness. In most cases the belief is held by a minority of one, although group delusions can arise (such as FOLIE À DEUX). Several major categories of delusion are commonly noted by mental health professionals: the *erotomanic* type, an unwarranted belief that one is loved by someone else, usually of higher status; the *grandiose* delusion that one is special, important or powerful in some way; the *jealous* type, in which one falsely thinks that a spouse or lover is unfaithful; *persecutory* delusions, perhaps the most frequent type; and *somatic* delusions, in which one erroneously believes that one's body is exuding foul odors, infested with parasites or malfunctioning. Many delusions have been reported which do not fit into the major categories—for example, LYCANTHROPY, the belief that one has turned into a nonhuman animal, and DEMONOMANIA, the belief that one is possessed by a spirit. *Bizarre* delusions are a special category, consisting of especially outlandish notions—for example, the idea that one's body has expanded to the size of the universe, or that aborted fetuses are being implanted into one's chest during sleep.

If a delusion is not bizarre and is unaccompanied by other signs of psychological illness, a person may be diagnosed with delusional disorder. The average age of onset of this illness is between 40 and 55. Recent immigrants to a foreign culture are prone to developing delusional disorders, which are sometimes resolved if the immigrant returns to the home society.

Delusions can be part of the symptom picture of several other types of psychological disorders, including ORGANIC MENTAL DISORDERs and SCHIZOPHRENIA.

See also CAPGRAS SYNDROME; FREGOLI'S SYNDROME.

For further reading: American Psychiatric Association; Oltmanns and Maher.

demonomania Coined by the 19th century psychiatrist Esquirol, this term refers to the belief that one is possessed by a spirit. There are two subtypes: cacodemonomania, possession by an evil spirit; and theomania, possession by a beneficent entity, such as God. Psychiatrists view demonomania as a type of DELUSION.

See also POSSESSION.

depersonalization This term refers to a type of disturbance in a person's relationship with their own body or mental processes. Ordinarily, it is beyond question that one's body and mind are real and that they belong to one's self. People experiencing depersonalization report that they feel like external observers of their own thoughts and behaviors. They may feel like their body is a robot, functioning automatically while they watch. BODY IMAGE DISTORTIONs and DEREALIZATION often accompany depersonalization. The experience may have a dreamlike or uncanny quality.

Occasional episodes of depersonalization are normal; up to 70% of adolescents report short bouts of it. Persistent or recurring depersonalization is sometimes a feature of EPILEPSY and it can be a symptom of a psychological disorder. If the depersonalized feelings are the main problem, one may receive a diagnosis of depersonalization disorder, classed as a type of DISSOCIATIVE DISORDER. Persistent depersonalization can also be associated with ORGANIC MENTAL DISORDER, SCHIZOPHRENIA and other disorders.

For further reading: American Psychiatric Association; Noll (1992a).

derealization The feeling that everything in the world is unreal. The environment may appear to be composed of dream images or insubstantial phantoms, or to be a movie one is watching. Many people have occasional short episodes of derealization. It is often accompanied by DEPERSONALIZATION. Persistent or recurrent and distressing feelings of derealization may be linked to a psychological or NEUROLOGICAL DISORDER.

devekut This Hebrew word, meaning "cleaving" or "adhesion," is the most common term for the MYSTICAL EXPERIENCE in the context of Judaism. Devekut refers to the practice of keeping one's attention fixed on God. The deity may be represented by his names, scriptures, symbols or ideas. The Jewish mystic (or kabbalist) who cleaves to God through his representations can experience his presence.

Idel (1989) noted that devekut has "a variety of meanings, from imitating divine behavior to the total fusion with the divine." Orthodox Jewish doctrine holds that God and humanity are distinct; people who claim that they are God are committing blasphemy. Some descriptions of devekut come perilously close to identifying the mystic with God, or even cross the boundary of orthodox thought. The 12th century kabbalist Abraham Abulafia, who taught many techniques of devekut, said that those who properly executed his methods would "become one entity" with God. Others describe devekut as an intimate encounter with God that falls short of complete fusion, as in the following description (quoted by Idel):

> the [divine] light overwhelmed him, and he gazed at it because of his great desire to cleave to it and to enjoy it without interruption, and after he cleaved to it he did not wish to be separated from the sweet radiance, and he remained immersed and hidden within it. And his soul was crowned and adorned by that very radiance and brightness.

Devekut, whether described as fusion or an intimate encounter, is said to transform the soul of the mystic, leading to a life of contemplation or compassionate action.

See also KABBALAH; UNIO MYSTICA.

For further reading: Idel (1988, 1989).

devil's jelly Reports of gelatinous blobs apparently descending from the sky have been recorded for centuries. Typically, the appearance of the mysterious stuff is heralded by a falling star, or METEOR. In some modern accounts the luminous entity is labeled a UFO. When witnesses investigate the site where the object seemed to land, they find a mound of jelly. The substance has been described as white, grey or green; almost invariably, it gives off a foul odor and tends to dissolve quickly, leaving no trace. Folk traditions have dubbed the substance devil's jelly, star jelly, star shot or star rot.

A poem by the 16th century poet John Suckling attests to the antiquity of the belief in devils' jelly:

> As he whose quicker eye doth trace
> A false star shot to a mark't place
>   Do's run apace,
> And, thinking it to catch,
> A jelly up do snatch.

Sir Walter Scott, in his novel *The Talisman*, states: "Seek a fallen star and thou shalt only light on some foul jelly, which in shooting through the horizon, has assumed for a moment an appearance of splendour." The experience that inspired these literary observations contin-

ues to be reported to the present day. An English account from 1978 (cited in Corliss), for instance, described a mass that "glided down about the size of a football and settled like a jelly. It was white, and [strawlike], but cellular. It did not appear to disintegrate, but had completely disappeared by the morning."

Most researchers doubt that the gelatin actually comes from the sky. Conventional meteorites are composed of rock, enabling them to survive the friction of penetrating the Earth's atmosphere; any soft masses entering the atmosphere from space would vaporize before reaching the surface. Instead, they suggest the origin of devil's jelly is terrestrial—huge colonies of bacteria, half-digested material vomited by animals or unusual plant secretions have all been suggested. What, then, accounts for the association between devil's jelly and meteors streaking through the heavens? Perhaps it occurs because people searching for meteorite fragments scrutinize the landscape more carefully than usual, discovering things—such as innocuous masses of gelatin—that ordinarily would pass unnoticed, then erroneously link their discoveries with the aerial lights.

See also FAFROTSKIES.

For further reading: Corliss (1983b).

dharma-megha samadhi Literally, the concentrative state of the "virtue cloud," this Sanskrit term refers to the highest meditative state in the system of RAJA YOGA. It is classified as a type of ASAMPRAJNATA SAMADHI.

dhyana A Sanskrit term meaning "meditation" or "absorption," dhyana is synonymous with the Pali word JHANA. In Indian Buddhism dhyana refers to states of consciousness, cultivated in meditation, in which the attention is completely concentrated on a single object—a task that the undisciplined ordinary mind finds almost impossible. In the Far East dhyana (in Chinese, *ch'an;* in Japanese, *zen*) is defined more broadly to include not just the advanced states

of concentration, but the preparatory meditations, undertaken by beginners, which eventually lead to those states. Dhyana Buddhism is
thus a general term for any Buddhist school that
emphasizes the practice of MEDITATION, rather
than the study of philosophical doctrines.

See also ABSORPTION; MINDFULNESS.

diabolical experiences Unpleasant experiences involving apparent contact with evil, supernatural forces were called diabolical
experiences by Spanos and Moretti. They included under this heading three categories: encounters with demonic beings; revelations from
evil spiritual beings; and feelings of being overwhelmed by evil forces, including demonic POS-
SESSION.

Individuals who have diabolical experiences
are also prone to MYSTICAL EXPERIENCEs. They
tend to score high on measures of ABSORPTION
and HYPNOTIZABILITY, and often show signs of
poor PSYCHOLOGICAL ADJUSTMENT. Absorption
and hypnotizability are both associated with a
tendency to have a wide range of unusual experiences. If people are emotionally upset when
they become absorbed or hypnotized, their feelings will probably affect their awareness; the
resulting negative experience is easily interpreted
as the operation of evil beings. Tellegen thought
that people with high absorption capacities had
the potential for psychotic-like experiences if
they were anxious or sad.

See also Appendix; BAD TRIP; NIGHTMARE;
NIGHT TERROR; OLD HAG EXPERIENCE; UFO AB-
DUCTION EXPERIENCE.

For further reading: Spanos and Moretti;
Tellegen.

dissociation Many psychologists and psychiatrists believe that thoughts, feelings and intentions can become split off from the major
functions of the personality and continue to
function independently. The process by which
such divisions in the mind are created is known
as dissociation. A limited amount of dissociation
seems to be part of normal life. Jung believed
that everyone had dissociated clusters of
thoughts and feelings called complexes, which
can manifest as inexplicable moods and fantasies. Dissociation has been mentioned in connection with many kinds of unusual experience.

AUTOMATISMS, or unwilled behaviors, have
long been explained as the acts of dissociated
parts of the personality. One of the most common procedures in hypnosis is to encourage the
subject to dissociate. For instance, if a patient is
suffering from a sore leg, the hypnotist may
encourage the patient to imagine that the leg
belongs to someone else, along with the pain. By
dissociating the pain from awareness, many people have experienced relief. Some types of AMNE-
SIA are understood to be dissociations of memory
contents so that they are no longer retrievable.

POSSESSION and OBSESSION have traditionally
been blamed on demons; but modern authorities
instead attribute these unpleasant occurrences to
the invasion of consciousness by dissociated
mental contents. A major category of mental
illness, the DISSOCIATIVE DISORDERs, is thought
to be caused by extreme dissociations.

For further reading: American Psychiatric
Association; Hilgard.

dissociative disorder Mental illnesses that
feature disruptive DISSOCIATION of the personality. In FUGUE, a person forgets their ordinary
identity and adopts a new one; after recovery,
the person can no longer recall his or her identity
during the episode. Psychogenic AMNESIA also
involves a sudden, extensive loss of memories
that are later retrieved, but it does not entail the
assumption of a new identity. Sufferers of MUL-
TIPLE PERSONALITY DISORDER behave as if two
or more distinct personalities control them in
turn; many clinicians believe that in such cases,
dissociated complexes of thoughts and feelings
have learned to function independently.

For further reading: American Psychiatric
Association; Shorter.

dogmatism Some studies have found that dogmatism, or the tendency to hold unquestioned rigid beliefs, can be associated with belief in ESP.

See also Appendix.

doppelganger This German term, literally meaning "double-walker," has been adopted into English literature to refer to APPARITIONs of living persons. The annals of folklore and psychical research are full of anecdotes in which people are observed in two locations at once; in some cases, individuals have reported that they have had the unnerving experience of encountering ghostly images of themselves!

In the lives of religious adepts such as saints and yogis, double appearances are frequently understood to be instances of BILOCATION, the literal reproduction of the material body. A common interpretation found in folk cultures is that the doppelganger is a person's wandering soul, or a denizen of the spirit world with a special attachment to the mirrored individual. In Irish tradition, seeing a "fetch" or doppelganger in the morning signifies long life; such an encounter in the evening warns of impending death. The English Romantic poet Percy Bysse Shelley reported seeing his doppelganger shortly before his accidental drowning. (Such correlations, even if accurately reported, do not necessarily provide evidence for PRECOGNITION; if people interpret doppelganger sightings in an ominous fashion, the resulting state of anxious distraction may well render them accident prone.)

In most instances of doppelganger sightings, neither the witness nor the person reproduced by the apparition deliberately sought to produce the phenomenon. The German literary figure Wolfgang Goethe reported that he was shocked to see the image of a friend of his, dressed in Goethe's own dressing gown, while he was walking on a country road. Goethe discovered, upon returning home, that his friend had dropped by in rain-dampened clothing and had borrowed Goethe's gown. Furthermore, the friend claimed that he had fallen asleep and dreamed that he had met Goethe on the road, at the same time the writer saw his double!

Perhaps the most widely witnessed doppelganger was that of Emilie Sagee, investigated by the 19th century psychical researcher Robert Dale Owen. Sagee was a school teacher who was forced to leave her employment on several occasions due to the disruption caused by her apparition. While she was inside the classroom, her students often reported that they could also see her in the yard beyond the window. This double would imitate her movements. On occasion, Sagee herself would be outside, and the doppelganger would be seen sitting at a desk inside.

In some accounts, doppelgangers seem to be deliberate productions. In the classic collection of doppelganger reports, *Phantasms of the Living*, Gurney described a case in which a man attempted to appear to friends who lived across town. They stated (supposedly without prompting or prior awareness of his intention) that they had witnessed his ghostly image at the time of his efforts. Gurney instructed the trio to repeat the experiment, which they did successfully. In this case, the man who projected his image described his experience as follows:

> Besides exercising my power of volition very strongly, I put forth an effort which I cannot find words to describe. I was conscious of a mysterious influence of some sort permeating my body, and had a distinct impression that I was exercising some force with which I had been hitherto unacquainted, but which I can now at certain times set in motion at will.

Although much of the traditional material on the doppelganger cannot transcend the status of folk tales, more recent investigations leave no doubt that apparitions of living persons are sometimes encountered. The spontaneous cases are likely produced by the same mechanisms that underlie other sorts of apparition; ILLUSIONs and HALLUCINATIONs are the most likely explanations. Concerning reports of the deliberate creation of doppelgangers, and those accounts in which information unknown to the viewer seems to be conveyed, other factors may come into play. If such reports are accurate, they are, at least, startling coincidences; the presence of an ESP factor would be suggested. However, accounts of doppelgangers are anecdotes; no matter how sincerely they are described or investigated, it is difficult to isolate the role of memory distortions or undetected normal explanations in the construction of the stories.

See also BODY IMAGE DISTORTIONs.

For further reading: Gurney, Myers and Podmore; Inglis (1986).

double consciousness   People with certain types of sleep disorders, such as narcolepsy, sometimes report that they see dream images superimposed on the real world during wakefulness. If they do not mistake the dream images for real external objects, this double consciousness is classified as a PSEUDOHALLUCINATION. If the viewers believe that the imagery is a true perception, they are suffering from HALLUCINATION.

See also DELIRIUM; HYPNAGOGIC STATE; HYPNOPOMPIC STATE.

drugs   A drug is a substance that can chemically alter the functioning of the body. It was long ago noticed that many drugs also affect the operations of the mind. Historically and cross-culturally, drug taking has been one of the primary gateways to the domain of unusual experiences.

The range of psychological effects produced by drugs, and the expanse of theories and values attached to these effects, is reflected in the diverse terminology currently in use to describe these effects. Perhaps the most general common term for mind-altering substances is *psychoactive*—"acting upon the mind." Another common term in North America sinces the 1960s is *psychedelic*, literally "mind expanding," giving a positive aspect to intense drug experiences. An adjective with a less optimistic aura, originating in the psychiatric literature, is *psychotomimetic*,

or "psychosis-mimicking." This term emphasizes the parallels between some drug-induced experiences and those of people with severe mental disturbances. *Intoxicant* highlights the fact that psychoactive substances disrupt the ordinary functioning of the central nervous system; in sufficient doses (which in some cases are quite low) they are toxic, with harmful or lethal effects. *Phantastica* is a popular European term, referring to the fantasy-enhancing effects of some drugs. Certain substances are renowned for causing people to regard mental images as percepts; they experience HALLUCINATIONs, hence the term *hallucinogen*.

Until very recently, humans derived their drugs primarily from plants. Botanists have noted that drug plants come from two main divisions within the plant kingdom: the angiosperms or flowering plants, and the fungi. There may be 500,000 species of angiosperms and 100,000 of fungi. Very few of these have been scientifically analyzed for their psychoactivity. Over the millennia, people have been observing and experimenting with plants and have discovered many that contain mind-altering potencies. Since 1806, when morphine was extracted from the opium poppy, many psychoactive chemicals have been isolated from plant sources, and methods invented to make synthetic variants. For instance, mescaline comes from the PEYOTE cactus; psilocybin was isolated from Psilocybe mushrooms, revered by the Aztecs as TEONANACATL; and LSD was synthesized during research on the ERGOT fungus.

The discovery of the powers hidden within certain plants must have come very early in the history of our species. McKenna has even argued that this discovery may be *responsible* for our species, that a psychoactive substance is "the real missing link" bridging nonhuman and human evolution:

> The impact of hallucinogens in the diet has been more than psychological; hallucinogenic plants may have been the catalysts for everything about us that distinguishes us from other higher

primates, for all the mental functions that we associate with humanness.

Drug-enchanced sensory acuity could have improved success in food gathering. Perhaps drug-taking with others led to increased community bonding and sexual activities, which produced more and better protected offspring. The otherworldly vistas revealed in hallucinations may have challenged primate verbal capacities, granting some adaptive advantage on those who developed language. McKenna advances the hallucinogenic mushroom Stropharia cubensis, still in use today by some Mexican shamans, as the botanical missing link.

Siegel suggested that the human fascination with psychoactive plants began at least 40,000 years ago. In their Ice Age environment, early people likely experimented with any available food source, and would have stumbled upon the surprising effects of certain plants. Siegel also believes that many discoveries were made by observing the behavioral impact of drug plants eaten by wild animals.

The use of plants to induce unusual experiences has been documented on every continent, with the possible exception of Australia. The aborigines were familiar with the hallucinogenic plant *Duboisia myropoides,* and probably used it to invite divinatory visions, although contemporary natives seem to have lost this knowledge. While the number and availability of psychedelic plants is roughly equal in the Old World and the New, anthropologists have noted that their use has been much higher among native groups in the Americas. Schultes and Hofmann speculated that this difference arose from cultural factors. Most Old World cultures have been distanced from hunting and gathering cultures for considerably longer than New World societies. Hunters and gatherers tend to use a wider range of food sources than town dwellers, perhaps keeping them in touch with the psychoactive potencies available in their environment.

In order to understand the role of drugs in producing unusual experiences, several influences must be considered. On the biological level, psychoactive materials affect the firing patterns of neurons in the central nervous system. The molecular shapes of the hallucinogens closely resemble those of neurotransmitters, the chemical messengers responsible for communication between neurons. The hallucinogen molecules occupy the receptor sites intended for the neurotransmitters, thus disrupting ordinary nervous system functions. Some features of drug experiences probably depend on the extent and nature of the disruption.

This biological impact is reflected on the psychological level by interference with habitual patterns of processing sensory information, thinking, imagining and feeling. The result is destabilization: with the familiar inputs altered, the conventional sense of self and world loses its anchor. Elements that normally do not enter awareness may be disinhibited. In drug ceremonies aimed at inducing unusual experiences, other destabilizing factors are often introduced to magnify this effect: the physical removal of the experimenter from familiar surroundings, and subjection to AUDITORY or PHOTIC DRIVING, for instance.

The experiences of the drug-altered mind are amenable to shaping by the forces of expectation and belief. Often these are reinforced by a ritual context, which reminds the experimenter what the drugged state is supposed to be like. The flickering geometric images called FORM CONSTANTS, caused by the disruption of visual system functioning, have been interpreted as the ghosts of ancestors and as the architecture of the City of God. Obviously, there is tremendous cultural variation in experiences with the same drug.

Many societies have used drug-induced experiences to create or reinforce cultural ideas. Interpreting hallucinations as perceptions of a supernatural realm has been extremely widespread; perhaps the most common use of hallucinogens has been to access the occult powers and knowledge thought to exist in that realm. This use of drugs is most prominent in cultures in which the differences in status and wealth between the highest and lowest members of the social order are not great. In more stratified societies, power is concentrated among the elite sectors, which try to protect their privilege. The democratic access to power seemingly granted by hallucinogens breaks the power monopoly of the elites, which usually act to suppress their use by other social sectors.

A central feature of the INITIATORY EXPERIENCE is liminality, or the dissolution of the ordinary sense of self. Psychoactive drugs can be potent aids in producing liminal states. They are utilized as part of initiation rites in many cultures. Influenced by expectations and further guided by rituals, the contents of psychedelic experiences during initiations serve to confirm the spiritual realities the initiates have been taught. On the basis of her comprehensive survey, Dobkin de Rios observed that "cultural identity is learned and reaffirmed by psychic productions under drug experiences in many traditional societies of the world."

The shaping of beliefs by a drug experience, which then seems to validate the truth of the belief, has played a role in supporting the traditions of societies under pressure from external forces. In west Africa and North America, native drug-taking societies (based on IBOGA and PEYOTE, respectively) have formed to promote cultural cohesion in the face of Western colonial influence.

Finally, among peoples that have lost the strength that comes from a coherent meaning system, drug experiences have been sought as temporary havens from bleak reality. With neither sanctioned rituals nor disciplined expectations to pattern the experiences, most of the potential usefulness of psychoactive drugs disappears, and the likelihood that personal anxieties will assume control is heightened. Sadly, and unnecessarily, this is the state of affairs among many sectors of modern Western society.

The potentially negative outcomes of unguided psychedelic use may have blinded contemporary society to the untapped potentials of these substances. Weil observed:

> In any area where emotion is a major element, distortions become very great; science becomes as distorted as anything else. . . . the quality of investigation in the area of psychoactive drugs is terrible [because of an] unconscious need to find damaging evidence against those substances. Experiments are then designed to produce information that seemingly confirms the seeded beliefs and fears.

The belief in a link between psychedelic drugs and the paranormal has persisted into the contemporary world. Studies have reported that modern Westerners with a history of taking psychedelics are more likely to report unusual experiences and to hold anomalous beliefs than those who have never used drugs.

See also Appendix; BAD TRIP; DATURA; ENTHEOGEN; FLY AGARIC; WITCHES' OINTMENT; YAJE.

For further reading: Dobkin de Rios; Lukoff, Zanger and Lu; McKenna; Schultes and Hofmann; Siegel (1989); Stafford; Weil.

drumming A widely used method for inducing an ALTERED STATE OF CONSCIOUSNESS. A repetitive drum beat can provide the RHYTHMIC SENSORY STIMULATION that disrupts the ordinary firing patterns of nerve cells in the brain.

See also SHAMANISM.

earth sound   In the noise-polluted environment of the late 20th century, sounds of unknown origin are usually dismissed without investigation as having ordinary sources. Urban dwellers in particular live in an acoustic sink of engine noises, gunshots and horns. Even in rural settings, listeners are never far from the auditory residue of modern technologies. In quieter times, however, strange sounds were occasionally heard to emanate from the earth itself. These noises were not ordinary earthquake rumblings—they were frequently described as percussive or even musical in quality. Even in the present day, anomalous sounds are sometimes detected over the artificial din.

Accounts of mysterious earth sounds date back many centuries. The region around East Haddam, Connecticut, was referred to by its native inhabitants as *Morehemoodus,* "the place of noises." White settlers dubbed the series of explosive noises that occasionally shook their houses the Moodus Noises. The intensity of the Noises is said to range from gentle throbbings in the floorboards to loud detonations that are audible in nearby towns. This phenomenon is still reported today. Other sites of recurrent earth sounds include the Scottish town of Comrie, a rural area in the Australian State of Victoria (where the noises are known as Hanley's Guns) and Jamaica. The *gouffres,* as the Jamaican noises are called, have been described as sounding like breaking glass.

Such odd experiences have given rise to folkloric explanations, generally involving the behavior of departed spirits. The Moodus Noises, for example, were said to signal the displeasure of native deities at the arrival of Christians in the vicinity. Geologists have speculated that layers of underground rock could snap percussively due to shifts in the earth. Gas bubbles circulating noisily in subterranean caverns have also been suggested. Seismic activity could also generate electricity from crystalline rocks, perhaps triggering the crackle of electrostatic discharges in underground pockets.

See also WATER GUN.

For further reading: Corliss (1983a).

ecstasy   This term is derived from the Greek *ekstasis,* which means "standing outside." Ecstasy refers to a class of experiences in which a person feels as if they have been transported out of their routine ways of feeling, perceiving and acting.

Various definitions of ecstasy have been offered. For some writers, the term is virtually synonymous with ALTERED STATE OF CONSCIOUSNESS or TRANCE. Most reports of ecstasy include descriptions of elation, purification and loss of worldly awareness, sometimes with a sexual connotation; Laski includes "desolation ecstasies," which feature intense emotions of despair.

A sense of new or mystical knowledge is another common aspect of ecstatic reports. Laski analyzed her survey of ecstasies into categories based on the value ascribed to this cognitive aspect. *Adamic ecstasies,* in Laski's terms, are joyful states in which self and world are felt to be purified and renewed; there is not a sense of knowledge gained. *Knowledge ecstasies* include a feeling of revelation, without direct contact with the source of wisdom. In *knowledge-contact ecstasies* there is an encounter with the source, variously described as a spirit or god. The most highly valued ecstatic type in Laski's classification is the *union ecstasy;* one does not merely make contact with the knowledge source, but fuses or unites with it. This category includes intense MYSTICAL EXPERIENCEs.

Some writers have used the term "ecstasy" in a quite restricted sense. St. Teresa of Avila, for instance, identified ecstasy as a specific stage in the ladder of spiritual experiences. It follows the mystic's first union with God and precedes the betrothal of the mystic's soul with Divinity.

Ecstasies may endure for a moment or last for several hours. Both the private experiences of individuals and mass behaviors—such as the medieval DANCING MANIA, the group writhings of the CONVULSIONARIES, or the possession of convent populations in 17th century France—have been labeled ecstasies.

See also ENSTASY; RAPTURE.

For further reading: Laski; Merkur; Peers; Sargant.

education   Some skeptics have argued that people who hold paranormal beliefs are ignorant or intellectually deficient. If this is so, then people with lower levels of education would be expected to have more paranormal beliefs than those better educated. Studies have not confirmed this theory. Tobacyk, Miller and Jones found a positive correlation between education level and global paranormal belief. The link between education level and specific types of anomalous belief has not been consistent across studies; for example, belief in ESP was found to increase with education levels in some surveys, but other researchers found a negative correlation. Belief in spirits and UFOs tends to decrease with education.

Other researchers have examined academic achievement, as measured by grade point averages, in relation to paranormal belief. Again, the results are inconsistent. Both positive and negative correlations between grades and beliefs have been reported.

It is possible that paranormal belief is not affected consistently by *general* education level, but specifically by the amount of scientific education or education about the psychology of unusual experiences. Singer and Benassi, who maintain that paranormal belief thrives on ignorance about science, have proposed that surveys of paranormal belief should be used as a measure of the effectiveness of science education in the United States. While some studies have found a negative relationship between the level of science education and anomalous belief, others have reported no relationship, and some (e.g. Salter and Routledge) have even found higher levels of paranormal belief among science students compared to humanities students.

Other studies have measured the effect on paranormal belief of courses specifically devoted to a critical examination of these unusual experiences. Most reported that such courses tend to reduce paranormal belief. Irwin, however, found that his course lowered belief in CRYPTICS, but slightly increased belief in PSYCHOKINESIS.

The correlations that have been found may not be related to the content of the education as much as to the attitude of the course instructors toward paranormal beliefs. In addition to learning information presented in class, students are often strongly influenced by the biases of their teachers. If education-related changes in paranormal belief are caused by the *information* learned in a course, students who learn more should show greater shifts in belief than students who learn less. If, however, the changes in belief arise from acquiring the instructor's *attitude* toward paranormal possibilities, there should be little relationship between the amount of information learned by a student and the degree of shift in belief. A study by Jones and Zusne reported a general decrease in paranormal belief among students taking a skeptically oriented course on anomalies; they noted that the belief changes were unrelated to the amount of information acquired by the students.

The results of the research on education and anomalous belief are hard to interpret, because the studies were conducted using different measures of belief, AGE groups and settings. Certainly, there is no clear support for the idea that only ignorant or stupid people hold paranormal beliefs.

See also Appendix; BELIEF, ANOMALOUS; INTELLIGENCE; REASONING SKILLS.

For further reading: Irwin (1990b); Jones and Zusne; Salter and Routledge; Singer and Benassi; Tobacyk, Miller and Jones.

eidetic imagery After viewing an object, some people can retain an almost photographically detailed mental image; every detail of the perceived object is said to be reproduced in the image. These eidetic images normally persist for a period of minutes, but they can recur vividly many years later.

The ability to produce eidetic images is relatively common among preschool children, but it usually disappears by adolescence and it is rare among adults. Most researchers believe that eidetic images are not a distinct type of experience, but are just exceptionally vivid visual memories.

It is noteworthy that eidetic imagers do not recall *everything* they see, as if their memory acted as a continuously rolling video camera. Indeed, although it is possible to improve memory significantly by using strategies called mnemonics, the much-vaunted photographic memory has never been demonstrated to exist.

See also PALINOPSIA.

electronic visual phenomenon The screen of a television set displays a randomly flickering light—often called "snow"—when tuned between channels. Some viewers have reported the appearance of images in the snow, including pictures of deceased individuals. Promoters of these experiences believe that spirits can send their own signals through TV sets. Jules and Maggie Harsh-Fischbach named this occurrence the electronic visual phenomenon. Baker noted that "Uncommitted observers who have witnessed the Fischbach's Electronic Visual presentations reported seeing only a few vague, ill-deformed [sic] shadows on the TV screen

snow as if the set was tuned to a station whose signal was much too weak for a clear and definite picture." Most of these televised ghosts are probably visual PAREIDOLIA: meanings projected into random stimuli by the minds of observers.

See also ELECTRONIC VOICE PHENOMENON.
For further reading: Baker (1992).

electronic voice phenomenon When listening to audiotapes of noise, such as the sound of static from a radio tuned between stations or the hum of an open telephone line, some people believe they have heard voice messages from departed spirits or extraterrestrials. These experiences are widely known as electronic voice phenomena or EVPs. Most researchers think that any meaning found in the random sounds is put there by the wishful thinking of the listeners—in other words, the voices are auditory PAREIDOLIA.

See also ELECTRONIC VISUAL PHENOMENON.

emotional arousal Both low and high levels of emotional arousal have often been noted in association with unusual or supranormal experiences. Other correlates of anomalous experiences, such as HYPNOTIZABILITY, are amplified by extremes of arousal. P. Nelson found that people who are prone to intense positive emotional states, featuring joy and excitement, tend to have more unusual experiences than calmer people. Spanos and Moretti observed that people who have DIABOLICAL EXPERIENCEs are often prone to unpleasant emotional conditions.

See also Appendix; ALTERED STATE OF CONSCIOUSNESS; PSYCHOLOGICAL ADJUSTMENT.
For further reading: P. Nelson; Spanos and Moretti.

emptiness The notion of emptiness (Sanskrit *shunyata*—also translated as "Void," "Plenum-Void" and "open dimension of Being") is one of the most misunderstood concepts in Buddhism. Emptiness is said to be the true nature of reality by the Buddhist schools. The direct experience of emptiness, through the mental faculty called

PRAJNA, is the means by which ENLIGHTENMENT is attained.

The two main surviving schools of Buddhism, Theravada and Mahayana, define the nature of emptiness somewhat differently. For the Theravada, emptiness refers to the insight that there is no such thing as a "self"—that is, a central core or essence of a person that persists through time. When one uses the tools of meditation to search for a self, one does not discover anything in existence that could be such a thing. Instead, reality is composed of continuously changing elements called *dharmas*. These entities, which resemble atoms, exist only for a moment. Reality, then, is empty of a "self of persons." Direct experience of this absence of stability in the personality could be devastating, if the mind is not anchored in the state of meditative calmness known as SHAMATHA.

For the Mahayana, the undermining of everyday experience implied in the notion of emptiness is even more sweeping. Not only is there no such thing as a personal self, the Mahayana teaches that absolutely nothing has any inherent existence. Even the momentarily existent dharmas of the Theravada are seen as illusory. The ultimate nature of all things, including ourselves, is emptiness.

Most people cannot perceive emptiness easily. To the untrained awareness, things do not seem to lack their own existence. A person must first develop an idea or *conceptual understanding* of emptiness, which can then be deepened through meditation into a *direct experience*. Buddhist texts present mental exercises to aid in gaining the correct conception. For instance, when someone looks at a car, it seems obvious that the vehicle is really there, that an object we call a car has some sort of independent existence. But where, exactly, is the car? If one analyzes the car into its components, it has a steering wheel, tires, an engine, a body, etc, but none of these are the "car." Is there anything other than these parts that make up the car? There is not. But the car seems to be greater than the sum of its parts,

and yet, when one searches for this additional element, we find nothing. It now appears that "car" is just a word used to refer to an object which is not there when carefully searched for. This analysis can be repeated for every element of awareness, without our finding any concrete thing to which our language points.

Everything, in other words, is empty. If we repeat such exercises, we can eventually gain a conceptual understanding of emptiness. Even the indirect awareness of emptiness one gains by fully grasping the concept can be "mind-blowing"—the current Dalai Lama compared the moment of comprehending emptiness as akin to being hit by lightning.

The Mahayana emptiness sounds as if it denies that anything exists. Indeed, many have misunderstood the idea and have accused Buddhism of being nihilistic. The Buddhist emptiness is the absence of *inherent* or independent existence, not the absence of existence of any kind. Things do exist, but in a *noninherent* fashion. Noninherent existence is a very difficult concept, as it denies a quality possessed by all of our normal experiences. The Middle Way or Madhyamika school of Buddhism feels that one can only speak of what reality is not—to discover what it is, one must have direct experience of it.

Other Buddhist schools have held that the Madhyamika way of describing emptiness in strictly negative terms is too easily confused with nihilism, and therefore they have tried to say something about what emptiness *is*. The Yogacara school, for instance, teaches that emptiness is the lack of a difference between the nature of the objects we experience and the nature of our own consciousness—in other words, that everything is mind. The Buddhist TANTRA also conveys a positive content to the ultimate void—in Kennard Lipman's phrase, that emptiness is "a radiant presence full of vivid imagery." The visualization practices of Tantric SADHANA are said to induce the experience of perceiving all beings as deities, all sounds as

MANTRAS and the entire world as a luminous palace, or mandala. Such an experience seems far removed from the frightening emptiness of existential angst, with which the Buddhist emptiness is often confused.

The experience of emptiness possesses the negative function of pointing out that our normal belief in the independent existence of ourselves and of objects is wrong; but it is also positive, in freeing us from the limitation and suffering produced by this mistaken belief. Andrew Harvey captured this double-edged quality of the "open dimension of Being":

> there are two ways of saying Sunyata [emptiness] . . . You can say it harshly, and you can say it gently. You can say it so that it sounds like the iron hand of death beating on the door, or like waves fanning out and whispering on the seashore. When you say it the first way you tremble slightly because you understand that to know Emptiness is the end of the Ego you have cherished and you are afraid; when you say it gently you are happy because in the experience of Emptiness is spaciousness and freedom, is Nirvana. To be freed from a false perception of the Self is the end of Buddhism; to realize that there is Nothing and No-one is also to understand that one is in everything and in everyone, that there is no death, no fear, no pain, no separation.

See also VIPASSANA.

For further reading: Harvey; Hopkins (1983, 1984); Lipman; Streng.

encounter prone personality This term was coined by Ring to describe the personality type that seems most likely to have NEAR DEATH EXPERIENCEs and UFO ENCOUNTERs. The hallmark of the encounter prone personality is ABSORPTION—a tendency to focus attention on mental images and thoughts to the exclusion of events in the outside world.

For further reading: Ring.

enlightenment The supreme spiritual realization in the Buddhist tradition, enlightenment is associated with a range of concepts, including BODHI and NIRVANA. Although the English word conjures images of light, "enlightenment" is not associated with visions or unusual light phenomena. Indeed, it does not designate any *particular* content of experience, but rather a transformation of *all* experiences. The path to enlightenment is marked by many exotic states and occurrences, such as JHANAs and NIMITTAs and its attainment might correspond with an unusual experience—but these must not be mistaken for enlightenment itself, say the Buddhist masters.

There are many schools of Buddhism, and each has a specific understanding of enlightenment. It is generally held that there are two main kinds of enlightenment—that of a Foe Destroyer (Sanskrit *arhat*) and that of a Buddha. Foe Destroyers are said to have trained their awareness to the point that they have uprooted the Great Foe: the ignorance which gives rise to suffering. This ignorance of the true nature of things is not just a false belief, but a false perception. The objects of ordinary experience appear to have a reality of their own, independent of our consciousness of them, and separate from other objects. Things appear in this way, according to Buddhism, because we do not correctly discern the truth: that nothing exists independently of the rest, that nothing is permanent or can give lasting satisfaction. A book, for example, seems to have its own existence apart from me; it seems to endure over time; and, if I like the book, I might have lasting happiness by owning it. The Foe Destroyer has realized this to be an illusion and is no longer subject to control by the passions arising from it.

This realization liberates the Foe Destroyer from the endless chains of cause and effect stirred by basing one's security in that which does not exist. However, the enlightenment of the Buddha is even more profound. In addition to ending the enslavement to illusion, the attainment of Buddhahood destroys the illusion itself.

The consciousness of the Foe Destroyer continues to perceive the false appearances, but is not fooled by them; the awareness of the Buddha perceives things as they actually are.

Hopkins compared our unenlightened everyday awareness to an illusion created by a magician. The magician through trickery can create the illusion that a pebble is actually a beautiful man or woman. Seeing the attractive image we become filled with desire—a desire that, because of the true nature of the object, can never be satisfied. Foe Destroyers perceive the beautiful image, but are not stirred by yearning; they know the trick. Buddhas see the pebble. This tradition claims that the quality of experience of enlightened beings of both kinds is drastically different from normal awareness.

In Zen Buddhism there are several different forms of enlightenment experience, although only one true enlightenment. Awakening to reality can occur in a partial (KENSHO) or more thorough (SATORI) fashion and it can be evoked gradually (ZENGO) or suddenly (TONGO).

For further reading: Diener; Fischer-Schreiber; Hopkins (1984).

enstasy Religious scholar Mircea Eliade coined this term to designate altered states of consciousness that are not appropriately placed under the alternate heading of ECSTASY. Most ecstatic conditions are said to involve a sense of stepping outside of oneself, even to the extreme of relocating consciousness apart from the body, as in OUT-OF-BODY EXPERIENCES. "Ecstasy" also has a connotation of blissful excitement. Many forms of altered awareness, especially meditative states, possess neither of these characteristics. Meditators frequently describe going within themselves in order to discover their true nature; and calmness, rather than excitement, more often accompanies meditation. Eliade labeled such states "enstasy"—literally, "standing within" oneself. The term has not achieved wide usage. Feuerstein employs "enstasy" as a translation of SAMADHI, the Sanskrit word for a state of concentrated attention.

For further reading: Eliade (1969); Feuerstein (1989).

entheogen Derived from the Latin *en theos*, meaning "god within" or "within god." This term was coined by Gordon Wasson, a pioneer in ethnomycology—the study of the use and meaning of fungi (including mushrooms) in various cultures. An entheogen is a psychoactive substance which can produce spiritual experiences when ingested. Wasson held that hallucinogenic mushrooms, especially the FLY AGARIC, were historically the most important entheogens.

For further reading: Wasson.

enthusiasm In modern popular usage, enthusiasm simply means strong motivation or intense desire, but in previous times the term referred to more dramatic phenomena. The word is derived from the ancient Greek *enthusiasmos*, the condition of having a god *(theos)* inside oneself. In antiquity, excited or inspired behavior was thought to signal the presence of a divine power. The most extreme type of enthusiasm was full POSSESSION, in which ordinary control and awareness was relinquished to the god or demon.

Orthodox Christianity rejected the spiritual value of possession. However, New Testament passages referring to people "filled with the Holy Spirit" (e.g. Acts 4:31) provided the justification for other forms of enthusiastic states. Throughout the history of Christian culture, individuals and groups have claimed that the Holy Spirit was active within them.

The Montanists, a second-century movement that rivaled the Catholic church in its popularity, practiced a type of mediumship in which the Holy Spirit spoke through trance specialists, prophesying the imminent end of the world. In the later Middle Ages, a heretical group called the Brothers and Sisters of the Free Spirit spread throughout western Europe. The Free Spirits claimed that the Holy Spirit dwelled within them, and that therefore they were above all earthly laws and could do as they pleased.

In the Reformation and its aftermath, many Christian sects formed. These experiments in religious practice and lifestyle produced many outbreaks of spontaneous enthusiastic behavior, usually attributed to the presence of the Holy Spirit. Ranters, Rollers, Jumpers, Shiverers, Shakers and Quakers, gripped by the feeling that a holy power greater than themselves had taken control, involuntarily or quasi-voluntarily performed the actions that gave them their names.

During the 18th century, reason and moderation became central values in western culture. "Enthusiasm" became a derogatory term, and enthusiastic behaviors of all kinds were viewed as pitiable losses of personal discipline. Nonetheless, from the mid-1700s throughout the 19th century, waves of the Christian Revival movement spread through western Europe and North America. Traveling preachers drew large crowds. Spell-binding orators described the horrors awaiting sinners after death and called down the Holy Spirit to enter the hearts of the faithful.

Enthusiastic behaviors, often thought to indicate that the performer was truly converted or saved, could grip entire congregations. One of the most potent preachers was John Wesley, the founder of Methodism. The enthusiasm he evoked was too intense for some; between 1739 and 1742, it was reported that 14 members of Wesley's audiences became temporarily insane, and nine were propelled permanently into madness.

See also MANIA.

For further reading: Knox; Sargant.

entoptic phenomenon The term "entoptic" derives from Greek, meaning literally "within vision." Entoptic phenomena, or entoptics, are sensations produced by the structure of the visual nervous system—the eyeball, the optic nerve and the parts of the brain dedicated to processing visual input. In an entoptic experience, one has visual sensations that do not correspond to an external visual stimulus (known as a "distal stimulus"). The most familiar entoptics are the "stars" seen when one receives a blow to the back of the head.

Entoptics are distinguished from VISUAL HALLUCINATIONs, in that the latter are not products of the visual system; rather, hallucinations are *mental* images, misinterpreted as external objects. An entoptic experience can lead into a hallucination in a susceptible person; for example, blue flashes caused by an entoptic process might be organized into a vision of a glowing blue monster by a paranoid individual.

Under the right lighting conditions, the eyeball can view features of its own structure. The lens of the eye contains fibers that radiate from its center. In defective lenses, these fibers can cause a starlike luster to appear around distant lights. Debris drifting in the vitreous body (the transparent liquid between the iris and the retina), can cast shadows on the retina; the resultant sensations are called FLOATERS. Sometimes, blood circulating through capillaries adjacent to the retinal light receptors can also be seen, an occurrence known as SCHEERER'S PHENOMENON. The eyes are constantly quivering, which can impart a sense of motion to these entoptic effects.

Mechanical pressure on the eyeball can cause retinal cells to fire, creating the sparkling displays called PHOSPHENEs.

Information from the retina is transferred, via the optic nerve, into the brain. Entoptic phenomena can also arise from disturbances in the optic nerve, or from the visual areas of the brain. Simple geometric images, such as lines, dots, zigzags and curves, can appear in the visual field. These entoptics, called FORM CONSTANTS can be triggered by a range of sensory, chemical and psychological influences.

As people of all ethnic groups, genders and historical periods possess almost identical visual systems, it is predictable that entoptic phenomena have been reported or depicted in virtually every culture. The biological origins of these experiences are little known by most people, even today. Many explanations have been devised for the mysterious sensations, most of them involving the perception of spiritual realities.

See also IDEORETINAL LIGHT; ISAKOWER PHENOMENON.

For further reading: Horowitz; Kluver; Siegel (1977).

entotic phenomena Meaning "within the ear," this phrase is a variant term for TINNITUS.

See also ENTOPTIC PHENOMENA.

epilepsy In ancient Greece, it was thought that the gods or spirits, for their own inscrutable reasons, would "seize" people's souls for short periods, leaving their victims' bodies flopping uncontrollably. Individuals who displayed this behavior were said to suffer from *epilepsia,* or "seizures." The term has come to designate a class of NEUROLOGICAL DISORDER that features these bouts of diminished control.

Even in ancient times, some thinkers suspected that epilepsy was of internal origin. The famous physician Hippocrates concluded that brain malfunctions, rather than spirits, were involved. But the majority viewed the disorder as a type of POSSESSION. A description of demonic possession by the fourth century church father Cyril of Jerusalem (quoted by Robbins) may well be an account of an epileptic seizure:

> [The Devil] throws down him who stands upright; he perverts the tongue and distorts the lips. Foam comes instead of words; the man is filled with darkness; his eye is open, yet his soul sees not through it; and the miserable man quivers convulsively.

Epilepsy today afflicts about 1% of the population. The causes of the brain sensitivity underlying the seizures are varied. Neural damage from head injury, oxygen deprivation, high fever and tumors have all been noted. In some cases, there may be a congenital defect in the production of chemicals that dampen the activity of nerve cells; in the absence of these substances, brain tissues become hyperexcitable.

Seizures often occur in response to environmental triggers. These vary, depending on the brain region affected. Some epileptics must avoid flashing lights; others shun the rhythms of music. Stress is a common trigger. Once activated, waves of electrical activity radiate from the damaged site in the brain, disrupting ordinary functioning. In some types of epilepsy, the seizures are relatively subtle—the individual may lose consciousness momentarily, the episode marked only by trembling eyelids. In others, consciousness may remain undisturbed, but body parts will move involuntarily. Sometimes, complex sequences of behavior are repeated; the sufferer can only witness his or her own actions. In the most dramatic forms of epilepsy, both consciousness and muscle control are lost. The epileptic falls into convulsions, followed by a period of coma. In severe cases, epilepsy can threaten the body's life support system. Fortunately, many epileptics can now control their condition by drug therapy.

Prior to the onset of the seizure, many sufferers experience a period of altered consciousness known as the epileptic "aura" (not to be confused with the glowing halo seen around the body by some psychics, also called an AURA). A great range of unusual experiences have been reported in connection with this period. Perceptual changes, including BODY IMAGE DISTORTIONS and HALLUCINATIONs, are common. The normal links between memories and feelings of recognition can be scrambled, producing sensations of DÉJÀ VU and JAMAIS VU. Feelings of INVISIBLE PRESENCEs are featured in some auras.

Emotions from anxiety to overwhelming joy are stirred by seizures, according to some epileptics. Shifts in the boundaries of the self can result in DEPERSONALIZATION, or even MYSTICAL EXPERIENCE. The Russian novelist Fyodor

Dostoyevski was one epileptic who had ecstatic auras. He observed (quoted by Sacks, 1985):

> You, all, healthy people, can't imagine the happiness which we epileptics feel during the second before our fit . . . . I don't know if this felicity lasts for seconds, hours or months, but believe me, I would not exchange it for all the joys that life may bring!

In some cases the brain discharges that cause epileptic auras occur without leading to seizures. If the neurological origin of these experiences remains undetected, it is easy to see how the aura might be interpreted as a contact with another world.

See also MIGRAINE; TEMPORAL LOBE ABNORMALITY; TOURETTE'S SYNDROME.

For further reading: Beyerstein; Mandell; Temkin; Robbins; Sacks (1985).

epiphany On January 6, Christians celebrate the Feast of the Epiphany (Greek for "manifestation") in memory of the meeting between the three wise men and the infant Christ. Joyce, in his novel *A Portrait of the Artist as a Young Man,* employed the term to refer to an experience of wondrous revelation, and this usage has become popular.

Epiphanies happen suddenly and uncontrollably. A person may be viewing a beautiful scene in nature or a work of art when, in Joyce's words, "The mind is arrested and raised above desire and loathing." For a moment, the person stops evaluating what is perceived in terms of what it is for him or her, i.e. whether it can harm or help. Stripped of one's judgment, the object shines forth in its naked reality, as it is in itself. The glimpse tends to be short-lived, as deep-seeded mental habits do not remain in abeyance for long, and the object quickly resumes its ordinary appearance.

The reality unveiled during this brief paralysis of judgment is frequently described in spiritual or even mystical terms. As Blake's famous passage in *The Marriage of Heaven and Hell* observes, "If the doors of perception were cleansed, every thing would appear to man as it is, infinite."

See also NUMINOUS EXPERIENCE; MYSTICAL EXPERIENCE.

For further reading: Campbell (1988).

ergot The Ergot fungus (genus *Claviceps*) has been responsible for a variety of chemically triggered unusual experiences, both deliberate and accidental, throughout European history. The fungus invades the kernels of cereal grasses, especially rye, replacing the endosperm with its own fruiting bodies. On ergot-infected grain, purplish "spurs" can be seen. These structures contain a type of lysergic acid, a hallucinogenic substance related to LSD.

Ergot intoxication was probably an important feature of the ancient religious rituals known as the Eleusinian Mysteries. The cult at Eleusis was centered on the figures of two Greek goddesses of vegetation, Demeter and her daughter, Persephone. The initiates of Eleusis included many of the greatest minds of Greece and Rome, such as Plato, Sophocles, Aristotle, Aeschylus, Pindar and several Roman Emperors. In their secret rites, they consumed kykeon, a liquid that caused trembling, dizziness, a cold sweat and, finally, a personally transforming experience of illumination. The composition of this substance was lost after the Mysteries were destroyed by orthodox Christian authorities in the fifth century. Modern researchers believe that *kykeon* consisted of water, mint and ergotized barley.

In 1039, in the Dauphine region of France, there occurred the first known mass outbreak of what came to be known as St. Anthony's Fire. Individuals afflicted with the "Holy Fire" suffered from intense burning sensations in the skin, confusion and hallucinations, and, not uncommonly, death. If the symptoms persisted, gangrene would set in. Then the fingers, toes, earlobes and nose would atrophy and drop off. At the time the malady was thought to be caused by demons or by God's wrath. In fact, ergotized rye had been milled into bread, spreading mass ergot poisoning. The decreased blood flow to the skin and extremities, a physical reaction to the ergot, resulted in gangrene and atrophy.

But the biological cause of St. Anthony's Fire was not discovered until 1676. Throughout the Middle Ages, ergotized rye with its telltale purple spurs was viewed merely as food of inferior quality, not as toxic. As a result, whenever there was a shortage of "clean" rye, the bread of the lower classes would be made from ergotized grain, as well as other psychoactive adulterants—vetch, which can cause depressed moods, and darnel grass, which can create disorientation and tiredness. St. Anthony's Fire was continuously breaking out in various parts of Europe. Pilgrimages to shrines of St. Anthony, the healing saint, often proved effective, probably because the pilgrims left their tainted food sources behind during their journeys. During much of the later Middle Ages, most of western Europe's poorer citizens were probably suffering to varying degrees from the mind-altering ingredients in their bread.

Once the cause of St. Anthony's Fire was discovered, bread makers were taught to discard ergotized grain. Occasional outbreaks of this chemically induced mass madness have continued into the 20th century, when ergot inadvertently slipped into the food supply. In 1929, outbreaks occurred in Ireland and the Ukraine; France and Belgium reported epidemics of ergot poisoning in 1953.

See also DRUGS.

For further reading: Bove; Schultes and Hofmann; Stafford; Wasson, Hofmann and Ruck.

ESP Popular acronym for EXTRASENSORY PERCEPTION, the alleged ability of the mind to acquire knowledge of the world without the use of the known senses.

exchange of hearts One of the CHARISMS, or seemingly supernatural phenomena associated with sanctity, recognized by the Roman Catholic Church. Catholic accounts of the lives of mystics and saints occasionally mention the appearance of an encircling ridge of flesh on the individual's finger. This is said to represent a ring, indicating that one has exchanged one's heart with that of Christ in heavenly marriage. Such bodily alterations often occur in conjunction with the STIGMATA, and may share an underlying physiological mechanism.

For further reading: Murphy; Thurston.

experience, unusual See UNUSUAL EXPERIENCE.

extrasensory perception This term, often known by its acronym ESP, came into use in the latter part of the 19th century and was popularized by the founder of modern PARAPSYCHOLOGY, J.B. Rhine. Perception is the process by which the mind acquires information about the world. Ordinarily, perception begins with sensation—receptors in a sense organ (eye, ear, skin, tongue, nose and the various sensory systems within the body) come in contact with energies originating in the world and transmit information about them to the brain in the form of neural impulses. People commonly report experiences in which perception seems to occur in the absence of sensory processes; in these cases, the mind apparently gathers information directly from an outer source. Some writers distinguish between extrasensory experiences (those in which perception without sensation seem to be happening) and ESP proper (referring to actual instances of paranormal perception); others simply refer to "ESP experiences," without committing themselves to a true paranormal occurrence.

Subsumed under the heading of ESP are a variety of phenomena, including telepathy, or gaining information directly from the mind of another; clairvoyance, paranormal knowledge of distant or concealed events; precognition, foretelling future events; and retrocognition, extrasensory awareness of past events.

ESP experiences have been reported in every known society and they are widespread today. The 1990 Gallup Poll on paranormal phenomena reported that 49% of adult Americans believe in ESP. Many other surveys in various countries have observed even higher levels of ESP belief and experience. The endurance of this belief in the face of official skepticism from the scientific elites is striking and points to a basis in common and compelling experiences.

Over the past century, two major approaches have been employed in investigating ESP: collecting and analyzing reports of spontaneous ESP experiences; and attempting to demonstrate the reality and characteristics of extrasensory functioning under controlled conditions. The study of spontaneous case collections dates back to the early years of the Society for Psychical Research, founded in 1882. Gurney, Myers and Podmore published a two-volume study based on over 700 reports of telepathy in 1886. This opus was followed by several other massive case collections. These researchers were attempting to prove the reality of extrasensory awareness by amassing cases that seemingly could not be explained in any other way. They sought ESP cases in which the unusual experience was documented prior to its verification—for example, a person who wrote a description of a dream about an accident before the accident happened.

One of the first discoveries made by the early psychical researchers was that ESP experiences were not only reported by the uneducated and unintelligent, but by people of every walk of life and degree of functioning. These investigators, most of whom belonged to the privileged classes themselves, believed that professionals and aristocrats were somehow more trustworthy witnesses than those in lower classes; so the finding that doctors, lawyers and scientists reported ESP experiences encouraged them in their search for definitive evidence.

The early researchers gradually came to realize that demonstrating the reality of ESP on the basis of spontaneous case reports is virtually impossible. No amount of checking the accounts could conclusively rule out normal explanations, such as misremembering, fraud and coincidence. The analysis of spontaneous cases has yielded much valuable information on the nature of the ESP *experience,* even if the paranormality of these experiences is not proven.

Perhaps the most valuable examination of spontaneous ESP cases was undertaken by L.E. Rhine. She admitted that such material could never be used to prove the existence of ESP. She believed, however, that the patterns she found by reviewing over 15,000 reports could be used to devise hypotheses about ESP that could then be tested under rigorous laboratory conditions. In addition, Rhine felt it was valuable to learn as much as possible about this ubiquitous category of human experience. Since she began to publish her findings in 1951, several other researchers have followed her lead of collecting ESP reports without attempting to determine their degree of paranormality. Much has been learned.

L.E. Rhine divided spontaneous ESP experiences into four categories. An *intuitive impression* consists of a simple feeling or hunch, without mental imagery, that occurs while one is awake. An example would be a sense that "something is wrong" felt by a traveler about to board a plane; trusting this intuition, he or she decides to postpone the trip, and the plane that was about to be taken later crashes. Rhine used the term *hallucination* to refer to waking ESP experiences accompanied by perceptions of objects that are not physically present; for instance, an apparition that appears at the moment a relative in a distant place unexpectedly dies. A *realistic dream* is an ESP experience involving vivid mental imagery that accurately portrays features of a distant, past or future event. This category refers both to dreams that happen while one is asleep and to imagery that appears when awake. Dreaming of receiving a package in the mail that unexpectedly arrives the following day is a typical example. Rhine's category of *unrealistic dreams* includes sleeping and waking ESP experiences in which information is presented to consciousness in the form of fanciful or symbolic depictions; for example, dreaming of rising in an elevator shortly before being surprised by a promotion.

The most common type of ESP experience in Rhine's collection was the precognitive realistic dream, comprising 60% of precognition reports. The remaining precognition reports broke down as follows: 19% were intuitive impressions; 15% were unrealistic dreams; and the remaining 6% were hallucinations. Concerning ESP experiences of presently occurring events (telepathy and clairvoyance), she noted that 35% took the form of intuitions, 25% were hallucinations, 21% were unrealistic dreams and 19% were realistic dreams. Retrocognition was reported too rarely for a meaningful analysis to be done. Most other surveys and case collections have yielded similar proportions.

Rhine considered these four forms of ESP experience with respect to their completeness of content—the degree to which the experience matched the details of the persons and events to which they seemingly referred. She found that realistic dreams had the highest degree of completeness (19%) and hallucinations were the least complete (32%). When ESP experiences are related to other people (as telepathy does by definition, and the other categories frequently do), they are generally individuals who are emotionally important to the experient.

Another significant feature of spontaneous ESP experiences was noted by Irwin. He found that 90% of the subjects in his survey reported that they were engaged in low levels of physical activity when the ESP experience occurred. About two-thirds of Irwin's subjects also recalled that they were alone at the time. Minimizing interaction with the external world seems to enhance the likelihood of an extrasensory experience.

Over the past 20 years, numerous studies have examined the relationships between ESP experiences, beliefs and other factors. Belief in the reality of ESP has been linked with a host of characteristics, including: GENDER (females are more likely to believe in ESP); FANTASY PRONENESS; HYPNOTIZABILITY; MAGICAL THINKING; SENSATION SEEKING; CREATIVITY; external LOCUS OF CONTROL; CONTROL NEEDS; low SOCIAL INTEREST; DOGMATISM; RELIGIOSITY; and DEATH CONCERNS. Research relating ESP beliefs to factors of EDUCATION has yielded contradictory results. The following characteristics have been reported to correlate positively with the tendency to have ESP experiences: TEMPORAL LOBE ABNORMALITY; history of HEAD INJURY; fantasy-proneness; hypnotizability; and ABSORPTION.

As noted above, the analysis of spontaneous case reports cannot be used to establish whether or not ESP truly exists. Although an ESP experience may convince the person who had it that the event cannot be explained in conventional terms, a skeptical observer can usually provide plausible alternatives to ESP. A major difficulty with spontaneous ESP cases is the possibility that the match between the experience and an event was sheer coincidence. If I dream about a man in a gorilla suit reading Shakespeare, and encounter such a person on the subway the next day, chance might seem like a unlikely explanation to me. But if I consider that each night on earth, our species generates many billions of dreams, it would seem likely that at least some of those dreams would correspond in detail to experiences on the following day by chance alone; and there is no way to be sure that my ESP experience was not one of those chance matchings. In order to gather evidence for ESP, it is necessary to find a way to calculate the probability that a correspondence between an ESP experience and an event is due to coincidence; if it can be demonstrated that these correspondences happen much more often than could be reasonably ascribed to chance, and all other possibilities can be ruled out, this finding could count as evidence for the reality of ESP.

Obviously, these requirements cannot be met in the everyday world where spontaneous ESP experiences happen. Thus, some researchers turned to the more controllable setting of the laboratory. As early as 1884, psychical researcher and Nobel laureate Charles Richet was conducting experiments in which subjects tried to use ESP to guess the suits of concealed playing cards. A list of subjects' guesses could be compared with the actual sequence of the target cards; the number of correct matches (or hits) expected if only chance was operating could be precisely calculated, and significant deviations from this figure could be taken as an indication that something other than coincidence was operating.

Over the next 50 years, a number of ESP experiments were undertaken, with unconvincing results. The contemporary era of experimental ESP research was inaugurated by J.B. Rhine in 1927. He started the first sustained research program of ESP experiments at Duke University in Durham, North Carolina. Rhine and a colleague, Karl Zener, developed the distinctive set of target cards that are popularly known as Zener cards. A deck of Zener cards consists of five each of the following symbols: circle, square, wavy lines, cross and star. In a typical experiment of Rhine's early years, a subject would try to guess the order of the cards as they were contemplated, one at a time, by a "sender" who would attempt to transmit the symbol. Simple statistics could be used to determine whether the number of hits obtained by the subject was substantially different from chance expectation.

Some of the early card-guessing studies by Rhine's laboratory reported that the number of matches between guesses and targets would occur by chance less than once in a million times. The researchers quickly realized, however, that in many of their experiments, it had been possible for subjects to acquire information about the target symbols through sensory means—the

symbols on some of the Zener card decks had been so heavily printed that they were faintly visible on the backs of the cards. If the subject could view the cards, even from the back, they might have been able to inflate their hit rate without using ESP. This problem was corrected, but it has remained a perennial issue in the evaluation of ESP research results. All possible sensory contact between subject and the targets, no matter how unlikely, must be eliminated before ESP can be advanced as an explanation for a correlation between guesses and targets. Serious ESP researchers no longer use cards for creating target sequences; instead, they are generated by computers, and are not seen by either experimenters or subjects until after the guesses have been made. (The problem of sensory cues is less important in precognition experiments, in which the sequence of targets may not be generated until after the subjects have finished their participation in the study).

Critical examination of early ESP experiments raised other important issues. One of these was the randomization of target sequences. Unless the targets were arranged completely without order, any patterns in the target sequence might accidentally match habitual patterns in the guessing sequence—for example, if a subject tended to guess "star" for every fifth target, and there happened to be such a nonrandom positioning of star cards in the target Zener deck, the number of hits would be artificially inflated. Researchers have gone to great lengths to eliminate this potential problem, and the highest quality experimenters routinely check the randomness of their targets using statistical methods.

ESP experiments in which there is a fixed set of targets to be guessed are known as forced choice studies. Such procedures bear little resemblance to spontaneous ESP experiences. Since the 1960s, many researchers have turned to an alternative method called free response that seems more relevant to ESP experiences as they happen in real life. In this approach, the target is not a sequence of symbols, but a picture, object or location. The subject is asked to imagine or intuit the characteristics of this target. A description of their impressions can then be statistically compared with the target, to discern whether there are more resemblances than chance would predict.

Even in ESP experiments in which the possibility of sensory cues and target nonrandomness have been satisfactorily addressed, many other potential problems remain. The person who compares the order of guesses and targets can make mistakes that can either inflate or decrease the number of matches; errors can be made in statistically analyzing the data; and, even in a perfectly designed, conducted and analyzed experiment, there is still the possibility of cheating on the part of the subjects and/or experimenters. Occasionally, the field of ESP research has been tainted by hoaxes, as has every other area of scientific research; but, given the controversial nature of the phenomenon under study, parapsychologists have had to take unusual precautions to reduce the possibility of fraud.

In the decades since Rhine's Parapsychology Laboratory began operating at Duke University, thousands of ESP experiments have been conducted and published by researchers around the world. A considerable number of these have reported results that differ significantly from chance expectations. In addition, a few weak patterns in ESP scoring have been recognized. The most consistent of these pertain to subjects' expectancies regarding ESP, and their state of attention. Schmeidler coined the term *sheep-goat effect* to refer to a tendency for believers in ESP to score above chance levels, and for nonbelievers to score at, or even significantly below, chance. A review by George suggested that individuals who are open-minded about the possibility of ESP may tend to score higher than either confirmed believers or nonbelievers.

Surveys of spontaneous ESP experiences suggest that ESP is more likely when a person's attention is withdrawn from the external world, and focused inward. This finding inspired researchers to examine the effect of internal attention states on scoring in ESP tests. Dozens of studies have reported that meditation, hypnosis, sensory deprivation and deep muscular relaxation practices all tend to enhance performance on ESP tests. Researchers who asked subjects to dream about targets have also claimed that the dream state seemed to be ESP-conducive.

Despite the body of experimental results amassed by ESP researchers, many remain skeptical about the existence of ESP. Parapsychologists have been unable to produce a repeatable ESP experiment—one that consistently yields significant ESP scores.

Repeatability is a widely accepted requirement for the acceptance of a phenomenon by the scientific community. In the absence of the repeatable ESP experiment, some skeptics argue that the significant results that have been obtained may be due to a combination of undetected sensory cues, experimenter errors or fraud. Others who have examined the current body of evidence are convinced that the reality of ESP has been established; they contend that while a perfectly repeatable ESP experiment may not exist, patterns such as the sheep-goat effect and the enhancement of ESP scores in internal attention states indicate that a real, albeit elusive, paranormal phenomenon is involved. And yet others have concluded that the results of the last 100 years of ESP research cannot be explained either by conventional science or by appeals to paranormal concepts. This school of thought defines ESP experiences and experimental findings as an anomaly—an unsolved mystery that can neither be dismissed nor resolved at present. The controversy—and the research—continues.

See also Appendix; GESP; PSYCHICAL RESEARCH.

For further reading: Akers; Bem; Bem and Honorton; Gallup and Newport; George (1984); Gurney, Myers and Podmore; Honorton; Hyman (1985, 1994); Hyman and Honorton;

Irwin (1989); Morris, Edge, Palmer and Rush; Rhine (1965); Schmeidler (1988).

eyewitness accounts of unusual experiences "I saw it with my own eyes!" Such statements are frequently used to establish the truth or accuracy of a reported experience. While it is certainly the case that the likelihood of distortions grows the further a story travels from its author, eyewitness accounts are themselves unreliable guides to past events.

Errors in eyewitness accounts can occur during the experiences themselves. Perception is strongly influenced by an observer's assumptions, expectations and needs. These factors can cause a person to misidentify a perceived object, especially if it is not something familiar. ILLUSIONs (the misperception of a stimulus) and HALLUCINATIONs (perception in the absence of a stimulus) can happen to anyone; they are not only experienced by the mentally ill.

Unless an observer records an experience immediately, his or her report of the event will be based on memory. The mind does not store and retrieve information passively; rather, memory is just as affected by beliefs and motivations as percepteion. Distortions of recognition and recall, known as PARAMNESIAs, compromise the usefulness of memory evidence unless there is corroboration from other sources.

Unfortunately, the frailties of perception and memory are not restricted to individuals. Groups can misperceive illusions, hallucinate, and suffer from memory distortions. If members of the group have the opportunity to communicate with each other during the experience, their misperceptions are likely to become similar, due to the GROUP DYNAMICS OF UNUSUAL EXPERIENCES. Communication following the experience can produce common inaccuracies in memory. Thus, consensus in multiple eyewitness accounts does not prove that events took place the way witnesses say they did.

Eyewitness accounts can also be tainted by deception. Eyewitnesses themselves have been the victims of hoaxes, which they have innocently reported as amazing phenomena; and researchers have been hoodwinked by tricksters posing as eyewitnesses. The possibility of pseudologia phantastica, or compulsive lying, must also be considered in this regard.

In the face of these threats to the accuracy of eyewitness accounts, many researchers have concluded that such reports are too unreliable to use as evidence for claims of anomalies. Parapsychologists in the 1920s decided that the only way to evaluate whether ESP was possible was to conduct experiments in a controlled laboratory setting; decades of collecting eyewitness accounts of extraordinary occurrences had not produced a single report that could not be explained by some speculative combination of deception, false perception or FALSE MEMORY, however unlikely the combination may be. Parapsy- chologists still study eyewitness reports in order to come up with ideas concerning the nature of ESP, which they then try to evaluate through experiments.

Although the unreliability of eyewitness stories would seem to call for an open mind in most cases, the temptation to leap to conclusions is hard to resist. Some researchers fill in the uncertainties with their own convictions that certain anomalies are impossible and decide—often without investigation—that any reports to the contrary must be false. Others find it easier to believe the sincerity of witnesses than the evidence that sincerity does not protect against the untruthfulness of perception and memory.

For further reading: Loftus (1979); Loftus and Ketcham; Rosenfield.

fafrotskies "It's raining cats and dogs!" Most people know better than to take this old saying literally. But many unexpected things—including living animals—have indeed been observed to rain from the sky. Unusual objects and substances that fall to earth are called fafrotskies. This term, coined by Sanderson, is an acronym derived from the phrase "*fallen from the skies.*"

Accounts of odd inorganic materials falling from above date back at least as far as the Middle Ages. Later medieval records describe rains of small crosses. Woodcut illustrations depict people catching these heavenly tokens in the folds of their garments. Such tales strain the credulity of the modern secular mind. It is possible, however, that these events were hailstorms—hail has been known to assume a cruciform shape.

More difficult to understand is the famous rain that fell on Nuremberg, Germany in 1561. In a clear sky witnesses viewed a ring around the sun, airborne crosses, blood red streaks and two cylindrical shapes. Such appearances could have been PARHELIA, optical effects created by atmospheric ice crystals. However, the forms then rained to the ground, and the image of an immense spear was seen overhead. It is impossible to sort out the phenomenon as originally witnessed from exaggerations and additions later included in the account. Evidently, however, an event occured that included an aerial display of some sort followed by fafrotskies.

More recently, the meteorological literature has recorded many accounts of inorganic fafrotskies. Rains of sand, coal, cinders, dust and salt have been well-documented. Downpours of sulphur have occasionally been reported, but the yellowish substance usually proves upon analysis to be pollen.

Animals have also dropped from the sky. Fish are the most frequently reported type of fafrotsky. In some cases, the fish are said to be frozen; but in others they are very much alive. A typical instance, which occurred on a windy, rainy day in Scotland, was described in an account collected by Corliss (1977):

> I was startled by something falling all over me—down my neck, on my head, and on my back. On putting my hand down my neck I was surprised to find they were little fish. By this time I saw the whole ground covered with them. I took off my hat, the brim of which was full of them. They were jumping all about. They covered the ground in a long strip of about 80 yards by 12 . . . My mates and I might have gathered bucketsful of them, scraping with our hands. We did gather a great many, about a bucketful, and threw them into the rain pool, where some of them now are.

Other creatures that have reportedly showered the earth include frogs, toads, snails, shellfish, worms, caterpillars, snakes, eels and, perhaps least surprisingly, birds.

Plant materials such as leaves, seeds, nuts, berries and seaweed have appeared as fafrotskies. Rains of hay, although perhaps unpuzzling, can be spectacular. On occasion, hundreds of clumps of windborne hay, looking like huge aerial spiders, have been sighted passing overhead. One Welsh account noted that a squadron of flying hay balls "caused much consternation while passing over the town."

Whirlwinds, tornadoes and waterspouts are the commonly proposed explanations for fafrotskies. Most fafrotsky objects are relatively small, well within the power of concentrated winds to bear aloft for considerable distances.

Some rains of sand and cinders seem to have coincided with meteors and may have an extraterrestrial origin.

Some features of the phenomenon suggest that the airborne objects plummet from very considerable heights. The pattern of impacts on the grounds is usually highly elliptical and restricted to a small region, up to a few hundred feet long. Such a distribution is typical of objects that fall from the upper levels of the atmosphere or from space. In one well-documented massive bird fall, the animals were found to have hemorrhaged lungs and ruptured livers, suggesting that they had been carried to extremely high altitudes—well above their ability to fly.

Even more mysterious is the fact that most rains of fafrotskies appear to have been carefully sorted. Materials deposited by whirlwinds are a combination of sizes, shapes and substances. In contrast, only a single species of animal is normally found in any given fafrotsky fall, and each individual is approximately the same size. The kind of debris that one would expect to be sucked up along with the fafrotsky material is absent. It is unclear what aerial filtering mechanism could produce the consistency and purity of fafrotsky deposits.

See also ANGEL HAIR; DEVIL'S JELLY; METEOR; THUNDERSTONE.

For further reading: Corliss (1977); Sanderson (1972).

fallacy of personal validation   Variant term for the BARNUM EFFECT—the perception of uniquely personal meanings in vague, general information.

false awakening   Dreaming that one has awakened from a dream, when one has not, is known as a false awakening. Only when one actually wakes up and remembers the dream is the error detected. False awakenings are most commonly associated with LUCID DREAMS. They are not identical with them: In the false awakening, one dreams that one has awakened; in the lucid dream, one becomes aware that one is dreaming. A false awakening necessarily terminates a lucid dream, as it entails the loss of awareness that the experience is a dream.

Even experienced lucid dreamers can be fooled by false awakenings. Van Eeden, the first modern researcher to explore lucid dreams, reported that:

> I had a lucid dream, in which I made the following experiment. I drew with my finger, moistened by saliva, a wet cross on the palm of my left hand, with the intention of seeing whether it would still be there after waking up. Then I *dreamt* that I woke up and felt the wet cross on my left hand by applying the palm to my cheek. And then a long time afterwards I woke up *really* and knew at once that the hand of my physical body had been lying in a closed position undisturbed on my chest all the while.

Rarely, dreamers have reported multiple false awakenings—they dream of awakening, later to dream of awakening again and again until eventually they truly do. Some have wondered if the ordinary state of consciousness we call "being awake" may not itself be a sort of false awakening. Perhaps it is possible to attain types of awareness compared to which everyday consciousness is a dream. Certain texts from the meditative traditions, such as the Buddhist *Diamond Sutra*, say as much:

> Thus shall ye think of all this fleeting world:
> A star at dawn, a bubble in a stream;
> A flash of lightning in a summer cloud,
> A flickering lamp, a phantom, and a dream.

See also METACHORIC EXPERIENCE.

For further reading: C. Green; Malamud; Price and Wong; Van Eeden.

false memory   Contrary to popular belief, the function of memory is *not* the storage and retrieval of accurate information about past experiences. Memory, like all psychological processes, aims to help a person adapt to present circumstances; and often, our adaptation is best supported by false recollections. Some previous experiences may be so grave a threat to our current self-esteem or cherished beliefs that re-membering them might be overwhelming; we completely block their recall, a phenomenon called psychogenic amnesia. Other memories might more effectively enhance our confidence if they are altered somewhat rather than totally suppressed. These distortions of information in memory are called PARAMNESIAs.

Most of us implicitly trust our memories. We are strongly motivated to do so. As Loftus and Ketcham observed: "Our memories are so valu-able because they are literally a part of us—they tell us who we are, what we have experienced, and how we should feel." A challenge to the veracity of our memory is felt to be an assault on personal integrity, both in the sense of truthful-ness and of the foundation of our sense of iden-tity. Nonetheless, research has demonstrated conclusively that human memory is a frail guide to the past.

Vivid memories seem more trustworthy than dim ones. Unfortunately, vividness is an unreli-able index of accurate recall. Vivid fantasies can be mistaken for memories, or vice versa; fre-quently, fantasy and accurate recollection merge seamlessly. The Swiss psychologist Jean Piaget recounted how, as an adult, he clearly remem-bered an assault that he supposedly witnessed when he was a child; he later learned that the incident he so vividly recalled had never hap-pened. Few of our certainties about the past are ever scrutinized; because of their vividness, they are presumed to be true. Bartlett was one of the first researchers to discern memory's true nature. He observed that:

> Remembering is not the re-excitation of innu-merable fixed, lifeless and fragmentary traces. It is an imaginative reconstruction or construc-tion, built out of the relation of our attitude towards a whole active mass of organized past reactions or experiences . . . It is thus hardly ever really exact, even in the most rudimentary cases of rote recapitulation, and it is not at all important that it should be so.

Imagination and memory cannot be distin-guished with certainty because they are not sep-arate processes; rather, memory is a type of imagination—one that creates a useful image of the past.

Bartlett discovered that memories change in predictable ways over time. With repeated rec-ollection, irrelevant or unfamiliar elements tend to drop out of memory (leveling); the central details become exaggerated (sharpening); and the memory is reinterpreted in terms of the person's beliefs and needs (assimilation). Con-sider a story in which a man is killed by debris from a satellite after seeing an ominous bird; at the moment of death, his soul escapes from his mouth as black smoke. A listener from a modern urban society, if asked to recall this story after one year, might forget about the bird (leveling), remember the satellite as a chunk of Skylab (sharpening) and recall the escaping soul as blood (assimilation). A listener from a tradi-tional rural culture might only vaguely recollect the satellite as "something from the sky" (level-ing), remember the bird as an owl (sharpening) and alter the smokey soul into a soul-spider, in accord with the beliefs of his people (assimila-tion).

What we remember also depends on the con-text in which we remember it. Loftus and Zanni showed a film clip of a traffic accident, following which they asked their subjects one of two ques-tions: "Did you see *the* broken headlight?" or "Did you see *a* broken headlight?" Twice as many viewers who were asked the first question remembered seeing a broken headlight, despite the fact that none was shown in the film clip.

These factors affect the recollection of all experiences, including unusual ones. Many in-vestigators insist that memories have little value as evidence for the occurrence of extraordinary events without corroborating information. The older the memory, the more likely it has been distorted in the ways noted by Bartlett. When psychical researchers began to collect anecdotes in the 19th century, they quickly discovered the fallibility of memory. Zusne and Jones recounted the case of Sir Edmund Hornby, a famous judge who reported an apparition nine years after the experience:

> One night in January, 1875, a newspaper editor known to the judge entered his bedroom, ignored the Judge's request to leave, sat down on the foot of his bed, and asked for information for his paper concerning a judgment made the previous day. The time was 1:20 in the morning, according to the Judge. The Judge finally gave in to the request for fear that an argument might wake up his wife. . . . After the visitor was gone, Lady Hornby awoke, whereupon the Judge told her about the visit. He repeated the story to her the next morning. That day, he also learned that the editor whom he had seen the night before had died about 1 o'clock in the morning. The inquest showed that he had died of a heart disease. . . . The Judge asserted that he had not been asleep but wide awake, that after a lapse of 9 years his memory was quite clear on the subject, and that he had not the least doubt that he had seen the man and that the conversation had taken place between them. . . . [Investigation revealed] that the editor had died at 9 in the morning of the day in question, that no inquest was held on his death, that there was no record of the judgment that figures so prominently in the story, and that Judge Hornby was not married at the time.

Children's recollections are not immune from false memories either, as demonstrated in 1891 by Varondeck (cited by Baker, 1992). When he asked 28 school children to identify the color of their teacher's beard, 19 could do so; only one recalled, correctly, that the teacher was beardless. By the 1980s, many seemed to have forgotten this lesson. The testimony of children concerning allegations of criminal acts by adults was regarded as especially reliable in some clinical and legal circles. The claim, still advanced by some, that "children never lie," is neither true nor relevant; children as well as adults can retrieve false memories with perfect sincerity.

One result of the contemporary ignorance regarding children's memory was the outbreak of mass accusations of Satanic child abuse in the United States and Canada. The best-known case involved the McMartin Preschool in Manhattan Beach, California, which was said to be a headquarters for devil-worshipping child abusers. The charges, which resemble those made by inquisitors during the European witch hunts of medieval times, were founded on memory reports elicited from children by adults searching for Satan stories; no substantiating evidence turned up, and the case was dropped.

It is true that the accuracy of memory can be improved. Techniques for improving the efficiency of storing and retrieving memory material are often taught in college study skills seminars. Witnesses of unusual events are sometimes subjected to HYPNOSIS to enhance their memories. Unfortunately, there is no evidence that hypnotized people have consistently better memories than unhypnotized ones; rather, hypnosis tends to increase *confidence* in one's ability to remember, rather than *accuracy*. A hypnotized person may thus be more likely to mistake a fantasy for a true recollection.

See also EYEWITNESS ACCOUNTS OF UNUSUAL EXPERIENCES.

For further reading: American Psychological Association; Baker (1992); Bartlett; Loftus (1993); Loftus and Ketcham; Loftus and Zanni; Zusne and Jones.

fana   Among the Sufis—Moslems who aspire to a direct experience of God—there is a cherished instruction: "Die before you die!" In other words, before the death of the body, the Sufi should experience the annihilation of his or her ordinary sense of self, in order to clear the way for contact with God. This moment of annihilation is called, in Arabic, *fana*—literally, "extinction." Glasse observed that the meaning of fana in the Moslem system corresponds to the idea of NIRVANA in Buddhism.

Fana is a high spiritual state, the attainment of which is usually preceded by much preparation. Through study of doctrine, adherence to social laws and contemplative practices, the Sufi brings about the extinction of inner obstacles prior to full fana—for instance, the deaths of the "soul that inclines to evil" (*an-nafs al-ammarah*) and the "soul that accuses" (*an-nafs al-lawwamah,* which produces unwholesome guilt).

Following fana, the Sufi, although spiritually transformed, is still alive. Such a person still functions on the level of everyday life, but now he or she has a sense of a deep relationship to God. There is still a sense of separateness from the divine, however. Some Sufi teachers speak of a more advanced experience—*fana al-fana,* or "extinction of the extinction." In this condition, even the awareness of the fana experience itself is removed, leaving nothing between oneself and God. This moment leads to the ultimate state of consciousness described in Sufism—BAQA.

See also RUYA'HA.

For further reading: Bakhtiar; Glasse; Schimmel.

fang-chung shu   A Chinese phrase meaning "arts of the inner chamber," fang-chung shu refers to meditations involving sexual intercourse that were practiced by some devotees of NEI-TAN, a Taoist system aiming to produce immortality. It was widely believed that health, as well as spiritual growth, depended on balancing the forces known as *yin* and *yang.* Yin manifests in the dark, negative, feminine and passive aspects of reality; yang in the light, positive, masculine and active features. Men required contact with yin to balance their yang, and vice versa for women. This requirement was taken literally, and acted out, by the devotees of fang-chung shu.

Most of the writings on these practices describe them from the male viewpoint. During foreplay, the man is encouraged to absorb the woman's yin by swallowing her "jade fluid" (saliva) and touching her breasts in ritually prescribed ways. During intercourse, the male partner acquires more yin through his penis, and the female takes yang through her vagina. At sexual climax, he should endeavor not to release any semen. Various techniques were taught for accomplishing this, including grasping the base of the penis, exhaling forcefully and grinding the teeth. It was thought that the ejaculate would then flow to the brain, where it was transformed into a youth-imparting energy.

The earlier texts on fang-chung shu recommend performing the act with as many partners as possible, especially young and attractive ones. The role model was the legendary Yellow Emperor, Huang-ti. He was reputed to have made love to 1200 women without losing any of his sperm. Orgies were organized for the convenience of fang-chung shu devotees. As the severe morality of Confucianism rose to public dominance around the seventh century, fang-chung shu became politically incorrect. It has continued to be practiced in secret, though. Other mystical schools have interpreted the "arts of the inner chamber" more figuratively, claiming that the union of yin and yang occurs within each individual.

See also TANTRA, HINDU.

For further reading: C. Chang; Fischer-Schreiber; Schipper.

fantasy proneness   Many children in Western societies display an ability to become involved in fantasy, such as make-believe games and IMAGINARY COMPANIONs, that seems beyond the capacity of most adults. Indeed, it is commonly believed that maturity entails reducing fantasy involvement in order to engage the adult challenges of the "real" outside world. A small group, comprising a few percent of the population, do not abandon the child's immersion in fantasy when they grow up. These individuals have been dubbed fantasy prone personalities, or fantasy addicts. Fantasy prone people report that they may spend most of their waking time attending to mental imagery.

People who fantasize a lot as adults tend to remember having an unusually rich fantasy life as children. Often, a significant adult such as a relative or teacher rewarded the child for his or her rich imagination, and encouraged make-believe games and the reading of fantastic tales. Many fantasy prone adults also recall being abused as children; such people could have honed their imaginal skills as a means of temporarily escaping from CHILDHOOD TRAUMAs.

Fantasy proneness has been linked to a wide variety of unusual experiences and beliefs. EXTRASENSORY PERCEPTION, OUT OF BODY EXPERIENCEs, MYSTICAL EXPERIENCEs, APPARITIONs and NEAR DEATH EXPERIENCEs are all more often reported by the fantasy prone. Wilson and Barber speculated that "individuals manifesting the fantasy-prone syndrome may have been overrepresented among famous mediums, psychics, and religious visionaries of the past." General paranormal belief, as well as specific beliefs in ESP, spirits and cryptic animals, are also more characteristic of fantasy prone personalities' world views. Some skeptics have suggested that fantasy prone personalities simply have trouble discriminating between perceptions and fantasies and so they are more prone to mistaking normal occurrences for paranormal ones and drawing false conclusions.

But the fact that vivid fantasizers tend to have unusual experiences does not necessarily mean that those experiences are fantasies. Possibly, fantasizers' sensitivity to the contents of the mind renders them more likely to detect anomalous events that others would miss.

Ring studied the relationship between two types of childhood experience and anomalous experiences as adults. He defined fantasy proneness as the childhood tendency to have vivid fantasies, and childhood alternate reality experiences as the tendency to have strange experiences that seemed real. Ring reported that fantasy proneness, as he defined it, was not associated with later unusual experiences, but that both NEAR DEATH EXPERIENCEs and UFO ENCOUNTERs were positively correlated with the alternate reality experiences. Most researchers would include Ring's "alternate reality experiences" under their definition of fantasy proneness.

Fantasy proneness is also associated with other personality traits: capacity for ABSORPTION, or completely focusing one's attention on a single object; and HYPNOTIZABILITY. Some researchers view absorption and fantasy proneness as identical, while others distinguish them. Wilson and Barber implied that hypnotizability and fantasy proneness were the same thing; more recent studies have found that they are related, but not identical. Some highly hypnotizable people are not fantasy prone, and vice versa.

Many fantasy prone individuals function very well in society. Fantasy proneness can confer certain benefits, such as the ability to generate orgasms through fantasy alone, without any physical stimulation. There is growing evidence that vivid fantasizers may be more vulnerable than others to some disorders. Pseudocyesis, or false pregnancy, is more common among the fantasy prone. Several studies have found that frequent fantasizers tend to report coping more poorly with stress, higher levels of anxiety and lower self-esteem than in frequent fantasizers. Irwin suggested that fantasizers might not actually be less well-adjusted than others; they might be more aware of their problems and thus more likely to report them in a survey. Or, childhood trauma might cause both fantasy proneness and psychological problems later in life; if so, fantasy proneness itself would not be the cause of the adjustment problems.

See also Appendix.

For further reading: Lynn and Rhue (1988); Ring; Wilson and Barber.

Fata Morgana According to legend, Morgan Le Fay was the fairy sister of King Arthur. She had the unpleasant habit of conjuring visions of cities and harbors in order to entice sailors to their ruin on jagged rocks. Her name has been given to a remarkable type of MIRAGE seen repeatedly in many parts of the world.

The classic report of a Fata Morgana was made in 1773 by Friar Minasi (quoted in Corliss). He noted a rare spectacle that occurred on mornings when the sea was calm, and he gazed across the Straits of Messina toward Sicily:

> . . . on a sudden he sees appear in the water . . . various multiplied objects, such as numberless series of pilasters, arches, castles well delineated, regular columns, lofty towers, superb palaces with balconies and windows, extended alleys of trees, delightful plains with herds and flocks, armies of men on foot and horseback, and many other strange figures, all in their natural colours and proper action, and passing rapidly in succession along the surface of the sea.

If a fog hovered above the water, Minasi noted, the images would also appear floating in the air. Three images of this Fata Morgana have been observed at once, one above the other.

This mirage is produced when conditions conspire to arrange the air over the Strait into a giant lens. Images of the rocks along the Sicilian coast are magnified and distorted; with a little imagination, they are perceived as the scenes described above.

Fata Morganas have been observed at other sites where atmospheric lenses sometimes develop. They are more common at cooler latitudes. The Firth of Forth, in Scotland, is the location of a recurring Fata Morgana. Corliss presented this description: from the water's surface there

> suddenly shot up . . . a huge perpendicular wall, apparently 800 or 900 feet high, with a smooth and unbroken front to the sea. On the east side lay a long low range of rocks . . . a beautiful columnal circle, the column seemingly from 20 to 30 feet high, appeared on the outermost rock. Presently the figure was changed to a clump of trees, whose green umbrageous foliage had a very vivid appearance. By and by the clump of trees increased to a large plantation, which gradually approached the main portion of the island, until within 300 or 400 feet, when the intervening space was spanned by a beautiful arch. . . . trees and towers, columns and arches, sprang up and disappeared as if by magic.

Fata Morganas seem to be composed of images magnified over a great distance and the fancies of the observer. The atmosphere is capable of refracting light from beyond the horizon, but the limits of this phenomenon are uncertain. The most fantastic reports of Fata Morganas concern the so-called "Silent City" of Mt. Fairweather on the Alaska Panhandle. A phantom city has repeatedly been seen at a glacier on the peak. Some have reported that the image corresponds to the city of Bristol, England, 4,000 miles away. Most researchers do not believe that the Silent City could be optically caused by Bristol.

For further reading: Corliss (1984).

Fatima apparitions In a rural hollow called the Cova da Iria, near the village of Fatima, Portugal, a series of odd occurrences took place in 1917 that have become one of the most famous mysteries of modern times. Over six months, tens of thousands of people witnessed events that they could not explain in ordinary terms.

The central figure in the Fatima story was Lucia Santos, a young shepherdess who lived with her family in Fatima. Her first unusual experience happened in 1915, when she was eight. While tending her flock, she and two companions saw a cloud in the shape of a man. Lucia witnessed this form in the sky on two other occasions that year. In 1916, Lucia and two cousins (Jacinta, aged six, and eight-year-old Francisco) encountered an apparition on three occasions while tending their sheep. Lucia and Jacinta heard the apparition speak; Francisco could see it, but not hear it. According to the girls, the form described itself as an "angel of peace." On its last visit, it administered Holy

Communion to the three children. None of the little shepherds told anyone about these incidents at the time.

On May 13, 1918, the trio were pasturing their flock by the Cova da Iria. They experienced a brilliant flash of light, which they took to be lightning. Fearing that a thunderstorm was near, they hurried into the hollow. As they passed a bush, they noticed the luminous image of a woman, dressed in white, hovering over it. Lucia later wrote that this image "radiated a light more intense than a crystal glass filled with sparkling water." The mysterious form instructed the children to say many rosaries and informed them that she would return to the Cova to visit them on the 13th of each month for the next five months. Then she vanished. As in the events of 1916, the two girls both saw and heard the apparition; Francisco saw, but did not hear.

The children vowed to each other not to tell a soul about their strange encounter. Jacinta, however, was convinced that the apparition had been the Blessed Virgin Mary; overcome with excitement, she blurted out the news to her family. Soon, everyone in Fatima knew of the children's encounter and the apparition's prediction of its return. Reaction ranged from extreme skepticism to reverent anticipation of the Virgin's next visit. Lucia's mother was convinced she was lying and beat the child in order to extract a confession. None of the children retracted their story, regardless of the pressures brought to bear on them.

On June 13 the trio returned to the Cova, accompanied by about 50 onlookers. By now, all three children had decided that the lady was indeed Mary. They knelt before the bush; soon, they saw the luminous image above it. While Lucia conversed with the apparition, the other two children looked on; the surrounding crowd could see nothing unusual, although those standing closest to the bush reported hearing "an indistinct whispering, or the loud buzzing of a bee" seemingly emanating from the bush. When Lucia announced that the Virgin was now going

away, many of the onlookers heard a loud noise, like "the explosion of a rocket," and watched a little white cloud rise above the bush.

By July 13, the date of the children's third appointment with the apparition, the events at Fatima were attracting national attention. Approximately 4,500 people followed the visionaries to the bush in the Cova that day. While the children had their apparitional experience by the bush, many onlookers also reported unusual phenomena. The sun seemed to lose its heat, and dimmed; a buzzing or humming sound was heard; and, at the conclusion of the children's encounter, the loud noise and white cloud were perceived.

The experiences of the eyewitnesses converted many skeptics to belief in the reality of the visitations. The Portuguese government, however, was becoming concerned. Government leaders were hostile to the Catholic church and probably suspected that the stories coming out of Fatima were a Catholic plot to excite the faithful. On August 13, the predicted date of the Virgin's fourth visit, the children did not go to the Cova; they had been kidnapped by a local official, who held them in a nearby town until the day passed. Undaunted, a crowd of 18,000 descended on the Cova. A large number of those present apparently witnessed strange happenings. Around the tree, there again occurred a noise and a cloud, accompanied by a flash. Many people saw rainbow-colored lights in the sky illuminating the ground and a spinning globe passing overhead. Several days later, the children, now released, reported that the Virgin had visited them again. There was only one onlooker at this unpredicted encounter.

When the seers kept their appointment with Mary on September 13, they were accompanied by about 30,000 people. As the children knelt before the tree, the crowd reportedly beheld a luminous sphere floating through the air. The light settled onto the tree and disappeared. The children evidently saw the Virgin at this time, and Lucia conversed with her. Many of the onlookers noticed a cloud of what they took to be white flower petals falling from the sky, but the material never reached the ground. One witness described this curious optical effect:

> As the people stare at this strange sight they soon notice that the falling, glistening globules, contrary to the laws of perspective, grow smaller and smaller as they near them. And when they reach out their hands and hats to catch them they find that they have somehow melted away.

The episode ended when the glowing sphere rose from the tree and disappeared into the glare of the sun.

The final predicted visit of the apparition on October 13 was anticipated throughout the nation. Major Portuguese newspapers, which had anti-religious orientations, sent journalists to Fatima in order to document that nothing extraordinary would happen that day. When the seers arrived at the Cova, they found an encampment of 70,000 people. Lucia and her cousins had trouble reaching the tree of the apparitions because people kept prostrating themselves in front of them, begging them to request a favor of the Blessed Virgin.

The children knelt before the tree. They became enraptured, as Lucia talked with the image that only the visionary trio could perceive. Then Lucia cried out to the crowd, "Look at the sun!" The onlookers gazed skyward. Then, by all accounts, including those of the skeptical journalists, a weird spectacle ensued. A disk appeared overhead, typically described as resembling "a dull silver plate." It was generally assumed to be the sun, but Rogo has noted that the reported location of the object in the sky did not match the location of the solar disk at that time. Next, in the words of Dr. Almeida Garrete of the University of Coimbra, a witness to the event:

> This chequered shining disc seemed to possess a giddy motion. . . . It turned on itself with an astonishing rapidity. Suddenly a great cry, like a cry of anguish, arose from all this vast throng. The sun while keeping its swiftness of rotation, detached itself from the firmament and, blood-red in colour, rushed towards the earth, threatening to crush us under the immense weight of its mass of fire. There were moments of dreadful tension.

The phenomenon was reported by observers as far as 40 kilometers from the Cova. Pereira, in a group of these distant witnesses, recorded the experience:

> I looked fixedly at the sun, which appeared pale and did not dazzle. It looked like a ball of snow turning on itself. . . . Then suddenly it seemed to become detached from the sky, and rolled right and left, as if it were falling upon the earth. Terrified, absolutely terrified, I ran towards the crowd of people. All were weeping, expecting at any moment the end of the world. . . . During the long minutes of the solar phenomena, the objects around us reflected all the colours of the rainbow. Looking at each other, one appeared blue, another yellow, a third red, etc. . . . After about ten minutes the sun climbed back into its place, as it had descended, still quite pale and without brilliance. When the people were convinced that the danger had passed, there was an outburst of joy.

The spectacle marked the end of the strange happenings in the Cova da Iria. Within two years, Jacinta and Francisco had both died of influenza. Lucia went on to become a nun and wrote a detailed account of her life and experiences.

The events of Fatima are important because they touch on a feature that most people rely upon to discern whether something is real—the shared experience of others. If, as some have argued, reality is what the majority of people experiences, then the witnesses of Fatima must have experienced a supernatural reality. Conversely, if consensus is an unreliable guide to the nature of things, and the thousands of onlookers at Fatima were all mistaken in what they saw, questions are raised concerning whether the "common sense" certainties of daily life might also prove to be false.

The shared aspects of the Fatima occurrences pose a challenge to conventional explanations. Regarding the descriptions of the apparition given by the children, Carroll noted that the accounts given by the trio became more divergent as more witnesses were present—their descriptions of the May encounter were virtually identical, whereas the apparitional display of October was described quite differently by each child. Carroll argued that any commonalities in the children's descriptions of the apparitions arose from discussions between the seers following each experience. As they compared what they saw and heard, they shaped their memories of the apparition accordingly. The growing number of onlookers would have reduced their opportunities for discussing the apparition among themselves before reporting their experiences to others, and so the differences between their reports grew. The basis of the shared apparitional experience, Carroll suspected, was merely a HALLUCINATION. During the first visitation on May 13, Lucia probably had the hallucination first and caused her companions to hallucinate also through suggestion.

Could such a mechanism also account for the common descriptions of unusual events given by the hordes of onlookers, who included avowed skeptics, on five separate occasions and, during the last episode, over a large geographical area? Experiments in social psychology have demonstrated that suggestion can induce common experiences among small groups of subjects. Perhaps the widely circulated stories regarding the occurrences at the Cova da Iria functioned as suggestions. As each encounter yielded more accounts of wondrous experiences, the expectations likely grew, culminating in the spectacle of October 13. If the spheres, discs, rainbow lights and petals viewed by so many were mass hallucinations caused by suggestion, then the malleability of public experience is much greater than most people realize.

Alternatively, this explanation may be inadequate. Vallee noted that the Fatima stories share a number of features with many reports of UFO ENCOUNTERs, and places the aerial displays over the Cova in that category. Many Roman Catholics to this day prefer the simpler explanation of supernatural intervention.

See also MARIAN APPARITION.

For further reading: Carroll; Nickell; Rogo; Vallee; Walsh; Zimdars-Swartz.

flagellation Whipping or beating a person in order to improve health or morals dates back to ancient times in western culture. Flagellation has also been employed to induce spiritually elevated states of consciousness.

In the later Middle Ages, so many people engaged in public self-flagellation that the practice took on the characteristics of a mass compulsion. During the 13th century, there was widespread expectation that a new Age of the Holy Spirit was about to begin. In Italy groups of "flagellantes" formed processions through the streets as they whipped themselves into ecstatic states. Such activities met with the disapproval of the orthodox religious authorities, but many members of the uneducated classes were impressed by the piety of the flagellants and rewarded them with honors.

Around the time of the Black Plague in the mid-14th century, Europeans felt a sense of helplessness and terror at the imminent end of the world. These factors fed public displays of compulsive behavior, such as the DANCING MANIA, as well as a resurgence of self-flagellation. The practitioners became loosely organized at this time. They adopted a distinctive mode of dress: a cloak and hood, marked with a red cross. Long lines of men, women and children snaked from town to town in Spain, Italy, Germany and the Netherlands. They would periodically strip to the waist and strike themselves with chains, rods and spiked thongs until blood flowed from the wounds. The spiritual intensity of the flagellants brought them a certain authority—excited bystanders would carry out any order they gave, including murder. Many mass killings of Jews resulted from the incitements of the blood-spattered penitents.

One remarkable Russian sect was known as the Khlysty (from the word *khlyst,* meaning "horsewhip"). The goal of the Khlysty, who appeared in the 17th century, was to transform themselves into perfected beings, or Christs. In their ceremonies, groups of men would perform frenzied dances around a boiling jar of water while being beaten by virgin girls dressed in white. The dancers would reportedly become possessed by the Holy Spirit. After the ceremony, the performers were thought to possess supernatural powers such as healing and clairvoyance. The notorious friend of the Romanovs, Grigori Rasputin, had belonged to the Khlysty for a while as a young man, according to some accounts.

The practice of flagellation for spiritual ends has endured to the present day. The flagellants' movement was carried to the New World by the Spanish conquistadores and has survived in the form of Los Hermanos Penitentes, a rural religious group in Colorado and New Mexico. Some Roman Catholics belonging to the organization called Opus Dei ("Work of God") whip themselves for purification and ecstasy. Some members of the modern witchcraft movement in England, particularly in the Gardnerian and Alexandrian branches, have included ceremonial scourging in their initiation rituals to symbolize that painful experiences can expand one's consciousness.

See also ALTERED STATE OF CONSCIOUSNESS; GROUP DYNAMICS OF UNUSUAL EXPERIENCES.

For further reading: Hill; Merskey.

flashback   A flashback is an involuntary memory of such intensity that it overwhelms one's perceptions of the present. The remembered material can appear so real that it forms HALLUCINATIONs. The term is used most commonly in connection with drug experiences, but it applies to any vivid and intrusive recollection. Proust's description of a flashback is one of the best known passages in modern literature:

> And so, mechanically, weary after a dull day with the prospect of a dull morrow, I raised to my lips a spoonful of the tea in which I had soaked a morsel of the cake. No sooner had the warm liquid, and the crumbs in it, touched my palate than a shudder ran through my whole body, and I stopped intent upon the extraordinary changes that were taking place. Undoubtedly what is thus palpitating in the depths of my being must be the image, the visual memory which, being linked to that taste, has tried to follow it into my conscious mind.

Proust's character is then flooded with childhood memories associated with the flavor of the tea-dipped cake.

Flashbacks are reported by about 10% of the general population. Although flashbacks are often memories of traumatic events, they can also be of pleasant things. As in Proust's example, in most cases the flashback is triggered by encountering some reminder of the occasion when the experience was stored in memory.

Among users of psychedelic drugs, the prevalence of flashbacks rises to 25%. A flashback of a previous drug experience may be cued by taking the drug again. Achieving intoxication using other substances, or even merely thinking about a drug experience, can sometimes reawaken the memory. Stress, fatigue and illness have also been linked to drug flashbacks. Tec reports the case of a man who was falsely led to believe that the wine he had just imbibed was spiked with LSD. He was revisited by old LSD hallucinations for the next 14 days.

It is generally easier to remember something if one is in the same state of mood, arousal or consciousness as when the memory was formed. Depressed, excited or inebriated people can most clearly recall their actions the next time they return to those conditions. Many drug flashbacks are probably examples of this phenomenon, known as state dependent memory. Fischer noted that drug flashbacks most likely occur when the person is in a similar state of arousal as the initial experience. These unbidden recollections can occur months or years following the last drug experience. In some cases of prolonged heavy drug consumption, flashbacks can become chronic. More typically, they become less numerous and intense over time.

Individuals prone to flashbacks have been found to differ in several ways from those who do not have them. Flashbackers tend to rate higher in HYPNOTIZABILITY, have higher resting heart rates, be more sensitive to drugs, be more sensitive to low levels of sensory stimulation and be less consistent in their measured reactions and behaviors.

See also BAD TRIP.

For further reading: Fischer; Panton and Fischer; Proust; Stafford.

floaters A common type of ENTOPTIC PHENOMENON. The eyeball is filled with a transparent liquid, the vitreous body, through which light passes on its way from the pupil to the retina. Blood cells can leak into this area; cells from the macula, or outer wall of the eyeball, can also become detached. Such debris, drifting through the path of the light traversing the vitreous body, casts shadows on the retina. One may then see small circles floating across the field of vision; sometimes, these forms appear in chains or tangles. Floaters tend to become more common as a person ages. They are most easily seen when the light entering the eye is relatively bright and steady, as when one looks into the sky on a cloudless day. Floaters have been interpreted as visions of spirits, manifestations of psychic energy or even as signs of impending madness. In fact, they are the result of normal wear and tear on the visual system.

See also SCHEERER'S PHENOMENON.

For further reading: Neher (1990).

fly agaric This mushroom, called by botanists *Amanita muscaria,* is found in northern temperate regions across Eurasia and North America. The best known variety is spectacular in appearance, with its blood red cap flecked with white; another important type of fly agaric, orange-capped with yellow flecks, grows in eastern and central North America. The fly agaric is a little factory producing the alkaloid muscimole; when eaten, it can cause HALLUCINATIONS. The impact of this mushroom on human history has been the subject of intense debate, but most authorities agree that it has been immense. Schultes and Hofmann consider the fly agaric to be "perhaps man's oldest hallucinogen." Wasson enthused that it was "the supreme ENTHEOGEN of all time."

In addition to visual hallucinations, ingestion of fly agaric has been associated with a range of other reactions. These include distortions in the perception of size (macropsia and micropsia), DELIRIUM and rapid mood swings. An unusual feature of fly agaric intoxication is that it often produces great restlessness and movement, whereas most hallucinogens create drowsiness. The mushroom's potency arises from the muscimole's disruption of central nervous system functioning, so overdosing can cause coma and death.

The native cultures of Siberia, who had very little contact with other societies until the 16th century, are thought to have preserved vestiges of extremely ancient religious practices. Several Siberian groups used the fly agaric as a gateway to the spirit world, for divinatory and diagnostic purposes, and for pleasure. Shamans among the Koryak, for example, would eat the mushroom prior to retiring into a totally darkened room. They often reported having OUT OF BODY EXPERIENCES in which they journeyed to the land of the dead and received instruction from ghosts. In social activities the Koryak took advantage of the fact that muscimole is not metabolized, but leaves the body in the urine. During parties of the rich, the less privileged men of the tribe would wait outside. When mushroom-intoxicated celebrants emerged from the huts to empty their bladders, they would be persuaded to pee into wooden bowls. The contents would then be quaffed to provide a "poor man's high." This process could be repeated for five cycles, it was said, before the urine lost its potency.

The role of cultural expectations on shaping the psychedelic experience is illustrated by the accounts of fly agaric intoxication among the Siberian Chukchee. They believed that the mushrooms were a tribe of spirits. One could expect the spirit of each mushroom to appear in a vision following its consumption. Chukchee artists have produced drawings showing the "mushroom men" carrying off their souls to visit spirit lands.

The practice of using the fly agaric may have been transferred to North America along with ancient migrants from Siberia. Shamans among the Dogrib tribe of northwestern Canada eat the fungus to contact spirits. One practitioner (quoted by Schultes and Hofmann) described his experience:

> Cleansed and ripe for vision, I rise, a bursting ball of seeds in space. . . . I have sung the note that shatters structure. And the note that shatters chaos, and been bloody. . . . I have been with the dead, and attempted the labyrinth.

The Ojibwa people who live near Lake Superior in the United States ingest the fly agaric as a sacrament at an annual festival.

Many scholars believe that reverence for this magic mushroom also diffused south from central Asia into India. The earliest religious text of Hinduism is the Rig Veda, composed around 1400 B.C. Of the 1,028 hymns in the Rig Veda, 120 refer to a substance called *soma,* which was so revered that it was addressed as a deity. Its euphoric and visionary effects were described rapturously:

> Where there is eternal light, in the world where the sun is placed, in that immortal imperishable world place me, O Soma. . . . Where life is free, in the third heaven of heavens, where the worlds are radiant, there make me immortal. . . . Where there is happiness and delight, where joy

and pleasure reside, where the desires of our desire are attained, there make me immortal.

Soma was a drink, made from a plant and consumed sacramentally. There are also references to urine drinking in soma rituals. The identity of the plant from which the hallucinogenic drink was made was long ago forgotten; but recent research, led by Wasson, suggests that it was none other than the fly agaric mushroom. (Some writers have argued for other candidates: McKenna suggested a different mushroom, *Stropharia cubensis;* and Flattery and Schwartz proposed the giant Syrian rue.)

Allegro, in his well-known work *The Sacred Mushroom and the Cross,* advanced the notion that the fly agaric played an instrumental role in the early history of Judaism and Christianity. Allegro "translated" the ancient Hebrew names of God and the patriarchs by comparing them to words in Mesopotamian languages. He found that they referred to a fertility cult centered on the worship of the fly agaric mushroom. He further argued that the Jesus stories in the New Testament were actually coded descriptions of secret ceremonies that involved ingestion of the psychedelic fungus. In short, Christ was a mushroom. Allegro's thesis provoked intense controversy and has not been widely accepted by scholars.

One piece of evidence suggests the remote possibility that some Christians of the Middle Ages may have attributed an esoteric significance to the magic mushroom. A fresco in the Romanesque Plaincourault Chapel in France portrayed the Edenic Tree of knowledge as a mushroom with a bright red, white flecked cap. The image closely resembles the fly agaric; but there is no consensus regarding the identity or meaning of the depicted plant.

See also BERSERK.

For further reading: Allegro; Flattery and Schwartz; McKenna; Schultes and Hofmann; Stafford; Wasson.

folie à deux A French phrase, meaning "madness of two"; the term for a DELUSION shared by two people. Folie à deux is one form of INDUCED PSYCHOTIC DISORDER.

foo fighters During the winter of 1944–1945, Allied pilots flying bombing runs over western Europe began to report that their planes were being visited by strange lights. Described as being spherical or disc-shaped and red, orange or white in color, the mysterious entities would follow the planes just beyond or behind the wing. Usually, but not always, they were seen at night by solitary pilots. Sometimes, the lights were observed apparently flying in formation; occasionally, they were photographed. Extant photographs depict patches of light corresponding well with the pilots' verbal accounts. The phenomena were dubbed "foo fighters," "foo" being a popular English distortion of *feu,* the French word for fire.

Allied bombers encountered foo fighters over Japan in 1945. The Allies suspected that the Axis forces were using some sort of psychological warfare technique in an attempt to distract their pilots; but, following the war, it was learned that German and Japanese pilots had also been visited by foo fighters and had thought they were Allied weapons! The glowing forms were occasionally reported by pilots during the Korean and Vietnam wars.

Several theories have been offered to explain the foo fighters. In some cases exhausted pilots may simply have experienced HALLUCINATIONs. The pilots' hallucination-proneness could have been enhanced by the fact that they flew in unpressurized cabins, thus undergoing the stresses of rapid altitude changes; this would explain why foo fighters are no longer reported by pilots today, whose cabins maintain a constant pressure.

A military team that investigated the Japanese sightings concluded that they were misidentifications of the planet Venus—having heard the stories from Europe, the fliers in the Pacific arena were primed to interpret any light that could not be immediately identified as foo fighters.

Menzel and Boyd noted that, by the closing stages of World War II, most of the bombers would have wings that had been damaged and repaired with patches. These irregularities on the wing surfaces would have interfered with air flowing over the wings, creating eddies through which ice crystals would swirl. Reflections of light from these ice vortices, Menzel and Boyd speculated, were the basis of the foo fighter sightings.

The appearance of foo fighters resembles natural electrical phenomena, such as BALL LIGHTNING or ST. ELMO'S FIRE, and might have been caused by similar mechanisms. Some have argued that the foo fighter sightings were actually UFO ENCOUNTERs. The modern interest in "flying saucers" or "UFOs" did not begin until 1947.

For further reading: Haines; Menzel and Boyd.

form constants Geometric images produced by the human visual nervous system itself, rather than by external stimuli, form constants comprise an important class of ENTOPTIC PHENOMENA. They appear so commonly in unusual experiences that Siegel (1989) commented, "the [form] constants are the staffs upon which the music of our intoxications is written. There are many individual variations, but the theme is distinctly human."

Unlike other species of entoptics, such as PHOSPHENEs, FLOATERS and SCHEERER'S PHENOMENON, form constants are thought to be produced by regions of the visual system beyond the eyeball. In ordinary vision, light from the external world shines onto sensitive receptor cells in the retina; the retinal cells send information to the thalamus and visual cortex of the brain, via the optic nerve. The brain constructs our visual perception of the world from this information. When the activity of cells in the optic nerve and visual cortex does not represent events and objects in the outer world, form constants are experienced.

Form constants can occur spontaneously; they have also been deliberately sought. Many conditions and techniques can cause entoptic visions. Anthropologists and psychologists have documented the following triggers of form constants: AUDITORY and PHOTIC DRIVING, fatigue, rhythmic movements, SENSORY DEPRIVATION, concentration, DRUGS, MIGRAINE headaches, hyperventilation and SCHIZOPHRENIA. They have also been produced by direct electrical stimulation of the visual cortex. Each of these factors disrupts the ordinary functioning of the visual system, causing cells to fire abnormally.

This neural firing is not random, however. Numerous researchers, starting with Kluver in 1926, have observed that form constants are usually geometric shapes, which fall into a limited number of classes. This restricted variety suggests that specific groups of cells in the brain are being activated, rather than a disorganized firing of neurons. Lewis-Williams and Dowson reported six major types of form constants, based on a review of the literature:

> These are (1) a basic grid and its development in a lattice and expanding hexagonal pattern, (2) sets of parallel lines, (3) dots and short flecks, (4) zigzag lines crossing the field of vision (reported by some subjects as angular, by others as undulating), (5) nested catenary curves . . . and (6) filigrees or thin meandering lines.

People undergoing one of the experiences that tend to produce form constants often report a sequence of phenomena. First, the geometric images themselves appear, flashing or glowing as they dart across the visual field. Siegel described the experiences of "psychonauts"—experimental subjects who had taken hallucinogenic drugs and then carefully reported their sensations. At the outset of the psychonautical voyage, a luminous, tunnel-like image appeared in the middle of the visual field. Then:

Initial black-and-white images began to take on colors. They started to pulsate, moving toward the center of the tunnel or away from the bright light. Some images rotated like pinwheels while others darted across the visual field. The accelerated movements brought many new geometric forms, including various tunnel and lattice arrangements. The lattices included gratings, fretworks, honeycombs, and chessboard designs. There were also multicolored kaleidoscopic forms bursting from the tunnel, like so many flowers from a magician's hat. These geometric forms frequently cloned themselves or combined into ever-changing structures.

As the entoptic visions continue, they begin to transform into more complex objects. Generally, these images represent things familiar to the person and are affected by expectations and emotional states. Thus, a Huichol Indian who had eaten peyote in order to induce a religious vision described "a big spiral and I saw the fire god in the center and rushing out toward me," Siegel reported.

In the third stage of entoptic experience, subjects may find themselves in the middle of a vortex or tunnel. This image marks a transition from the sensation of form constants to frank HALLUCINATIONs. Against a background of entoptic forms, frequently manifesting as an immense lattice of squares like a giant checkerboard, complex images arise. This display can be so vivid and emotionally charged that it is felt to be a perception of the external world. The attention of experients is now fully absorbed; they may believe themselves to be in another world.

Because form constants appear to be a basic response of the human visual system to unusual stress or stimulation, it is not surprising that descriptions or depictions of them are virtually universal. Pictures of form constants may be found among the very earliest works of art. Geometric designs painted in caves by the Old Stone Age people of Europe and Australia have been recognized as representations of entoptic phenomena. Lewis-Williams and Dowson speculated that the depicted form constants were experienced by practitioners of SHAMANISM during their otherworldly journeys. And, indeed, Reichel-Dolmatoff reported that the Amazonian Tukano people decorate their villages with motifs based on form constants they observe during drug-induced shamanic trances.

The form constants and their transformations can easily be interpreted as glimpses into a spiritual domain. It has been suggested that the dazzling geometric images described by the medieval visionary HILDEGARD OF BINGEN, and regarded by her as perceptions of the City of God, were migraine-induced form constants. Some researchers have similarly interpreted the vision of traveling through a tunnel, frequently reported in NEAR DEATH EXPERIENCEs.

For further reading: Kluver; Lewis-Williams and Dowson; Reichel-Dolmatoff; Ripinsky-Naxon; Sacks (1970); Siegel (1977, 1989).

formication The HALLUCINATION of feeling hordes of small creatures, such as insects, crawling over one's skin. This profoundly unpleasant experience often occurs in states of withdrawal from addictive drugs, such as the DELIRIUM TREMENS of alcohol withdrawal.

fox fire Phosphorescent glow sometimes seen on rotting logs and stumps at night. The light is emitted by types of fungus, notably *Armillaria mellea* and *Panus stipicus,* as they digest the wood. This phenomenon contributes to the haunted nocturnal atmosphere of the forest. Fox fire has been suggested as the cause of some reports of GHOST LIGHTs and WILL-O'-THE-WISPs.

Fregoli's Syndrome In this disorder, one becomes convinced that someone familiar is able to inhabit and control the bodies of others. When a sufferer of Fregoli's Syndrome encounters someone unknown, he or she may be gripped by the conviction that the familiar person inhabits the body of the stranger. This condition is classed as a PSYCHOSIS because the sufferer has clearly lost touch with ordinary reality. The syndrome takes its name from an early 20th century actor named Fregoli. In the first reported case of the disorder, a woman felt that Fregoli was persecuting her by possessing people she would meet. Fregoli's Syndrome may be an extreme version of DÉJÀ VU—the feeling that someone or something never seen before is familiar.

See also ILLUSION DES SOSIES.

frenzy In modern parlance, a state of uncontrollable excitement and activity. Some writers refer to the four types of MANIA recognized by the ancient Greeks as the "Four Frenzies."

fugue In current psychological and psychiatric usage, the fugue state is regarded as a psychological disorder. In the current diagnostic manual of the American Psychiatric Association (DSM-IV), fugue is defined as a type of DISSOCIATIVE DISORDER, with four defining characteristics: sudden, unexpected departure from the conditions of one's ordinary lifestyle, such as job, home and family; assumption of a new identity, which might include a new name and vocation; inability to recall one's previous identity; and the absence of such causes as ORGANIC MENTAL DISORDERs.

Fugue states were noted by mental health professionals in Europe and North America during the 19th century. American neurologist Silas Weir Mitchell observed the condition among soldiers traumatized during the Civil War. Mitchell predicted, correctly, that fugue states would manifest among soldiers in future wars also.

The classic case of fugue state was that of Ansel Bourne. One morning in January 1887, Bourne, a carpenter who lived in Rhode Island, disappeared. It was discovered that he had withdrawn all his money from the local bank. The mystery of Bourne's fate was solved in March; he had moved to a small town in Pennsylvania and was operating a small variety store which he had rented. He had seemingly taken on the identity of one Albert J. Brown of New Hampshire and had no knowledge of a man named Ansel Bourne. One morning, Bourne reported that he had spontaneously recovered his former identity and had no idea what he was doing in Pennsylvania or who Albert Brown was! Bourne's experience was investigated by the great psychologist William James, as well as by Silas Mitchell. James discovered that Bourne recovered his identity as Brown while hypnotized, but continued to behave normally as Bourne at other times. Later commentators have speculated on the stresses that might have triggered the fugue of Ansel Bourne. Some sort of domestic trouble seems likely.

In the hellish front line conditions of World War I, some soldiers would be found wandering around, seemingly unable to identify themselves properly. At first, military authorities assumed that this behavior indicated malingering in order to escape from soldierly duty, and the offenders were summarily shot. However, men who were recognized as among the bravest fighters also displayed these mysterious lapses. Eventually, British physicians attached to the troops realized that they were dealing with cases of incipient fugue state. It was felt that such a diagnosis would stigmatize the soldiers, so instead the sufferers were labeled as victims of "shell shock."

The British psychologist Halse Rivers viewed the fugue state in an evolutionary context, believing it to be related to behaviors observed in other species. Many animals, when under conditions of extreme perceived danger, will freeze or "play dead." This reaction increases the animal's chance of surviving, if the source of threat is a predator who loses interest when the intended victim stops moving. Rivers argued that the radical inhibition of normal behavior, even to the point of assuming a new identity and environment, was just a more complex expression of the same basic protective maneuver. Rivers' theory

provides an important clue for the treatment of fugue state—removal of the threat should produce a reversion to normal behavior. Indeed, this often seems to be the case. Danger to a human is often more difficult to identify than a threat to an animal, however. People are menaced not only by physical danger, but by threats to self-esteem, social position, financial security, spiritual certainty and innumerable other possibilities. Thus, alleviating the fugue state may not always be a simple matter.

The fugue state resembles other types of unusual experience. In psychiatric literature MULTIPLE PERSONALITY DISORDER also involves individuals who claim to be other people than their ordinary historical identity. In such cases the idea that personal needs (attracting attention, escaping from painful truths) are being served by the strange behavior are frequently discussed—a point of convergence with the fugue state.

States of POSSESSION by spirits may also be related to the fugue state. Social anthropologists have noted that socially isolated or marginal people are often most prone to possession. The strange behaviors of possessed people are frequently terminated when they undergo rituals of exorcism. Such performances bring the community together in an expression of concern for the possessed individual, and it may be this demonstration of caring that serves to remove the threats associated with social marginality. Again, as with the fugue state and multiple personality disorder, behaving in a highly uncharacteristic manner might be the only way a person believes that the threat can be removed.

For further reading: American Psychiatric Association; Inglis (1989); Kenny; Rivers.

furor   This term usually refers to an agitated, noisy or uncontrollable situation. Some writers use the phrase "Four Furors" as a variant term for the four MANIAS of classical Greece.

gelatinous meteorite Variant term for DEVIL'S JELLY.

See also METEOR.

gender Many surveys examining belief in anomalous phenomena have found that women show higher levels of general belief than men. Women are also more likely to endorse some specific beliefs, such as ESP and the existence of spirits of the dead, according to some studies. Women's greater tendencies toward anomalous belief are probably cultural in origin. Zusne and Jones wondered if the greater encouragement of boys to become educated in science might be the cause of the gender difference, as the level of scientific education has often been found to correlate negatively with anomalous belief level.

Men are more likely than women to endorse some categories of anomaly: belief in UFO encounters, and in cryptic animals. No one knows why these beliefs should part from the general tendency toward greater anomalous belief among women. Culturally determined interest patterns are probably involved; Pekala, Kumar and Cummings noted that males more than females reported enjoying science fiction movies and books, a genre that often features spacecraft and monsters.

Findings on gender differences in unusual experiences have been inconsistent. Pekala et al. found in an American sample that women are more likely to report encountering spirits and communicating with the dead; males reported more near death experiences. Nelson (1989), studying Australians, reported a slightly greater likelihood of unusual experiences among women; women reported considerably more near death experiences than men.

See also Appendix.

For further reading: Irwin (1993); Pekala, Kumar and Cummings; P. Nelson; Zusne and Jones.

geophysical influences Unusual experiences do not occur at random, either in time or space. Sightings of strange phenomena often cluster in certain locales, and many types of anomalous report happen in waves. Some researchers believe that these patterns are caused in part by the electrical and magnetic energies of the earth.

Persinger (1974) was the first to report that anomalous experiences are more frequently reported in regions where geological fault lines lie below the surface. Hilly areas rich in quartz, and not prone to earthquakes, seem especially "haunted." Persinger speculated that the fault lines put pressure on the quartz deposits; in the absence of a major release of strain via an earthquake, the stressed quartz could only vibrate with small tremors. Vibrating or compressed crystals generate a weak electric field; this phenomenon, called the piezoelectric effect, was harnessed in crystal radio sets. A quartz-generated field could, under certain circumstances, ionize the air above the rock deposit, Persinger suggested, producing the luminous masses known as PLASMA. Glowing balls of plasma might fly through the air above the fault lines, dissipating before a witness could make careful observations. Such mysterious stimuli could serve as a basis for reports of UFO ENCOUNTERs and APPARITIONs.

Tributsch suggested other possible geophysical influences. He studied the behavior of animals prior to earthquakes. Many animals seemed to be responding to invisible processes that precede a tremor. Tributsch suspected that positive ions were emerging from the ground and were absorbed by nearby animals. These particles would disturb the normal chemical activities in their brains, inducing fear behavior. Perhaps human brains could be similarly disturbed by concentrations of ions from the earth. Tributsch suggested further that luminous mist can leak out of the ground near fault lines. These mists could serve as another stimulus of unusual experiences.

Another geophysical mechanism that has been implicated in anomalous events is the magnetic field of the planet. The intensity of this global field fluctuates, in part because of the "solar wind," a stream of plasma radiating from the sun which deforms the earth's own magnetic halo. Persinger and Schaut noted that reports of TELEPATHY increase on days of low geomagnetic activity that were preceded by days of unusually high activity. Randall and Randall reported a positive correlation between reports of HALLUCINATIONs and magnetic disturbances caused by the solar wind. Some parapsychologists have reported that subjects in ESP experiments tend to score more highly on days of low geomagnetic activity; higher PSYCHOKINESIS scores, however, have been linked to periods of intense magnetic activity. Perhaps these shifts in field strength are affecting the brains of susceptible people, such as those with signs of TEMPORAL LOBE ABNORMALITY, speculated Persinger.

See also GHOST LIGHT; MOUNTAINTOP GLOW; OCEAN LIGHT.

For further reading: Gissurarson; Persinger (1974; 1988a,b); Persinger and Lafreniere; Persinger and Schaut; Randall and Randall; Tributsch.

GESP Acronym for "General ESP," This term refers to both TELEPATHY and CLAIRVOYANCE. It was coined by J.B. Rhine, the founder of modern parapsychology, when he realized that it was impossible to separate the two types of alleged psychic phenomena. In any experiment designed to test for telepathy, there has to be a "sender" and a "receiver." The sender attempts to transmit a message to a receiver by psychic means. If the receiver does get the message, there is no way of knowing whether the receiver "read the mind" of the sender (which would be telepathy) or psychically detected the state of the sender's brain (which would be clairvoyance) and deduced the message from that information.

See also EXTRASENSORY PERCEPTION.

ghost This word is derived from the Saxon *gaste,* meaning "spirit." In common usage a ghost is the soul of a dead person that becomes visible to the living. Psychical researchers reserve the term to refer to a recurrent APPARITION. Unlike other classes of apparition, ghosts tend not to display awareness of their environment; rather, they seem to behave automatically, repeating their path and activities like a figure on a film loop. A 1990 Gallup poll estimated that 25% of adult Americans believe in ghosts, and 9% claim to have seen one.

See also HAUNTING.

For further reading: Gallup and Newport; Haining.

ghost light Things that glow in the night seem to be a universal source of fear and wonder. An immense amount of folklore has grown around recurrent nocturnal luminosities, known as ghost lights. Some ghost lights are so regular and widely known that they have become tourist attractions. A range of mechanisms has been suggested for this phenomenon. The explanations remain speculative, however; no one has ever managed to control a ghost light, or create one in a laboratory.

A large number of ghost lights are reported in mountainous regions. Perhaps the best known of all ghost lights are the Brown Mountain Lights, which haunt this summit in the Blue Ridge Mountains of western North Carolina. The first journalistic account of the spectacle appeared in 1913, but folklorists believe that these lights may have been seen as far back as 1850. From several vantage points in this rugged terrain, a variety of unidentified glows regularly disturb the gloom around Brown Mountain. Most often reported are bobbing globes, variously described as bluish-white to reddish, visible for as long as 15 minutes. A diffuse white light, illuminating several acres of the mountain's forested ridge, has also been noted. There are no reliable reports of anyone getting close to the lights; campers on Brown Mountain generally see nothing unusual.

Many travelers along the old Inca tracks in the Peruvian Andes have observed the famed "money lights"—flickering bluish forms that disappear when approached. It is believed that the lights indicate the sites of buried Inca treasure. The trails in this region are pocked with holes dug at the behest of the money lights.

Another well-known ghost light has often been seen on a peak in the Chinati Range of southern Texas. Gaddis described this light as resembling a star that "glitters like a weird eye" from the side of the mountain. It is sometimes bright enough to be seen 50 miles away.

Another type of ghost light favors roads and tracks at lower elevations. An account from 19th century Bolivia, cited by Corliss (1982), described how a group of soldiers tried to apprehend a ghost light that frequented a track near their encampment:

> the military were posted around the square, and we waited from 10 o'clock till 12 or 1 in an atmosphere bathed in the brilliancy of a full moon . . . we caught sight of it as it directly, but gently, approached along the road, upon which, running to intercept it, and stumbling at every step over rough and swampy ground, we managed to arrive within 3 yards of the glowing vision as it slowly glided at about 5 feet above the level of the earth. It presented a globular form of bluish light, so intense that we could scarcely look at it, but emitted no rays and cast no shadows; and when about actually to grasp the incandescent nothingness, suddenly elongating into a pear-shape tapering to the ground, it instantly vanished; but on looking round up

it rose again within 50 yards, but this time we could not overtake it, as it bounded over a hedge, then over trees, and finally disappeared in an impenetrable swamp.

The Maco Light has regularly been seen along a stretch of railroad track near Maco, North Carolina. A luminous sphere weaves back and forth, about three feet above the track. The approach of a train seems to trigger the light; many engineers have braked in response, believing that they were being signaled. Local tradition ascribes the phenomenon to Old Joe Baldwin, a conductor who was decapitated in an accident on the spot in 1867; Old Joe is said to wander the tracks at night, searching for his head.

The Ozark Spooklight appears on a country road near Joplin, Missouri. Like the Maco Light, it is evoked by oncoming traffic. Gannon, who investigated the Spooklight in 1965, offered a clear description (quoted by Corliss, 1977):

> Ahead of us a golden light flashed into view, as though someone a half mile away had switched on a reading lamp. It seemed to jiggle, to wobble back and forth, diminishing and brightening. When I let myself, I could imagine it was rushing at me, then quickly receding. It *did* look like a ball of fire; the edges were blurred and constantly changing. We could see its reflection in the car hood. It jiggled around for a few minutes, then blinked out.

Ghost lights have also been sighted over water. Perhaps the best known is the Baie Chaleur Fireship, observed from the coast of New Brunswick. Prior to storms, a luminous hemisphere is sometimes observed over the water. This shape can gradually change into an array of shimmering columns.

A single explanation is not likely sufficient to explain the diversity of phenomena that are dubbed ghost lights. Some of the nocturnal radiances are almost certainly MIRAGEs. Many investigators of the Brown Mountain Lights, for instance, have concluded that the bobbing globes are the lights of towns and automobile headlights, refracted over the mountain by air layers of varying density. The various hues of the lights could be due to the amount of dust in the air; and their movements may be caused by turbulence in the refractive layers, or perhaps by an AUTOKINETIC illusion. (It is noteworthy that the refraction spectacle known as a FATA MORGANA, or phantom city, has also been seen near Brown Mountain). Gannon concluded that the Ozark Spooklight was created by refracted light from car headlights.

This explanation seems not to apply to the Maco Light. Following the suggestion that the Light was caused by headlights on a nearby highway, the thoroughfare was closed one night as an experiment. But Old Joe's lantern appeared anyway. Some researchers have suggested that certain ghost lights that are triggered by the approach of a vehicle might be the result of a piezoelectric effect. The oncoming vehicle could vibrate quartz crystals in the ground, causing them to generate an electric field. This electrical activity might be capable of ionizing the air above the crystalline deposits, creating luminous balls of PLASMA. Attempts to generate ghost lights deliberately by exploding dynamite near their wandering grounds have not been successful.

Without a doubt, a number of ghost lights are types of ST. ELMO'S FIRE, a slow discharge of electricity from the earth into the air. Some elevated regions like the Andes are prone to the massive diffuse discharges called MOUNTAINTOP GLOWs; ghost lights viewed in these areas are probably smaller scale productions of the same mechanism.

The combustion of naturally occurring gases such as methane and phosphine has also been advanced as an explanation for some ghost lights. This process is generally thought to underlie WILL-O'-THE-WISPs. Corliss suggested that the Baie Chaleur Fireship might be caused by natural gas escaping from the sea floor.

Glimpses of phosphorescent fungi, either gleaming as FOX FIRE on rotting logs or bedeck-ing the feathers of nocturnal BIRDS, might account for some ghostly glows. CEMETERY LIGHTs—ghost lights that frequent graveyards—could be luminous products of bodily decay.

Some researchers believe that these mundane notions fail to explain the apparently *intelligent behavior* of many ghost lights. The lights at times have seemed to exhibit curiosity and playfulness as they invite observers on chases through the night. Some view ghost lights as a type of UFO ENCOUNTER—Gaddis entitled his chapter on ghost lights "UFOs that haunt."

Indeed, the occasional witness claims to have made contact with the intelligence behind the ghost lights. Ralph Lael insisted that one night on Brown Mountain he followed the lights, which led him into an underground city populated by aliens. Later, they took him on a holiday to Venus. After that, he opened the "Outer Space Rock Shop Museum" near Brown Mountain, where he sold souvenirs and copies of a book about his adventure.

For further reading: Corliss (1977, 1982); Gaddis.

ghost rockets In 1946, hundreds of observers in Sweden and Finland began to report strange objects traveling through the sky. Dubbed "ghost rockets," the objects were often described as shaped like cigars or fireballs. Sometimes they were seen to drift slowly across the heavens; at other times, they darted overhead at speeds far beyond those of any airplane. Aerial maneuvers, such as loops and sharp turns, were also described. Explosions were sometimes heard to emanate from the objects, but no debris was ever found.

At the time, there was widespread concern that the Russians had continued developing Nazi military rockets at captured German research installations. Many assumed that the ghost rockets were Russian experiments. Investigators at the Swedish defense ministry concluded that most of the sightings were misidentifications of natural events, but they could not explain about 20% of the reports.

Ghost rockets were also seen in southern Europe, Turkey and North Africa through 1947 and 1948, when the reports gradually died down. It seems likely that GROUP DYNAMICS OF UNUSUAL EXPERIENCES played a role in the ghost rocket phenomenon. People across this region feared a Russian attack using advanced rocket technology. Their anticipation caused them to interpret any aerial event that was not easily identified as a rocket. As ghost rocket stories circulated south from Scandinavia, more and more people would be primed with this perceptual bias.

See also UFO ENCOUNTER.

For further reading: Bartholomew (1993); Sachs.

glossolalia   This term derives from the Greek roots *glossa,* "tongue," and *lalia,* "speech." Glossolalia, or "speaking in tongues," is the act of speaking in what seems to be a language unknown to the speaker. Since ancient times, this practice has usually been interpreted in terms of divine inspiration or paranormal ability. Some subtypes of glossolalia are distinguished in the literature on the subject: pure glossolalia, or speaking in a language that is apparently unknown to anyone; and XENOGLOSSY or xenolalia, speaking in a language unknown to the speaker, but identifiable by others as a known tongue. A related phenomenon, known as heteroglossolalia, is said to involve a person speaking in a language known to them, which is perceived as a different language known by the hearer.

Glossolalia occurred in some Christian communities of the first century A.D. In his First Letter to the Corinthians, Paul compared glossolalia to the practice of uttering intelligible prophecies:

> he who speaks in tongues is talking with God, not with people, for no one understands him;

he speaks mysteries in a state of inspiration. But when someone prophesies, he speaks to people and gives them spiritual strength, encouragement, and comfort. The person who speaks in tongues gives spiritual strength to himself, but the prophet gives spiritual strength to the community . . . The prophet is greater than the one who speaks in tongues—unless he can interpret, so that the congregation may receive spiritual strength. (14:2–5)

At the time the letter was composed (around 56 A.D.), the church had both Jewish and Greek members. The Jewish Christians were more comfortable with inspired speech that they could understand, in the tradition of BIBLICAL PROPHECY; the cultural background of the Greek Christians led them to expect that God would inspire unintelligible, ecstatic utterances in the manner of the classical oracles. Paul, being of Jewish descent, leaned toward the preference for prophets, but was also working to attract Greeks to the new faith. His solution to this potential clash of religious expectation was to acknowledge both prophecy and glossolalia as legitimate, but to rank the former above the latter. Later in his epistle, Paul states that, whereas glossolalia involves only a person's spirit, prophecy engages both the spirit and the interpreting mind, and therefore is a more mature spiritual expression.

The best known glossolalic incident is recounted in the New Testament's Book of Acts. The apostles gathered together at Pentecost, "And there appeared unto them cloven tongues like as of fire, and it sat upon each of them. And they were all filled with the Holy Ghost, and began to speak with other tongues, as the Spirit gave them utterance." (2:3–4) Some scholars believe that this story, written perhaps 15 years later than Paul's first Corinthian letter, was invented to strengthen the Greek spiritual mode within mainstream Christianity.

Despite their legacy of textual references to glossolalia, orthodox Christians came to discourage the practice. This move may have been motivated by the glossolalic performances of ancient competitors to orthodoxy. One such group, the Montanists, interpreted the utterances of their seers to mean that the Catholic church should not be supported. Another heretical movement, the Gnostics, were also fascinated by seemingly meaningless vocalizations, as shown in this song of praise from the *Gospel of the Egyptians* (quoted by Miller):

> O glorious name, really truly, aion o on, iiii eeee eeee oooo uuuu oooo aaaa, really truly ei aaaa oooo, O existing one who sees the aeons! Really truly, aee eee iiii uuuuuu oooooooo, who is eternally eternal, really truly, iea aio, in the heart, who exists, u aei eis aei, ei o ei, ei os ei!

By the Middle Ages, glossolalia was firmly associated with heresy. During the days of the Great Witch Hunt in the Renaissance/Reformation period, speaking in unknown tongues was likely to be taken as a sign of demonic POSSESSION. Glossolalics were apt to receive an exorcism, or even an accusation of consorting with devils, as reward for their "inspiration."

In the modern era, glossolalia is most often found among Pentecostal and Holiness congregations, and in marginal groups such as the Quakers, Shakers and Mormons. A number of New Age channelers have produced sounds which purport to be the language spoken by beings from other planets.

Researchers have studied audiotape recordings of glossolalic utterances. Even if the meaning of a language is unknown, analysis can reveal whether the flow of sounds shows a structure consistent with meaningful language. Analyses of pure glossolalic utterances recorded at Pentecostal meetings have detected repetitive sounds and rhythms, but no true language structure. It seems likely that, in most cases, glossolalic sounds are not intrinsically meaningful, but rather are expressions of strong emotional arousal.

Zusne and Jones noted similarities between the sounds of glossolalia and those emitted by severely brain-damaged individuals. They suggested that the excitement of religious fervor can dissociate the speech-producing centers of the brain from the faculties of thought.

Indeed, in many cases glossolalics are obviously highly aroused by their religious rituals, which frequently involve rhythmic singing and dancing. However, a study by Spanos, Cross, Lepage and Coristine demonstrated that the ability to produce language- like sequences of sound can be deliberately learned under calm circumstances. The researchers played one minute taped segments of Pentecostal glossolalia to subjects who had never heard such things before. Thirty percent of the subjects were immediately able to give a fluent imitation of what they had heard. With further exposure, 70% of the subjects could convincingly "speak in tongues." In actual Pentecostal settings, similar opportunities for learning are provided. Newcomers are not expected to speak in tongues, but are first encouraged to observe others doing so, and to practice silently.

For further reading: Luck; Spanos, Cross, Lepage and Coristine; Miller; Nickell; Zusne and Jones.

goseki In Zen Buddhism, it is said that following a spiritual awakening (KENSHO or SATORI), one may display self-conscious or artificial behaviors, as if trying to display one's changed awareness to others. The insight gained in the ENLIGHTENMENT experience has not been fully integrated into the person's life. This residual impact is called goseki, or the "stink of enlightenment." After a time, the goseki vanishes, and the person acts normally, although his or her consciousness has been forever altered. Full enlightenment leaves no such residue—the completely awakened person behaves in a natural manner, devoid of peculiar features.

See also AKU-BYODO; MAKYO; ZEMBYO.

group dynamics of unusual experiences When an unusual experience is reported by an individual, many find it easy to dismiss the account as the result of some personal malfunction or deviousness. But when an anomaly is experienced by a group, dismissal becomes more difficult, as people are accustomed to depend on consensus as an index of reality. Proponents of paranormal explanations often regard multiple-witness cases as major challenges to the conventional world view. However, research in social psychology has demonstrated that perceptions, like diseases, can be transmitted from person to person. The infectious experience may bear little relation to the objective conditions. When the shared perception is strange, or if it seems to violate mainstream beliefs concerning the nature of reality, this transmission process is often called "hysterical contagion." The term is misleading—one does not have to be suffering from one of the psychological disorders traditionally labeled HYSTERIA to be affected by it.

Humans are social animals who rely on those around them for cues as to how to make sense of the world. Subtle communication between observers guides their experiences toward agreement. This reliance is known as *informational social influence*. When an object of perception is unfamiliar or ill-defined, the reactions of others strongly affect what one experiences. Sherif's experiments with the AUTOKINETIC EFFECT, for instance, demonstrated how informational social influence causes groups of observers to agree in their perceptions of an illusory movement.

Anomalous experience reports frequently occur in waves—a few initial reports are followed by a steadily growing number of sightings, which then gradually taper off. Many categories of anomaly, from sightings of strange HUMANOIDS and UFO ENCOUNTERs to demonic POSSESSION and MARIAN APPARITIONs, show this pattern. The waves might reflect the presence of a stimulus which triggers such experiences. The pattern can also be explained as the signature of hysterical contagion, the infectious perception rippling through a population of observers. The famous WINDSHIELD PITTING EPIDEMIC that swept through Seattle in 1954 showed that

the contagion process can operate in the absence of any unusual stimuli. Other examples have since occurred. In 1990 a rumor spread in Nigeria that evil sorcerors were stealing people's penises or breasts by casually touching them. Riots flared in crowded streets and markets, triggered by someone "discovering" that one of their body parts was missing. Teenaged Egyptian girls were afflicted by a swooning epidemic in 1993. In one incident, 150 girls in a train station fainted when they heard a (false) report that a previous victim had just died in hospital.

Stewart used a theory of collective behavior, originally developed by Smelser, to understand waves of unusual experience reports. He considered six factors that play a part in such phenomena. First, regional conditions must be conducive. In order for a rash of Bigfoot sightings to occur, the geography must permit the creature to make sudden appearances and then to evade capture—very few Bigfoot encounters are reported in urban settings. Also, channels of communication must be available for the reports to spread. Our age of mass media may be especially susceptible to the psychological contagion process.

Second, Stewart noted the importance of strain and uncertainty in the community. Social and economic stress, as well as a lack of faith in authorities, predispose people to embrace unconventional interpretations. If everyone simply accepted the pronouncements of skeptics concerning UFOs, there would doubtless be fewer reported sightings.

Every culture has marginal traditions that offer alternative explanations for various experiences. Stewart identifies these traditions as important sources for the ideas that structure contagious perceptions. Anyone strolling on the shore of Loch Ness who knows the lore about the lake's monstrous inhabitant is primed to see any odd movement in the water as the stirrings of the beast.

A triggering episode often serves as the pebble that commences the avalanche of reports, according to Stewart. In the cases of mass demonic possession among 17th century French nuns, a single nun first fell victim; her example was then followed by others in her convent, and sometimes the mania spread to other centers as well.

As stories of strange happenings are transmitted through the community, people begin actively to seek the experience and, not surprisingly, many are successful. Stewart describes a wave of Bigfoot sightings in South Dakota which led to nocturnal Bigfoot hunts in the woods. Even without looking for strange creatures, walking through the woods at night can produce unnerving experiences.

Finally, as Stewart notes, outbreaks of unusual manifestations are aided by breakdowns in official control of public expression. The more tolerant a society is regarding a particular unconventional idea, the more likely it is that this idea will influence anomalous experiences. The notion that UFOs are extraterrestrial vehicles is not endorsed by many scientists, but there are no laws against believing it.

The existence of contagious perceptions complicates matters for those who prefer unconventional explanations of mass-witnessed anomalies. It should, however, provide no comfort to those who hold that all violations of conventional belief are thereby explained away. After all, the "consensus reality" itself is subject to the same social processes that create hysterical contagion. If a person never has an experience that challenges consensual beliefs, it may be that informational social influence is simply preventing them from noticing any anomalous events.

For further reading: Kerckhoff and Back; Levy and Nail; Rosnow and Fine; Sherif; Sirois; Smelser; Stewart.

gustatory hallucination   A taste experience that occurs without stimulation of the mouth's taste receptors. Gustatory HALLUCINATIONs sometimes happen in connection with mental illnesses like SCHIZOPHRENIA, and brain disorders such as EPILEPSY.

hakushi Literally "white paper" in Japanese, this term refers to a spiritual experience that can arise in the practice of Zen meditation. In order to perceive one's true nature—the goal of Zen—all distractions must be eliminated. When, in ZAZEN practice, all perceptions, thoughts, feelings and images fade away, leaving the mind as blank as a sheet of white paper, the meditator may glimpse the basic quality of awareness itself. The state of hakushi should not be confused with merely having a "blank mind" in the ordinary sense. Normally, when one's mind seems blank, attentiveness is simply so dull that one is unaware of mental activities. In the "white paper" state, awareness is extremely sharp, and mental processes are utterly calmed.

hallucination This term derives from the Greek *hyalein,* which means "to wander in mind." The word "hallucination" was first used by Lavater in 1572 to describe encounters with "ghostes and spirites walking by nyght"—that is, APPARITIONs. The 19th century psychiatrist Esquirol formulated the definition that still prevails today: A hallucination is a sensory experience that occurs in the absence of any external object, generally as a feature of mental illness. Hallucinations are involuntary mental images that are mistaken for perceptions of the physical world.

Hallucinations should be distinguished from several related phenomena. ILLUSIONs, like hallucinations, are mistaken perceptions; but unlike hallucinations, they are not purely *mental* images, but are misperceptions of actual physical stimuli. ENTOPTIC and ENTOTIC PHENOMENA are not mental images either; rather, these sensations are caused by illusions and malfunctions in

the parts of the nervous system that process information from the eyes and ears.

Hallucination can be hard to distinguish from perception itself. In many cases, people have unusual experiences when they are alone; it may be difficult to know whether or not an actual stimulus caused the strange perception. Many researchers measure these occurrences against their own assumptions about reality—if someone reports a perception that is beyond the researcher's belief, it is assumed to be a hallucination or other mistake. This approach can lead to a blind refusal to consider anything that does not conform to one's prejudices. Others rely on consensus; checking the accuracy of reports by individual witnesses may be impossible, but if multiple witnesses observe essentially the same thing, then a physical object is assumed to have been present. Consensus, however, is not as reliable a guide as most people think. Collective hallucinations can be caused by the GROUP DYNAMICS OF UNUSUAL EXPERIENCES.

Further problems arise in distinguishing hallucinations and perceptions if one considers the possible existence of objects that are not real in a physical sense. Throughout history, most people have believed in nonphysical realities, such as spirit worlds. If one accepts the possibility of alternative realities, distinguishing between a false perception of the physical world and a true perception of some nonphysical reality becomes a formidable challenge.

Hallucinations are widespread among ordinary people. Several surveys in western countries over the past century have found that between 10 and 27% of the general population experience occasional hallucinations. Posey and Losch surveyed American college students, 71% of whom reported hallucinations. Children are prone to hallucinate IMAGINARY COMPANIONs. The link in the popular mind between hallucinations and mental illness makes most people reluctant to admit publicly having had them.

A great number of conditions can trigger hallucinations in ordinary people. These include states of physical stress, such as food, water or sleep deprivation; HYPNOSIS; emotionally stressful circumstances like bereavement, assault or kidnapping; SENSORY DEPRIVATION; transitions between sleep and wakefulness, the HYPNAGOGIC and HYPNOPOMPIC STATEs; and ingestion of hallucinogenic drugs. Individuals who suffer the amputation of limbs or breasts often persist in feeling PHANTOM LIMB SENSATIONS. Brain disorders like EPILEPSY can also produce false perceptions.

Ongoing or recurrent hallucinations are found most often among the mentally disturbed. They can occur in connection with almost any type of psychological disorder, perhaps because all such conditions are immensely stressful. Hallucinations are most closely associated with SCHIZOPHRENIA; a majority of schizophrenics report them.

Hallucinations can mimic any of the senses. There are false perceptions of sound (auditory), taste (gustatory), smell (olfactory), touch (tactile), sight (visual), muscle sensations and movements (kinesthetic) and internal organs (cenesthetic). The content of hallucinations depends largely on the hallucinator's expectations and motivations, as well as on external circumstances. A prisoner may hallucinate a doorway to freedom; a paranoid schizophrenic may hear threatening voices; an adolescent on an initiatory VISION QUEST may encounter a spirit helper.

Horowitz observed that the transition from ordinary perceptions to hallucinations typically follows one of two paths. The process can begin with the appearance in the mind's eye of unusually vivid fantasy and memory images. These forms become more intense and insistent, taking on a greater sense of reality. At this point, a person may use strategies to test the reality of the images, such as closing the eyes or looking away. If the images become so clear that they resemble perceived rather than imagined objects, one may try the defense of reciting to oneself, "This can't be real," or "This is only a dream." In the final stage, the ability to distinguish image and percept is lost; one is hallucinating. This sequence is most common among mentally disturbed hallucinators.

Hallucinations can also begin with changes in perception—the colors or borders of everyday objects are intensified, halos are seen, movements appear blurred or streaked. Next arise entoptic forms such as spots, flashes and geometric shapes. Finally, the entoptics transform into more complex images; if these are judged as externally real, one is hallucinating. Deprivation states, brain disorders and drugs most often produce this transition pattern.

In both perception and hallucination, images are created by the mind. Perceptual images are based on information carried to the brain by the senses; hallucinated images are constructed from internal sources, such as memories and fantasies. The invasion of mental images into the fields of perception seems to depend on a disruption of ordinary sensory input. West offered the following model of the process. Picture:

> a man in his study, standing at a closed glass window opposite the fireplace, looking out at his garden in the sunset. He is absorbed by the view of the outside world. He does not visualize the interior of the room in which he stands. As it becomes darker outside, however, images of the objects in the room behind him can be seen reflected dimly in the window glass. For a time he may see either the garden (if he gazes into the distance) or the reflection of the room's interior (if he focuses on the glass a few inches from his face). Night falls, but the fire still burns brightly in the fireplace and illuminates the room. The watcher now sees in the glass a vivid reflection of the interior of the room behind him, which appears to be outside the window.

The glassy surface represents conscious awareness; the objects seen through the glass are perceptions of the outside world; the objects within the room, seen reflected on the glass, are the materials of memory and fantasy. When the intensity (the sunlight) of sensory input is greater, we perceive an outer object; but when the imagined input is more vivid (the firelight), mental images dominate awareness. If one mistakes an interior reflection on the glass of awareness for a view of the outer world, that person is experiencing an hallucination. All of the triggering conditions mentioned above shift the balance between outer and inner sources in this direction and impair the ability to distinguish mental images and percepts.

Researchers have studied bodily processes connected with hallucinations. Asaad suggested that a mechanism exists in the brain stem that controls both sensory and imagery functions. During the phase of sleep called the REM stage, this mechanism stimulates the brain to create dreams. Hallucinations may be caused by the intrusion of the REM stage into wakefulness. Schatzman studied the electrical activity in the brain of a woman who could hallucinate at will. The regions of her brain responsible for ordinary vision reacted to hallucinated figures as if they were actually present in front of her. When she hallucinated a figure blocking her view of a test stimulus, her brain activity shifted as if the stimulus had been occluded by an external object.

See also PALINACOUSIS; PALINOPSIA.

For further reading: Asaad; Horowitz; Posey and Losch; Schatzman; Siegel (1977); L. West.

hallucinosis   This term refers to any condition in which a person is prone to HALLUCINATIONS, but without other disturbances of consciousness like DELUSIONS or thought disorders. The condition can be caused by organic brain disorders such as EPILEPSY, as well as prolonged drug use or withdrawal. Sometimes, as in ALCOHOL HALLUCINOSIS, this problem can be chronic.

haunting   A haunting is an ongoing disturbance, of seemingly paranormal origin, that is associated with a particular location. Hauntings are often contrasted with POLTERGEISTS, which are disturbances usually linked to a person rather than a place. Typical features of hauntings include mysterious sounds (knockings, groans and sighs, footsteps, creakings and rustlings), atmospheric phenomena like drafts and sudden temperature changes, the movement of objects without apparent cause and lights of unknown origin. APPARITIONS, called ghosts, are frequently part of a haunting. The phenomena can persist for decades and tend to be more active at night. They are traditionally believed to be the activities of unhappy spirits.

Hauntings are not new. An ancient Egyptian papyrus, preserved in the Cairo Museum, recommends that victims of hauntings should deposit a scroll requesting that the disturbances cease on the tomb of the suspected culprit. The Roman writer Pliny the Younger recounted the story of Athenodoras, a philosopher who rented a haunted house. Athenodoras encountered the ghost of a man in chains, who pointed to a spot on the floor; excavation uncovered a chained skeleton, the proper burial of which ended the haunting, wrote Pliny.

Every culture and historical period has reported hauntings. Western Europe and especially Britain, dotted with evocative castles and mansions, has accrued perhaps the greatest number of haunting stories. But today, shopping malls and trailer parks are equally likely settings for a haunting outbreak. A 1990 Gallup poll indicated that 29% of adult Americans believe in hauntings and 14% have experienced one.

Psychical researchers have long been fascinated by hauntings. As Flammarion noted in his classic volume, *Haunted Houses,* "What diversified observations we have to examine! The study of haunted houses is an immense mosaic." When the Society for Psychical Research (SPR) was founded in 1882, one of its first mandates was the investigation of hauntings. Researchers would collect the testimony of witnesses and try to discern if any normal explanations would suffice. Over the years, many cases have proven to be based on the activities of rodents in the walls, the settling of house foundations, ILLUSIONs, HALLUCINATIONs and trickery.

But some have not been easily dismissed. In 1982, the SPR published a centenary commemoration series of reports, including a summary by MacKenzie of 100 years of haunting investigations. One of the most impressive cases in that record involved a haunted house in Cheltenham, England. At the site, the ghostly figure of a woman in black was attested by 17 witnesses over a seven year period. The apparition was sometimes viewed by several observers simultaneously and it appeared during the day or night. Over 20 witnesses also testified that they heard unaccountable footsteps, knockings on bedroom doors, and movements of untouched door handles. Intriguing as such accounts are, they must always be studied with the unreliability of eyewitness testimony in mind. Anecdotes, no matter how striking, cannot serve as proof that things happened the way they are remembered.

Perhaps the most famous haunted house in modern history was Borley Rectory in England. For several decades prior to its destruction by fire in 1939, the rectory was the setting for an immense number and range of ghostly experiences. Apparitions included a phantom coach and horses, a headless man, a lady in white and a nun; objects were said to levitate, knockings were heard, beds ejected their occupants and pencil writing appeared on the walls. Unfortunately, the psychical researchers involved conducted an incompetent investigation, and controversy continues regarding whether anything other than fraud, unusual acoustics and an infestation of noisy mice were responsible for Borley Rectory's chilling reputation.

Many well-known haunting tales turn out, on investigation, to be nothing more than legends; others are fabrications, such as the American tale of the "Amityville Horror," marketed (lucratively) as non-fiction.

In recent years some researchers have used sophisticated techniques in the study of haunted houses. Infrared film has been taken of haunting sites, without notable results. Maher and Hansen took a device known as a random event generator, often used in parapsychology experiments, to a haunted apartment building in New York to see if its functioning would alter significantly—it did not. Maher and Schmeidler developed a procedure in which a floor plan of a haunting site is divided into a grid. After walking through the site, research subjects are asked to mark on the grid where they think a ghostly experience is likely, and their marks are compared with the reported locations of haunting phenomena. Studies of this type have noted some correspondence between the impressions of the experimental subjects and those of the witnesses. Such agreements are not necessarily evidence that the subjects were sensing the presence of ghosts, the investigators have pointed out; it may simply be that certain spots, by virtue of their poor illumination or other features, seem "spookier" than others. These would be the places where jittery or otherwise suggestive individuals would have haunting experiences.

For further reading: Flammarion; Haining; Mackenzie; Maher and Hansen; Maher and Schmeidler.

head injury A blow to the head can damage the delicate tissues of the brain, causing changes in thought and perception. Even small injuries can change brain functioning in subtle ways; it is thought that "minimal brain damage" from impact or fever may be much more common in the general population than is commonly thought. There are many anecdotes about PSYCHICs acquiring their powers (or at least their belief in their powers) following a head injury. Fenwick and his colleagues examined the relationship of head injury and a range of unusual experiences. He found that people who believed they were psychic were more likely to have had a serious head injury than those who did not claim to be psychic. Fenwick also noted that having had a head injury was positively associated with later experiences of ESP and contact with spirits, and there was a slight trend linking head injury and MYSTICAL EXPERIENCEs.

See also Appendix; TEMPORAL LOBE ABNORMALITY.

For further reading: Fenwick et. al.

heiligenschein   When a person's shadow falls on a dew-soaked lawn or field at dawn, a luminous white halo can sometimes be seen around the head of the silhouette. If a group of people view their shadows under these conditions, the glowing ring—known as heiligenschein—is visible to each observer only around the head of his or her own shadow. The effect is caused by the morning light refracting and reflecting from dewdrops. At a certain angle in all directions from each person's point of observation—the eyes—the radiance from the dew overlaps, creating a circular band of intensified light.

See also BROCKEN SPECTRE.

hesychasm   This meditative tradition developed in the Byzantine Empire between the 11th and 14th centuries, although its roots lie in ancient Palestine and Egypt. Hesychastic practices are associated with the MYSTICAL EXPERIENCEs of Eastern Orthodox Christianity.

The central practice of hesychasm is the recitation of the Jesus Prayer: "Lord Jesus Christ, Son of God, have mercy on me a sinner," or in its shortened Greek version, "Kyrie eleison." This prayer dates from the time of the first Christian monks, who dwelled in the Egyptian desert during the first centuries A.D. Hesychasts use it in the manner of a MANTRA, ceaselessly reciting it as a means of raising their awareness beyond the realm of ordinary appearance. In the words of Sorskij, hesychastic practice allows one to view "a light that the world does not see"—the luminous presence of God. Hesychasts have always been fond of expressing their mystical experiences in terms of light.

Divine illumination is to be found, say the hesychasts, in the depths of one's own mind. Focusing the attention on the prayer thus removes the distractions of sensation, emotion and fantasy (in Greek, hesychia means "inner silence"). St. Nilus put it this way: "He who wishes to see what his mind really is must free himself of all thoughts; then he will see it like a sapphire or the hue of heaven."

Diligent practice of hesychastic meditation leads one through a series of mystical experiences, resembling the UNIO MYSTICA of the Western Christian tradition, culminating in THEOSIS—full union with the divine light. Hesychasm is a living tradition. It is still practiced in some Eastern Orthodox retreat centers. The best known site of hesychastic practice today is the monastery complex atop Mount Athos, in northern Greece.

See also METANOIA; THEOPTIA.

For further reading: Chirban; Matus; Pelikan.

high dream   Users of psychedelic drugs sometimes report intensely pleasant experiences known as "highs." These states usually feature an enhanced appreciation of sensory beauty and often a feeling of access to great wisdom. When similar experiences happen in a dream, it is called a high dream. Faraday (1973) described a typical example:

> [In the dream,] I was standing on the veranda of my parents' house looking out at the garden, which was in full bloom. Suddenly, the whole garden became filled with a quite new kind of life. The flowers and trees literally pulsated with energy and radiated exotic color, and my own body seemed to join in the dance of nature. The experience seemed to last only a minute or two, and then the garden reverted to its normal very beautiful state, and I woke up.

Tart, who first identified this phenomenon and coined the term, found that high dreams happen most frequently to people who have had prior experience with drug-induced highs; in these cases the high in the dream is likely based on memories of the waking highs. In some high dreams, the sleeper dreams of ingesting a drug, following which he or she experiences the psychedelic effects.

High dreams have also been reported by people without prior psychedelic drug experience. At a later date, some "drug-naive" high dreamers have taken psychedelics and found the drug-triggered experience to be very similar to the high dream. Such reports suggest that the non-drugged sleeping brain may be able to create the changes in neural activity that are ordinarily produced by psychoactive substances.

See also LUCID DREAM.

For further reading: A. Faraday; Tart (1969).

Hildegard of Bingen, visions of This medieval German visionary has provided us with "the most complete documentation of a mystical illumination experience in the history of the human race," according to Hozeski. Almost forgotten for centuries, modern students of religion and unusual experiences are beginning to rediscover the significance of her accounts.

Hildegard was born in 1098, in the town of Bermersheim by the Rhine River. She was the youngest of ten children. To relieve her overburdened household, she was placed in a convent attached to the monastery of Disibodenberg at the age of eight. Hildegard worked in the infirmary; at 38, on the death of the abbess, Hildegard was selected to be her successor. Until the age of 42, Hildegard was apparently not viewed as unusual, aside from the fact that she suffered from a mysterious recurrent illness that periodically confined her to bed. Then, in her own words,

> When I was forty-two years and seven months old, a burning light of tremendous brightness coming from heaven poured into my entire mind. Like a flame that does not burn but

enkindles, it inflamed my entire heart and my entire breast, just like the sun that warms an object with its rays.

As a result, "All of a sudden, I was able to taste of the understanding of the narration of books. I saw the psalter clearly and the evangelists and other Catholic books of the Old and New Testaments." After this revelation, she realized that she had a prophetic mission to share her spiritual insights with the world.

Unbeknownst to anyone except those closest to her, Hildegard had been having VISIONS since she was a child. Now, she felt compelled by God to write about her experiences. As she was a devout Roman Catholic, she interpreted them according to Catholic doctrine. Her visions were declared authentic by St. Bernard, who was probably the most influential man in Europe at the time; the pope, Eugenius, proclaimed her an inspired prophetess.

The official recognition of the church's highest officials gave Hildegard a degree of influence almost unprecedented for a woman living in that misogynistic age. Claiming the direction of God, she insisted that she be allowed to found her own convent on the nearby site of Rupertsberg, near Bingen. She informed the abbot of Disibodenberg that he had to release to her all the dowry funds donated to the monastery for the support of her nuns, or he would be eternally damned. She got the money.

In the new convent, surrounded by a community devoted to her, Hildegard continued to have visions. These experiences inspired her to become perhaps the greatest creative individual of the later Middle Ages. Hildegard composed dozens of hymns in a novel and beautiful musical style; she supervised the creation of a series of astounding illustrations based on her visions, which transcended the artistic conventions of the day; she invented the dramatic genre of the morality play; she wrote books on theology, natural history and medicine, as well as intensely poetic descriptions of her visions; she went on four preaching tours—unheard of for an orthodox woman; and she was asked for political advice by, among others, both the emperor and the pope. After a long and unique life, Hildegard died in 1179.

What was the nature of Hildegard's experiences? Although she is widely known as a mystic, it appears that she rarely had a MYSTICAL EXPERIENCE in the strict sense of the term, as referring to an experience of union with God. Rather, she reported revelations that occurred while her ordinary sense of self was intact, in an everyday waking state:

> I truly saw those visions; I did not perceive them in dreams, nor while sleeping, nor in a frenzy, nor with the human eyes or with external ears of a person, nor in remote places; but . . . while I was awake and alert with a clear mind, with the innermost eyes and ears.

The experiences typically consisted of a visual and an auditory component, according to her report. Common visual elements included points or streaks of brilliant light, intense colors, glowing circles or spheres, human forms and strange combinations of imagery. A disembodied voice often explained the significance of the vision to her. Following is a typical example, from her text *Scivias*:

> I saw a very bright light, and inside it there was a person who was the colour of a sapphire. This person was completely surrounded by a very pleasant fire of reddish colour. The very bright light completely surrounded this fire of reddish colour, and at the same time this fire completely surrounded the light. Both the fire and the light surrounded the person, existing as one light with one force of potentiality. Then I heard the living light speak to me.

Hildegard interpreted this experience in orthodox terms: the light, fire and person symbolize the Father, Son and Holy Spirit.

Hildegard apparently did not induce her visions through spiritual techniques such as fasting, meditation or the ingestion of drugs. Her biography contains no hint that she had a psychosis. The mechanism that produced these bizarre audiovisual phenomena remains unclear. Oliver Sacks suggested a possible neurological origin of the visions. Noting Hildegard's recurrent spells of illness, he speculated that she suffered from MIGRAINE headaches. Some migraine sufferers report unusual visual phenomena prior to the onset of the headache, caused by a temporary drop in oxygen supply to the cerebral cortex. The geometric forms that characterize these migraine auras resemble those described by the German seer. Sacks argued that Hildegard's experiences "provide a unique example of the manner in which a physiological event, banal, hateful, or meaningless to the vast majority of people, can become, in a privileged consciousness, the substrate of a supreme ecstatic vision." One feature of Hildegard's case seems not to fit Sack's ingenious suggestion. She reported that her pain would disappear when she expressed the vision she had received. Unfortunately, migraine sufferers have not found that describing the contents of their auras ends their headaches.

For further reading: Hozeski; Sacks (1970); Zum Brunn and Epiney-Burgard.

holy blood miracles Since the later Middle Ages, Roman Catholic communities have reported strange occurrences involving the preserved blood of saints. The earliest and best known of the holy blood miracles centers on vials containing a substance which is said to be the blood of St. Januarius, a fourth century martyr. The vials are stored in a crypt in Naples. Three times each year, on festival days, the vials are displayed in public. Usually, the solid masses within the containers apparently liquefy during the displays, an event easily interpreted as miraculous by the adoring throng. Accounts of this blood miracle date back to 1389. Several other miraculous blood relics have been reported in southern Italy, also dating back to the late 14th century.

Until recently, the odd behavior of St. Januarius' blood eluded explanation in non-supernatural terms. Perhaps the first person to undertake research on the problem was Cardinal Lambertini, prior to becoming Pope Benedict XIV in 1740. Assuming that the substance was actual blood, he obtained human blood samples and tried to recreate the coagulating and liquefying behavior of the St. Januarius material. He could not discover any conditions under which blood could react in this manner and concluded that the events in the Neapolitan church were truly miraculous.

In 1890 Albini tried to concoct simulated "blood" that would liquefy when shaken or gently heated. One of his mixtures—composed of powdered chocolate and sugar in water—formed a viscous glob when still which liquefied when agitated. However, it eventually separated into layers and would not resolidify. (Also, 14th century Europeans did not possess chocolate). Other attempts were even less successful.

Epstein and Garlaschelli described a better simulation of the holy blood miracle in a 1992 report. Garlaschelli synthesized a gel of iron hydroxide, which forms a dark colored solid when undisturbed, but becomes a liquid when shaken. The gel maintains this capacity over repeated cycles of agitation. The authors of the study argued that the creation of this substance would not have been beyond the capacity of an alchemist in the 14th century. Until the guardians of St. Januarius' blood relics permit a chemical analysis of the substance, solutions to the mystery remain speculative.

Many reports exist in church annals of blood appearing on the bread wafers used in the eucharist. In Catholic dogma the bread changes into Christ's flesh during the Mass; the miracle of the bleeding host is thought to be a glimpse of a normally invisible process. Alternatively, some reports of bleeding hosts may have been due to a bacterial growth called *Serratia marcescens*. Colonies of this organism, which thrives on bread, appear as bright red patches.

For further reading: Epstein and Garlaschelli; Nickell; Rogo; Sox.

humanoids, anomalous Stories about beings that resemble members of our species, yet are unmistakably different, are found in every culture and time period. World folklore is rife with humanoids of all shapes and sizes, from diminutive fairies to towering giants. Reports of humanoid encounters continue to be part of modern life. The most commonly noted types of contemporary humanoids include those associated with UFO ENCOUNTERs (usually assumed to be the occupants of the mysterious crafts) and the hairy humanoids spotted in natural settings. Other important series of sightings such as those of MOTHMAN and SPRINGHEEL JACK, do not fit into either category.

In the most widely used classification system for UFO sightings, humanoids are featured in Close Encounters of the Third and Fourth Kinds (CE-III and CE-IV). The latter class includes reports of UFO abductions, in which the witness alleges to have been kidnapped by humanoids and often mistreated. Bullard and others have noted the similarities between such cases and traditional accounts of abductions by fairies, suggesting that the contemporary wave of CE-IVs is somehow a continuation of the older phenomenon.

Most of the hairy humanoid sightings are studied by cryptozoologists—researchers of "unknown animals"—rather than UFO investigators. It is generally assumed that if the hairy humanoids exist, they are some form of animal either unknown to biology or thought to be long extinct. The occasional cases in which hairy humanoids are seen in conjunction with UFOs tend to embarrass both the naturalists and the UFOlogists.

The best known of the hairy humanoids are the North American forest creature known as the Sasquatch or BIGFOOT, and the Asian mountain dweller called the ABOMINABLE SNOWMAN or Yeti. But variants of these beasts have been reported in many other locations. Brazilians occasionally spot the Mapinguary, and Argentinians the Ucumar. Western Africans wandering in the deepest jungles have encountered the Sehite, a pygmy-like race covered in reddish fur. Aside from the central Himalayas, home of the Yeti, several Asian mountain ranges are haunted by hairy humanoids: the Yagmort of the Urals, the Almasty of the Caucasus and the Dev of the Pamirs, among others. The Yowie is believed by many to inhabit the wilder regions of Queensland and New South Wales in Australia. Even in small, densely populated Japan, the Hiba-gon has sometimes been glimpsed in the woods.

Sightings of the Sasquatch are concentrated in British Columbia and the northwestern United States, although reports have been filed from almost every American state. On the basis of over 1,000 Sasquatch sightings, Green reported the following typical characteristics of this creature: generally heavier and taller than humans, height estimates averaging well above seven feet; almost always seen individually; the hair seems more animal than human; the proportions of the limbs are humanlike, but the head has striking simian qualities; omnivorous; largely nocturnal; inactive in cold weather; and attracted to lakes and streams. He noted that Russian accounts of hairy humanoids fit this picture, except that the Eurasian creatures are described as of normal human height.

Sasquatch encounters seem to predate the advent of European cultures in North America. Stone sculptures found in the Columbia River area of Oregon depict the head of an apelike creature and may date back as far as 1,500 B.C. The lore of many Native groups of the Northwest coast feature hairy humanoids; the term "sasquatch" is a name for such a creature in the Halkomelem language, spoken by the Coast Salish of southern British Columbia. According to the Salish, seeing a sasquatch could cause a person to go crazy, pass out or undergo "soul loss", a dangerous condition requiring the aid of a shaman.

Sightings by non-Natives have been recorded in the late 19th and 20th centuries, peaking in a great wave of reports during the 1970s. At the height of interest, the Sasquatch became a pop culture sensation, inspiring a spate of books, B-movies, Halloween costumes, advertising appearances, "Bigfoot-long" hotdogs and even footprint-shaped pastries with toenails of chocolate icing.

In the Himalayas, belief in the Yeti is deeply rooted in the indigenous cultures. In ritual performances depicting the acts of gods and spirits, dancers representing the Yeti wore caps said to be scalps of the beast (although they appeared to be made of goatskin). The Yeti is the national animal of the tiny mountain state of Bhutan, and has been featured on Bhutanese postage stamps. Natives discern three kinds of Yeti—the small *yehteh*, the midsize *mehteh* and the huge *dzuteh*. Several international mountaineering operations in the region (including the 1951 Mount Everest Expedition) have reported spotting the Yeti or its tracks in the snow.

There is no conclusive evidence that any life form corresponding to the Sasquatch or Yeti exists outside of the imagination. All of the physical traces allegedly left by the creatures are ambiguous. Many oversized footprints have been discovered in mud or snow and preserved via photographs and plaster casts. Most of the snowprints are suspect, because they are indistinguishable from ordinary sized animal or human prints that have enlarged through melting around the edges. During the late 1980s, there was some excitement concerning "dermal ridges" detected in some American Bigfoot mudprints. Dermal ridges are subtle irregularities in the skin surface; some researchers felt it was beyond the power of a hoaxer to duplicate this feature in a fake footprint, but others disagree.

Occasionally, photographic evidence for hairy humanoids is produced. The most famous recent picture was taken in 1986 by English adventurer Anthony Wooldridge. He photographed a Yeti standing in deep snow in a Himalayan pass, from a distance of several hundred feet (he was unable to get closer because of a snow slide). A later visit to the site revealed that the "Yeti" was a rock outcropping.

Most of the hairy humanoids that have been caught on video are obvious fakes. The most interesting Sasquatch film was shot by Roger Patterson in northern California in 1967. The footage seemingly shows a humanoid covered in brown fur, 6 feet 8 inches tall, over 400 pounds, with large, sagging breasts, as it saunters across a clearing and into the woods. Exhaustive analysis of Patterson's film has not demonstrated that it was a hoax; but it is hard to tell a hirsute humanoid from a human in a hair suit.

In Asia, Africa and South America, apes and monkeys briefly or distantly observed probably account for a number of hairy humanoid reports. In North America, bears might sometimes be misidentified. Even other humans could serve—during a wave of Bigfoot sightings in South Dakota in 1977, hunting parties were shooting at each other in attempts to bag the elusive beast.

Some skeptics believe that the hairy humanoid phenomenon is adequately explained by a combination of misperceptions and hoaxes. Other researchers are impressed by the consistency and endurance of the reports, but are puzzled by how a sustainable population of such creatures could continue to exist without yielding a single carcass for study. With hairy humanoids, as with murder investigations, no final scientific conclusions can be reached without a body.

For further reading: Bullard (1987); J. Green; Halpin and Ames; Krantz; Napier; Sanderson (1961); Stewart.

hypermnesia It has often been claimed that memory is improved in various unusual states. An increase in general memory ability while in an ALTERED STATE OF CONSCIOUSNESS is known as hypermnesia. Many practitioners of HYPNOSIS have noted improved recall in hypnotic subjects; on occasion, police investigators have tried hypnotic techniques to unearth lost details from the memories of crime witnesses. Although sometimes a person in an altered state will remember something that they had forgotten, there is little experimental evidence that any altered states feature *consistently* improved memory. Attempts to produce hypermnesia through hypnosis do not often succeed; instead, the hypnotized person's ability to distinguish true memories from fantasies may be reduced, leading to increased confidence and decreased accuracy of recall. Thus, false hypermnesia is much more common than true improvement in memory abilities.

It is true that one may be better able to remember what one did during a previous episode of altered consciousness by reentering that state. This phenomenon is called state-specific memory. An example is the person who loses his or her keys while intoxicated; he or she may not be able to recall where the keys are until they become inebriated again. Claims of hypermnesia go beyond state-specific memory; the hypermnestic person is said to have better access to all memories, not just those of experiences in a particular mental state.

It is also true that one can improve memory by learning methods of enhancing the encoding and recovering of information in memory. These techniques are called mnemonic strategies. Unlike claims of hypermnesia, the use of mnemonics does not depend on attaining an altered state.

See also AMNESIA; FALSE MEMORY.

For further reading: Baddeley; Lynn and Rhue (1991).

hypnagogic state Each night, as our brains shift from ordinary wakefulness to sleep, we pass through the hypnagogic state. This condition is typified by an upsurge in spontaneous mental content and especially by an increase in vivid sensations that are not produced by external sources.

Mavromatis and Richardson summarized several surveys of hypnagogic imagery reports. In most studies around three-quarters of the respondents indicated that they had, at least occasionally, experienced visual sensations while drifting off to sleep. One of the most common hypnagogic experiences is seeing FORM CONSTANTS, the visions of geometric shapes caused by cells firing in the visual system whenever the normal waking state is disrupted.

Vivid visual imagery is also common during the hypnagogic transition. Hypnagogic images typically do not occur in a narrative sequence, as in dreams; rather, a series of disconnected pictures appear. Brief images of unknown faces are most often reported. Children are sometimes frightened by this experience. Other solitary images can also arise. They may depict events of the previous day or they may be drawn from older memories.

Auditory sensations are also typical in the hypnagogic state. Hearing one's name called is the most frequent such experience. Music, both well-known and unfamiliar, is another common hypnagogic sound. The German composer Richard Wagner, among others, was inspired in his works by hypnagogic music.

Poetry, gibberish and crashing sounds in one's head have also been reported. Hypnagogic smells are not uncommon, ranging from fetid stenches to floral scents.

Kubie believed that hypnagogic imagery is more useful than dream imagery for purposes of learning about oneself:

> It is probable that in this partial sleep, in this no-man's land between sleeping and waking, a form of dissociation occurs which makes it possible to by-pass the more obstinate resistances which block our memories in states of full consciousness, and which contribute to the distortion of memory traces in dream.

The notion that the defenses of the unconscious are reduced in the hypnagogic state is also endorsed by many practitioners of HYPNOSIS. The moments before falling asleep are thought to be particularly good times for people to give themselves hypnotic suggestions for change.

Some people have reported that they have been able to establish control over hypnagogic imagery if they become aware that the images are not real. They can then guide the experience in pleasant or useful directions. This balancing act between wakeful control and the intense imagery of the dream state resembles lucid dreaming.

A person can slip into a hypnagogic state without being aware of it. The visions and sounds might then be confused with perceptions of the external world. Such hypnagogic hallucinations are most likely when one has been deprived of sleep for long periods. Occasionally, however, the intrusion of hypnagogic material into the waking state occurs for no known reason. Hufford suspected that the OLD HAG EXPERIENCE is probably a kind of "hypnagogic attack."

Baker noted some characteristics of hypnagogic hallucinations. They are often accompanied by changes in the experience of the body—one may find oneself paralyzed, or have an OUT OF BODY EXPERIENCE. The content of the hallucination is typically bizarre—apparitions, strange humanoids and monsters. Following the hallucination, which may be startling in its apparent reality, the witness generally falls quickly to sleep.

See also HYPNOPOMPIC STATE.

For further reading: Baker (1991); Hufford; Mavromatis and Richardson.

hypnopompic state As one awakens from sleep, one passes through an intermediate condition known as the hypnopompic state. Auditory and visual mental images of great vividness can occur during this time. McKellar found that 21% of surveyed college students reported occasional hypnopompic experiences. Hypnopompic visions and sounds can be so intense that they can be mistaken for perceptions of external events. However, such HALLUCINATIONs are often accompanied by telltale features that reveal their imaginal nature: the hallucinator usually feels paralyzed; and frequently, the hallucinator quickly falls asleep again following the experience.

The content of hypnopompic imagery often anticipates the expected events of the coming day, as if the mind is preparing itself for the tasks ahead—one may hear an alarm clock before it goes off, or imagine commuting to work. A hypnagogic image might on occasion closely match an event that occurs later. If the image is remembered, it might be taken as an instance of PRECOGNITION. If the hypnopompic experience is forgotten, the event might still seem strangely "familiar" when it happens. Forgotten hypnopompic correspondences with events may thus explain some instances of DÉJÀ VU.

Hypnopompic experiences can also be quite unlike ordinary life. Many cases of bedside encounters with strange creatures and ghosts are probably hypnopompic hallucinations. Baker described the following example of a nocturnal ghostly meeting, which displays the telltale signs of a hypnopompic event:

> I went to bed and went to sleep and then sometime near morning something woke me up. I opened my eyes and found myself wide awake but unable to move. There, standing at the foot of my bed was my mother, wearing her favorite dress—the one we buried her in. She stood there, looking at me and smiling and then she said: 'Don't worry about me, Doris, I'm at peace at last. I just want you and the children to be happy.' What did you do then? Nothing, I just closed my eyes and went back to sleep.

See also HYPNAGOGIC STATE.

For further reading: Baker (1991); Hufford; McKellar.

hypnosis *Hypnos* was the Greek god of sleep. Braid coined the term "hypnosis" in 1852 to refer to the sleep-like state he could induce in his surgical patients merely by talking to them. In fact, hypnosis and sleep are entirely different conditions. Many definitions of hypnosis have been advanced, reflecting the multitude of theories concerning its nature. Most researchers agree that hypnosis involves a reduction of external awareness and a decrease in critical or analytic thinking; these changes enable the hypnotized person to respond to inner phenomena, such as mental images and thoughts, as if they were real. Individuals with a strong capacity for hypnotic responding (hypnotizability) can experience dramatic alterations of mood, perception, memory and biological functioning while hypnotized.

There are three types of circumstances within which hypnosis occurs. The best-known is *heterohypnosis,* in which one person, the hypnotist, provides another with hypnotic suggestions, usually in the form of words. In *self hypnosis,* an individual gives the suggestions to himself or herself. *Spontaneous hypnosis* also happens, in which one enters a hypnotized condition unintentionally. In so-called "highway hypnosis," for instance, a driver may become so absorbed in thought that he pilots the vehicle automatically, unable to later remember parts of the journey. The same process is being tapped in all three hypnotic circumstances—an inward focusing of attention. The common belief that in heterohypnosis the hypnotized person falls under the control of the hypnotist is unfounded. A hypnotist acts as a guide to help steer the experience, but does not "take over" the hypnotic subject any more than a football coach "takes over" the players on the field.

Procedures for inducing hypnosis were developed in ancient times. A Roman magician, Clearchus, used a "soul dragging wand" to cause numbness; the wand fixated the subject's attention, reducing awareness of other sensations. Apuleius described boys "lulled to trance by spells," which sounds like a verbal hypnotic induction. During the era of Christian domination in Europe, hypnotic procedures, such as ritual magic, were kept alive in subcultures.

Hypnosis resurfaced in the late 18th century. A French physician, Franz Mesmer, proclaimed that the universe was suffused with a kind of living magnetic fluid. This "animal magnetism," as he called it, was especially concentrated in the human body. Mesmer developed techniques for manipulating the fluid and found that many ill people reported dramatic relief from his ministrations. For a short while, "Mesmerism" became quite popular. Mesmer, dressed in a purple robe, presided over his clinic. Patients would sit around a barrel filled with iron filings and "magnetized water," gripping iron rods that protruded from it. When Mesmer touched his patients, or passed his hands over them, many would go into convulsions thought to be caused by the flow of animal magnetism; when they recovered, their symptoms had sometimes abated. An investigation into Mesmerism was commissioned by King Louis XVI and headed by Benjamin Franklin. The study concluded that animal magnetism did not exist; the effects of Mesmerism were due to the imagination of the patients, many of whom had psychological rather than physical disorders.

Braid resurrected Mesmerism, under its modern name, in the 1850s. He demonstrated that hypnosis improved the outcome of surgical amputations among injured soldiers. Braid correctly deduced that a key feature of hypnosis was a shift in attention; although the alteration in hypnosis was psychological, it could produce significant changes in bodily processes. Since that time, hypnosis has been intensively investigated. Although Mesmer's theory was dismissed over 200 years ago, a link between hypnosis and occultism persists in many minds.

Contemporary psychological research indicates that two factors contribute to the experience of hypnosis: the capacity to produce vivid fantasy images; and the capacity to narrow the attention, or to make the mind blank. Although many people, including some researchers, believe that hypnosis is an ALTERED STATE OF CONSCIOUSNESS, this notion is misleading. It is impossible to tell whether or not a person is hypnotized by measuring physiological changes. There do not appear to be any special processes occurring in hypnosis that do not also happen during ordinary wakefulness. Dramatic hypnotic phenomena are simply intense versions of everyday experiences—amnesia, hallucinations, and pain reduction, for instance, do not require an unusual state of consciousness for their occurrence. A firm line cannot be drawn between hypnotized and unhypnotized experience; some researchers believe that brief episodes of spontaneous hypnosis may happen, unnoticed, several times each day.

Currently, hypnosis is used for entertainment by stage magicians and as a method of treatment by health care professionals. Conditions that often respond to hypnosis include migraine and tension headaches, allergies, warts, asthma and persistent pain. The effectiveness of hypnosis for these disorders depends mainly on the hypnotizability of the sufferer. The vivid imagery of hypnosis can also be used as a "practice space," in which a person can safely try out new behaviors and solutions to problems. Such imagined rehearsal can build confidence in skill in actual performance.

Mental imagery can affect the flow of blood in the body; embarrassing thoughts can cause blushing, and sexual fantasies can shift blood to the genitals. Hypnotic enhancement of blood flow control can create astonishing effects among highly hypnotizable people. Barber documented cases in which hypnosis cured intractable skin diseases, minimized the effect of burns, produced inflammation and blisters, and even caused permanent enlargement of adult female breasts. According to Barber, these changes resulted from a fine-tuned channeling of blood to the skin.

Since the days of Mesmer, claims have been made that hypnosis magnifies paranormal abilities. The followers of Mesmer noted four types of "higher phenomena": transfer of the senses, including "dermal vision," or the ability to read text with the fingers; community of sensation, in which stimuli applied to the hypnotist would be felt by the hypnotized person; mental suggestion, a linkage of mind that allowed the hypnotist to send suggestions, and even to hypnotize, even when separated from the hypnotic subject; and psychic abilities like CLAIRVOYANCE and TELEPATHY. Stanford reviewed a number of studies by parapsychologists and found that subjects tend to score higher on ESP tests when they are hypnotized. Some critics contend that this effect may be due to the enhancement of the subjects' abilities to detect subtle sensory cues concerning the target material, rather than an increase in ESP.

See also FALSE MEMORY.

For further reading: Barber; Lynn and Rhue (1991); Spanos and Chaves; Stanford (1992).

hypnotizability   It has long been known that people differ in their responsiveness to HYPNOSIS—a few individuals cannot be hypnotized, some people have profound responses and most of us react moderately to hypnotic inductions. Hypnotizability (also called hypnotic susceptibility) is a person's capacity for becoming involved in his or her own imagination in response to suggestions given by a hypnotist. Hypnosis taps this capacity by encouraging people to experience their thoughts and fantasies as if they were real.

Researchers measure hypnotizability using one of several standard susceptibility scales. These scales consist of a series of suggestions given following a hypnotic induction. Some scales are administered individually, while others can be presented to a group. The suggestions are brief phrases instructing subjects to create imaginary situations and perform the corresponding behaviors—for instance, "your arm is light as a feather, you can feel it floating off the table." The test suggestions are presented in order, from "easy" to "difficult." Most people respond to some degree to easy suggestions, such as arm levitation. Difficult suggestions, like hallucinating a kitten sitting in one's lap and petting

it, are fully and consistently achieved only by highly hypnotizable people.

Children generally score higher on hypnotizability scales than adults. It is likely that extensive use of fantasy play among many children reflects their easy access to the imagined world. Why adults tend to lose much of their hypnotic ability, and whether this loss is found among adults of non-western societies, is still unclear.

Adults who retain their hypnotic capacity from childhood are the high hypnotizables. Such people tend to report significant levels of childhood trauma, such as abuse or family breakups. Perhaps they intensified their involvement with fantasy to escape from the unpleasantness around them. High levels of hypnotizability are also positively correlated with ABSORBTION—the tendency for attention to become completely focused on a single object—and FANTASY PRONENESS.

While people with high hypnotic ability can enter into hypnosis easily under most circumstances, individuals with moderate or even low ability can do so under certain conditions. Most people become more hypnotizable when they are very aroused, very relaxed or while experiencing SENSORY DEPRIVATION.

Hypnotizability is linked with a variety of unusual beliefs and experiences. High hypnotizables tend to have greater levels of paranormal beliefs in general, as well as specific belief in ESP. As Irwin noted, "These results suggest that paranormal belief is linked to a cognitive style of fantasizing."

Hypnotic ability is correlated with a general tendency to report anomalous experiences. Specific types of unusual experience that are more often reported by high hypnotizables include: ESP; OUT OF BODY EXPERIENCE; MYSTICAL and DIABOLICAL EXPERIENCE; LUCID DREAM; NEAR DEATH EXPERIENCE; AURA; and PAST LIFE RECALL. According to some skeptics, high hypnotizables have more strange experiences because they are prone to mistaking vivid fantasies for external perceptions. A study by Lynn, Weekes and Milano found, however, that hypnotic ability does not lead to a confusion of the inner and outer worlds; high hypnotizables may experience fantasies as "real," but this quality of "reality" is different from that of objects they perceive with their senses.

Hypnotizability seems to play a role in the development of some physical and psychological disorders. Wickramasekera (1986) reported that people who have extremely high or low hypnotic ability are prone to developing stress-related physical disorders. He speculated that high hypnotizables may damage themselves because of their hypersensitivity to environmental and internal signals, whereas low hypnotizables may be less aware of the harmful effects of stress until harm has already occurred. High hypnotizables also are more vulnerable to developing hysterical disorders. Sufferers of MULTIPLE PERSONALITY DISORDER are almost always highly hypnotizable.

A person's hypnotic ability can also affect how well he or she responds to therapy. Hypnotic treatment of phobias, allergies, migraines, warts, burns and asthma works better with high hypnotizables; the effectiveness of hypnotic therapy for bad habits and addictions is less influenced by the patient's hypnotic ability. Even nonhypnotic therapies may have greater impact on high hypnotizables, if the treatments involve the use of deep relaxation procedures and mental imagery.

See also Appendix.

For further reading: Lynn and Rhue (1988); Lynn, Weekes and Milano; Wickramasekera (1986, 1991).

hysteria   This term is Greek for "uterus." The ancients believed that a woman's womb could become loose and wander through the body, producing strange experiences and behaviors. In the 19th century "hysteria" was widely employed in medical circles as a diagnosis encompassing a wide range of physical and mental disorders. Although "hysterical" symptoms were no longer attributed to a dislodged uterus, it was widely believed that uterine disease could disturb the functioning of organs and nerves throughout a woman's body, including her brain. According to this doctrine, women were considered to be, in Shorter's words, "uterine-driven automata," incapable of resisting the crazed impulses emanating from their wombs. This notion persisted into the 20th century. The term is falling out of usage by mental health professionals today, because many women feel insulted by its historical connotations. Contemporary labels for disorders that formerly were grouped under the heading of hysteria include DISSOCIATIVE DISORDERs, the SOMATOFORM DISORDER called "conversion disorder," and the stress-induced breakdown of mental functioning known as "brief reactive psychosis." The term "hysteria" is still widely used by laypersons to refer to excited or irrational behavior.

For further reading: American Psychiatric Association; Shorter.

iboga This shrub, known to botanists as Tabernanthe iboga, flourishes in the undergrowth of tropical forests in West Africa. Its roots contain three alkaloid substances that powerfully stimulate the central nervous system. Psychoactive effects can range from dreamy sensations to florid HALLUCINATIONs. Iboga has become the focus of an important religious movement in Zaire and Gabon, especially among the Fang people.

Prior to the impact of European colonists in West Africa, iboga was generally consumed in small quantities for its invigorating and aphrodisiacal properties. By the late 19th century, French activities in the region were severely straining the fabric of Fang culture. Traditional religious attitudes toward the spirit world were under particular attack by Christian missionaries. Secret societies were formed in order to preserve Fang beliefs and rituals. These groups embraced the practice of iboga eating as a method of gaining direct experience of the world of spirits.

Accounts differ concerning how the Fang learned about the hallucinogenic powers of iboga. Some reports indicate that the potency of iboga roots was discovered by Pygmies, who then taught Fang elders. Others have suggested that hunters observed the disturbed behavior of wild boars, porcupines and gorillas after these creatures ate iboga roots and then tried it themselves.

The iboga cult, known as Bwiti, has functioned as a rallying point for Fang traditionalists during the present century, serving to promote tribal solidarity in the face of foreign influence. In many villages the Bwiti temple is one of the largest and most important structures, featuring elaborate decorations derived from the drug-induced visions of initiates. Although Bwiti has acted as a counter to Christian proselytizing efforts, Christian symbols have been incorporated into the Bwiti system. For instance, the Virgin Mary has become identified with the primordial First Woman who gave birth to the universe.

In order to join the cult, one must first "see the Bwiti"—that is, one must have a vision of a god associated with the realm of the ancestors. The experience is induced by "breaking open the head" through eating large quantities of iboga during an initiation ceremony. The plant can be drunk in powdered form or ingested in its natural state.

As the iboga trance sets in, the candidate may appear to be gripped by seizures. Guien witnessed a Bwiti initiation (quoted by Dobkin de Rios):

> Soon all his sinews stretched out in an extraordinary fashion. An epileptic madness seizes him during which, unconscious, he mouths words which when heard by the initiated have a prophetic meaning and prove that the fetish has entered him.

Prior to the ceremony, the candidate has learned what to expect. These beliefs structure the drug experience, thus confirming the spiritual authority of the cult leaders. Ndong Asseko, a Bwiti initiate, described his iboga journey (quoted by Schultes and Hofmann):

> When I ate [iboga], I found myself taken by it up a long road in a deep forest, until I came to a barrier of black iron. At that barrier, unable to pass, I saw a crowd of black persons also unable to pass. In the distance. . . . it was very bright. I could see many colors in the air. . . .

Suddenly my father descended from above in the form of a bird. He gave me then my [iboga] name and enabled me to fly up after him over the barrier of iron.

The visionary trips can last for several hours. If the Bwiti is not seen, the candidate is fed more iboga. Many deaths from overdoses have been recorded. Candidates who survive the ordeal often collapse, remaining immobilized for up to seven days.

Periodically, members of Bwiti gather in their temples for dances, representing their alliance with the ancestor spirits. Small quantities of iboga root are consumed at these meetings. The low dosages trigger feelings of floating, which are said to enable the performers to "fly" while dancing, in a manner pleasing to the spirits.

For further reading: Dobkin de Rios; Fernandez; Schultes and Hofmann; Stafford.

idea of reference   This is an incorrect belief that events in a person's environment have a special meaning for him or her. For instance, a person viewing the hand gestures of strangers in a restaurant might get the notion that the strangers are sending hand signals to them; or someone listening to the radio may feel that the songs contain secret messages specifically for him or her. Momentary feelings of this kind probably happen occasionally to many people and they pass quickly without incident; but if they persist or recur, they could be symptomatic of a mental disorder. Sufferers of SCHIZOPHRENIA commonly have ideas of reference. This symptom is less fixed and enduring than a DELUSION.

ideophany   An uncommon term for a HALLUCINATION or PSEUDOHALLUCINATION experienced by a single person.

ideoretinal light   Flashes of light or color that appear in the field of vision in the absence of sensory stimulation. Ideoretinal light is often observed in the HYPNAGOGIC STATE. This occurrence is likely a type of ENTOPTIC PHENOMENON.

ignis fatuus   A name for WILL-O'-THE-WISPs, coined by the ancient Romans and still used today. In Latin the phrase means "fool's fire"—unwary travelers, assuming that the flickering nocturnal lights signaled the presence of settlements, have been lured into treacherous swamps to their deaths.

illusion   An illusion is a mistaken perception of an object. Illusions are theoretically distinguished from HALLUCINATIONs: In the case of illusions, an object is actually present, but perceived as something else; hallucinations are perception-like experiences in the absence of any corresponding external object. In practice, however, it is often impossible to separate illusion and hallucination. An experience can start as an illusion (a flapping curtain is misperceived as a ghost) and transform into a hallucination (the witness hears the ghost speak). Commonly, the stimulus of an unusual experience remains unknown (some sightings of Bigfoot might have been misperceived bears; others could have been sheer hallucination).

Illusions are also theoretically distinct from ordinary perceptions. Again, in practice this division is hard to sustain. Although in normal perception it seems as if one perceives the world "as it really is," in fact every sensation is filtered through the expectancies, assumptions and habits with which the mind organizes its input into a coherent experience. The objects of normal perception appear to be solid, independent, enduring things; but physics tells us that they are not. The qualities of solidity, independence and endurance are not present in the stimulus, but are added by the mind. Thus, in a strict sense, all perceptions have illusory qualities.

There are two main types of illusion. *General illusions* are those that affect almost everyone. Certain types of stimulation can trick the mind into creating incorrect images of the world. A commonly noted example is the moon illusion—many people have observed that the full moon appears larger when it is just above the horizon than when it is high overhead. In fact, the image of the lunar disk that reaches the eye from either location is identical in size. When viewed near the horizon, the mind automatically compares the apparent size of the moon with visible distant objects on the earth's surface; the moon, seen to be farther away than the most distant terrestrial object, is judged to be huge. This judgment affects the perception of the horizon moon, granting the image a sense of immensity. The moon viewed overhead cannot easily be compared to the apparent size of things on the ground. The mind is left to judge the true size of the overhead moon with fewer distance cues than are available for the horizon moon. As the image of the moon in the sky is about the size of a quarter held at arm's length, the mind is biased to perceive the overhead moon as small. Psychologists have discovered hundreds of such perceptual tricks.

Another form of general illusion is caused by the influence of human needs on perception. In order to continue functioning in an uncertain, often tragic, world, most people distort their perceptions in optimistic directions. Taylor observed that ordinary perceptions are biased toward seeing oneself as more admirable, more in control and with a more positive future than is actually the case. People who do not create these self-affirming illusions are vulnerable to mental illness.

Idiosyncratic illusions are caused by the biasing effects of less widely held motivations and expectations. When we need or expect to perceive something, we are predisposed to find it. Horowitz noted that:

> the same ambiguous round shape on initial perceptual representation can be 'illusioned' into an orange (if the subject is hungry), a breast (if he is in a state of heightened sexual drive), a cup of water (if he is thirsty), or an anarchist's bomb (if he is hostile or fearful).

Or, one might add, the round shape could be a UFO (if one has just read a tabloid story about alien spacecraft) or the Blessed Virgin Mary (if one is a devout believer in divine apparitions).

The more ambiguous the stimulus is, the more influence these factors have in constructing the experience. The ideal conditions for the occurrence of idiosyncratic illusions are as follows: illumination levels are dim; the stimulus object is not clearly viewed; the object is seen only briefly; the observer is in a state of impaired perceptual functioning, such as extreme stress, excitement or tiredness; and the observer is primed by relevant beliefs or desires. Many of these conditions are prevalent in reports of unusual experiences.

Idiosyncratic illusions are not restricted to individuals. Collective illusions can occur via "hysterical contagion" if a group of people share common motivations or expectations. If witnesses communicate with each other during or after the experience, they can unintentionally "fine tune" their mutual interpretations, creating closely matching illusionary perceptions. On the largest scale, cultures act as massive perceptual biases—members of each culture are led to conform their perceptions with those of their neighbors. As noted above, some illusions may be normal, or even universal.

See also GROUP DYNAMICS OF UNUSUAL EXPERIENCES.

For further reading: Baker (1992); Horowitz; Taylor; Zusne and Jones.

illusion des sosies   In a classical myth, the god Mercury takes on the appearance of Amphitryon's servant, Sosie. The French phrase "illusion des sosies," or "illusion of doubles," refers to a condition in which someone becomes convinced that a familiar person has been replaced by an identical replica. This delusion is also called Capgras Syndrome. The "illusion des sosies" may be an extreme variant of JAMAIS VU— the perception of a well-known object without a feeling of recognition.

In most cases, a close friend or family member of the person suffering the illusion is thought to have been replaced. The sufferer develops a belief system to explain why the replacement has happened and resists all efforts to demonstrate the error of this conviction. Such loss of contact with reality is categorized as a PSYCHOSIS.

Twentieth century victims of "illusion des sosies" tend to blame aliens or secret government experiments for the replacement of their loved ones. In premodern times it was widely believed that fairies loved to kidnap humans, especially infants, and substitute replicas called changelings. "Illusion des sosies" would naturally be explained in these terms, sometimes with horrifying results. In 1897, in the village of Clonmel, Ireland, an incident occurred that has been called the last witch burning in Europe. Michael Cleary became convinced that his wife Bridget had been replaced by a changeling. In attempting to extract a confession of her fairy identity, he roasted her to death in the hearth fire. Afterward, he set off for a local hill reputed to be a fairy haunt, brandishing a kitchen knife, intent on rescuing his wife from the kidnappers. Concerning the murder victim, Cleary later said to friends, "Have you no faith? Did you not know that it was not my wife, she was too fine to be my wife, she was two inches taller than my wife." Cleary was convicted of manslaughter and sentenced to 20 years of hard labor.

See also FREGOLI'S SYNDROME.

For further reading: Enoch and Trethowan; Noll (1990).

imaginary companion Developmental psychologist Piaget observed that children under three years of age do not distinguish between mental images and perceptions of the outer world. Between three and six, they realize that fantasies and perceptions are different, but consider the two phenomena to be distinct kinds of external reality. Older children realize the "mental" aspect of mental images—that they occur in an inner, subjective realm. During the second stage in the development of attitudes toward fantasy, some children acquire imaginary companions.

Children who are isolated, lonely or especially creative are most likely to have imaginary companions. They may talk to these invisible beings, play with them, set a place at the table for them and otherwise acknowledge their reality. Some parents worry that this behavior may be unhealthy and try to discourage it. Most researchers have concluded that imaginary companions are usually harmless. They may even be valuable, as they permit children to fill a gap in their social environment.

In later childhood, imaginary companions usually fade away. Sometimes INNER VOICES persist until adolescence, but the child recognizes their imaginal quality and does not confuse them with external sounds. For some individuals, however, the imaginary companions of childhood persist well into adulthood. This phenomenon is most common among FANTASY PRONE PERSONALITIES. Such people usually keep the persistence of their companion a secret, justly fearing persecution.

Although modern western society teaches its children that imagination is unreal and defines any disagreement as immature or pathological, this has not been the case in most cultures and historical periods. Many cultural traditions emphasize the importance of acquiring new imaginal companions—generally called spirits or deities—when entering adulthood. Such is the aim of the VISION QUESTs of native North Americans, for example. Religious specialists known as SHAMANs were required to maintain relations with spirits, in some cases entering into marital bonds with them. Socrates had an invisible guide, his *daimon*. Many practitioners of Sufism, the mystical branch of Islam, claim to have been taught by al-Khadir, a visitor from the imaginal world. Magicians through the ages have cultivated links with the domain of the spirits. Even in the modern West, there is a marginal tradition of deliberate concourse with nonmaterial beings. For instance, the influential psychiatrist Carl

Jung stated his indebtedness to a winged man named Philemon, with whom he would walk in his garden, discussing profound matters.

Imaginary companions can also appear to adults without being sought. Stress and isolation are predisposing factors. Members of mountaineering expeditions in the Himalayas have frequently reported sensing the presence of helpful entities, sometimes seeing them—in these instances, mild oxygen deprivation may also have been involved. Arctic explorers and sailors alone at sea have often noted imaginary companions. A famous case was that of Joshua Slocum. While sailing alone, Slocum became ill, and his boat was overtaken by an ocean storm. He saw the pilot of Columbus' ship *Pinta* steer his boat into calmer waters. On several occasions during Slocum's journey, the pilot reappeared to offer assistance, and Slocum held conversations with him.

See also RUYA'HA.

For further reading: Piaget; Plank; Reed (1988); Trismegistus.

incendium amoris   This experience of the "fire of love" is recognized by the Roman Catholic church as one of the CHARISMS, or occurrences frequently associated with sanctity. Subjectively, the incendium is experienced as intense sensations of heat; there are also reports of external manifestations, ranging from feverish skin to warmth radiating from the body, and even the appearance of heat blisters on the skin and the scorching of clothing.

In the records of investigations prior to the canonization of saints, there are many accounts of the incendium amoris. Typical is the case of Philip Neri, a 16th century Italian saint. In 1544, this pious man had a vision. The Holy Spirit, in the form of a globe of fire, entered his mouth, lodging in his heart. For the rest of his life, he periodically experienced strong feelings of heat and swelling in his breast. Thurston reports of this heat:

it sometimes extended over his whole body, and for all his age, thinness and spare diet, in the coldest days of winter it was necessary, even in the midst of the night to open the windows, to cool the bed, to fan him while in bed, and in various ways to moderate the great heat . . . Even in winter he almost always had his clothes open from the girdle upwards, and sometimes when they told him to fasten them lest he should do himself some injury, he used to say he really could not because of the excessive heat he felt. One day, at Rome, when a great quantity of snow had fallen, he was walking in the streets with his cassock unbuttoned; and when some of his penitents who were with him were hardly able to endure the cold, he laughed at them and said it was a shame for young men to feel cold when old men did not.

After Philip's death in 1595, an autopsy was performed. It was discovered that two ribs over his heart had been broken and pushed outwards. The injury had evidently been sustained many years prior to his demise. This finding suggests that the saint had indeed suffered from some sort of physical trauma, perhaps disturbing his thermal regulation.

Aspects of the incendium amoris accounts are reminiscent of other forms of unusual experience. Descriptions of the inner heat sensations closely resemble phenomena associated with some Eastern meditation practices, such as KUNDALINI Yoga and the Six Yogas of NAROPA. The skin disturbances may be related to the dermatological oddities of the STIGMATA, which are also often associated with religious devotion. Heat damage to materials such as clothing is not convincingly documented; if such effects do occur, their cause may be similar to that of another alleged thermal phenomenon, SPONTANEOUS HUMAN COMBUSTION.

For further reading: Murphy; Thurston.

incubus nightmare   In traditional European lore an incubus is an evil spirit that invades a woman's bedroom at night, mounts her chest, has sexual intercourse with her and gives her nightmares. (Men were said to be visited by the incubus' female equivalent, the succubus.) An experience that lent credence to this belief was the incubus nightmare.

Unlike ordinary nightmares, the incubus nightmare does not begin in the dreaming phase of sleep (the REM stage) but in deep, dreamless sleep. Breathing and heartbeat slow dramatically, as if the sleeper were approaching death. The REM stage then begins, accompanied by menacing dreams, a feeling of paralysis and the sensation of a great weight crushing the chest.

The incubus nightmare may be caused by the activation of a neurological relic of human evolution—the diving reflex. Seabirds and aquatic mammals that dive for food possess a reflex that inhibits breathing and heartbeat while submerged, allowing them to remain below for longer periods. This mechanism is of no use to humans, but it is thought to persist as a vestige in the nervous system. When activated in babies, the diving reflex may be a cause of SIDS (sudden infant death syndrome, or "crib death"); in adults, the reflexive suppression of life support functions could be the basis of the incubus nightmare.

See also OLD HAG EXPERIENCE.

For further reading: Hufford; Zusne and Jones.

induced psychotic disorder   It is not unusual for people who spend a lot of time together to develop similar views. A special case arises when one member of a couple or a group harbors DELUSIONs, or fixed false beliefs, and his or her partner(s) also become delusional. This phenomenon has been called "contagious insanity," or more formally, "induced" or "shared psychotic disorder."

In most instances, the delusion is shared by two people. This condition has been dubbed "folie à deux," or the "madness of two." Enoch and Trethowan recounted a typical case: a 79-year-old woman convinced her 72-year-old brother, with whom she was living, that their neighbors were trying to harm them. According to the deluded couple, the neighbors had accused them of two crimes—murder, and sexual acts with dogs. They worried that they were being poisoned and thought that strange influences were being directed at them through the heating ducts. Eventually, the couple had to be hospitalized.

This case has several standard features of folie a deux. The delusion originated with one member of the couple (the sister), who was the dominant member in the relationship; she "induced" the delusion in her brother, who was used to complying with her wishes. They lived relatively isolated lives, away from ordinary social influences that would have tended to highlight the oddness of their belief. Once it had taken root, however, the delusional idea resisted all attempts to dispute it.

Delusions can also be induced in entire families. Waltzer described the most extreme case on record, a "folie à douze" ("madness of twelve")—a family of two parents and ten children, all of whom lived in a shared delusional world. As Noll commented, "Psychosis is a game the whole family can play."

See also GROUP DYNAMICS OF UNUSUAL EXPERIENCES.

For further reading: Enoch and Trethowan; Noll (1990); Waltzer.

infrasound   The human ear cannot register sound waves below 15 to 20 cycles per second. There is some evidence, however, that infrasonic stimulation does affect people. Infrasounds are generated by a variety of natural phenomena, including thunderstorms, earthquakes, strong winds and volcanoes. Because of their low frequency, infrasounds can travel great distances from their point of origin. Stephens, quoted by Corliss, noted the following possible effects of exposure to infrasound: "nausea, disequilibrium, disorientation, blurring of vision, lassitude. Internal damage may occur due to the fact that infrasonic waves easily penetrate deeply and may induce resonant effects on organs." He also reported that statistics reflecting impaired performance, such as absenteeism and accident rates, have been positively correlated with storms happening up to 2,000 miles away. It is possible that infrasound contributes to the feelings of unease that many people experience when a thunderstorm is approaching.

For further reading: Corliss (1977).

initiatory experience One of the most widespread of human perceptions is the sense that the course of life is divided into stages. In each stage, expectations and beliefs—largely acquired from one's culture—determine a person's sense of self, social roles and world view. What it means to be a child, adult, spouse and elder are thus defined. In addition, new phases in a life commence when one enters certain specialized positions, such as those of a shaman or a professional. The experience of transition between life's stages is called initiation.

In most of the world's societies, the initiation experience is structured by ritual. Arnold Van Gennep noted that *rites of passage,* as he designated them, usually consist of three phases. In the first phase, called *separation,* those to be initiated are removed from their ordinary surroundings. They are "kidnapped" by the initiators and carried off into the woods or they are forced to leave the world of daylight and descend into deep caves. In such ways, they are separated from all of the familiar experiences that anchored the self definition they possessed in the life stage that is drawing to a close.

Van Gennep called the second phase *marginality.* Persons undergoing initiation have been taken beyond the edges of the familiar world within which they dwelled. Far from the stabilizing features of everyday life, the initiates experience uncertainty concerning who they are, and about what is real. They may glimpse the unfixed and arbitrary nature of cultural features that formerly appeared to be absolutely true. The old concept of self breaks down, in preparation for the installment of a new identity for the next life stage. In many instances of shamanic initiation, this destruction is experienced as being literally torn apart by the spirits. Marginality is dangerous—one could become lost in the strangeness, forgetting who one was and failing to find out who one could become.

The phase of marginality is often marked by the occurrence of unusual experiences. This is unsurprising, as many of the techniques traditionally used to disrupt the anchors of the self concept interfere with a range of perceptual and cognitive functions. These methods include torture, starvation, SENSORY DEPRIVATION or sensory overstimulation, sleep deprivation and ingestion of DRUGS. In many cases unusual experiences are deliberately sought as evidence of contact with the world of spirits—for example, the native North American VISION QUEST.

In Van Gennep's final phase, known as *aggregation,* initiates are provided with their new self concept. They are taught the knowledge and given the symbols appropriate to their new rank; they may receive a new name and a new dwelling place. Following the initiation when they return to the society, they are, in a sense, "reborn." In addition, they may experience the world they live in as similarly transformed, for they have had old truths canceled and new ones revealed.

Individuals who have spontaneous unusual experiences frequently report that such occurrences are personally very meaningful. Those who undergo NEAR DEATH EXPERIENCEs or UFO ABDUCTIONs often describe enduring changes in their senses of self and reality. Thompson suggested that many spontaneous unusual experiences display the same threefold structure of separation, marginality and aggregation that Van Gennep found to structure rites of passage. Encounters with the unknown seem to trigger the initiatory pattern in many people, resulting in varying degrees of personal transformation.

Some have gone further, speculating that many strange occurrences might be deliberate attempts to provoke initiatory shifts in observers, or in the entire culture. Raschke, discussing UFO ENCOUNTERs, noted that:

> Such experiences tend to be convulsive, perplexing, and *outre* and to conflict strikingly with the habitual thought patterns of the subject. A meeting with a UFO is apt to leave the witnesses' world in upheaval. One must remain curious, therefore, whether the *purpose* of UFO sightings and contacts is mainly to undercut the ingrained human longing for secure knowledge and faith, rather than to gratify it. . . . UFOs can be depicted as what I would call ultraterrestrial agents of deconstruction.

The aim of this deconstruction, in the words of Ring, would be "a gradual but inexorable dismantling of the commonly held structures of thought and values in order to permit a new, more fluid, and open way of being in the world . . . a nonrigid openness to experience itself." In other words, UFO encounters, as well as other seeming violations of conventional assumptions about reality, could serve to propel us into marginality. Perhaps we would emerge from this initiation with less constricted definitions of self and world.

For further reading: Raschke; Ring; Thompson; Van Gennep.

inner voice For most people, the notion of "hearing voices" is associated either with sanctity or sickness. It is true that AUDITORY HALLUCINATIONs are a common symptom of severe mental disorders such as SCHIZOPHRENIA. Many famous religious figures have indeed described encounters with the divine that involved hearing voices—Moses, Joan of Arc and St. Teresa of Avila arc but a few noteworthy examples. The phenomenon has also occurred, sometimes with regularity, to many who are neither saints nor psychotics.

The inner voice is an auditory experience that seems to come from within oneself. It is thus distinguished from the auditory hallucination, which is perceived to arise from the external world. The two kinds of experience have in common the sense that the voice is *autonomous*—that is, it seems to originate from a source beyond one's conscious control and knowledge, unlike ordinary thoughts, which typically feel deliberately generated by oneself.

Because the inner voice is autonomous, it can also be unpredictable, saying things that can surprise the "hearer." The psychiatrist Carl Jung experienced an imaginal being named Philemon, which manifested as both a vision and an inner voice: "I observed clearly that it was [Philemon] who spoke, not I . . . I understood that there is something in me which can say things I do not know and do not intend."

Attitudes toward inner voices have depended on what they say and on the prevailing beliefs of the time. In the premodern West, inner voices saying unpleasant things have usually been construed as the statements of demons; as they seem to arise from within, they were often taken as evidence of demonic POSSESSION. Inner voices with positive or helpful content could be understood as good spirits or angels; or as a ruse of devils, seeking to mislead the unwary. Modern psychology does not generally accept the possibility that interior phenomena could originate from spirits. Instead, voices are thought to be produced by one's own psychological operations, functioning outside of one's awareness—as Heery put it, "Just as the external voice communicates between one human being and another, the inner voice may communicate intrapsychically between one level of the psyche and another."

The vividness of the inner voice experience can vary. At one end of the range is the feeling that "something is telling me to do this." Although the impulse does not clothe itself in words, there is nonetheless a verbal quality to it, as if one is receiving a suggestion or command. If this urge pertains to the direction our lives should take, we speak of having a "calling" or vocation. As Jung noted, "To have vocation means in the original sense *to be addressed by a voice.*"

Inner voices also express themselves in actual language. The famous "daimon" of Socrates may have been an experience of this type. Socrates told of an inner voice (which he attributed to a spirit guardian) that periodically forbade him from putting himself into dangerous situations. Mahatma Gandhi described an advisory voice, which once told him: "You are on the right track, move neither to your left, nor right, but keep to the straight and narrow."

While the inner voice often arises spontaneously, it has also been sought. As the voice is autonomous, it cannot be compelled to occur. But various procedures have been devised in attempts to invite the hidden source to speak. Seeking the inner voice has played a part in alternative reality traditions. For instance, in the 17th century Martin Rulands (quoted in Fabricius) encouraged the devotees of ALCHEMY to practice meditation, which he defined as "an internal talk of one person with another who is invisible, as in the invocation of the Deity, or communion with one's self, or with one's Good Angel." Several schools of modern psychotherapy suggest that people cultivate an ability to attend to the flow of inner experience, merely listening to one's thoughts without trying to cause or change them. Autonomous contents, such as inner voices, may be detected and even engaged in dialogue; "talking to yourself" in this fashion can produce insights into personal issues, practitioners report.

Little research has been conducted on the inner voices of those who are not suffering from mental disorders. Heery analyzed the accounts of 30 normal subjects who had inner voice experiences. She found that the reports tended to fall into three categories. In some cases, inner voices seemed to express aspects of the person that had become disconnected from ordinary consciousness, and that were striving to be reintegrated. The second category included voices that gave guidance regarding personal growth and fulfillment. A third type of voice, reported only by people who regularly practiced meditation, tried to guide the person toward a spiritual view of life, of "the I being part of a larger process."

For further reading: Heery; Jung; Raphael-Staude; Sedman.

insects By far the most numerous multicellular animals on this planet, insects rarely attract people's attention unless they are pestering us or eating our crops. When passing through a region of high electrical activity, such as a storm front or an area in which crystalline rocks create a piezoelectric effect, insects can become luminous. By a process similar to that which produces ST. ELMO'S FIRE, pointed structures on the insects' exoskeletons attract concentrations of electricity. The current is discharged into the air, causing tiny flares. Callahan and Mankin demonstrated this phenomenon in the laboratory—photographs of predatory stink bugs placed in an electric field show brilliant discharges of red, blue and green light.

Insects sometimes travel in swarms, up to 16 miles long and 64 miles wide. A swarm flying into an electrically charged area could suddenly become visible as a humming cloud of millions of glowing specks. As it leaves the charged region, the swarm would disappear from view. It has been suggested that some reports of UFO ENCOUNTERs might have been sightings of electrified bugs. Two common features of UFO accounts—the instant appearance and disappearance of the object, and the disruption of electromagnetic devices such as radio and television during the encounter—are consistent with this theory.

See also GEOPHYSICAL INFLUENCES.

For further reading: Callahan and Mankin; Sachs.

intelligence Disbelievers in the paranormal often regard believers as unintelligent. Very few studies have examined the relationship between anomalous beliefs and performance on intelligence tests. Several researchers have noted that people who score low on IQ tests tend to be more superstitious. Jones, Russell and Nickel reported that *high* IQ scores were associated with greater levels of global paranormal belief. Thus, there is little evidence to support this common prejudice among paranormal skeptics.

See also Appendix; CREATIVITY; EDUCATION; REASONING SKILLS.

For further reading: Irwin (1993); Jones, Russell and Nickel.

invisible presence The uncanny feeling that one is not alone is familiar to many. Nelson's (1989) Australian survey found that 36% of the respondents had "felt the presence of someone who was not there in a physical way." Generally, this sensation occurs when one is unaccompanied and thus cut off from the reassurance of others that there are no such things as invisible beings.

Conditions of quiet and darkness permit one to detect faint stimuli that are ordinarily masked; these are interpreted in accord with a person's expectations and fears. Thus, in environments with a reputation for invisible presences, such as an abandoned house or a graveyard, one's worries can transform innocuous sights and sounds into hints of hidden menace.

The sense of presence can precede the onset of a more dramatic experience, such as seeing an APPARITION. When an invisible presence is felt upon awakening from sleep, it may well be a HALLUCINATION produced in the HYPNOPOMPIC STATE. If a presence is felt to be friendly, the individual might enjoy the feeling and invite the presence back for further visits. In this way, an invisible presence could turn into an IMAGINARY COMPANION.

Mountaineers are especially prone to reporting invisible presences. "Altitude sickness," oxygen deprivation caused by failure to adapt to the thin air in high places, predisposes the brain to play such a trick. In some remote areas, the combination of isolation, silence, altitude and expectancy based on folklore create nearly irresistable conditions for the experience of invisible presences. For instance, Reed described:

> the 'giant spectre' of Ben Macdhui (4296 feet), the highest of the Cairngorm peaks in Scotland. This particular legend is of quite recent origin, dating back only to the late 1920s when a story related by a veteran climber and respected scientist reached the newspapers. Professor N.J. Collie, F.R.S., had recalled when he felt he could 'hear' footsteps in the snow as though somebody or 'something' was accompanying him. The feeling became so overwhelming that he fled from the peak. Since then the invisible 'thing' has stalked many lonely walkers over the snowy, featureless top of Macdhui and among its vast cliffs and desolate lochans.

Some people are more prone than others to sense invisible presences. Persinger reported that individuals who have unusual metabolic activity in the temporal lobe of the brain's right hemisphere are more likely to report a history of encountering invisible beings. He suggested that aspects of a person's own sense of self are generated in this brain region; when it becomes unusually active, the self-image of the right hemisphere intrudes upon the left hemisphere, which interprets it as the presence of an unseen external entity.

A common reaction to an unnerving sense of presence is to make noise, by whistling or humming a tune. The person thus drowns out the faint sounds that can be elaborated into frightful stirrings and provides a reminder of the ordinary world in which people are not snatched by unseen creatures. It is interesting that we take invisible presences seriously enough to feel fear; yet we deliberately increase our vulnerability by trying to ignore possible warning sounds. Such paradoxical behavior suggests that people who sense invisible presences are caught between mental sets representing incompatible world views: a reality in which unseen spirits can inflict harm; and a universe in which such beings are harmless figments of the imagination.

For **further reading:** P. Nelson; Persinger (1993); Reed (1988).

Isakower phenomenon   During the transition between wakefulness and sleep—the HYPNA-GOGIC STATE—some people have reported an impression of a round or amorphous shape that seems to loom momentarily in front of their eyes and then recede. Psychiatrist Otto Isakower regarded the experience as an infantile memory of the mother's breast; more likely, it is a type of ENTOPTIC PHENOMENON. It has been suggested that the Isakower phenomenon could be responsible for some accounts of apparitions or UFO occupants appearing at one's bedside.

For further reading: Isakower.

jamais vu   This French phrase, meaning literally "never seen," refers to a disorder of recognition—the perception of a familiar object, accompanied by the feeling that one has never before encountered it. Jamais vu is the opposite of the more common déjà vu, in which a novel experience seems intensely familiar.

Jamais vus can occur suddenly and spontaneously; they can also be induced rather easily. If one repeatedly says a well-known word, such as one's own name, the connection between the sound and meaning of the word soon becomes "overloaded." For a short period, the word fails to evoke the meaning and registers in the mind as a meaningless grouping of syllables. Many people have noted that if they stare intently at the reflection of their own face in a mirror, under a dim light, they eventually cease to recognize themselves; although the facial features may not appear to alter, the face in the mirror no longer seems to be their own. Some reincarnationists believe that this technique allows them to see their faces in previous lives.

In some cases jamais vus may occur when a familiar setting or person has changed slightly, as when an old friend has changed her hair color, or a single book has been inserted upside down in a bookcase. We may not be able to identify the altered detail, but we notice that *something* is different; unrecognition may pervade everything we experience at that moment. The normal electrical activity of the brain can be disrupted, either by neurological illnesses like EPILEPSY, or by brief misfirings of nerve cells in the brain. These disturbances can confuse the relation between perception and recognition, causing déjà vus; similar processes may be responsible for some jamais vus.

In jamais vu the feeling of unrecognition is false. One might conclude, however, that the feeling is correct—the supposedly well-known object actually is novel to us. Some have concluded, on the basis of jamais vu, that their spouse has been replaced by a clever replica. This error is known as ILLUSION DES SOSIES.

See also CRYPTOMNESIA; PRESQUE VU.
For further reading: Reed (1988).

jet lag syndrome   After a long journey across several time zones, many travelers crave a good sleep. Upon awakening from their first rest at their destination, some people experience an episode of paralysis, accompanied by auditory and visual HALLUCINATIONs. The stress of travel is thought to disturb the body's regulation of its normal sleep/wake cycle. The symptoms of the jet lag syndrome may be an invasion of wakefulness by the sleep stage known as REM sleep, which features paralysis and vivid dreams.

See also HYPNOPOMPIC STATE.

jhana   One of the most important types of meditative state mentioned in the literature of Buddhism, "jhana" in the Pali language is the equivalent of the Sanskrit *dhyana,* the Chinese *ch'an* and the Japanese *zen.* A jhana is a state of unusually concentrated attention. The term is sometimes translated as "absorption" or "trance."

In Buddhism, concentration is not developed for its own sake, but as a tool for reaching the goal of ENLIGHTENMENT. This supreme achievement is based on cultivating awareness through meditation practice. One of the essential tools of meditative attainment in Buddhism is SHAMATHA, or calm abiding. The practice of the jhanas exercises the faculty of shamatha; the meditator is instructed to develop the ability to run through the jhanas as if they were musical scales, in order to become a virtuoso of consciousness. In addition, attainment of the jhanas is said to combat certain disordered emotional conditions which pose obstacles to spiritual progress.

The early Buddhist writings identify varying numbers of jhanas; most commonly, eight or nine are listed. The first five jhanas differ from each other with respect to the condition of the meditator's consciousness; in each of the second four jhanas, the factors of consciousness are identical, but the objects on which the meditator focusses are different. The distinction between the two sets of jhanas has led modern historians to suggest that originally they were separate meditation systems of non- Buddhist origin. If so, they must have been combined very early in Buddhist history, perhaps by the Buddha himself.

In order to begin the practice of the jhanas, the meditator can choose to focus on any object, internal or external; the classical texts list objects that have specific effects in addition to serving merely as targets for concentration. Focusing on a rotting corpse, for instance, understandably tends to nullify uncontrollable lust.

Prior to attaining the sharp concentration of the first jhana, a preliminary stage, known as "access concentration," has been noted. In this state of consciousness, the mind is dominated, but not filled, with the object of meditation. The meditator remains aware of the external world, bodily sensations and the ordinary background chatter of the mind. Sometimes, blissful feelings, alterations in body image, and visions of light are reported.

In the first jhana, the mind rests continuously on the meditation object. This state of absorption is unstable at first, lasting only for a moment; with practice it can be held for long periods. According to the Buddhist psychological system called ABHIDHARMA, the first jhana is characterized by the presence of five mental factors: initial thought about the object; sustained reasoning about the object; rapture; happiness; and one-pointed concentration. The first two factors are not the same as the undisciplined thoughts that are found in ordinary experiences, but a calm sense of comprehending the meditation object through reasoning. Rapture is an intense delight, which can manifest as surges of joy or pleasurable vibrations in the body; happiness is a quieter, more sustained feeling. These five factors sweep awareness clean of laziness, doubt, hatred, worry and greed. Mastery of the first jhana is required for the attainment of the supernormal powers called ABHIJNAS.

By noting the superiority of the first jhana over the less focussed states of ordinary consciousness, meditators can propel themselves into deeper modes of concentration. In the second jhana, the factor of initial thought about the object ceases. The energy of this factor is absorbed by one-pointed concentration, sharpening the meditator's awareness of the object. In a similar fashion, the meditator can move through the next three jhanas: In the third jhana, sustained reasoning ceases; rapture is eliminated in the fourth jhana; and in the fifth jhana, happiness disappears, leaving only a sharp one-pointed concentration, focused, laser-like, on the object of meditation.

One cannot be conscious without the presence of concentration to some degree; so the four higher jhanas also possess the extreme concentration achieved in the fifth jhana. In the higher jhanas, the objects of meditation are "formless." The nature of these objects is difficult to comprehend by anyone other than advanced meditators. In order to develop the sixth jhana, the meditator imagines the meditation object expanding until it is infinitely large; this allows the practitioner to focus on "the infinity of space." In the seventh jhana, the meditator's own consciousness becomes identified with space; the object then becomes "the infinity of consciousness." The eighth jhana emphasizes that space itself has no shape or form; space is not a thing, and this quality gives the object of the jhana its name—"no-thing-ness." In the most refined jhana, the ninth, the meditator's consciousness has turned away even from the awareness of the absence of form, to "the ultimate limit of perception." This state is not unconsciousness, but rather is beyond description in terms of whether the meditator is or is not perceiving anything; hence another title for the ninth jhana, "neither perception nor nonperception."

Although the jhanas are said to be capable of destroying the hindrances to enlightenment mentioned above, they cannot uproot the seeds of these hindrances in the mind. Because of this limitation, the jhanas by themselves cannot produce the liberation from suffering that is the goal of Buddhism. The shamatha which is strengthened by jhana practice must be coupled with special insight (VIPASSANA) in order to reach that lofty goal. Unlike non-Buddhist practitioners of jhana, the Buddhist who has mastered shamatha and vipassana can launch into the state called NIRODHA from the ninth jhana. In this condition, which reportedly can last for up to seven days, all mental activity ceases, and even bodily functions slow to the point where they are undetectable.

See also ABSORPTION.

For further reading: Buddhaghosa; Goleman; Govinda (1974).

jivan-mukti In Hinduism, the ultimate spiritual state is called "release while alive," or jivan-mukti. Through the development of profound insight concerning the nature of the Self, one can be released from bondage to illusion, and the fear, desire and hatred that arise from ignorance. The sublime state of awareness that characterizes jivan-mukti is SAHAJ SAMADHI. Jivan-mukti is contrasted with VIDEHA-MUKTI, or "release at death."

jobutsu In Japanese this term literally means "becoming a Buddha"; it refers to the attainment of complete ENLIGHTENMENT in Zen Buddhism. According to the Zen tradition, in a sense one cannot *become* a Buddha, because all sentient beings already possess Buddha-nature. However, few beings are aware of their enlightened nature. Achieving full awareness of the Buddha-nature is jobutsu.

joshin In the practice of ZAZEN, the central meditative activity of Zen Buddhism, the meditator attempts to transcend the feeling that he or she is separate from the object of meditation. If one is meditating on the breath, one merges with the breath. The state of effortless concentration in which the self is not distinguished from the object is known as joshin, which means "a collected mind."

Kabbalah   Kabbalah is the central mystical tradition of Judaism. Over the centuries, kabbalists developed and borrowed a range of practices for inducing unusual states of awareness. The goal of these states was to gain knowledge of God, or even a vision of Him. Some kabbalists even dared to aspire to a complete union with the divine being; these mystics were usually declared heretics.

The roots of Kabbalah may be found in Jewish mystical schools of the first centuries A.D. Members of these groups used visualization and chanting to trigger OUT OF BODY EXPERIENCEs, during which they would journey through the heavens to glimpse God's throne. In the 12th and 13th centuries, the classical Kabbalistic tradition appeared in Spain and southern France. While many of the kabbalistic texts from this time were mainly philosophical, they hint at meditation practices borrowed from the Moslem mystics known as Sufis.

The most renowned character of the classic period was the Spaniard Abraham Abulafia, who lived in the late 13th century. Abulafia became notorious for proclaiming himself the messiah and for attempting to convert Pope Nicholas III to Judaism, for which effort he narrowly escaped with his life. He also outraged more conservative kabbalists with his innovative and open teaching of techniques for changing consciousness. Abulafia authored 26 meditation manuals. His primary method was the "Way of Names," which involved visualizing, intoning and manipulating the letters in various names of God while practicing certain postures.

After the expulsion of the Jews from Spain in 1492, many Jewish refugees settled in Palestine. There, kabbalists gathered in the town of Safed, where the tradition developed further. The Hasidic movement, which originated in the Ukraine in the early 18th century and spread throughout the Jewish communities of eastern Europe, was a popular form of Kabbalah. Jewish intellectuals of the 1800s tended to reject Kabbalah as superstition. During the present century, however, interest in kabbalistic teachings is again growing among Jews.

The influence of Kabbalah has extended beyond the boundaries of Judaism. As early as the 15th century, scholars of the Italian Renaissance tried to adopt kabbalistic ideas and practices into a Christian world view. Elements of the Kabbalah significantly enriched the occult traditions of ALCHEMY and RITUAL MAGIC.

For further reading: Hoffman; Idel (1988); Kaplan; Scholem.

kaivalya   The goal of the Hindu meditation system called RAJA YOGA is liberation from bondage to mental habits, attachments and aversions. The state of complete freedom is called *kaivalya*—a Sanskrit term literally meaning "aloneness." Freedom is thus designated because it is achieved by disentangling the real self from its identification with mental contents. When one realizes that he or she is not concepts, memories, roles or possessions, but rather pure awareness (*purusa*) itself, a person can isolate this awareness from the constant churning of mental machinery (*buddhi*). Then, one is no longer subject to the pervasive suffering of ordinary experience.

In kaivalya, awareness stands alone. The mind can continue to operate, forming thoughts, images and emotions. These shapings of buddhi are illuminated by the light of purusa, but the source of illumination—the self—remains unperturbed. Yoga writings indeed compare the isolated Self to "a flame in a windless place."

Kaivalya is often used as a synonym for MOKSHA, the supreme spritual achievement in Hinduism. Some writers state that kaivalya refers to liberation that does not involve God, whereas moksha is the experience of liberation through God.

The attainment of kaivalya is only possible after the meditator has ascended through the range of concentrative states (SAMADHIs), refining concentration until the mind is stilled (SAMPRAJNATA SAMADHI) and even the seeds of future actions are destroyed (ASAMPRAJNATA SAMADHI). The possibility of kaivalya is directly experienced in the visionary state known as VIVEKA-KHYATI. This condition must not be mistaken for total "aloneness," but can serve as a motivating factor to spur the meditator's efforts toward the goal.

For further reading: Feuerstein (1989, 1990); Friedrichs; Zaehner.

kaleidoscopic sun   The sight of the solar disc trembling in the sky, then multiplying, while radiating beams of various colors "seems well beyond the capacity of atmospheric optical theory to explain," according to Corliss (1977). Reports of kaleidoscopic suns are rare. The following account from Ireland, cited by Corliss, is typical:

> A friend shouting to me to hurry out, I saw the sun behaving in a most unusual fashion; now surrounded by bright red, flashing rays in all directions, then changing to yellow in which the body of the sun, though more clearly visible, appeared to dance and shift about here and there in a radius of about 5 degrees; again changing to green, the rays flashing as in the red—all these changes taking place in less time than it takes to write. . . . Of all the beauties seen I should think the quickly changing mock suns the most beautiful as they flashed here and there faster than it was possible to count them.

Kaleidoscopic suns might be caused by the refraction of sunlight as it passes through sheets of airborne ice crystals. Alternatively, the light might be bent by encounters with AERIAL BLOBs, air pockets of varying temperatures, densities and moisture contents.

Kaleidoscopic suns, as described in the meteorological literature, closely resemble the dancing sun phenomena associated with the apparitions of FATIMA and MEDJUGORJE. In the Fatima case, it would be a truly astonishing coincidence if the unusual atmospheric conditions that produce the kaleidoscopic effect coincided, in time and place, with the "miracle" predicted by a vision of the Blessed Virgin Mary several months previously. If the dancing sun of Medjugorje is actually a kaleidoscopic sun caused by atmospheric refraction, it is unclear why the effect recurs at the site of the Marian visions, and why only some of those present report seeing it.

See also MOCK SUN.

For further reading: Corliss (1977, 1984).

kensho   A Japanese term meaning "seeing one's own true nature," kensho refers to the experience of ENLIGHTENMENT in Zen Buddhism. One's true nature is that of a Buddha, but very few people realize this; instead, people identify with various roles and labels, such as family status, nationality, gender or profession. When one is led, through the practice of meditation, to the realization that one is Buddha, the experience is so removed from normal assumptions that it may be very difficult to describe or even to recognize it for what it is. For this reason, when Zen practitioners have powerful experiences, they discuss them with a Zen master, who is said to have the ability to discern the authentic kensho. The term "kensho" is technically a synonym for another Zen word, SATORI. However, it is customary that initial "breakthrough" experiences—glimpses of one's Buddha nature—are called kensho, whereas more complete realizations are designated satori. Michael Diener has compared the attainment of enlightenment to breaking through a wall; kensho is a small hole in the wall, and satori is knocking the wall down.

For further reading: Diener; Kapleau.

kinesthetic hallucination False sensations of the body's skeletal muscles. This category of HALLUCINATIONs includes experiencing movements of limbs that are not actually in motion. An extreme type of kinesthetic hallucination occurs among sufferers of phantom limb syndrome—they may feel the movement of body parts that have been amputated.

See also BODY IMAGE DISTORTION; PHANTOM LIMB SENSATIONS.

koan A koan is a word, phrase, question or story used as an object of meditation in Zen Buddhism, especially in the Rinzai school. The aim of koan practice is to "solve" the koan; however, the solution cannot be reached by the use of reason. Koans are not riddles, but nonrational problems designed to frustrate ordinary methods of problem-solving. The mind is thereby propelled into unusual modes of perception, aiding the practitioner toward ENLIGHTENMENT. Zen master Philip Kapleau described the koan as "an exceptionally wieldy scalpel for extirpating from the deepest unconscious the malignant growth of 'I' and 'not-I' which poisons the Mind's inherent purity and impairs its fundamental wholeness."

The koan is normally assigned to the meditator by the master after the student has developed some skill in mental concentration. While the range of possible koans is limitless, most koans in use today are taken from one of several collections. The best known of these is the *Mumonkan* of Zen master Mumon Ekai. Famous koans include: "What is the sound of one hand clapping?"; "What did your face look like before your parents were born?"; and the syllable "Mu."

Initially, the meditator will probably try to solve the koan using familiar patterns of thought. Each attempted solution is presented to the Zen master, who judges its quality. However, habitual approaches inevitably fail, being compared to "trying to smash one's fist through an iron wall." Again and again, answers are rejected, and the meditator is admonished to practice more intensely. This painful struggle is valuable; as the practitioner despairs of finding the answer through known methods, he or she is forced to rely on possibilities arising from spontaneous levels of the mind. At these levels, one is completely free, and becoming fully conscious of this freedom is the goal of Zen.

Eventually, the disciplined meditator will lose the feeling of trying to solve the koan and will experience a sense of merging with it—the "I" of the meditator and the "not-I" of the koan disappear. An answer acceptable to the master may then occur. This moment is often described as a spiritual breakthrough, the enlightenment experience called KENSHO. The solution to a koan could take any form—a statement, a gesture or laughter. But it must convey to the master that the student has made contact with his or her own enlightened nature.

Solution of a koan does not necessarily indicate that the meditator is fully enlightened. In most cases a series of koans is assigned in order to deepen and stabilize the spiritual awareness. One 20th century Zen master, Yasutani, required his students to answer a sequence of 546 koans before their training was pronounced complete.

For further reading: Diener; Kapleau; Shibayama.

kokushittsu A Japanese phrase, literally meaning "bucket of black paint." In Zen Buddhism kokushittsu refers to the state of darkness, doubt and futility that often occurs prior to a spiritual breakthrough (SATORI). The Zen student in this condition is abandoning his or her most cherished illusions, but has not yet glimpsed the treasure of realization.

See also ALCHEMY; DARK NIGHT OF THE SOUL.

kundalini "Snake" or "serpent power" in Sanskrit, this term originally referred to a type of meditation practiced in Hindu TANTRA. Recently, kundalini has become a label for a variety of experiences that involve sensations of energy moving vertically in the body.

According to the tantric tradition in Hinduism, spiritual realization comes about in the union of consciousness and life-energy, symbolized by the sexual embrace of the deities Shiva and Shakti. In each individual, Shiva is said to be located atop the head, while Shakti, in the form of a sleeping snake, lies coiled at the base of the spine. The task of the tantric meditator is to awaken the kundalini. This energy will rise through the body along the central energy channel, experienced as a surge of energy ascending the spinal column. At the crown of the head, the aroused Shakti merges with the essence of consciousness. Specialized techniques of breathing, body posture, visualization and recitation of MANTRAs are taught in order to stimulate the kundalini.

Along the pathway of the kundalini's ascent are located the CHAKRAS, psychic structures that correspond to aspects of human personality. Various schools enumerate various numbers and kinds of chakras. As the snake of power rises, it stimulates each chakra. The aim of the tantric practitioner is to prevent the kundalini from falling below the level of the heart chakra; the lower chakras represent self-centered appetites, whereas the higher ones embody spiritual aspirations.

Experiences associated with the kundalini in tantric Hinduism are diverse. Classical texts state that Shakti's energy climbs the central channel in one of five ways: creeping like an ant scaling a tree trunk; like a fish swimming in an ocean; like a monkey that leaps from the spinal base to the head in a single bound; in the manner of a bird, hopping from branch to branch; or undulating, like a snake. Metaphors used to describe the sensation of kundalini frequently combine liquid and luminous qualities, in phrases such as "flowing light" or "liquid fire."

Other experiences reported by kundalini practitioners range through pronounced alterations in thinking, visions, BODY IMAGE DISTORTIONS, OUT OF BODY EXPERIENCEs, amplified sex drive, hypersensitivity, motor AUTOMATISMs and pain. Traditionally, these phenomena are taken to indicate the spiritual immaturity of the experient; when consciousness is perfectly united to the life force, one is not disturbed by uncontrolled experiences such as these. A famous 20th century practitioner of kundalini meditation, Gopi Krishna, reported that he was tormented for 12 years following his first kundalini experience by a barrage of agonizing psychological problems before he was able to stabilize the energies he had awakened. Eventually, he claimed, he became "a pool of consciousness always aglow with light," able to write prolifically about his experiences.

Psychiatrist Lee Sannella collected accounts of "kundalini-type" experiences that have occurred spontaneously. Typical is the following:

> Then a tingling started to move from her pelvis up her back to her neck. She began to see light inside her head. She was amazed to find that she could see this light all the way down her spine as well. The energy and tingling moved over her forehead and became focused under her chin. She felt as if there were a hole in the top of her head. Sleep was very difficult, and for the next six weeks meditation was the only thing that helped her. She felt that if she did not meditate, the heat flowing in her body would grow so intense as to damage her. Other people could feel excessive heat when they touched her lower back.

Sannella and others in the TRANSPERSONAL PSYCHOLOGY movement have suggested that the kundalini practices of Hindu Tantra may be a culturally specific way of attempting to harness a universally occurring phenomenon. When people are at a period of crisis in their lives, they may be especially prone to feel unusual surges of energy along the axis of the body. These feelings correspond to the breaking down of old expectations and habits. Such sensations, and the experiences that typically accompany them, can be very frightening, and could even be taken as symptoms of PSYCHOSIS. In fact, some transpersonal psychologists argue, the spontaneous kundalini experiences signal an opportunity for tremendous spiritual growth, not merely a collapse of ordinary functioning. In 1980, Christina Grof established the Spiritual Emergence Network in California to serve as a resource and support system for individuals undergoing such crises.

See also NAROPA, SIX YOGAS OF.

For further reading: Avalon; Grof and Grof; Krishna; Sannella.

levitation   The belief that material bodies can hover or fly in the air without ordinary means of propulsion is primordial and widespread among human cultures. There is little doubt that the nucleus of the belief in levitation consists of experiences—witnessed acts of apparent levitation and personal experiences of one's own body floating in the air.

Since prehistoric times, expectations of levitation have featured as an aspect of spiritual practices. Among the shamans of various cultures, it is thought that the journey to the spirit world can involve the actual transportation of the body; shamans of the Tungus people employ an assistant who firmly grasps a chain wrapped around the shaman's waist during rituals, in order to prevent the shaman's body from being sucked into the sky.

Stories of levitation figure prominently in historical religious traditions. In Eastern faiths the ability to levitate is said to be available to spiritual adepts as one of the psychic powers or SIDDHIS. The most ancient religious document in India, the *Rig Veda,* seems to describe a deliberately induced levitation experience:

> These sages, swathed in wind, put dirty red tatters on. When gods get in them, they ride with the rush of the wind. . . . He sails through the air, seeing appearances spread out below. The sage, this god and that his friend, friendly to all that's well done.

Stories of levitation are found very early in Christian history. St. Paul himself wrote of a trip to heaven, but he was unable to decide whether it was an OUT OF BODY EXPERIENCE or a levitation. An ancient legend recounts how the magician Simon Magus was able to fly through the air with the aid of demons. The prayers of St. Peter banished the devilish helpers, and Simon crashed to his death.

Over the centuries, tales of saintly levitation were so common that the phenomenon was acknowledged as a CHARISM, or possible sign of holiness, by the Roman Catholic church. Unlike the stories from Eastern traditions, the levitations of western sages were generally portrayed as spontaneous. Deliberately to seek such indications of grace would be viewed as arrogant, so the accounts often emphasize the surprise, and even the resistance, of the uplifted individual. A typical description of the experience was written by Sister Maria Villani, a 17th century Italian nun (quoted by Murphy):

> On one occasion when I was in my cell I was conscious of a new experience. I felt myself seized and ravished out of my senses, so powerfully that I found myself lifted up completely by the very soles of my feet, just as the magnet draws up a fragment of iron, but with a gentleness that was marvelous and most delightful. At first I felt much fear, but afterwards I remained in the greatest possible contentment and joy of spirit. Though I was quite beside myself, still, in spite of that, I knew that I was raised some distance above the earth, my whole body being suspended for a considerable space of time.

The best known historical case of purported levitation is that of St. Joseph of Copertino. Joseph was known during his life in the 17th century as "the flying friar." Over 100 eyewitness accounts of his spontaneous levitations were recorded. Many of these incidents happened in public places and were attested by multiple witnesses. His case was personally explored by Prosper Lambertini, who later became Pope Benedict XIV, the man who codified strict standards for the investigation of alleged miracles. Lambertini was deeply impressed by Joseph, for he decreed the flying friar's beatification—the first step toward full canonization, or declaration of sainthood. Dingwall summarized one of the reports concerning Joseph:

> one day a priest, Antonio Chiarello, who was walking with him in the kitchen-garden, remarked how beautiful was the heaven which God had made. Thereupon Joseph, as if these words were an invitation to him from above, uttered a shriek, sprang from the ground and flew into the air, only coming to rest on the top of an olive tree where he remained in a kneeling position for half an hour. It was noticed with wonder at the time that the branch on which he rested only shook slightly as if a bird had been sitting upon it. It appears that in this case Joseph came to his senses whilst still on the tree, as the Rev. Antonio had to go to fetch a ladder to get him down.

Not all reports of levitation were associated with holiness in the eyes of the Catholic church. TRANSVECTION, or flight to the WITCHES' SABBATH, was thought to be a reality by many church leaders during the Renaissance and Reformation periods. It is possible that some individuals did have flying experiences, caused by the absorption of hallucinogenic substances contained in the WITCHES' OINTMENT.

Levitation reports became a major theme in the seances of Spiritualism, a movement that had millions of followers during the 19th and early 20th centuries. In the darkness of the seance room, objects would be observed floating in the air, supposedly elevated by the hands of the spirits; in many cases, hidden devices or accomplices were responsible for the fraudulent effects.

The most renowned report of a levitation in the literature on Spiritualism involved the medium D.D. Home. During a seance one evening in London, attended by three highly respected English gentlemen, Home announced that he would leave the room, float out of a window of an adjacent room, and re-enter the seance room through its window. The witnesses all stated that, after Home left the room, they could hear him in the next room; shortly afterward, he appeared, hovering in the air, beyond the window of the seance room, through which he entered. Some have viewed this episode as evidence for the physical reality of levitation, because of the credibility of the three witnesses and because throughout his spectacular mediumistic career Home was never caught employing trickery. Skeptics have suggested a host of non-paranormal explanations. Home could have jumped to the windowsill of the seance room, or conveyed himself there with ropes; or, he might have crept back into the dimly lit seance room unobserved and perched in front of the window *inside* the room, creating the appearance of floating outside; hallucination and blackmail of the witnesses have also been suggested.

Claims and investigations of levitation have continued into the late 20th century. In 1977, the Transcendental Meditation (TM) organization announced that it had developed a levitation training program, based on traditional Hindu yoga techniques. Photographs of alleged levitators were produced, showing cross-legged people seemingly floating several inches off the floor. Analysis suggested that the depicted individuals had simply propelled themselves upwards using leg and arm muscles, and were hovering momentarily at the apogee of their jump. TM leaders have consistently refused to demonstrate their astonishing powers to researchers.

Benson investigated reports that Tibetan Buddhist lamas continue to practice the age-old meditations that granted levitatory abilities. Directed by the Dalai Lama to two masters, he witnessed an activity in which a meditator would snap into a cross-legged position while standing upright and crash heavily onto the ground. There was, however, "no floating or hovering." Benson queried the lamas as to:

whether it was possible to stay up in the air. The younger monk said his great-grandfather had been able to do so, but he knew of no one doing it today. I then asked the older man if he knew of anyone who could carry out such a feat. He said it was an ability that was present many hundreds of years ago, but not today. I asked the old monk if he would like to levitate, and with a twinkle in his eyes, he responded, 'There is no need. We now have airplanes.'

Most people today are familiar with levitation through the stage acts of magicians. These performances are, of course, tricks—the apparently levitating body is supported by a concealed platform, rods or wires. The techniques for creating this illusion were imported to the West from India in the early 19th century.

The experiential basis for the venerable belief in levitation probably includes phenomena involving no movement of the physical body. The drastically altered bodily sensations which are interpreted by some as an out of body experience might be construed by others as literal levitation. Feelings of lightness or floating occur to many people in a variety of contexts. Horton reported that eight out of 30 subjects who entered deeply relaxed states experienced an illusion of levitation. One subject clung to her chair, and another abruptly ended the exercise, in order to prevent liftoff!

Obviously, interpretations of bodily sensations cannot account for eyewitness reports of others' levitations. If such things actually occur, they would be considered as instances of PSYCHOKINESIS. However, the anecdotes concerning the sages, saints and mediums are all subject to many factors—from misperception and undetected fraud to inaccuracies of memory—that render them unreliable as evidence for extraordinary phenomena.

For further reading: Benson; Dingwall; Irwin (1989); Murphy.

lightning   Among the many electrical processes that stir the Earth's atmosphere, lightning is the most common and familiar. The range of lightning's behavior is greater than most people realize, and encounters with the rarer forms can be startling. Lightning is caused by the development between two regions of largely different electric charges. Typically, this difference evolves between storm-disturbed air and the ground beneath it. Driven to equalize the concentration of electrons, a concentrated burst of electricity flows rapidly between the regions, which is visible as a lightning bolt.

The actual discharge occurs in stages that happen too quickly for the human mind to discriminate between them. The first, a downward stroke called the leader, is a high voltage surge lasting about a millionth of a second. Usually it is invisible, but audible—it heats the air in its path so rapidly that a shock wave radiates outward, sensed by the ear as thunder. The initial stroke is immediately followed by an upward flow of current, which retraces the path of the downstroke. Atoms along the edge of the electrical channel are excited into a streak of light, producing the display detected by the eye.

Most lightning discharges occur between differently charged areas within clouds; these sparks are normally veiled from sight, but their thunder may be heard. Occasionally, observers have noted "rocket lightning"—discharges flowing upward from cloud tops into the upper atmosphere. The upper terminal regions of rocket lightning are invisible, and their formation is poorly understood.

Even more mysterious are reports of horizontal discharges. Sometimes, lightning erupts sideways out of a storm cloud, and can carve a path for several miles through the air before finally grounding; at that distance, local inhabitants may be enjoying clear skies and be unaware of the nearby storm when suddenly visited by the discharge. Electrons flow toward the closest "sink" for them to fill; and this path typically carries them between the most adjacent points of earth and cloud. In cases of horizontal lightning, unseen aerial processes, likely involving airborne particles with conductive properties, are involved.

Horizontal discharges do not account for all reports of "bolts from the blue"—in many instances of lightning during clear weather, all storm activities are far too distant to have produced the discharge. In such cases some unknown process must have created an electrically charged region in the air without the concentration of moisture that usually accompanies it.

The paths chosen by the flowing electrons are sometimes so odd that they have been labeled lightning's "pranks." Gaddis noted that:

> Bolts have fused metallic objects such as zippers, necklaces, earrings, and watch bands on human bodies without otherwise seriously harming the persons. They have popped bags of popcorn, cleared clogged drains in kitchen sinks, and turned iron chains into solid rods. One bolt split a forty-foot tree and ripped away three sides from a baby carriage beneath the tree, yet left the infant occupant unharmed. . . . [Lightning discharges] have pulled keys out of locks and knitting needles from the hands of women, melted shot in a gun without igniting the powder, and thrown persons out of bed unharmed while the bed was broken into pieces.

Corliss described a house struck by lightning in Iowa, after which it was discovered that every other plate in a stack of 12 dinner plates had been shattered by the discharge.

The movement of electrons is always accompanied by a magnetic field. This field can mould the shape of lightning's discharge channel, even pinching it into segments. When this happens, a lightning bolt can break up into a string of disconnected glowing patches—a phenomenon called "bead lightning." Although the beads ordinarily last only momentarily, some researchers believe that, under some conditions, these luminous pellets could endure for extended periods, giving rise to sightings of BALL LIGHTNING. Many thousands of observers have reported electrified spheres floating through the air. Some of these entities have been photographed. Technically,

ball lightning is not lightning; it is not rapid electrical discharge, but a slowly discharging pocket of plasma.

See also AURORA; MOUNTAINTOP GLOW; ST. ELMO'S FIRE.

For further reading: Corliss (1982, 1994); Gaddis.

lilliputian hallucination Named after the tiny people in *Gulliver's Travels,* a type of VISUAL HALLUCINATION in which a person views small human figures. It can occur in a wide range of toxic drug reactions, neurological disorders and mental illnesses. Lilliputian hallucinations are the probable source of many old tales of encounters with the fairy folk. Anne Jeffries, a 17th century Cornish peasant, was seen on one occasion to suffer a seizure of some kind; when she recovered, she described how she had just been assaulted by a troop of little men. They had swarmed over her body, kissing her, before she was whisked to a palace and seduced by a fairy man, she recounted.

For further reading: Asaad; Briggs.

Loch Ness Monster Loch Ness is the largest freshwater lake in the British Isles. It is 24 miles long, over a mile across at its widest point and ranges in depth from 450 to nearly 1,000 feet. The waters of the Loch are rendered virtually opaque by suspended particles of peat. For at least the last 1,500 years, something strange has occasionally been seen to emerge from its depths. Today, the Loch Ness Monster is the best known of the world's CRYPTICS, or "impossible animals."

An account dating from 565 A.D. describes how St. Columba chastened a monster that had threatened a swimmer in Loch Ness. The historical truthfulness of the tale is dubious, of course, but it doubtless reflects a contemporary belief that the waters of the Loch harbored an uncanny presence. Over the following centuries, other sightings were made. But few people spent much time in the region until 1933.

In that year the shores of the Loch were cleared for a road. On April 14, Mr. and Mrs. John Mackay reported the first modern encounter with the monster; as they drove along the new road, they watched for about a minute as an enormous creature rolled and splashed in the Loch. Their story was published in the newspaper in nearby Inverness; and, before long, there were more sightings. From then until now, many thousands of visitors to Loch Ness have claimed glimpses of the monster.

Perhaps the most prolific reporter of sightings was Alex Campbell, who lived on the Loch and was responsible for regulating the salmon fishery there. Campbell published the following description of the beast, which typifies many others:

> It had a long, tapering neck, about 6 feet long, and a smallish head with a serpentine look about it, and a huge hump behind which I reckoned was about 30 feet long. It was turning its head constantly.

Usually, the monster is spotted in the water; sometimes, an unaccountable wake has been taken as a sign that something large was moving about just beneath the surface. There are also rare reports of the monster being met at night, wandering across the road on flippers.

Most of the eyewitness accounts of meetings with the monster are consistent with misidentifications of driftwood, birds, otters and boat wakes, amplified by the expectations of the witnesses. Expectations, however, cannot be photographed. One of the unique features of the Loch Ness phenomenon is the abundance of photographic and video evidence purporting to show the monster. The first photo was taken in 1933. The picture shows a blurry black line on the water's surface (which, as Randles pointed out, appears strangely like a swimming dog with a stick in its mouth).

The best-known Loch Ness Monster photograph was taken the following year. Robert Wilson, a respected English physician, released a picture to the press apparently showing the head and neck of a creature rising from the Loch. Decades later, analysis revealed that the object in the photo could not have been more than two feet long. An associate of Wilson who died in 1993 confessed on his deathbed to the hoax— the "monster" had been a toy submarine, fitted with a plastic head and neck.

Over the ensuing decades, a small gallery of images has been submitted by Loch visitors, showing the raised head or hump of the beast, with varying degrees of ambiguity. Some are evident frauds; others are likely blurry pictures of ordinary objects floating in the water.

One of the most impressive photos was taken by Anthony Shiels in May 1977. The neck of the creature rises above the water, bearing a head with distinct mouth and one visible eye. A computer enhancement analysis found that the object was partially transparent—water ripples behind the "creature" can be seen through the neck.

The first Loch Ness Monster video was shot in 1960. A small dark object moves across the Loch's surface, leaving a wake. Analysis of the footage by photographic experts at the Royal Air Force concluded that the object responsible for the effect was likely a living creature, and could have been up to 90 feet long. Their conclusions have been challenged by others, but they served to give some credibility to the continuing reports of monster encounters.

Since 1970, several scientific expeditions have combed the Loch for definitive proof of the monster's existence. While these efforts have failed to secure solid evidence, they have yielded enough tantalizing data to keep monster lovers hopeful. In 1972, an automatic underwater camera photographed what *could* be a flipper about 7 feet long. Another underwater camera took two interesting photos in 1975: a murky shape that *could* be a head; and another, perhaps the best evidence to date, that does look rather like a long neck attached to a bulbous body.

In recent years, Loch Ness has been subjected to ever more sophisticated scrutiny. In 1987, an armada of 20 sonar-equipped boats systematically swept the Loch and found no monsters. In 1992, researchers studying the Loch's geology and ecology took 7 million sonar depth readings, mapping the lake bed in detail. These efforts yielded some unexplained sonar contacts in the middle of the Loch, which some analysts feel may have been shoals of fish.

Believers in the reality of the Loch Ness Monster are challenged by the usual difficulties besetting cryptics. How could a breeding population of large animals survive in the Loch without being much more visible? Why have no bodies or bones ever been recovered? And what sort of animal could the monster be? The descriptions of witnesses do not correspond to any known living species. The monster's profile is similar to some animals thought to be long-extinct—the plesiosaur and the zeuglodon. But these creatures are thought to have died out 65 million years ago and 20 million years ago respectively. It is hard to fathom how either could have survived, unconfirmed, in Loch Ness to the present.

See also MOKELE-MBEMBE.

For further reading: Eberhart; Mackal (1976); Meurger and Gagnon.

locus of control A person who feels that the outcomes of events in life are usually determined by external forces beyond control is said to have an *external* locus of control; the belief that one's own abilities and decisions create most outcomes indicates an *internal* locus of control. Psychologists measure this trait using questionnaires. Several studies have examined the relationship between locus of control and paranormal beliefs. Individuals with an external locus of control are more likely to report general paranormal beliefs, as well as specific beliefs in spirits and cryptic animals. One study found that external locus was associated with belief in ESP, but another reported that people with an internal locus were more likely to hold ESP beliefs. External locus of control is also associated with low PSYCHOLOGICAL ADJUSTMENT.

See also Appendix; CONTROL NEEDS.

locutions The experience of divine illumination in the form of inner words or statements. Often, locutions are accompanied by VISIONs, which seem to be the source of the words. Locutions are included in the list of CHARISMs, or supernaturally originating phenomena recognized by the Roman Catholic church.

See also INNER VOICE.

Loudun nuns, possession of One of the best known instances of mass possession occurred at a convent in the French town of Loudun in 1633. It is likely that the incident began as a hoax. A local priest, Father Urbain Grandier, had made a disparaging remark about the powerful Cardinal Richelieu. The cardinal's aides, doubtless inspired by the mass possession of Aix-en-Provence earlier in the century, persuaded some nuns at the convent to simulate demonic possession and to accuse Grandier of witchcraft.

Several nuns, including the mother superior, Jeanne des Anges, soon began to display strange behaviors. These included convulsions, erotic movements, breath holding and blasphemous utterances. At Aix, a priest accused of sending demons to possess nuns had been burned to death. Sadly, the same end befell Grandier. His fate was sealed when, at his trial, the prosecutors presented as evidence a pact supposedly signed, not only by the accused, but also by several devils, including Lucifer and Beelzebub.

After Grandier's death at the stake, the unexpected happened. The possessed nuns were not cured, but became more bizarre in their actions. Witnesses recorded that they threw their heads from their chests to their backs very rapidly, as if their necks were broken. They performed seemingly impossible bodily contortions, while "Their tongues issued suddenly from their mouths, horribly swollen, black, hard, and covered with pimples." Sometimes the nuns were overtly sexual in their movements and speech—"their acts, both in exposing themselves and inviting lewd behaviour from those present, would have astonished the inmates of the lowest brothel in the country," noted one observer.

Evidently, what had been initiated as a political plot had developed its own momentum. The nuns' behavior undoubtedly served as an outlet for otherwise inexpressible erotic urges. They continued to receive a great deal of attention, the convent at Loudun virtually becoming a tourist attraction. In addition, they had been granted a pension to compensate for their suffering at the hands of the witch Grandier. When Cardinal Richelieu, seeing no further advantage to be gained, discontinued the pension, the nuns' behavior gradually returned to normal.

See also AIX-EN-PROVENCE NUNS, POSSESSION OF; AUXONNE NUNS, POSSESSION OF; LOUVIERS NUNS, POSSESSION OF.

For further reading: Huxley (1961); Robbins.

Louviers nuns, possession of This case was the third instance of the mass POSSESSION of nuns in France during the 17th century. The behavior of the nuns at Louviers were undoubtedly influenced by the widely known earlier cases, involving the nuns of AIX-EN-PROVENCE and LOUDUN.

Father Mathurin Picard served, seemingly without incident, as chaplain to the convent of Loudun between 1628 and his death in 1642. He was assisted by Father Thomas Boulle. Following the demise of Picard, some of the nuns began to display unusual behaviors. They would fall into convulsions, howl like animals and shout the names of demons. Possession was strongly suspected, and exorcists were called in.

Lengthy exorcisms, lasting up to four hours a day, were undertaken. The ceremonies were conducted in church. The spectacle of the possessed women struggling with the exorcists attracted crowds of onlookers. Gradually, investigators pieced together a weird tale from the utterances of the demoniacs. For decades, the convent had supposedly been the center of a secret cult led by Fathers Picard and Boulle and their predecessor, a Father David. The main practices of the cult were said to include nudity, all manner of sexual acts, performance of the Black Mass and the consumption of human flesh. Such activities attracted evil spirits, of course—one of the nuns described how she had been repeatedly raped by a cat with "a huge penis just like a man's."

Although the existence of a Satanic cult in Louviers at the time is highly unlikely, there may well have been a basis of truth in the claims of the nuns. There were Christian heresies in western Europe that promoted nudity. It is not impossible that the chaplains were involved with such beliefs. And sexual abuse by Catholic priests is certainly within the realm of possibility. The women of the convent, in a socially powerless position, might well have experienced themselves living in a hellish world; there may have been no other route available to express their emotional injuries than the display of demoniacal symptoms.

The behaviors of the Louviers nuns were rewarded by sympathetic attention and by action. Father Boulle was tortured and burned alive as a witch; the body of Father Picard was exhumed and dishonored. One of the nuns, Madeleine Bavent, had been accused by the others of sending devils. She was imprisoned and died after being brutalized by the guards. The possessed nuns were dispersed to other convents.

See also AUXONNE NUNS, POSSESSION OF.

For further reading: Robbins.

lucid dream In lucid dreams, sleepers are aware that they are dreaming. Many people who have had lucid dreams report them to be an exhilarating experience in which the dream imagery can be deliberately controlled to some extent. The following typical example was reported by Anne Faraday:

> In the dream, she was informed that she could choose either to have intercourse with a fantastic dream lover and be strangled by him afterward, or never to have sex again. Her growing

desire for a life lived to the full rather than a living death led her to choose the former, and as she was being led into the arena she suddenly became lucid. Instead of waking herself up or changing the scene, she decided to trick them all and go along with the game; and as she laughed to herself as how she would get up and walk away at the end, the environment expanded, the colors deepened, and she was high. Then the scene changed and she found herself flying in an extraordinarily high state, going through walls and windows without difficulty, and although she had been looking forward to the sex, now her deprivation did not seem to matter because she was enjoying other even more exhilarating exeriences.

Lucid dreams have been a topic of intense interest among many non-western cultures. In modern times, lucid dreaming was first noted in 1913 by Van Eeden, who coined the term.

It is not the case that dreams are either lucid or nonlucid; rather, this quality can be present in degrees. Most dreams are *nonlucid*—the question of whether or not the experience is a dream never arises. *Prelucid* dreams are those in which the dreamer wonders whether or not he or she is dreaming. Prelucidity can lead into more fully lucid dreams, if the question is answered affirmatively.

Malamud described two subtypes of lucid dreams. In *intellectually lucid* dreams, the dreamer is aware of the imaginal nature of the experience but still finds the content irresistably compelling. For instance, dream dangers still evoke fear in the intellectually lucid dreamer. *Experientially lucid* dreams feature complete awareness of the dream's nature, and an expanded choice of dream actions. The example dream presented above belongs to this category.

Among the general population, surveys have found that about 50% have had lucid dreams. A number of studies attempting to relate the occurrence of lucid dreams to personality traits, intelligence, abilities and features of waking mental imagery have produced few consistent results. There seems to be a tendency for lucid dreamers

to be good at visual tasks such as assembling puzzles, to be higher in HYPNOTIZABILITY, and to be superior in activities requiring balance, like walking on a balance beam.

Some dreamers are able to signal to the waking world when they are experiencing dream lucidity. These specially trained subjects, in the dream lucid state, can cause their eyeballs to move in an agreed upon pattern that is detectable by researchers. This feat has permitted studies of brain functioning at the precise moments of lucidity. This research has found that lucid dreams happen during the REM stage of sleep, the same stage that produces ordinary dreams. Lucidity can be attained at the onset of a dreaming period, or when a dream is already in progress. The normal REM period is punctuated by brief moments of awakening; some episodes of lucid dreaming begin from these "micro-awakenings."

Lucidity in dreams commences in a variety of ways. Commonly, a dreamer becomes lucid during a nightmare; cornered by a terrifying monster, the dreamer suddenly realizes that "this is just a dream!" It is likely that the fear arousal has brought the dreamer close to awakening; the dreamer remains asleep, but "borrows" some awareness from the waking state.

Dream lucidity often arises from noticing impossible features or inconsistencies in dream content. Noticing the absurdity of a bizarre object like a purple kangaroo or a walking mountain can jolt the dreamer into awareness. Most people are dyslexic in dreams—the printed word is blurry or changes shape. Frustration at their sudden illiteracy has triggered lucidity in many dreamers. Van Eeden reported that he would conduct experiments in lucid dreams, in order to test the dream world's ability to mimic physical reality:

> I dreamt that I stood at a table before a window. On the table were different objects. I was perfectly well aware that I was dreaming and I considered what sorts of experiments I could make. I began by trying to break glass, by

beating it with a stone. I put a small tablet of glass on two stones and struck it with another stone. Yet it would not break. then I took a fine claret-glass from the table and struck it with my fist, with all my might . . . yet the glass remained whole. But lo! when I looked at it again after some time, it was broken. It broke all right, but a little too late, like an actor who misses his cue. This gave me a very curious impression of being in a *fake-world,* cleverly imitated, but with small failures.

Some people have realized they were dreaming simply by noticing the strange, unreal atmosphere of the dream, literally, its "dreamlike quality." This type of lucid dream onset is often connected with micro-awakening episodes in REM sleep.

Lucid dreams can end in one of two ways: dreamers either lose the dream and wake up, or lose their lucidity and continue having a nonlucid dream. Lucid dreamers are sometimes fooled by a FALSE AWAKENING—they dream they have awakened, when actually they have slipped back into nonlucidity.

For thousands of years, lucid dreams have been deliberately sought. The fourth century yoga Sutras of Patanjali recommended "witnessing the process of dreaming." Among the classical Tibetan meditation practices called the Six Yogas of NAROPA are exercises for attaining realization in dreams. In the 12th century, the Sufi master Ibn el-Arabi taught that "a person must control his thoughts in a dream. The training of this alertness will produce great benefits for the individual. Everyone should apply himself to the attainment of this ability of such great value." The Senoi of Malaysia have long prized lucid dream skills and teach them to their children for defense against nightmares.

Contemporary researchers, drawing on traditional sources as well as their own findings, have developed several training programs for the induction of lucid dreams. A key feature of these methods is creating an expectation that one will have lucid dreams. Expectancy also seems to affect the content of dreams—if one believes that in a lucid dream it is impossible to pronounce one's name or to have sex, then it probably will be. Practices that have been found to promote lucid dreaming include: frequently asking, "Is this a dream?" during wakefulness; habitually looking for surprising or inconsistent events; and suggesting to oneself while falling asleep that one will have a lucid dream. Presenting cues to someone while they are dreaming, such as playing an audiotape that states "This is a dream," has also been successful.

Many benefits have been suggested for lucid dreaming. One can act out fantasies, indulge in forbidden or physically unsafe pleasures or rehearse new behaviors without the consequences that would follow in waking life. Although a few writers have worried that interfering with the normal nonlucid course of dreams might have unhealthy results, none have been reported.

Some believe that the lucid dream experience has spiritual value. As there are degrees of lucidity in dreaming, so also in wakefulness—we spend much of our waking time befogged by worries, hopes and irrationalities. Cultivating lucid dreams, it has been suggested, enhances lucid wakefulness.

For further reading: A. Faraday; C. Green; Laberge and Gackenbach; Malamud; Van Eeden.

lung-gom Buddhist traditions claim that many supernormal powers, or SIDDHIs, can be achieved through meditation practice. Among Tibetan Buddhists, one of the most commonly reported abilities is lung-gom: the ability to run extremely quickly over difficult terrain. Masters of lung-gom are said to skip across rocky ground like a stone skips on the surface of water. This power is allegedly produced by a particular meditative exercise involving control of the breath.

See also ABHIJNA.

lycanthropy This term is derived from Greek roots meaning "wolf-man." Lycanthropy refers to the DELUSION that one has been transformed into a predatory animal, such as a wolf. While the "wolfman" or "werewolf" (an Anglo-Saxon word meaning "man-wolf") are horror movie staples, lycanthropy is also a historical reality. Records describing individuals who believed themselves to be animals exist from the fifth century B.C., and the phenomenon is probably much older. Some people have succumbed involuntarily to the belief in shape-shifting; others have sought the power of transformation.

Lycanthropy has been noted in many cultures. In Japan, belief that one can become a fox has often been noted, while in other parts of Asia, the tiger is favored. Secret societies centered on ritual transformation into hyenas or leopards (often followed by murderous attacks on enemies) were once widespread in Africa. Shamans in the New World have practiced identification with jaguars, snakes, fish and birds.

In the West, lycanthropy may date back to archaic times. Ginzburg presented evidence for an old shamanic practice that may have survived from the Old Stone Age into the 17th century in remote regions of Europe. In this rite, men entered a trance state in which they became animals and fought evil magicians who threatened the livelihood of their villages. Evidently, the Scandinavian BERSERKrs, who were active in the 11th century, preserved old traditions that instructed them how to turn into bears during battles. Burkert described an ancient Greek cult of human sacrifice in which the participants identified themselves with wolves. And, in the Old Testament, an incident is described in which the Babylonian king Nebuchadnezzar believes himself to be an ox: "Nebuchadnezzar . . . was driven from men, and did eat grass as oxen, and his body was wet with the dew of heaven, till his hairs were grown like eagles' feathers, and his nails like birds' claws" (Daniel 4:33).

Although the ancient pagans tended to view involuntary lycanthropy as a type of "melancholy" or mental disorder, Christians saw it as an act of the devil. In the dangerous days of the Great Witch Hunt (15th through 17th centuries), many incidents of lycanthropy were reported, especially in France, where they were called *loup-garous*. Some of these individuals, in the belief that they were wolves, killed and cannibalized their victims. Several reports suggest the existence of a folk tradition that taught how to transform oneself into a wolf. The procedure involved rubbing one's body with an ointment containing hallucinogenic plants such as belladonna, mandrake and DATURA, and donning a belt of wolf-skin. The lycanthropic paste resembles the WITCHES' OINTMENT that allegedly aided witches in their flights to the sabbath.

As belief in flying Satanists declined at the close of the witch hunting period, so too did belief in the notion that people could literally change themselves into animals. With the rise of psychiatry, lycanthropy again became viewed primarily as a mental illness. The 19th century psychiatrist Esquirol coined the term "zoanthropy" for the delusion of animal transformation. Cases occasionally appeared in the medical literature and continue to do so. Noll reviewed psychiatric journals in English and French published between 1975 and 1992. He found 17 reports of lycanthropy: six people believed themselves to be wolves; four were dogs; two were cats; and there were also a tiger, a gerbil, a rabbit and two unspecified creatures. Delusions of animal transformation are most often associated with the disturbance of mood and thinking called bipolar disorder (formerly called "manic depression"). Sufferers of major depression or SCHIZOPHRENIA have also succumbed to lycanthropic beliefs. The most common treatment described in contemporary accounts is drug therapy.

Some reported cases of lycanthropy may have a physical basis. Illis suggested that sufferers of a rare disorder known as congenital porphyria were persecuted as werewolves. Victims of the disease become painfully sensitive to light, so that they shun the day and only go out at night. Their teeth turn red or reddish brown; their skin becomes yellow and ulcerated; and they are subject to abnormally thick growth of body hair. The disorder can damage the nervous system, producing unstable behavior. In a society where belief in animal transformation thrives, it is easy to see how the neighbors of people with porphyria, as well as the sufferers themselves, might conclude that the victims were changing into hairy beasts.

Deliberately inducing a state of identification with an animal is still practiced today. Canizares described a lycanthropic technique practiced by a certain Mexican shaman. After drinking an infusion made of mushrooms and roots, the practitioner concentrates on a nearby animal, while chanting incantations. Then, his informant stated:

a person's will can virtually enter into an animal, so that such a person can actually see through that animal's eyes and walk, fly, or swim inside the animal; it is as if, by some psychic mechanism, the animal acts as a television camera; whatever it sees is transmitted to you. In other words, it's a case of total identification with a particular animal.

This method seems to be a type of deliberate OUT OF BODY EXPERIENCE.

See also MANIA; POSSESSION.

For further reading: Burkert; Canizares; Ginzburg (1985); Illis; Noll (1992b); Otten.

macropsia A kind of perceptual distortion in which nearby objects are seen as very large. Macropsia can occur as an effect of psychedelic drugs, as well as a variety of NEUROLOGICAL DISORDERs.

See also MICROPSIA.

magical thinking The mainstream modern world view assumes that objects or persons cannot influence each other unless energy is transferred between the cause and the effect. The belief that causal relations can occur without physical energy transfer is called magical thinking. A common magical concept is the idea that objects which resemble each other are connected, and that manipulating one object can affect the other. In this belief, one might stick pins in a doll resembling someone in an attempt to harm that person. The notion that things that were in contact with each other at one time remain linked, even when separated, is another magical idea. An article of someone's clothing, or a clipping of their hair, is used in some magical spells to direct occult influences at them. Many cultures have a magical view of the universe—it is believed that behind the world of appearances is a hidden network of forces that can be tapped through spells and rituals. Often, these forces are personified as spirits.

Members of modern western society may engage in magical thinking for a variety of reasons. Some belong to subcultures that teach magical views, such as the New Age movement. Others simply do not know the conventional explanations for certain phenomena, so they invent magical causes—young children might attribute the sound of thunder to "God's coughing," because they do not yet understand the cause of light-

ning. Magical thinking also features in severe mental illnesses like SCHIZOPHRENIA. One schizophrenic patient noticed that the sun rose each morning after he raised the blinds in his room and concluded that he was able to control the sun's movements through his actions.

In psychological research, magical thinking tendencies are most often measured using the Magical Ideation Scale created by Eckblad and Chapman. The scale is a set of items requiring a "true or false" response, such as "I have felt that I might cause something to happen just by thinking too much about it" and "I have sometimes felt that strangers were reading my mind." High scores on the Magical Ideation Scale have been linked with proneness to schizophrenia. Several studies have also found that magical thinking is often associated with a wide range of anomalous beliefs, such as ESP, spirits and CRYPTIC animals. Also, Thalbourne reported that people who score highly on the Magical Ideation Scale are more likely than others to report MYSTICAL EXPERIENCEs.

Some researchers observed that many items on the Magical Ideation Scale concern belief in phenomena that may be unusual, but not necessarily magical, such as TELEPATHY. Even when these items were deleted from the scale, however, the correlation remained between magical thinking and paranormal beliefs.

See also Appendix; PSYCHOLOGICAL ADJUSTMENT.

For further reading: Eckblad and Chapman; Thalbourne (1991); Zusne and Jones.

mahabba Arabic for "love," mahabba refers specifically to the state of being lost in the love of God. In the path of spiritual development outlined by the Sufis or Moslem mystics, this ecstatic experience is preceded by MAKHAFAH, the fear of God; it can lead to a more intimate divine contact called MA'RIFAH, or knowledge of God. The mahabba experience has been called the dividing line between the mass of Moslem believers and the spiritually advanced Moslem.

makhafah Arabic for "fear," makhafah refers to the fear or awe of God. A feeling of God's vastness and power is one of the first spiritual experiences on the path of Sufism, the mystical branch of Islam. Makhafah purifies the seeker, preparing him or her for higher states like MAHABBA and MA'RIFAH. This experience is the Moslem equivalent of the "mysterium tremendum" aspect of the NUMINOUS EXPERIENCE.

makyo A Japanese term deriving from the roots *ma*, meaning "devil," and *kyo*, or "world," makyo refers to illusory experiences. There are two types of makyo, the general and the specific. Generally, the entire lifespan of the ordinary person is makyo, in the sense that everything experienced does not exist as it seems. From the Buddhist perspective, the apparent solidity and independent existence of external objects, for instance, is illusory; the essence of things is not solidity, but EMPTINESS. In this general sense, only those who have attained BUDDHAHOOD have completely dispelled makyo. More specifically, makyo refers to the illusory experiences that arise during the practice of meditation.

All serious meditators are familiar with the intrusion of unusual experiences during their practice. If one is meditating facing a wall, random cracks or lines may suddenly appear to be depictions of faces or animals (PAREIDOLIA). One may have visual or auditory HALLUCINATIONs. The body image may distort, causing the practitioner to experience the feet or hands growing to gigantic proportions. The meditator might become very hot or cold. Sometimes, spontaneous movements of the body can occur. These events are all regarded as makyo.

Such experiences can seem demonic, as they tend to distract the person from the meditation practice. Some meditators become frightened, believing that they are literally being assaulted by devils, or losing their minds. Others become excited, in the belief that these phenomena are profound spiritual experiences.

In the Zen Buddhist tradition, the appropriate reaction to makyo is simply to ignore them and continue with the assigned meditation practice. The aim of Zen is the attainment of Buddhahood; chasing after strange experiences, or struggling to suppress them, is viewed as a deviation from the path to the highest goal. The 14th century Zen text *Zazen Yojinki* dismisses makyo as the result of "a maladjustment of the mind with the breath"—the meditator should ensure that the breathing is calm and regular.

Although the occurrence of makyo in meditation is not a spiritual accomplishment, neither is it necessarily a sign of ineffective practice. Tradition holds that, just prior to attaining enlightenment, the Buddha himself was plagued by makyo—he saw visions of a vast demon army attacking him, followed by beautiful women who tried to seduce him from his practice. He allowed these images to pass and finally achieved awakening.

For further reading: Diener; Kapleau.

mandala In Sanskrit, *mandala* literally means "circle." Some scholars have argued that the term derives from the roots *manas*, mind, and *dala*, "to dilate"—hence, "mind expander." The circular images called mandalas have been used as potent means of altering consciousness, especially by practitioners of Buddhist TANTRA.

Generally, a deity is depicted at the center of the Tantric Buddhist mandala. This being is not a god in the western sense; rather, it represents an aspect of buddha consciousness, which is potentially present within everyone. In concentric rings surrounding this central figure, other spiritual beings and objects are portrayed. Frequently, the mandala is divided into four quadrants, each of a different color and populated by different kinds of beings. The entire image represents the palace of the central deity. At the same time, it symbolizes the universe. In tantra and other forms of Mahayana Buddhism, the world of enlightenment and the phenomenal world are thought to be the same place, viewed in different ways. The world, viewed spiritually, is a mandala.

In the main tantric meditation practice, the SADHANA, the meditator identifies with a deity in order to awaken the corresponding aspect of enlightened awareness. The mandala is often incorporated into sadhana practice. The meditator studies the mandala until every detail can be reproduced in the imagination. Then the practitioner merges with the central deity, acquiring its powers and characteristics. The universe is visualized as the mandala, one's own divine palace, filled with deities and surrounding one in every direction. Such a practice is not considered a mere escapist fantasy; rather, the mandala portrays the truly divine state of the world and oneself, which is hidden by our ignorance.

The 20th century psychiatrist Carl Jung believed that the circular form of the mandala represented the human personality's instinctive drive toward wholeness. Whereas in Asian religion mandalas were deliberately visualized for their spiritual effects, Jung thought that they could also appear in consciousness spontaneously. Jung reported that his patients would often experience visions, fantasies or dreams in which a circle appeared, when their personal integrity was threatened:

> As a rule a mandala occurs in conditions of psychic dissociation or disorientation, for instance in the case of children between the ages eight and eleven whose parents are about to be divorced, or in adults who, as the result of a neurosis and its treatment, are confronted with the problem of opposites in human nature and are consequently disoriented; or again in schizophrenics whose view of the world has become confused, owing to the invasion of incomprehensible contents from the unconscious.

The mind spontaneously creates a round figure in an effort to compensate for the psychic disruption caused by the crisis. Jung found that encouraging his patients to draw or paint mandalas often had a calming effect. One of Jung's most radical ideas was his suggestion that UFO ENCOUNTERs, which are often seen as circles in the sky (so-called "flying saucers"), are visions of mandalas. The integrity of western civilization itself has become threatened by the challenges of the present century; in a mass effort to compensate for the fragmentation of modern life, UFO-mandalas are now appearing to millions of people.

For further reading: Rhie and Thurman; Storr; Tucci.

mania In modern parlance, a mania is a state of excited obsession; we speak of a philatelist's mania for stamp collecting or of an intense popular interest in UFOs as a UFOMANIA. In ancient Greece, "mania" was the word for "madness." The Greeks believed in two kinds of madness: mundane and divine. Mundane madness was often thought to be due to assault or POSSESSION by hostile spirits. Such cases would often be viewed with awe, because the sufferers had been touched, however destructively, by supernatural forces. Physical causes, such as excessive drinking or imbalances in the "humours" of the body, were also recognized by more sophisticated thinkers.

Divine madness was potentially valuable as an avenue of contact with the gods. Socrates is quoted by Plato in the *Phaedrus* as saying: "Our greatest blessings come to us by way of madness, provided the madness is given us by divine gift." Socrates goes on to provide a fourfold classification of divine madness: prophetic, telestic, poetic and erotic. These types are sometimes mentioned in English literature as the "Four Frenzies" or "Four Furors."

Prophetic madness is caused by Apollo, deity of the sun and of reason. He was held to be extremely knowledgeable, because of his intellectual powers and his vantage point; sometimes, he would deign to share his knowledge with mortals. The oracle at Delphi was the best known center where prophetic madness was regularly induced for purposes of divination. Priestesses of Apollo would prepare themselves to function as mediums for their god through purification rituals, drinking the blood of sacrificed animals or chewing laurel leaves (a plant sacred to Apollo). The legend that the Delphic oracle would inhale a vapor seeping from the earth is an unfounded, late invention. The mediumistic utterances would often make little sense and would require interpretation by attendants. Their interpretations were frequently just as ambiguous as the original proclamations. Dodds suggested that prophetic madness received widespread support in ancient Greece because Apollo served as a father-figure who offered a sense of security about the future.

Telestic madness was possession of the spirit by Dionysus, god of wildness. Groups of devotees would congregate in the countryside, and drinking and dancing, abandon themselves to spontaneous joy. Rohde (quoted in Oesterreich) offered a vivid reconstruction of these performances:

> The ceremony took place on mountain heights at dead of night, by the flickering light of torches. Loud music resounded; the clashing of brazen cymbals, the deep thunder of great hand-tympani and in the intervals the 'sounds luring to madness' of the deep-toned flutes. . . . Excited by this wild music the crowd of revellers dances with piercing cries. We hear nothing of any song; the fury of the dance leaves no breath for it. . . . in a frenzied, whirling, and violent round the ecstatic crowd hastens upwards over the mountain-sides. It is mostly women who turn to the point of exhaustion in this giddy dance. Strangely clothed: they wear . . . long flowing garments made, it seems, from fox-skins sewn together; over these roebuck skins,

> and horns upon their heads. Their hair flies wild, their hands grasp snakes, . . . they brandish daggers or thyrsi with hidden lance-heads under the ivy. So they rage until every emotion is excited to the highest pitch and in the 'holy madness' they fling themselves upon the animals destined for sacrifice, seize and dismember the assembled booty and with their teeth tear the bloody flesh which they swallow raw.

According to Dodds, these debauches served to discharge the impulses that make people vulnerable to the GROUP DYNAMICS OF UNUSUAL EXPERIENCES; thus, paradoxically, relinquishing one's self-control in the Dionysian ritual might strengthen it in other settings.

The third type of divine madness, the poetic mania, was the domain of the Muses. These beings were held to be responsible for creative ideas that appear in a person's mind. The poet can undergo certain preparations, such as singing hymns to the Muses (this is the origin of the word "music"); but whether or not they answer the call is beyond human control. The involuntary aspects of creativity are well-explained by this belief. Inspiration often does not come as the result of a logical train of thought, but "out of the blue," so it is well-labeled as a type of madness. Most artists have experienced being "gripped" by an idea, and feeling almost compelled to develop it; here, the mad quality of the Muses' interventions is most evident.

The gods Eros and Aphrodite are responsible for erotic madness. Like creative thoughts, the compulsions of love often seem driven by powers outside of oneself, and they certainly do not obey the strictures of rational behavior. Plato saw a special importance in erotic madness: love brings together the most divine aspects of a person with the earthiest, animal levels. The intensity of this union can give rise to an impulse to seek the highest delight—the transcendent knowledge of the True, the Good and the Beautiful.

See also DANCING MANIA.

For further reading: Dodds; Luck; Oesterreich.

manna from heaven "Then said the Lord unto Moses, Behold, I will rain bread from heaven for you" (Exodus 16:4). Thus, according to the Old Testament, were the wandering Israelites alerted to the edible substance that appeared mysteriously "upon the face of the wilderness" (Ex. 16:14). They were to subsist on this "manna" for 40 years. The Exodus account describes manna as white in color, and with a sweet taste. Unlike most Biblical miracles, falls of manna have continued to be reported throughout history. The appearance of the miraculous bread has been reported in northern Africa and western Asia.

Most researchers have concluded that manna exists, but that it does not descend from the sky. Instead, it is created on earth, but its source is so mysterious, and its nutritious properties so wonderful, that it is ascribed a heavenly origin.

One candidate for the identity of manna is nostoc. This primitive plant is a land alga that shrivels into nearly invisible threads when dry, but swells into a gelatinous mass in the presence of moisture. It is noteworthy that the manna of Exodus was noticed following the evaporation of the morning dew, which could have activated the nostoc.

The secretion of a lichen species, *Lecanora esculenta,* has also been proposed as the true manna. The lichen, which grows in arid regions, produces small, yellowish spheres which are filled with a sweet white syrup. In parts of Turkey, a delicious bread is made with this substance. A region of 19th-century Persia is said to have become covered with a layer of the lichen almost an inch deep. Animals and humans ate it eagerly. Local belief held that this manna had been deposited by a whirlwind.

Another possible source of manna is tiny insect parasites on tamarisk shrubs. Aphids and scale insects that infest these desert plants excrete a sweet fluid. This material dries into white granules on the branches and the ground underneath.

See also DEVIL'S JELLY.

For further reading: Corliss (1977).

mantra This Sanskrit word derives from the roots *manas,* "mind," and *tra,* "protection." Thus, a mantra is a "mind protection." Mantra meditation is important in both the Hindu and Buddhist traditions, especially among the schools of TANTRA.

Mantras are sounds that can be uttered aloud or recited silently. When the meditator's attention is focused on a mantra, the mind is "protected" from being occupied by the trains of thinking and fantasizing that normally consume mental energies. Through mantra practice, it is claimed that the mind is lifted to a higher plane, where unusual powers and experiences can be induced.

In ancient India, it was widely believed that Sanskrit was a sacred language. Unlike other languages, in which words had been invented to designate things, Sanskrit words were thought to be the mystical sounds emitted by the things themselves, audible only to the sages. Knowledge of an object's name gave one magical control over it. Throughout history, people have used mantras composed of Sanskrit words as magical spells to control weather, attract love and money, kill enemies and achieve other goals. This practice closely resembles, in theory and practice, the use of "words of power" in the western magical tradition.

The best known use of mantras is for the attainment of spiritual goals. The power of the mantra to cause transformations of consciousness is said to derive from two features. First, certain so-called "seed syllables" (*bijas*) naturally move the mind in certain directions. For instance, the syllable OM, when allowed to resonate in the center of the body, causes a sensation of expansion into the universe. Another bija, HUM, stimulates a feeling that vast forces are being harmonized within oneself. Second, some of the words used in mantras have symbolic connotations. Perhaps the most famous Buddhist mantra—OM MANI PADME

HUM—contains two Sanskrit words, *mani* (jewel) and *padme* (lotus). Such words evoke powerful associations from the meditator's memory—the preciousness and luminosity of a jewel, the continuous unfoldment and purity of a flower. When combined and recited in prescribed ways, mantras are viewed as tools for altering awareness in quite specific directions. In both Hindu and Buddhist traditions, mantras have been crafted to guide the practitioner toward spiritual insights.

In tantric meditations (SADHANAs), recitation of a mantra is frequently accompanied by visualization of a symbolic form such as a deity. Various syllables can also be visualized vibrating and radiating light within the practitioner's body. In addition, the meditation teacher may instruct the student to regard all sounds as mantras—that is, as meaningful expressions of spiritual reality. Through such comprehensive means, it is claimed that mantras can be used speedily to transform ordinary consciousness into the mind of a Buddha.

Although researchers attempt to analyze the contents of mantras in order to deduce their historical origins, the actual use of a mantra does not involve any attempt to decipher a literal meaning. The power of mantra practice is more akin to the effects of poetry or song, which cannot be reduced to finite meanings.

Mantras vary greatly in length. The shortest are single syllables, usually bijas such as OM, AH, HRIH, DHIH, etc. Perhaps the longest is the 100-syllable mantra of Vajrasattva: OM VAJRASATTVA SAMAYA MANU PALAYA VAJRASATTVA TWENOPA TEESHTHA DRIDO ME BHAVA SUTO KYO ME BHAVA SUPO KYO ME BHAVA ANURAKTO ME BHAVA SARVA SIDDHI ME PRAYACCHA SARVA KARMA SUKHA ME CHITTAM SHRIYA KURU HUM HA HA HA HA HO BHAGAVAN SARVA TATHAGATHA VAJRA MA ME MUNCA VAJRI BHAVA MAHA SAMAYA SATTVA AH. The meditation teacher usually prescribes a specific number of repetitions, which are counted off by the meditator using a rosary. In the foundation practices of Tibetan Buddhist meditation, for example, the Vajrasattva mantra is to be recited 100,000 times while visualizing the diamond body of Vajrasattva, who represents the intrinsic purity of the awakened mind.

See also KUNDALINI.

For further reading: Blofeld; Govinda (1969).

Marian apparition Appearances of the Blessed Virgin Mary comprise one of the most enduring classes of unusual experience in Western history. Belief in visitations of Mary has been the most popular positive meaning attached to apparitional encounters over the past thousand years (demonic encounters being the most popular negative meaning). Recent research into Marian apparitions has suggested that, whether or not stimuli of supernatural origin are involved, psychological and social processes shape the experiences and govern their public impact.

Reports of Marian apparitions are found throughout the span of Christian history, but their frequency, geographical distribution and characteristics are not constant. The earliest recorded visit of Mary occurred in the third century A.D., when St. Gregory Thaumaturgus stated that she appeared to him in a VISION. During the third and fourth centuries, the role of Mary as an intercessor in heaven on behalf of the Catholic faithful was first defined. Until the 12th century, however, Marian apparitions were relatively uncommon—Christ and the saints were more popular objects of devotion and were the favored interpretations of apparitional experiences. In the later Middle Ages, there was a tremendous upsurge in reverence for Mary and belief in her power. This shift in religious attention was reflected not only in the dedication to her of every cathedral built in the Gothic period, but also in the perception of apparitions.

The major source of information on Marian apparitions in the later medieval period is the

Dialogus Miraculorum, composed by Caesarius of Heisterbach around 1223. He collected 64 accounts of visionary encounters with the Virgin. The amount of editing done by Caesarius or others is unknown, so we cannot take these stories as accurate records of personal experience. However, we can deduce from them the general features of the typical Marian apparition of the time. In all cases the seers were pious Roman Catholics; in most instances, they were monks belonging to the Cistercian Order (as was Caesarius). The vast majority of these medieval encounters occurred to individual visionaries, in private settings. In the rare instance when someone saw Mary on more than one occasion, the second encounter was unexpected. The apparitions usually appeared during times of personal or community crisis; Mary frequently acted to prevent divine punishment for sinful behavior, allowing people a second chance at living an upright Christian life.

In 1507, Mary visited Alsace to resolve a religious dispute. Local Franciscans were promoting the doctrine of Mary's immaculate conception. They were opposed by the Dominicans, who insisted that she had been conceived in original sin. The Blessed Virgin appeared to Brother Letser, a Dominican, and confirmed the accuracy of the Dominican position. Shortly afterward, one of the heads of Letser's priory was discovered costumed as the apparition; the good brother had been the victim of a hoax. The tricksters were soon dispatched to meet their maker, courtesy of the Inquisition.

There was a sharp drop in Marian apparition reports, beginning in the early 16th century. The Protestant Reformation, with its rejection of the Catholic Mary cult, was doubtless a factor; so also was the interest of the Inquisition in examining all unusual experience reports for the influence of the Devil. But occasional reports of the Virgin's visits continued. Pope Benedict XIV formulated the official attitude of the church toward Marian apparitions in his *De Servorum Dei Beatificatione et Beatorum Canoniziatione* (1734–38). He stated that reports of Marian appearances should not be automatically accepted or rejected; rather, they should be subjected to rigorous examination under the auspices of the bishop within whose diocese the events happened. If church approval is given, it is permissible to believe in the divine origin of the apparition and to publicize its occurrence. However, Catholics are not *required* to believe in the divinity of Marian appearances, even if the church has approved of them.

The modern period of Marian apparitions began in the early 19th century and continues today. For the past 200 years, Mary's visits have displayed important differences from the standard accounts of the Middle Ages. Zimdars-Swartz has noted that many modern apparitions have been serial—occurring to the same visionaries on several occasions, the return visits often being predicted by the apparitional figure itself. Also, a large number of contemporary occurrences have been public—the visionaries have been accompanied by others during their encounters.

The modern cases frequently have other features which are rare or unknown in earlier reports. For instance, modern seers frequently state that Mary has given them a secret, often concerning an imminent world catastrophe that will happen unless people repent of their sins. Many of those who witness the visionaries during their encounters report unusual experiences themselves—seeing strange lights or clouds, observing the sun "dancing" in the sky, hearing a mysterious buzzing sound, finding that the beads on their rosaries have changed color, etc.

During the modern era, seven Marian apparitions have been approved by Catholic bishops, according to the standards set by Pope Benedict: four in France (Paris, 1830; La Salette, 1846; Lourdes, 1858; and Pontmain, 1870); one in Portugal (FATIMA, 1917); and two in Belgium (Beauraing, 1932; Banneux, 1933). In addition, there have been thousands of cases, some of which have involved hundreds of thousands of people, that have not received church approval. Most significant of the unapproved cases include the phenomena of ZEITOUN, Egypt (1968–1971) and MEDJUGORJE, Bosnia (1981–present).

The frequency of Marian apparitions seems to have peaked in the mid 20th century. Between 1947 and 1954, about 14 cases per year were being reported to Catholic authorities. Devotional and theological attention to Mary was also high during that time, culminating in 1950, when the bodily assumption of the Virgin into heaven was proclaimed a dogma of the church by Pope Pius XII. Thereafter, Marian apparitions have declined somewhat, in parallel with the reduced official emphasis on devotion to Mary among Catholics. However, the shrines associated with the sites of famous Marian appearances continue to thrive; each year, Fatima welcomes almost two million visitors, Lourdes over four million and the Mexican shrine at Guadalupe 12 million.

Regarding the geographical distribution of Marian apparitions, there is a general pattern of concentration in countries where Roman Catholicism has been the dominant religion for the longest period of time. The country most haunted by Mary is Italy—in various surveys, the proportion of Marian apparitions reported in Italy varies from 30 to 43% of the world total—followed by France and the Catholic regions of Germany and Austria. Where the idea of a visit from the Virgin is most plausible and has the deepest historical roots, it is most likely that this interpretation will be given to an apparitional encounter.

A significant exception to this rule is Spain, a region that has had a devoutly Catholic population since the early Middle Ages. Marian apparitions are *not* common in Spain at any period. Instead, there is a wealth of reports of unusual occurrences associated with statues or pictures of Mary—images that talked, bled, perspired, cried, gestured or materialized. William Christian, who reviewed Marian phenomena in Spain during the late medieval and Renaissance period,

has suggested that the political situation within the Spanish church distorted the general pattern of Marian apparitions found in other parts of Catholic Europe. Spanish Catholic leaders in the cities wished to retain control of the churches in rural areas. The site of a Marian appearance tended to attract a certain prestige and independence, so the urban bishops were not predisposed to approve reports of Marian appearances in the countryside. Apparition reports by poor peasants could be easily disregarded and could even provoke a visit from the notorious Spanish Inquisition. Miracles associated with physical images were more difficult for the urban authorities to dismiss. The statue or painting quickly became the focus of a shrine, and the odd behavior of the image could be seen as ongoing proof of divine activity. As a result, the Spanish countryside became dotted with shrines built around "miraculous" images rather than sites of Marian apparitions. The implication of Christian's view is that the occurrence, or at least the reporting, of Marian apparitions is determined in part by the degree to which the visionary's community is rewarded for the sighting.

In some cases, the stimulus which the visionary interprets as Mary seems to be internal; in others, the stimulus is a feature of the external world. Michael Carroll, taking a non-supernatural position, describes these two types of Marian vision as instances of HALLUCINATION and ILLUSION respectively. In the cases he believes were hallucinations, there was no evidence for the presence of unusual visual stimuli in the vicinity of the apparition; in almost all such cases, the visionaries not only saw Mary, but also heard her speak (auditory effects do not normally occur in connection with visual illusions, but hallucinated voices are not uncommon in the psychiatric literature). In the cases Carroll suspects were illusions, ambiguous visual stimuli, such as lights of uncertain origin, seem to have been present; in every such case, the Virgin was seen, but was not heard. In both types of case, the visionaries render the mysterious stimulus meaningful by interpreting it in accord with their assumptions and expectations about unusual encounters, that is, by resolving the ambiguity into the supernatural figure of Mary.

In cases where more than one person views the Marian apparition, new questions arise. In cases of multiple seers, there is often a great deal of reported agreement concerning the features of the apparition. If Marian apparitions are merely the interpretations of ambiguous stimuli, why would groups of people (sometimes numbering in the thousands) have similar experiences? Another analysis of modern Marian apparitions by Carroll suggests that similar perceptions may arise in part because of communication between the seers. In many serial apparition cases, the number of onlookers (those accompanying the visionaries, but not experiencing the visions themselves) tends to increase through the series. The more onlookers are present, the less opportunity the seers have to discuss their visions with each other before describing them to the onlookers. Carroll found that as the number of onlookers increases, the accounts of the seers tend to diverge in their details. In the Beauraing case, for instance, during the first apparitional encounters there were few onlookers, and the descriptions of the Virgin's behavior by the five visionaries were nearly identical. By the time of the last appearance in the series, there were several thousand onlookers; in this episode, the seers had no chance to discuss their experience among themselves and reported strikingly different utterances by the apparitional figure. This is not to say that visionaries who report similar experiences are deliberately imitating each other; rather, they are being affected by the reports of the other seers in making sense of their own encounter.

In summary, the following conditions appear to be favorable for the occurrence of a Marian apparition report. First, deeply rooted expectations should exist among the visionaries and their community that a visit from the Virgin Mary is possible. Second, an ill-defined stimulus, external (such as a mysterious light) or internal (a mental image), should be present. The interpretation of this stimulus as Mary is drawn from the visionary's beliefs. Third, the Marian interpretation should serve a need of the visionaries or their community—the resulting attention and reverence given to the seers or the village would tend to reinforce the experience. The scientifically inclined can regard Marian apparitions as hallucinations and illusions; people who are less committed to natural explanations may believe that the mysterious stimuli have a divine origin.

For further reading: Carroll; Christian; Nickell; Rogo; Zimdars-Swartz.

ma'rifah   In Arabic this term means "knowledge"; the Sufis, or mystical Moslems, use it to refer to an experience in which one has knowledge of God. The knowledge of ma'rifah is neither conceptual, like information from a book, nor perceptual, like seeing something outside of oneself; it is a direct link between the soul of the Sufi and God. The full attainment of ma'rifah must be preceded by MAKHAFAH (purification through the fear of God) and MAHABBA (drawing near through the love of God). Ma'rifah can lead to the most spiritually exalted states recognized by Sufism—FANA and BAQA.

meditation   Meditation is one of the most widespread practices associated with unusual experiences. Shapiro offered the following definition:

> Meditation refers to a family of techniques which have in common a conscious attempt to focus attention in a non-analytical way, and an attempt not to dwell on discursive, ruminating thought.

The origins of meditation are lost in prehistory. The earliest clear evidence for meditation was unearthed in the remains of Mohenjodaro, an ancient city located in what is now Pakistan. A 4,000-year-old seal depicts a human figure seated in the classical cross-legged meditation posture.

In Asia, Buddhism, Hinduism and Taoism prominently feature meditation as part of the spiritual path; but such practices have also been significant in Middle Eastern and western religious traditions. Moslems, especially those belonging to the mystical branch of Sufism, utilize chanting and the famous whirling dances of the dervishes to fix their attention on higher things; the Jewish path of KABBALAH offers meditation on various symbols and names of God as a spiritual ladder.

Christianity has a rich history of prayer going back to its inception. Christian literature distinguishes meditation and CONTEMPLATION. Meditation is "discursive" prayer in which the mind actively explores the meaning of a theme, such as a Bible story. Contemplation involves stilling the mind, fixing awareness on an image, thought or idea of God. Technically defined, Christian "contemplation" fits Shapiro's general definition of meditation better than does Christian "meditation."

There are two main types of meditation, with innumerable variants. In *concentrative meditation,* the attention is fixed on a specific object. This object can be external, such as a statute or candle flame; it can be a bodily sensation, like breathing or muscular movement; or it can be internal, such as a mental image. In *expansive meditation,* one attends to whatever is happening in the present moment, without trying to select one object over another. The key to this practice is MINDFULNESS—remaining sharply aware of what one is sensing, rather than becoming lost in thought, feeling or fantasy. Some meditation techniques combine or alternate the concentrative and expansive approaches.

Smith suggested that three psychological skills are involved in meditation: *focusing* the beam of attention; *letting be,* or putting aside unnecessary mental activity; and *receptivity* to the experiences of meditation, however peculiar or disturbing they may be. As Smith observed:

These skills may well be displayed in a meditation session. One diverts attention from hectic everyday concerns to, say, the simple flow of breath. One focuses. One puts aside attempts to force a particular pattern of breathing or analyse the breathing process, and so on. One maintains a stance of letting be. And one dispassionately accepts whatever changes may transpire such as images, unexpected feeling states, and the like. One remains receptive.

Formal meditation practice often involves adopting a special posture; but meditation can also be done while walking, eating or engaging in any other activity. In many traditions, advanced meditators are said to remain in an aware state continuously, with the distinction between practice and non-practice no longer existing.

While the basic types of meditation are widespread, the aims of meditation depend on the cultural tradition within which it is practiced and on individual interest. In some cases, meditation is used as a self-help tool. For instance, acquiring supernormal abilities has often been claimed as an effect of meditation. In contemporary settings, meditation is used as a relaxation technique to promote calmness and healing. Many traditions teach that meditation can also be a means of self exploration and spiritual development.

The relationship between meditation and unusual experiences has been variously interpreted. Sometimes, visions or other phenomena experienced by the meditator may be taken as signs of progress toward the goal—for instance, the NIMITTA of Buddhist tradition. Zen, on the other hand, emphasizes that unusual experiences arising in meditation are mere distractions (MAKYO) and should be ignored. Spiritually oriented meditation generally aims not for transient alterations of awareness, but for a permanent transformation of consciousness into a higher condition. To the less advanced meditator, glimpses of these higher states in meditation can occur as MYSTICAL EXPERIENCES.

Since the 1960s, several hundred scientific research papers have been published on meditation. The scientific method is necessarily restricted to examining only a few aspects of meditation, and only those that can be measured. Critics have wondered if such a fragmentary approach may miss how these aspects work together as a whole to create the truly important features of meditation practice. Most studies have examined people who were relatively inexperienced meditators; more advanced practitioners may not always be comparable. The diversity of traditional meditation methods is not represented in the experimental literature, so important differences in the effects of the methods and contexts of practice may not be detected. Nonetheless, the body of research on meditation has yielded some interesting findings.

While many people dabble in meditation for a short period, relatively few include meditation as a regular part of their lifestyle. There seem to be consistent differences between people who become serious meditators and those who do not. Beginning meditators who go on to maintain their practice often score highly on measures of ABSORPTION and HYPNOTIZABILITY. These factors reflect an ability to maintain attentional focus. Both absorption and hypnotizability have been linked with a tendency to have a broad range of unusual experiences, including ESP, MYSTICAL EXPERIENCEs and OUT OF BODY EXPERIENCEs; these factors may partly explain why many people have such experiences while meditating. Some studies have reported that people who drop out of regular practice after starting tend to have lower levels of PSYCHOLOGICAL ADJUSTMENT and higher levels of personal defensiveness than meditators who continue their practice.

During meditation while sitting, oxygen consumption and heart rate tend to decrease; electrical activity in the brain reflects a deepening state of wakeful relaxation. There is no consistent evidence that meditators enter a particular ALTERED STATE OF CONSCIOUSNESS. Experienced meditators do show certain physiological changes that are rarely seen in new meditators, according to some researchers, Kasamatsu and Hirai noted that the presence of theta waves (an electrical rhythm of 4–6 cycles per second) in brain activity during meditation tended to increase with years of Zen meditation practice. The meaning of these differences is unknown.

Meditation has been shown to produce lasting psychological effects in some practitioners. Meditating regularly can increase a person's ability to relax; however, it seems to be no more effective in this regard than many other forms of relaxation practice. Significantly decreased levels of anxiety and enhanced well-being have also been linked with regular meditation. A few studies have reported uncomfortable effects of regular practice for some meditators, including increased anxiety, tension, confusion, boredom and depression. Such discomforts may sometimes reflect the "growing pains" of self awareness.

The most significant effects of meditation, however, can probably be understood only within the context of the tradition followed by the meditator. Many spiritually valuable experiences discussed by meditation schools, such as NIRVANA and MOKSHA, are still beyond the reach of scientific measuring instruments.

For further reading: Holmes; Kasamatsu and Hirai; Jevning, Wallace and Beidebach; Shapiro; Shapiro and Walsh; Smith; M. West.

mediumship A medium is a person who is thought to "mediate" between the worlds of the living and the dead. The term is sometimes used broadly to include practitioners of SHAMANISM, but it usually refers to TRANCE specialists belonging to Spiritualism and allied movements.

Spiritualism began in 1844 when an American, Andrew Jackson Davis, fell into a trance and experience vistations from departed spirits. Davis stirred interest in the possibility of spirit communication through his lectures and writings. In 1848, Margaret and Kate Fox became the first professional mediums. The Fox sisters held seances at which mysterious rapping sounds were heard, apparently produced by discarnate sources. (Many years later, Margaret stated that the rappings were fraudulent, made by cracking the joints in their toes. Kate denied the allegation.) Private seances and public demonstrations by touring mediums became very popular. During the latter half of the century, the Spiritualist movement had attracted millions of followers in Europe and the Americas. The desire to investigate scientifically the stories of paranormal events associated with mediums was a prime motivation for the founding of the Society for Psychical Research in 1882. Spiritualism continues today. Its prominence has largely waned in Europe and North American, but a variant called *espiritismo* or spiritism is still widely practiced in Latin America.

A typical seance involves a group of up to several witnesses (called "sitters") assembled around a table with the medium.

Some of the sitters may wish to make contact with specific deceased friends or relatives. Following a prayer or hymn, the medium lapses into silence, sitting motionless with eyes closed. After a time, the medium begins to breathe heavily, perhaps groaning and twitching. Then, the manifestations of the spirits commence.

Mediumistic phenomena are often divided into two categories: mental and physical. Mental mediums can see and hear the dead and can relay messages to the living. Often, they will relinquish control of their own bodies, allowing the spirits to speak and act directly through them—a form of voluntary POSSESSION. Or, only partial control is allowed, allowing the production of AUTOMATISMs such as automatic writing or the use of a sliding pointer (called a planchette) to spell out words.

The spirit messages transmitted via mental mediumship are frequently vague and prosaic and utterly unconvincing as evidence for the presence of a discarnate intelligence. More likely, such material consists of fragments of memory and fantasy, loosely woven together by the constructive processes of the medium's own mind. Occasionally, however, there have been reports of more impressive demonstrations. Mediums have been said to mimic deceased people whom they allegedly never knew in life with great accuracy and to provide intimate details known only to those closest to the departed. Some sitters have left seances convinced that they had encountered a dead relative through the medium.

Several mundane explanations must be considered in this regard. The history of mediumship is rife with fraud; some mediums have secretly researched prospective sitters, in order to acquire information to feed back to them during a seance. The majority of practicing mediums have been sincere Spiritualists, and fraud is not involved in most seances. The BARNUM EFFECT can also play a role—a rather general mediumistic utterance that could apply to any number of persons could be heard by a sitter as being more specific than it actually is, especially if the sitter is eager to communicate with the spirit. A third factor is the CLEVER HANS EFFECT. People emit information about themselves and their interests constantly and uncontrollably; a medium can learn details about a sitter without the awareness either of the medium or the sitter and package the information in the form of a spirit revelation. A medium may also have learned about the deceased at some point in the past and then forgotten about it. The knowledge can re-emerge in the guise of contact with a spirit (CRYPTOMNESIA), and its origin in memory rather than the afterlife will be sincerely denied by the medium.

Some well-documented episodes in the history of mental mediumship are explainable in conventional terms only by some elaborate version of these mundane factors, if they are conventionally explainable at all. The famous case of the "cross- correspondences" began shortly after the death in 1901 of the last of three classical scholars—Henry Sidgwick, Edmund

Gurney and Frederic Myers. During their life, these men had been intensely curious about the possibility of survival after death—indeed, all three were founders of the Society for Psychical Research. During the 30 years after their demise, about a dozen mediums around the world received messages allegedly from one of the three men. Many of these messages contained fragments or allusions deriving from obscure Latin and Greek sources. Individually, the messages made no sense; but, when fitted together like a jigsaw puzzle, their meanings became evident. As the mediums were distributed from India through Egypt, England and America, a fraud would have been a massive undertaking; and psychological processes like cryptomnesia cannot explain how people who have never met or communicated with each other could produce parts of a single message. Some commentators have opted for an explanation involving ESP—the mediums were psychically connected on an unconscious level. Psychical research E.J. Dingwall, however, remained unimpressed with the cross-correspondences. He suspected that the more striking matches in the jigsaw of messages might have been due to rearrangement and selection of the mediumistic material by one of the main investigators, J.G. Piddington.

In physical mediumship, the spirits indicate their presence not merely through the medium's behavior, but by affecting the seance environment directly. The range of odd phenomena reported from seance rooms includes rappings; the movement or levitation of objects on the table, the table itself, and the medium; flashes of light; breezes; temperature changes; writing and drawing on slates; the playing of musical instruments; the creation of wax casts of spirit hands, including fingerprints; the teleportation of objects between the seance room and other locations; and the materialization of visible spirit bodies. Sometimes, a whitish substance called ectoplasm was said to emerge from the body orifices of the medium, mould itself into various shapes and perform acts such as lifting tables and blowing trumpets.

Seances are traditionally conducted in dim or no lighting, so as not to deter the spirits. Such a setting is ideal for two processes that probably account for most of the phenomena of physical mediumship—the misinterpretation of poorly perceived stimuli and deception. A group of expectant people sitting in the dark is primed to perceive confirmation of their hope and to influence each other toward consensus via the GROUP DYNAMICS OF UNUSUAL EXPERIENCES.

Many of the best known physical mediums during Spiritualism's heyday were caught in fraud. Samples of ectoplasm, when obtained, usually proved to be cheesecloth or muslin regurgitated by the medium. Some mediums employed assistants who hid nearby until the lights went down; under cover of darkness, and clad in black, they would then produce the show. The technology of hoaxing has continued to evolve—the *Master Index to Magic in Print* lists three pages of citations on methods to create fake rappings. There have been few reports of dramatic physical mediumship during the last 40 years. Not every physical medium was caught cheating; whether there was ever anything more going on in the Spiritualist seance rooms is a matter of continuing debate.

See also CHANNELING.

For further reading: Gauld; Hansen (1992b); Kerr.

Medjugorje apparitions The best known recurrent APPARITION case of recent times was centered in the village of Medjugorje, Bosnia (in 1981, when the phenomenon began, Bosnia was part of Yugoslavia). In several respects, the occurrences at Medjugorje resembled the FATIMA APPARITIONS of 1917: the witnesses were a group of children; the visions were MARIAN APPARITIONs, which recurred predictably; the Virgin Mary imparted a series of secret messages to the seers; and many people who came to witness the visionaries themselves reported unusual experiences. Unlike the Fatima events, which happened monthly for half a year, the apparition of Medjugorje continues to appear daily to some of the seers.

In June 1981, six children (then aged from 10 to 17) began to claim that they were meeting the Virgin Mary on a hilltop near the village. Mary wore a grey dress and white veil, they stated, and spoke to them in fluent Croatian (their own mother tongue). Some of the witnesses who accompanied the seers to these early encounters reported viewing a white light on the hill, but neither seeing nor hearing the Virgin. Carroll suggested that some sort of unusual visual stimulus of natural origin was present at the time. The seers, who were all devout Catholics, could have interpreted the stimulus as a holy visitation.

The stories that the Virgin was visiting Medjugorje on a daily basis quickly aroused interest. The devout and the curious began to flock to the village to see for themselves. Factions within the Catholic church accused each other of trying to exaggerate or suppress the reports in maneuvers of ecclesiastical politics. The Communist government was displeased, suspecting an attempt by the church to whip up religious feeling. Authorities barred the seers from visiting their vision site on the hill.

The children received permission to meet each day in a small room in the parish church. There, the visions and voices continued. When the phenomenon began to receive international attention, the number of onlookers grew steadily; between the onset of the apparitions in 1981 and the commencement of the Bosnian civil war in 1992, several million visitors from around the world traveled to Medjugorje.

The visionary episodes themselves became embedded in a daily ritual. Each evening, a few preselected visitors—generally clergy—were admitted into the room of the apparition along with the seers. Outside, a vast throng recited rosaries. A light would be turned on within the room, visible from outside, signaling the crowd to be silent while the Marian visitation took place. At some point, the children would all suddenly kneel and stare at a blank spot on the wall while speaking noiselessly. Afterward, each visionary would describe to a priest what the Virgin had said to them. Messages from Mary intended for the public would later be posted on a bulletin board.

Most of the messages consisted of injunctions to repent and pray. The messages not shared with the public were said to comprise material of personal relevance to the seers, as well as advice for the church and prophecies of impending disasters. At least one of the seers also received visions of heaven and hell and recognized deceased acquaintances there.

Many of the pilgrims to Medjugorje, immersed in the atmosphere of religious excitement, had unusual experiences themselves. One of the most commonly reported was the temporary ability to stare straight into the sun without damaging the eyes, while the solar orb appeared to flicker and dance in the sky. Many others reported visions of Christ and Mary in the clouds, or on the hill where the apparition first appeared. Some claimed that the links of their rosaries had been suddenly transmuted into gold.

The Virgin, via the seers, granted scientific research teams access to the children during their visionary episodes. The primary scientific investigator has been Henri Joyeux. He attached a variety of physiological sensors to the seers' bodies to monitor the physical aspects of the visionary ecstasies. Joyeux reported that the electrical activity of the seers' brains during the visitations was dominated by alpha waves, indicating a relaxed, attentive state of awareness. There was no evidence of epileptic seizure activity or of dreaming. Joyeux was puzzled by the fact that the seers were activating their larynxes and moving their mouths normally during the apparitional conversations, and yet they produced no sound. He was also struck by the perfect synchronization of each seer's eye movements during the arrival and departure of the

Virgin, as if they were viewing the movements of an object.

Other observers were impressed by the coordination of the seers' conversations—when one child stopped silently verbalizing, another would begin, without any obvious sensory cueing between them. It is well established, however, that people can communicate, unintentionally and without awareness, through very subtle cues such as slight shifts in breathing or posture.

The events at Medjugorje have spawned enthusiastic devotional groups, especially in the United States. Occasionally, visionary phenomena inspired by Medjugorje happen in these groups. In 1988, a church in Lubbock, Texas became the focus for such an occurrence. Local parishioners, who had visited Medjugorje, announced that Mary would cause miracles to occur at the church on August 15. On that date, 15,000 people gathered; many of those present reported "sun miracles" and visions of Jesus and Mary in the sky.

Recent political upheavals have made Medjugorje virtually inaccessible to the pilgrim. But in late 1992, one of the original seers went on an international tour, sponsored by a religious magazine. He claimed to have been visited by the Virgin while he knelt on an auditorium stage in each city on the itinerary, and relayed her divine words to the audience.

For further reading: Carroll; Cornwell; Kraljevic; Laurentin and Joyeux; Nickell; Zimdars-Swartz.

metachoric experience Celia Green coined this term for an experience in which the entire environment is replaced by HALLUCINATION. The transition between ordinary awareness and the completely hallucinated world of the metachoric experience can occur imperceptibly; if the metachoric world is a replica of the physical one, the hallucinator may not even realize that anything unusual has occurred. Metachoric experiences can happen while one is awake or in an ALTERED STATE OF CONSCIOUSNESS. They can

be brief or last for hours. FALSE AWAKENING, LUCID DREAMs, NEAR-DEATH EXPERIENCEs, OUT-OF-BODY EXPERIENCEs, WAKING DREAMs and some APPARITIONs are classified as metachoric experiences. Many other kinds of unusual experiences might be unrecognized instances of metachoric experience.

For further reading: C. Green.

metagnomy Variant term for EXTRASENSORY PERCEPTION.

metakinesis Variant term for PSYCHOKINESIS—the direct influence of the mind on the environment, or "mind over matter."

metanoia A Greek word, referring to the experience of choosing to begin the quest for God. The nature of spiritual growth is understood in Eastern Orthodox Christian tradition on the basis of the Biblical passage: "And God said, Let us make man in our image, after our likeness" (Genesis 1:26). The "image" is defined as the potential within each person to reach God; the "likeness" is the yearning to achieve the highest spiritual state, THEOSIS. Metanoia is the moment at which a person begins to move from latent possibilities of "image" toward their complete expression in theosis, impelled by the motive energy of "likeness."

Metanoia can simply be a dawning conviction in the reality of God, and a commitment to make progress toward Him. The metanoic moment is sometimes accompanied by visions or intense emotional upheavals. Symeon the New Theologian, a Byzantine saint of the 10th and 11th centuries, described a metanoia that happened while he was listening to the preaching of his teacher (quoted by Matus):

> I drew near to him with penitence and faith, and as I clung to his feet, at once I felt a supernatural warmth, then I perceived a faint, radiating luminosity, then I sensed in his words as it were a breath of God, then a fire came forth from him and entered into my heart, causing tears to

spring forth in endless flow, and then a fine ray flashed through my spirit faster than lightning. What appeared to me next was like a torch in the night or like a small, flaming cloud which rested upon my head, as I lay face down in prayer. Then the cloud flew off, and shortly after I saw it in the heavens.

See also HESYCHASM; THEOPTIA.

For further reading: Chirban; Matus; Pelikan.

meteor Tumbling through interplanetary space can be found a great number of rocky debris known as *meteoroids*. Most of this material is thought to originate from the crumbling of colliding asteroids and from the disintegration of comets. When a meteoroid encounters the earth's atmosphere, the tremendous friction ionizes the air around it, producing the characteristic luminous streak called a "falling star" or, scientifically, a *meteor*. Some meteors bounce off the upper atmosphere and return to space, like a stone skipping on the surface of a pond. Most meteoric material is completely vaporized between 75 and 40 miles above the earth. But some meteors reach the surface, and are then called *meteorites*.

Meteorites range in size from invisibly small dust particles to mammoth "Apollo objects," such as the ones that gouged out the Arizona Meteor Crater and Crater Lake in Quebec. About 65 million years ago, the impact of a massive meteorite off the Yucatan Peninsula is thought to have led to the extinction of the dinosaurs. In terms of composition, there are three main types of meteorites: low density stones, the most abundant kind; stony-irons, made of iron embedded in stone; and iron meteorites.

Humans have always been intrigued by meteors and wonderstruck at meteoritic "rocks from heaven." The Roman Emperor Heliogabalus honored a meteorite with a procession through streets strewn with gold dust. Prior to the time of Mohammed in the early seventh century, a black meteorite fell near Mecca. The rock was built into a corner of the central Meccan shrine, the Ka'bah, where it is still revered by Moslems today (the stone's blackness is said to symbolize the condition of FANA—the extinction of the ordinary self concept, in order to become filled with God). Christians too have sensed a divine connection to meteorites—when a 260-pound rock fell near the Swiss town of Ensisheim in 1492, it was displayed in the local church as a sacred relic.

Orthodox science did not accept the existence of meteorites until 1804, despite the vast accumulation of reports. Eminent scientists, in fact, vehemently denounced meteorite stories. The phenomenon did not fit the prevailing models of the universe, and therefore was impossible. Their reaction serves as a cautionary tale for those who dismiss without investigation the significance of unusual experiences on the grounds that the reported occurrences contradict the truths established by science.

Meteors and meteorites are today firmly accepted. The "rocks from heaven" can still surprise us, however. The more a meteor deviates from expected meteoric behavior—the fast, silent, linear streak in the night sky—the greater the likelihood that the event will be misidentified, or leave the observer puzzled, perhaps to file a report of a UFO ENCOUNTER.

Most meteors follow a straight path across the sky. Some, however, have been observed to wobble, or even to change direction. Meteors that skip off the upper atmosphere can create a glowing arc before heading back into space. An irregularly shaped rock, rotating as it falls, may undulate. Pockets of gas encased in meteoric rock can be heated by atmospheric friction, causing them to explode and throw the meteor into a different trajectory.

Meteors are typically silent. If the plummeting rock is exceptionally near, or unusually large, auditory effects can occur. Hissing, rumbling and detonating sounds arise from the disintegration of the meteor. These are normally heard shortly after the meteor is seen, as sound waves travel more slowly than light. In some cases, however, observers have stated that a sound caused them to look up, and then they saw the meteor. Corliss (1977) wondered if an incoming meteor might produce an electromagnetic influence that could operate on a human nervous system, inducing an auditory sensation. More prosaically, perhaps these anomalous sounds were created by meteors that immediately preceded the observed ones.

Most meteors brighten the sky for a fraction of a second before either vaporizing completely or coming to earth. Some meteors are visible for longer periods. Massive rocks meet with more atmospheric resistance than smaller ones; the larger meteors may be considerably slowed by friction as they descend, producing a brilliant fireball that can last for several seconds. Meteoroids travelling through space in approximately the same direction as the Earth can also appear to move very slowly. Some meteoroids, moving faster than the planet, catch up to it from behind; just as a slightly faster vehicle seems to drift past the slower one on the highway, these meteors move across the sky at a leisurely pace. Meteoroids moving ahead of the Earth in its orbit can be overtaken by the planet, to similar effect. "Lazy" meteors, as they are called, can remain in view for as long as 30 seconds.

On an average night, a keen-eyed observer can expect to spot about seven meteors in an hour, this frequency increasing after midnight. Occasionally, "showers" of meteors appear when hundreds of streaks appear in the sky each hour. Some meteor showers are predictable—they happen in the same region of the sky and at the same part of the year. Regular showers occur because certain areas of the earth's orbital path are densely strewn with meteoroids. Showers can also happen without warning, as the planet encounters a swarm of space rocks that were not there during its previous circuit. One especially awesome such event was viewed from central Canada to Brazil on February 9, 1913, when a number of massive fireballs seemed to fly in formation. As the date was the Catholic feast day of St. Cyril, the fiery visitors became known as the Cyrillids. According to one witness, quoted by Corliss:

> There were probably thirty or thirty-two bodies, and the peculiar thing about them was their moving in fours, threes, and twos, abreast of one another; and so perfect was the lining up, you would have thought it was an aerial fleet maneuvering after rigid drilling. About half of them had passed, when an unusually large one hove in sight, full ten times as large as the others. Five or six would appear in two detachments, probably five seconds apart; then another wait of five or ten seconds, and another detachment would come into view. We could see each detachment for probably twenty or twenty-five seconds. The display lasted about three minutes. As the last detachment vanished, the booming as of thunder was heard—about five or six very pronounced reports.

Almost 2,000 tons of meteoritic material falls to earth every day, almost all of it in the form of dust. Indeed, the average household dustball, when analyzed, is found to contain some particles from outer space. Sometimes, meteorite dust may be responsible for unusual phenomena. History reports several instances of dry fogs of unknown origin that blanketed large parts of the world. In 526 A.D., a reddish haze covered the Eastern Roman Empire. In May 1783, a luminous blue fog descended on Sweden. By year's end, it had spread from Syria to central North America. A similar event occurred in 1831. These occurrences were not associated with major volcanic activity. It has been suggested that the earth encountered concentrations of meteoric dust on these occasions. In 1908 a space object—now thought to have been a stony meteor about 98 feet in diameter—flattened a large area in central Siberia. For weeks afterward, the night sky glowed around the world, almost certainly because of dust from the vaporized rock.

See also THUNDERSTONE.

For further reading: Corliss (1977, 1986, 1994); Chyba, Thomas and Zahnle.

micropsia   A form of perceptual distortion in which nearby objects are seen as very small, as if looking through the wrong end of binoculars. Micropsia has been reported as an effect of psychedelic drugs and as a symptom of a NEUROLOGICAL DISORDER.

See also LILLIPUTIAN HALLUCINATION; MACROPSIA.

migraine   This affliction is the most common NEUROLOGICAL DISORDER, found in up to 10% of the population. In addition to the agonizing pain and nausea that makes the disorder so feared, many migraine sufferers report disturbances in perception that precede the onset of the headache.

The susceptibility to migraine attacks appears to be genetically based. A variety of factors, including stress, hormonal changes, air pressure fluctuations and food sensitivities, can trigger the migraine process in vulnerable people. First, the blood vessels in the head constrict, reducing blood flow to brain tissues. As a result, the neurons in the brain receive inadequate oxygen. They temporarily malfunction, giving rise to the unusual experiences. This period is known as the migraine "aura" (not to be confused by the AURA sometimes seen around the body by psychics). The vessels then rebound, like a rubber ball that is squeezed and released; as the walls of the vessels stretch, the migraine pain begins. The ensuing headache can persist for hours or days.

Visual changes are the most commonly reported feature of the migraine aura. Luminous halos appear around objects, and light seems brighter. Blind spots can form in the visual field. Pulsating patches of color and streaks of light are also frequent. Some migraineurs experience BODY IMAGE DISTORTIONs, DEPERSONALIZATION, DÉJÀ VU and HALLUCINATIONs.

These striking phenomena can easily be interpreted in spiritual rather than neurological terms. Some people experience the aura without a subsequent headache; in such cases the underlying migraine mechanism may be unsuspected, and the perceptual changes taken as a revelation from an external source. Sacks and Beyerstein have argued that the spectacular visions of the medieval mystic HILDEGARD OF BINGEN were actually her interpretations of migraine auras.

See also EPILEPSY.

For further reading: Beyerstein; Sacks (1970).

mindfulness   The practice of mindfulness is one of the central meditations in Buddhism. The normal state of consciousness is characterized by extreme habituation—most of our mental and physical functions are carried out automatically, beyond our awareness. According to Buddhism, suffering is caused by our habits of greed and hatred, which in turn are based on an incorrect view of reality. None of these sources of suffering can be ended as long as we are largely unconscious of our own activities. Mindfulness meditation, practiced by all schools of Buddhism, aims to retrieve the meditator's life from the deadening encrustation of habit.

In the *Satipatthana Sutta,* the Buddhist text that outlines mindfulness practice, the meditator is taught to focus attention on four domains of experience, in increasing order of difficulty—the body, feelings, mental states and phenomena. In mindfulness of the body, the breath is typically the first meditation object. One simply allows one's attention to remain on the breathing, guiding the awareness back to the breath sensations whenever it wanders. There is no attempt to modify the breathing rhythm. This process leads naturally into a greater awareness of other bodily sensations. In order to increase mindfulness, the meditator may analyze the body into 32 components and systematically focus the attention on each one. Initially, mindfulness is practiced in a standard sitting meditation posture, but the awareness must eventually be sustained while walking, standing and lying as well. Traditionally, Buddhists would visit burial grounds to meditate on rotting corpses, in order to increase mindfulness of the body's transient nature.

An acute awareness of the body leads the meditator into noticing the continuous changes in the realm of feelings. Mindfulness of feeling is cultivated by noticing whether the present feeling is pleasant, unpleasant or neutral, and whether it pulls one toward the external world or away from it.

Our ever-changing feelings have as their backdrop states of mind, which can be hard for the inexperienced meditator to detect. Practitioners of mindfulness notice whether the present state of mind has the qualities of greed, hatred or delusion.

After much practice, mindfulness eventually becomes sensitive enough to notice the moment-by-moment changes in all phenomena, external and internal. By perceiving the momentariness, essenceless nature, and ungraspability of all things, our enslavement to greed and hatred is lessened. Gautama Buddha taught that mindfulness can lead one to attain NIRVANA.

See also DEAUTOMATIZATION.

For further reading: Snelling; Thera.

mirage When a beam of light passes through materials of different densities, it bends or refracts. Air can function as a refracting medium, creating the range of optical phenomena known as mirages. For most people, the most familiar type of mirage is the shimmering strip seen hovering above road surfaces on hot days. Light reflecting from the road ahead is redirected toward the observer's eye by a layer of warm air; the shimmering, easily mistaken for swirling water, is produced by air turbulence. The refractive powers of air can cause many more surprising effects.

The light from ordinarily recognizable objects can be distorted into weird appearances by passing through sheets of air of varying densities and temperatures. Bright stars and PLANETS near the horizon sometimes seem to move erratically, because of shifts in the configurations of the intervening refractive layers. The rather common tendency to report the sighting of a star or planet as a UFO encounter may sometimes be explained by this effect.

If more than one refractive layer is present in the atmosphere, the result can be multiple mirages. For instance, several images of a distant shoreline have been observed hovering over the water, stacked one above the next. Multiple refractive layers, arranged in an as yet poorly understood fashion, can sometimes act as lenses, magnifying far points in a deceptive fashion. Atmospheric lenses are thought to cause the aerial cities called FATA MORGANAs.

More mysterious are lateral mirages, in which the image appears horizontally displaced from the depicted object. "Double suns" have been reported, in which a phantom sun can be seen to one side of the real thing; the phantom gradually merges with the solar disc. (Lateral solar mirages are different and much rarer than MOCK SUNs, which appear in pairs and are due to refraction by airborne ice crystals.) Sideways bending of light requires a sheet of air that is vertically oriented; no one has yet explained how such an atmospheric structure could endure turbulence and gravity for more than a moment, but lateral mirages can persist for up to ten minutes.

Strangest of all are "mirror mirages." Several cases have been collected by Corliss in which the image of an object has appeared in the opposite direction from the original, as if an immense mirror had been erected in the sky. This very uncommon sight tends to be seen from ships at sea; the imaged object may be a distant lighthouse or another ship. Mirror mirages still await even a rudimentary explanation—as Corliss (1977) noted, "This type of mirage is not recognized by most meteorologists, for it seems to contradict the principles of atmospheric optics."

See also GHOST LIGHT.

For further reading: Corliss (1977, 1984).

missing time   The inability to remember events for a period of time is a common occurrence. Most people have driven along a familiar route, absorbed in thought, suddenly to realize that they recall nothing about the traffic maneuvers—stopping at lights, making turns—that they must have executed a short time before. When attention is strongly focused on internal events like thoughts and mental images, routine information from the outside world may not be stored in memory. The expected data evoke habitual responses and are discarded. Gaps in recall are often given a more exotic interpretation when they are linked to unusual experiences.

Recollection failures are an important feature in many accounts of UFO abduction; one of the most widely read books on the subject, by Hopkins, is entitled *Missing Time*. Typically, an individual notices a gap in memory, accompanied by signs of emotional disturbance such as anxiety spells and nightmares. Suspecting that something traumatic occurred to cause their amnesia, they consult someone whom they believe to be an authority in such matters: a therapist or researcher of anomalies. The authority uses various prompting techniques, especially HYPNOSIS, to retrieve the missing memories. In response, the forgetful person begins to have mental images, which are interpreted by the authority—and by the person themselves, in many cases—as repressed memories of an encounter with beings from a UFO.

A similar scenario applies to many instances in which an adult recollects long-repressed memories of horrific abuse suffered as a child. Spontaneous recall of abuse at the hands of Satanic cult members usually occurs in response to intensive therapeutic probing, including hypnosis.

When confronted by a severely unpleasant event, some people develop *post-traumatic stress disorder*. They try to avoid anything that reminds them of the painful incident and often struggle not even to think about it. These protective efforts can become automatic, producing an inability to recall features of the trauma.

It is rash, however, to conclude that every episode of missing time contains a hidden trauma. In some cases the time gap could have occurred in the ordinary fashion as uninteresting experiences were not encoded into memory. The signs of emotional stress that provoke a person to wonder about the "missing time" could have causes unrelated to the gap in recall. The blank space in the memory record serves as a perfect screen upon which to project FALSE MEMORIES—fantasies mistaken for accurate recollections. The use of hypnosis to excavate buried traumas merely increases the likelihood that the retrieved material will conform to the expectations of the hypnotist.

It is almost certain that many of the UFO abduction stories that fill in time gaps are tainted by false memories—generally, investigators who believe that the aliens are friendly retrieve accounts of beneficent visitors, and investigators who are convinced of their hostile intent uncover tales of terror.

For further reading: Bullard (1989); B. Hopkins; Klass (1988); Rosenfield.

mock moon   On nights when light from the moon passes through a layer of atmospheric ice crystals on its way to earth, an observer can sometimes view a pair of false images of that celestial body, appearing a short distance to either side of it. Like their solar counterpart, MOCK SUNS, mock moons (also known as moon-dogs) are caused by ice crystals refracting light to the observer's eye that ordinarily would not reach it. Mock moons appear at those points in the sky from which light is being refracted to the observer's location. Because of the shape and orientation of the crystals, light is redirected toward the observer from areas to either side of the true moon image. Mock moons are more rarely seen than mock suns. They could sometimes be mistaken for UFOs.

See also PARASELENAE.

mock sun   As they drift through the atmosphere, ice crystals can act like tiny prisms, altering the path of light that passes through them. Under certain conditions, this process can create duplicate images of the sun known as mock suns or sundogs.

Most commonly, mock suns appear in pairs, flanking the actual solar disc. The inner edges of these images are often reddish, while the outer edges are bluish or violet. If the air is calm, the ice crystals tend to lie in the atmosphere with their axes oriented vertically. This orientation produces mock suns at 22 degrees on either side of the sun. If the crystals are randomly oriented, another pair of mock suns may appear at 46 degrees.

More complicated atmospheric conditions can arrange the ice crystals into multiple layers, with varying axial orientations. These configurations can create other mock sun effects. Rarely, single sundogs are reported. Mock suns above or below the sun's disc, rather than beside it, have also been noted, although optical theory cannot easily account for such images. On one occasion, a spectacle of eight mock suns was observed.

It is easy to understand how people who believed that the sky was the abode of supernatural forces could regard mock suns with awe. In modern settings mock suns have probably led to reports of UFO ENCOUNTERS. Like rainbows, mock suns seem always to maintain the same distance from the observer. If a pilot notices a mock sun and attempts to approach the "object," the image seems to "evade interception" by maintaining its distance.

Near Salt Lake City in 1961, a pilot chased a silvery disc through the sky. Menzel and Taves suggested that the disc was a mock sun.

See also MOCK MOON; PARHELIA.

For further reading: Corliss (1984); Menzel and Taves.

mokele mbembe   This term is the name given to a swamp monster by the people of Central Africa. Sightings of the beast have been recorded since the 19th century, when European explorers first penetrated the area. Cryptozoologists have undertaken a series of expeditions to determine the validity of the reports concerning the mokele mbembe. Dr. Bernard Heuvelmans, president of the International Society of Cryptozoology, described the mokele mbembe hunt as "the zoological craze of the 1980s."

One of the earliest serious accounts of the swamp monster was offered by Captain Freiheer von Stein zu Lausnitz, who journeyed through the Congo in 1913 and 1914. In the Likouala swamps, he collected eyewitness descriptions of a creature as big as an elephant, with a long, slender neck and a single great tooth or horn. The mokele mbembe was said to live in clay caves hollowed out of river banks.

The first serious research effort devoted to the swamp monster accounts was undertaken in 1932. A. Monard, a Swiss zoologist, attempted unsuccessfully to track the creature in isolated regions of Angola where it had been sighted. Monard said that the survival of a dinosaur from the Mesozoic Age in such a remote area might be possible.

During the same year, cryptozoologist Ivan Sanderson was traveling in Africa. Sanderson reported finding mysterious giant tracks in the jungle, later encountering a very large creature which briefly poked its head out of the water near his boat.

Intrigued by these stories, another expedition was mounted in 1980. It was directed by Roy Mackal, a biologist at the University of Chicago, and James Powell, a herpetologist (specialist in reptiles). They trekked to the Likouala swamp and Lake Tele region in the People's Republic of the Congo, which was the source of the most detailed mokele mbembe sightings. During their stay, they searched in vain for the beast itself, but met and interviewed many witnesses. Mackal and Powell formed the hypothesis that the animal was a very small sauropod, the class of dinosaur to which creatures like the brontosaurus belonged.

A return expedition mounted by Mackal in 1981 again failed to yield any direct contact with the elusive mokele mbembe. However, near Lake Tele Mackal did discover a track of disturbed vegetation, as if an enormous mass had moved through, leaving large, unidentifiable footprints.

Shortly thereafter, Herman and Kia Regusters, two Americans who had been part of Mackal's crew but had decided to strike out on their own, reported that they had succeeded in observing and photographing the mokele mbembe. The Regusters' claim is not taken seriously by some members of the cryptozoological community. Unfortunately, their photographic evidence is quite ambiguous.

In 1983, Congolese zoologist Marcellin Agnagna and two other witnesses reported a group encounter with the mokele mbembe. They stated that they sighted the back, neck and head of the animal protruding from the water of Lake Tele and actually waded in to get a closer look. The creature was in continuous observation for about 20 minutes before it submerged. Although the expedition had photographic equipment, they reported incredible bad luck—in the excitement of the moment, they forgot to adjust the focus of the video camera and also neglected to remove the lens caps from the still camera! And so, the biggest "one that got away" did it again.

The most recent attempt to verify the existence of the mokele mbembe occurred in 1986, when British cryptozoologist Bill Gibbons led an expedition to Lake Tele. Again, only large footprints, strangely damaged vegetation and more stories from the locals were reported.

Curiously, Mackal and Powell collected stories of native encounters with other strange creatures in the region. Some of these accounts sound like descriptions of other species of dinosaurs, including an animal with planks growing out of its back (stegosaurus?) and a beast with a single

horn that could kill elephants (monoceratops?). The Likouala-Tele area has changed relatively little since the age of the dinosaurs and is only sparsely populated. It has been suggested that some saurians could conceivably have survived in such an environment.

The evidence supporting a saurian survival in the modern Congo consists of anecdotes, which are subject to all of the well known distortions inherent in the processes of memory, and some ambiguous physical traces (blurry film, old footprints, disturbed vegetation). Without much more solid evidence than currently exists, the possibility that the mokele mbembe is a dinosaur remains highly speculative.

See also CRYPTIC; CRYPTOZOOLOGY; LOCH NESS MONSTER.

For further reading: Mackal (1987); Randles; Sanderson (1972).

moksha Literally "liberation" in Sanskrit, moksha is the aim of all spiritual practice in Hinduism, the equivalent of ENLIGHTENMENT in the Buddhist traditions. Although it is sometimes taken to be an escape from the world to another realm, such as a heaven, moksha is actually a permanent alteration in consciousness. One who has attained moksha has transcended the appearance of the ordinary world, seeing that the diversity of phenomena revealed to the senses is misleading; in truth, there are no distinctions between the essences of things. In light of this insight, one is said to be liberated from the pains of desiring and rejecting; one's own self is not different from the self of the universe, so there is no need to defend it. Moksha is regarded as the highest of the four main goals in Hindu culture (the other three being money, pleasure and doing one's duty).

See also JIVAN-MUKTI; SAHAJ SAMADHI.

For further reading: Feuerstein (1989); Friedrichs.

Mothman Point Pleasant, West Virginia was the center of a wave of strange experiences during 1966 and 1967. The primary figure was the "Mothman," a winged humanoid that was reported by over 100 witnesses. This entity was frequently seen in flight; sometimes, aerial lights were observed first, out of which the form of the Mothman seemed to emerge. It was said to be about six feet tall, with a wingspan of 10 feet, and gray in color; there was no detectable head, but a pair of bright red eyes were visible between the shoulders. Some witnesses heard its voice—a squeaking sound, like that of a mouse.

The Mothman was fond of appearing to drivers and could not be eluded—some observers reported accelerating above 100 m.p.h., only to find the creature cruising along beside them. Unaccountably, the Mothman was especially likely to be seen by menstruating women.

Eventually, the Mothman furor subsided. Thirteen months to the day after the first Mothman sighting, the main bridge linking Point Pleasant to Ohio collapsed into the Ohio River, with great loss of life. Some witnesses claimed they saw mysterious lights above the bridge, leading others to wonder if the winged visitor was somehow involved.

See also GROUP DYNAMICS OF UNUSUAL EXPERIENCES; SPRINGHEEL JACK.

For further reading: Keel.

mountaintop glow High places, so far removed from the arenas of ordinary life, have been associated with strange forces for millennia. The sense of mystery has undoubtedly been fed by the sight of lights weaving among mountain peaks at night. The best known example of this phenomenon is the "Andes lights," which have been viewed in Bolivia, Chile and Peru. Brilliant flashes of yellow and red, as well as immense sheets of flame, dance on the highest peaks and ridges. On some evenings, gigantic pillars of light have been observed projecting into the sky from the pinnacles. Like huge searchlights in appearance, they have been visible 300 miles from the mountains. These displays produce no sound and can occur during clear weather. The Andes lights were powerfully stimulated during the great earthquake of 1906 in central Chile; eyewitnesses described great jets of light seemingly igniting the entire sky.

Mountaintop glows of the Andes type have also been noted periodically in the Alps and in the heights of Mexico and Lapland. Ships approaching the island of Madeira have reported strings of brilliant white flashes glittering across the island's mountainous profile. Although the conditions required for the production of such displays are not perfectly understood by scientists, it seems that any elevated area could produce luminous effects, given the right state of the atmosphere.

Most researchers believe that mountaintop glows are greatly amplified examples of ST. ELMO'S FIRE. Electricity tends to become concentrated on pointed structures, such as steeples, towers or mountain peaks. The discharge of electrons from the point of concentration into the atmosphere creates a lightning-like radiance. Because of the slow and continuous nature of the discharge, in contrast to the abruptness of conventional lightning, the air surrounding the path of discharge does not slap together; thus, very little sound is produced. The enhancement of the Andes lights by earthquakes could be due to the piezoelectric effect: when quartz crystals within the mountains are stressed, they could generate an added electric charge.

Other unusual visual phenomena often seen in the vicinity of mountains include ALPENGLOW, FATA MORGANAs and GHOST LIGHTs.

For further reading: Corliss (1982).

mukti This Sanskrit term, meaning "release," is a variant term for the condition of MOKSHA—complete liberation from suffering and illusion.

See also JIVAN-MUKTI; VIDEHA-MUKTI.

multiple personality disorder This mental illness, commonly called "split personality," is one of the best known types of severe psychological disorder. It is classified as a type of DISSOCIATIVE

DISORDER called "dissociative identity disorder" by mental health professionals. Frequently confused with SCHIZOPHRENIA, multiple personality disorder (MPD) is an unrelated illness. Prior to 1980, MPD was rarely diagnosed; but in recent years, many thousands of people have received this diagnosis.

The essential feature of the disorder is the apparent presence of two or more distinct personalities within one person (in some cases, 40 or more personalities have been reported). The various personalities are displayed through unique patterns of speech and behavior; the MPD sufferer often first comes to the attention of health care professionals because of the dramatic inconsistencies in his or her daily actions.

Noll described a typical case of MPD. A frantically disturbed young woman was brought to the psychiatric hospital where Noll worked as a psychologist. His careful interviewing uncovered the following personalities: "Beverley," depressed and fragile; "Jumpin' Joanie," who took over during stressful times, including menstruation (as "Beverley" was afraid of blood); "Jennifer," who said she was six years old and embodied the patient's innocence; and "We," the patient's conscience, who attempted to oversee the other personalities.

Most sufferers of MPD report horrendous histories of CHILDHOOD TRAUMA, involving severe physical or sexual abuse. Often, some of the personalities state that they are unaware of the existence of the others. These personalities may have amnesia for the periods when another personality is in control and be puzzled by evidence of their own activities during those times. One MPD sufferer, who owned a bridal shop, was angered by repeated deliveries of gaudy fabrics that she would never have ordered—until she was shown the signatures, in her own handwriting, on the requisition forms.

Some clinical researchers believe that MPD is caused by DISSOCIATION—a splitting off of mental contents from mainstream awareness. According to this theory, mental fragmentation can occur in response to the stresses of repeated child abuse. A victim may find the feelings of hatred toward an abusive parent so overwhelming that they are partitioned from ordinary consciousness. In time this segregated material can develop a degree of independent functioning and identity. From this perspective, effective therapy for an MPD sufferer would require that each personality be identified and then "integrated" to form a whole person again. HYPNOSIS is frequently used to map out the "family" of personalities thought to reside within the MPD patient.

Other researchers do not accept the dissociation theory of MPD. They prefer to view the disorder as a case of multiple *roles,* rather than a literal fragmenting of the personality. This school of thought argues that, as a child, the abuse victim learned that adopting various roles made life easier. Acting passive when threatened by punishment, and eager when offered rewards, helped the person avoid the punishments and garner the rewards. In some cases this role-taking developed into the extreme form of MPD. The multiple roles theory suggests that trying exhaustively to map every alleged "personality" that exists in the MPD patient might make the problem worse—by rewarding the patient with continued attention for each new personality, the therapist could inadvertently encourage the patient to continue generating more and more roles. Instead, according to multiple roles theory, the therapist should help the patient to find healthier ways to experience a rewarding life than the dramatically inconsistent actions of MPD. This approach does not imply that MPD sufferers are simply pretending to have multiple personalities; they may create more roles as an unconscious response to punishments and rewards. The controversy over the two viewpoints about MPD is still unresolved.

For further reading: Bliss; Hacking; Noll (1990); Spanos et. al. (1986).

myoclonic jerk The relatively common experience of the involuntary jerking of one's muscles while drifting off to sleep. The effect resembles being startled. The myoclonic jerk is caused by a general signal sent to the muscles from the brain region that controls movement; in most cases, it is a harmless misfiring of nerve cells. In some rare nervous system disorders, these discharges can happen repeatedly, causing the limbs to flail and even propelling the person out of bed.

The myoclonic movement can feel as if one has been touched or grabbed. Some reports of nocturnal visits from spirits or UFO occupants likely arise from such misinterpretations.

myroblutai A Greek term meaning "unguent spouters," this name was given by members of the early Christian church to individuals who secreted "holy oils" from their bodies. The belief that saintly people exude a special substance from their bodies—variously described as sacred blood, milk, oil or "manna"—is featured in the life stories of devout Christians to the present day. The phenomenon of the myroblutai is included in the list of CHARISMs, or supernatural phenomena associated with holiness as recognized by the Roman Catholic church. If there is anything more to such stories than religious propaganda, they may reflect extraordinary metabolic processes connected to intense religious devotion and practice.

See also ODORS OF SANCTITY; STIGMATA.

mysterium fascinans Latin for "fascinating mystery"; a term coined by Otto referring to the compelling attraction to the sacred presence felt in the NUMINOUS EXPERIENCE.

mysterium tremendum Latin for "awesome mystery"; Otto used this term to refer to the feelings of humility and fear evoked by a NUMINOUS encounter with a supernatural presence.

mystical experience In Greek the adjective *mystikos* refers to something that is secret or hidden. The English adjective "mystical," which derives from the Greek, has been used to describe anything that is mystifying, confusing or occult. Since the 17th century, "mysticism" has referred to a type of unusual experience that, while difficult to understand for those who have not had it, is not necessarily mystifying or occult. A mystical experience is characterized by the feeling that, despite the apparent diversity in the world, everything forms a unity. This feeling can be vague and fleeting; or, in a fully developed mystical experience, it can eliminate all other mental activity, and last for hours.

Stace has identified some common characteristics of the mystical experience. The unity of all things is not just perceived; perceptions can be misleading. Rather, it is sensed as certain knowledge, compared to which the apparent separation of objects in the world seems illusory. While some mystics have described aspects of their experience as painful or burning, overall the mystical experience is described in overwhelmingly positive terms. For many who have had it, the apprehension of an underlying unity is the most meaningful moment in their lives.

Another common characteristic is the inability to describe the experience in words. Ordinary language has developed in order to describe the world of distinct objects; the unity glimpsed by the mystics cannot be captured using words that highlight the separateness of things. Thus, many mystics have employed language in a paradoxical manner to hint that the essence of their experience transcends the distinctions of language—"the fullness of the void," "the brilliant darkness," "dying into life."

According to Stace, two subtypes of the mystical experience can be distinguished: introvertive and extravertive. The introvertive mystical experience features a sense of being beyond space and time, and a dissolution of all mental contents into the feeling of unity. Even the mystic's sense of being a distinct self disappears. The English poet Alfred Lord Tennyson attempted to convey what his introvertive mystical experiences were like (quoted by James [1958]):

a kind of waking trance—this for lack of a better word—I have frequently had, quite up from boyhood, when I have been all alone. This has come upon me, as it were out of the intensity of the consciousness of individuality, individuality itself seemed to dissolve and fade away into boundless being, and this not a confused state but the clearest, the surest of the surest, utterly beyond words—where death was an almost laughable impossibility—the loss of personality (if so it were) seeming no extinction, but the only true life. I am ashamed of my feeble description. Have I not said the state is utterly beyond words?

In the extravertive subtype of the mystical experience, the world of separate things does not disappear; rather, the unity is sensed *within* the diversity of ordinary appearances. Often, there is a feeling that everything—even inanimate things like rocks and waves—possesses an inner life. While viewing a beautiful sunset, the Indian poet Rabindranath Tagore had such an experience (quoted by Happold):

> As I was watching it, suddenly, in a moment, a veil seemed to be lifted from my eyes. I found the world wrapt in an inexpressible glory with its waves of joy and beauty bursting and breaking on all sides. The thick cloud of sorrow that lay on my heart in many folds was pierced through and through by the light of the world, which was everywhere radiant. . . . There was nothing and no one whom I did not love at that moment. . . . [The activities of the people], their forms, their countenances seemed strangely wonderful to me, as if they were all moving like waves in the great ocean of the world. . . . I seemed to witness, in the wholeness of my vision, the movements of the body of all humanity.

Many people who have mystical experiences interpret them in religious terms. Believers in theistic religions generally talk of experiencing the presence of God, or even of union with God. Buddhists, who do not rely on the concept of a creator or savior deity in their spiritual lives, refer to a direct perception of EMPTINESS, the impersonal reality.

The occurrence of mystical experiences in all of the world's major faiths indicates that these belief systems are simply different versions of the same message, different gateways to the same mystical reality, according to some scholars. Others disagree, pointing out that the meaning given to mystical experiences differs dramatically across religions—a Christian experiencing mystical marriage with Christ cannot be equated with a Hindu realizing the unity of the personal and universal soul without doing violence to the basic tenets of both belief systems. Even atheists have mystical experiences. Evidently, there must be some common cause—whether biological, environmental, or spiritual—involved in mystical experiences, which are then patterned by the beliefs and expectations of the mystic.

It has long been thought that mystical experiences were uncommon. Religious authorities believed that only saints and other spiritual achievers were likely to be graced with an awareness of the divine presence. Many psychiatrists, including Freud, observed that some mentally disturbed people reported mystical experiences, speculating that pathological rather than spiritual forces were involved. Many surveys have refuted the rarity of the mystical experience—most studies report that 30 to 40% of respondents affirm that they have had it.

It seems that some people are more likely to have mystical experiences than others. Several psychological traits have been associated with mystical reports, including ABSORPTION, FANTASY PRONENESS, HYPNOTIZABILITY and tolerance of AMBIGUITY. These correlations suggest that the capacity to focus one's attention in unusual ways may be involved. Fenwick noted that individuals with a history of HEAD INJURY are more likely to have mystical experiences. And Thalbourne reported an association between mystical reports and MAGICAL THINKING, which has been taken as a sign of proneness to SCHIZOPHRENIA. Although these findings are consistent with the link between mysticism and malfunction observed by psychiatrists, several studies have found that people who report mystical experiences tend to be mentally healthier than the average person, showing higher levels of PSYCHOLOGICAL ADJUSTMENT. The mystical feeling of unity may in some cases be connected with mental or physical problems, but in most instances there is no evidence of this.

Mystical experiences can occur spontaneously. A partial list of reported triggers of mystical moments includes drugs, sex, fever, religious worship, natural beauty, music, the death of others, the prospect of one's own death, suicidal feelings, the sight of a garbage dump, slime, excrement, derelict buildings, a dead chicken, fog and hearing a whistle wailing in the dark. It seems that almost anything can set off a mystical experience in a predisposed individual. Hood (in Spilka, Hood and Gorsuch) wondered if the key ingredient is the sudden and surprising onset or termination of stress. If one is unexpectedly confronted with beauty or ugliness, danger or excitement, one's everyday habits of attention may be derailed. A person can then pay attention to things in unusual ways. If the attention focuses strongly on the commonalities between objects rather than their differences, a powerful sense of unity—the hallmark of the mystical experience—may arise. This feeling is then interpreted in light of the mystic's beliefs.

As the mystical experience has been so highly valued as a glimpse of reality, it is not surprising that people have tried to induce it. Many spiritual practices, ranging from meditation to contemplation and prayer, aim to open a person to contact with truth; often, these contacts are associated with mystical experiences. Few if any people can produce such an experience at will. Mystical practices can, at best, prepare a person; the actual occurrence is beyond the control of the human will, which is why it is frequently regarded as caused by the will of God.

See also Appendix; DARK NIGHT OF THE SOUL; DEAUTOMATIZATION; NUMINOUS EXPERIENCE; PANENHENIC STATE; UNIO MYSTICA; ZERO EXPERIENCE.

For further reading: Fenwick et. al.; Happold; Hood; James (1958); Spilka, Hood and Gorsuch; Stace; Thalbourne (1991).

narcissism A personality trait characterized by a grandiose exaggeration of self-importance and a lack of empathy with others. Some studies have found that narcissistic individuals are more likely than people who have low levels of narcissism to believe in ESP and spirits.

See also Appendix; BELIEF, ANOMALOUS.

Naropa, Six Yogas of Among the most important meditation practices of Tibetan Buddhism, the Six Yogas are attributed to the famous 11th century master of Buddhist TANTRA, Naropa; it is unlikely, however, that he invented them. The origin of the Yogas is unclear. Some researchers have suggested that they combine traditional Buddhist meditations with material derived from the practices of SHAMANISM. The goal of the Yogas is to transform the ordinary body and mind into the body and mind of a Buddha. Vivid visualization of energy processes within one's body and training oneself to regard everything as having the ultimate nature of EMPTINESS are the two key mental skills in Naropa's practices.

The first Yoga is the practice of *Dumo*, a Tibetan word meaning "Fierce Woman." The aim of Dumo meditation is to generate an inner heat which incinerates bodily impurities, as well as mental obstacles to ENLIGHTENMENT. The meditator is instructed to imagine the physical body as hollow; then, an energy body, composed of nodes (CHAKRAS) and channels, is visualized. In connection with certain breathing techniques, the practitioner learns to control the flow of energy in this visualized circulatory system. The energies are brought together in the vicinity of the navel. They ignite, forming a flame which shoots up the center of the body. In a controlled fashion, this flame is enlarged until it engulfs the body in a fireball.

Tibetan monks, who used to spend long periods meditating in frigid mountain caves, have reported that the Dumo Yoga can keep a person warm in the coldest temperatures. They have also told of competitions among Dumo practitioners. David-Neel described the practice:

> The neophytes sit on the ground, cross-legged and naked. Sheets are dipped in icy water, each man wraps himself in one of them and must dry it on his body. As soon as the sheet has become dry, it is again dipped in the water and placed on the novice's body to be dried as before. The operation goes on in that way until daybreak. Then he who has dried the largest number of sheets is declared the winner of the competition.

Research conducted at Harvard Medical School by Benson and his colleagues discovered that Dumo meditators were capable of increasing the temperature of their fingers and toes by as much as 8.3° Centigrade (14.9° Fahrenheit).

The second of Naropa's practices is the Yoga of the Illusory Body. Its aim is to penetrate the false appearances of things. Although it seems as if the objects of awareness, including one's own body, are entities possessing their own independent existence, Buddhism teaches that, in fact, their true nature is empty. Meditators are taught to contemplate their reflection in a mirror, and to listen to echoes of their voices. Reflections and echoes have no existence of their own, apart from their sources; so also, bodies and sounds themselves do not exist apart from the mysterious reality of the void. Visualization exercises are also used. An image of a Buddha, for instance, is developed in the mind until it is more vivid than an object perceived with the senses; then, by dissolving it, the insubstantial nature of the image is revealed. This exercise leads the meditator to see that perceived objects also lack any solid existence. As G.C.C. Chang notes, "During this practice, the yogi will feel strongly that nothing really exists. This experience will continue to deepen until one reaches full Enlightenment."

The Dream Yoga is the third of Naropa's practices. Meditators train themselves first to remember dreams, then to attain consciousness while dreaming (LUCID DREAMING) and then to assume control of dreams. Eventually, one is able to journey in the dream state to the abode of the Buddhas, and to receive teachings from these wise beings. Visualization practices, said to affect the circulation patterns within the energy body, are the central technique of this Yoga.

Light Yoga, Naropa's fourth practice, requires the mastery of the preceding Yogas. The Light is actually the experience of emptiness, the ultimate reality of all things. Techniques of breathing, posture and visualization are taught in this Yoga to enable the practitioner to hold the perception of this Light in every state of consciousness, including sleep.

Next, the BARDO Yoga, or practice of the intermediate state, is discussed. In this context, the Tibetan term *bardo* refers to the states of awareness that are said to occur between death and rebirth. The condition of being between lives is said to be full of opportunities for attaining liberation from the endless cycle of reincarnation, which is pervaded by suffering. Studying the various experiences to be expected after death, as described in texts such as the *Tibetan Book of the Dead*, is helpful preparation. Thinking that one is already in the bardo, that everything one experiences is a post-mortem apparition, is also recommended. Practice of the Illusory Body, Dream and Light Yogas train the mind to recognize the reality of the void; if this recognition occurs in the after-death bardo, one is immediately liberated.

The last practice in Naropa's collection is the Yoga of Consciousness Transference. In this meditation the practitioner first visualizes a hollow tube, like a bamboo stalk, running up the middle of the body. A tiny sphere of light sits in this tube. The meditator places his or her awareness in the sphere and shoots it through the top of the head. During life, the technique can be used to leave the body and journey to other places; at the moment of death, the meditator visualizes a Buddha and projects the sphere of consciousness into this image, thus ensuring a rebirth in the spiritual world of the Buddha. It has been reported that mastery of this Yoga is indicated by the appearance of an actual small lesion or lump in the scalp at the point where the sphere exits.

See also MEDITATION.

For further reading: Benson et. al. (1982); G.C.C. Chang (1974); David-Neel; Namgyal.

near death experience People who come close to death and later revive sometimes report memories of unusual experiences they had while apparently unconscious. These memory accounts are often said to be recollections of "near death experiences" (NDEs). Stories of returning from the brink of death with tales to tell are widespread and may be universal. The earliest overt description of a near death experience was given by Plato in *The Republic*. He recounts how a soldier named Er was taken for dead and placed on a funeral pyre. Er suddenly revived and told of leaving his body and journeying to an otherworldly place of judgment. It seems likely that even earlier writings on what the newly dead can expect to encounter, such as the Egyptian Book of the Dead, were based in part on NDEs.

This phenomenon has been noted throughout the history of the West. In the sixth century, Pope Gregory the Great published a collection of unusual experience accounts, including three NDEs. Another such collection, compiled by Caesarius of Heisterbach in the 13th century, also contained NDEs. The experiences recorded by orthodox Christian sources invariably conform to the prevailing dogmatic pictures of the afterlife. Whether the NDEs themselves fit so neatly into the requirements of the church or whether pious editors had reworked the original stories for propaganda purposes is unknown.

With the rise of the modern scientific world view, it became popular to dismiss NDE stories along with many other sorts of unusual experience accounts as superstitions or signs of madness. Serious interest began to return in the late 19th century. In 1892, Heim published an article entitled "The Experience of Dying from Falls." Heim had interviewed 30 mountain climbers who had fallen from cliffs and nearly died. He reported a surprising finding—the experience of approaching death had been peaceful and happy: "They had, so to speak, fallen into heaven." In the present century, occasional publications in the medical and psychical research literature addressed NDEs; but the floodgate of popular fascination was thrown open by the 1975 massive bestseller *Life After Life* by Raymond Moody. Since then, several surveys and case collections of NDEs have been undertaken, and a *Journal of Near Death Studies* established. (It is noteworthy that Moody no longer recommends his own books to people wanting to learn about the NDE; he encourages them to consult the more recent and better scientifically grounded works of others).

Recent studies have revealed that many people who are brought close to death—through injury or illness—do not report NDEs after being revived. Estimates of the proportion of those who have been near death and recounted NDEs range from 7% to 72%; this variance may be explained in part by the reluctance of some survivors to admit that they remember an NDE. Compared to others, people who report NDEs are more likely to state that they had experienced CHILDHOOD TRAUMA; they also tend to display a capacity for ABSORPTION, FANTASY PRONENESS and HYPNOTIZABILITY. (Ring disputes that NDE informants are fantasy prone; but his descriptions of the CHILDHOOD ALTERNATE REALITY experiences of NDE informants would be considered by other researchers as evidence for fantasy proneness.)

Several studies have confirmed that certain elements occur commonly in NDEs. These elements are sometimes described as "stages," which is misleading as they do not happen in every NDE and do not always occur in the same order. The most common element, recalled by a majority of informants, is a feeling of calmness and joy. Another feature noted by at least half of the informants in most studies is an OUT OF BODY EXPERIENCE. Dying persons can suddenly find themselves observing their physical bodies from an external vantage point and may see or hear events—such as the banter of a surgical team laboring to save the patient's life—that are later confirmed as an accurate memory of what transpired at the time. Some writers have pointed to this occurrence as evidence that a center of awareness—a "soul" or "self"—had actually detached itself from the unconscious body. Numerous studies have shown, however, that comatose or anaesthetized people can store and later retrieve some information presented to them verbally, despite their unconscious state.

About one-quarter of the informants described a "passage through darkness," which can take the form of floating along a tunnel toward a distant light. Although this element has become the stereotypic feature of the NDE in popular culture, it is, in fact, reported by a relatively small number of NDE informants.

Almost one-third of NDEs involve the appearance of a brilliant light, frequently golden in hue. Nearly half of the informants reported an encounter with a nurturing, supportive "presence." This encounter is sometimes felt rather than seen; but often it takes the form of a religious figure such as Christ, or an unidentified "being of light."

Most surveys have found that about 25% of informants described a review of their lives flashing past during the NDE. This experience has been compared to viewing a film of one's existence since birth, very rapidly. Others have described a series of bright images of their life's highlights and turning points.

A final common NDE element, noted by up to 54% of the informants in the surveys, is a visit to a heavenly realm. Most frequently, splendid lawns and gardens are recalled; palatial architecture has also been observed. These accounts resemble the descriptions given by people in the throes of DEATHBED VISIONS.

Most NDEs are said to end suddenly with the awakening of the informant. Sometimes, a figure in the otherworldly setting indicates the end of the experience by telling the informant to return to the body.

Most of the informants in the major surveys and case collections mentioned above were raised in the modern West. Cross cultural and historical research into the NDE suggests that the experience is less uniform than is commonly stated. Zaleski compared modern NDE accounts with those of the Middle Ages and found consistent differences—for instance, visits to hell and purgatorial settings figure prominently in the medieval stories, but are extremely rare in modern NDEs. Zaleski detects the fingerprints of cultural influence on the modern accounts, which she describes as "shaped throughout by optimistic, democratic, 'healthy-minded' principles that transparently reflect a contemporary ideology and mood."

Pasricha and Stevenson have collected NDE accounts from India and reported systematic differences from western NDEs. The typical Indian NDE involves the informant being escorted to another world by spirit messengers, confronted by a "man with a book" (often said to be Yama, Lord of the Dead) who discovers that an error has been made in bringing the informant there and sent back to life by the messengers or by deceased relatives. Viewing one's own body from without is extremely rare in Indian NDEs, and the panoramic life review is unknown. These comparative findings suggest that the experience

itself, the remembering of it and/or the reporting of it is being crafted by the forces of personal expectation and need.

The lack of uniformity among NDEs poses problems for those who wish to take the NDE literally as a glimpse of the afterlife. Why would the otherworld change as a function of the informant's century and society? Many researchers believe that the NDE is caused by processes in the body of the endangered individual, rather than originating from without. Seizures and cerebral oxygen deprivation can happen to a person who is severely stressed or injured, and both of these factors can cause HALLUCINATIONS. Certain features of NDEs resemble FORM CONSTANTS—geometric images produced by the visual system when its normal functioning is disrupted. A common form constant is the cone or tunnel. Siegel suggested that this image was the basis for the tunnel journey noted in some NDEs. The body in stress can release quantities of endorphins, a substance that can cause feelings of serenity similar to the most commonly cited element in NDEs.

Typically, these biological processes trigger bizarre, disorganized experiences, unlike the coherent narratives of many NDEs. Seizures, lack of oxygen, visual system malfunctions and endorphins may explain some features of NDEs, but not their overall structure. Some have suggested that the NDE is a defense against the terror of life's end; the dying mind organizes the elements of the NDE into a comforting fantasy that implies the survival of death. All such theories are speculations; and, barring an experiment in which volunteers are brought to the verge of death and then revived while subjected to physical and psychological manipulations, they are likely to remain so.

Regardless of the ultimate causes of NDEs, their impact on survivors is often dramatic. Commonly noted effects include an enhanced sense of life's preciousness, and a rise in compassion and religious feelings. Most NDE informants report a strengthened conviction that the self survives death. A noteworthy exception is Ernst Rodin, a neurologist who had an NDE that he described as "one of the most intense and happiest moments in my life," and then proceeded to explain it as the result of insufficient oxygen reaching his brain tissues. Rodin lamented that he will fall for the illusion again when he dies: "despite my current awareness that these visions and beliefs will be utterly false, I know that I will accept them as full truth when the time comes."

See also METACHORIC EXPERIENCE.

For further reading: Heim; Irwin (1989a); Kellehear; Moody; Pasricha (1993); Pasricha and Stevenson; Ring; Rodin; Siegel (1980); Zaleski.

negative hallucination In a regular HALLUCINATION, one perceives something that is not physically present; in a negative hallucination, one fails to perceive something that is present and available to the senses. Strictly speaking, all hallucinations involve a negative hallucination; in order to hallucinate an object, one must block out what is actually occupying the area filled by the hallucination. Negative hallucinations can be created using HYPNOSIS and are often found among sufferers of DISSOCIATIVE DISORDERs. In these instances, the phenomenon is simply an exaggerated form of refusing to pay attention to something. Negative hallucinations can also arise from neurological causes, as in some cases of EPILEPSY.

nei-tan Some branches of the Chinese philosophy called Taoism have as their aim the attainment of immortality. Nei-tan is the Taoist meditative process that is said to produce this lofty goal. In theory, each person is composed of three vital energies: essence (*ching*), identified with the sexual juices; breath (*ch'i*); and spirit or consciousness (*shen*). These elements are not merely physical, but are connected with the spiritual forces that give rise to the universe. By transforming ching into ch'i, and ch'i into shen,

an immortal "sacred embryo" (also known as the Golden Flower) forms within the body. During the formation and gestation of the embryo, a host of unusual experiences occur.

Some Taoists have insisted that the first step in nei-tan is the practice of sexual meditations called FANG-CHUNG SHU. Intercourse, when properly conducted, is said to propel the sexual emissions to a spot in the brain, where they can be transmuted into ch'i. The moral climate changed in China around the seventh century, and such practices were frowned upon. Many devotees of nei-tan dispensed with this step, but some have continued to practice it in secret.

The central meditations of nei-tan involve the visualization of light circulating within the body. First, the meditator concentrates on imagining sensations of energy flowing from the heart region, through the abdomen, to the kidneys. This is known as the "lesser celestial circulation." If the meditator practices diligently, the coursing of the energy can actually be felt; it no longer has to be imagined.

When the lesser circulation is clear, the meditator goes on to the "greater celestial circulation." Attention is focused on energy sensations flowing from the base of the spine to the top of the head, and down again through the front of the body. Men start the energy moving by concentrating on a spot below the navel; women begin at the middle of the chest. At various stages of practice, concentration is fixed on certain points in this circulating path. The entire process resembles the meditations on the CHAKRAS of Hindu and Buddhist TANTRA.

As the sacred embryo grows, it requires nurturance via a special breathing technique, the "embryo breath." The meditator learns to hold the breath for prolonged periods, during which the ch'i energy is visualized circulating through the body, flowing into an umbilical cord and pervading the form of the embryo.

If the nei-tan has been done correctly, the meditator will have the feeling that he or she has become integrated with the cosmos. At death, the embryo will leave the corpse behind. The practitioner will have become one of the Immortals, legendary beings who possess magical powers.

Like most intensive spiritual practices, the nei-tan meditations can produce unexpected experiences. Chang Chung-yuan wrote of a novice who had begun to study with a nei-tan master:

> One night, as the young man walked along the mountain path, he felt a sudden lightning circulate within him and there was the roar of thunder at the top of his head. The mountain, the stream, the world, and his very self vanished. The experience lasted for 'about the time it would take five inches of incense to burn.' Thereafter he felt like a different man, purified by his own light. The student was told that this lightning must be put aside. The Master, having experienced it frequently during his thirty years of meditation, no longer paid attention to it.

The most familiar esoteric Taoist text to Westerners is *The Secret of the Golden Flower,* a 17th century work. The psychiatrist Carl Jung wrote an essay on this work, which combines ideas of nei-tan with those of Zen Buddhism.

See also KUNDALINI.

For further reading: C. Chang; Fischer-Schreiber; Schipper; Storr.

neurological disorder   Every known facet of human experience involves the activities of the brain. When normal brain functioning is affected by illness or injury, all kinds of unusual experiences can result. Some researchers have suggested that occasional brain malfunctions (especially TEMPORAL LOBE ABNORMALITIES) occur in many members of the general population, giving rise to otherwise unexplainable reports of strange events. Among the major neurological disorders, EPILEPSY, MIGRAINE and TOURETTE'S SYNDROME are well-known for their association with unusual experiences.

For further reading: Beyerstein.

New Jersey Vegetable Monster   A humanoid resembling a giant stalk of broccoli, reputedly seen one night by a drunk in the New Jersey Pine Barrens. The case has entered the folklore of anomalistic studies as representing the least evidential type of unusual experience report.

nightmare   In premodern times, frightening dreams were thought to be caused by evil spirits who climbed onto the chests of sleepers and "rode" them—hence the term "nightmare." These terrifying experiences occur in REM stage sleep, the same phase that produces innocuous dreams. Most nightmares arise during the second half of the sleep period, when the dreamer spends more time in relatively light stages of sleep. The primary difference between a nightmare and other dreams lies in the unpleasant content of the nightmare and the intensity of emotional reaction to it. Indeed, the fear evoked by nightmares is often disturbing enough to awaken the sleeper—often to his or her relief.

Nightmares usually portray apparently life-threatening situations, such as being pursued by a ravenous monster or falling off a cliff. Dreaming of one's own death in a nightmare is very rare. The occurrence of nightmares is often linked with stressful periods in one's life. They can also be a side effect of some medications.

Occasional nightmares are normal, especially before age 20. Recurrent frightening dreams are afflicting about 5% of the population at any given time; a further 6% report having had repeated nightmares in the past. Repetitious distressing dreams are classified as *dream anxiety disorder*. In children this disorder is not associated with any mental disorder. Among adults, recurrent nightmares are more often found in those suffering from a range of psychological disturbances. This association may be explained by the stress evoked by mental illness. Some studies have suggested a link between repeating nightmares and artistic creativity.

The nightmare is usually distinguished from another unpleasant sleep phenomenon, the

NIGHT TERROR (although some terminological confusion remains in the literature). These events occur in different stages of sleep. The nightmare is a dream, consisting of a sequence of images, and is usually remembered upon awakening; the night terror is commonly a single image and is usually forgotten completely. The fear arousal of the night terror is typically more intense than that of the nightmare.

See also HYPNAGOGIC STATE; HYPNOPOMPIC STATE; OLD HAG EXPERIENCE.

For further reading: American Psychiatric Association; Coleman; Dement; Hartmann; Hufford.

night terror An episode of night terror strikes in dramatic fashion—a sleeping person suddenly sits upright in bed and emits a blood-curdling scream. Drenched in perspiration, with pounding heart and ragged breathing, the victim can remain agitated and confused for up to 10 minutes. Attempts at consolation by worried family members are usually futile during this period. The individual may not be able to say what was the source of the fright; or he or she might report a single, terrifying image. After the terror subsides, the person can normally return to slumber. The following morning, he or she may not even recall the episode.

Night terrors usually happen during the first half of the sleeping period. The sleeper is not in the condition known as the REM stage, when dreams occur, but in the dreamless stages of deep sleep. The night terror is thus distinguished from the NIGHTMARE, which is a frightening dream.

Many people, especially children, have occasional experiences of night terror without any lasting ill effect. Up to 4% of children between the ages of 4 and 12 suffer from recurrent night terrors. Repeated episodes have also been known to torment adults, although much more rarely than in children. Prolonged recurrent night terrors are classified as *sleep terror disorder*. The origin of this condition is unclear. Some studies have indicated that individuals who have been ill with high fevers are more likely to suffer from it. People with sleep terror disorder can be propelled into a night terror episode merely by being suddenly awakened.

The interference with breathing connected with night terrors has been described as a sensation of great weight crushing the chest. In the Middle Ages, this feature gave rise to the interpretation that the experience was caused by demons called incubi and succubi. These spirits were believed to creep into bedrooms at night and perch on sleepers' chests. A succubus would visit men; assuming a female form, it would sexually stimulate the sleeper and drain semen from him. Then, the devil would transform into a male form, or incubus. Mounting sleeping women in this guise, it was said to inseminate them. (Some writers regard the INCUBUS NIGHTMARE as a phenomenon related to the night terror, but caused by a different mechanism).

See also OLD HAG EXPERIENCE.

For further reading: American Psychiatric Association; Coleman; Dement; Hartmann; Hufford.

nimitta In the Pali language of ancient India, this word literally means "sign." Buddhists use the term to refer to certain visual phenomena that arise during the course of meditation practice. In one meaning of the word, the nimitta is a deliberately induced mental image of an external object. For example, if one is meditating on a colored disc, the visualized image of the disc is the nimitta. The term also refers to spontaneous images that can accompany states of concentrated attention. In the practice of *anapanasati*, or meditation on breathing, practitioners sometimes report seeing their breath as a stream of starlight, smoke, a silver chain or a garland of tiny flowers. Such nimittas signify the attainment of nondistracted focusing on the meditation object. They can become distractions, however, if the meditator is excited by the experience and forgets to continue the assigned meditation.

See also MAKYO; MEDITATION.
For further reading: Buddhaghosa.

nirananda-samapatti "Merging without bliss," a meditative state discussed by some practitioners of RAJA YOGA. It is classified as a type of SAMPRAJNATA SAMADHI.

nirasmati-samapatti "Merging beyond the feeling of 'I am'," a state of concentration in the RAJA YOGA map of consciousness. It is classified as a type of SAMPRAJNATA SAMADHI.

nirodha This Sanskrit term, which means "destruction" or "cessation," designates a state of consciousness said to be attainable only by those who have mastered Buddhist meditation practices. Nirodha is the highest goal of the sequence of mental concentrations known as the JHANAS.

The jhana meditations are employed by Buddhists to develop the capacity called SHAMATHA, or calm abiding. When a profoundly calmed mental condition is attained, the meditator can practice VIPASSANA, or insight, to explore the nature of reality. The state of nirodha is accessed from the most concentrated jhana, the ninth, when calm abiding and insight are both present.

Prior to entering nirodha, meditators must decide how long they wish to remain in the state and program themselves to emerge following the selected duration. This preparation is necessary because there is no sense of time when in nirodha. Buddhist texts claim that the heartbeat and breathing of a person in nirodha slow to undetectable levels. A meditator is said to be able to remain in this condition for up to seven days.

In addition to physiological quiescence, mental activities are said to cease completely in nirodha. Buddhist schools differ over whether nirodha can even be called a state of consciousness. However, all agree that all manifestations of the emotional disturbances that pose obstacles to ENLIGHTENMENT are suppressed; nirodha therefore can serve as a powerful cleansing of the mind.

Although some sources equate nirodha with the Buddhist goal of NIRVANA, most Buddhists make an important distinction between the two states. While the jhanas and their pinnacle, nirodha, counteract the *occurrence* of the afflictive emotions, the seeds of these disturbances are left untouched. Thus, the benefits of nirodha are temporary—when the meditator returns to less exalted states of awareness, the afflictions can blossom again. The *First Bhavanakrama* (quoted by Sopa) notes: "Even though one has developed trance [jhana] through meditation, this does not destroy the perception of a self. The passions will ripen again for him." Nirvana, by contrast, destroys not only the afflictions of greed, hatred and delusion, but the fundamental error—belief in an enduring self—which produces all suffering.

For further reading: Buddhaghosa; Goleman; Sopa.

nirvana A Sanskrit word, nirvana derives from the term *vana*, meaning "to burn," coupled with the negative prefix *nir*. The classic metaphor for nirvana, probably invented by the Buddha himself, is the extinguishing of a flame. Nirvana, according to every school of Buddhism, is the highest goal of meditation. The meanings given to the term, however, are many.

The attainment of nirvana is connected to the practice of meditation. In Buddhism, two faculties—calm abiding (SHAMATHA) and insight (VIPASSANA)—must be fully developed and used to examine the nature of one's experience. Through this process, the meditator will discover that no object in any possible world can produce lasting satisfaction. One may, however, glimpse a reality which has no inherent characteristics at all. This glimpse is nirvana. The ultimate reality apprehended in nirvana is understood according to the conceptions of the various schools of Buddhism. Theravada Buddhists speak of the "unborn, unconditioned peace"; Mahayana Buddhism denotes the object of nirvana as EMPTINESS. Nirvana is difficult to describe because no ordinary mental processes occur while in this state.

As a result of this contact with reality, however conceived, one can free oneself from attachment to the sources of suffering in the phenomenal world, according to Buddhism. Thus, the burning emotional afflictions of greed, hatred and delusion are extinguished, like the snuffing of a flame, in nirvana.

Some texts indicate that there are degrees of reaction to nirvana which mark stages on the path to the final liberation.

The more highly evolved the level of insight immediately prior to entering nirvana, the more thorough is the resulting destruction of the sources of suffering. After the first experience of nirvana, one is freed from the following obstacles to enlightenment: belief in the existence of any type of permanent self; doubt concerning the effectiveness of Buddhist insight; and addiction to rules and rituals. Those who have attained this state are known as "stream-enterers," for they have joined the stream of experience that eventually produces liberation; it is said that they will become enlightened within seven lifetimes.

As one's insight matures, repeated entry into nirvana can produce further benefits. The meditator perceives ever more clearly the absence of self, permanence and satisfactoriness in all phenomena. As a result, one becomes less enslaved by angry and lustful impulses. Someone who has attained this level of wisdom is called a "once-returner," in the belief that only one more incarnation will be required before liberation is achieved.

The next stage of development is that of the "non-returner," one who will not need to be reborn. As a result of their nirvana, such beings are thought to be freed from anger and sensual desire. The fully liberated being is known as the "foe destroyer" (arhat), because every obstacle to freedom has been extinguished by the fully matured nirvana. No longer is one controlled by cravings for experiences, even those of extremely refined meditative states; pride, restlessness and the illusions that produce suffering are fully uprooted, never to return.

In the Theravada school of Buddhism, the nirvana of the foe destroyer is called the "nirvana with remainder." Although the sources of suffering have been destroyed, their effects persist as a kind of karmic momentum. Therefore, some degree of suffering continues until the karma of past actions is exhausted, and the foe destroyer dies. At this point, the "nirvana without remainder" is attained. The foe destroyer enters nirvana and will not reincarnate.

Mahayana Buddhism holds that individuals who feel compassion for their fellow beings can choose to delay their final departure into nirvana, in order to work for the liberation of all. Such a person, called a *bodhisattva,* renounces the static nirvana of the foe destroyer for an "active nirvana." In this condition the bodhisattva is free from the chains of greed, hatred and delusion and is able to reincarnate at will in order to assist others toward this freedom. Eventually, the supreme ENLIGHTENMENT of a Buddha is attained. Buddhas are said to be not only liberated, but omniscient, and are therefore extremely powerful helpers.

See also NIRODHA.

For further reading: Fischer-Schreiber; Goleman; Snelling.

nirvicara-samapatti "Merging without reflective thought," a concentrative state discussed in the RAJA YOGA system. It is classified as a type of SAMPRAJNATA SAMADHI.

nirvicara-vaisharadhya "Clear awareness without reflective thought," a meditative state discussed by practitioners of RAJA YOGA. It is classified under the heading of SAMPRAJNATA SAMADHI.

nirvikalpa samadhi This form of SAMADHI, or state of concentrated attention, is viewed as a high spiritual achievement among meditators following the Vedanta tradition of Hinduism. It is known as "without (*nir*) concepts (*vikalpa*)" because thinking ceases. When one thinks, one has the sense that his or her thought is different from the object of the thought—the idea of a sandwich is not an actual sandwich. In Nirvikalpa Samadhi, all forms of separateness, including thoughts, are eliminated. The meditator experiences his or her own deepest self as not differentiated from the self of the universe, or God.

Goleman quotes the following description of Nirvikalpa Samadhi:

> an avalanche of indescribable bliss sweeps away all relative ideas of pain and blame . . . All doubts and misgivings are quelled forever; the oscillations of mind are stopped; the momentum of past actions is exhausted.

This profound state is accessed through meditation practice and can only be maintained while the body is perfectly still. Metabolic functioning slows to the point that respiration and heart beat are said to be imperceptible. It is claimed that the meditator can remain in this condition for up to three months, although such a feat has never been demonstrated under controlled conditions.

According to an important meditation text, the *Mandala-Brahmana-Upanishad,* the ability to enter Nirvikalpa Samadhi drastically reduces the need to sleep and eliminate waste.

This state also reduces attachment to the concept of oneself as a limited being, a major obstacle to the attainment of full self realization. When the awareness that one's self and the universal self are not different can be maintained during everyday activities, then the static condition of Nirvikalpa Samadhi has been transformed into the highest spiritual state—SAHAJ SAMADHI.

For further reading: Feuerstein (1989, 1990); Goleman.

nirvitarka-samapatti "Merging without thought," a concentrative state identified in the RAJA YOGA system. It is classified as a type of SAMPRAJNATA SAMADHI.

numinous experience The Latin word *numen* refers to the feeling of being in the presence of an impersonal supernatural force. Otto derived the term "numinous experience" to designate states of religious awe. The numinous is often experienced in natural settings, when one is overwhelmed by the grandeur of the universe, or when a spiritual presence is sensed in the stillness of a church. The numinous feeling can mark the onset of a MYSTICAL EXPERIENCE.

According to Otto, the essence of the numinous experience is a feeling of encounter with something that is "wholly other" than oneself and all ordinary objects. He noted two types of emotional reaction to this encounter. In the *mysterium tremendum,* one's own sense of insignificance, powerlessness and incomprehension in the face of a vast divinity is highlighted. The tremendum:

> may at times come sweeping like a gentle tide, pervading the mind with a tranquil mood of deepest worship. . . . It may burst in sudden eruption up from the depths of the soul with spasms and convulsions, or lead to the strangest excitements, to intoxicated frenzy, to transport, and to ecstasy. . . . It may become the hushed trembling, and speechless humility of the creature in the presence of—whom or what? In the presence of that which is a *mystery* inexpressible and above all creatures.

Otto named the other reaction to the numinous encounter the *mysterium fascinans.* The presence of the sacred mystery can evoke a compelling fascination and a burning desire to pursue the experience after it has faded. Otto argued that the numinous experience was the origin of religion: various taboos arose out of respect and fear for the power sensed in the tremendum; prayers and ceremonies can be seen as attempts to satisfy the urge toward the numinous that characterizes the fascinans; and the myriad beliefs concerning gods and spirits are ways of explaining the nature of the "wholly other" sensed in the encounter.

Otto's emphasis on the "wholly other" in the numinous experience has been criticized as having an orthodox Judeo-Christian bias. The mainstream Jewish and Christian tradition has always emphasized that God and humanity are distinct. Anyone claiming that he or she was God was viewed as a blasphemer. In some non-western traditions, and in certain unorthodox Christian movements, however, the true nature of the self was identified with God. Numinous experiences can sometimes feel like encounters with "wholly Self"—the awesome and fascinating depths of one's own being. In this vein, Carl Jung considered dreams and fantasies in which a person comes into contact with the deepest layers of the unconscious mind to be numinous experiences. Abraham Maslow noted that PEAK EXPERIENCEs, or glimpses of one's highest potential, had numinous qualities.

For further reading: Maslow (1968, 1976); Otto; Storr.

obsession In traditional Catholic thought, an obsession is an attack by a devil from outside of one's body (the term is derived from the Latin *ob sedere,* "to sit outside"). Obsessions were distinguished from POSSESSIONs, in which the evil spirit invaded the body. The truly virtuous were held to be immune to the indignity of possession; so, the saints were portrayed as suffering obsessions only (typically in the form of visions of seductive women). In the mid-19th century, "obsession" was adopted as a psychiatric term. Today, it no longer refers to external assaults, but to the uncontrollable contents of one's own mind. A thought, impulse or fantasy that recurs and cannot be suppressed is a hallmark of obsessive-compulsive disorder, and also afflicts some sufferers of SCHIZOPHRENIA.

See also AUTOMATISM.

For further reading: Reed (1985); Robbins.

oceanic feeling Freud coined this phrase to refer to the experience of losing one's personal boundaries and being "flooded" with blissful emotion. The oceanic feeling has frequently been interpreted in religious terms, as contact with or immersion in God. St. Catherine of Genoa described her MYSTICAL EXPERIENCE in oceanic terms (quoted by Laski):

> I am so placed and submerged in His immense love, that I feel as though in the sea entirely under water, and could on no side touch, see, or feel anything but water.

St. Francis of Sales reported an experience in which "the soul lets herself pass or flow into What she loves—gently glides, as a fluid and liquid thing—The outflowing of a soul into her God."

Laski, who studied a number of accounts of oceanic feelings, suggested that the experience involves changes in breathing. Oceanic feelings are often preceded by taking a deep breath and accompanied by holding the breath. Whether altered respiration is a cause or an effect of the experience is unknown.

Freud and other psychoanalysts have interpreted oceanic feelings as camouflaged memories of very early experiences. The sensations of the unborn fetus, still "immersed" in its mother, and the inability of a newborn baby to distinguish its own body from the rest of the world, may be the vaguely recalled origins of oceanic feelings. Most researchers now reject the psychoanalytic theory, as the nervous system of an infant has not yet developed the ability to store and retrieve conscious memories.

See also CRYPTOMNESIA.

For further reading: Laski.

ocean lights The play of colors that grants the sea much of its beauty is usually caused by light reflecting from the surface or from particles in the water. In a broad stretch of ocean around Asia, from the Indian Ocean to the South China Sea, and less often in other waters, mariners have reported luminous phenomena originating in the sea itself. These spectacles assume various forms: diffuse glows pervading a large area; stationary or moving bands of light; huge rotating luminous wheels; and other shapes.

Encounters with a "milky sea," in which the entire water surface radiates light, have been noted for centuries. The following vivid description of an oceanic spectacle south of Java dates from 1854 (quoted by Corliss, 1977):

The whole appearance of the ocean was like a plain covered with snow. There was scarce a cloud in the heavens, yet the sky . . . appeared as black as if a storm was raging. The scene was one of awful grandeur; the sea having turned to phosphorus, and the heavens being hung in blackness, and the stars going out, seemed to indicate that all nature was preparing for that last grand conflagration which we are taught to believe is to annihilate this material world.

The British Meteorological Office has collected 235 sightings by seafarers of the milky sea since 1915. Analysis by Herring and Watson indicates that most of the sightings are clustered in the northwestern Indian Ocean, east of the Horn of Africa. The favored month of the phenomenon is August, followed by January. The occurrence of milky seas seems unrelated to the depth of water or distance from shore.

Sometimes, ocean lights display a structure. Probably the most common of these forms is the stationary luminous belt, which has been observed in waters around the world. Ships may pass over the glowing band without affecting it. The radiance is sometimes described as steady, although in other reports it is said to flicker rhythmically. Many sailors have reported several belts of submarine light, spaced at regular intervals. The belts can stretch to the horizon in both directions.

Sometimes, the luminous bands move through the water. Moving bands are mostly observed in the circum-Asian marine regions. This striking report is from the Gulf of Oman, 1906 (quoted by Corliss, 1977):

shafts of brilliant light came sweeping across the ship's bow at a prodigious speed, which might be put down as anything between sixty and two hundred miles an hour. . . . It was just as if a large gun with a rectangular muzzle were shooting bars of light at us from infinity. These light bars were about twenty feet apart and most regular; their brilliancy was dazzling. . . . an intervening ship had no effect on the light beams.

Then there are the reports of vast marine light wheels. In many cases the form consists of luminous spokes that converge at a hub, like a cartwheel. The extent of the wheel can cover the entire water surface visible from a ship. The spokes may be straight, as if the bands of light described above had all joined at one end. Gently curving spokes have also been seen. These structures can appear in groups, with overlapping spokes. Sometimes, they are seen to spin slowly, occasionally stopping and changing rotational direction.

In addition to belts and cartwheels, a variety of other luminous shapes have surprised mariners off the shores of Asia. Spinning patches of light, glowing crescents and expanding phosphorescent rings, as well as zigzag flashes, are some of these rarely viewed types.

The explanation usually offered for ocean lights is that they are swarms of luminiscent marine microorganisms. Waters sampled from the glowing displays have often shown high counts of such creatures. Puzzling features remain, however. Herring and Watson noted that only marine bacteria would be capable of generating the strong, steady light that characterizes milky seas; samples taken from these displays have not been found to contain them.

How great numbers of phosphorescent organisms could become coordinated into large structures such as bands and wheels is also unclear. Some researchers have suggested that underwater vibrations, perhaps from earthquakes, could clump the organisms together. Corliss speculated that electromagnetic influences in the atmosphere might also be involved. His suggestion helps to make sense of some occasionally reported features of ocean light. In a number of cases, glowing shapes composed of mist were seen *above* the ocean's surface. In other accounts, activating a ship's radar has stimulated lights in the ocean, pointing to an unseen cause sensitive to electromagnetic impulses.

For further reading: Corliss (1977, 1982); Herring and Watson.

odors of sanctity Reports of mysterious, pleasant fragrances associated with holy persons date back to the first centuries of the Christian era. It was said that a divine scent accompanied Polycarp of Smyrna, who was martyred in 155. Accounts of this phenomenon have persisted to the present century. In the presence of Padre Pio, considered by many to be a modern saint, a strong perfume comparable to violets or fine incense has often been reported.

A number of accounts suggest that odors of sanctity can be transferred from the originating person to other persons, places or objects. Concerning Sister Giovanna Maria della Croce of Roveredo, who lived in 17th century Italy, her biographer (quoted by Thurston) wrote that her sacred scent:

> exuded not only from her body but also from her clothes long after she had ceased to wear them, from her straw mattress and from the objects in her room. It spread through the whole house and betrayed her comings and goings and her every movement.

After a visit from a pious woman, Margaret Reilly, who died in 1937, the nuns at Reckshill in New York claimed that a delightful fragrance persisted in their chapel for many days.

Odors of sanctity are frequently described in conjunction with other CHARISMS, or seemingly supernatural phenomena associated with holy people in the Roman Catholic tradition. This link is especially evident in cases of STIGMATA. Of St. Veronica Giuliani, it was recorded (quoted by Thurston) that:

> When the [stigmatic] wounds were open, they emitted so delicious a fragrance throughout the whole of the convent that this alone was sufficient to inform the nuns whenever the stigmata had been renewed, and on several occasions the religious were convinced by ocular demonstration that they had not been deceived.

Odors of sanctity have sometimes been reported emanating from the ringlike ridge of flesh that appears in another Catholic charism, the EXCHANGE OF HEARTS.

Although mysterious scents are best known in the context of orthodox Christianity, they are sometimes reported by practitioners of other spiritual disciplines. Bayless described an incident that occurred while he was interviewing a yogic adept. He suddenly experienced a sweet odor, apparently coming from the yogi's chest. Bayless stated:

> He opened his shirt at my request, and I was able to determine that it was pouring from a small area on his chest exactly as though a faucet which provided scent had been turned on. The odor became so powerful that his entire studio became saturated with it. Then, as suddenly as it came, it ceased.

At the moment of death of the spiritual teacher George Gurdjieff in 1949, those present noted that the room became filled with the scent of violets. Mysterious fragrances have often been reported at Spiritualist seances, supposedly indicating the presence of spirits. Flowery odors of unknown origin also feature in many accounts of POLTERGEIST outbreaks.

It thus appears that the Catholic "odor of sanctity" may be an instance of a broader class of unusual experience and not restricted to that religious tradition. Most cases are linked to individuals with extraordinary levels of spiritual commitment. In the case of poltergeist odors, the focal person, around whom the phenomena appear to center, may be the source.

Stories of mysterious odors suffer from the same evidential weaknesses as do all anecdotal accounts—expectations can induce witnesses to have olfactory HALLUCINATIONs, fraud and misperception could have occurred in some instances, and memory may have sharpened the unusual features of the experience. If a supernatural origin is insisted on for odors of sanctity, it would have to be of a nature not restricted to Catholic, or even to Christian, recognition. Owen (1970) speculated concerning the possibility that the odors are not illusory, but have a natural explanation:

> Agreeable odours are occasionally reported by physicians in connection with various maladies; and it is not inconceivable that profoundly religious temperaments may be correlated in some degree with metabolic effects in which both biochemical and psychosomatic factors participate.

This possibility might also apply to the "extrascentsory" activities of some mediums and poltergeist foci.

For further reading: Bayless (1971); Murphy; Owen (1970); Thurston.

Old Hag experience   On occasion, the normal boundary between the waking and sleeping states blurs, giving rise to strange experiences. The American theologian Henry James, Sr. (father of the psychologist William James and the novelist Henry James, Jr.) reported such an occurrence in 1844. James was relaxing one afternoon in a chair, apparently awake; he was suddenly gripped by "a perfect insane and abject terror, without ostensible cause." He found himself temporarily paralyzed and sensed the presence of an invisible, evil being. Others who have had such experiences also reported HALLUCINATIONs of terrifying forms, shuffling sounds and musty odors.

Hufford surveyed these experiences in Canada and the United States more than a century after James' account. He estimated that about 15% of the general population has had them. In Newfoundland folklore such events are described as visits of the "Old Hag." Hufford used the designation "Old Hag experience" to refer to the general phenomenon. Some of the Newfoundlanders interviewed by Hufford described a curious custom known as "hagging." Supposedly, if a person says the Lord's Prayer backward while kneeling naked, and then calls out "Hag, good Hag," their enemy will be visited by the Old Hag that night.

Ellis noted the similarity between the Old Hag's visits and accounts of nocturnal UFO abductions. Many purported UFO victims awaken suddenly to find themselves paralyzed and realize in horror that strange creatures have invaded their bedroom.

The bodily paralysis and convincing imagery of the Old Hag encounter are also found in the states that bridge waking and sleep. Ordinarily, when a person dozes off he or she briefly enters the HYPNAGOGIC STATE; a similar realm, the HYPNOPOMPIC STATE, marks the passage from sleep to wakefulness. It is likely that the Old Hag is produced by an intrusion of these transition states into normal waking consciousness. The cause of this short-lived neural misfiring is unknown. There is no evidence that the Old Hag experience is a sign of mental or physical disorder.

See also INCUBUS NIGHTMARE; NIGHTMARE; NIGHT TERROR.

For further reading: Ellis; Hufford.

olfactory hallucination   A false perception of smell. Olfactory hallucinations can feature in EPILEPSY and SCHIZOPHRENIA, but are most often reported by sufferers of HYSTERIA. Mysterious odors are sometimes sensed in the HYPNAGOGIC STATE.

See also ODORS OF SANCTITY; POLTERGEIST.

organic mental disorder   Ongoing psychological problems caused by an identifiable bodily malfunction are diagnosed as organic mental disorders. A range of disturbing unusual experiences can accompany these ailments, including AMNESIA, DELIRIUM, DELUSIONs and HALLUCINOSIS. Frequently, a disruption of blood flow in the brain is the underlying cause. Strokes, head injury and Alzheimer's Disease are among the most common medical conditions giving rise to organic mental disorders. Mental health professionals recognize two types of mental disorders with known organic origins: those due to medical conditions such as disease or injury; and those due to the ingestion of toxic substances.

It is important to distinguish organic mental disorders from NEUROLOGICAL DISORDERS. Although both classes of illness are caused by abnormal physical states, sufferers of neurological disorders are not considered mentally ill; rather, they are subject to uncontrollable behaviors and distorted perceptions which are often mistaken by others as signs of mental illness.

For further reading: American Psychiatric Association; Lishman.

out-of-body experience Ordinarily, a person experiences the world from a vantage point seemingly located within the physical body. As George Tyrrell has noted, however, personal consciousness is not actually located *anywhere*—awareness does not take up space, has no physical properties such as size or shape and cannot be observed residing at any point in the material universe. The "location" of awareness is therefore an aspect of experience that each individual invents, undoubtedly based partially on the fact that much of the content of consciousness comes from the sense organs, which *are* located in the world—on the physical body. Our ordinary perceptions are filled with cues suggesting that our awareness resides within our heads, behind the eyes. However, there is no reason that someone could not produce an impression that awareness is elsewhere, particularly when attention is not occupied by normal sensations and perceptions. When a person experiences the location of consciousness as being external to the material body, this is known as an out-of-body experience, or OBE.

The OBE is one of the most commonly reported kinds of unusual experience. Survey-based estimates of OBE incidence in the general population range from 8 to 15%, and among subpopulations such as college students, it is much higher, up to 48% in some samples. Although psychologically disturbed individuals sometimes have OBEs, so do many normal peo-

ple; the occurrence of an OBE in itself is not an indication of mental problems.

A rich record documents the occurrence of the OBE throughout history and across cultures. Many nonliterate peoples have developed methods to induce the OBE deliberately, in order to utilize it for the benefit of the community. For instance, part of the repertoire of many Shamans (adepts who establish relationships with spirits) is projection of the soul from the physical body into the realm of spirits. Shamans use this technique to consult spirit beings concerning the future and distant events and to retrieve the souls of sick people, thus aiding them back to health.

There was a great interest in OBEs in the ancient world. The stream of Jewish literature known as the Pseudepigrapha, composed during the centuries preceding the birth of Christ, featured vivid accounts of out of body travel by Hebrew prophets. For instance, in the Book of Enoch, the adventures of Enoch as he journeys through the many levels of heaven are recounted. There may be such an account in the New Testament itself. In Paul's second letter to the Corinthians (12:2–4), he wrote:

> I know a man in Christ who fourteen years ago was caught up into the third heaven—whether in the body or out of the body I do not know, God knows. And I know that this man was caught up into paradise—whether in the body or out of the body I do not know, God knows— and he heard things that cannot be told, which man may not utter.

Some schools of the spiritual movement known as Gnosticism, which flourished in the Roman Empire during the first few centuries A.D., believed that the physical world, including the body, was a prison. The Gnostics developed meditative procedures by which they could escape their material confinement and transmit their souls to a distant realm of light.

Another wave of interest in OBEs was recorded during the Middle Ages. The medieval accounts usually feature monks who left their bodies and viewed heaven and hell. Caesarius of Heisterbach, in his work of 1223 entitled *Dialogue on Miracles,* preserved many such stories. Deliberately inducing OBEs was not condoned, because such probing into God's mysteries would have been seen as involving the sin of *curiositas,* the desire to know unnecessary things.

During the Great Witch Hunt of the Renaissance and Reformation periods, many reports were made of witches flying through the air at night to attend the diabolical sabbath. Some demonologists of the time held that the witches left their physical bodies behind and traveled in spirit form during their nocturnal flights. Most of these tales were invented by innocent victims of the witch hunt during torture sessions in attempts to tell their interrogators what they wished to hear. However, in at least some instances, it appears that OBEs were at the root of the rumor concerning night-flying witches.

For example, in 1560 a witch offered to demonstrate her flying abilities to the scholar Giambattista Porta. The woman passed into a trancelike state of insensibility and remained so for a while. Upon recovering, she reported that she had flown a great distance, while Porta had been observing her motionless body.

In 1575, in an isolated corner of Italy, inquisitors searching for witches stumbled upon what seems to be a survival from pre-Christian times of a tradition involving the deliberate use of OBEs. Some of the peasants in this region would periodically induce altered states of consciousness, in which they would leave their bodies to do battle with evil sorcerers whom they believed were menacing their crops.

With the decline of the supernatural world view and the rise of science, interest in OBEs waned again. But by the mid-19th century, involvement in the spirit world had returned once more, most notably in the forms of Spiritualism and Theosophy. The spiritualist movement, which began in the 1840s and became popular throughout the western world for several de-

cades, centered around the activities of MEDIUMSHIP. While most mediumistic activities involved the POSSESSION of the medium by a spirit, or the manifestation of paranormal phenomena such as the mysterious movements of objects, some mediums reported OBEs.

One such Spiritualist medium was a Swiss woman named Catherine Muller, better known by her pseudonym, Helene Smith. She was investigated by one of the first psychologists, Theodore Flournoy. Smith reported that in trance states her soul was able to travel to Mars. She observed that the red planet was populated by plants, animals and human-like creatures, and she was able to write in the Martian language. As little was known at that time concerning conditions on Mars, Flournoy was unable to check the accuracy of Smith's accounts. He was able, however, through careful study of the Martian script, to deduce that the alien language was closely modeled on French, Smith's mother tongue. Flournoy concluded, to Smith's displeasure, that the Martian experiences were an elaborate fantasy concocted by her unconscious mind.

The Theosophical Society was founded in 1875 and it enjoyed a large following during the last years of the century. Theosophy employed many concepts derived from Hinduism and Buddhism in their complex world view, including the belief that humans have other, subtle bodies nested within the coarse physical form. Theosophists experimented with techniques for projecting the astral body, which could travel far from the coarse body, remaining attached to it by a silver cord. If the cord was cut, they taught, the person would die. The astral body has endured as a popular concept in many 20th century esoteric systems. Several techniques for the induction of an OBE have been described in the occult literature. One entrepreneurial occultist, Robert Monroe, has even developed a technology, called "Hemi-Sync," which he claims can produce OBEs.

Scientific research into the OBE was relatively neglected for many decades, largely because of the occult connotations the phenomenon had acquired. As researchers realized that many people who had no interest in occultism had OBEs, another prejudice surfaced. As early as 1886, physical researchers had begun to discuss OBEs; Edward Gurney, in the classic work, *Phantasms of the Living*, classified the OBE as "a known form of pathologic experience, or,—as I should regard it—of hallucination." Such a view was still being advanced in 1952, when Rawcliffe stated that OBEs were linked to HYSTERIA and SCHIZOPHRENIA. The idea that the OBE is a sign of mental illness was plausible before it was known how common the experience is among the normal population. It is no longer a defensible opinion today.

Over the last 25 years, a sizable amount of research has been conducted into the OBE. Researchers have tried to illuminate such questions as the following: What are the typical features of the OBE? What kind of person has OBEs, and under what circumstances? What is the nature of the OBE? These questions have been pursued utilizing surveys, case report studies and experimental work in the laboratory.

Irwin (1989) has summarized the major findings concerning typical features of the OBE. The majority of experients have reported that the OBE begins and ends instantaneously—they suddenly find themselves "outside" their physical bodies, and later just as abruptly discover themselves back "within" it. However, up to 40% of the sample noted peculiar sensations associated with departure and re-entry, particularly buzzing or clicking sounds and feelings of bodily vibration.

Most people who have a spontaneous OBE report that they view their physical bodies from a nearby vantage point, such as the ceiling. One's center of awareness frequently seems to travel in the local environment and sometimes covers great distances (as in the case of Helene Smith). Individuals who deliberately induce OBEs are more likely to begin their experience in the vicinity of the physical body and then to travel to realms that do not seem to be earthly locations at all—domains populated by the dead or by astral beings, for instance.

OBEs are most commonly described as being quite vivid and realistic, without the shifting, blurred nature of dreams. However almost half of those who reported OBEs noted that effects in the out-of-body environment would occur if the experient simply willed the effect to happen, or if the focus of attention was shifted—features reminiscent of the dream world.

More than half of those who experienced OBEs reported that consciousness resides in a nonphysical body, separate from the material form, during the experience. This structure is known as the parasomatic body. Reports of the silver cord described by theosophists are rare and are usually found in the stories of people familiar with the idea of the cord from reading occult books.

The majority of OBE experients firmly believe that they were literally out of their bodies during the experience. About 15% claimed that they acquired information about distant occurrences during the OBE that they could not have obtained if their senses had been restricted to the immediate vicinity of the physical body, as they ordinarily seem to be.

Several research projects have considered the personal characteristics and circumstances associated with OBEs. Most OBEs occur when a person is calm and still, meditating or lying on a bed. Some OBEs begin when the individual is highly excited and active (a shamanic drumming performance, for instance), and others occur when the experient is engaged in a habitual activity to which minimal attention is being paid (a sentry after several hours on guard duty). These varied scenarios have in common the feature of not paying attention to ordinary bodily sensations—because of the monotony of low arousal, the overload of high arousal or habituation. Such circumstances permit the mind to focus on mental imagery without distraction.

The research literature indicates that OBEs can happen to people of any age and either sex, regardless of education, social class or religious convictions. Several studies have compared the personality characteristics of those who reported OBEs with those who claimed never to have had the experience. Several results emerged from these comparisons. OBE experients tended to have significantly greater than normal capacity for ABSORPTION—that is, for becoming so concentrated on something that ordinary distractions cannot interrupt one's attention. Furthermore, OBE experients were significantly more likely than nonexperients to display a need for absorbing experiences. (Absorption has been found to be linked with several other categories of paranormal experience.)

People who report OBEs are also more likely to experience LUCID DREAMs, practice meditation and score higher on measures of HYPNOTIZABILITY than nonexperients. Although the ability to produce vivid mental images does not seem to differ between OBE experients and nonexperients, the former group is better able to imagine what an object looks like when viewed from various angles.

Some experiments have examined the bodily functioning of individuals while they were having OBEs. (These subjects had previously developed the skill of deliberately inducing OBEs). The bodies of the OBE experients in these studies displayed deep relaxation, and brain wave monitoring suggested that the subjects were awake and paying attention to something. There were no indications of a unique OBE "state."

Several theories have been advanced to explain the nature of the OBE. The oldest, and intuitively obvious, theory states that the OBE is what it appears to be: the separation of the soul or self from the material body. This view, known as the ecsomatic theory, is embraced by almost all occultists, and by very few scientists, because of the differing metaphysical commitments of the two groups. Another theory was suggested by parapsychologists such as Tyrrell: that the OBE is a fantasy which sometimes contains information about the world acquired using ESP. It would appear to be impossible to distinguish empirically between the ecsomatic and ESP theories, although some have tried, unconvincingly.

Both of these theories claim that the OBE can contain information which is not obtained using the senses. Is there any evidence for this possibility? A few studies have been conducted to explore this issue. Most of these experiments were inconclusive, or failed to rule out the possibility of sensory acquisition of information about the target. However, some puzzling results have emerged. For example, Smith and Irwin reported that the greater the similarity an experimentally induced OBE showed to the features of spontaneously occurring OBEs, the more accurate was the description of a distant target object the OBE experient produced. Further research is called for to confirm this result.

The currently dominant theories regarding the OBE do not consider the possibility that anything other than known psychophysiological processes are involved in the experience. Some theorists believe that the OBE arises from a temporary disturbance in cortical functioning, similar to an epileptic seizure. There is little evidence to support such a view.

Several other theories hold that the OBE is a type of mental imagery. These theories observe that feeling that the self is located within the body is maintained by the influx of ordinary perceptions and body sensations. When these anchoring inputs are disrupted, the flow of mental imagery may become unusually vivid in consciousness. Individuals with a high capacity for becoming absorbed in imagery can find that images of scenes viewed from positions outside of the body can produce the experience of actually being located at those positions. Blackmore suggested that the realm through which the awareness of the OBE experient travels is actually the mental map of the world, stored in the brain, which people use to orient themselves when moving physically in the material world.

See also Appendix; AUTOSCOPY; BODY IMAGE DISTORTION; DEPERSONALIZATION; EXTRASENSORY PERCEPTION; METACHORIC EXPERIENCE; NEAR-DEATH EXPERIENCE.

For further reading: Alvarado (1982, 1992); Couliano; Flournoy (1963); Ginzburg (1985, 1991); Gurney, Myers and Podmore; Irwin (1985a, 1989a); Rawcliffe; Robbins; Smith and Irwin; Stanford (1987); Tyrrell.

palinacousis   A rare condition in which a person hears vivid echoes of voices, music or other noises for a time after the triggering sound has stopped. Sometimes, only a part of the original sound is repeated. The cause of this annoying experience is unknown; it is likely related to some type of NEUROLOGICAL DISORDER.

See also PALINOPSIA.

palinopsia   The recurrent visual images of objects long after they have been removed from sight. Palinopsia is linked to several types of NEUROLOGICAL DISORDER, including tumors and epilepsy. This condition is distinct from EIDETIC IMAGERY. In palinopsia the images are symptomatic of a disease and occur involuntarily; most who have it are adults. Eidetic images are unrelated to illness, under voluntary control and most commonly reported by children.

See also PALINACOUSIS.

panenhenic state   This term derives from Greek, meaning "all is one." Zaehner coined the phrase to refer to a MYSTICAL EXPERIENCE in which a person perceives the natural world as a harmonious whole or unity. Christian tradition often calls such experiences "pantheistic"—"all is God." Zaehner preferred the term "panenhenic" because not everyone who has had the experience has interpreted the natural unity as God. Reid described a typical panenhenic experience:

> It was as if I had never realized before how lovely the world was. I lay down on my back in the warm, dry moss and listened to the skylark singing as it mounted up from the fields near the sea into the dark clear sky. No other music ever gave me the same pleasure as that passionately joyous singing. It was a kind of leaping, exultant ecstasy, a bright, flame-like sound, rejoicing in itself. And then a curious experience befell me. It was as if everything that had seemed to be external and around me were suddenly within me. The whole world seemed to be within me. It was within me that the trees waved their green branches, it was within me that the skylark was singing, it was within me that the hot sun shone, and that the shade was cool. A cloud rose in the sky, and passed in a light shower that pattered on the leaves, and I felt its freshness dropping into my soul, and I felt in all my being the delicious fragrance of the earth and the grass and the plants and the rich brown soil. I could have sobbed with joy.

See also COSMIC CONSCIOUSNESS; NUMINOUS EXPERIENCE; OCEANIC FEELING.

For further reading: Reid; Zaehner.

panic   The ancient Greek god Pan was said to spend much of his time dancing with nymphs in woodland glades. When annoyed, however, he had the power to create feelings of terror. The Athenians revered this deity, because it was thought that he had caused "panic" among invading Persian troops that helped the Greek soldiers to victory. Pan was closely associated with another god, Dionysus; and panic resembled the frenzied state of "telestic MANIA" that befell Dionysus' worshippers.

Pan's name has become attached to any overwhelming feelings of fear. In a typical panic attack, one experiences several of the following: difficulty in breathing; dizziness; pounding heartbeat perhaps with chest pain; trembling; sweating; choking; nausea; feelings of DEPERSONALIZATION or DEREALIZATION; numbness or tingling; flushes or chills; and fear of dying or going crazy. Panic is triggered by the sense that one has lost control in the face of some imminent threat. Sometimes a person becomes panicky for no apparent reason; a careful collection of the episode usually reveals that the individual had a frightening thought or fantasy that set off the body's alarm reaction. Sufferers of repeated panic attacks may be diagnosed as having a mental illness, "panic disorder."

For further reading: American Psychiatric Association; Beck and Emery.

paramnesia A general term for distortions of memory. Types of paramnesia include: failure of recall (AMNESIA); mistaking a memory for a non-memory (CRYPTOMNESIA); mistaking a non-memory for a memory (FALSE MEMORY); false recognition (déjà vu), and its pathological extreme, FREGOLI'S SYNDROME; failure of recognition (JAMAIS VU), and its pathological extreme, ILLUSION DES SOSIES; and false sense of prediction (PSEUDO-PRESENTIMENT). A clear distinction between ordinary memory and paramnesia cannot be made, because normal memory processes do not provide reliably accurate information about the past.

Some writers employ the term "paramnesia" to refer to a specific kind of memory error: believing that a present event is *identical* to a remembered event in the past, when in fact the present event is merely *similar* to the past one. A person may have a vague dream about a ship, lacking in detail, and become convinced that a ship seen the following day matches perfectly the dreamed ship. Someone who makes this type of mistake could think that they possess the power of precognition, or predicting the future.

For further reading: Baker (1992); Zusne and Jones.

paranoia A false belief that one is being persecuted or that one has special powers or importance is known as a paranoid DELUSION. Many people have momentary thoughts of a paranoid nature, which pass harmlessly. If the idea becomes fixed, however, it could signal the onset of a mental disorder. People who have paranoid delusions without other disturbing symptoms such as HALLUCINATIONs might be diagnosed with a "delusional disorder." Bizarre delusions in association with other symptoms (usually AUDITORY HALLUCINATIONs) are often symptoms of SCHIZOPHRENIA.

For further reading: American Psychiatric Association; Noll (1992a).

paranormal Literally, "beside the normal," a paranormal event is one that violates the boundaries of space and time, or cause and effect, as they are normally understood. For instance, PRECOGNITION, TELEPATHY and CLAIRVOYANCE, all considered impossible according to conventional science, are paranormal phenomena. Whether or not paranormal events ever occur has been hotly debated for ages. A paranormal experience is one that appears to involve a paranormal event.

See also PARAPSYCHOLOGY; PRETERNATURAL; PSYCHICAL RESEARCH; SKEPTICISM; SUPERNATURAL.

paranormal hallucination An HALLUCINATION with seemingly PARANORMAL content, such as an APPARITION of the dead or a visual PREMONITION. People who deny the possibility of paranormal events assume that every apparently paranormal experience is either a paranormal hallucination, a misinterpreted normal event or a hoax.

parapsychology This widely used (and misused) term was coined by German psychical researcher Max Dessoir in 1889. The prefix "para," meaning "beside," denotes a field of study pertaining to fringe areas of psychology. As Morris defined it, parapsychology is "the study of apparent new means of communication or interaction between an organism and elements in its environment." Parapsychology has come to focus on two types of purported phenomena—EXTRASENSORY PERCEPTION (ESP) and PSYCHOKINESIS (PK). The field is characterized by its use of scientific experiments, conducted in controlled laboratory settings, which assess the reality and functioning of ESP and PK.

Unfortunately, the meaning of the term has become blurred in popular usage. Psychics, exorcists and mediums advertise themselves as "parapsychologists"; and the entire range of occult and anomalous topics, from astrology to witchcraft, is sometimes lumped together under the heading of "parapsychology." These are confusing abuses of the word, which refers strictly to laboratory experiments concerning PSI (a blanket term for ESP and PK).

Some writers assert that parapsychology has demonstrated the existence of psi. For instance, Berger and Berger stated that, "Parapsychology asks us to accept behavior that simply does not fit into the time-space-energy-motion picture of the world that physical science has painted for us." Others prefer to define the subject matter of parapsychology in terms of psi as an anomaly—that is, as a category of human experience that remains unexplained in conventional terms. The latter position, championed by Palmer, does not necessarily imply that psi *cannot* be explained, but merely that the explanation for apparent instances of ESP and PK remains unknown at present.

Parapsychology is frequently viewed as a subdivision of the broader field of PSYCHICAL RESEARCH. Since the late 19th century, psychical researchers have studied claims of PARANORMAL occurrences using a range of approaches, including field investigations of HAUNTINGS and POLTERGEISTS, collecting and analyzing case reports of APPARITIONS, scrutinizing the performance of mediums and conducting experiments in ESP. Parapsychologists are the experimentalists of psychical research.

Although psychical researchers had been conducting ESP experiments even before the founding of the Society for Psychical Research in 1882,

it was not until 1927 that the first ongoing parapsychological research program was established. In that year, J.B. Rhine began his famous ESP experiments at Duke University, in Durham, North Carolina. Rhine published his results in the classic work *Extra-sensory Perception* in 1934; in that year, he began his experimental studies of PK, the results of which were published in 1943. In 1935, Rhine founded the Parapsychology Laboratory at Duke University; following his retirement in 1962, the Laboratory became a private research establishment, the Institute for Parapsychology. Housed in the same building as the Institute is Parapsychology Press, which has published one of the premier journals in the field, the *Journal of Parapsychology,* since 1937.

Although the research of Rhine and his colleagues failed to establish the reality of ESP and PK to the satisfaction of many, it stimulated wide interest in parapsychology. Since the founding of the Parapsychology Laboratory, other parapsychological research programs have appeared (and, after a time, disappeared for lack of funds) around the world. Following World War II, the first university chair in parapsychology was established at the University of Utrecht, Netherlands; another was established in 1985 at the University of Edinburgh. In 1957, an international organization of professional parapsychologists was founded, named the Parapsychological Association (PA). Twelve years later, the PA was accepted as an affiliate member of the prestigious American Association for the Advancement of Science.

Most parapsychological research is supported by private funds; thus the vitality of the field has ebbed and flowed several times in this century with the level of public interest. Parapsychology has so far failed to provide a reliably repeatable demonstration of a psi effect. This has allowed some skeptics to claim that the field has not progressed, because its subject matter—psi—does not exist. While few would hold that the paranormal has been conclusively demonstrated in the laboratory, all but the most extreme debunkers acknowledge that some of the results of parapsychological research are not easily explained. And so, research continues.

For further reading: Alcock; Berger and Berger; Broughton; Druckman and Swets; Kurtz; Morris; Morris, Edge, Palmer and Rush; Palmer (1992).

parascopy Variant term for EXTRASENSORY PERCEPTION.

paraselenae As moonlight descends through the earth's atmosphere to bathe the nighttime landscape, it can encounter airborne substances that produce unusual displays for observers. Such phenomena are called paraselenae, a term derived from the Latin roots *para,* "near," and *selene,* "the moon." The refraction of moonlight by atmospheric ice crystals creates the best known paraselenae, such as circular lunar halos, arcs and MOCK MOONs. Mixtures of crystal shapes, or multiple layers of crystals, are thought to explain much rarer lunar spectacles, such as elliptical and teardrop shaped halos. In one case a square halo around the moon was reported. Mock moons—circular images that appear in pairs, one on each side of the true lunar image— can be distorted by rare atmospheric conditions into cone-shaped bands of light that seem to project from the sides of the moon.

See also PARHELIA.

For further reading: Corliss (1984).

pareidolia Random stimuli, such as the shapes of clouds or rust on an old car, sometimes seem to take on meaningful forms. These images are known as pareidolia. Few adults believe that the perceived shapes are actually there—rather, the meaning is imposed on the stimulus by the mind, which seeks constantly to organize sensory input into an experience of a coherent world. Once a pareidolic interpretation is made, it tends to persist; thus, once one notices that a blood stain resembles an accusing hand, it will prove diffi-

cult to see the stain as anything else. Some psychologists and psychiatrists still use the Rorschach inkblot test during personality assessments. In this procedure, patients are asked what they "see" in random splashes of ink on cards; the pareidolia reported by the viewers are thought to reveal the unconscious motivations that influence their perceptions. Pareidolia are probably involved in a range of unusual experiences.

Many traditional methods of divination, or accessing hidden knowledge, involve meditating on seemingly random sensations. Diviners contemplate flickering candlelight glinting off a crystal ball or the shimmering surface of water. They glimpse images which they take to be visions of distant events (clairvoyance) or future happenings (precognition). Most of the visualized forms are likely pareidolia.

Pareidolia are sometimes considered to be miracles. Devout individuals who are constantly thinking about divine "signs" on earth are primed to interpret ambiguous stimuli in religious terms; when they encounter water marks on a basement floor, or see dust swirling in a sunbeam, they are more likely than others to construct a spiritually meaningful perception. In 1978, a woman in New Mexico accidentally scorched a tortilla; she concluded that its burned underside was an image of Christ's head, rimmed with a crown of thorns. The scorch pattern can indeed be seen in this way; to an uncommitted observer, however, it resembles a lot of other things too. Nonetheless, she reverently preserved the tortilla under glass, and it became an object of pilgrimage for thousands of believers.

Pareidolia can occur in any sensory modality. If people listen intently to a recording of a meaningless sound, such as the noise of water spraying against a shower curtain, many will eventually believe that they can detect occasional messages embedded in the hiss. In 1959 a Swedish film producer, Fredrik Jurgenson, noticed faint voices on a recording he had made of bird songs. Jurgenson came to believe that the voices were those of departed spirits. One of his students, Konstantin Raudive, set out to catch the spirit voices deliberately. Raudive ran blank tapes through a tape recorder in quiet settings, recorded the static from a radio tuned between stations or attached a diode to an aerial and recorded its output. He was able to hear voices uttering short phrases, including that of his deceased mother. Critics have suggested that in addition to pareidolic interpretations of meaningless noises, Raudive may have inadvertently picked up broadcasts from faraway radio stations with some of his procedures.

Another source of unpatterned sound is the telephone. Rogo and Bayless collected dozens of reports of ostensible spirit voices using this modern medium in their book, *Phone Calls From the Dead.* The electronic hum of an open phone line or the crackle of a bad connection make ideal templates for auditory pareidolia. Recently bereaved persons are predisposed to interpret ambiguous stimuli in terms of their loss, and are also susceptible to HALLUCINATIONs and PSEUDOHALLUCINATIONs. It is thus likely that most "phone calls from the dead" are not what they seem to be.

The existence of auditory pareidolia has not discouraged some people from continuing the attempt to communicate with the spirit world using modern media. In 1982, an association called Electronic Voice Phenomena was formed in the United States to promote conversations with the dead, and with extraterrestrials, using tape recorders and telephones. Shepanek, in Estep, provided these instructions for making a call to the beyond:

A telephone recording control (available from Radio Shack) and a telephone jack adaptor [are required]. To convert your existing telephone jack to a "two holer," you jack the device into the telephone wall jack along with your telephone and also into the mike and remote input of a cassette recorder. The method is as follows: Put the recorder into RECORD mode (it will not be activated until you lift the telephone

receiver), lift the phone receiver, and dial any single digit. Make a brief announcement as you would in any tape session. You will have thirty-four seconds of clear line before the taped offer of assistance breaks in. Hang up and repeat the procedure. The obvious shortcoming is the brevity of the clear line time. An alternative is to arrange with a friend (preferably one acquainted with your strange life style) to call at a pre-set time and leave his/her telephone off the hook for whatever period is agreed upon.

If one wishes to record the voices of the dead, it might make sense to go to where they congregate—a cemetery. Many who have sat silently in a graveyard with tape recorder running have claimed to detect phantom voices upon replaying the tape. As Hines noted:

The tape recorder, while it is recording is picking up stray sounds from the environment and, especially, the sound of the breeze or wind passing over the microphone. When played back, these noises do sound strange and, at least to me, rather peaceful. If one expects to hear voices, constructive perception will produce voices. The voices, not surprisingly, are usually described as speaking in hoarse whispers.

The dead may also be seen wandering through cemeteries, especially at night. Vague luminous stimuli can serve as the basis for visual pareidolia under these conditions, explaining some accounts of GHOST LIGHTs.

During the 1980s, American fundamentalist Christians became concerned that some popular musicians were embedding Satanic or nihilistic messages in their songs. One purported technique, called backmasking, involved recording the message backward; the conscious mind, it was claimed, could not hear the message, but it would affect the listener insidiously. In fact, the fundamentalists were simply hearing their own fears, projected into the music and then perceived as auditory pareidolia. There were no backmasked voices in the contentious music. In any case, research has demonstrated that voices played backward are incomprehensible to listeners and have no effect on them.

See also ELECTRONIC VISUAL PHENOMENON; ILLUSION.

For further reading: Baker (1992); Begg, Needham and Bookbinder; Estep; Hines; Zusne and Jones.

parhelia   Derived from the Latin roots *par,* "near," and *helios,* "the sun," this term refers to unusual optical effects that occur in the vicinity of the solar disc. As sunlight penetrates the atmosphere, it sometimes encounters sheets of ice crystals. These particles act like prisms, bending and splitting the light into surprising luminous displays. The most commonly noted parhelic effects are images of the sun, called MOCK SUNs, that appear adjacent to the actual solar disc.

A less frequently observed spectacle is the solar cross. In this effect, two immense beams of light stretch across the sky, intersecting at the sun. This awesome spectacle was viewed over Illinois in 1880, as reported by Davenport (quoted by Corliss, 1977):

> There appeared . . . two very brilliant mock suns intersected by a well defined, slightly iris-colored, bright circle, having the sun as its center. This circle was divided into quadrants by four brilliant rays of white light, radiating apparently from the sun, two horizontally and two vertically, the horizontal rays intersecting the mock suns and extending some distance beyond. . . . The most remarkable part of this interesting phenomenon was the appearance of a brilliant inverted crescent near the zenith . . . The colors were disposed in prismatic order and as brilliant as those of the most beautiful rainbow I ever saw; the red outside, toward the sun; the violet inside.

The horizontal arm of the cross was likely a mock sun effect, the refracted light being scattered between the solar disc and the mock suns. The vertical arm was the result of light reflecting from airborne crystals. The cross is a sacred symbol in many cultures; the impact of a sky-born cross of light on most people unaware of the optical mechanisms producing it would be profound. Menzel and Taves suggested that the visions of Ezekiel described in the Old Testament were observations of such parhelia.

In addition to mock suns and solar crosses, various arrangements of aerial ice crystals can create other parhelic sights. These include halos around the sun, sometimes occurring multiply and in colors; arcs of light, at various orientations to the sun; and parhelic circles, rings of white light passing through the sun and paralleling the horizon.

Corliss described a range of parhelia that are not easily accounted for by conventional optics. Offset and elliptical solar halos and bands of light have been viewed. Rarely, observers have noted "jumping halos" that appear suddenly to expand or contract around the sun. Perhaps complex interactions between the positions and shapes of ice crystals can generate these weird effects.

See also PARASELENAE.

For further reading: Corliss (1977, 1984); Menzel and Taves.

past life recall   See REINCARNATION MEMORY.

Pavor Nocturnus   Variant term for NIGHT TERRORs.

peak experience   The American psychologist Abraham Maslow coined this term to refer to occasions when people sense their own highest potentials. Maslow's interest in peak experiences arose from his concern that modern Western culture does not have an image of human perfection to inspire our efforts at self improvement:

> Every age but ours has had its model, its ideal. All of these have been given up by our culture; the saint, the hero, the gentleman, the knight, the mystic. About all we have left is the well-adjusted man without problems, a very pale and doubtful substitute. Perhaps we shall soon be able to use as our guide and model the fully growing and self-fulfilling human being, the

one in whom all his potentialities are coming to full development, the one whose inner nature expresses itself freely, rather than being warped, suppressed, or denied.

Maslow proposed that human motivation could be understood as a hierarchy of needs. Only when the lower needs are met can the higher ones be properly pursued. At the bottom of this motivational pyramid are the basic physiological and safety needs; next are our requirements for love and self esteem; and, at the top, are self-actualization needs, based on an urge to live up to our greatest possibilities as individuals. Peak experiences are associated with movement toward the ideal condition of complete self actualization.

Maslow studied the lives of people he believed to be self actualized. He found that the peak experiences they reported had several common characteristics: blissful feelings; focused attention on the here and now; freedom from anxieties, doubts and inhibitions; spontaneous, effortless functioning; and a sense of being merged or harmonized with one's environment. Maslow recognized that peak experiences can sometimes be triggered in people who are not especially self-actualized, particularly through the use of psychedelic drugs.

Some features of the peak experience can only be described in paradoxical language. Maslow noted that the feeling of transcending the ordinary limits of the self, of fusing with the world, is attained through a strengthened sense of personal identity. One who is not yet emerged as an individual from the blind social impulses of the crowd cannot transcend himself or herself. Paradoxical expressions are typical of MYSTICAL EXPERIENCEs; and, indeed, Maslow felt that the great mystics of all religions were self actualized persons. The core of every major spiritual tradition is the peak experience, Maslow believed.

The idea of the peak experience became very popular among the American counterculture of the 1960s. Some of the excesses of this period led Maslow to issue a warning:

Out of the joy and wonder of his ecstasies and peak-experiences he may be tempted to *seek* them, *ad hoc*, and to value them exclusively, as the only or at least the highest goods of life, giving up other criteria of right and wrong. Focused on these wonderful subjective experiences, he may run the danger of turning away from the world and from other people in his search for triggers to peak-experiences, *any* triggers. . . . In a word, he may become not only selfish but also evil. My impression, from the history of mysticism, is that this trend can sometimes wind up in meanness, nastiness, loss of compassion, and even in the extreme of sadism.

Self actualization requires the solid ground of ordinary experiences, as well as the soaring leaps of peak experiences.

See also PLATEAU EXPERIENCE.

For further reading: Friedman; Maslow (1968, 1976).

peyote   This small, spineless cactus grows in the Rio Grande Valley and adjacent regions of Mexico and Texas. Its name derives from the Nahuatl *peiotl,* the term by which it was known to the Aztecs. The crowns of the peyote cactus contain the powerful alkaloid hallucinogen mescaline. The ingestion of these crowns, called "mescal buttons" or "peyote buttons," has been one of the most widely used chemical pathways to unusual experiences in native North America.

Following the consumption of peyote, many people have reported two distinct phases of reaction. First, there is often a period of relaxation and contentment, accompanied by enhanced perceptual sensitivity. Then, as the effects of the mescaline deepen, ENTOPTIC PHENOMENA, especially the appearance of the geometric images called FORM CONSTANTs, frequently occur. HALLUCINATIONs in all sensory modalities are also common. The specific contents and meanings of peyote-induced experiences are structured by the beliefs and expectations of the individual. Peyote has usually been taken within the context of religious rituals, in order to steer the experiences in a spiritually meaningful direction.

Archaeologists have discovered samples of peyote from caves and rock shelters in Texas dating back more than 3,000 years. At the site of the ancient city of Monte Alban in central Mexico was found a ceramic snuffing pipe in the form of a deer with a peyote in its mouth, from the sixth century B.C. Evidently, the relationship between humans and peyote long predates the arrival of Europeans in the Americas.

The earliest historical account of peyote use was provided by the 16th century chronicler Sahagun. He noted its use among the Chichimecs, the ancestral group from whom the Aztecs arose (quoted in Dobkin de Rios):

> Those who eat or drink it see visions either frightful or laughable. This intoxication lasts two or three days and then ceases. It . . . sustains them and gives them courage to fight and not feel fear nor hunger nor thirst. And they say that it protects them from all danger.

Some reports claimed that Cortes, the conqueror of the Aztecs, fed his own troops peyote in order to help them endure long marches. In general, however, the Spanish reaction to the magic cactus was violently hostile. Jesuit writers associated peyote use with "heathen rituals and superstitions," "horrible visions" and "diabolic fantasies." The eating of peyote was ruthlessly suppressed in Mexico, and most of the religious lore connected to it in pre-Columbian times was lost.

The peyote persecutions did not significantly affect the Huichol and Tarahumara tribes, who lived in remote areas in the mountains of northern Mexico. These groups have continued to the present day to utilize the peyote as a means of accessing divine realms.

Once a year, a group from the Huichol tribe is sent into the desolate regions where the cactus grows. This pilgrimage involves traveling 200 miles from the Huichols' homeland—a trek that was formerly made on foot, and today with the help of the automobile. The peyote hunt is itself a sacred performance. The land of the peyote is viewed as a paradise, and entry into it must be preceded by acts of purification and confession. While the hunters fan across the landscape, filling large baskets with harvested mescal buttons, they eat peyote in order to make contact with the spiritual forces of the place. The Huichols sell some of the peyote they collect to the Tarahumaras and retain the rest for their own use.

The use of peyote among the Huichol and Tarahumara occurs within a ritual context. Participants dance, sing and are exposed to continuous drumming while eating mescal buttons. This combination of stimuli serves to destabilize ordinary habits of attention and to dispose the peyote eaters to interpret unusual sensations as the presence of spiritual forces. The peyote rites are believed to promote good crops, healing and insight into the meaning of one's life. A Huichol shaman (quoted in Schultes and Hofmann) instructed:

> Speak to the Peyote with your heart, with your thoughts. And the Peyote sees your heart. . . . And if you have luck, you will hear things and receive things that are invisible to others, but that god has given you to pursue your path.

Among the Huichols, the peyote experience has also given rise to a unique artistic tradition. Their intensely colored yarn paintings, depicting peyote visions and myths, are eagerly sought by art collectors.

In the latter part of the 19th century, religious use of peyote began to diffuse northward from the growing region of the cactus. In the United States and Canada, native culture was under great pressure from the encroachment of Eurocentric society; as in the case of IBOGA cults in western Africa, the use of a hallucinogen to strengthen traditional beliefs in personal access to spiritual forces proved very appealing.

The peyote religion that developed among the Plains Indians took on distinctive forms as it spread from reservation to reservation. The most common ceremonies were nocturnal gatherings, at which the participants sang and ate mescal buttons throughout the night. A crescent-or horseshoe-shaped altar was constructed, on which was displayed the largest available button, called the Father Peyote. The peyotists meditated on Father Peyote and received spiritual guidance.

The North American peyote religion soon absorbed elements of Christian belief. Peyote experiences were understood as giving practitioners direct communion with the Christ about whom they heard so much in the missionary churches. As J.S. Slotkin observed, "The white man goes into his church house and talks *about* Jesus; the Indian goes into his teepee and talks *to* Jesus." Such nondeferential attitudes, however, did not endear the peyotists to the authorities—they were targeted for persecution by both state and federal governments in the United States.

In an attempt to foster a united front among peyotists and to demonstrate their legitimacy as a religious group, practitioners in Oklahoma founded the Native American Church in 1918. Among the stated aims of the new Church was "to foster and promote the religious belief of the several tribes of Indians in the State of Oklahoma, in the Christian religion with the practice of the Peyote Sacrament as commonly understood and used among the adherents of this religion." The Church spread to reserves across the U.S. and Canada. Its legal representatives fought successfully to establish the right of Church members to ingest peyote during sacred rites.

The interaction of drug effects and culture is not always positive, as in the case of the Mescalero Apaches. After peyote was introduced to this tribe, incidents of violence during peyote ceremonies began to be reported. The problem grew so severe that most Mescaleros rejected its use. In every other tribal group, peyote practice was consistently serene. Why

was the Mescalero reaction exceptional? Boyer, Boyer and Basehart noted that traditional Mescalero religious rites emphasized the importance of a single shaman's experiences, rather than those of a group, as in peyote ceremonies. Unused to the psychedelic democracy of the peyote session in which everyone experienced contact with the divine, Mescaleros at peyote rites ended up competing against each other for group influence, and hostilities often resulted.

Currently, the Native American Church is incorporated in 17 American states and represented in the Canadian provinces of Manitoba, Saskatchewan and Alberta. Membership estimates range from 100,000 to 225,000. Peyote is still used as a sacrament. Church groups far from the Rio Grande growth area receive their supply of mescal buttons via the U.S. postal service.

For further reading: Boyer, Boyer and Basehart; Dobkin de Rios; Hirschfelder and Molin; Myerhoff; Schultes and Hofmann; Slotkin; Stafford.

phantom breasts   About 23% of women who undergo mastectomy report that they continue to sense the missing breast. Often the phantom sensations are itchy or painful. Phantom breasts are more common among younger women and among those who became depressed following surgery. This phenomenon is probably caused by the same processes that create PHANTOM LIMB SENSATIONS.

For further reading: Asaad.

phantom limb sensations   Phantom sensations are feelings that occur in the absence of any sensory input from the limb. A large number of amputees report vividly experiencing the missing part, even though the limb may have been removed decades ago. Phantoms are also described by those who have suffered disconnection of the nerves connecting a limb to the body, even though the limb itself remains attached. If an arm is made insensitive by cutting off the circulation using a pressure cuff, that person can experience a phantom arm after about 30 minutes.

The phantom limb phenomenon seems so extraordinary that the first scientist to explore it, the 19th century neurologist S. Weir Mitchell, was afraid to publish his findings in a research journal. Instead, he wrote a piece of fiction describing a phantom limb experience for the *Atlantic Monthly,* to test his colleague's reactions.

Phantom limbs can appear immediately after the removal or neural disconnection of a limb, but days, months or years can pass before they manifest. Even those born without limbs report phantoms: A young boy, born with an arm that ended at the elbow, described phantom fingers that emerged from the stump. Often, phantom sensations are not constant, but appear and fade unpredictably. The most striking feature of the phantom is the unshakeable sense that the ghostly limb is part of one's own body. Phantoms have been said to feel more intensely real than the existing limbs.

The range of phantom sensations is as great as that of ordinary experience. One of the most commonly noted sensations is phantom pain, reported by up to 70% of amputees. These discomforts include feelings of burning, cramping or shooting pain. Phantom itching is another common complaint—sometimes, pretending to scratch where the limb used to be provides relief! Sensations of heat, cold, pressure, warmth and dryness have also been noted.

Phantom limbs tend to move like ordinary limbs. A phantom arm, for instance, will swing normally as a person walks; a phantom leg will bend when one sits down. Some phantom limbs feel frozen in unusual positions. A man with a phantom arm that projected straight out from his body would pass sideways through doors so he would not bump into the walls. If only part of a missing limb reappears as a phantom—a phantom foot of an amputated leg, for example—the separated part will stay in its correct location relative to the body. If an artificial limb is attached, a phantom will usually mimic its motion.

The cause of phantom limb sensations is uncertain. Some occultists take the phantoms as evidence for the existence of an astral body, dwelling within the physical body like a hand in a glove; a phantom limb is like a finger protruding after the glove's finger is torn off. Medical researchers have suggested that phantom sensations are caused by abnormal firing of nerve cells in the limb stump, or the spinal cord. Surgery to these areas, however, normally does not permanently eliminate the phantom.

Most researchers now believe that phantom sensations are created largely by the brain itself. Melzack has suggested that the normal experience of the body—the body image—is constructed by a complex circuit of several brain regions, which he calls the *neuromatrix.* Nerve cells firing continuously in the neuromatrix maintain the sense that one has a body. Sensory input from the body does not create the neuromatrix, but modifies the firing patterns of its cells so that one's bodily experiences correspond to changes in the body. In the absence of sensory information from a limb, the neuromatrix remains active. The nerve cells, now uncontrolled by input, fire spontaneously; they may also try to send messages to the absent limb. It is this neural activity, Melzack believes, that causes phantom limb sensations.

Sufferers of phantom limb pain are often desperate for relief. While no one treatment has proven effective for all patients, many have been helped by acupuncture, relaxation, hypnosis and drug therapies.

Phantom limb sensations, as Mitchell long ago realized, challenge some basic assumptions of ordinary experience. Melzack noted:

One such assumption is that sensations are produced only by stimuli and that perceptions in the absence of stimuli are psychologically abnormal. Yet phantom limbs . . . indicate this notion is wrong. The brain does more than detect and analyze inputs; it generates perceptual experience even when no external inputs occur. We do not need a body to feel a body.

See also BODY IMAGE DISTORTION; CENESTHETIC HALLUCINATION; KINESTHETIC HALLUCINATION; OUT OF BODY EXPERIENCE; PHANTOM BREASTS; PHANTOM VISION.

For further reading: Katz and Melzack; Melzack.

phantom vision   About 15% of people who lose all or part of their vision from eye injury or eye diseases experience this phenomenon. In phantom vision the person "sees" very realistic objects, even though visual information about the world is not reaching the brain. Most commonly visualized are normal-sized people and buildings; tiny people and animals are less popular. These images are not mere memories as phantom visions of things never before seen can occur. A typical case was noted by Melzack:

> A woman in one of our studies who had lost much of her vision because of retinal degeneration reported being shocked when she looked out a window and saw a tall building in what she knew to be a wooded field. Even though she realized that the building was a phantom, it seemed so real that she could count its steps and describe its other details. The building soon disappeared, only to return several hours later. The phantom vision continues to come and go unexpectedly . . .

Generally, people with phantom vision do not confuse the phantom forms with true percepts; in these cases, the visions are classed as PSEUDO-HALLUCINATIONS. Individuals who confuse their phantoms with perceived objects are having HALLUCINATIONS and are diagnosed as suffering from Anton's Syndrome.

See also BLINDSIGHT.

For further reading: Asaad; Melzack; Schultz and Melzack.

phosphene   A variety of ENTOPTIC PHENOMENON. When a person presses or rubs the eyes, the squeezing of the eyeballs can cause the light receptors in the retina to fire, and the person may then see bright flashes and swirls of light. These sensations are called phosphenes. Some people have interpreted phosphenes as being bursts of psychic energy or images of spiritual forces. Some writers employ the term "phosphene" broadly, including not only mechanically produced retinal effects, but also FORM CONSTANTs.

See also FLOATERS; SCHEERER'S PHENOMENON.

photic driving   The electrical activity of the cells in the brain's cortex usually follows a rhythmic pattern. The wavelike tracings of the electroencephalogram, or EEG, display this feature of neural activity. When a person is exposed to regular pulses of visual stimulation—a flickering candle or a flashing stroboscope—the electrical rhythms of the brain tend to mirror the frequency of the visual input. This phenomenon is called photic driving. Individuals subjected to this interruption of ordinary neural functioning often report a range of unusual experiences.

Photic driving was first studied in the laboratory by Walter and Walter and has since been examined by several other researchers. Jilek summarized the most commonly reported effects of photic driving:

1. Visual sensations with characters not present in the stimulus, that is: (a) Colour; (b) Pattern; (c) Movement.
2. Simple sensations in other than the visual mode: (a) Kinaesthetic (swaying, spinning, jumping, vertigo); (b) Cutaneous (tingling, pricking); (c) Auditory (rare); (d) Gustatory and Olfactory (doubtful); (e) Visceral (probably connected with (a)).
3. General emotional and abstract experiences: (a) Fatigue; (b) Confusion; (c) Fear; (d) Disgust; (e) Anger; (f) Pleasure; (g) Disturbance of time sense.
4. Organized hallucinations of various types.

5. Clinical psychopathic states and epileptic seizures.

Photic driving may have played a part in the ritual induction of unusual experiences in non-technological cultures. Someone staring at a bright fire while people danced around it, for instance, could be exposed to sufficient rhythmic input to produce the effects.

More recently, researchers have experimented with contemplation of flickering strobe lights and have reported striking experiences, including exceptionally vivid production of the geometric images called FORM CONSTANTs. Horowitz found that the most intense visual experiences could be produced by gradually varying the frequency of the stroboscope between 10 and 80 flashes per second. Several studies observed that people most prone to photic stimulation effects were those with a history of experiencing mental images during the HYPNAGOGIC STATE.

Neher described an extremely simple method of photic driving:

> All that is necessary is to face an extremely bright light (the sun is ideal if you are careful) with your eyes closed. Then spread the fingers of one hand and pass your fingers back and forth a few inches in front of your eyes. This causes a rhythmic stimulation of your eyes that will produce a changing array of patterns and colors. By moving your fingers faster or slower, you can modify the sensation.

Individuals who are prone to epileptic seizures should not attempt to induce photic driving; anyone should terminate the exercise at the first sign of discomfort.

See also AUDITORY DRIVING; RHYTHMIC SENSORY STIMULATION.

For further reading: Horowitz; Jilek; Neher (1990); Walter and Walter.

PK Popular acronym for PSYCHOKINESIS—the alleged power of the mind directly to influence outer events, or "mind over matter."

planets The Earth shares the solar system with eight other planets, five of which—Mercury, Venus, Mars, Jupiter and Saturn—are visible to the unaided eye. Although they can be hard to distinguish from stars, planets tend to shine with a steadier light. They are always to be found along the track of sky traveled by the sun and moon, called the ecliptic. Planets, like all extra-terrestrial objects, rise in the east and set in the west because of the earth's rotational direction. Most modern members of Western culture, particularly those who live in cities, pay little attention to the night sky. They can thus easily misidentify a planet as something else—such as a UFO. Sightings of planets are the most common explanation for UFO ENCOUNTERs.

When a planet is at its closest approach to the Earth, its unusual brilliance could easily seem to be coming from an object within the Earth's atmosphere. The identity of a planet can be further masked by other factors. As the light from a planet passes through the air, it can be refracted or reflected by aerial substances. As this light encounters the boundaries between air masses, or sheets of floating ice crystals, the image of the planet can appear to pulsate, change shape or color or move back and forth in the sky. Furthermore, a planet can seem to move suddenly due to the AUTOKINETIC EFFECT—the sensation that an observed object is changing position, when actually only the observer's eyeballs have moved. Other illusory effects can arise when planetary light is viewed through glass, such as a car windshield.

From the earth's surface the most spectacular planet is Venus, our nearest neighbor in space (after the Moon). At its brightest, Venus' light can cast shadows. This planet is so often reported as an unidentified object that it has been nicknamed "Queen of the UFOs." Because of its orbit near the sun, it is only visible low in the sky before sunrise or after sunset. The visible light from Venus therefore reaches the atmosphere at a low angle and passes through a greater amount of air than light from sources overhead. The appearance of Venus is thus especially susceptible to distortion by atmospheric effects. Shaeffer reported that the UFO observed by American president-to-be Jimmy Carter in 1969 was actually Venus.

The next closest planet in the solar system, Mars, has also been responsible for a host of unusual experiences. Some UFO researchers have reported that UFO sightings tend to increase when Mars is nearest to the Earth. Supporters of the hypothesis that UFOs are space vehicles have suggested that the craft come from Mars and take advantage of the reduced traveling distance; the skeptically inclined feel that the increased luminosity of Mars when it is nearby produces more misidentifications.

For further reading: Corliss (1994); Sachs.

plasma Matter has four known states: solid, liquid, gas and plasma. The plasma state occurs when the electrons within the atoms of a substance become so energized that they separate from the nucleus. The result is a cloud of positively charged nuclei (called ions) and negatively charged electrons. Energy exchanges between the particles cause this cloud to glow. Plasma is similar to gas, except that it is a good electrical conductor and reacts to magnetic fields. Naturally or accidentally occurring plasmas are being continually created in the Earth's atmosphere. Encountering them has provided the basis for many unusual experiences.

The most common source of plasma is high tension power lines. The high voltages can ionize the air around the wires or transformers, causing the luminosity known as corona discharge. This phenomenon resembles ST. ELMO'S FIRE, a related type of electrical discharge event. Sometimes plasmas have been seen to detach from the power lines and float through the air. The initial cloud can break up into smaller pockets which drift together as if they were flying in formation. Plasmas created in this manner dissipate quickly, which could create the appearance of a luminous object or "fleet" that instantly vanishes.

Klass suggested that a great number of UFO ENCOUNTERs are actually sightings of plasma. The increased number of UFO sightings since the 1940s correlates positively with the growing voltages and quantities of power lines; the interference with radios and car batteries often reported near UFOs would be expected in the proximity of plasma. As the mass media spread the notion that UFOs may be visiting spaceships, observers would more likely interpret the mysterious glowing forms in accord with this idea, "seeing" features such as windows and landing gear where none actually existed. Not everyone is convinced by this theory. Doubters have pointed out that plasmas created by electrical equipment only last a few seconds, whereas many UFO sightings last considerably longer. Friedman (cited by Sachs) admitted that many features of UFO experiences are caused by plasmas—but then proposed that these plasmas are created by alien spacecraft!

Another widely reported plasma phenomenon is the so-called BALL LIGHTNING, also known as globe lightning or kugelblitz. These naturally formed plasmas are not true lightning. In the case of lightning, electricity is discharged rapidly, usually between clouds and earth; ball lightning has been observed continuously for as long as 20 minutes and thus must be a slow discharge event.

Although most reports of ball lightning describe spherical plasmas, other shapes have also been noted. Many observers have seen rod-or cylinder-shaped plasmas. Rarely, luminous electrical ribbons are reported. Colors range from bluish-white to reddish- orange, the typical hues of ionized nitrogen and oxygen. In size, ball lightning can be as small as a pea or larger than a bus.

Ball lightning usually appears during thunderstorms. Occasionally, plasmas have been sighted in clear weather, far from any power lines; the forces that create these entities remain unknown. Sailors have observed plasma balls rise from the surface of the water and dissipate in the sky.

They can also materialize in enclosed spaces, such as houses, or even inside planes. Often, their disappearance is associated with a thunderclap; a lightning discharge evidently disrupts whatever process holds the plasma together. Ball lightning has been known to do considerable damage to property and animals—the rod-shaped variant is thought to be especially destructive—but accounts of harm to humans are extremely rare.

Some features of ball lightning resist conventional explanation. The trajectory of the plasma is often erratic and sometimes seems purposeful—although what the purpose of the object's "behavior" could be is unclear. A typically strange display was witnessed by the Reverend John Lehn, cited by Gaddis:

Seated during an electrical storm . . . a ball or globe of lightning came through the screen in the otherwise open window without in any way damaging or affecting the screen . . . and descended to the floor. It was about the size of a grapefruit and yellow in color, similar in hue to sodium flame, though it did not dazzle my eyes. It swiftly and deliberately rolled about my feet and then hopped up into the bowl of the wash basin and melted into two portions the steel chain holding the rubber stopper and then disappeared, I presume down the drain. It made no sound at any time. The whole event took but a few seconds.

Several weeks later I was standing in the same bathroom . . . during another electrical storm. Exactly the same kind of event occurred. The ball of fire of approximately the same size and color circled my feet after it had come through the screen with no visible effects on the wire. After the globe of fire circled my feet, it went beyond for some short distance and then hopped up into the bathtub and, as it descended, it melted into two pieces the steel chain that held the rubber stopper.

Plasma created in the laboratory dissipates immediately unless it is contained in a "magnetic bottle," a pocket created by magnetic fields. Ball lightning sometimes survives for many minutes, while moving continuously. The nature of the force that prevents natural plasmas from dispersing quickly is a great puzzle. Similarly, WILL-O'-THE-WISPs are thought to be clouds of luminous gas which mysteriously resist dispersion; perhaps there is a link between these two classes of unusual phenomena.

Chemist David Turner (cited by Zimmer) has proposed a model of ball lightning that could explain many of its mysteries. He noted that most of the ions that form plasma in the air are highly unstable and would not survive long enough to produce the spectacular displays of ball lightning. Three kinds of ions likely to be part of an aerial plasma are relatively stable—nitrites, nitrates and positive hydrogen. Turner calculated that these substances would interact to form a spherical "skin" of cool steam, preserving the hot interior of unstable ions and causing the object to wander. The ball would disappear when the heat leaked away, or when the protective skin was ruptured.

In addition to corona discharges and thunderstorms, crystalline rocks have been suggested as a possible generator of plasmas. Quartz crystals, when vibrated or stressed, create electrical fields. This phenomenon, known as the piezoelectric effect, is the basis for the old crystal radio sets. If rock formations containing large quantities of quartz are shaken—perhaps by earth tremors or by a nearby train—they could ionize the air above them, producing plasmas. Some GHOST LIGHTS—luminous forms that are repeatedly seen at certain spots—have been thought to be caused in this fashion.

See also GEOPHYSICAL INFLUENCES.

For further reading: Corliss (1982, 1994); Grigor'ev, Grigor'eva and Shiryaeva; Sachs; Klass (1974); Zimmer.

plateau experience Maslow claimed that every person has a need to develop to his or her highest potential. This process of psychological growth is called self actualization. During the developmental journey, brief glimpses of the self actualized state can occur, known as PEAK EXPERIENCEs. Maslow also mentioned another, lesser known phenomenon, the plateau experience. This condition is attained only by those who are advanced on the path of self actualization, the fruit of a lifetime of disciplined spiritual seeking. The plateau experience is a calm and clear perception of oneself and the world. One feels serenely in control during the plateau, which can evolve into a constant state of being. By contrast, the peak experience can be emotionally excited rather than calm, it can be artificially triggered with drugs even in people who are not self actualized, and is transient rather than lasting.

For further reading: Maslow (1976).

poltergeist In German, *polter* means a noise or uproar, and *geist* means "spirit." Thus, a poltergeist is literally a "noisy spirit." The term is used to describe an outbreak of unexplained events that is commonly ascribed to the actions of occult beings.

Poltergeist accounts date back to the first century. The Roman historian Livy described an incident in which people were pelted by mysterious "showers of stones." Many accounts of poltergeists were recorded in the Middle Ages, when they were attributed to demons; later, during the Renaissance and Reformation, poltergeist occurrences often led to witch hunts. A famous poltergeist witness was the leading Protestant Martin Luther. He recounted that one day he had received as a gift a sack of nuts; that night, while in bed, "it seemed to me all at once that the nuts had put themselves in motion; and, jumping about in the sack, and knocking violently against each other, came to the side of my bed to make noises at me." Luther believed he had been visited by a devil.

The first book published in English to discuss poltergeists was Ludwig Lavater's 1572 classic, *Of Ghostes and Spirites Walking by Nyght, and of Strange Noyses, Crackes, and Sundry Forewarnynges.* Despite his suggestive title, Lav-

ater took a skeptical position, suggesting that many people embroider the sounds of passing cats and weasels, and the fretting of worms in the walls, into supernatural events. More than a century later, however, eminent thinkers were still blaming evil spirits. In 1682, a "stone-throwing devil" visited New Hampshire; for several months, rocks, bricks and tools rained down on the house of George Walton, according to Increase Mather, clergyman and president of Harvard.

Although belief in witchcraft was in decline by the 18th century, encounters with poltergeists continued. The family of the founder of Methodism, John Wesley, endured two months of knockings and groanings of no known origin; although a small animal like a badger or rabbit, "which seems likely to be some witch," was spotted in the house on a few occasions.

Poltergeist phenomena have persisted to the present day. Investigating such reports has been an important activity of psychical researchers. Several books have surveyed the poltergeist cases collected by the investigators. Gauld and Cornell undertook a statistical analysis of 500 cases reported since 1800. Most outbreaks last between two weeks and two months, but about one-quarter of the episodes in Gauld and Cornell's survey persisted for over a year. The most commonly reported feature is the mysterious movement of small objects, pebbles, glasses, ashtrays and the like. Sounds of unknown origin, such as rapping, pounding, footsteps, scratching, rattling, panting and popping noises are typical. Heavy things like refrigerators and linen chests are alleged to move occasionally. Some poltergeists have shown a penchant for unstoppering bottles. In many instances, the trajectories of the flying objects are described as unlike that of thrown objects; they are said to veer erratically or to float.

The mysterious disappearance or reappearance of small objects is often noted. Less common poltergeist phenomena include starting fires and mysterious seepages of water from the walls or ceiling. APPARITIONs are sometimes seen in connection with poltergeist outbreaks. Inexplicable odors, ranging from stenches to the scent of violets, have been noted. Occasionally, a poltergeist has been said to assault someone. Pinches, scratches and bites have been claimed to appear on the victim's body. In an account from 1598, a playful poltergeist pestered a convent of nuns by tickling them "nearly to death."

Case collections suggest that most poltergeist outbreaks occur in the general vicinity of a particular individual, known as a "focal person." The person at the center of the poltergeist storm is usually under 20 and female. Typically, there is evidence of emotional conflict in the focal person—he or she is often not living with the natural parents and is in a situation where severe constraints are placed on emotional expression. Some focal persons have shown clear signs of mental or NEUROLOGICAL DISORDERs.

A range of theories has been advanced to explain the poltergeist. The most widespread and ancient explanation is that there is actually a "noisy spirit" involved. It is noteworthy in this regard that, according to Catholic annals, exorcism is notoriously ineffective against poltergeists.

Following Lavater, many researchers believe that at least some poltergeists can be explained in normal terms. A little vigilance reveals that the average living environment is filled with sounds of uncertain cause; with some imagination, these could be interpreted as the acts of a noisy ghost. Small earth movements and the shifting of building foundations can sometimes cause objects to move unaccountably.

The prominence of a focal person in many cases has raised suspicions of trickery. In a few instances fraud has been uncovered. Threads attached to small objects can send them flying when tugged; holes bored in walls can be used to knock things over; and, if witnesses can be momentarily distracted, a hoaxer can simply throw something. The strange paths of the flying objects in poltergeist reports is not easily explained simply in terms of hoaxing; but the trickery of witnesses' memories must also be considered.

Fodor speculated that the focal person is seething with unexpressed sexuality (a not atypical condition for an adolescent, as so many focal persons are). If ordinary outlets for these feelings are not available, "a sidetracking of the sexual energies in a maturing body may be responsible for the explosive manifestation." This sidetracking could take the form of deliberate fraud, or of the unconscious production of rappings and object movements via AUTOMATISM. Some researchers have suggested that the focal person may cause the poltergeist phenomena, not by tricks, but by PSYCHOKINESIS (PK). They refer to poltergeists as "recurrent spontaneous psychokinesis," or RSPK.

In order to investigate the PK hypothesis, focal persons have been invited to parapsychology laboratories to participate in PK experiments. No significant results have been produced. Roll, investigating a poltergeist outbreak in Miami in 1966–1967, carefully mapped the paths of the flying objects with respect to the location of the focal person at the time of the movements. He discovered that most of the objects moved in a counter-clockwise direction around the focal person's body; also, the further from the focal person an object was at the beginning of its flight, the greater distance it moved. Roll speculated concerning a "psi field" of PK energy that might radiate from the focal person's body during the disturbances. More studies of this kind would be invaluable.

Investigating poltergeists is a difficult business. Researchers frequently learn about an outbreak through reports in the media; and by the time a serious investigator arrives, the phenomena have often either stopped or fallen prey to the encouragments of sensationalism. About three poltergeist cases a year continue to surface. And so, for those worried about "noisy spirits," the famous old anti-poltergeist prayer may thus still be worth knowing: "From ghosties and ghoulies and long-legged beasties and *things that go bump in the night,* may the good Lord deliver us."

For further reading: Christopher (1970); Fodor; Gauld and Cornell; Owen (1964); Roll.

possession Possession is a form of TRANCE behavior that is understood, both by the possessed person and by others, to be caused by the displacement of the individual's soul or self by that of an alien entity. Usually, although not always, the possessed person afterward reports amnesia for the period of possession. Dramatic behavioral changes can accompany the entity's occupancy of its human host. Oesterreich and others have claimed that these behavioral features are relatively constant across time and cultures and probably reflect an underlying physiological mechanism activated in possession. Consider, for instance, the following description of a man possessed by a demon, given by the fourth century Christian writer Zeno of Verona (quoted by Oesterreich):

> His face is suddenly deprived of colour, his body rises up of itself, the eyes in madness roll in their sockets and squint horribly, the teeth, covered with a horrible foam, grind between blue-white lips; the limbs twisted in all directions are given over to trembling; he sighs, he weeps; . . . he confesses his sex, the time and place he entered into the man, he makes known his name . . .

Compare with the following account of a "demoniacal attack," described over 1500 years later by the French psychiatrist Richer (quoted by Oesterreich):

> Suddenly terrible cries and howlings were heard; the body, hitherto agitated by contortions or rigid as if in the grip of tetanus, executed strange movements; the lower extremities crossed and uncrossed, the arms were turned backwards and as if twisted, the wrists bent, some of the fingers extended and some flexed, the body was bent backwards and forwards like a bow or crumpled up and twisted, the head jerked from side to side or thrown far back above a swollen and bulging throat; the face depicted now fright, now anger, and sometimes madness; it was turgescent and purple; the eyes widely open, remained fixed or rolled in their sockets, generally showing only the white of the sclerotic; the lips parted and were drawn in opposite directions showing a protruding and tumefied tongue.

Not all possessions are so vividly enacted; among those experienced in possession, the shift in behavior can be quite subtle.

The trance states that are interpreted as possession are probably universal. The interpretation itself is remarkably widespread. According to Bourguinon's massive survey, belief in possession by spirits was found in 74% of world cultures. Furthermore, she reported that 52% of the world's societies maintain an institutionalized deliberate practice of possession. Deliberate possession is most common in Asia, where it occurs in 72% of the sampled cultures; it is rarest among native North American societies, where it is found in only 25% of Bourguinon's sample. A 1990 Gallup poll found that 49% of adult Americans believe in the reality of possession by demons.

A prominent example of possession harnessed for the benefit of society is the state oracle of Tibet. The oracle is a man who is selected for possession by a spirit counselor named Dorje Drakden. The office of the oracle has advised Tibet's leaders on important matters of state for over a millennium. When a consultation is requested, the oracle must don the elaborate costume of a legendary hero. This garb consists of eight layers of clothing, weighing over 100 pounds, a helmet that weighs another 30 pounds, and a backpack radiating metal poles from which flags and banners hang. Thus encumbered, the oracle induces a trance by visualizing himself as a deity at the center of a MANDALA. Unlike the paroxysmal possessions described above, the oracle is serene when possessed by Dorje Drakden. Questions are whispered into his ear, to which he gives quick answers. The present Dalai Lama, currently in exile from his occupied country, decided to leave Tibet in 1959 on the advice of the oracle, whom he still consults today.

In the West, both spontaneous and deliberate possession are found throughout history. In classical Greece the Manias were seen as possessions by the gods. The ancient Mesopotamians and Hebrews dreaded invasions of evil spirits; the New Testament speaks often of demonic possession and exorcism. Mainstream Christianity discouraged possession, viewing it as the work of Satan. In part, this rejection might have been based on the enthusiasm for possession by angels and the Holy Spirit among heretical groups.

Relatively little was written about possession during the early Middle Ages; but in the later medieval period, there seems to have a surge both in reports of possession and the fear of it. Europe's building anxiety about the pervasiveness of evil spirits, which would culminate in the Great Witch Hunt (15th through 17th centuries), made the possession interpretation of unusual behaviors very popular. The paranoid mentality of the time was fanned by the circulation of tales such as the one described by Boguet (quoted by Robbins). Cautious townspeople dunked an apple into a river before eating it; the apple "gave out a great and confused noise; it cannot be doubted that this apple was full of devils, and that a witch had been foiled in an attempt to give it to someone."

With the decline of official belief in demons following the Scientific Revolution (unofficially, demon beliefs are still widely held today), the Great Witch Hunt ended. Involuntary possession continued, however. During the 19th century, explanations of possession behavior in terms of invasive spirits were replaced by diagnoses of mental illness. Esquirol labeled possession DEMONOMANIA and considered it a type of DELUSION. In an article on demonic possession in the 17th century, Freud wrote that "what in

those days were thought to be evil spirits to us are base and evil wishes, the derivatives of impulses which have been rejected and repressed." Only a small minority of mental health professionals have continued to entertain the possibility that truly alien entities may play a part in possession.

The 19th century saw the return to popularity of deliberate possession, which had been marginalized in the West since ancient times. The Spiritualist movement, which at its height captured the attention of millions in Europe and the Americas, featured the idea that individuals called MEDIUMs could permit themselves to function as mouthpieces for departed souls.

Spiritualism's popularity began to ebb after World War I; but, toward the end of the present century, voluntary possession rose again in the heart of the New Age movement, where it is called CHANNELING. Instead of spirits, many channelers serve as vehicles for extraterrestrials. The 20th century has also seen the massive growth of the African diasporic faith (variants include Voodoo, Santeria, Lucumi, Candomble, Umbanda and others). The spiritual climax of these religions involves possession by gods or spirits during ceremonial gatherings.

From the medical standpoint, there are several new labels for phenomena that were likely interpreted as involuntary possession in the past. In MULTIPLE PERSONALITY DISORDER, individuals act as if they have two or more distinct personalities; sufferers often report that the personalities are unaware of each other to varying degrees. It is easy to see how such a behavior pattern would not surprise a person who believes in possession; the extra personalities are simply regarded as intruders. Conversion disorder, in which body parts that are ordinarily under conscious control can seem to acquire a "will of their own," was probably regarded in the past as a sign of possession.

Some psychiatrists have suggested that the cluster of behaviors and beliefs that comprise possession is sufficiently distinct from other disorders to merit its own psychiatric diagnosis—"Possession Syndrome." Allison offered this working definition of Possession Syndrome:

> a dissociative disorder in which the patient unconsciously believes he is possessed by evil spirits who act out his forbidden wishes. The manifestation depends upon his view of what demonic spirits are like and how they should act.

Two features have been claimed to distinguish Possession Syndrome from multiple personality disorder: A possessed person, unlike a multiple, knows of the existence of the demonic personality; and the alternate personalities of the multiple are no known person and represent psychological conflicts within the sufferer, whereas the alternate personalities in possession identify themselves as gods or spirits. Possession Syndrome is still not recognized as a distinct psychological disorder by the mainstream psychiatric community.

Physical illnesses have probably been blamed on demonic possession in previous times. Some descriptions of possession in premodern records resemble the seizure behaviors of EPILEPSY sufferers, or individuals with TOURETTE'S SYNDROME. Today, these maladies are blamed on disorders of the nervous system.

Deliberate possession, in most cases, probably has nothing to do with illness—as Gordon Melton (quoted in Klimo) observed, "There doesn't seem to be anything pathological about mediums. They are in all respects fairly normal people who happen to go into trance." What, then, is voluntary possession, if not the result of a disorder? Sargant noticed that many of the procedures used to induce possession involve bombarding the brain with a massive amount of stimulation, in the form of vigorous dancing, drumming, chanting and ingestion of drugs. He argued that possession is an interpretation given to the maneuvers of an overloaded nervous system to protect itself, a phenomenon called *transmarginal inhibition*. In one of the stages of

inhibition, known as the ultraparadoxical phase, a person's ordinary response patterns are reversed—loved ones are rejected, previously despised foods are craved. Such "uncharacteristic" behaviors would seem to confirm the presence of an alien character in the possessed person's body.

Anthropologists, noting the presence of institutionalized possession in diverse cultures, have suggested a variety of social functions for possessed behaviors. Possession happens most frequently among members of society who have little economic or political power—Lewis noted its prevalence among "women and other depressed categories." Acting out the roles of powerful and prestigious spirits can give meaning and a sense of control to lives that may otherwise seem unimportant and helpless. Possession may at times actually improve social standing—a peasant who provides effective counseling or healing while possessed can receive enough gifts and respect to become upwardly mobile.

For further reading: Allison; Bourguinon; Gallup and Newport; Klimo; Lewis; Lewis-Fernandez; Noll (1992b); Oesterreich; Sargant.

posthallucinogen perception disorder A psychiatric term for FLASHBACKs following the ingestion of hallucinogenic drugs.

prajna One of the most important achievements of Buddhist meditation practice is the cultivation of prajna, a Sanskrit term often translated as "wisdom" or "discriminating awareness." Prajna is the antidote to the false understanding of reality which, according to Buddhism, gives rise to suffering. This wisdom slices through the obstacles to ENLIGHTENMENT; hence, it is frequently symbolized by a flaming sword. Prajna is a direct seeing of reality, and the eye of wisdom is another of its symbols.

In Buddhist theory, effective meditation brings together two mental functions: SHAMATHA, or calm abiding, and VIPASSANA, or insight. On this basis, the meditator examines the nature of reality. Prajna, the deepest vision of what is real, is nurtured through meditation practice. Unlike other types of knowledge, the wisdom of prajna does not concern the details of the object on which the meditator's attention rests, but on its ultimate nature. For instance, if one is meditating on a statute, prajna is not concerned with the color, material, or features of the statute, but with what the statue essentially is. Under the scrutiny of the prajna-eye, the solidity of reality as it appears to ordinary consciousness is revealed to be an illusion.

The "ultimate nature" that is the object of prajna is defined differently according to the various schools of Buddhism. The Theravada school views the direct perception of the "three marks" (the absence of a self, the impermanence of all phenomena and the unsatisfactoriness of ordinary experience) as the reality revealed by prajna. In the Mahayana schools, prajna is the wisdom that realizes that all objects are empty of any kind of free-standing or inherent existence. This truth is called *shunyata,* or EMPTINESS.

It is foolish to attempt to grasp onto things or states of mind if they are all impermanent or empty, yet this is what people try continually to do, so say Buddhists. Prajna's revelation helps one to see the uselessness of these attempts. The more clearly one perceives the unnecessary pain one causes oneself and others because of false views, the stronger one's motivation becomes to break free of these delusions. When wisdom is so great that one no longers falls into the habit of grasping at the objects of experience, a person is freed from suffering. He or she can then either escape from the phenomenal world into NIRVANA, or devote oneself to helping others become free.

For further reading: Hopkins (1983); Snelling.

prayer This term is most often used in a Christian context to refer to the practice of orienting the mind toward God. Unusual experiences that occur during prayer are almost always interpreted in a religious light. Roman Catholicism has an elaborate classification system for types of prayer. The act of praying can be either vocal or mental. Vocal prayer can be performed individually or communally. Mental prayer has two subtypes. Ordinary mental prayer includes CONTEMPLATION (non- discursive) and MEDITATION (discursive), as well as devout emotional states. Extraordinary prayer includes MYSTICAL EXPERIENCEs and CHARISMs.

preaching sickness Northwestern Europe has been subject to this curious phenomenon since the 18th century. First reported in Finland in the 1770s, the preaching sickness is characterized by the onset of a sleep-like or trance state, in which the individual proclaims religious doctrines. The sermons of the "sleeping preachers" were sometimes quite eloquent. Children as well as adults were subject to this loss of voluntary control. Mass outbreaks of preaching sickness continued periodically in Finland until the 1930s. Sweden was visited by epidemics of the preaching sickness on several occasions in the 19th century.

See also GROUP DYNAMICS OF UNUSUAL EXPERIENCES; MEDIUMSHIP; POSSESSION.

precognition The alleged ability directly to know the future without the use of inferences or guesswork. Precognition is a major category of EXTRASENSORY PERCEPTION. The most common type of precognitive experience, comprising about three-quarters of survey and case reports, is the dream that seems to contain information about events that later occur.

premonition Variant term for PRECOGNITION.

presque vu This French phrase, meaning "almost seen," refers to a yearning for a feeling of completion that seems imminent, but remains just beyond attainment. The intense poignancy of presque vu has generally eluded description in prose; Lovecraft tried to convey the flavor indirectly, by evoking the settings in which "it" can arise:

It is in sunsets and strange city spires,
Old villages and woods and misty downs,
South winds, the sea, low hills, and lighted towns,
Old gardens, half-heard songs, and the moon's
fires. But though its lure alone makes life worth
    living,
None gains or guesses what it hints at giving.

Presque vu sometimes features in MYSTICAL EXPERIENCEs as a powerful longing to achieve union with the divine presence. In Judeo-Christian traditions which hold that the creator and his creatures always maintain some degree of separateness, mystical presque vu is taken as a foretaste of future intimacy with God in heaven.

Presque vu can occur in psychedelic drug experiences. The feeling of tantalizing nearness to perfection may be accompanied by appropriate HALLUCINATIONs. Naranjo reported "a vision of innumerable snail shells, each with a little piece missing," linked with presque vu.

Frequently, the object of yearning is unknown—one simply has an ill-defined sense that the ordinary world is not one's true home, of being a "stranger in a strange land." In presque vu one can feel on the verge of remembering a long-forgotten truth about oneself and the universe. The feeling can seem to be a hint of that which one has been unknowingly seeking all one's life, rendering all finite achievements and joys pale consolations. This experience has convinced some that their soul is in exile from a higher realm. Religious movements that promise to teach methods for the soul's return to its homeland, such as Gnosticism, sprout from the experiential seed of presque vu. Naranjo suggested that the idea of purgatory—a state in which the soul must undergo purification before being allowed into heaven—might be linked to the presque vu experience.

Studies in perception have demonstrated that people have a tendency to see complete figures, even if the stimulus itself contains gaps. For instance, many observers fail to notice the space caused by a single burned out bulb in an illuminated sign. This drive to fill in sensory blank spots is known as closure. Interference with the mind's striving for closure could cause some episodes of presque vu.

See also DÉJÀ VU; JAMAIS VU.

For further reading: Kluver; Lovecraft; Naranjo.

preternatural   A preternatural event is one that seems to originate from a SUPERNATURAL source. Examples include: apparent encounters with spirit beings like gods, ghosts, angels or devils, as well as experiences that seem to involve a journey of the soul through a spiritual realm, such as OUT OF BODY EXPERIENCEs, NEAR DEATH EXPERIENCEs and the entranced travel of SHAMANS. Use of the term "preternatural" does not imply that these experiences are truly supernatural, merely that they seem to be.

See also ANOMALY; PARANORMAL.

pseudohallucination   A sensory experience that is as vivid as an actual perception, but which the person having it knows to be unreal. Pseudohallucinations differ from HALLUCINATIONs only in that the hallucinator believes the experience to be real. A pseudohallucination may be so intense that it provokes an emotional reaction, such as fear or delight; but the observer is still unfooled, as one who responds to a film does not believe the actors to be actually present. Voices or visions of deceased persons, experienced by 50 to 65% of the bereaved, are the most common type of pseudohallucination.

For further reading: Asaad; Horowitz.

pseudologia phantastica   This Greek phrase, which means "elaborate false speech," refers to pathological lying. It is normal to distort memory in a self-serving fashion to support one's sense of personal importance and control. In some forms of personality disorder, individuals report memories of extreme self-aggrandizement, containing elements so improbable that no one takes them seriously. When challenged, they add further details that are usually even more outlandish. The deception in such cases is not necessarily conscious. The liar's need for attention may be so great that the false information is blended with the memories themselves, and the lie assumes the aura of truth.

Pseudologia phantastica complicates matters for researchers of unusual experiences. Whenever a dramatic event is described in the media, people with pathological lying tendencies are prompted to claim that they were somehow involved. Investigators of unsolved crimes are plagued by people offering patently impossible "confessions." Sensational accounts of UFO ENCOUNTERs or sightings of CRYPTICs elicit similar responses, inflating researchers' estimates of the number of actual witnesses.

See also FALSE MEMORY.

For further reading: Reed (1988).

pseudo-nirvana   This state, although exalted, is considered a danger to advanced practitioners of MEDITATION, according to the Buddhist literature. The pseudo-nirvana has several characteristics: the vision of a brilliant light; feelings of rapture, devotion and happiness; serenity, combined with vigourous energy; and clear mindfulness of each moment. The experience is so attractive that meditators might abandon their efforts to develop wisdom and compassion; they might even mistake it for NIRVANA itself. In true nirvana there is freedom from any craving for experiences; in pseudo-nirvana there is a subtle attachment to the state's pleasures.

pseudo-presentiment   The false feeling of having predicted an event that one is currently perceiving. Unlike precognition, in which a person has an experience that matches a future occurrence, a pseudo-presentiment is *not* the fulfillment of any prophecy, for no prediction was made; rather, it is the sense that one *did* predict the event, although one did not. An example of

apparent precognition would be dreaming about a purple bus, which one then sees the following day. A pseudo-presentiment would be seeing a purple bus and being gripped by the feeling that one predicted this event, when in fact one had never before thought about it. Pseudo-presentiment is closely related to DÉJÀ VU, which also involves false feelings of recognition.

For further reading: Reed (1988).

psi   *Psi* is the first letter in the Greek word *psyche,* which means "mind" or "soul." Thouless proposed that the word "psi" be used to refer to two categories of PARANORMAL phenomena—EXTRASENSORY PERCEPTION and PSYCHOKINESIS. He objected to the term "extrasensory perception" because it is not known if ESP experiences actually involve any form of perception. Similarly, "psychokinesis" implies that the mind causes the movement of objects, and it is not known whether this is how PK experiences are produced either. In contrast to these widely used terms, "psi" does not carry such unproven implications—it is neutral.

Thouless' term has been generally adopted by parapsychologists to refer to the subject matter of their discipline. Some use it to designate events that they believe involve actual paranormal influences; for others, psi events are simply occurrences that *appear* to be paranormally produced, but which may eventually be explained in conventional terms. In popular usage "psi" is sometimes taken as a synonym for PSYCHIC abilities, as in "She has psi, so she can predict the future."

Thouless and Wiesner later proposed two subtypes of psi: "psi gamma," corresponding to ESP; and "psi kappa," or PK. These distinctions have not come into general use.

For further reading: Thouless.

psychic   This widely used word, which can be an adjective or a noun, derives from the Greek *psyche,* meaning "mind" or "soul." As an adjective, psychic is often used synonymously with PARANORMAL. Any event that appears to challenge conventional assumptions regarding the limits of possibility is designated a psychic phenomenon. For instance, "psychic healing" refers to medicinal practices that do not employ procedures or substances recognized as therapeutic by contemporary western medicine. "Psychic abilities" are powers viewed as unproven by many scientists, such as ESP, reading auras, and communicating with the spirits of the dead.

As a noun, the term "psychic" normally refers to individuals who believe themselves to possess psychic abilities. They are also known as "sensitives," implying that psychic influences are always present, but remain undetected by the less attuned people. Almost every known culture has people who are supported by their communities in return for their psychic services; foretelling the future, conversing with the departed, finding lost objects, solving crimes, healing, cursing and resolving problems of love have been perennial issues. In modern western society, professional psychics continue to thrive. Although their powers are not acknowledged in the mainstream world view, psychics are consulted—and often richly remunerated—by people of every background and walk of life.

Several factors may be involved in the enduring ability of psychics to impress their clients. The BARNUM EFFECT is the tendency to perceive a vague and general personality description as uniquely relevant personal information. If the client is highly motivated to believe in the psychic's powers, the client may feel that even statements applying to almost everyone ("You sometimes worry about money") display supernatural insight. In the CLEVER HANS EFFECT, a person unknowingly provides information to an observer, who then feeds it back as a psychically acquired revelation. For example, someone who has obviously been crying may be told "You have recently lost something that was dear to you." The trance states and various divining methods (concentrating on Tarot cards or a crystal ball) used by psychics may in fact sharpen their ability to detect sensory cues being emitted by the client. The Barnum and Clever Hans effects can operate outside the awareness of the psychic and the client—they both may think that psychic abilities are operating, rather than these subtle relational processes.

While the vast majority of psychics are sincere practitioners who believe in their own psychic abilities, there have always been "fake psychics" who have made money from the credulous and naive. Manuals exist that explain how to create the illusion that one has paranormal insights. The Barnum and Clever Hans effects are well known to fake psychics, who try to maximize their impact. Two main methods are discussed in the fake psychic literature. The technique called the *psychological reading* emphasizes the Barnum effect, while another procedure, the *cold reading,* relies primarily on the Clever Hans effect. If the fake psychic knows the identity of the client in advance of the reading, they may conduct research to learn as much as they can about them, later to package the results of their detective work as paranormally obtained. Fraudulent psychics who pretend to commune with spirits use a sophisticated technology of tricks to create the appropriate effects, like rappings, materialization of ghosts and mysterious lights and sounds in the seance room. Honest psychics have been brought into disrepute by such shenanigans.

Some skeptics have argued that our susceptibility to misleading processes like the Barnum and Clever Hans effects, combined with the occurrence of fraud and the occasional lucky guess, fully explains the persistent popularity of psychics. Others leave open the possibility that there remains an unexplained factor—that *sometimes, some* psychics might actually acquire information through paranormal means.

See also PARAPSYCHOLOGY; PAREIDOLIA.

For further reading: Christopher (1970, 1975); Hansen (1992b); Hyman (1989); Marks and Kammann.

psychical research While interest in psychic phenomena—occurrences that seem to indicate the existence of powers or dimensions beyond the conventional modern view of reality—has existed in every culture and historical period, the systematic study of these events is relatively recent. In the West prior to the 17th century, claims of miracles or demonically caused phenomena were easily accepted without investigation by most people, because they made sense—given the almost universal belief in supernatural beings, occasional signs of their presence were expected.

Joseph Glanville, a 17th century Englishman, has been called "the father of psychical research." He was perhaps the first person to engage in a systematic study of a paranormal report. In 1662, a house in Tedworth was plagued by a "phantom drummer"—a drumming sound of unknown origin was repeatedly heard in and around the house. Glanville interviewed "ear-witnesses" and heard the sounds himself. He was unable to come up with an explanation, but published an account of the case in his famous book on supernatural phenomena, *Saducismus Triumphatus*. Glanville also founded a group that met regularly to discuss reports of APPARITIONs, HAUNTINGs and POLTERGEISTs and to test those who claimed they could converse with spirits.

The most important psychical researcher of the 18th century was Prosper Lambertini, who became Pope Benedict XIV. Before his promotion, Lambertini was in charge of investigating reports of VISIONs, CHARISMs and other miracles among devout Catholics. He formulated strict rules of evidence and was aware of the misleading powers of excitement, imagination and trickery. As the pope, he established the criteria for evaluating miracle claims in his *De Servorum Dei Beatificatione et Beatorum Canonizatione*.

By the 19th century, the mechanistic world view of modern science had largely come to dominate the thinking of the educated classes. Belief in the powers of witchcraft was widely held to be a relic of a superstitious past, stories of ghosts were increasingly ridiculed and even the existence of God was beginning to be doubted openly. Perhaps in reaction to this demystification, there arose social movements based on anomalous experiences. Mesmerism was established in the late 18th century and it continued to attract attention well into the 19th. Mesmerists used the procedures that have come to be called HYPNOSIS. In addition to claiming that they could accomplish healing with their techniques, Mesmerists reported that their entranced patients had demonstrated telepathy, clairvoyance and out of body travel.

Even more influential than Mesmerism was the rise of Spiritualism in the 1840s. This movement centered on mediums who claimed to be able to contact the dead. Their seances and public demonstrations were filled with apparent psychic phenomena. So-called "mental mediums" displayed knowledge that seemingly could not have been obtained via normal means, suggesting either the help of spirits or the existence of human psychic abilities. In the vicinity of "physical mediums," objects reportedly moved when no one was touching them. To many, either spirit intervention or "mind over matter" seemed to be the only explanations. Spiritualism attracted millions of followers in the Americas and Europe.

Depending on one's emotional leanings, it was easy either to embrace or reject the mysteries of Mesmerism and Spiritualism without investigation. These responses did not appeal to a group of European intellectuals who, in 1882, established the Society for Psychical Research in London, England. The first president of the SPR was Henry Sidgwick, a prominent British classical scholar and philosopher.

The activities of the society were devoted to a critical investigation of psychical claims. These included mediumistic phenomena, but also reports of unsought paranormal experiences, including TELEPATHY, CLAIRVOYANCE and PRECOGNITION, as well as the sorts of cases that concerned Glanville, the Society's 18th century predecessor. Projects of the SPR included the first major collections of paranormal reports. In their efforts to prove that the incidents happened as reported, researchers learned about the vagaries of human memory; and, in their investigations of mediums and other psychics, about the frailty of human observational skills, as well as the cleverness of tricksters.

By the late 1920s, the opinions of the SPR membership had become divided. One faction held that the evidence for the reality of the paranormal, collected over the past 40 years, was overwhelming, and could not be explained by recourse to conventional notions. Many members of this group were Spiritualists. The skeptical faction was more impressed by their inability to prove any such thing. The believers mostly left the SPR around this time. The SPR continues to this day. It publishes two important periodicals—the *Journal* and the *Proceedings of the Society for Psychical Research*. As is noted at the front of each issue of the *Journal,* the Society's mandate continues to be "to examine without prejudice or prepossession and in a scientific spirit those faculties of man, real or supposed, which appear to be inexplicable on any generally recognized hypothesis."

Inspired by the founding of the SPR, a group of Americans, led by William James and William Barrett, established the American Society for Psychical Research in 1885. The scope of the Americans' activities was similar to that of their British counterparts; and, by the 1920s, they had arrived at the same troubled condition. The more and less skeptically inclined parted ways, and the ASPR fissured, not to be reunited until 1941. Today, the ASPR is headquartered in New York, where it publishes the *Journal of the American Society for Psychical Research.*

Perhaps the most important legacy of the early work of the SPR and ASPR was the realization that merely investigating reports of unusual experiences was not likely ever to produce convincing evidence for the existence of para-

normal processes—in the world of everyday perception and memory, it is just too difficult to rule out every possible conventional explanation. This discovery produced growing interest in trying to capture paranormal events in the controlled circumstances of a scientific experiment. In the laboratory setting, it was hoped, explanations in normal terms could be excluded. This interest led, in the late 1920s, to the beginning of the first program of experimental psychical research—or PARAPSYCHOLOGY—headed by J.B. Rhine at Duke University in Durham, North Carolina.

Another outcome of the activities of the SPR and ASPR has been the proliferation of psychical research organizations throughout the world. Many national and regional societies now conduct investigations into anomalous claims and reports. Some of these groups are extremely skeptical and aim at "debunking" such claims; others lean toward credulity and employ psychics and exorcists in an uncritical manner; and some groups maintain an open-minded skepticism.

For further reading: Inglis (1977); Mauskopf and McVaugh (1980).

psychogenic death Literally "mind-caused death," the possibility that a person can die as the result of a psychological process was first considered by social scientists under the name voodoo death. Researchers observed in many cultures that individuals who were cursed, or who violated a taboo, frequently died shortly afterward in the absence of obvious physical causes. The classic description is that of Basedow (cited in Cannon). He observed the reaction of an Australian aborigine who had just had a cursing bone pointed at him by a sorceror. The victim:

> stands aghast, with his eyes staring at the treacherous pointer, and with his hands lifted as though to ward off the lethal medium which he imagines is pouring into his body. His cheeks blanch and his eyes become glassy and the

expression on his face becomes horribly distorted. . . . He attempts to shriek but usually the sound chokes in his throat, and all that one might see is froth at his mouth. His body begins to tremble . . . he sways backward and falls to the ground . . . writhing as if in mortal agony. After awhile he becomes very composed and crawls to his [shelter]. From this time onwards he sickens and frets, refusing to eat and keeping aloof from the daily affairs of the tribe.

Unless a counter-spell is done quickly, death may be imminent.

Three possible explanations can be considered for this dramatic phenomenon: magic; a subtle physical effect of some sort; and a psycho-physiological effect, in which the victim's psychological reaction to the perceived threat interferes with the basic life-supporting functions of the body. The latter explanation is known as "psychogenic death."

The magical explanation is the one offered in most societies in which the phenomenon occurs. Usually, it is said that the soul of the victim has been driven from the body; in the absence of this life-force, the body breaks down. Few modern researchers take this explanation seriously.

Some scholars have suggested purely physical mechanisms to explain death in response to a cursing ritual. In many traditional societies, cursed persons are considered to be "as good as dead." Consequently, they may be deprived of the essentials of life and die of starvation or dehydration. In addition to their magical skills, many sorcerors are renowned for their knowledge of poisons. The potency of curses is often assisted by the administration of toxins.

Most researchers accept that deprivation and poisoning are sometimes involved in the tragic outcome of curses. However, the medical literature clearly suggests that psychological reactions *can* produce lethal effects—in effect, that one can be scared to death. Cases are on record in which seemingly healthy people suddenly expired when shot at with an unloaded gun, while stepping onto a stage to give a speech, when nearly being hit by a car, while viewing a solar eclipse (in the belief that the world might soon end) and upon exposure to a startling noise. In one instance, when a healthy bank teller suddenly died during a robbery, the robber was convicted of murdering her through fear.

Laboratory research has suggested a possible mechanism underlying such anecdotes. Dogs injected with massive doses of catecholamines, chemicals that are secreted in response to stress, die from lesions of the heart muscle. Autopsies performed on people who suddenly died under stress revealed identical damage to the heart. If a person fervently believes that they are about to die by magic, their terror will likely trigger a massive release of catecholamines, leading quickly to the fulfillment of their fear. Other studies have found that some laboratory animals react to excessive stimulation by slowing their metabolism to dangerous levels—another possible contributing factor to psychogenic deaths in humans.

For further reading: Cannon; Davis (1988); Eastwell; Engel.

psychokinesis Psychokinesis (often denoted PK) is the apparent ability of a person (or other organism) to influence the environment without using any of the known conventional means such as muscular action. The term is compounded of the Greek roots *psyche* ("mind" or "soul") and *kinesis* ("movement"). Thus, it implies that the mind is acting directly on the external world; hence the popular phrase for PK—"mind over matter." Along with EXTRASENSORY PERCEPTION, PK is one of the main alleged phenomena studied by parapsychologists.

PK has been offered as an explanation for many unusual experiences that are traditionally viewed as either miracles or the action of spirits. In his collection of strange phenomena associated with Catholic saints, Thurston reported many incidents in which the holy wafer of the Mass allegedly rose from the altar and deposited itself into the mouth of the communicant. The devout may consider such an event to be a divine act; but some have argued that it would more likely be caused by PK on the part of the priest or the communicant. Similarly, stories of LEVITATION, POLTERGEISTS, the effects of RITUAL MAGIC, and the seance room occurrences known as physical MEDIUMSHIP, are ordinarily attributed to disembodied beings, but could equally well be explained by PK influences from living humans.

Indeed, it is difficult to say what PK *cannot* accomplish, if it exists. Most theorists believe that PK likely operates to fulfill the desires of the PK source. But we may not be conscious of everything we desire, and it has been suggested that coincidences such as surprise encounters with old friends on the street might be caused by the guiding influences of "unconscious PK." Philosophers who believe that the mind and the body are distinct entities (a position called dualism) have suggested that PK is the link between mind and brain; when the mind wills the lifting of the left arm, for instance, PK manipulate the appropriate cortical neurons to bring about this behavior. Others have speculated that PK is unaffected by the distance between its source and its target and may even transcend the barriers of time—the possibility of "retro-PK," or psychokinetic influence upon past events, has been discussed in the parapsychological literature.

Whether or not "mind over matter" is possible, belief in it is not uncommon. A 1990 Gallup poll estimated that 17% of Americans believe in the reality of PK, and 7% believe they have experienced it. L.E. Rhine collected almost 200 reports of spontaneous PK occurrences. Most of the PK events in her collection involved two people: one who reported witnessing the PK, and one who was undergoing a crisis of some sort at the moment of the event. In the typical case, the crisis was death. At the time of someone's demise, a faraway friend or relative notices a mysterious occurrence—a vase tumbles from a secure place on a shelf, a watch or clock suddenly stops, a mirror or window breaks unaccountably. The witness may state that they did not even know of the crisis at the time. In these circumstances many witnesses assume that the PK influence originated from the person undergoing the crisis, and that the PK effect was an attempt to send a message to them.

As evidence for the reality of direct mental influence on the environment, case reports and surveys are not conclusive. Windows break and clocks stop all the time; only occasionally does such an event coincide with a personal crisis, leading a witness to believe in a link between the event and the crisis. But a certain number of such coincidences would be expected by chance, even if PK did not exist, and it is impossible to say whether a particular PK experience was a chance matching of crisis and event, or whether some paranormal connection was involved. Furthermore, most case reports rely on the memories of witnesses, who may be reporting experiences they had long ago, and human memories are not always reliable accounts of what really happened. A conclusive demonstration of PK would require an effect that was so dramatic and well-documented that it could not be explained as a coincidence, a misperception, a misremembering or a fraud—for instance, a levitation of a large object in public, witnessed by many, under conditions precluding fraud, recorded by video and repeatable on demand. No one has ever achieved such a feat.

An alternative approach to providing evidence for the existence of PK is to try to produce it in the controlled conditions of a research laboratory. Again, no large scale PK of the sort described above has ever been documented in conditions that ruled out other explanations.

Since 1934, however, experiments have been conducted which have demonstrated the reality of PK at least to some researchers' satisfaction. In that year parapsychologist J.B. Rhine met a gambler who claimed to be able to influence the fall of dice by will power alone. Although the gambler's attempts to demonstrate his abilities were unconvincing, the incident suggested to Rhine that extremely small PK effects might be detectable by studying tasks like dice throwing. With an six-sided die, each particular die face should come up an average of 10 times per 60 throws, if nothing other than chance is affecting the die's behavior. If, over a large number of die throws, a large departure from this chance expectation is observed, the presence of an influence upon the die should be suspected. If cheating and errors in observing and record keeping can be eliminated, and the die is unbiased and tumbling randomly, such a result would constitute evidence for PK, Rhine argued.

Early experiments by Rhine tried to rule out the possibility of cheating and unsound dice by using dice-rolling machines rather than throwing the dice by hand, and alternating the die faces which the subjects were instructed to "will" to face up. Rhine and his colleagues reported very significant deviations from chance expectation in the dice-rolling experiments, which seemed to be evidence of a PK influence on the dice. Some critics continued to doubt whether more conventional explanations could be dismissed. And some simply rejected the results as impossible. If researchers could have produced the alleged PK effect reliably, the criticisms and blanket dismissals would have been muted. But this proved difficult to do. If PK existed, it seemingly could not be prompted to perform on command.

Since 1970, a large number of studies have been conducted using more sophisticated technology in an attempt to demonstrate PK effects more clearly than the earlier research. Instead of dice-rolling, a more certain source of randomness was harnessed: radioactive material. According to physics, the emission of particles from radioactive substances occurs at thoroughly random intervals—the length of time between clicks on a Geiger counter cannot in principle be predicted. If subjects in an experiment were able to demonstrate the ability to cause particles to be emitted nonrandomly from a radioactive source, this would be evidence of PK.

American parapsychologist Helmut Schmidt pioneered the new approach to PK research. He devised a system that has come to be known as a "random event generator," or REG. A radioactive source is put in proximity to a device that detects particle emissions; this device is connected to a visual display, such as an array of lights. In the absence of anomalous influences, the lights should come on at random, reflecting the randomness of the radioactive emissions. In PK experiments, subjects are asked to observe the display and to attempt to affect the sequence of lights through mental means—by visualizing the desired outcome, by sheer force of will or by trying other psychological strategies. The recording and analysis of the REG's activity can be automated, eliminating the possibility of scoring errors by an experimenter. Nonradioactive electronic sources of randomness have also been used as the basis of an REG. The visual display can be designed in ways that will increase the interest and motivation of the subjects; for instance, the scores obtained in a computer game can be determined by an REG, and the subjects instructed to maximize their scores in the game.

A substantial number of REG-based experiments, conducted at many laboratories, have reported significant deviations from randomness. The ideal of a reliably repeatable PK effect remains elusive, however. Some critics allege that conventional factors can explain the results of the PK experiments—the REG was not really random, the experimenters erred in various ways, the significance of the published data would disappear if all the unpublished experimental results were to be included or someone cheated. Others feel that PK has been demonstrated by any reasonable standards; they note that no experiment in all of science produces identical results each time, and that the level of repeatability in PK studies is equivalent to that of many generally accepted phenomena in other research areas. As in ESP research, the conclusions of those who examine the results of PK experiments may depend largely on their own preconceptions about the possibility of paranormal phenomena.

See also Appendix.

For further reading: Gallup and Newport; Rhine (1970); Robinson; Schmeidler (1990); Thurston; Zusne and Jones.

psychological adjustment　Many anomalies researchers have wondered whether a link exists between psychological health and the tendency to have unusual beliefs and experiences. Severely disturbed people such as schizophrenics often do have strange perceptions and viewpoints. There are several ways in which a person's ability to adjust to life's challenges might be related to anomalous belief and experience propensities—anomalous reports could be *symptoms* of mental illness, *causes* of poor adjustment, *supports* for psychological health or signs of *personal potential*.

Some skeptics have argued that anomalous reports indicate a loss of contact with reality; if so, even nonpsychotic people who have anomalous beliefs or experiences are likely to have psychological problems. Strange experiences might also cause adjustment problems—unusual events can be very stressful and could strain some witnesses' ability to cope, making them more prone to psychological difficulties. Schumaker (1990), who thinks that all paranormal beliefs are false, suggested that these beliefs help people escape from the horrors of reality, such as the certainty of death. Schumaker's viewpoint predicts that believers generally would function better in everyday life than nonbelievers, who lack the protection of comforting paranormal falsehoods. In many traditional cultures anomalous experiences are taken to indicate that a person possesses special talents which should be cultivated. Practitioners of SHAMANISM, for instance, often receive their calling to master the spirit world during a period of mental disturbance.

The most commonly used measure of psychological adjustment in research is Eysenck's Neuroticism Scale. This questionnaire asks subjects for a true/false response to items like "Do you ever feel 'just miserable' for no good reason at all?" and "Do you often feel disgruntled?" Individuals scoring high on this scale tend to be more emotionally unstable and have more social problems. Other widely used measures of general adjustment are similar to Eysenck's scale.

Studies comparing scores on psychological adjustment scales with levels of anomalous belief and experience have produced inconsistent results. Most of the studies examining paranormal beliefs and adjustment reported a negative correlation: higher levels of belief were linked to lower levels of adjustment. Schumaker (1987) reported the opposite finding; better adjusted people had more paranormal beliefs. (Irwin [1991b] noted that Schumaker seems to have made mistakes in analyzing his data). Some studies have found no correlation between adjustment and paranormal beliefs in general.

Concerning unusual experiences, people who report MYSTICAL EXPERIENCEs tend to score high on measures of psychological adjustment (with the possible exception of measures of MAGICAL THINKING); DIABOLICAL EXPERIENCEs are associated with lower adjustment; and OUT OF BODY EXPERIENCEs are unrelated to adjustment.

See also Appendix; EMOTIONAL AROUSAL; NARCISSISM.

For further reading: Irwin (1991b, 1993); Schumaker (1987, 1990).

psychosis　A psychosis is a mental disorder characterized by a loss of contact with reality as it is normally defined. Persons suffering from psychosis often report delusions (unrealistic beliefs) and hallucinations (false perceptions), and their behavior can be unpredictable and incomprehensible. The most common type of psychosis is SCHIZOPHRENIA, which occurs in about 1 in every 100 people. Many normal individuals who have unusual experiences fear to mention them to others, for fear of being labeled psychotic.

For further reading: American Psychiatric Association; Noll (1992a).

qurb An Arabic term meaning "nearness," Qurb refers to the experience of God's presence. This state is brought about by intense concentration on God, according to the teachings of Sufism, the mystical branch of Islam. Qurb can be a prelude to more intimate experiences of the divine, such as MAHABBA.

Raja yoga The tradition of Royal Yoga is a grand synthesis of Hindu methods of transforming consciousness. By developing awareness through exercises for the body and mind, the path of Raja Yoga is said to lead to the ultimate achievement—freedom through self-realization. The most influential text of the school—the *Yoga sutras* of Patanjali—was composed sometime between the second century B.C. and the fifth century A.D., although it contains material dating from much earlier times.

Patanjali's Royal Yoga is closely associated with an ancient philosophical system called Sankhya. The Sankhya philosophers analyzed the mind into two main parts. The *purusa* is pure awareness. It is the essence of the self. The contents of the mind—all of our perceptions, concepts, feelings and fantasies—are manifestations of a substance called *buddhi*. This substance is not conscious; rather, it is illuminated by the purusa, which becomes aware of it (when I think of a house, for instance, the image of the house is not conscious; rather, my awareness illuminates the image). Most people normally identify themselves with the buddhi—I am my interests, my social roles, my memories. However, in the philosophy associated with Raja Yoga, this identification is a mistake. "I" am not buddhi, but purusa. The path of Raja Yoga aims to disentangle purusa and buddhi, so that one clearly experiences the difference, and realizes the self as pure awareness.

In order for the two mental elements, purusa and buddhi, to be separated, the continuous activity of the buddhi must be quietened. Raja Yoga teaches eight "limbs," or practices, to pacify the buddhi—thus, this branch of yoga is often called *Ashtanga Yoga,* or "eight-limbed" yoga.

The first two limbs promote calmness in one's style of life. The limb of *yama,* or restraint, encourages the yogi to be nonviolent, truthful, chaste, without greed and frugal in diet. *Niyama,* the second limb, emphasizes development of the correct attitude: keeping one's mind continually pointed toward the "supreme reality," instead of dwelling on material things. The foundation of a wholesome lifestyle is essential for the successful practice of the higher limbs—if outer events are continually arousing the mind, it will be impossible to still it.

Practice of the next three limbs helps to calm the body. The practice of yogic posture (*asana*) eliminates chronic muscle tension and combats distracting illnesses, while special breathing techniques (*pranayama*) balance the subtle bodily energies. The posture and breathing practices are also called *Hatha Yoga.* Most of what passes for yoga in the West today consists of these two limbs. While these activities may well promote physical health, and occasionally evoke some unusual experiences, they cannot contribute substantially to spiritual progress without the other six limbs, say the Ashtanga yogis.

The fifth limb is *pratyahara,* or withdrawal of the senses from the outside world. The practitioner is trained to regard every sight, sound, taste, touch and smell as one's own self, which helps the senses to abandon these objects and focus within. The classic image of pratyahara is found in the *Goraksha-Paddhati:* "As the tortoise retracts its limbs into the middle of the body, so the yogi should withdraw the senses into himself."

The final three limbs of Ashtanga Yoga (known collectively as *samyama,* or mental constraint) aim directly to pacify the mind. *Dharana* is the process in which attention is fixed on an internal object. The texts mention various appropriate objects for this practice, including visual or auditory mental images, and locations within the body. In the next limb, *dhyana,* attention can be maintained on the object for sustained periods of time. This practice leads to the final limb—SAMADHI, or concentration on the object to the point where a sense of distinction between the observer and the observed is no longer present.

In Raja Yoga, the development of samadhi, supported by the other limbs, is the key to liberation. Yogic writings describe a scale of consciousness to be ascended by the meditator. As concentration deepens, the buddhi's constant squirming slows, and its energy is harnessed to sharpen the attention even more. The lower stages on the scale are called SAMPRAJNATA SAMADHIs. From the most refined of these, the meditator can launch into the higher states, the ASAMPRAJNATA SAMADHIs. Eventually, the buddhi is pacified, and even the habits that would drive future activity are erased. Purusa can now be clearly distinguished from the inert buddhi. The meditator, having identified with pure awareness, is no longer mesmerized by the flow of experience. This is the ultimate state of freedom, or KAIVALYA.

Samyama is also said to produce supernormal powers, or SIDDHIs. These abilities are the last temptations on the path of Raja Yoga. If the meditator becomes attached to the development of powers, he or she will again become enslaved by the play of the mind and its illusory rewards.

For further reading: Eliade (1969); Feuerstein (1989, 1990); Larson and Bhattacharya; Mishra.

Ramanujan, Srinivasa This Indian thinker, who lived at the turn of the 20th century, has two claims to fame. First, Ramanujan is regarded as one of the most creative mathematical theorists of modern times. Second, he reported that he "received" his breakthroughs in mathematics through a process seemingly akin to CHANNELING.

Ramanujan was born in 1887, in a small, isolated Indian village. He received relatively little formal education. When he was 16, he acquired an old mathematics textbook and became fascinated. After memorizing it, Ramanujan wished to explore the subject further, but had no access to the higher levels of institutional learning.

At this time, Ramanujan stated, he began to sense the presence of two deities—Namagiri, a local goddess, and Saraswati, the well-known Indian deity of logic. He reported that these beings taught him how to discover new mathematical theorems. Working alone, completely unconnected to the academic world of his day, Ramanujan received tutoring from the goddesses and produced a series of ingenious mathematical theorems.

Eventually, Ramanujan mailed his work to eminent mathematicians in England, who quickly recognized his brilliance. Concerning the novelty of his formulas, Godfrey Hardy of Cambridge University commented, "They must be true, because if they were not true nobody could have had the imagination to invent them." Unfortunately, this unique mind was active only briefly—Ramanujan died in 1920, aged 33.

Although many scientific discoveries have been associated with nonlogical processes such as dreaming and reverie, Ramanujan's example is unusual. There may be no other modern case in which a researcher has reported receiving verifiably correct, novel and important information directly from supernatural beings. The esoteric literature is filled with such claims, of course, but channeled information is usually vague and poetic, in contrast to the precise quality of Ramanujan's mathematical theorems.

For further reading: Harman and Rheingold; Hastings.

rapture From the Latin *rapere,* "to seize," a state in which one feels carried away by profound emotion. Rapture is sometimes used synonymously with MYSTICAL EXPERIENCE. Some fundamentalist Christians use the term to refer to the carrying off of the righteous prior to Christ's second coming.

reading of hearts Traditional Christian term for telepathy—direct knowledge of another person's thoughts or feelings without reliance on inference or sensory cues. The ability to read hearts has frequently been reported of saints. It is recognized as a CHARISM, or typical accompaniment of holiness, by the Roman Catholic church.

reasoning skills Belief in paranormal concepts has often been called "irrational" or "credulous" by some skeptics. It is possible that poor reasoning skills could lead a person to embrace incorrect views about the nature of things. It is also the case that most people find it difficult to question their own deeply held beliefs; people who hold anomalous beliefs might be expected to have trouble thinking critically about them.

Research into the relationship between reasoning skills and paranormal beliefs has usually measured reasoning abilities by presenting logical problems for subjects to solve; beliefs are assessed with a questionnaire. The results of these studies are varied and offer no clear support for the idea that most paranormal beliefs are simply the result of incorrect thinking. Some studies have reported that lower reasoning abilities are associated with higher general levels of anomalous belief, as well as specific belief in ESP and spirits. Other researchers have found no such correlations, however. Studies examining whether people reason more poorly about paranormal topics than non-paranormal ones have also produced inconsistent results.

Irwin (1993) noted that the studies which found an association between uncritical thinking and paranormal belief were all conducted by avowed skeptics. He suggested that the more critically skilled subjects in these experiments could have discerned the experimenters' negative attitudes toward paranormal beliefs and responded by minimizing their admission of such beliefs; subjects with poorer reasoning skills might have been less perceptive and not reduced their endorsement of paranormal beliefs.

See also Appendix; EDUCATION; INTELLIGENCE.

For further reading: Irwin (1991b, 1993).

reincarnation memory The belief that one has lived before is almost as widespread as the notion that one will live again in a spiritual world. Reincarnation is a central doctrine in Asian systems such as Hinduism and Buddhism, but it is not foreign to the West. Ancient thinkers like Pythagoras endorsed the idea, as did the Druids among the Celts. Reincarnation was commonly believed by early Christians; church fathers like Origen, as well as heretics such as the Gnostics, promoted the doctrine. In the Middle Ages, the Bogomil and Cathar heretics resurrected the Christian reincarnation belief. Esoteric Judaism, or KABBALAH, teaches reincarnation. In the New World too, belief in rebirth is widespread—many Inuit groups, the Hurons and Algonquins of eastern North America and the Tlingit and Carrier tribes of the West Coast were all traditional reincarnationists. This broadly distributed and persistent belief is based in part on the experience of reincarnation memories.

Recollections of past lives reported by children have been widely noted. Stevenson, the most industrious researcher in this field, has examined over 2,000 reincarnation reports of children from the following countries: Brazil, Burma (Myanmar), Canada, India, Lebanon, Thailand, Turkey, Sri Lanka and the United States. The prevalence of reincarnation memories among children is hard to estimate accurately. Generally, more reports are made in societies with mainstream reincarnation beliefs. In some cultures such reports are met with interest and approval; in others, they are taken as omens of disaster or mental illness. The relationships between conventional belief in reincarnation memories, attitudes toward children reporting them and the actual frequency of their occurrence have not been clearly disentangled.

Many childhood reincarnation stories are easily dismissed as immature fantasies. Chari considers past life personalities as the Asian equivalent of the IMAGINARY COMPANIONs that cheer up lonely and bored Western children. In some cases, however, the child seems to possess knowledge derived from past life experiences. The best known instance is the story of a young Indian girl, Shanti Devi. Christie-Murray recounts:

Kumari Shanti Devi, born in October 1926 in Delhi, from the age of about four talked of her former life in Muttra, about a hundred miles away, saying that she had been a Chaban by caste, that her husband, a cloth merchant, had been named Pt Kedar Nath Chaubey, and that her house had been yellow. Chaubey was found actually to exist in Muttra. His cousin interviewed the girl, who recognized him and convincingly answered questions concerning intimate details of her former life. In 1935 the husband with his second wife and former wife's ten-year-old son came to Delhi. Shanti, deeply moved, recognised him, answering more intimate questions convincingly. A few days later she, her parents and three investigators visited Muttra, where she identified her husband's elder brother and her father-in-law. She told the driver the correct route to her former house, mentioning that it had not been asphalted when she knew it, pointed out various buildings erected since her death, and in her own house identified the *jai-zarur*, a local name for a privy not understood by Delhi-ans. Led away to a newer house now occupied by Chaubey, she recognised her former brother, now aged twenty-five, her uncle-in-law and other details, and later picked out her former parents in a crowd of over fifty people. The first wife, Lugdi, had died aged twenty-three in October 1925 after the birth of a son. The intermission was therefore about three months.

A review of Stevenson's data indicates that children begin to report past life memories between the ages of two and four and have usually lost the memories by age eight. The average time between the death of the supposed preincarnation and the present life ranges from almost none among some native American groups through 9 months (Turks), 14 months (East Indians), 21 months (Lankans) and 48 months among the Tlingit.

In societies that believe in the possibility of sex changes between lives, many children remember a past life of the other gender; in cultures where the gender identity of the soul is constant, one's previous sex normally matches the present one. Cross-sex rebirth reports are almost unheard of in Turkey, comprise about 15% of American accounts, and rise to 20% in Burma and Thailand. In some cases a child's sense of being preincarnated in an opposite gendered body is reflected by an interest in transvestism (cross-dressing). (It is noteworthy that anxiety about interlife sex change partially motivated orthodox Christianity to suppress the reincarnation doctrine. St. Jerome wrote that the worst part of Origen's teaching was that "we may have to fear that we who are now men may afterwards be born women").

The frequency of apparent reincarnation within families also varies across cultures. Among the Tlingit, 85% of the remembered preincarnations were family members; in Asia, this figure drops to about 2%. In societies where family reincarnation is uncommon, the alleged previous incarnation lived an average of 15 miles from the remembering child; the distance is almost never greater than 100 miles.

Prior to a child's birth, the mother or other female relative often has a dream revealing the child's previous life; the announcing dream is especially prevalent among the Burmese, the Turks and the natives of North America's west coast. Ancient tradition holds that Queen Maya, the mother of Gautama Buddha, had an announcing dream revealing her son's significance.

Among cultures with significant wealth gaps between social classes, downward mobility between existences is the norm; in most cases children recall being richer in their previous lives. Recollections that the previous identity died violently are found in all samples; such reports are uncommon among Lankans, while they form a sizeable majority among Lebanese and Americans. Birthmarks on the child are frequently related to remembered past life behaviors, including the mode of death; over half of the Tlingit children with reincarnation memories have such marks.

Spontaneous recollections of past lives are less common among adults. The most frequent adult experience that tends to be interpreted in reincarnationist terms is the DÉJÀ VU—a feeling that something one is now perceiving has happened before. Some people assume that the déjà vu event occurred during a previous existence. The inexplicable fascination with particular cultures or historical periods that grip many people at some point in their lives has also been taken as a hint of previous identities. The most spectacular report of spontaneous past life recall among adults was reported by Guirdham. He described a group of people, some of whom were connected with each other only through distant acquaintances, who began to experience dreams, INNER VOICEs and AUTOMATISMs regarding the Cathar heretics of 13th century France. The group concluded that they were all reincarnated members of that medieval movement.

Various techniques have been developed for the deliberate awakening of past life memories. Asian meditation systems like the Yoga Sutras of Patanjali have practices for this aim, and past life recall is frequently mentioned as a by-product of intensive meditation practice.

In modern times, HYPNOSIS has been the most commonly used procedure to access previous lives. The technique of hypnotic age regression, in which the subject receives suggestions to experience himself or herself at an earlier age of the present life, was first reported by Colavida in 1887; regression into previous lives may first have been done by Stark in 1906. Since that time, several variants of hypnotic past life regression have become popular. In one simple technique, subjects are asked to visualize a thick book, representing the record of all their existences. Once one locates one's present life in the book, one can leaf backward to see depictions of prior lives. The Christos technique, which combines relaxation, visualization and massaging the forehead and feet, is another popular trigger for past life recall.

Wambach surveyed 1,088 American subjects who underwent past life regression. She reported that most of the recalled previous lives were lower class individuals, and that the gender division of past lives was close to the proportions found in the living population. These findings do not conform to the reports of spontaneous past life memory among children, suggesting that deliberate adult recollections may be caused by different mechanisms. Spanos found that people who are highly hypnotizable and who have a strong capacity for ABSORPTION in fantasy tend to report the most vivid memories of prior lives.

Since the 1960s, reincarnation recall has been the basis for a brand of psychotherapy, past life therapy. People who suspect that difficulties such as phobias or persistent bad moods may derive from traumas in previous lives are hypnotically encouraged to remember the hurtful incident. Reliving the event with greater understanding allegedly helps with the present problem. Wambach surveyed over 18,000 patients of past life therapy and reported that a majority found the treatment beneficial.

The occurrence of apparent recollections of past lives is indisputable. The explanation for this experience is hotly debated. Believers in the doctrine of reincarnation generally have no difficulty accepting the past life memory at face value. Others have suggested that cases in which the individual displays knowledge seemingly acquired in another life may actually have gathered the information during the present life using

ESP, or that the person was possessed by a spirit with the relevant knowledge.

Theories that do not rely on paranormal hypotheses have also been advanced. It is impossible for anyone to distinguish with certainty between accurate recollections and FALSE MEMORIES consisting of imagined material; the distinction is blurred further by hypnosis. Hypnotized subjects tend to produce the experiences desired by the hypnotist, and most hypnotists working in the past life field are searching for memories of prior existences. Baker demonstrated that reports of hypnotic regression to past lives are influenced by the hypnotist's attitude toward the phenomenon: When subjects were given an enthusiastic presentation about past life memories prior to the regression, 85% went on to remember a past life; after a neutral presentation, 60% recalled a past life; only 10% admitted to past life recall following a negatively toned presentation. The fantasies of children are also susceptible to manipulation through rewards and punishments; it has been suggested that the preponderance of wealthy previous lives among child recollectors may reflect their desires, or those of their families, to form a link with a higher social class.

The correlation between cultural expectations and features of past life memories, such as cross-sex incarnations and rebirth within families, is consistent with the idea that remembrances of prior lives are fantasies, molded by personal motivations and beliefs. It could be argued that the culturally distinct patterns are the cause of the differences in belief, not their effects. Likely, the influence between belief and experience is mutual.

Baker found that 90% of the people who can hypnotically regress to *previous* lives can also progress into *future* lives. If one accepts regression reports as sufficient proof for reincarnation, one is faced with the challenge of comprehending how one's future lives are preplanned.

In many cases the accurate historical information that appears in past life memories could have been learned in the present incarnation. The inability to recognize an ordinary memory for what it is, without knowing where one learned it, is a common process called CRYPTOMNESIA. In adult cases it is almost impossible to prove that verifiable facts contained in past life recollections were never encountered at some earlier point in the person's present life.

Cryptomnesia can also occur among children. In most cases of children's past life recall, the families of the child in the present life and the alleged past life have met before any investigator has arrived on the scene. There is usually no way of knowing how much information has already been exchanged between the "preincarnate" family and the child, and how much the details of the case may have been exaggerated, intentionally or otherwise.

The idea that most past life memories are imaginative constructions is plausible and consistent with the evidence. Whether a truly anomalous process such as ESP or reincarnation might happen alongside the more prosaic mechanisms is a topic of continued controversy.

See also UFO ABDUCTION EXPERIENCE; XENOGLOSSY.

For further reading: Baker (1982); Chari; Christie-Murray; Guirdham; Irwin (1989a); Matlock; Pasricha (1990); Spanos (1991); Stevenson; Wambach.

religiosity   Given that most religions teach the existence of spiritual, divine or demonic influences that can affect human life, it is natural to wonder whether religious people are more likely to hold other types of anomalous beliefs as well. Studies on religious affiliation have generally noted no differences—members of various denominations and religions tend to endorse global belief in the paranormal at about the same levels. Concerning religious behaviors, most studies have found no relationship between frequency of church attendance and general anomalous beliefs; both rare and frequent attenders report more MYSTICAL EXPERIENCEs than those who go to church a moderate amount, however. A survey of Icelanders by Haraldsson found that people who pray are more likely to believe in ESP. The strongest religious correlation with paranormal belief is the degree of one's professed religious feelings, regardless of denominational commitment or other behaviors. People who express intense religious feelings are more likely to endorse paranormal beliefs in general and ESP in particular; however, they are less likely to believe in ghosts or UFOs.

See also Appendix; DEATH CONCERNS.

For further reading: Haraldsson (1981); Irwin (1993).

retrocognition The alleged ability of the mind to obtain information directly from the past without the use of ordinary sources such as historical accounts. Retrocognition is the reverse of the more commonly reported precognition, or direct knowledge of future events. Retrocognition is included as a type of EXTRASENSORY PERCEPTION. This phenomenon is rarely reported. Retrocognitive experiences usually take the form of visual and auditory HALLUCINATIONs. For instance, in 1951 two visitors to the vicinity of Dieppe, France, reportedly heard the sounds of the raid on the town by Allied forces nine years earlier. Some reports of retrocognition may actually be instances of CRYPTOMNESIA—a failure to recognize one's own memories as such. Someone who read a lot of books about medieval knights as a child may be gripped by vivid mental images of knights when first visiting a European castle and interpret the experience as a psychic glimpse into the distant past.

For further reading: Inglis (1986).

retrospective hallucination Mistaking the memory of a fantasy for the memory of an actual event. Piaget reported a personal example: As an adult, he could clearly recall an assault and robbery he supposedly witnessed when he was a young child. Later in life, he learned that the event he so vividly remembered had never taken place. As a child, however, he had been informed about the alleged incident and had probably visualized it while being told the story. Subsequently, he remembered his own fantasy, believing it to be an accurate memory.

See also CRYPTOMNESIA; FALSE MEMORY.

rhythmic sensory stimulation When the brain receives rhythmic input through any of the sensory channels, the electrical activity of the cells in the cortex tends to adopt the pattern of the sensory input. This occurrence, called sensory driving, disrupts ordinary brain functioning and is associated with a range of unusual sensations and emotional reactions. Rhythmic sensory stimulation has been deliberately employed in rituals for thousands of years to induce altered states of consciousness. Flashing lights or patterned sounds, such as drumbeats, can trigger the effects. Pulses of electric current to the muscles of the face and eyes, and direct electrical stimulation of the cortex, produce similar experiences.

See also AUDITORY DRIVING; PHOTIC DRIVING.

Further Reading: Ludwig; Neher (1961, 1962).

riddhi Prominent among the ABHIJNAs, or supernormal powers believed in by Buddhists, is the class of bodily transformations known as riddhi. Through the concentrative ability attained through the meditative states called JHANAs, the practitioner is said to acquire the ability to cause changes to the body in accordance with the mind, or to generate a mind-made body. It is likely that this process is related to what modern psychologists would call the deliberate induction of the OUT OF BODY EXPERIENCE.

According to a classic text, the *Visuddhimagga*, the following experiences are associated with the attainment of riddhi: the production of multiple bodies (BILOCATION); passing through walls and even mountains as if they were open spaces; diving in and out of the ground; walking on water; traveling through the sky like a bird while seated cross-legged; rising to touch and sun and moon, and even ascending to the highest heaven. Another abhijna, the Divine Eye, must also be cultivated along with riddhi, so that the space traveler will not bump into invisible objects and beings.

The riddhi experiences are justified in Buddhist literature by stories that describe how the Buddha and other masters used them. For example, in the ancient collection called the *Samyutta Nikaya,* an incident is recorded in which the Buddha wished to cross the Ganges River on a ferry boat. The boatmen requested a fee; the Buddha, owning only a begging bowl and robe, could not pay and was denied boarding. Then, he flew through the air, arriving on the other shore in an instant. The origin of the belief in riddhi is certainly pre-Buddhist. Riddhi is probably related to the magical flights described in the primordial traditions of SHAMANISM.

See also LUNG-GOM.

For further reading: Buddhaghosa.

ritual magic   According to magicians, another world lies beyond the domain of the senses. In this occult dimension, the ordinary boundaries of time and space can be bypassed. Objects that are separated in the everyday world may be linked in the hidden realm; thoughts and fantasies can affect physical things directly; and life forms exist without physical bodies. Magicians are those who manipulate the secret connections and spirit beings, in order to cause changes in the world and themselves. In physics and cooking, one must follow certain patterns of activity to produce a desired result; so also in magic, where the prescribed activities are called rituals.

Ritual magic is found around the world, but the term is ordinarily used to refer to an occult tradition that has existed at the margins of western culture since ancient times. Catholic Christianity has always insisted that the only proper bridge between the visible and spiritual worlds is the church. In the later Middle Ages, however, some clerics developed rituals so they could make direct contact with spirits. These practices

were derived from ancient Jewish magic, remnants of pre-Christian paganism, some Moslem ideas and elements of mainstream Christian rites like the mass and exorcism. The books containing the instructions for conjuring the spirits were called "grimoires." These writings and their authors were roundly condemned by orthodox authorities.

The grimoires often advised lengthy preparations involving fasting and praying. These preliminaries allowed the magician to build a sense of expectation that the ceremony would work. The rituals themselves required meditating upon *sigils*—symbols representing each spirit to be called. The magician also chanted long passages laced with magical words and "names of God," most of which would have made no sense at all to the chanter. Quantities of incense smoke (some of which may have had psychoactive effects) were inhaled; sometimes, animals were sacrificed. All of this would have propelled the magician into an ALTERED STATE OF CONSCIOUSNESS in which mental images would become extraordinarily vivid. The expectancies established prior to the rite could then shape these fantasies into the forms of the spirits.

Detailed descriptions of the appearance of various spirits are given in the grimoires, along with their specialties. Such lists enabled the magician to select the appropriate helper and to visualize them correctly. The *Lemegeton,* for example, depicts the spirit Amon as:

> a strong and powerful marquis, who appears like a wolf with a serpent's head and vomiting a flame. When so ordered, he assumes a human shape, but with the teeth of a dog. He discerns past and future, procures love and reconciles friends and foes.

Successful visualization was taken as a sign that contact had been made with the unseen world. The spirit was then commanded to do the magician's bidding.

Ritual magic survived the fires of the Inquisition and the scorn of modern science. There was a revival of interest in these practices in the 19th century. At this time, some magicians began to interpret the old texts in a psychological light—the spirits could be understood as forces within oneself, as well as independent beings in an occult dimension. Magical rituals were not simply deluded attempts to achieve one's wishes, but techniques of contacting and integrating unconscious aspects of the magician's own being. Ritual magic could be viewed as a path of personal and spiritual growth. (Actually, such an understanding of magic was not new; it had been held by some pagans in ancient times, but was lost with the advent of orthodox Christianity). The great Irish poet and ritual magician W.B. Yeats, among others, held this view.

The practice of ritual magic continues to this day. Techniques of consciousness alteration derived from eastern traditions and SHAMANISM, as well as psychedelic drugs, have entered the tradition. The theory of magic has also kept pace with changes in mainstream thinking. The world of spirits is equated with the "collective unconscious" by many modern magicians. A recent development is "chaos magick," based loosely on mathematical chaos theory.

See also ALCHEMY.

For further reading: Kieckhefer; Seligmann; Waite.

RSPK Acronym for "recurrent spontaneous psychokinesis"; a term used by some psychical researchers to refer to a POLTERGEIST.

ruya'ha Islamic tradition attributes to the prophet Mohammed the following saying: "When we live, we sleep, and when we die, we wake." In other words, in our ordinary waking state of consciousness, we are profoundly unaware of the reality that provides the context of our lives. The Arabic term ruya'ha—literally, "dreams" or "visions"—refers to experiences in which living beings are said to glimpse the world of the normally unseen. Ruya'ha provide inspiration for the Moslem spiritual seeker and also assistance in the form of knowledge.

The Moslem belief in ruya'ha is anchored in the Koran. (This scripture itself resulted from an experience of Mohammed while he was meditating in a cave around 610 A.D. The angel Gabriel appeared to him and began to dictate the text). Prior to the peace treaty between Mohammed's followers and the rulers of Mecca, he dreamed that he would enter the Sacred Mosque at Mecca without encountering resistance. This came to pass. Referring to the incident, the Koran noted that "God has already fulfilled in truth the dream [ar-ru'ya] for His Prophet" (48:27).

Ruya'ha have played an especially important role among the devotees of Sufism, the Islamic methods and doctrines that promote a direct experience of God. Between the world of the senses and the domain of the spirit, according to Sufi thinkers, exists an intermediate realm—the 'alam-i-mithal, dubbed by Corbin the "mundus imaginalis," or imaginal world:

> The mundus imaginalis is a world of autonomous forms and images, forms in suspense, that is, not inherent in a material substratum like the colour black in a black table, but 'in suspense' in the place of their appearance, in the imagination, like an image suspended in a mirror. It is a perfectly real world, preserving all the richness and diversity of the sensible world but in a spiritual state. The existence of this world presupposes that it is possible to leave the sensible state without leaving physical extension . . . Neither the physical senses nor the pure intellect are the organs apprehending this world; it is grasped by 'suprasensible senses,' essentially an imaginative consciousness. . . . It is not fantasy.

A sharp distinction is made between the merely imaginary—daydreams and other mundane mental images—and the imaginal—perceptions of the 'alam-i-mithal. Ruya'ha are synonymous with the latter.

In the Sufi tradition, a guide on the mystical path of return to God is deemed essential. While human teachers are revered, many of the most renowned Sufis have insisted that divine guides, who can be contacted in the imaginal realm, are best. Sufis who are led only by invisible masters are called Uwaysis, after Uways, the first such figure. The most famous Sufi of all, Ibn 'Arabi (1165-1240), was taught throughout his life by an imaginal being named al-Khadir, "The Green One." Khadir has reportedly appeared to many Sufi meditators, before and since.

Some Sufis have developed practices aimed to induce a ruya'ha of a spiritual guide. The following description, by Najmoddin Kobra (d. 1221), suggests, in Zen-like fashion, that the visionary teacher is one's own true nature. It begins by concentrating on the sensations of one's face (quoted by Bakhtiar):

> When the circle of the face has become pure, it gives off light like a spring emptying water, so that the mystic has a feeling of flashing lights irradiating from his face. This flashing appears between the eyes and the eyebrows. It continues until it covers the whole face. When this happens, there appears before you, facing your face, another Face, equally of light. It also radiates light, while behind its transparent veil a sun becomes visible which appears to be animated by oscillation. Actually this Face is your own face, and the sun is the sun of the Spirit who comes and goes in your body. Later, purity submerges all your person, and behold you see before you a person of light from which lights also irradiate. . . . The opening of interior vision, the vision's organ of light, begins with the eyes, continues to the face, followed by the breast, finally by the entire body. It is this person of light before you who is called the suprasensible guide . . .

See also BAQA; FANA.

For further reading: Bakhtiar; Corbin; Glasse; Schimmel.

S

sadhana The central meditation practice of Buddhist Tantra, the sadhana combines a variety of mental skills into a potent induction of transformative experience. Tantric teachers claim that proper performance of the sadhana is the quickest means to attain full ENLIGHTENMENT.

According to tantric theory, every thought, feeling, image and perception already contains the energy of a spiritually awakened mind; also, the human body comprises not only the physical body known to all, but a subtle body which is the body of a buddha. However, few people realize that each person possesses all the ingredients of enlightenment. Rather, people habitually define ourselves as unenlightened beings, very far from the exalted status of BUDDHAHOOD. The methods of sadhana help one to recognize the enlightened features of one's mind and body.

One will be unable to cultivate already enlightened features as long as one clings to the belief that one is far from Buddhahood. In order to detach from the ordinary self concept, tantric meditators practice experiencing themselves as deities. Identifying oneself with a deity is accomplished through visualizing oneself as inhabiting the deity's body and possessing the deity's power, reciting the MANTRA that represents the deity's essence, and imagining the universe as the deity's splendid palace, or MANDALA.

Tantric deities are not to be understood as external to oneself. Rather, they represent aspects of the enlightened mind. The tantric tradition has developed a vast range of deities. Some are peaceful, buddhas seated on lotus flowers; others are raging embodiments of wrath, possessing many heads and dancing upon the corpses of demons in a halo of flames. Often, pairs of deities are visualized as locked in a sexual embrace. This configuration represents the union of wisdom (the direct awareness of EMPTINESS) with compassionate action, the distinctive characteristic of Buddha consciousness. Identification with various deities, assigned by the meditation teacher, stimulates the awakening of the meditator to his or her own enlightened nature.

Sadhana practices are divided into two stages, called the generation stage and the completion stage. In the stage of generation, one vividly imagines oneself to be the deity. The imagination is intensified to the point where, in the stage of completion, one's latent buddhahood emerges—one is actually transformed, body and mind, into the deity. Masters of sadhana emphasize that merely pretending to be the deity is not the correct practice—the meditator must really experience himself or herself as that aspect of enlightened consciousness in order for the desired result to occur. And, of course, identification with a deity is very different from merely believing that one is a great person. A puffed-up self concept leads to selfishness; true awakening to one's enlightened nature produces great compassion and boundless wisdom, say the tantrics. The achievements of sadhana practice are said to be marked by tremendous feelings of bliss.

See also KUNDALINI.

For further reading: Cozort; Hopkins (1984); Yeshe.

sahaj samadhi This state of concentrated attention, or SAMADHI, is viewed as the highest condition of consciousness by meditators of the Vedanta school of Hinduism. *Sahaj* literally means "born together." In Sahaj Samadhi one is aware of two dimensions of existence at the same time: the realm of Absolute Reality, in which there are no distinctions, only Being, Consciousness and Bliss; and the Relative Reality of things, persons and everyday life. Sahaj Samadhi is attained through mastery of a spiritual state called NIRVIKALPA SAMADHI, in which one realizes the nonduality of one's own self and the universal Self.

One who functions in sahaj samadhi is completely free of bondage to fears, desires or habits of any kind. Any state of consciousness can be entered at will. Such a person is said to have attained the ultimate condition of a living being —JIVAN-MUKTI.

The 19th-century Indian mystic Sri Ramakrishna was reputed to dwell in Sahaj Samadhi. His biographer, "M," described his state of awareness:

> he is devoid of ideas of 'I' and 'mine', he looks on the body as a mere shadow, an outer sheath encasing the soul. He does not dwell on the past, takes no thought for the future, and looks with indifference on the present. He surveys everything in the world with an eye of equality; he is no longer touched by the infinite variety of phenomenon [sic]; he no longer reacts to pleasure and pain. He remains unmoved where he—that is to say, his body—is worshipped by the good or tormented by the wicked; for he realizes that it is the one Brahman [Self of the universe] that manifests itself through everything.

See also ENLIGHTENMENT.

For further reading: Feuerstein (1990); Friedrichs; Goleman; M.

St. Anthony, visions of This fourth century Egyptian hermit was one of the first Christian monks. His VISIONs were recorded in a biography written by Bishop Athanasius, who may have edited the material to promote the spread of orthodox Christianity. There is no doubt, however, that Anthony did have many unusual experiences while meditating alone in the desert. His legendary association with disturbing expe-riences caused him to be called upon by Catholics through the centuries who believed they were suffering from demonic assault.

St. Anthony lived from 251 to 356. He was born to a Christian family and his deep piety led him to spend most of his life in solitude, engaging in spiritual purification. In isolated caves and on mountaintops, Anthony was repeatedly tormented by visions of grotesque demons. These creatures tempted him to sin, especially to violate his celibacy. He reported great suffering as he firmly resisted his devilish afflictions.

The story of St. Anthony's visionary temptations and resolve remained popular for many centuries after his death. The belief spread that virtuous Christians were surrounded by demons, who constantly sought their moral downfall. Monks who undertook austere practices often reported visions of these evil spirits and took St. Anthony as their role model.

Among the populace, Anthony became the saint to whom one prayed when suffering from NEUROLOGICAL DISORDERs such as EPILEPSY, attributed to the workings of demons. The saint was so frequently entreatied to cure another mysterious torment, in which large numbers of people would develop intense burning discomfort and sometimes go mad, that it became known as ST. ANTHONY'S FIRE.

For further reading: Schultes and Hofmann; White.

St. Anthony's fire In the Middle Ages, this term was used to refer to the symptoms of ERGOT poisoning, which afflicted many members of the poorer classes. The burning sensations and HALLUCINATIONs caused by the toxin were mistakenly attributed to the attacks of demons or to God's displeasure over sinfulness. St. Anthony, who was famous for his legendary ability to resist demonic assaults, was the object of prayer and pilgrimage by the sufferers of the "Holy Fire." The saint is frequently depicted holding a torch, symbolizing his power over the affliction.

See also ST. ANTHONY, VISIONS OF.

St. Elmo's fire Erasmus was a Catholic bishop, martyred in the fourth century. Very little was recorded concerning his life; so, following his death, legends grew to fill the spaces. One tale had it that St. Erasmus—or St. Elmo, as his name was deformed over time—continued to preach even after being struck by lightning. His immunity to the harmful effects of electricity appealed to seafarers, who were frequently menaced by it. St. Elmo became the patron saint of sailors.

During storms at sea, sailors noticed plumes of light that would appear atop the mast and other projections of the ship. Sometimes the glow would even surround a sailor's head. Although the flames softly crackled and hissed, they did no damage and came to be seen as signs of St. Elmo's protective presence.

St. Elmo's fire has also been observed on land, flickering from church steeples, radio towers and even from fingers held aloft during unsettled weather. Long sparks, taller than a person, have been observed radiating from the tops of sand dunes. During a thunderstorm in France in 1879, an entire forest became a swirling sea of St. Elmo's fire.

The peaks of mountains are favored locations for the appearance of St. Elmo's fire. Dey, a signal officer on Pike's Peak, described an intimate encounter with the friendly glow (quoted by Corliss, 1977):

> In placing my hands over the revolving cups of the anemometer—where the electrical excitement was abundant—not the slightest sensation of heat was discovered, but my hands instantly became aflame. On raising them and spreading my fingers, each of them became tipped with one or more beautiful cones of light, nearly three inches in length. The flames issued from my fingers with a rushing noise . . . The wristband of my woolen shirt, as soon as it became dampened, formed a fiery ring around my arm, while my mustache was lighted up so as to make a veritable lantern of my face.

The spectacle of St. Elmo's fire is produced by the tendency of electrons to become concentrated at pointlike surfaces. If this concentration becomes intense enough—as occurs in an electrically active environment such as a thunderstorm—the electrons will slowly flow from the point into the air, causing the gentle luminosity. Snow storms and sand storms can also create the conditions for the fire to manifest, as the blowing particles trigger electrical discharges from the earth to the air. These surprising effects are probably the basis for some reports of UFO ENCOUNTERs and APPARITIONs.

See also MOUNTAINTOP GLOW.

For further reading: Corliss (1977, 1982); White.

St. John's Dance In 1374, a DANCING MANIA broke out in Germany, Belgium and the Netherlands. Those afflicted were called St. John's Dancers. The association between the dancers and St. John is obscure. Some historians have suggested that the mania may have first appeared during the celebration of the Festival of St. John the Baptist in midsummer, 1374. The summer solstice was a major event in the calendar of pre-Christian Europe; the pagans had marked the festival by wild dancing, and these performances were transferred to the Christianized St. John's celebration. Some of the celebrants of 1374 might have found themselves unable to stop dancing. Other researchers have speculated that the mania was named after St. John because he died following the dance of Salome.

For further reading: Merskey.

St. Vitus' Dance The Rhineland and Belgium was the site of a DANCING MANIA in 1418. The sufferers were taken to chapels of St. Vitus, a third century martyr and patron saint of epileptics, dancers and actors, in hope of a cure, hence the name given to this outbreak. "St. Vitus' Dance" has become a popular term for the NEUROLOGICAL DISORDER more properly called Sydenham's Chorea.

samadhi   This term is a Sanskrit word meaning "stabilization" or "firmness." Samadhi refers to any state of consciousness in which the attention is concentrated on an object. States of concentration are associated with the acquisition of unusual wisdom and powers in spiritual traditions worldwide. Many kinds of samadhi are discussed in the meditation literatures of Buddhism and Hinduism.

In Buddhism, samadhi is one of the three "higher trainings" that lead to ENLIGHTENMENT. Buddhist concentration is a condition of total absorption, in which any sense of distinction between the observer and the object is eliminated. In samadhi, one does not experience oneself meditating on a tree, for instance; there is just the tree. The ability to attain samadhi is required in order to establish the mental condition known as SHAMATHA, or calm abiding. A series of increasingly focussed states of concentration, called JHANAs, are discussed in Buddhist writings. Meditation masters are said to be able to enter NIRVANA directly from the most concentrated state.

Samadhi also plays a vital role in the various schools of Hindu meditation. As long as mental activity is scattered and undisciplined, as in ordinary consciousness, there is little chance to discover the true nature of the self. In samadhi, the mind is quietened, and becomes transparent, like a still pool of water. Then, realities that are normally hidden beneath the turmoil of thoughts, images and emotions can be viewed. Within Hinduism, samadhis are classified into a variety of systems. For instance, the RAJA YOGA school identifies two main types of concentrative state: SAMPRAJNATA SAMADHI, in which mental activity of a highly refined sort continues; and ASAMPRANATA SAMADHI, without mental stirring of any kind. Each type of samadhi is divided into many subclasses. The school called Vedanta, associated with other kinds of yoga practice, offers a similar division of states into SAVIKALPA SAMADHI and NIRVIKALPA SAMADHI.

In both Buddhist and Hindu traditions, the attainment of samadhi is said to give the meditator access to supernormal abilities of various kinds. These powers are called ABHIJNAs or SIDDHIs.

See also BHAVA-PRATYAYA SAMADHI; TANTRA, HINDU.

For further reading: Buddhaghosa; Feuerstein (1989, 1990); Fischer-Schreiber; Friedrichs; Goleman.

samapatti   This term, which means "attainments" in the Sanskrit and Pali languages of India, is a variant term for the states of meditative concentration called JHANAs. Sometimes, samapatti also refers to the condition of absolute stilling of the mind and body, known to Buddhists as NIRODHA.

samprajnata samadhi   In the Hindu meditative system of RAJA YOGA, the practitioner is taught how to concentrate the mind in order to attain states of focussed awareness called SAMADHI. Yoga texts delineate a range of concentrated states, generally divided into two parts. The lower section of this scale of consciousness consists of the *samprajnata samadhis,* "concentrated states with conscious content." In these samadhis, the attention is focused on an object. The object can be coarse (the shapes and colors of a deity's image, for instance), subtle (the inner or psychic features), the functioning of one's sense organs or even the feeling that one exists. The meditator is not aware of himself or herself as separate from the object; rather, the object fills awareness, and the meditator merges with it. The samprajnata samadhis are regarded as the equivalent of the SAVIKALPA SAMADHI of the other major Hindu school, the Vedanta. They are also comparable to the lower JHANAs in the Buddhist mapping of concentrative states.

In the traditions associated with the most important Yoga manual, the *Yoga Sutra,* the ascent up the ladder of samprajnata samadhi commences with the state called *savitarka-*

samapatti, or merging in the presence of thought. Here, attention is focused on the coarse or superficial features of an object. The object's appearance stirs spontaneous thoughts in the mind.

As concentration deepens, the next state—*nirvitarka-samapatti,* or merging without thought—is reached. In this condition, thought processes are no longer aroused by the presence of the object.

Next on the scale of awareness is *savicara-samapatti,* merging in the presence of reflective consciousness. Sharpened concentration allows the meditator to experience inner or psychic features of the object that are invisible to ordinary perception. Thoughts of a deep kind are activated by this experience. The meditator reflects on questions such as "Who am I?" and "What is the world?" with great intensity. As a result, attachment to worldly things is reduced.

In *nirvicara-samapatti,* the practitioner merges with the subtle features of the object without activating reflective thoughts. According to some teachers, this state leads to *nirvicara-vaisharadhya,* or clear awareness without reflective thoughts, the threshold of the higher concentrative states called ASAMPRAJNATA SAMADHIs.

The famous ninth century Yoga text *Tattva-Vaisharadi* by Vacaspati Mishra identifies four kinds of samprajnata samadhi above nirvicara samapatti. Many other authorities on Yoga do not recognize these states. According to Vacaspati, after reflective thinking ceases, the meditator can turn the attention to the activity of the sensory channels. This maneuver produces a temporary experience of bliss; hence the name of this state (*ananda-samapatti,* or merging with bliss). When the bliss subsides, one is merged in *nirananda-samapatti.*

After this attainment, the practitioner can focus on the mere sense that he or she is present, without any other mental content. This state is *asmita-samapatti,* merging with the feeling that "I am." When even this extremely faint object fades from awareness, one is in *nirasmita-samapatti,* the merging beyond anything that corresponds to the conventional experience of the self. Further refinement of concentration enables the meditator to penetrate the realm of asamprajnata samadhi.

See also VIVEKA-KHYATI.

For further reading: Feuerstein (1990); Mishra.

samyama In the meditative tradition of RAJA YOGA, this term refers to three mental skills required for achieving spiritual states. The meditator must be able to fix the attention on an object (*dharana*), maintain this focus (*dhyana*), and calm the mind to the point that awareness is fully absorbed in the object (*samadhi*). If the proper foundation of a pure lifestyle and healthy body has been established, the practice of samyama can lead to KAIVALYA, the supreme state of consciousness. By directing samyama at various objects, one can also acquire the supernormal powers called SIDDHIs, according to the yogis.

Sasquatch The name given by the Coast Salish Natives of British Columbia to a hairy HUMANOID sometimes encountered in the forest. The word has been adopted into mainstream North American usage.

See also CRYPTIC.

satori This term designates an important experience in Zen Buddhism. "Satori" is derived from the Japanese verb "satoru," meaning "to know." Thus, satori is a type of knowledge. However, unlike other forms of knowledge, in the satori experience there is no sense of distinction between the knower and that which is known; it is a nondualistic perception of ultimate reality. Satori does not result from reasoning, because reasoning requires a separation between the thinker and the object of thought. As such, little can be said to describe it. Nonetheless, some of the attempts to convey the satori experience in words are moving. The following example is from Kapleau's collection of satori accounts:

> At midnight I abruptly awakened. At first my mind was foggy, then suddenly that quotation [a saying of a Zen master] flashed into my consciousness: 'I came to realize clearly that Mind is no other than mountains, rivers, and the great wide earth, the sun and the moon and the stars.' And I repeated it. Then all at once I was struck as though by lightning, and the next instant heaven and earth crumbled and disappeared. Instantaneously, like surging waves, a tremendous delight welled up in me, a veritable hurricane of delight, as I laughed loudly and wildly: 'Ha, ha, ha, ha, ha, ha! There's no reasoning here, no reasoning at all! Ha, ha, ha!' The empty sky split in two, then opened its enormous mouth and began to laugh uproariously: 'Ha, ha, ha!'

In traditional Mahayana Buddhist terms, satori is the direct cognition of EMPTINESS by the exercise of PRAJNA. The occurrence of satori marks the ENLIGHTENMENT of the meditator.

See also KENSHO.

For further reading: Kapleau.

savicara-samapatti "Merging in the presence of reflective thought," a meditative state discussed in the RAJA YOGA literature. It is considered a type of SAMPRAJNATA SAMADHI.

savikalpa samadhi In the Hindu psychology of Vedanta, savikalpa samadhi is a MYSTICAL EXPERIENCE in which the meditator encounters the presence of God, who is the self of the universe, as well as his or her own true self. This variety of SAMADHI, or state of concentrated attention, is called "with (*sa*) concepts (*vikalpa*)," because the mystic is able to think during the experience. The thoughts that arise in this state are much clearer and more profound than those of ordinary consciousness. Savikalpa samadhi is viewed as a lower form of spiritual experience, because the meditator still perceives

himself or herself as distinct from God. This sense of distinction is eliminated in the higher state known as NIRVIKALPA SAMADHI.

savitarka-samapatti "Merging in the presence of thought," a state of concentration according to the RAJA YOGA school of Hindu meditation. It is classified as a type of SAMPRAJNATA SAMADHI.

Scheerer's phenomenon A type of ENTOPTIC PHENOMENON, or sensation arising from the structure of the visual system. In order to reach the light-sensitive receptor cells at the back of the retina, light must first pass through several intervening layers of retinal cells. These cells are nourished by a network of capillary blood vessels. When the light entering the eye is bright and steady, it is sometimes possible to see streaking points of light and shimmering webs in the field of vision, caused by the blood flow in front of the receptors. Alternately straining and relaxing the facial muscles can cause the specks of light to accelerate and slow. Scheerer's phenomenon can also be enhanced by circulation disturbances within the eye. Individuals unfamiliar with the biological origin of the light sensations have tended to regard them as perceptions of spiritual phenomena. Zusne and Jones suggested that the psychic "vitality globules" reported by the theosophical writers Besant and Leadbeater were actually intraocular blood cells. Neher (1990) observed a clairvoyant group which believed that the flecks of light they saw were psychically magnified air molecules.

See also FLOATERS; PHOSPHENES.

For further reading: Asaad; Neher (1990); Zusne and Jones.

schizophrenia Schizophrenia is the most common of the conditions known as psychoses—psychological disorders that feature a loss of contact with what most people regard as real. It afflicts about one person in a hundred. "Schizophrenia" is derived from Greek, and literally means "split mind." Unfortunately, this terminology has led many people to confuse schizophrenia with a different ailment, MULTIPLE PERSONALITY DISORDER or "split personality." The two disorders are unrelated; multiple personality disorder is not even classed as a psychosis.

The "splitting" in schizophrenia is not merely of the personality, but can involve a disintegration of the whole range of mental functions. The ability to think in a coherent manner may be lost, to be replaced by a barely meaningful flow of ideas; or, the false beliefs called DELUSIONs can come to dominate thought. MAGICAL THINKING is often displayed by schizophrenics. Contact with the external world can be disrupted in a variety of ways: the slightest sensation may become amplified, overwhelming the sufferer with a barrage of impressions; the world may appear to be an unreal or dreamlike place (DEREALIZATION); trivial events may become intensely meaningful (IDEAS OF REFERENCE), and relevant events become devoid of significance; the sensory fields may be invaded by HALLUCINATIONs, especially of the auditory variety. Emotional responses often become flattened or inappropriate. Many schizophrenics are also tormented by BODY IMAGE DISTORTIONs and feelings of DEPERSONALIZATION. Their behavior can become bizarre and unpredictable.

The onset of these dramatic symptoms is usually preceded by a period of gradual deterioration in social functioning. Relatives, friends or colleagues may notice that the individual has become more withdrawn, or sometimes speaks or acts in uncharacteristic, puzzling ways; or, the first signs of onset may only be noticed in retrospect, after it has become obvious that something is seriously amiss. The acute phase of the disorder can last from one week to years, during which the more extreme departures from consensus reality occur. In western cultures most schizophrenics are hospitalized for this period. Drug therapy and counseling are the most common treatments for schizophrenia today; elec-

troconvulsive therapy ("shock treatment") and brain surgery were common practices earlier in the century, but are rarely used to treat schizophrenia now.

Many schizophrenics manage a partial recovery. A full return to the level of functioning prior to the onset of the disorder is uncommon. Often, medications are recommended even after the acute phase has passed, in order to reduce the chances of a relapse.

The causes of schizophrenia remain a mystery. In the past it has often been suggested that schizophrenics are driven into psychosis by disturbed family relationships; in particular, domineering mothers (so-called "schizophrenogenic mothers") were blamed. Research has so far failed to support these views. More recently, many researchers have suggested that schizophrenia is a brain disease with a genetic component. A number of studies have found evidence for brain abnormalities in some schizophrenia sufferers, but proof of a biological cause for the disorder is still lacking. Today, the diagnosis of schizophrenia is still based on the strange behaviors of its victims, not on family patterns or biological tests.

There are many myths concerning schizophrenia and unusual experiences. Writers have often asserted that the shamans of traditional societies are schizophrenics, because they engage in magical thinking and have experiences that do not fit with the reality beliefs of the modern world. Noll (1983) and others have shown that this equation of shamans and schizophrenics is incorrect. Unlike schizophrenics, shamans control their experiences and generally use them for the benefit of their communities.

Another prevalent falsehood is that unusual experiences of any kind, and particularly HALLUCINATIONS, are probably signs of the onset of schizophrenia. While it is true that schizophrenia can produce every imaginable kind of unusual experience, it is also true that people with no psychological disorders can occasionally experience almost anything as well, including hallucinations. As a result of this misunderstanding, many people rarely discuss their unusual experiences with others for fear of being labeled crazy. The high incidence of many odd experiences among the normal population, revealed in anonymous surveys, is thus unknown by most of the people who have them.

For further reading: American Psychiatric Association; George and Neufeld; Noll (1983, 1992a).

scientism The belief that the methods of scientific research are capable of solving every problem and answering every question about the world. Adherents of scientism generally fail to acknowledge that every world view, including that of modern science, is based on unprovable assumptions; none of the conclusions of science can be regarded with certainty as being forever beyond revision. Philosophical questions involving meaning and value also cannot be addressed by empirical science; as it is often said, science can help us understand *how* something happens but not *why*. People with scientistic biases reject the possibility that some aspects of unusual experiences may never be explainable in scientific terms. Scientism is sometimes confused with SKEPTICISM.

See also ZETETICISM.

sensation seeking This personality trait has been found to correlate with a tendency to hold anomalous beliefs and have unusual experiences. Sensation seekers are easily bored by routine. They are drawn to novel, thrilling and adventurous activities, are more likely to take psychoactive drugs, tend to have more sex partners and often score higher than average on tests of creativity. Psychologists measure sensation seeking using questionnaires.

Zuckerman, who created the most widely used measure of sensation seeking, observed that:

the sensation seeker is attracted to ideas that go beyond the bounds of current scientific verification. It is more exciting to believe in the existence of mysterious forces than to accept the more parsimonious limitations of present-day knowledge.

Research has confirmed that sensation seeking is positively associated with global tendencies to believe in paranormal concepts, as well as with specific beliefs in ESP and spirits. Sensation seekers also report more unusual experiences on surveys than less adventurous types. The anomalous beliefs held by many sensation seekers may cause them to interpret more experiences as anomalous, or perhaps their pursuit of thrills puts them more often in situations (such as seances or haunted houses) where unusual experiences are more likely to occur.

See also Appendix.

For further reading: Kumar, Pekala and Cummings; Zuckerman.

sensory deprivation Decreasing sensory stimulation is a widely used method of inducing an ALTERED STATE OF CONSCIOUSNESS. The waking mind is ordinarily bombarded by sensations that demand attention, drowning out the subtler images and thoughts originating from within. When the "noise" of the outer world is turned down, the "signals" from the inner domains are more easily detected. In conditions of sensory reduction, BODY IMAGE DISTORTIONs, vivid, dreamlike imagery, ENTOPTIC PHENOMENA, enhanced suggestibility and HALLUCINATIONs often occur.

Sensory deprivation has traditionally been used to access the spirit world. Some shamans wore hoods, stared into fires or reclined in lightless tents, and drowned out extraneous noises by loud drumming. Native North Americans engaged in VISION QUESTs would isolate themselves in remote, featureless settings, far from the sights and sounds of daily life, and stare into the sky. Buddhist meditators in Tibet used to have themselves walled up in caves, leaving open only a small, S-shaped tunnel through which food could be passed.

In ancient Greece, individuals who wished to conjure APPARITIONS of the dead would enter a torch-lit underground chamber called a "psychomanteum." There they would contemplate a reflective surface such as a crystal, polished metal object or bowl of liquid. Recently Moody has resurrected this procedure. The modern psychomanteum is a dimly-illuminated, windowless room hung with black velvet curtains. The seer sits in an easy chair and gazes into a large angled mirror on the wall for about 45 minutes. In Moody's initial study, 55% of those who entered the psychomanteum reported visionary experiences of departed loved ones. Everyone who had such an experience reported it to be positive. The possible usefulness of the psychomanteum technique in bereavement counseling is being explored.

Since the mid-1950s, scientists have studied the effects of sensory deprivation. John Lilly and his colleagues made extensive use of the "sensory isolation tank," a kind of enclosed bathtub containing salt water, within which the participant floated. A less elaborate way to reduce sensations is the "ganzfeld" (German for "complete field") procedure, developed by Witkin and Lewis. In this method the participant rests in a reclining chair or on a mat. Headphones play white noise, a monotonous hissing sound, and halved ping-pong balls are placed over the eyes, so that only diffuse, unstructured light can reach them. After a short period, the mind adapts to the unvarying sensory input and the participant is no longer aware of it.

Using the isolation tank or the ganzfeld procedure, researchers have asked participants to describe their experiences during or after the sensory deprivation session. Most people find sessions of up to 45 minutes pleasant and relaxing. Psychologists (Best and Suedfeld; Cooper) have found that short sensory deprivation sessions can help smokers and alcoholics reduce their addictive behaviors.

Parapsychologists have examined whether the ganzfeld procedure increases scoring on ESP tests. Dozens of such studies have reported positive results, and many parapsychologists rank the ganzfeld research among the strongest evidence for the existence of ESP. Skeptics have criticized this line of research for possible errors in analyzing the data and flaws in the design of the studies.

See also RHYTHMIC SENSORY STIMULATION.

For further reading: Best and Suedfeld; Cooper; Honorton; Hyman (1985); Hyman and Honorton; Lilly; Moody (1992); Witkin and Lewis.

shamanism *Shaman* is a word in the Tungus language of Siberia. It means "one who is excited, moved, raised." Among the Tungus are spiritual specialists who enter a TRANCE state characterized by dancing and shaking. This practice is part of a worldwide tradition of harnessing altered states for the benefit of the community, which anthropologists have named shamanism.

Shamans are found in hunter-gatherer and simple agricultural societies in Asia, Europe, the Americas and Australia. It is likely that shamanism is the world's oldest spiritual tradition. According to Noll, "the shaman's goal is enhanced mental imagery." Shamans enter into unusual conditions of consciousness in which the vividness of images is increased. These images are understood to be the world of spirits. Shamans, unlike ordinary dreamers or the mentally disturbed, are not at the mercy of this imaginal world; rather, they have trained to acquire mastery over the spirits and can commute between the spirit realm and that of ordinary perception at will. As the spirits are held to have special knowledge and abilities, shamans' spirit mastery gives them great power.

Not everyone can be a shaman. The potential for shamanism is usually first seen at the onset of puberty. Shamanically gifted people often experience mysterious symptoms at this time—

bodily pains, HALLUCINATIONs and disturbances of thought and emotion. These phenomena are believed to be the call of the spirits to the shamanic vocation. If the chosen people do not learn how to control the experiences through shamanic training, they may sicken and die. In many cultures acquiring the proper relationship with a spirit may require a VISION QUEST.

Initiation into shamanism involves learning the lore of the spirit world and using this knowledge to pattern the trance experiences. Most shamanic societies have a similar view of the otherworld. There are three domains: a subterranean realm; the world of normal human experience; and a sky realm. The domains are connected by a central axis, often viewed as a tree. Shamans learn to journey between the worlds by visualizing the tree and traveling along it. This practice, known as "soul flight," may in some cases be an OUT OF BODY EXPERIENCE. However, in a typical out of body journey, the physical body is still; whereas many shamans enact the soul flight by dancing or climbing onto the roof of their hut and may report the otherworldly experiences as they are occurring.

While the soul flight is the most typical shamanic behavior, other types of relation with the spirits are frequent. Some shamans engage in MEDIUMSHIP, in which a spirit is allowed to animate their body and speak with their vocal apparatus. Zoanthropy, or embodying animal spirits, is very common. The female shamans of the Asian Tadjik peoples are said to maintain ongoing sexual relationships with spirits.

Over the millennia, shamans discovered a great array of methods for inducing their visionary states. The use of drumming is widespread in shamanic cultures. Siberian shamans consider the drum to be a horse that carries them into the spirit lands. The drum's rhythmic stimulation induces AUDITORY DRIVING, a disruption of the brain's ordinary activity patterns, allowing extraordinary patterns to be imposed. Dancing around a flickering fire can cause PHOTIC DRIVING, to similar effect. Shamans may have been the first to use psychedelic drugs for spiritual purposes. Some practitioners wear blindfolds or lie in a darkened tent; the resulting SENSORY DEPRIVATION is conducive to unusual experiences.

The master of spirits fulfills many important functions in his or her society. Shamanic cultures believe that many illnesses are caused by a person's soul becoming lost or captured in the spirit world, or by a malign spirit inhabiting the body. Shamans can retrieve lost souls from the otherworld and can persuade invading entities to leave the bodies of the sick. They can also consult the spirits regarding future events, the location of game or the identity of a criminal. Noll observed that shamans, with their highly developed mental imagery skills, functioned as the "memory" of the community. Shamanic cultures are mostly nonliterate, so the shamans are responsible for preserving and transmitting the myths that organize their understanding of the world.

Shamanism has tended to disappear in more complex societies. The diverse roles of the shaman become divided among specialists—priests, exorcists, psychics, counselors, physicians, scholars. In progress-oriented western culture, the shaman became the symbol of backwardness and superstition—in parts of Europe it has been a criminal offense to own a shaman's drum until quite recently. Currently, there is a minor revival of serious interest in shamanism. Some urban Westerners have been attracted by the shaman's intimacy with nature and respect for the power of the imaginal. Traditional shamanic societies are striving to retain their lore in the face of modernism. Ironically, some cultures are turning to western anthropologists to help them recreate their own lost shamanic traditions. For instance, the Lapps of northwestern Europe have requested American anthropologist Michael Harner to give them workshops on shamanism.

For further reading: Eliade (1964); Harner (1980); Heinze; Noll (1985); Ripinsky-Naxon; Schmidt.

shamatha This Sanskrit word, meaning "calm abiding," refers to one of the mental abilities necessary for the attainment of ENLIGHTENMENT in Buddhism. A brief period of self observation reveals that one's ordinary state of consciousness is rarely calm; rather, each person is subjected to a continuous storm of uncontrolled thoughts, images and emotional reactions. Such turbulence makes a poor foundation on which to base a disciplined search for reality, which is the task of Buddhism. Therefore, many types of Buddhist meditation promote the development of calm abiding.

The attainment of shamatha requires sharply focused concentration, or SAMADHI. Calm abiding is more than mere concentration, however. A concentrated mind can be rigidly fixed on its object; the mind in shamatha, although it rests steadily on its object, displays a great dexterity—it can shift effortlessly in any way the meditator directs. The condition of shamatha is therefore an ideal condition for the investigation of the nature of experience. In Buddhism, shamatha is used in accompaniment with a kind of analytic probing called VIPASSANA, or insight. Together, shamatha and vipassana nurture the wisdom that leads to accurate comprehension of reality.

Shamatha is sometimes compared to a lamp emitting a steady light; vipassana is the use of this stable illumination to explore the contents of a dark room. Or, shamatha is a perfectly calm lake, in which the fish of vipassana swims as it studies the formations on the lake bottom.

Buddhist teachers say that the discoveries made through vipassana (the nonexistence of the self, the absence of any permanent things and the unsatisfactoriness of all phenomena) would profoundly upset the mind if it was not anchored in shamatha. When one has mastered vipassana, however, these insights are deeply understood and actually help to induce calm abiding.

Calm abiding is initially cultivated by meditations in which practitioners hold their attention on specific objects, such as the process of breathing, a statue of a Buddha or an internal image.

The attention must be disciplined, but not strained. Shamatha is a condition of balance between two extremes—an overly excited mind (symbolized by a restless monkey) and a state of sluggish fixation (represented by a sleepy elephant). Abiding continuously between the monkey-mind and the elephant-mind is difficult. The perfect attainment of shamatha takes a great deal of practice for most people. Increasing proficiency in concentration can take the meditator into the altered states of consciousness called the JHANAS. Practice in the jhanas can improve mental dexterity, but is not in itself a goal of Buddhism.

For further reading: Hopkins (1984); Sopa.

shikan-taza A Japanese phrase meaning "just sitting," shikan-taza is an important meditation practice in Zen Buddhism, especially in the Soto school. In this practice, the meditator does not direct the mind to any particular object; rather, he or she merely attends to whatever perceptions or sensations occur. Zen master Hui Hai advised: "When things happen, make no response. Keep your minds from dwelling on anything whatsoever." The state of mind cultivated in shikan-taza has been compared to that of someone during a duel of swordsmanship: extraneous thoughts are dispelled, and attention is absorbed fully in the details of the present moment. Eventually, such practice is said to uproot all obstacles to ENLIGHTENMENT, as these obstacles thrive on concerns about the past and future.

For further reading: Kapleau.

siddhi This Sanskrit term, meaning "perfect abilities," is used in Indian traditions to refer to supernormal powers acquired through the practice of meditation. These abilities are said to be associated with unusual states of concentrated attention called SAMADHIs or JHANAS.

Meditation manuals frequently display ambivalence concerning the value of the siddhis. On the one hand, their attainment signifies that the meditator has made substantial progress in gaining mastery over the meditative states; the powers can also be used to help others. However, the quest for unusual abilities can lead the meditator astray. The goal of most spiritual teachings is not the acquisition of worldly powers, but the attainment of an exalted consciousness—variously called self-realization, liberation, ENLIGHTENMENT, etc. Chasing after special powers can distract the meditator from the single-minded pursuit of the highest aim. Thus, most texts warn the student against becoming attached to the siddhis, and many even encourage meditators to avoid them.

In Hinduism the two schools most commonly mentioned in connection with the siddhis are RAJA YOGA and TANTRA. The Raja yogis cultivate a type of concentration called SAMYAMA. They claim that unusual effects can be obtained by directing their attention at various objects while practicing samyama. For example, focusing on the throat removes sensations of hunger and thirst; contemplating the features of someone's body can reveal that person's mental condition; samyama directed at memories produces past life memories; attending to the relationship between one's own body and the surrounding space can lead to LEVITATION. It is even claimed that a meditation master, via samyama focused on a student, can enter the student's body in order to destroy some of the obstacles to improved meditation practice.

Hindu tantra purports to access the siddhis through meditation on special locations within the body known as CHAKRAS. When the three highest chakras, at the throat, forehead and crown, are activated, the entire range of psychic abilities are said to be awakened.

In Buddhism, the jhana states are associated with the special abilities called ABHIJNAs. As in Hinduism, Buddhist tantra is closely linked with the siddhis. The most commonly mentioned powers in this tantric tradition include: production of an invincible sword; the ability to see deities; the power to run extremely quickly; invisibility; eternal youth; magical flight; the ability to project healing energies into pills; and control over spirits. Each of these powers may be understood not only literally, but as metaphors for types of spiritual achievement.

The crowning attainment of Buddhism—enlightenment—is sometimes called the "supreme siddhi." The biographies of the 84 *mahasiddhas,* individuals who became enlightened, preserve many entertaining tales about the use of siddhis. The mahasiddhas reportedly could even cause rivers to flow backward and stop the sun's movement in the sky. These masters were said to use their astonishing powers to deflate the pretensions of others, and to dispel spiritual ignorance. For example, the mahasiddha Saraha's biography describes an episode in which Saraha converted a king and his courtiers to Buddhism by immersing himself in boiling oil and drinking molten copper without harm.

For further reading: Eliade (1969); Feuerstein (1990); Fischer-Schreiber; Friedrichs.

skepticism   The Skeptics were a school of philosophers in ancient Greece. Human perception and thought are so error prone, they argued, that nothing can be known for certain. Since that time, the skeptical position has meant an absence of belief, coupled with a willingness to question all assertions of truth or certainty. Throughout history, skeptics have raised doubts concerning explanations for unusual experiences, especially if these explanations involved paranormal beliefs.

The Hindu and Buddhist traditions are rife with claims of extraordinary abilities—the ABHIJNAs, SIDDHIs and others. In ancient India, the philosophical school called Mimamsa questioned the possibility of obtaining knowledge without the use of the senses; another group, the Carvakas, rejected the siddhis as delusional.

The famous Roman author and orator Cicero wrote a skeptical treatise on PRECOGNITION. Although belief in the possibility of foretelling the future was held by almost everyone of his time, Cicero noted that gullibility is also a widespread trait. Many who consulted specialists in divination, such as the Delphic Oracle, were impressed by the diviners' accuracy. Cicero observed that the prophecies were usually so vague that they could mean anything, and that people read their own expectations into these utterances. In response to tales of auguries (a type of divination) that gave clear and accurate information about the future, Cicero rejected them on the grounds that precognition violates the beliefs about the world held by intellectuals: "In trying to prove the truth of the auguries, you are overturning the whole system of physics."

With the triumph of Catholic Christianity over paganism, the paranormal beliefs of the pagans had to be dealt with. Some of these were absorbed into the Christian world view (many locations sacred to the old gods became church sites); others were changed in value (the deities of the pagan pantheons were labeled demons). Skepticism regarding certain pagan paranormal beliefs was also promoted. Early medieval churchman Regino of Prum insisted on the falsity of a common belief (quoted by Flint):

> Wicked women . . . seduced by the phantasm and illusions of demons believe and declare that they can ride with Diana the pagan goddess and a huge throng of women on chosen beasts in the hours of night.

Anyone holding this belief was encouraged to be more skeptical by a prescription of 40 days of penance on bread and water during Lent, for seven consecutive years.

During the later Middle Ages and Renaissance, official skepticism regarding a host of pagan-tainted supernatural events was reversed. Inquisitors' needs to foster support for their witch hunting activities prompted them to spread fear about the supposed malign powers of the witches. Disbelief in these powers removed the justification for the hunt; so by 1486 when the major instruction manual on the witch persecutions, *Malleus Maleficarum,* was pub-

lished, skepticism about the paranormal abilities of witches and demons was viewed as heresy.

Nevertheless, some brave individuals continued to voice doubts about the idea of an evil supernatural conspiracy. The best known skeptic of this period was Reginald Scot. His 1584 book, *The Discoverie of Witchcraft,* was described by historian Henry Lea as having "the honor of being the first of the controversial works which resolutely denied the reality of witchcraft and the power of the devil." King James I of England ordered all copies of Scot's work to be destroyed.

Another notable skeptic of the "Burning Times" was the 17th century German priest Friedrich von Spee. He served as confessor to individuals charged with witchcraft and became convinced of the baselessness of the accusations. Von Spee wrote and argued against the validity of confessions extracted by torture, which were the heart of the inquisitorial proceedings. When asked why his hair had greyed prematurely, he replied: "Grief has turned my hair white—grief on account of the witches whom I have accompanied to the stake."

With the advent of the modern, scientifically rooted world view, the skepticism of brave souls like Scot and Von Spee concerning the witch hunt became general. As the political power of the church gradually weakened, individuals who claimed to possess paranormal abilities, such as psychics, were able to promote themselves openly. Some conjurors and clairvoyants attracted loyal (and lucrative) support from aristocratic circles; their activities were met by skeptical publications. From 1784, Henri Decremps issued a series of books revealing the methods of fraudulent occultists.

The Scottish philosopher David Hume published his essay, "Of Miracles," in 1825. This work inaugurates the modern era of skepticism and is still quoted regularly by skeptics today. In it, Hume tried to prove the impossibility of paranormal events, which he called "miracles." A report of a miracle, by definition, flies in the face of all ordinary experience; if chairs levitated in everyday life, no one would consider levitation to be miraculous. "A miracle is a violation of the laws of nature; and as a firm and unalterable experience has established these laws, the proof against a miracle, from the very nature of the fact is as entire as any argument from experience can possibly be imagined." Hume asserted that any evidence for a paranormal occurrence should be rejected, unless the falsity of the evidence would be more miraculous than the reported paranormal event itself.

Hume's view, taken to an extreme, could prevent a person from considering possibilities that do not fit snugly into preconceived notions. This dogmatic mentality has been expressed by some skeptics. Donald Hebb, after considering the ESP research conducted by J.B. Rhine, stated: "Personally, I do not accept ESP for a moment, because it does not make sense. . . . Rhine may still turn out to be right, improbable as I think that is, and my own rejection of his views is—in a literal sense—prejudice." The danger that Hume's approach can merely reinforce biases provoked Rao to attack "Hume's fallacy" on logical grounds: "[Hume's] argument that there could be no proof of a miracle because by definition miracles do not exist is patently circular. He assumes what he attempts to prove."

A more reasonable implication that many have drawn from Hume is summarized in the popular skeptical slogan "Extraordinary claims require extraordinary evidence." The further removed from established views and experience is a claim, the stronger the evidence must be before the claim is accepted. And the onus of proof is on the claimant. Thus, the reported discovery of a new species of warbler in a remote forest is more readily acceptable than an account of a UFO abduction, because the existence of the new warbler would be less disruptive to accepted beliefs. As personal biases can strongly influence one's ability to evaluate evidence, the slogan should be accompanied by a corollary: Extraordinary claims require extraordinary self-vigi-lance on the part of investigators. The weirder the claim, the more likely that one's own prejudices—pro or con—will affect judgment about it.

The mid-19th century saw the rise of Spiritualism. The astonishing reports emanating from seance rooms and meeting halls where touring mediums performed attracted skeptical comments and investigations. In 1874, Marvin recommended that mediums should be hospitalized and given purges to cure them of "mediomania." The Society for Psychical Research was founded in 1880 in order to apply scientific methods of investigation to Spiritualist claims, among other phenomena.

The vast amount of mediumistic deception uncovered by investigators fueled the skeptical attitude toward the paranormal in the first part of this century. Hansen (1992a) noted that the modern skeptical scene is dominated by three groups: stage magicians, psychologists and "rationalists/atheists." Performing magicians are well-versed in the methods of trickery and have often exposed frauds. (It is noteworthy, however, that surveys indicate that belief in the paranormal is much more common among magicians—82% in one American poll—than the general population.) Psychologists are well aware of the fallible nature of perception, which inclines them away from accepting paranormal accounts at face value. Also, many psychologists are philosophically committed to a materialistic world view that seems to preclude such phenomena as ESP. The rationalist camp includes some promoters of "secular humanism" who are hostile toward any unsubstantiated paranormal claims, including those of religion.

The most prominent skeptical body in the West today is CSICOP—the Committee for the Scientific Investigation of Claims of the Paranormal. This group was founded in 1976 and publishes the widely circulated journal *Skeptical Inquirer*. A number of prominent scientists, magicians and atheists are members or supporters of CSICOP.

Strictly speaking, skepticism entails neither *belief* nor *disbelief* in the possibility of a phenomenon, but an *absence* of belief without proof. In fact, many people who call themselves skeptics are passionate disbelievers in the paranormal. Intellectual commitment to a world view is a matter of belief, regardless of whether that world view is conventional or supernatural. When disbelief occurs as a belief system, the skeptic is subject to the same psychological forces that are associated with any other belief. Truzzi regards "disbelieving skepticism" a contradiction in terms, and labels those who hold this position "pseudo-skeptics."

Belief systems guide perception so that experience tends to confirm the beliefs. Skeptics have noted that believers in the paranormal are more likely to have apparently paranormal experiences. By the same token, paranormal disbelievers are unlikely to have such experiences, reinforcing their view that all reports of paranormal occurrences must be based on fraud or error.

Belief systems tend to serve the needs of the believers. Commentators have speculated that paranormal disbelief can sometimes be a strategy of managing fear. Irwin found that skepticism toward parapsychological research was associated with a fearful attitude toward the paranormal.

People who are emotionally invested in their beliefs tend to feel threatened by disagreement. Believers often act to defend their certainties and may attack those who view things differently. Some skeptics have behaved in this fashion. Nisbet (quoted in Wade), an executive director of CSICOP, proclaimed that paranormal belief is "a very dangerous phenomenon, dangerous to science, dangerous to the basic fabric of our society" and advocated the aggressive promotion of disbelief. CSICOP members have attempted to pressure colleges and universities to ban sympathetic discussions of paranormal concepts. The editorial policy of *Skeptical Inquirer* allows the use of ridicule, sarcasm and other offensive devices in its articles; Lasagna compared the attitude expressed in one article he reviewed with that of the Spanish Inquisition. It has even been alleged that the CSICOP leadership attempted to suppress the results of a study on astrology when it became apparent that the findings suggested an astrological influence of Mars on sports ability; this incident caused several CSICOP members to resign in protest.

At its best, skepticism is an attitude of considering all evidence, and raising every question. Skeptics should be skeptical of their own ability to remain neutral, and should be continuously vigilant regarding the subtle power of their own biases. At its worst, skepticism can solidify into a rigid "disbelief," founded on assumptions that are defended with religious fervor. In this case, questioning becomes constricted to suit one's own agenda. A danger sign of the lapse from true skepticism into dogmatism is an inability to respect those who disagree.

See also ANOMALY; SCIENTISM; ZETETICISM.

For further reading: Flint; Hansen (1992a, 1992b); Hebb; Hume; Irwin (1989a); Lasagna; Lea; Rao; Robbins; Truzzi; Wade.

sleek Astronomers and other watchers of the night sky have periodically noted the unusual streaks of light known as sleeks. They resemble the trails of METEORs, but move extremely rapidly, and have the disturbing quality of seeming to be very close to the observer. Sleeks also do not display heads, trains or other features that careful observers familiar with meteors frequently note.

Some researchers have suggested that sleeks are caused by some sort of electrical discharge in the atmosphere. There is evidence, however, that in at least some instances, sleeks are actually ENTOPTIC PHENOMENA—sensations caused by activity within the nervous system that falsely appear to represent external objects. In the following case, cited by Corliss, an astronomer observed a sleek in his bedroom:

I was lying in bed, in a darkened room, when I saw a bright streak of light to my extreme right. Had I seen this streak in the sky, I would undoubtedly have called it a meteor . . . However, it started from just below the ceiling and disappeared before it reached the floor. It did not move with my eye, but carried on falling as I looked up at it. I have seen minor bright spots and flashes before and have always regarded them as mere optical defects, but this streak was very real and in fact its appearance startled me.

Corliss noted that astronauts often report seeing streaks of light while in space, even with their eyes closed; the usual explanation for this effect is that cosmic rays passing through the astronauts' heads are somehow triggering neural activity in their visual systems. He suggested that terrestrial sleeks also might be "visible cosmic rays."

For further reading: Corliss (1982).

sleep drunkenness Although a period of grogginess upon waking from sleep is normal, some people are prone to becoming trapped between the two states. Unable either to return to unconsciousness or to become fully aroused, they are disoriented and behave in an uninhibited manner. Occasionally, sufferers of sleep drunkenness have committed acts of aggression, including murder. When they manage to awaken completely, they have little or no memory of the episode. Monitoring the electrical activity of the "sleep drunk" brain has confirmed that the condition combines waking neural processes and those of deep sleep.

See also HYPNOPOMPIC STATE.

For further reading: Coleman; Dement.

sleepwalking Most people assume that mental activity is virtually absent during deep sleep because they remember nothing when awakened from this state. The performance of complex, goal-directed behaviors while deeply asleep dramatically challenges this belief. The behavior of many sleepwalkers is clearly motivated. Chil-

dren who crawl into bed with their parents while asleep, for example, appear to be responding to an infantile desire. And consider the case of an Ontario man with a history of sleep disorder, who drove one night to his in-laws' house and killed them; he was acquitted of murder on the grounds that he was asleep during the commission of the crime. (Aggressive acts by sleepwalkers are extremely rare.)

Sleepwalking and other sleep activities occur during the nondreaming stages of sleep; sleepwalkers are not "acting out" their dreams. Episodes of sleep behaviors generally last for up to a half hour. First, the sleeper performs meaningless, repetitive acts, such as picking at the pillow or bedsheets. This phase is followed by more mobile activities, such as walking, dressing and eating. They may wander about with a blank, staring face. Sleeptalking sometimes occurs, but it is usually slurred or garbled. It is a myth that sleepwalkers cannot hurt themselves; they can stumble or amble into dangerous places, such as rooftops or fire escapes.

The sleepwalking episode can end in a variety of ways. The sleepwalker may simply stroll back into bed and wake the next morning with no knowledge that the previous night's adventures took place. Wandering sleepers sometimes curl up and continue their rest far from where they fell asleep; they will awaken without knowing how they got there. Contrary to popular belief, it is not hazardous to awaken a sleepwalker deliberately; it may be difficult, however, as the person is in a deep stage of slumber.

Sleepwalking usually begins between the ages of 6 and 12 and is uncommon after the teenage years. If an adult without a childhood history of sleepwalking begins this behavior, it will likely become chronic. Individuals who are fatigued or under stress are more likely to sleepwalk. There is some evidence for a genetic component; certainly, sleepwalking tends to run in families. Dement described a patient with recurrent sleepwalking; one night during a Christmas family reunion, he found himself in his grandfather' dining room, surrounded by all his relatives—fast asleep.

See also AUTOMATISM.

For further reading: Coleman; Dement.

social interest Some people are highly motivated to seek out and respond to the needs and wishes of those around them. Others are more inclined to dismiss their social environment, preferring to focus on their own needs. The trait of social interest has been found to correlate with the level of belief in paranormal phenomena. Individuals who have low social interest are more likely to hold general paranormal beliefs, as well as specific beliefs in ESP, spirits and cryptic creatures. Low social interest is also associated with problems in PSYCHOLOGICAL ADJUSTMENT.

See also Appendix; CONTROL NEEDS; NARCISSISM.

somatoform disorder This class of mental illness features a disturbed relationship between body and self in the absence of any diagnosed physical ailments. The somatoform disorders comprise a major drain on the health care system, as its sufferers generally seek inappropriate medical treatment, rather than the psychiatric or psychological help they need. It is important to note that those afflicted with these disorders are sincere in their complaints; the psychological sources of their experiences are unconscious. Thus, victims of somatoform disorders must be distinguished from malingerers or "con artists," who deliberately pretend to be ill for their own purposes.

Mental health professionals recognize several different types of somatoform disorder. In *body dysmorphic disorder,* the victim becomes obsessed with an imagined physical imperfection; or, if a small departure from bodily perfection is present (as it always is), the victim's concern about it is grossly exaggerated. An example would be someone with a nose of normal proportions who frets constantly that the nose is hideously large. A person with *hypochondriasis* spends a great deal of time in physicians' offices, complaining about physical sensations that most people would ignore or dismiss. To the hypochondriac, a momentary tingling, muscle spasm or gaseous pressure surely indicates the presence of a life-threatening illness, and negative medical findings provide no comfort. *Pain disorder* involves the persistent reporting of bodily discomforts in the absence of an identified cause. This class of somatoform disorder is controversial, as many health care workers believe that modern procedures may not be capable of detecting all organic sources of pain.

In some kinds of somatoform disorder, there are dramatic alterations in bodily sensations or functions. *Somatization disorder* is a long-standing pattern of various unpleasant sensations that have no detectable medical basis. A sufferer of this mental illness may complain of persistent vomiting, aches, shortness of breath, dizziness, double vision, urinary difficulties, loss of voice and other problems. Sufferers of *conversion disorder* experience a psychologically caused loss or change of function of a body part. An arm can become numb or rigid, the legs can refuse to walk, blindness or deafness can occur. These symptoms often happen after a traumatic episode. Conversion symptoms often fulfill a purpose for the victim on an unconscious level—the rigidity of the arm, for instance, may prevent the person from lashing out in fury at a loved one who has caused disappointment.

See also BODY IMAGE DISTORTION.

For further reading: American Psychiatric Association; Shorter.

somnambulism This is a traditional term for HYPNOSIS; some old sources refer to hypnotized individuals as "somnambules." In current usage, somnambulism is a variant term for SLEEPWALKING and related complex behaviors performed by sleepers.

spontaneous human combustion Stories of people being incinerated by flames from within date back over 200 years. Folkloric beliefs of this sort are undoubtedly much older. One of the earliest cases on record occurred in Rheims, France in 1725. The charred remains of a woman were found on her kitchen floor. Her husband was initially charged with murder, but the courts concluded that she had been a victim of spontaneous combustion.

Several other accounts of spontaneous human burning can be found in the legal and medical literature of the 18th and 19th centuries. In the mid 1800s, the debate concerning the reality of the phenomenon was fanned by the publication of Charles Dickens' novel *Bleak House,* in which a character, Mr. Krook, meets his death by spontaneous fire. Scientists of the day criticized Dickens for fostering superstition.

Despite orthodox skepticism, reports of "human fireballs" have continued throughout the present century. In some poorly documented accounts, bystanders were said to have witnessed the beginning of the immolation; but, in the best known instances, the victims were alone when they were set ablaze, and their remains were discovered sometime later.

In a substantial number of cases, the victims were known to be heavy drinkers; the elderly also appeared to be at special risk for the fiery fate. It was frequently reported that the bodies of victims had obviously been subjected to very high temperatures, while nearby objects showed little or no heat damage.

A variety of theories have been advanced to explain the mysterious burning deaths. Some have suggested that the key to the puzzle was the high alcohol levels in the bodies of many victims—perhaps they had become so perfused with the flammable liquid that the friction of ordinary movements set them alight. But no one could drink enough alcohol to alter the combustion properties of human tissue.

More esoteric writers such as Harrison have wondered if the flames are produced by some sort of PSYCHOKINESIS. Noting that some POLTERGEIST occurrences involve mysterious outbreaks of fire, and that often an emotionally disturbed or frustrated individual is at the hub of poltergeist events, Harrison concluded that sometimes strong emotions can psychically manifest as fire. In the case of spontaneous human combustion, the common causal emotions seem to be loneliness, despair and suicidal urges. It is noteworthy that one of the Six Yogas of NAROPA, a classic Tibetan meditation practice, is the generation of Dumo or "inner fire"; students are warned that improper technique can lead to spontaneous combustion.

Nickell and Fischer surveyed 30 reports of spontaneous human combustion. They found that the amount of bodily destruction correlated positively with the amount of available fuel sources, such as wooden flooring and chair stuffing. Furthermore, they noted that, in most cases, a source of ignition, like an open hearth or candle, had been near the body. Nickell and Fisher found no evidence for unknown processes in human combustion cases. Typically, they reported, the victim had probably handled fire carelessly (often because they were inebriated), and had set themselves alight; because they were alone, no one could come to their aid. As the body usually lay undiscovered for several hours, there was ample time for a small fire gradually to consume the remains, fueled by adjacent materials and by the victim's own body fat.

These investigators examined in detail the best-documented case of spontaneous combustion, that of the "cinder woman" Mary Reeser, who died in Florida in 1951. The remains of this 67-year-old widow had been found almost completely turned to ashes, except for a lump of bone thought to be her skull and one slippered foot. Nickell and Fischer discovered that Reeser had last been seen sitting in her overstuffed chair, wearing a flammable night dress, smoking a cigarette. She was known to be a heavy consumer of sleeping pills. The most probable explanation for her death was that she had passed out and ignited her gown with the cigarette. The researchers noted that most of the popular journalistic accounts of the "cinder woman" case contained inaccuracies that served to mystify what, apparently, was a simple tragedy caused by careless smoking.

For further reading: Gaddis; Harrison; Nickell and Fischer.

Springheel Jack   During 1837 and 1838, many residents of London reported encounters with a mysterious humanoid. These meetings often occurred in alleyways or on doorsteps, and always at night. The being was seen to leap clear across streets in a single bound, and hence was dubbed "Springheel Jack." Descriptions of Jack were mostly consistent; the following, from Vallee, is typical:

> The intruder was tall, thin and powerful. He had a prominent nose, and bony fingers of immense power which resembled claws. He was incredibly agile. He wore a long, flowing cloak, of the sort affected by opera-goers, soldiers and strolling actors. On his head was a tall, metallic-seeming helmet. Beneath the cloak were close-fitting garments of some glittering material like oilskin or metal mesh. There was a lamp strapped to his chest. Oddest of all, the creature's ears were cropped or pointed like those of an animal.

Contact with Springheel Jack was usually brief. He would loom suddenly from the shadows, or present himself when someone answered a ringing doorbell. Then, he would try to scratch the witness' face with his claws, as his chest lamp flashed rapidly. He would then spring back into the night, sometimes after spraying the witness with an anesthetic gas.

The authorities ignored the odd reports at first. As public unrest grew, nocturnal horse patrols were mounted and a reward was posted for information leading to the apprehension of Springheel Jack. No evidence turned up.

Jack turned up again in Aldershot, England, in 1877. He was spotted flying overhead by two sentries. They opened fire, with no effect. They reported that Jack paralyzed them with gas, and escaped.

Many sightings of Springheel Jack were noted in Liverpool in 1904, as he leaped from rooftop to rooftop. A figure fitting Jack's description was reported in Mattoon, Illinois in 1944. He was seen peering into windows at night. Investigators have recorded appearances of Jack as recently as 1975, when a witness in London's East End observed a man jump from pavement to pavement across a street. Sightings of quasi-human forms behaving in absurd ways occur in waves from time to time. The extent of Springheel Jack's appearances, in time and space, is remarkable. The reward for information about Jack has not yet been claimed.

See also HUMANOIDS, ANOMALOUS; MOTHMAN.

For further reading: Vallee.

stigmata   The phenomenon of the stigmata provides a dramatic demonstration of the intimate relationship between the mind and the body. Stigmata are eruptions on the skin that symbolize a belief held by the stigmatic. During the past eight centuries, over 300 cases have been reported. In most accounts, stigmatics have been devout Roman Catholics, and the marks have represented the wounds received by Christ—whip marks on the back from the flogging, nail wounds on the hands and feet, pricks on the head from the crown of thorns and the spear wound in the side. Occasional reports have been made of Moslems displaying stigmata symbolizing the battle wounds of Mohammed. The marks can take a variety of forms: a reddening of the skin; the appearance of blisters or welts; and the oozing of blood or clear serum from apparently unbroken skin.

In the New Testament letter to the Galatians (6:17), Paul wrote: "From henceforth let no man trouble me; for I bear in my body the marks [in the original Greek, *stigmata*] of the Lord Jesus." Believers in the divine origin of stigmata point to this passage as Biblical justification for their faith. It is unlikely that Paul actually had stigmata in the modern sense of the term; he may have been referring to injuries received as a result of persecution. The only other hint of possible stigmatic phenomena prior to the 1200s is found in the Book of Kells, a ninth century Irish illuminated manuscript in which St. Matthew is depicted with red marks like nail wounds on his feet.

A broadly accepted tradition holds that the first stigmatic was St. Francis of Assisi. Two years before his death in 1226, Francis undertook a spiritual retreat in a hut on Monte La Verna. His practices involved fasting to the point of starvation, and other acts of self-mortification. One morning, he was meditating on the experience of Christ on the cross. Then, according to the *Fioretti* (a near-contemporary biographical source, translated by Sherley-Price):

> While he was thus inflamed by this contemplation, he saw a seraph [angel] with six shining, fiery wings descend from heaven. This seraph drew near to St. Francis in swift flight, so that he could see him clearly and recognize that he had the form of a man crucified. . . . As St. Francis gazed on him he was filled with great fear, and at the same time with great joy, sorrow and wonder. . . . Then after a long period of secret converse this marvellous vision faded, leaving . . . in his body a wonderful image and imprint of the Passion of Christ. For in the hands and feet of St. Francis forthwith began to appear the marks of the nails in the same manner as he had seen them in the body of Jesus crucified.

The marks were said to stain Francis' clothing with blood and to prevent him from walking. They remained visible on his corpse.

By the end of the 13th century, at least 31 other cases of stigmata were recorded. Six of these occurred in a single convent in Freiburg, Germany. Without a doubt, a desire to emulate the beloved saint was responsible for this upsurge. Over the ensuing centuries, reports of the

phenomenon have continued. The Catholic church includes stigmata in their list of CHARISMs, or experiences that may be associated with holiness. In themselves, however, stigmata are not viewed as foolproof signs of sanctity—saints may have stigmata, but not all stigmatics are saints.

Since the 19th century, scholars have attempted to organize and analyze the accounts of stigmata. The first comprehensive study was undertaken by Imbert-Goubayre. He published his findings in a two-volume work, *La stigmatisation,* in 1894. Another important early researcher was Thurston, whose papers were published posthumously in 1950 as *The Physical Phenomena of Mysticism.* Reviews of the literature on stigmata have shown that the case of St. Francis possesses many features which recur in more recent instances. Non-Catholic examples of stigmatics are very uncommon; and, Catholic or not, almost all stigmatics display an extraordinarily intense religious devotion. Imbert-Goubayre's survey of 321 cases found that almost two-thirds of the stigmatics in his sample belonged to religious orders.

A previous history of traumatic experience, either accidental or self-inflicted, is characteristic of stigmatics since St. Francis' time. One was gored by a bull; another fell into a sawpit; another had a premature baby who strangled on the umbilical cord while she gave birth to him on a toilet. Many stigmatics were fond of torturing themselves as acts of spiritual devotion. Typical was the 19th century stigmatic Teresa Higginson, who slept on an old sack studded with knitting needles and sharpened sticks, and who rubbed hot coals on her breasts.

St. Francis was also typical in that the onset of his stigmata was preceded by deep meditation on the events of the crucifixion. Many of the more recent stigmatics have seemed almost obsessed with the cross, decorating their dwellings with many crucifixes.

Another common feature found in the Franciscan model is the occurrence of a vision associated with the commencement of the stigmata. In an account from 20th century Canada, a young woman was asked to mind an absent relative's house for a night. She became very nervous, fearing intruders, and was unable to sleep. She reported that a vision of Christ appeared to her, after which she felt reassured and fell asleep. Upon awakening the next morning, she found she had developed stigmata on her hands. These marks persisted for one year, vanishing on the anniversary of their appearance.

Although the prototypical stigmatic saint was a man, there have been about seven female stigmatics for every male. The precise location of the marks have varied greatly, seemingly in line with the specific beliefs of the individual stigmatics. In the case of Anne Emmerich, a Y-shaped cross appeared on her breast which resembled the cross she had contemplated as a child; and "lash marks" on the shoulders of St. Gemma Galgani corresponded to those on a favorite crucifix.

How are the mysterious markings formed? In some cases, the explanation appears to be mundane: self-mutilation. For instance, the 14th century stigmatic Lukardis of Oberweimar "would strike violently the place of the wounds in each palm; delivering another fierce blow in the same spot, the tip of her finger seeming somehow to be pointed like a nail." In order to attract the adoration of believers, some individuals are capable of wounding themselves. Such behavior need not be conscious fraud—sufferers of DISSOCIATIVE DISORDERs have frequently been observed to mutilate themselves and later deny any knowledge of the cause of their injuries, with apparent sincerity. A skin disorder called dermographia, most often found among dissociative sufferers and persons who have undergone extreme stress, renders the skin so sensitive that a mere gentle touch can cause discoloration or even welts.

In many instances, however, some other mechanism seems to be responsible for the occurrence of stigmata. Cases in which blood has emerged through intact skin are reasonably well-documented, and the issuance of blood from a stigmatic limb while encased in a plaster cast has also been reported. The possibility that a psychological process could *directly* cause physiological changes producing stigmata is not implausible. Even under normal circumstances, mental states can influence the distribution of blood in the body: embarrassment causes flushing of the skin; sexual excitement shifts blood to the genitals. Dermatology journals have recorded a phenomenon known as psychogenic purpura, in which skin inflammation and the hemorrhage of blood from capillaries occurs in response to stress.

The most dramatic evidence that stigmata can occur without external injury to the skin was reported by Lechler in 1933. He produced and photographed the swelling of blood from the feet, hands, forehead and eyelids of a hypnotic subject who was under continuous observation. No self-mutilatory behavior was detected. Although further confirmations of this bizarre phenomenon would be desirable, our current knowledge suggests the likelihood that strongly held beliefs can drastically affect the flesh.

For further reading: Barber; Murphy; Nickell; Owen (1970); Ratnoff; Sherley-Price; Wilson.

subsun   From a plane or elevated land, an observer can sometimes look down at the upper surface of clouds. If the clouds contain sufficient amounts of ice crystals they can become reflective, mirroring images of light sources above them. The most prominent luminous source is, of course, the sun. Subsuns, as reflections of the sun from clouds are called, can mimic the circular shape of the solar disc or be distorted into ellipses. Sightings of subsuns are thought to account for some UFO ENCOUNTERs. Occasional cases in which pilots have chased elusive glowing discs might have involved subsuns.

See also COUNTERSUN.

supernatural   The supernatural is a realm beyond nature as it is ordinarily understood. Unusual experiences of many kinds have traditionally been explained as the actions of beings from this realm. These entities are commonly called gods, spirits or demons. Contemporary science rejects supernatural explanations, preferring to seek answers in terms of physical, psychological and social forces.

See also ANOMALY; PARANORMAL; PRETERNATURAL; RITUAL MAGIC; SUPERNORMAL.

supernormal   Literally, "above or beyond" the normal. This term is sometimes used in relation to performances that are beyond the normal range of human abilities, such as an amazingly high jump or fast run. It is also used as a synonym for PARANORMAL or SUPERNATURAL.

swamp gas   The combustion of gases from decaying matter is thought by many researchers to explain sightings of luminous phenomena in marshy terrain, including UFO ENCOUNTERs and WILL-O'-THE-WISPs.

synesthesia   Experiencing one sensory modality in terms of another—visualizing a pastoral scene in response to peaceful music or appreciating the harmony of a painting—is not uncommon. Synesthesia occurs when such "cross-talk" between the senses is so vivid that stimulating one sense triggers actual perceptual experiences in the other. Auditory-visual synesthesia is most often reported—one's visual field may be invaded by sparks of light in response to a sudden noise, for example. Qualities of the stimulus detected by one sense may be represented in the other—harsh, grating sounds can appear as jagged streaks, and smooth sounds as gently curling spirals.

Synesthesia is sometimes induced by taking psychedelic drugs. The synesthetic effects can add to the transformative impact of drug use during religious rituals. Andritzky described his experiences after ingesting YAJE, or ayahuasca, a hallucinogenic vine employed for visionary purposes by many South American cultures:

> During the ayahuasca intoxication all of nature seems converted into an anthropomorphic drama, and the myths sung by the shaman are experienced multisensorially as absolute reality. The hallucinogenic vitalization and the synesthetic perception of the mythological events by various sensory systems immensely strengthen the power of symbols to reorganize the personality . . . the legends are not only heard, but seen in their full vitality and experienced with their emotional impact!

RHYTHMIC SENSORY STIMULATION, another method commonly used among traditional societies to disrupt ordinary states of consciousness, also frequently causes synesthesia.

Individuals suffering from the onset of SCHIZOPHRENIA, and those with certain types of brain tumors, have also reported this sensory leakage. Union of the senses can also be part of the MYSTICAL EXPERIENCE—a great number of famous mystics, including St. John of the Cross, St. Catherine of Siena and St. Teresa of Avila, described their sublime states in synesthetic terms. Some normally functioning people report that synesthesia is their usual way of experiencing things.

This phenomenon may have a neurological origin. Cells in the brain stem, called bimodal neurons, transmit signals from receptors in the eyes and the ears to higher brain centers. Changes in brain chemistry, or pressure from tumors, could irritate these neurons, causing them to activate both sensory channels when receiving messages in either modality.

See also ENTOPTIC PHENOMENON; HALLUCINATION; TINNITUS.

For further reading: Andritzky; Asaad; Cytowic.

tactile hallucination Also called haptic hallucination, it is a sensation of touch in the absence of any stimulus. The tactile hallucination of insects crawling over one's skin, known as formication, is common in states of withdrawal from addictive drugs. Among the mentally disturbed, false feelings of touch are most prevalent among sufferers of SOMATOFORM DISORDERs and SCHIZOPHRENIA.

Tantra, Buddhist *Tantra* is a Sanskrit word meaning "weaving" or "continuum." The tantric tradition represents the final great innovation in the psychology and spiritual practice of India. It affected both Buddhism and Hinduism, weaving together orthodox beliefs with perspectives and techniques that had survived outside the mainstream for thousands of years. These elements, which date back to the period before the emergence of either religion, provided meditators with powerful methods for the induction of unusual experiences. Influences from neighboring Afghan and Persian cultures can also be detected in the tantric synthesis.

The first tantric texts were composed by Buddhists. They appeared around the fourth century A.D. Hindus soon developed Hindu tantric practices, and over the following centuries, the two streams continued to borrow from each other. Buddhist Tantra became the dominant tradition in Tibet and it also had strong schools in China, Japan and Java.

The aim of Buddhist Tantra is the same as that of all the schools of Mahayana Buddhism—that is, the drastically altered state of awareness called BUDDHAHOOD. The other Mahayana schools hold that the achievement of this lofty goal requires meditative training extending over

three aeons, and almost countless reincarnations. Tantra claims that its methods are much more powerful, capable of establishing the full ENLIGHTENMENT of a buddha within a single lifetime. The force of tantric methods renders them very dangerous, however. Incorrect practice is said to produce effects ranging from uncontrollable arrogance and insanity to literal self-destruction in the form of SPONTANEOUS HUMAN COMBUSTION. For this reason, the tantric tradition emphasizes the importance of practicing the techniques under the close supervision of a qualified master.

The basic idea on which tantric methods are based is that the world of ordinary awareness and the world of enlightenment are not different locations; rather, they are the same world, but experienced in different ways. Normal awareness is controlled by our ignorance of the fact that people are already Buddhas; they habitually think of themselves as impure, limited beings, far from the exalted condition of enlightenment. This narrow self-concept blocks their perception of the divine nature of themselves and others. Even states of greed, hatred and delusion, seemingly so far from the wisdom and peace of Buddhahood, actually contain the potential of enlightenment. (The ordinary mind is *continuous* with the awakened mind, not radically separated from it—this is the meaning of tantra as continuum). Therefore, rather than trying to *destroy* the emotional turbulence and confusion which block our spiritual awakening, tantra attempts to *transform* these phenomena directly into Buddhahood.

In order to explode the normal self-concept which denies that one is a Buddha, the tantric adept employs a great range of techniques. The sound meditations known as MANTRAs are often used, to cultivate the experience that all sounds are divine; visualization of oneself and others as deities, and of the universe as a magnificent jeweled palace (MANDALA), is also a common practice. These approaches are combined in the central tantric meditation practice, the SADHANA.

If the techniques are used skillfully, tantrics claim, one can eventually transcend the feeling that one is merely imitating a Buddha, and one then realizes that one *is* a Buddha. The five "poisons," or emotional patterns tainted by the narrow self-concept, are transformed into the five kinds of Buddha-wisdom: anger becomes the Mirror-like Wisdom; pride is transmuted into the Wisdom of Equanimity; lust changes into Discriminating Awareness; jealousy is purified into the All-Accomplishing Wisdom; and mental dullness is sharpened into the Wisdom of All- Encompassing Space.

There are four main levels of practice in Buddhist Tantra. The levels are based on the spiritual maturity of the practitioner—in particular, on one's capacity for using pleasurable experiences to propel oneself toward enlightenment, rather than falling into the self-centered habits usually evoked by such experiences. The lowest tantra, Action Tantra, requires the ability to work with pleasure as intense as that which arises from looking into the eyes of a lover. In the next level, Performance Tantra, emotional energies as powerful as those experienced when laughing together with a lover are involved. The third level, Yoga Tantra, entails the mastery of feelings such as those stirred by holding a lover's hand or body. Energies as strong as those connected to sexual intercourse with a lover are harnessed in the most refined level of practice, Highest Yoga Tantra. These examples of arousal are simply benchmarks of intensity; they are not literally part of the spiritual exercises in most cases.

Much misunderstanding has occurred because the tantric tradition expresses certain of its teachings in the language and imagery of sex. In addition to the classification of tantric exercises in terms of arousal intensity, the union of wisdom and compassion which characterizes the enlightened state is frequently symbolized in tantric art by the sexual embrace of male and female deities. Christian missionaries who first encountered tantra in the 18th century spread the false view that this tradition is mainly concerned with orgies and sophisticated sexual techniques. In fact, practices involving actual sexual contact are quite rare in Buddhist Tantra. However, the bliss of sex (like all other kinds of experience) is thought to be, in reality, a manifestation of enlightenment. Therefore it is not condemned as sinful. Sex is accepted as a potential vehicle of Buddhahood, although it is considered a very difficult experience to use properly.

Buddhist Tantra's acceptance of pleasurable experiences as valid means of spiritual development, and the encouragement to view oneself as a deity, could very easily lead to grandiose selfishness rather than Buddhahood. In order to counter this possibility, practitioners are instructed to keep in mind the pure motivation of true tantric practice: to attain the wisdom and power of an enlightened being in order to help others become free of suffering. Although the experiences of tantric attainment are said to be supremely blissful, the goal of tantra is vast generosity, not self indulgence.

See also BARDO; CHAKRAS; NAROPA, SIX YOGAS OF; TERMA.

For further reading: Cozort; Govinda (1969); Guenther; Yeshe.

Tantra, Hindu The word "tantra" has many connotations, including "loom," "weaving" and "continuum." The traditions known as tantra weave together elements from a wide range of ancient Indian religious practices, forging powerful techniques for the alteration of consciousness. Although the methods of tantra probably existed outside the mainstream of Hindu and Buddhist spirituality for many centuries, perhaps deriving ultimately from shamanic roots, the first tantric writings appeared among the Buddhists in the fourth century. Buddhist Tantra stimulated some Hindus to adapt the tantric approach to their own goals.

Hindu tantric schools have in common an emphasis on the creative power of the universe, which they personify as a female divinity, Shakti. The source of all life and movement, tantrics believe that the mighty energy of Shakti can be utilized to reach the spiritual aim shared by other Hindus: the sublime condition of self-realization, variously known as MUKTI, MOKSHA, SAHAJ SAMADHI, etc.

In the symbolism of Hindu Tantra, everything arises from the union of the life force with pure consciousness. This merging of power and awareness is represented by the sexual intercourse of Shakti with the god Shiva. In each person's life, there is consciousness and energy. If these two factors can be brought together within oneself, one can achieve the profoundly energized meditative state, or samadhi, that leads to self-realization. The classic Hindu text, the *Kulacudamani Tantra*, advises, "United with the Shakti, be full of power."

Unlike many other religious traditions, tantrics hold that the body is not merely an obstacle to spiritual progress, but the very vessel within which it takes place. Pleasurable sensations are not rejected, but harnessed in the cause of uniting Shakti and Shiva within oneself. Tantra has become notorious in the West for its inclusion of sex as a meditation method. While many schools of Tantra do not engage in literal intercourse with a partner, some do. The aim is not ordinary pleasure; indeed, orgasm is often avoided entirely. Rather, the male identifies himself with Shiva, and the female with Shakti, in an attempt to merge these potentials inside themselves. Kissing is not part of the performance. During the phases of the act, the tantric chants various phrases to reinforce the sense of uniting the deities. The delightful feelings of sex are considered a diluted form of the great bliss that accompanies self-realization.

Among tantrics (of the so-called "left-hand path") that practice the sexual rites, identification with the deities is aided by the deliberate violation of certain of the social restrictions of Hindu society. A deity, after all, is not expected to follow the norms of conventional culture. The violations are not undertaken impulsively, but form part of a formal ritual. These are usually summarized as the five "M"s: consumption of the taboo foods *matsya* (fish), *mamsa* (meat) and *mada* (wine); taking *mudras,* or supposed aphrodisiacs such as parched kidney beans; and the meditative sex act (*maithuna*) with an illegal partner. Again, the aim of these practices is not mere indulgence, but the liberation of consciousness.

A central feature of Hindu tantric theory is the idea that the physical body people perceive is only the heaviest, crudest aspect of the human form. There are many subtler structures and currents of activity which interpenetrate and interact with the coarse body. The main interfaces between the coarse and subtle physiologies are called CHAKRAS. The main chakras are arranged along a central channel, paralleling the spinal cord. At the base of this channel is the personal embodiment of the Shakti; at the top of one's head is the location of the Shiva. An important branch of tantra called KUNDALINI yoga aims to merge the two, thus producing samadhi, by causing the Shakti to rise through the central channel to the Shiva's domain. Meditations on the chakras and the kundalini process utilizing visualization, MANTRA recitation, and special manipulations of the posture and breathing, are said to produce a range of unusual experiences. The skillful pracitioner of tantra knows how to employ these occurrences in the service of spiritual development.

For further reading: Avalon; Bharati (1975); Tucci.

tarantism In the 14th and 15th centuries, the Apulian region of Italy was visited by a unique form of DANCING MANIA. The strange behaviors of those afflicted were blamed on the bite of the tarantula spider. Individuals who believed that they had been bitten displayed dramatic alterations in movement. At times they would sink into a depressed state, during which they might become mute and insensitive to the external world. At other times they would be gripped by a compulsion to leap about violently, sometimes hurting themselves or others. They also developed strong sensitivities to colors. Most commonly, the Tarantist was abnormally attracted to red objects; many carried red pieces of cloth, which would fascinate them.

The Tarantists were powerfully affected by music. When they heard the sound of a fife, clarinet or Turkish drum, they would perform an energetic dance. It was believed that the dances would distribute the spider's poison throughout the body, so that it could be excreted through the pores. The modern dance form called the "tarantella" arose from the performances of the Tarantists.

As no one could be sure that they *hadn't* been bitten by a tarantula while asleep, no one was safe from the spell of Tarantism. In areas gripped with excitement about the dancers, any unusual physical sensation was liable to be interpreted as signaling the onset of the disorder. Groups of Tarantists began to appear in public, accompanied by musicians. By the 16th century, the phenomenon had spread beyond Apulia to other parts of Italy and continued to break out periodically into the 18th century.

See also: GROUP DYNAMICS OF UNUSUAL EXPERIENCES.

For further reading: Cavendish; Gloyne; Merskey.

te lapa Polynesians traveling by boat between the dispersed islands in the south Pacific Ocean scrutinized the marine environment for navigational cues. They called one of their strangest discoveries *te lapa*—"underwater lightning." Traditional seafarers occasionally saw flashes, streaks and other luminous forms emanating from beneath the ocean's surface. They believed that the te lapa always pointed in the direction of distant islands. This phenomenon is likely related to other types of OCEAN LIGHTs occasionally reported by sailors around the world, although only the Polynesians have used such displays for navigation.

For further reading: Corliss (1977).

telekinesis Variant term for PSYCHOKINESIS, the direct influence of the mind on objects or events, or "mind over matter."

telepathy Often called "mind reading," telepathy is the alleged ability to obtain information directly from the mind of another person. We are constantly inferring the contents of others' minds on the basis of sensory cues like posture, behavior, and utterances. In contrast to such indirect access, telepathy is said to involve the transfer of another's thoughts or feelings directly into one's own mind. Telepathy is commonly subsumed under the heading of EXTRASENSORY PERCEPTION. A Gallup poll of adult Americans, conducted in 1990, found that 36% of the respondents said they believed in telepathy.

See also GESP.

For further reading: Gallup and Newport.

teleportation The movement of an object or body between locations without traversing the intervening space. Physicists have discovered that subatomic particles can behave in this fashion. There have been many reports of teleported objects connected with POLTERGEIST outbreaks and the seances of MEDIUMs, but nothing of the sort has ever been demonstrated in scientifically adequate circumstances. Saints and meditation masters have often been said to possess the power of teleporting themselves to distant sites.

See also BILOCATION; CHARISM; LEVITATION; SIDDHI.

telepsychosis Variant term for TELEPATHY: obtaining information directly from another's mind, or "mind reading."

temperature inversion Under ordinary conditions, the air cools with increasing height. When cool air is found beneath a layer of warmer air, it is called a temperature inversion. An inversion can be produced by local geography; cooler air can be trapped in depressions ringed by hills or mountains, as happens frequently in Vancouver, Los Angeles and Mexico City. A rapid drop in ground temperature can cool the surface air quickly, leaving warmer air above it. Alternating layers of warm and cool air sometimes form. The boundaries between air masses distort light, sound and radar waves passing through them. Light from the sun, moon and planets can be deformed into unrecognizable displays, giving rise to reports of UFO ENCOUNTERs. Sounds from distant sources can bounce off these layers, causing AIRQUAKEs. Temperature inversions wreak havoc on radar by bending signals earthward, creating airborne radar images of earthbound objects.

 For further reading: Menzel and Boyd; Sachs.

temporal lobe abnormality The outer layer of the brain consists of a wrinkled sheet of nerve cells called the cortex. Processes within the cortex are closely linked with perception and thought. The cortex is divided into a pair of symmetrical structures, the left and right hemispheres. Each hemisphere is composed of smaller structures known as lobes. The temporal lobes, found on the sides of the brain, comprise about 40% of the cortical surface. Malfunctions in the temporal lobes have long been suspected of being a cause of UNUSUAL EXPERIENCES and ANOMALOUS BELIEFS.

 Damage to the temporal lobes can certainly produce drastic alterations in thought and perception. These changes are demonstrated before and during seizures by sufferers of epilepsy,

many of whom have injuries to the temporal regions. Researchers have suggested that the malfunctioning cortex of epileptics may render them susceptible to unusual experiences *between* seizures; however, surveys by Mungas and by Sensky and his colleagues found that the frequency of reported non-seizure anomalous experiences among epileptics was about the same as that for the general population.

 Several studies of non-epileptics have provided evidence for a link between unusual experiences and the temporal lobe. Nelson (1970) examined the electrical activity patterns (EEG) in the brains of 12 mediums; he reported abnormalities in the temporal lobes of 10, far above the population average. Neppe, using a questionnaire that inquired about symptoms that are often associated with temporal lobe malfunctions, found that individuals with possible temporal lobe symptoms were more likely to report anomalous experiences.

 Persinger and his colleagues also found evidence for a link between indications of temporal lobe disturbances and likelihood of reporting unusual experiences. Persinger suggested that a number of otherwise normal people have temporal lobes that are vulnerable to disturbance by environmental forces, such as electromagnetic fields; they may be prone to "microseizures" which can cause all manner of unusual experiences, from MYSTICAL EXPERIENCEs to UFO abductions.

 Fenwick and his associates compared individuals who believed they were psychic "sensitives" with alleged "nonsensitives," using a battery of tests that clinicians employ to determine the site of damage in head injury cases. Fenwick found that subjects who said they had experienced ESP or spirits were more likely to show signs of damage to the right temporal lobe than those who denied such experiences.

 See also Appendix; GEOPHYSICAL INFLUENCES; INVISIBLE PRESENCES; MIGRAINE; TOURETTE'S SYNDROME.

For further reading: Fenwick et. al.; Mungas; G. Nelson; Neppe (1983a,b, 1990); Persinger (1984); Roberts; Sensky; Skirda and Persinger.

teonanacatl   In the Nahuatl language spoken by the Aztecs, this term means "flesh of the gods." The word was used to refer to several types of psychedelic mushroom that have featured prominently in the induction of altered states among Mexican and Central American peoples. Fungi of several genera have been called teonanacatl, including *Psilocybe, Conocybe, Panaeolus* and *Stropharia*. While some authorities assert that the use of *Stropharia* mushrooms predates the arrival of Europeans in the New World, others have suggested that *Stropharia* was introduced to the Americas from the Phillipines by the Spaniards; it was subsequently incorporated into the mushroom practices of the native Mexicans, they believe.

Descriptions of the effects of eating the "divine flesh" suggest a common sequence of experiences: the onset of intoxication is marked by relaxation and withdrawal; the visual geometrics called FORM CONSTANTs then appear; these images gradually give way to full HALLUCINATIONS, the details of which are determined by the cultural expectations of the participant.

Munn describes the experiences of a Mexican shaman:

> One who eats the mushroom sinks into somnolence during the transition from one modality of consciousness to another, into a deep absorption, a reverie. Gradually colors begin to well up behind closed eyes. Consciousness becomes consciousness of irradiations and effulgences, of a flux of light patterns forming and unforming . . . At this initial moment of awakening, experiencing the dawn of light in the midst of the night, the shaman evokes the illumination of the constellations at the genesis of the world. Mythopoetical descriptions of the creation of the world are constant themes of these creative experiences.

Here, the shaman suggests to himself or herself contents of the visions derived from native mythology. In contrast, Schultes and Hofmann quoted a person with a Christian cultural background who found that his teonanacatl experience evolved according to a different theme, commencing with:

> geometric patterns, angular, in richest colors, which grew into architectural structures, the stonework in brilliant colors, gold and onyx and ebony, extending beyond the reach of sight, in vistas measureless to man. The architectural visions seemed to be oriented, seemed to belong to the . . . architecture described by the visionaries of the Bible.

Archaeological evidence suggests a widespread reverence for mushrooms in what is now southern Mexico, Guatemala and El Salvador during ancient times. Hundreds of mushroom forms made of stone and pottery have been found in these regions, some of which date back earlier than 1000 B.C. While many scholars suspect that the Maya, in particular, utilized mushrooms as sacred hallucinogens, no depictions of actual mushroom ingestion have yet been found. However, some of the artifacts clearly suggest that the consciousness-altering properties of the fungus were known to these ancient artists. The stems of the stone mushrooms are often in the form of seated humans, apparently in meditative or ecstatic states. A ceramic piece from Mexico shows four people joyfully dancing around a gigantic mushroom.

Mushroom shapes in gold were crafted in ancient Colombia, but whether they point toward mushroom eating practices is far from certain.

There is no doubt that teonanacatl played a central role in Aztec society. A stone sculpture of the Aztec plant god, Xochipilli, depicts him seated on a pedestal, singing in ecstasy; the sides of the pedestal are decorated with the caps of the hallucinogenic mushroom *Psilocybe aztecorum*. The Spanish destroyers of this civilization reported a variety of traditional uses—for entertainment, divination and communion with the gods. At the enthronement festivals of the Aztec emperors, the new ruler and his associates would consume teonanacatl for several days, while they watched the massive human sacrifices taking place to mark the event.

As Dobkin de Rios noted, the Spaniards were "culturally mycophobic"—that is, they were mushroom haters. The Roman Catholic insistence that the path to salvation lay in obedience to the church clashed with the Aztec belief that one could establish a direct link with the divine through teonanacatl visions. Spanish propaganda associated the fungus with Satan: "They called these mushrooms . . . 'God's flesh', or of the Devil whom they worshipped, and in this wise with that bitter victual by their cruel God were they houseled." The 16th century chronicle of Sahagun portrays a small, beaked devil dancing on mushroom caps, clawed hands beckoning to the unwary.

The violent suppression of the mushroom cult by the Spanish was very effective. It was not until the early 20th century that researchers discovered the continuing use of teonanacatl by native groups, particularly among the Mazatec tribe in the Mexican state of Oaxaca.

Modern Mazatec shamans employ mushrooms in divinatory and healing rituals which last all night. These ceremonies feature prolonged rhythmic chanting and clapping, which likely amplifies the drug effects through AUDITORY DRIVING. The profound sense of access to knowledge is often expressed in vividly poetic terms. The famous healer Maria Sabina (quoted by Schultes and Hofmann) stated:

> The more you go inside the world of Teonanacatl, the more things are seen. And you also see our past and our future, which are there together as a single thing already achieved, already happened. . . . I saw stolen horses and buried cities, the existence of which was unknown, and they are going to be brought to light. Millions of things I saw and knew. I knew

and saw God; an immense clock that ticks, the spheres that go slowly around, the inside the stars, the earth, and entire universe, the day and the night, the cry and the smile, the happiness and the pain. He who knows to the end the secret of Teonanacatl can even see that infinite clockwork.

See also PEYOTE.

For further reading: Dobkin de Rios; Munn; Schultes and Hofmann; Stafford.

terma In the literature of Tibetan Buddhism, there are thousands of texts known as termas. This word indicates that the books were not composed by ordinary means, but were "discovered" after being hidden by a master of former times. The most famous terma is the *Bardo Thodol*, known in the West as the "Tibetan Book of the Dead." Most termas are attributed to Padma Sambhava, the legendary eighth-century figure who established the Buddhist faith in Tibet. Those who discover termas are known as *tertons*.

Termas, according to this tradition, were originally deposited by Padma Sambhava in the deepest level of the minds of his most advanced disciples. The termas were transmitted through the generations of meditators who followed the teachings of this master's school, remaining outside the conscious awareness of those involved until the time was ripe for their revelation.

There are said to be three main types of terma, based on the kind of stimulus that triggers the retrieval of the text from the mental recesses of the terton. These are known as earth termas, pure vision termas and mind termas.

Earth termas are found in response to an external stimulus. Sometimes, actual scrolls of writing, supposedly deposited by Padma Sambhava in a cave or under a rock, are found by the terton, causing the rest of the text to emerge from his or her mind. Often, the stimulus is a pattern in the clouds, on the bark of a tree or the surface of a stream, supernaturally arranged to release the terma from the terton's memory.

Pure vision termas arise in response to imaginal displays thought to be sent by external entities. The visions frequently take the form of a visit from Padma Sambhava or a spirit who guarded the terma until the appropriate moment. The pure vision terma must be distinguished from the other visionary teachings mentioned in Tibetan Buddhism; the revelation is designated a terma only if the knowledge is thought to have been hidden within the visionary, rather than conveyed to him or her from an outside source.

Mental termas are held to be the highest form of terma discovery. In this category, the text emerges as the result of a mental content originating within the terton, perhaps a pattern of thought or a fantasy. It is as if the terma itself is requesting its own discovery. The possibility of distorted transmission is thought to be lessened in mind termas, compared to the other two categories.

One does not choose to become a terton; one is selected for the role by spiritual forces. Often, the call comes in the form of a dream or a strange event. The 17th-century terton Terdag Lingpa recounted how he was visited in a dream by a beautiful young woman, dressed in silk and adorned with glittering ornaments. They made love. Afterwards, she removed a ring, and placed it in his cup as a memento. When he awoke, Terdag Lingpa found in his cup a small red scroll, which activated the buried terma. Another famous terton, Ratna Lingpa, described a visit from a mysterious old man clad entirely in yellow. Ratna Lingpa offered his guest a meal. After dining, the stranger (who was actually Padma Sambhava) instructed him on the discovery of termas, and then vanished.

Tertons are very rarely monks; most are married householders. The presence of a spouse or other consort is held to be essential for the discovery of termas. If a terton fails to retrieve the terma, he or she becomes ill, and can even die. These features of the terma tradition suggest a pre-Buddhist origin. Contact with the spirit world in order to receive revelations is a theme of SHAMANISM, one possible source of the terma lore; although the notion that one's own mind is the site of the buried treasure is quite unusual.

In the terma tradition, unusual experiences are taken as opportunities for collaboration between the conscious mind and forces outside of awareness for creative ends. In this sense, it resembles modern practices such as CHANNELING and other types of AUTOMATISM.

For further reading: Evans-Wentz; Thondup.

theomania   In psychiatry, theomania refers to the belief that one is possessed by a good spirit, angel or deity. It is viewed as a feature of mental illness in the medical context; in religious settings, such a belief is often a valued spiritual experience. Theomania is a subtype of DEMONOMANIA.

See also POSSESSION.

theophany   From the Greek for "God's manifestation," a traditional Roman Catholic term meaning a VISION of God. Traditionally, theophanies were believed to be actual physical manifestations of the Deity that were perceived by human beings. In the Old Testament, God appears as a burning bush, a human form and a voice, among other things; in the New Testament, theophanic occurrences include the transfiguration and ascension of Christ.

See also THEOPTIA.

For further reading: Meier.

theoptia   In the Eastern Orthodox meditative tradition called HESYCHASM, progress on the path of spiritual development is often marked by the occurrence of the "vision of God," or theoptia. Most frequently, these divine encounters are described in terms of fire or light. In less mature versions of the theoptia, God is experienced outside of oneself, but advanced hesychasts describe Him within themselves as well. The theoptia can culminate in a full-blown MYSTICAL EXPERIENCE. The Byzantine saint Symeon the New Theologian left a vivid account of his holy visions. The following is typical of Symeon's theoptia (quoted by Matus):

> I sat in my cell and the light of a lamp shone on me, casting light on the shadows and darkness of night. It seemed bright to me as I attended to my reading, examining each word and analyzing each phrase. Then, O Lord, as I dwelt on these things, suddenly you appeared from above, far greater than the sun, and you shone forth from the heavens down to my heart. I saw everything else plunged into deep darkness, and in the midst a pillar of light cutting through the air all the way down from heaven to my poor self. . . . Have mercy on me. O Lord!

See also METANOIA; THEOSIS; VISION.
For further reading: Chirban; Matus.

theosis A Greek word meaning "deification" or "union with God," theosis is the highest type of MYSTICAL EXPERIENCE recognized in Eastern Orthodox Christianity. The mystic does not literally become God, as it would be heresy to claim that the creator is identical to one of his creatures. Rather, God's presence transforms the mystic's soul into a divine state. Afterwards, the deified person sees God's light everywhere and is said to radiate a strange luminosity. Matus stated that:

> The saints are like the moon on a winter night, surrounded by a halo; the unwaning light within penetrates their very being, makes them free from passions and surrounds their integrated body as it were with an aureole of invisible light.

See also AURA; HESYCHASM; METANOIA; THEOPTIA.
For further reading: Chirban, Matus.

therianthropy Variant term for LYCANTHROPY: the belief that one has been transformed into an animal.

thorybism Variant term for a POLTERGEIST, a series of disturbances, allegedly of a paranormal nature, that center around a person.

thunderstones For centuries, most scientists refused to accept the idea that rocks can fall from the sky. The reality of METEORs that reach the earth's surface—known as meteorites—is now firmly established. Meteorites originate in space and their composition is different from terrestrial rocks. Thunderstones, on the other hand, are rocks of ordinary terrestrial composition that apparently plummet from the heavens. They were formed on this planet, not in space. How, then, did they become airborne?

Most thunderstones are seen to fall during violent storms, or else they are discovered in craters afterward. Both single and multiple falls have been reported. The moment of impact is often marked by a clap of thunder.

The most widely accepted explanation for thunderstones is that they never took flight at all; rather, they were shallowly buried in the earth and became exposed by a lightning strike. Observers, discovering a hot rock in a hole, assumed that the stone had descended with the lightning. Alternatively, some thunderstones could have been created by lightning fusing materials in the ground at the site of the strike.

Mechanisms by which earth rocks can become levitated have also been suggested. Whirlwinds are capable of raising moderately sized stones and dropping them elsewhere. Huge meteorites have been known to collide with the earth in the distant past; perhaps these impacts propelled surface material into space, which would eventually drop back down. This theory does not account for the link between thunderstones and thunderstorms, however.

For further reading: Corliss (1977).

time gap phenomenon Variant term for MISSING TIME.

tinnitus Most people occasionally hear "noises in the head." These sensations, known as tinnitus, commonly include crackling, humming, buzzing, clicking, whistling, hissing and popping. Tinnitus usually persists for only short periods and does not interfere with ordinary hearing. The cause of tinnitus is unknown. The spontaneous firing of nerve cells in the inner ear, or in the auditory nerve that conducts information from the ear to the brain, is the most likely origin of tinnitus.

People with high blood pressure or hearing loss sometimes report disturbingly loud internal sounds. Persistent tinnitus is also a side effect of some medications and of withdrawal from addictive drugs.

Tinnitus can sometimes combine with sounds stored in memory, resulting in AUDITORY HALLUCINATIONs. Melzack recounted:

> A woman who had been a musician before losing her hearing says she 'hears' piano concertos and sonatas. The impression is so real that at first she thought the sounds were coming from a neighbor's radio. The woman reports that she cannot turn off the music and that it often gets louder at night when she wants to go to sleep. Another woman, who had lost much of her sight and hearing, experienced both phantom sight and sound. In one instance, she delightedly described seeing a circus and hearing the music that accompanied the acts.

The persecuting voices that evolve from inner sounds in sufferers of ALCOHOL HALLUCINOSIS are another example of this process.

See also PHANTOM VISION.

For further reading: Gross, Halpert, Sabot and Polisoes; Melzack.

tongo Japanese term for "sudden enlightenment." The notion that spiritual realization occurs in a breakthrough experience (called KENSHO or SATORI) is especially characteristic of the Zen Buddhist tradition, which originated in southern China. Tongo is contrasted with ZENGO, or gradual enlightenment, taught by the schools in northern China. However, Buddhists hold that the distinction is superficial—there is only one kind of ENLIGHTENMENT, regardless of what sort of experience conveys it.

tongues, speaking in Traditional Christian phrase for the phenomenon of GLOSSOLALIA.

Tourette's Syndrome Gilles de la Tourette's syndrome is an uncommon NEUROLOGICAL DISORDER that is still sometimes viewed as a kind of demonic POSSESSION. The disease is characterized by involuntary movements and vocal outbursts that grip the sufferer many times a day. The sensation experienced by the sufferer is of an external power taking control of the body.

The movements most often take the form of facial tics, grimaces, eye blinking or rolling and tongue protrusion. People with Tourette's Syndrome can be seized by an uncontrollable urge to make animal noises such as grunting, growling and barking, or to shout obscene or blasphemous phrases. One of Louis XIV's courtiers, who suffered from the disease, was known to stuff things into his mouth to prevent himself from barking at inopportune moments.

The exact cause of Tourette's Syndrome is still unknown. It appears to involve a chemical imbalance in the regions of the brain responsible for emotional expressions and movement. In many cases, the symptoms can be reduced through drug therapy. It is easy to see, however, how the association between this syndrome and spirit tormentors arose. (Tourette's patients who have undergone exorcisms have reported no relief.)

For further reading: Beyerstein; Friedhoff and Chase; Pitman.

trance This term derives from the Latin verb *transire*, meaning "to go across" or "to pass." Traditionally, trances were thought to be states in which the soul undergoes a passage to the spirit world. In modern parlance the term has a variety of meanings. Some writers equate trance with the whole range of ALTERED STATES OF CONSCIOUSNESS while others are more precise. The definition offered by Pattison, Kahan and Hurd is typical:

> Trance states are a mode of consciousness in which the person is conscious, but seemingly unaware or unresponsive to usual *external and internal stimuli*. Such persons act as if they are 'in their own world' apart from the immediate context of the external reality of the world about them.

Trance behavior may range from immobility, as in the typical hypnotic trance, to the vigorous activity seen in the trance dances of many non-literate societies. Some researchers prefer to view the trance as a type of social role adopted by the entranced person, rather than as a distinct type of consciousness—as actors remain in the waking state when they assume character roles, but their patterns of expression and responsiveness alter. Rossi noted that the ordinary waking state is frequently invaded by a trancelike condition, which he named the "common everyday trance":

> The housewife staring vacantly over a cup of coffee, the student with a faraway look in his eyes during the middle of a lecture, and the driver who automatically reaches his destination with no memory of the details of his route, are all varieties of the common everyday trance.

In her world survey of altered states of consciousness, Bourguinon noted two broad types of trance: possession trance, interpreted by the society as the occupation of the trancer's body by a foreign spirit, and trance not so interpreted. The second category, often called visionary trance, consists of experiences in which the trancer is visited by spirit forces, or journeys in an imaginal or spiritual world. Bourguinon reported that 90% of the 488 cultures in her sample deliberately practiced one or both types of trance. There is a tendency for visionary trance to be dominant among simpler societies, such as migratory or seminomadic groups.

Many of the activities of SHAMANISM fall under the heading of visionary trance. Possession trance is most common among relatively complex cultures, with elaborate social class systems and fixed settlements. Societies in which both trance types are found tend to be intermediate in social complexity. Researchers are unsure of the reason for this link between trance type and the structure of society. In the more complex cultures, people are more likely to have several different roles to play in their lives; perhaps this diversity allows them occasionally to adopt the role of a possessing spirit more readily than individuals from simpler societies, who have not developed the capacity for playing a range of roles.

Trances of either kind obviously fulfill important functions in cultures that deliberately cultivate them. These benefits include healing, receiving guidance from the spirits and permitting people to act out roles that otherwise would not be available to them. In modern western culture, trance is used in some mainstream therapies, such as HYPNOSIS; but, for the most part, deliberate trance phenomena are confined to marginal groups. Pentecostal Christian congregations become entranced through spirited hymn-singing, dancing, and sometimes by the excitement of exposing themselves to danger by handling snakes or drinking poison. Magicians, meditators, channelers and other spiritual explorers may also enter trances deliberately.

See also ECSTASY.

For further reading: Bourguinon; Evans; Pattison, Kahan and Hurd; Rossi; Sargant.

transpersonal psychology   The following definition was offered by Lajoie and Shapiro:

> Transpersonal psychology is concerned with the study of humanity's highest potential, and with the recognition, understanding, and realization of unitive, spiritual, and transcendent states of consciousness.

Adherents of this branch of psychology believe that there is more to being human than is recognized by the other main approaches in the field. Transpersonal psychology contrasts with perspectives that reduce human experiences to strictly personal terms.

Consider, for example, the MYSTICAL EXPERIENCE from the vantage of various schools of thought in psychology. A behaviorist might study it in terms of the social rewards and punishments given to the person who reports the experience. A cognitive psychologist would consider the beliefs and thought habits of the mystic. A psychoanalyst would view it as a regression to an infantile stage of development. A humanistic psychologist would ponder how the experience is connected to the values of the individual. The transpersonal approach acknowledges the importance of these perspectives as aspects of the mystical experience; but, in addition, transpersonalists consider what the experience says about the part of being human that goes beyond all of our normal definitions of self.

Transpersonal psychologists have shown great interest in the experiences and practices of the great religious traditions, particularly in MEDITATION. Another important topic has been ALTERED STATES OF CONSCIOUSNESS. In both cases, transpersonalists have avoided judging the reported phenomena by the standards of normal awareness; rather, they consider whether certain unusual states point to human possibilities that are superior to ordinary functioning.

The Swiss psychiatrist C.G. Jung is often named the "father of transpersonal psychology." He suggested the existence of a "collective unconscious"—a deep level of the mind that is shared by everyone and that seems to transcend time and space. Abraham Maslow, an American psychologist who explored the extraordinary states called PEAK EXPERIENCEs and PLATEAU EXPERIENCEs, was another transpersonal pioneer.

Today, California is transpersonal psychology's center of activity; its main forum, the *Journal of Transpersonal Psychology,* began publication in 1968. Critics condemn transpersonal psychology as a spiritual movement disguised as a science, but others praise it as an acknowledgment of the irreducible richness and mystery of human life.

See also ABNORMAL PSYCHOLOGY; ANOMALISTIC PSYCHOLOGY; PARAPSYCHOLOGY.

For further reading: Lajoie and Shapiro; Maslow (1968, 1976); Storr.

transvection Variant term for LEVITATION. The word "transvection" is usually used to describe the flight of witches through the air at night to attend the WITCHES' SABBATH, a central idea of the Great Witch Hunt which flourished during Renaissance and Reformation times. The belief in nocturnal flight might simply have been a fantasy of the witch hunters. Some researchers have suggested that ritually induced OUT OF BODY EXPERIENCEs might occasionally have been the origin of the reports; others suspect that hallucinogenic substances contained in the WITCHES' OINTMENT produced some of the accounts of transvection.

Turiya An ancient Hindu analysis of consciousness identifies four primary states of awareness: waking, dreaming, dreamless sleep and a fourth condition known as *turiya* (literally, "The Fourth" in Sanskrit). Attainment of Turiya was possible only through the practice of meditation. It was viewed as an important clue to the nature of consciousness.

In meditations to reach Turiya, the activities of thinking and imagining are allowed to die down completely, leaving consciousness to reflect upon itself. Turiya resembles dreamless sleep, in that both states are blissful. Whereas awareness in dreamless sleep is very dim, in Turiya it is exceedingly bright. In its clarity, Turiya is said to resemble the transient, spontaneous mystical experience called ANANDAMAYA.

One of the oldest and most important texts in the Hindu tradition, the *Mandukya Upanishad,* describes Turiya as follows (Prabhavananda and Manchester translation):

> The Fourth, say the wise, is not subjective experience, nor objective experience, nor experience intermediate between these two, nor is it a negative condition which is neither consciousness nor unconsciousness. It is not the knowledge of the senses, nor is it relative knowledge, nor yet inferential knowledge. Beyond the senses, beyond the understanding, beyond all expression, is The Fourth. It is pure unitary consciousness, wherein awareness of the world and of multiplicity is completely obliterated. It is ineffable peace. It is the supreme good. It is One without a second. It is the Self. Know it alone!

For most people, the perfect knowledge of one's self-nature available in Turiya is obscured in the other states of consciousness. When one is able to retain this knowledge under all circumstances, one has attained the condition known as *turiya- atita* ("the state beyond The Fourth"), which is synonymous with living liberation—JIVAN-MUKTI.

For further reading: Feuerstein (1989, 1990); Friedrichs; Prabhavananda and Manchester.

UFO abduction experience Stories of people being kidnapped by nonhuman beings from UFOs have attracted great attention in recent years. In Hynek's classification system of UFO ENCOUNTERs, these experiences are designated as "close encounters of the fourth kind," or CE IVs. The most common features of alien abduction reports were summarized by Bullard (1987):

I. At night in a remote area or at home, a witness sees a UFO and tries to flee. II. He enters a zone of strangeness as surroundings lose normal appearance, machines misbehave, his volition is impaired and his memory blanks out. Strange humanoid beings appear and float or carry him inside the UFO. III. He enters a uniformly lighted operating room where one or more alien beings subject him to a medical examination, sometimes of a painful character. IV. Afterwards he may see long tunnels and other parts of the ship, or travel a great distance in a short time to a dark and desolate other planet, then to a light and airy realm, both of which have buildings. Among the aliens he may also see a human being, and receive messages. On returning to earth, he finds a memory gap and injuries, and may receive later visits and extranormal manifestations.

Few abduction reports contain all of these features, but most have many of them.

Although it is generally believed that UFO abduction experiences are a quite recent phenomenon, some researchers have pointed to similarities between modern accounts and reports from earlier historical eras. For instance, Vallee unearthed a report by Agobard, a bishop of Lyons in the early ninth century. Agobard wrote that he saved four people threatened by a lynch mob. The four had been seen alighting from a "cloud ship," and witnesses assumed they were the associates of sorcerors. They themselves claimed, however, that they had been kidnapped by "miraculous men." (Agobard presumed that the entire episode had been delusional.) Throughout premodern times, tales were told of individuals who were borne away by fairies, or who were captured and tormented by demons. Perhaps abductions by cloud ship pilots, fairies and demons were the same basic type of experience as modern UFO abductions, expressed in the language and concepts of the time.

One of the first modern cases of UFO abduction was that of Antonio Villas-Boas. This Brazilian farmer reported that one night in 1957 he was forced inside an egg-shaped craft, where blood samples were taken from him and he was compelled to have sex with a beautiful female alien who barked like a dog. Curiously, a medical examiner reported that Villas-Boas was suffering from radiation poisoning, of unknown origin.

The Villas-Boas account did not attract wide attention outside the community of UFO enthusiasts. The case of Barney and Betty Hill, who claimed they were abducted in 1962, received enormous media coverage. It became the prototype with which all later abduction reports would be compared. The Hills were driving in the northeastern United States one evening and became alarmed by a mysterious aerial light that seemed to be following their car. Later, they found that they could not account for about two hours of their journey; Betty began to have nightmares. A psychiatrist used HYPNOSIS on them in an attempt to uncover any hidden memories of their MISSING TIME. While hypnotized, the Hills recounted how they were taken aboard a UFO, had telepathic conversations with UFOnauts, and were subjected to painful physical manipulations.

Based on the Hills' recollections of the stars in the sky on the fateful evening, researcher Robert Sheaffer concluded that the "mysterious light" had actually been the planet Jupiter. The Hills, believing themselves to be pursued by a UFO, had become lost on back roads when they tried to evade the "object"; their detours delayed them from their destination by two hours. The hypnotically retrieved "memories" must be mere fantasies, concluded many skeptics—including the psychiatrist who conducted the Hills' hypnotic sessions.

The 1970s saw an upsurge of UFO abduction reports, especially in the U.S. In the following decade, the phenomenon had become a media sensation and the central focus in the debate over the nature of UFOs. Budd Hopkins and Leo Sprinkle, relying heavily on hypnosis to "unblock" the memories of people who reported episodes of missing time, published detailed stories of alien kidnappings. Hopkins discovered that the UFOnauts were up to no good—they purportedly stole sperm and ova, and even fetuses from pregnant women, for use in genetic experiments. Sprinkle, however, found that his abductees were generally much better treated; he has concluded that the alien encounters are part of an "educational program for humankind on planet earth." In 1987, Strieber's description of his UFO abduction experiences became a bestseller in the nonfiction category.

Unlike many cases in the other classes of UFO encounters, CE IVs cannot be regarded as simple acts of misperception. A number of researchers have concluded that the best explanation for UFO abduction reports is that the stories are, for the most part, accurate recollections of encounters with beings from another world—or a hidden dimension of this world. They point to the fact that some abductees display physical injuries consistent with their stories. In no case, however, has physical evidence been docu-

mented that could not have been produced by less exotic causes. The differences in the kinds of abductions found by Hopkins and Sprinkle are difficult to explain if the experiences are understood in a strictly literal fashion.

Klass argued that the use of hypnosis to explain missing time was responsible for creating many of the abduction stories. Hypnosis is an unreliable method for enhancing memory; in fact, a more consistent effect of hypnosis is to decrease the hypnotized person's ability to distinguish accurate memories from fantasies. Hypnotic subjects also tend to respond in accordance with what they believe the hypnotist wants. Considerable care is required on the part of the hypnotist to minimize these unintentional suggested effects. Klass has noted that most of the hypnotists working in the UFO abduction field are not professionally qualified in hypnosis and are believers in the literal reality of abduction reports; some hold that they themselves have been abducted. These researchers could have influenced susceptible subjects to fantasize about the sorts of abduction events they were expecting, through prior discussions and leading questions; the subjects may then have believed these fantasies to be retrieved memories.

In order to assess the importance of the biasing factors noted by Klass, Bullard (1989) analyzed his large collection of abduction reports. He compared material according to the experience level of the hypnotist, and whether the hypnotist believed or disbelieved in the literal reality of abductions. Bullard found the same basic features in the stories, regardless of the hypnotist or the procedure; he concluded that "hypnosis makes far less difference than critics have claimed."

Believers in the literal reality of UFO abductions have also responded to Klass' observations by noting that many abduction "memories" have surfaced without the use of hypnosis. The effects of suggestion are not restricted to formal hypnotic procedures, however. Indeed, they can even occur without a hypnotist. Fictional material that one reads or watches on television can later be retrieved from memory without recalling its origin in fiction (CRYPTOMNESIA). Several researchers have argued that many of the details of abduction accounts have arisen in precisely this way. Randles, for example, recounted a case in which a woman awoke with a memory of being taken up a ramp into a UFO; inside, she was medically examined by aliens who smelled of cinnamon and had leathery skins. One of the aliens was named Gerard. These elements matched those of an episode of the television show Dynasty which featured a UFO abduction; the "abductee" had viewed the episode the evening before her experience. Kottmeyer (cited by Thompson) has documented close parallels between modern UFO abduction experiences and B grade science fiction films of the 1950s, such as *Killers from Space* and *Invaders from Mars*. Meheust has done similar detective work in the domain of science fiction literature. Perhaps these culturally available ideas were incorporated in the fantasies of predisposed individuals, who then mistook them for memories of UFO abductions. Alternatively, Sprinkle (cited by Klass) suggested that the fictional treatments of UFO encounters may themselves have been the result of alien influences—part of the "educational program" being secretly conducted by the UFOnauts.

A study by Ballester Olmos further supported the idea of a link between popular culture and UFO abduction experiences. He charted the frequency of abduction reports worldwide from 1957 to 1985, and found that increases in such reports were generally preceded by a spate of sensationalistic magazine and newspaper articles, books and television shows on the subject.

Neurological malfunctions have been mentioned as another possible contributor to UFO abduction experiences. According to Klass, Strieber's descriptions indicate that he might have temporal lobe EPILEPSY, which can produce hallucinations. Persinger has theorized that everyone has varying degrees of "temporal lobe

sensitivity"—a tendency for that region of the brain to produce unusual experiences—and that this tendency can be amplified by exposure to strong electromagnetic fields. UFO abduction experiences are one of the phenomena Persinger believes can be caused by temporal lobe activity.

Thompson found that UFO abduction experiences appear to have the same basic structure as INITIATORY EXPERIENCEs. Many abductees report that their sense of self and world is transformed by their alien encounters. Perhaps this initiatory aspect of UFO abductions indicates that the reality behind UFOs is deliberately acting to change human consciousness, or it may simply be a common reaction to any mysterious event.

In the persistent absence of evidence for the physical reality of UFO abductions, researchers have begun to study the psychological features of those who report these experiences. The results of these studies have been subject to varying interpretations. An early clinical study of nine abductees by Slater, reported by Bloecher, Clamar and Hopkins, concluded that "a battery of standard tests failed to detect any psychopathology that could be reasonably expected to be a cause for UFO abduction reports." Others have noted that mental illness is not required for a person to have a FALSE MEMORY—in fact, it is normal to do so. Furthermore, Slater's subjects did not seem to be a typical cross-section of normalcy; for instance, they tended to have unusually low self esteem, a lack of emotional maturity and mildly paranoid thinking. Whether these features point to personalities that would be prone to delusions of UFO abduction or whether they could be the result of traumatic encounters with aliens is the subject of continuing debate.

Similarly contentious findings were reported by Sprinkle and Parnell. The responses of abductees on a psychological assessment battery suggested to these researchers that their subjects were generally free from neurotic or psychotic symptoms. However, their observation that

UFO abductees tend toward suspiciousness and schizoid thinking could be interpreted in other ways.

Lawson wondered if UFO abduction stories could be experimentally produced in people who did not claim to be abductees. He subjected 20 volunteers, who reported no interest in UFOs, to a hypnotic induction; then, he asked them to imagine they had been abducted by aliens and to describe the experience. Lawson initially reported that the "imaginary subjects under hypnosis report UFO experiences which seem identical to those of 'real' witnesses." This conclusion is consistent with the idea that many abduction accounts are based on imagination rather than accurate memory. On re-examining his data, however, Lawson felt that there were crucial differences between the "imaginary" and the "real" accounts—in particular, the latter's emphasis on the physical effects of the abduction experience. Most recently, Lawson suggested that the core of the UFO abduction experience is a trace memory of the abductees' own births, elaborated with fantasy elements.

Ring included an unspecified number of UFO abductees among the subjects in his comparison study of UFO encounters and NEAR DEATH EXPERIENCEs. He reported no significant differences between the abductees and people who had reported other types of UFO encounters. Those whose lives had been touched by the aerial mysteries reported that they had endured significantly greater amounts of illness, neglect and abuse during childhood than subjects who were interested in the topic of UFOs but who had not had UFO experiences. More reports of other types of unusual experience, and greater tendencies toward DISSOCIATION, also characterized the former group. These findings indicate the existence of an ENCOUNTER PRONE PERSONALITY type, Ring suggested.

Spanos and his colleagues noted that UFO witnesses who reported intense contacts with UFO occupants, including abduction, tended to be higher in FANTASY PRONENESS than UFO witnesses who merely saw unidentified lights or distant objects in the sky. Intense contacts were also more likely to occur while the witnesses were in a HYPNAGOGIC, HYPNOPOMPIC or sleep state, conditions known to be conducive to HALLUCINATIONs.

For further reading: Ballester Olmos; Bloecher, Clamar and Hopkins; Bullard (1987, 1989); Hopkins; Hynek; Jacobs (1992); Klass (1988); Lawson (1980, 1988); Meheust; Parnell; Persinger (1989); Randles; Ring; Sheaffer; Spanos, Cross, Dickson and Dubreuil; Sprinkle; Strieber; Thompson; Vallee.

UFObia The irrational tendency to deny the possibility that some UFO ENCOUNTERs are actual contacts with nonhuman intelligences. Some UFO skeptics, under the banner of reason, engage in extreme contortions of logic and distortions of fact in order to fit all UFO reports into conventional terms. The motivation for these procrustean efforts, believe some of those who support unconventional explanations, is fear of the unknown.

See also UFOMANIA.

UFO encounter The term "unidentified flying object," or UFO, was coined by American Air Force captain and anomalies researcher Edward Ruppelt to refer to mysterious aerial phenomena reported by thousands of observers during the 1940s and 1950s. "UFO" is preferred by many to the older phrase "flying saucer," because many of the reports do not involve saucer-shaped forms. The newer term has its own inadequacies, however—in many cases, it is not at all clear whether the phenomena are "flying," or even if they are "objects." Some researchers have tried to promote more neutral terminology, such as "anomalistic observational phenomena," or AOPs. "UFO" dominates popular usage at present. Hynek established the standard definition of a UFO:

the reported perception of an object or light seen in the sky or upon the land, the appearance, trajectory or general dynamics and luminescent behavior of which do not suggest a logical, conventional explanation and which is not only mystifying to the original percipients but remains unidentified after close scrutiny of all available evidence by persons who are technically capable of making a common sense identification, if one is possible.

UFOs have almost become part of mainstream culture. A 1990 Gallup poll estimated that 47% of adult Americans believed in the reality of UFOs (meaning, presumably, that UFOs are some sort of unconventional object). Fourteen percent reported that they had seen one themselves.

UFOs of almost every imaginable shape, size, color and behavior have been reported. This diversity has prompted the development of classification schemes. The most widely used system, created by Hynek, sorts UFO encounters under two main headings—UFOs that seem to be distant from the observer, and close encounters. Distant observations are subdivided into three categories: nocturnal lights, discs viewed in daylight and anomalous radar traces. There are also three categories of close encounters. *Close encounters of the first kind* (CE-I) involve UFOs that leave no physical traces and are not associated with sightings of "occupants" or "entities." In *close encounters of the second kind* (CE-II), the UFO is said to leave physical signs of its presence. Reports of *close encounters of the third kind* (CE-III) include descriptions of apparent life forms connected with the UFO. More recently, another category has come into usage; *close encounters of the fourth kind* (CE-IVs) entail the abduction of humans by UFO occupants, and/or sexual contact between humans and UFOnauts. Some cases fall into more than one category, or do not fit neatly into any of them.

The domain of UFO encounters is so complex that a number of research disciplines are needed to map its richness. Swords noted that four major avenues of study are involved in attempting to understand UFO encounters: history; biological sciences; physical sciences; and personal and social studies.

The "modern era" of UFO sightings began on June 24, 1947. Kenneth Arnold, a search and rescue pilot, saw nine disc-shaped aerial objects while he was flying in the vicinity of Mount Rainier, Washington State. Arnold stated that the objects moved through the air "like a saucer would if you skipped it across the water," which gave rise to the expression "flying saucer." But Arnold's report was not the first recorded instance of an encounter with unexplained things in the sky—indeed, such sightings have occurred in every culture and recorded historical period. UFO researchers disagree as to whether the post-Arnold UFO encounters constitute a new phenomenon, or are the continuation of an age-old occurrence. Much of the difficulty in resolving this question arises from the fact that observers of unusual events, struggling to make sense of their experiences, tend to describe them in terms drawn from the world view of their own culture. When a medieval peasant recounted a meeting with a fairy who rode a cloud-ship, and a modern witness states that she encountered an extraterrestrial who piloted a spacecraft, it is unclear whether a similar stimulus is being described in two different, culturally appropriate ways, or whether two unrelated phenomena were involved.

The earliest known UFO report is found on a papyrus scroll dating from the reign of the Egyptian pharaoh Thutmose III in the 15th century B.C. "Circles of fire," shining brighter than the sun, were described floating through the sky. The Greek philosopher Aristotle wrote of "heavenly discs" and claimed to witness an object that landed on earth, then rose again and landed at another spot. The Roman scholar Cicero was another famous UFO witness of ancient times. He reported that on one occasion the sun was seen in the sky at night, accompanied by flying spheres. Many UFO students have speculated that some of the Bible stories, from the visions of Old Testament figures like Ezekiel and Elijah to the star of Bethlehem, might have been based on UFO encounters.

The early histories of non-Western cultures also bear witness to strange events in the sky. The Japanese record is especially rich in sightings of flying drums and "earthenware vessels" cruising overhead, leaving luminous trails. In 1235, aerial lights were seen looping through the night sky for several hours. A team of Japanese scholars commissioned to investigate the episode solved the mystery to their satisfaction—"It is only the wind making the stars sway!" they concluded.

The annals of premodern Europe describe many unexplained sightings of cloudships, flying hats, shields, balls, dragons, torches, pillars and armies clashing in the air. In the intellectual context of the time, these spectacles were usually interpreted as omens of imminent events, or signs concerning the will of God. UFO reports persisted after the rise of the scientific world view in the 17th century. The wave of AIRSHIP SIGHTINGS across the United States at the end of the 1800s is widely held to be an immediate precursor of today's UFO phenomenon. The FOO FIGHTERS spotted by World War II pilots would today be labeled UFOs.

Since the Arnold sighting, UFO encounters have been reported around the world. It is hard to determine if there are geographical differences in the frequency of UFO encounters, because the efficiency of national reporting systems varies greatly; there seems to be somewhat fewer UFO reports from south Asia than elsewhere, but this dearth may reflect poor communication rather than a paucity of experiences. It is clear that UFO sightings are not evenly spaced in time. Rather, they occur in clusters. A concentration of UFO reports over a short time period, from a limited geographical area, is called a *flap;* an increase in reports lasting for several months over a wider area is designated a *wave.* Since 1947, dozens of flaps and waves have occurred.

UFO encounters of both the distant and close varieties have continued without pause through the modern era; but there have been significant shifts in theme. Starting in the mid-1950s, some individuals began to claim that they had made contact with the UFO occupants, who had given them important messages for humankind. Most of these "contactees" have reported that extraterrestrials are concerned about the warlike and polluting ways of our species; some contactees warn that we are on the verge of destroying ourselves, while others proclaim that the "space brothers" will save at least some of us. By the early 1960s, reports of UFO abductions started to appear. These CE-IVs became more prominent during the 1970s and had become a major focus of media interest by the mid-1980s.

There have also been changes in fashion concerning explanations for UFO encounters. Throughout the modern era, skeptics have argued that UFO reports are produced by a range of familiar mechanisms, including misidentification of ordinary stimuli, mental illness and fraud. Most researchers agree that a majority of UFO reports do arise in this way. Some skeptics view the remainder as "not yet explained, but not necessarily unexplainable" by ordinary means; others deny even the possibility of a true mystery underlying some UFO reports, irrationally arguing that "absence of evidence is evidence of absence." For many skeptics, the matter seemed settled by the negative conclusion of the 1969 Condon Report. This document was produced by a committee at the University of Colorado, commissioned by the American government to determine the nature of UFOs. The report was discredited in the eyes of many when it was discovered that Edward Condon, who directed the committee, and Project Coordinator Robert Low, had reached the conclusion that "there's nothing to [UFOs]" even before investigations began.

An early hypothesis regarding UFOs, still popular today, is that UFOs are spacecraft, visiting our planet from other worlds. More recently, there has been considerable speculation that UFOs are manifestations of another dimension of reality here on earth, or perhaps some sort of atmospheric life form that only occasionally becomes visible to human eyes. Nazis, demons and American spies have also been suggested as the true identities of the UFO pilots.

Another theory of UFOs was proposed by the psychiatrist Carl Jung. He suggested that the disks seen in the sky are MANDALAs, or symbols of wholeness. These forms are frequently seen in dreams during times of personal crisis and represent the possibility of growth; during periods of mass social strain (such as the present century), the mandala may be witnessed communally as a sign of the peaceful integration that the population is yearning for. Jung was noncommittal as to whether there actually were saucer-shaped objects flying through the air, or whether the phenomena were entirely subjective—indeed, he believed in a deep layer of the mind, called the psychoid level, at which the mental and physical worlds merged.

Those who hold that some unidentified flying phenomena are indeed objects point to cases in which the UFO apparently left physical traces of its presence. Reported physical and biological effects of UFOs include crushed or burned vegetation where a UFO was seen to land, photographic images, debris from UFOs that seem to explode or crash, interference with the functioning of radios and automobile engines, farm animals said to be surgically mutilated, and effects on witnesses: temporary numbness and paralysis, and skin burns and rashes. Although some of these effects are not easily explained in conventional terms, no one has yet turned up any physical or biological traces that cannot have been made in ordinary ways. Stories of people being permanently abducted or killed by UFOs are not well substantiated.

Given the persistent inability of UFO researchers to make much progress on the physical front, some have turned to studying the psychological and social aspects of UFO reports. Research into normal perceptual and memory processes has revealed that both kinds of psychological activity are much less reliable than is commonly assumed. The tendency for individuals to misperceive or misremember unusual stimuli, especially if they have prior expectations concerning them, is quite high. The majority of UFO sightings are explainable as honest misidentifications of planets, clouds, airplane lights and a host of less common atmospheric phenomena. These stimuli can be altered almost beyond recognition by the filtering effects of witnesses' beliefs and expectancies. Hence, many psychologically normal people have reported viewing an object darting in the sky, changing color, with structures such as windows and fins, which has proven upon investigation to be the planet Venus.

Such expectation effects can influence groups of witnesses as well as individual observers. The GROUP DYNAMICS OF UNUSUAL EXPERIENCES can cause a perceptual bias to spread through a population like an infectious disease, provided there are channels of communication through which the bias can be transmitted. Some researchers have interpreted flaps and waves of UFO reports in these terms. An increase in sightings within an area may not reflect a rise in the presence of strange objects, but a change in mass attentional habits—as stories of UFO encounters circulate, people become more vigilant than usual and anticipate spotting a UFO. Any aerial event they had never noticed before is likely to be psychologically amplified into a mysterious object.

Although some UFO sightings are probably HALLUCINATIONs caused by mental illness, the vast majority of UFO witnesses are not suffering from psychopathology. Ring undertook a study to determine whether people who report UFO encounters differ from those who are interested in the subject, but who have never seen one themselves. He found that UFO witnesses were significantly more likely than nonwitnesses to report the following background information: anomalous experiences during childhood; serious childhood illness; sexual abuse and neglect as a child; and tendencies toward DISSOCIATION. Ring argued that traumas in early life predispose people to focus more intensely on inner events such as mental images (ABSORPTION), and to dissociate from unpleasant experiences as a means of escape. These tendencies toward dissociation and absorption constitute an "encounter-prone personality." Later in life, such individuals are more likely to witness UFOs. Ring found no marked differences between witnesses who reported CE-IVs (abductions) and those who had other sorts of UFO encounters. Ring's findings could be interpreted as evidence that many UFO witnesses are predisposed to confuse perception and fantasy; alternatively, Ring suggests that encounter-prone personalities are more sensitive to the multidimensional reality from which the UFO arises than are less inner-attuned people.

Ring's subjects also reported dramatic shifts in personal values because of their UFO encounter. Their attitudes tended to shift toward greater appreciation for life, increased self acceptance, and a stronger orientation toward spiritual issues and matters of planetary welfare. These results suggest that the UFO encounter is acting as an INITIATORY EXPERIENCE for some witnesses.

Spanos and his colleagues compared UFO witnesses with nonwitnesses on a variety of psychological measures. They found no significant differences between these groups in FANTASY PRONENESS, INTELLIGENCE or PSYCHOLOGICAL ADJUSTMENT.

At present, there is no consensus among UFO researchers regarding the true nature of the phenomenon, when it started, the validity of the physical and biological evidence and the role of social and psychological factors. The area has attracted a number of hoaxers and spiritual visionaries over the years, which has made research more difficult. Matters are clouded further by unsubstantiated rumors that governments are withholding information about UFOs from the public. Whether or not there exists a truly anomalous signal amongst all this noise remains a mystery.

For further reading: Cross, Dickson and Dubreuil; Gallup and Newport; Hynek; Jacobs (1975); Klass (1974); Menzel and Boyd; Menzel and Taves; Ring; Sachs; Spanos, Cross, Dickson and DuBreuil; Storr; Swords; Thompson.

UFOmania   A derogatory term referring to the credulous tendency to label every aerial phenomenon as a UFO without considering conventional explanations. To the UFOmaniac, every meteor, airplane tail light and symmetrical cloud is a UFO. Such people can be found among the followers of the small religious movements based on the UFO idea.

UFOria   A skeptical term denoting the mass excitement that accompanies—and perhaps contributes—to a wave of UFO sightings. In such an atmosphere, the GROUP DYNAMICS OF UNUSUAL EXPERIENCES are likely to operate, biasing observers to misidentify conventional phenomena as anomalous.

unio mystica   This Latin phrase, meaning "mystical union," has been used to designate the MYSTICAL EXPERIENCE as it occurs within the context of the Christian faith. The experience of a unity underlying the apparent diversity of worldly things is shaped by the beliefs of the mystic; when Christians have mystical experiences, they interpret them as an encounter with God. Many Christian mystics have described this encounter as a "union" with the divine.

The term "unio mystica" was first used in the 17th century, but the phenomenon has been reported by Christians in every historical period. A statement by St. Paul in the New Testament sounds mystical: "I am crucified with Christ: nevertheless I live; yet not I but Christ lives in me" (Galatians 2:20). Christian mystical experiences are not uniformly distributed in time, but tend to occur in waves. Underhill identified three peaks of Christian mystical activity in the third, 14th and 17th centuries. She interpreted this pattern in a very positive light:

> the great periods of mystical activity tend to correspond with the great periods of artistic, material, and intellectual civilization. As a rule, they come immediately after, and seem to complete such periods: those outbursts of vitality in which man makes fresh conquests over his universe apparently producing, as their last stage, a type of heroic character which extends these victories to the spiritual sphere. When science, politics, literature, and the arts . . . have risen to their height and produced their greatest works, the mystic comes to the front; snatches the torch, and carries it on. It is almost as if he were humanity's finest flower; the product at which each great creative period of the race had aimed.

According to another interpretation of this historical rhythm, the surges of mystical activity may reflect the amount of stress felt by members of the society. After a period of cultural creativity has run its course, the general level of stress rises; people grapple with problems that no longer yield to the old approaches. The onset or termination of stress is a common trigger of mystical experiences.

The unio mystica is generally understood as part of a process of spiritual development called the Mystic Path or Mystic Way. Mystical experiences do not happen continuously, but mark episodes of contact with God as the mystic progresses. Underhill noted five major phases of the Christian mystical life. First comes the *awakening* to the reality of God, and the urge to strive toward the holy presence. This change of awareness can occur suddenly, as in religious conversion, and may take the form of a mystical experience.

Next comes *purgation*—in order to eliminate the attachments and distractions that interfere with the mystic's relationship with God, spiritual disciplines are undertaken. The mystic may live on minimal food, water and sleep, retreat from worldly activities and even engage in FLAGELLATION and other forms of self-torture. These practices are usually stressful; the mystical experiences that are thus triggered can inspire the mystic to endure the ordeals of deprivation.

The trials of purgation are followed by the joys of *illumination*. During this stage, the mystic feels a growing confidence in the presence of God. Mystical experiences of overwhelming bliss can happen. VISIONS and voices of supernatural beings, which in a secular context would be called HALLUCINATIONS, also characterize the phase of illumination.

Beyond this phase lies another great ordeal, dubbed the DARK NIGHT OF THE SOUL by St. John of the Cross. God becomes unavailable. The mystic, who may have come to expect that the delights of illumination would last forever, now experiences nothing but the agonizing absence of the divine. No matter what acts of prayer, meditation, contemplation or mortification are undertaken, there is no hint of the unio mystica. The purpose of this phase is to complete the purification of the mystic. The impotence of the human will, and the delusions of spiritual pride, are here sharply demonstrated; and the final phase of the Mystic Way cannot begin until the lessons of humility are learned.

The pinnacle is the phase of *union*. The mystic, freed of mundane attachments and pride, is again blessed with the awareness of God's presence. Intense mystical experiences may still occur, but some mystics have noted that they are less frequent in this phase than in the previous ones. Rather, the presence of God becomes the constant undertone of *all* experience, the foundation of a holy lifestyle dedicated to loving acts. Only the greatest mystics of the Christian tradition—individuals like Richard of St. Victor, Catherine of Siena, and Teresa of Avila—are said to have reached the completion of the Mystic Way.

Chirban described a sequence of experiences in the mystical literature of Eastern Orthodoxy that corresponds closely to Underhill's pattern, which was derived primarily from Western sources. First, Chirban noted, is metanoia—an experience of conversion to the mystical quest for God. Then comes apatheia, or purification; illumination; and finally theosis, or union with God. Some Eastern writers, such as St. Gregory of Nyssa, mention a period of "clouds" or "darkness" preceding the attainment of union, perhaps matching the dark night of the soul.

According to Christian orthodoxy, the creator and his creation (which includes people) are distinct. Individuals who claim that they are God are guilty of heresy. The mystics' preference for describing their experience as "unio mystica" was theologically dangerous, as this phrase could easily sound heretical. Mystics who wished to remain orthodox were spurred to develop interpretations of the union with God that did not violate the essential distinction between God and creature. Some mystics were too daring, and suffered the consequences. One such was Meister Eckhart, a brilliant German preacher of the 14th century: "Between man and God, however, there is not only no distinction, there is no multiplicity either. There is nothing but one." "The eye with which I see God is the eye with which God sees me." Eckhart's works were condemned by the Vatican.

Mystical Christians who managed to stay on the right side of the theological law expressed the unio mystica using clever metaphors combining the ideas of union and distinctness. Many mystics wrote of a "spritual marriage" of the soul and God. In a marriage, the two individuals are united, but do not literally fuse. Jan van Ruysbroek, who was "blessed" by the church, noted that sunlight pervades the air without *becoming* air; an iron ball can be heated until it glows, and the heat does not transform into iron;

and so it is, he said, with God and the mystic's soul.

Another mystic reconciled the unio mystica with orthodoxy so successfully that he was proclaimed a saint. John of the Cross declared that the mystic union was a perfect alignment of the mystic's intentions with those of God: "the will of God and the will of the soul are conformed together neither desiring aught repugnant to the other." Such a situation occurs (ideally) in a labor union—a unity of intention, but not a loss of individual identity among the members.

See also NUMINOUS EXPERIENCE.

For further reading: Chirban; Dupre and Wiseman; McGinn; Stace; Underhill.

unlikely virtue   An unlikely virtue is a behavior or attitude that is rare among the general population. Psychologists measure people's tendency to claim unlikely virtues by including items such as, "My opinions are always completely reasonable" on true-false questionnaires. Agreement with many such items could reflect the actual presence of the virtues or, more likely, the presence of a tendency toward grandiose delusions about oneself. P. Nelson reported that people who scored either very high or very low on a measure of unlikely virtues tended to report more paranormal experiences than moderate scorers.

See also Appendix.

For further reading: P. Nelson.

unusual experience   The perception of an event that appears to violate conventional assumptions about reality is called an unusual experience. In modern Western culture, phenomena such as APPARITIONs, ESP, MYSTICAL EXPERIENCEs, OUT OF BODY EXPERIENCEs, NEAR DEATH EXPERIENCEs, CRYPTIC animals and UFO ENCOUNTERs are defined as unusual or anomalous, because none of them seem to fit easily into the prevailing scientific world view. Unusual experiences are often not what they appear to be, however; events that are explainable without invoking extraordinary concepts are frequently misinterpreted as paranormal occurrences. Any experience, anomalous or normal, is caused by an interaction of the following factors: the environment; the psychological traits and states of the observers; their physiological traits and states; and the outcome of the experience.

Certain environmental conditions are conducive to anomalous experiences. In darkness, familiar objects can be unclearly perceived or misperceived as anomalous. Unfamiliar objects can also be easily misinterpreted. For example, few people have much experience with ionized air, or PLASMA; glowing balls of plasma, created by electrical events in the atmosphere, have probably led to some UFO reports.

Dangerous or otherwise stressful circumstances also increase the chances of having an anomalous experience. Stress can disrupt ordinary ways of thinking and perceiving, temporarily permitting an observer to experience the world in a strange, new way. Environmental stimulation can be arranged to create this effect deliberately, as in the use of AUDITORY and PHOTIC DRIVING.

Another important environmental feature is the presence of other people. If alone, a person's own hopes, fears and expectations have free rein to affect the perception of events; and if that person is inclined to have anomalous experiences, he or she quite possibly will. If, however, others are present, their statements about what is happening may be influential; if all the other witnesses insist they saw the table levitate, one person's uncertainty about it can waver. Or, if everyone else ridicules the idea that a table can move by itself, an individual is more likely to dismiss as a perceptual error the sight of the table rising slightly.

Some individuals are more prone to anomalous experiences than others. Those who believe in anomalous concepts report more unusual occurrences than nonbelievers. People with a history of CHILDHOOD TRAUMA or psychedelic drug use, and those with certain personality traits such as ABSORPTION capacity or SENSATION SEEKING are more likely to experience anomalous events.

Anomalous experiences often occur when observers are in unusual states of attention. Intense focusing on external or internal phenomena, as in MEDITATION, is conducive to such experiences as are the transitions between states of consciousness, such as the HYPNAGOGIC and HYPNOPOMPIC STATES that happen between sleeping and wakefulness.

Unusual conditions of the brain are associated with at least some types of anomalous experience. Sufferers from brain disorders like EPILEPSY often have disturbed perceptions prior to seizures. Some studies have linked signs of damage to the brain's TEMPORAL LOBEs, and history of HEAD INJURY, to anomalous experiences. Malfunctions of the sense organs or the nerve cells that transmit sensory information to the brain can produce peculiar sensations, which may be interpreted in anomalous terms. Short-term interference with habitual brain functioning caused by fever or drugs can also be a factor. People in extremely high or low states of arousal report more unusual experiences than the moderately aroused.

An anomalous experience that meets a personal need of the witness, or one that is socially rewarded, can prompt that person to seek out the conditions under which the experience is likely to recur. Someone who sees a ghost of a beloved dead relative may feel relieved by this apparent validation of the belief in life after death, and may start attending seances to make more contacts with the spirit world. A person who is treated with reverence for having a vision, rather than being locked up as a crazy person, may practice rituals or take drugs to induce more visions.

See also AMBIGUITY; Appendix; CONFORMITY; EMOTIONAL AROUSAL; FANTASY PRONENESS; GENDER; GROUP DYNAMICS OF UNUSUAL EXPERI-

ENCES; HYPNOTIZABILITY; PSYCHOLOGICAL AD-
JUSTMENT; UNLIKELY VIRTUE.

For further reading: Evans; Ludwig; Neher
(1990); Tart (1975); Zusne and Jones.

verbigeration   A type of AUDITORY HALLUCI-NATION in which nonsense phrases are heard repeated over and over. Verbigeration is often immensely distracting and tormenting for the sufferer. The condition occurs most frequently in connection with SCHIZOPHRENIA. Kraepelin (quoted by Noll [1992a]) described a patient who heard the following phrase, endlessly repeated: "For we ourselves can always hope that we should let ourselves pray other thoughts. For we ourselves wish to know who would let the swine's head be tormented to death with us foolishly."

For further reading: Noll (1992a).

videha-mukti   The literal meaning of this Sanskrit term is "release without a body." In most cases videha-mukti refers to the achievement of the spiritual goal of Hindu mysticism—self realization and liberation from suffering—at the moment of death. Some sources also use the term to designate the experience of union with God or Absolute Reality during meditation. In this condition, the meditator loses awareness of his or her own body.

Vinum Nostrum   "Our Wine," a mysterious drink mentioned in some of the texts of AL-CHEMY. Some researchers believe that the Vinum Nostrum was a hallucinogenic drug, ingested by alchemists in order to bring revelatory visions.

vipassana   A word in the ancient Pali language of India, vipassana is variously translated as "insight," "special insight" or "higher vision." (The Sanskrit equivalent, less often seen in English publications, is *vipashyana*.) Vipassana is one of the two mental abilities, along with SHAMATHA, said by Buddhists to be required for the attainment of ENLIGHTENMENT. While shamatha can be developed by non-Buddhist meditators, vipassana is distinctively Buddhist.

Before the faculty of insight can be properly employed, the mind must first be stabilized in the condition of shamatha. Only then is it possible to explore the nature of one's experiences with clarity, in order to discover what is real and what is unreal in the ceaseless flow of consciousness. As meditation master Namgyal Rinpoche put it, the mind must be calmed (shamatha) and then awakened (vipassana).

According to Buddhism, the exercise of vipassana enables meditators to make their own discoveries concerning the true nature of the world. They are discouraged from relying merely on the reports of others, because such blind faith does not produce liberation from suffering. Nonetheless, some Buddhist texts do contain descriptions of the kinds of experience noted by advanced practitioners.

Initially, the vipassana meditator often notices that each object of experience seems to exist only for a moment; each content of consciousness arises and disappears very quickly, with virtually no period of being in existence. (Indeed, the Buddha reportedly could perceive 17×10^{21} arisings and fadings "in the wink of an eye.") And yet, our normal awareness seems to be filled with objects which persist over time. The result of this observation could be the realization that, in reality, things are not as they seem to be to the untrained consciousness. One may then be spurred on to deeper study of awareness.

As vipassana intensifies, impermanence is found to characterize every object of the physical and mental domains. Now the self, as one ordinarily conceives of it, is the enduring "core" or "essence." When the Buddhist meditator searches for such a self, none is found, just the ever-flickering stream of awareness. Nothing is permanent; and there is no self. The realization may dawn that much of the suffering in our lives is caused by trying to grasp onto states and objects which exist only for a moment, and from attempting to defend a nonexistent self against threat. Every experience which is tainted by these efforts is bound to be frustrating. These three discoveries of vipassana—impermanence, absence of self and intrinsic frustration—are known as the three marks of conditioned existence.

Buddhist teachers caution that our first glimpses of these truths can be overwhelming. Cherished self-identity is an illusion; everything one clings to is constantly dissolving; all of one's mundane goals are guaranteed to bring suffering. Unless the mind is anchored in shamatha, the result of these insights could be a complete loss of mental balance.

However, Buddhism assures, one can move beyond this terror. Understanding one's ordinary condition can enable one to be freed of it, and to attain liberation from suffering. Eventually, vipassana can uproot the false beliefs that fearfully deny the three marks. When no longer deluded by this ignorance, one can escape the control of greed, hatred and delusion. The thorough destruction of ignorance, which is the goal of vipassana, is achieved in the condition called NIRVANA.

Even after the meditator has refined vipassana to the point of clearly perceiving the three marks, however, there are pitfalls. The texts at this stage warn of a PSEUDO-NIRVANA. The practitioner might experience tremendous feelings of joy and peace and see visions of splendid light. If meditators become attached to these delightful experiences, they are again trapped in suffering; for wondrous meditative states also are impermanent. The experiences will end, leaving the meditator painfully yearning for their return.

Following the path of vipassana all the way to liberation is said to be the task of many lifetimes.

See also PRAJNA.

For further reading: Buddhaghosa; Goleman; Sopa.

vision   This term has been traditionally used in the West as a label for many types of unusual experience. In modern parlance, visionary phenomena would fall under such headings as HALLUCINATIONS, ILLUSIONS, OUT OF BODY EXPERIENCES, NEAR DEATH EXPERIENCES and APPARITIONS. The meanings and social impact of supranormal experiences, including visions, is largely determined by the framework of beliefs held by the culture in which they occur; care must therefore be taken not to lose the traditional significance of visions in modern interpretations.

Early orthodox Christianity inherited the tradition of BIBLICAL PROPHECY, which included belief in visions as possible communications with the divine. However, early heretics, particularly the Gnostics, cultivated visions. Based on their revelations, these groups promoted alternatives to the mainstream doctrines. Orthodoxy, therefore, was unable to reject all visions as false, because of Biblical precedent; at the same time, the subversive potential of visions to undermine the Catholic monopoly on spiritual authority had to be dealt with. The resultant tension surrounding reports of visions has characterized the Christian tradition for its entire existence.

Despite the suspicion in which visions were held, they continued to be reported throughout the pre-medieval Christian period by orthodox writers. The content of the visions was quite broad—figures of Christ and the saints, holy symbols such as the cross, angels and devils, heaven and hell. Frequently, sources do not specify whether the visionaries were asleep, in an ordinary waking state or some other state of consciousness. Whether the experients believed themselves to be inside or outside of their bodies at the time is often equally obscure. Most of the

visions were portrayed as occurring spontaneously—as the deliberate pursuit of such experiences smacked of heresy.

Several visionary events during the ancient
period influenced the development of Christian
belief. The demonic assaults on St. Anthony
established the notion that virtuous Christians
may be subjected to intimidation attempts by the
Evil One; the text known as the VISION OF PAUL
founded the tradition of using terrifying descriptions of sinners suffering in hell to encourage the
obedience of believers; and the vision of the
Roman Emperor Constantine may have ensured
the victory of Catholic Christianity over its heretical and pagan rivals.

The most important writer concerning visions
(and most other matters) in ancient Christianity
was the fifth century church leader St. Augustine. He discussed three categories of vision. In
the first, *corporeal vision,* one perceives the spiritual world *through* the ordinary sense of sight.
This type of vision seems to be a feeling of
appreciation evoked by seeing the beauty of
God's creation. The next type, called *spiritual* or
imaginative vision, involves the perception of
nonmaterial forms through mental imagery.
This category includes spiritual images occurring in God-sent dreams, as well as waking
visions. Augustine's final category, the *intellectual vision,* refers to the direct perception of
nonmaterial truths and beings, without mixing
them with sensory imagery, through the mind.
Each category of vision in this scheme was considered to be more spiritually advanced than the
preceding one.

In addition to Augustine, the pagan writer
Macrobius influenced later Christian thinking
concerning visions. Macrobius described five
kinds of visionary phenomena. Three of these
are types of dreams. The other two, the *visum*
(apparition) and the *visio* (prophetic vision),
occur during wakefulness. Macrobius defined
the visum as a mere figment of the seer's imagination, but the visio could be a true glimpse of
the future. All five of Macrobius' visionary types

fall within Augustine's category of imaginative
vision.

The most intense visionary activity in western
history occurred during the Middle Ages. Medi-
evalist Carolly Erickson has observed:

> The medieval past is full of visions. Extraordi-
> nary appearances—unusual natural configura-
> tions, visual portents, dream messages from the
> dead, divine and infernal warnings, intellectual
> illuminations, visions of the future—every-
> where complemented ordinary sight.

At the dawn of this era, in the seventh century,
Pope Gregory the Great published an important
collection of unusual experience reports. Visions
of the other world confirmed Gregory's teachings regarding the existence of purgatory, and
the need for virtuous living to avoid eternal
damnation. There is no way to determine if or
to what extent Gregory edited the reports to
conform to his doctrinal program. In his use of
vision stories to lend credence to orthodox
views, Gregory was careful not to encourage the
general acceptance of visions as valid revelations; most such experiences, he warned, are
illusions or a result of indigestion. Only holy
people, through "a certain inner awareness,"
can distinguish authentic visions from false ones.

In the later Middle Ages, important shifts
occurred in the content of Christian visions.
From the 12th century, there was a dramatic
increase in reports of MARIAN APPARITIONs, in
conjunction with the magnified role that the
Virgin Mary began to play in Catholic popular
devotion. Vision accounts by Catholic mystics,
carefully conforming to offical dogma, also
flourished, perhaps the best-known case being
that of HILDEGARD OF BINGEN. In addition, there
appears to be a rise in visions of evil spirits. At
this time, the early medieval optimism regarding
the continued triumph of Catholic Christian civilization was challenged by a series of events: the
emergence of powerful heretic movements like
the Cathars, the stresses of the Crusades and the
powerlessness of prayer against the Black Death

(bubonic plague). The anxieties of the age seem to be reflected in the tendency to interpret unusual visual and auditory phenomena in terms of demonic presences.

Kroll and Bachrach collected 134 vision reports from medieval sources. They found that only four were associated with indications of alcohol intoxication or modern criteria for mental illness. Of the remainder, 61 occurred while asleep, or in a HYPNAGOGIC STATE; 29 happened during physical illness; 15 were associated with intense stress; and 7 were linked with fasting or starvation. Eighteen cases seemed to happen in the absence of any identifiable triggering factors. In the Middle Ages, as in modern times, supranormal experiences frequently occurred to people who were not suffering from psychological disorders.

It is also noteworthy that, in Kroll and Bachrach's sample, only one case was viewed by the medieval chroniclers as indicating mental illness. The most heavily favored interpretation (in 126 cases) was contact with the divine or infernal realms, or PRECOGNITION. In six instances, the vision reports were regarded with skepticism. While there were no formal standards by which to sort true from false visions, reports by individuals of higher social status were generally granted more credence.

The most important visionary theorist of the later Middle Ages was Roger Bacon. He was a keen student of optics and used optical analogies to categorize the types of vision. We can perceive light in three ways, Bacon pointed out: by directly viewing the source; by refraction, when the light passes through an intervening medium; and by reflection, as in a mirror. The holiest people can have direct visions of spiritual truth; ordinary Christians may experience refracted or distorted images of the otherworld; while sinners can only see the world of the senses, which is a pale reflection of the divine reality.

The tendency to interpret visions as demonic activity rose to a tragic crescendo during the period of the Great Witch Hunt (15th through 17th centuries). The classical Christian world view and feudal social structure were shattered, to be replaced by the image of the world as a machine, as promoted by empirical science. There was no place in this clockwork universe for a domain of spirits; and, as this implication of the new world model became clear, the spiritual interpretation of visions began to be marginalized.

An important transitional figure in this regard was the 17th century philosopher Thomas Hobbes. He was a Christian and therefore retained a belief in a spiritual dimension. He was also a materialist; he held that all substances in the universe were composed of matter. As there was no such thing as a "spiritual substance" in Hobbes' world, the objects revealed in visions could not be substantial entities; rather, they were:

> nothing but supernatural apparitions of the fancy, raised by the special and extraordinary operation of God, thereby to make His presence and commandments known to mankind, and chiefly to His own people. (*The Leviathan*, 1651)

Later thinkers, such as Walter Scott in his *Letters on Demonology and Witchcraft* (1830), eliminated the "extraordinary operation of God" from the explanation of visions. The result was the modern understanding that visions are essentially hallucinations, without basis in substantial or spiritual reality, generally signaling the presence of a physical or mental disorder.

For further reading: Erickson; Kroll and Bachrach; Merkur; Pagels; Sarbin and Juhasz.

Vision of Paul   In a letter to the Christian community at Corinth, the first century religious leader St. Paul hinted about a vision he had experienced (2 Corinthians 12:1–4). Paul wrote that he had traveled "up into the third heaven," but refused to provide further details, stating that he had "heard things that cannot be told, which man may not utter." By the third century

A.D., however, a text was circulating that claimed to provide a more complete account of Paul's vision. According to legend, Paul buried this book, along with his shoes, in a marble box beneath his house in Tarsus. An angel revealed its existence to a pious man who dwelled in the house long after Paul's death.

The *Vision of Paul* (or *Apocalypse of Paul,* as the work was sometimes called), was originally composed in Greek. It was translated into Latin at an early date and was read throughout the Christian world. The text provides one of the earliest descriptions in Christian literature of the joys of heaven and the sufferings of hell. Paul recounts how sinners are judged after death and then cast into realms of eternal torment: some are suspended by their ears from flaming trees; others are immersed in a river teeming with piranha-like monsters; the worst sinners are sealed into a nightmarish pit, to choke forever from the foul stench.

Whether the imagery of the *Vision of Paul* was entirely fictional or was based on an experience cannot be determined today. St. Augustine denied the authenticity of the *Vision* on the grounds that it contradicted Paul's reticence in his New Testament letter. Modern scholars agree with Augustine that the text was not written by Paul. Nonetheless, early church leaders in general promoted the work as authentic; they had recognized that the "fire and brimstone" accounts of sinners' fates were effective tools for promoting piety, repentance and obedience among their followers. The *Vision* can be seen as the beginning of the Christian tradition of afterlife terror propaganda.

By the Middle Ages, the *Vision* had become enormously popular throughout Christian Europe. It was translated into many vernacular languages, including English, French, German, Welsh, Provencal, Danish, Bulgarian, Serbian and Romanian. The imagery of the *Vision* and its imitators was used by medieval individuals who had OUT OF BODY EXPERIENCEs to interpret these events. As a result, their accounts seemed to provide "eyewitness" corroboration of the *Vision*'s otherworld descriptions.

See also VISION.

For further reading: Zaleski.

vision quest   Practiced by many native groups in North America, a vision quest involves a solitary individual seeking contact with the spirit world. The quest may be undertaken for a variety of reasons: as part of an initiation into a new phase of life; to fulfill a vow; for healing; to acquire the relationships with the spirits necessary to become a SHAMAN; or to receive guidance about difficult personal decisions. In many cultures, but not all, the vision quest is an exclusively male activity.

A typical vision quest practice is the *hanbleceya* ("crying for a vision"), one of the Seven Sacred Rites of the Lakota tribe. After receiving instructions from a holy man, the seeker undergoes purification in a sweat lodge ceremony. He then retires to a pit dug on a hill or mountaintop, where he will remain in solitude for up to four days. During this time, the seeker fasts and calls to the spirits. The Lakota vision quest, like other such practices, uses physical deprivation and the anxiety of being alone to derail ordinary habits of perception. Thus the seeker is opened to sensing things in unusual ways. It is hoped that this altered state will yield a vision.

If the quest is successful, the seeker receives visions and other signs that a spirit is present. They may be taught songs, dances and symbols in order to recall the spirit when necessary in the future.

Not every quest ends in success. In some societies this is taken as a sign that the spirits have rejected the seeker; the purpose of the quest—healing, initiation, etc.—cannot be fulfilled. In others the vision quest can be repeated at another time.

Many vision quest sites across the continent were in use long before the arrival of the Europeans. Successful seekers would make paintings (pictographs) or carvings (petroglyphs) of their visions on rock surfaces at the site. In addition to humanoid shapes, visionary rock art contains a lot of geometric figures. Some researchers believe that these images depict entoptic phenomena—visual displays created by the nervous system under the impact of drugs or other stresses. The largest known accumulation of such visionary art can still be seen in what is now Writing-on-Stone Provincial Park in Alberta, where a quest site was in continuous use for at least 3,000 years. Members of the Shoshone, Sioux, Assiniboine, Gros Ventre and Blackfoot tribes would travel great distances in order to seek visions at this valley, which is filled with weirdly eroded sandstone forms.

A Christian parallel to the native North American vision quest can be found in the activities centered on St. Patrick's Purgatory, a cave on an island in Lough Derg, Ireland. From the 12th to the 18th centuries (when the cave was destroyed), pilgrims converged on this site from across Europe, "crying for a vision" in Christian terms. Pilgrims had to prepare through extensive praying and fasting; on arrival at the Purgatory, they lay in the cavern, imitating the state of death, while the appropriate rites for the dead were said over them by a priest. Then they were locked in the lightless space to continue their pilgrimage into the afterlife. Many reported meeting the saints, witnessing the torments of the damned and being purged of their own sins.

For further reading: Hirschfelder and Molin; Jilek; Zaleski.

visual hallucination In common parlance, visual hallucinations are "seeing things," mistaking visual images in the mind for perceptions of external reality. Visual hallucinations are the most common form of HALLUCINATION reported by normal people. Several studies have demonstrated that many individuals can produce visual imagery of nearly hallucinatory vividness in response to simple suggestions. Barber and Calverly instructed normal volunteers to visualize a cat sitting in their lap. Thirty-one percent reported seeing the cat; nearly 3% stated they believed the cat existed.

Among people with mental disorders, false visual perceptions are widespread. They are also typical responses to psychedelic drug ingestion. It is a modern assumption, unshared by most cultures and periods, that all visual sensations without corresponding physical objects must be false; in the pre-modern West, many VISIONs were held to be perceptions of nonphysical realities.

For further reading: Asaad; Barber and Calverly.

viveka-khyati "Vision of discernment" in Sanskrit, this term refers to a type of transformative experience discussed in the literature of RAJA YOGA. In this vision, the fundamental difference between the true nature of the self and that of everything else (including the contents of the mind—thoughts, feelings and images) is seen. When the self is not identified with the mental contents, it does not suffer from desire or fear. Viveka-khyati can occur in the highest stages of the meditative condition known as SAMPRAJNATA SAMADHI.

volcanic experiences Under the influence of psychedelic drugs, some people have reported a state characterized by intense ecstasy combined with an overwhelming sense of suffering. Grof named this state the volcanic experience. During the eruption of feeling, the body may react with sexual arousal, loss of sphincter control, nausea, hot flashes or chills, involuntary muscle twitches, breathing difficulties, pain or ringing in the ears. Visions can also occur. Naranjo listed the following visions as typical:

titanic battles, archetypal feats, explosions of atomic bombs, launching of missiles and spaceships, exploding volcanoes, earthquakes, tornadoes and other natural catastrophes, bloody revolutions, dangerous hunts for wild animals, discoveries and conquest of new continents.

Grof believed that the core of the volcanic experience is the dim memory of struggling through the birth canal. Although it may seem to be merely a BAD TRIP, this emotional upheaval can also signal the breakdown of outmoded habits and the emergence of a fresh new attitude.

For further reading: Grof; Naranjo.

voodoo death Term used by anthropologists to designate death in response to a seemingly nonphysical cause, such as a curse or the viola-tion of a taboo. Instances of lethal cursing have been observed among the Haitian adherents of the Voodoo religion, and the phenomenon is widespread; field workers have reported examples from traditional cultures of South America, Africa, Australia and New Zealand as well. Voodoo death is often thought to be caused by poisoning, by depriving the victim of life's necessities or by a psychophysiological mechanism—PSYCHOGENIC DEATH.

For further reading: Cannon; Davis (1988).

waking dream   A state of consciousness that has characteristics of both wakefulness and dreaming. Some researchers use the term as a synonym for LUCID DREAM, a dream in which one is aware that one is dreaming. Others refer to HALLUCINATIONs occurring in the transitions between sleep and wakefulness (the HYPNA-GOGIC and HYPNOPOMPIC states) as waking dreams.

Another type of waking dream is a state in which an awake person becomes highly absorbed in fantasy, and experiences the images appearing before the mind's eye as if they had a will of their own. Imagined figures that appear in this state can behave in unpredictable ways; they may even provide the waking dreamer with insights or advice concerning his or her problems. For this reason, some schools of psychotherapy encourage their clients to cultivate the ability to have waking dreams. This practice was called "active imagination" by the Swiss psychiatrist C. G. Jung, who learned of it while studying the texts of ALCHEMY and other occult traditions.

Green uses the term "waking dream" to refer to an experience in which a conscious person loses contact with the sensory world and enters a completely hallucinated world, without knowing it. She provided the following example:

> On arrival a lady in charge took us through the entrance hall, and opened a door on the far side, right on the banks of the river. As we stood in the afternoon sunshine, suddenly everything was black and rain seemed to be slanting down, and there was a small boat, and seven or eight figures in flapping black clothes, hurrying to get into the building—there was a great feeling of

fear. I was surprised to find shortly that I still stood in the afternoon sun.

Such profound invasions of imaginal material into ordinary awareness have received little attention from researchers, so the incidence of this type of waking dream is unknown.

See also METACHORIC EXPERIENCE.

For further reading: C. Green; Watkins.

water gun   Coastal dwellers around the world have periodically heard mysterious sounds, apparently emanating from some unseen occurrence offshore. These sounds are often described as muffled explosions. They can occur singly or in series. Nowadays, most hearers would think of sonic booms generated by aircraft. Reports of these auditory puzzles—collectively known as water guns, as they have frequently been compared to the sound of a detonating cannon—far predate the flight of any artificial objects capable of breaking the sound barrier, however.

Water guns are known by various names. The French call them *mistpouffers*—"fog dissipators." To the Italians, they are *marinas* or *brontidi*. The Japanese hear *uminari*. In localities that are prone to water gun reports, regional terms have arisen. The best known recurrent water gun phenomenon is the Barisal Guns. For over a century, residents and visitors of the Ganges Delta area have described explosive sounds of unknown origin which roll in over the water. The sound of the guns sometimes seems to arise over rivers; at other times, it comes from the open sea into which the arms of the delta drain. The quality of the noises ranges from deep, muffled booms to sharp reports comparable to pistol shots.

Inland lakes have also been home to water guns. Seneca Lake, one of the Finger Lakes in upstate New York, is the site of water guns that have been reported since records were first kept in the area; Indian legends concerning the sounds suggest that they may predate the arrival of Europeans. Lough Neagh in Northern Ireland is another location of recurrent water guns.

In some cases the mysterious sounds may simply be thunderclaps from distant storms. Distant thunder can be heard almost anywhere on earth; the clustering of water gun reports in certain locales suggests that another factor is at work. Many researchers have suggested that large bubbles of natural gas can leak from cavities in the submerged shelves rimming the continents; when these bubbles break the surface, they could ignite, causing the explosive sound of a water gun. Gas-bearing strata certainly exist beneath the oceans and are also found in lake bottoms. Oceanographers have found that the continental shelves are pocked with small craters, perhaps marking the exit of gas bubbles. No one has ever witnessed the eruption of such a bubble, however. How the bubbles would ignite on contact with the air still requires explanation.

See also AIRQUAKE; EARTH SOUND.

For further reading: Corliss (1983a).

will-o'-the-wisp These luminous bubbles and flames, seen at night in marshy regions, have proven so alluring yet impossible to grasp that their name has come to represent all manner of things enticing and unattainable. Records of their appearance date back to Roman times. Will-o'-the wisps take on a range of forms. Most common are flames, bluish or yellowish in hue. Some observers have noted hundreds of flames dancing above the ground. These lights can move vertically in a hopping motion, as if beckoning to the observer, and can also swoop and curve gracefully. Glowing balls that drift several feet in the air, sometimes merging or dividing, have also been seen. The movement of the luminous forms is unpredictable; they can disappear in one place and suddenly materialize in another, leading observers on a wild chase through the marsh.

Various meanings have accrued to will-o'-the-wisps through the centuries. Russians believed that the nocturnal lights were the souls of stillborn children; a widespread European view was that they were spirits who were too sinful for heaven but not evil enough for hell, condemned to wander lonely places of the earth bearing hot coals. A number of UFO ENCOUNTERS, including some of the famous wave of sightings in Michigan in 1966, have been attributed to will-o'-the-wisps.

No one has managed to produce a will-o'-the-wisp under laboratory conditions. As Corliss (1977) noted, "Serious scientific studies are nonexistent." Most commentators believe that the phenomenon is due to the combustion of gases emitted by decaying vegetable matter. The folklore that will-o'-the-wisps are omens of bad weather has been explained by the notion that changing barometric pressure prior to a storm forces the gases from the swampy soil.

One common gas of decay is methane. This substance, if ignited, can produce small, short-lived flames that could be carried a few feet by the wind before being extinguished. Burning methane gives off heat, however. People who have managed to pass their hand through a will-o'-the-wisp uniformly report no heat sensations. Also, it is unclear what feature of the swamp environment could ignite the methane, or how it could remain lit for long unless it were somehow prevented from dissipating in the air, and will-o'-the-wisps have been observed continuously for as long as 30 minutes.

Another swamp gas, phosphine, can combust spontaneously. But again, how mobile glowing forms of even short lived stability could be formed of a freely circulating gas is far from clear.

See also FOX FIRE; GHOST LIGHT; IGNIS FATUUS; PLASMA.

For further reading: Corliss (1977, 1982); Gaddis.

windshield pitting epidemic In 1954, a mysterious force seemed to be harassing the motorists of Seattle, Washington. Local newspapers had reported that small pits were suddenly and unaccountably appearing on car windshields. Thousands of car owners soon noticed the pits on their vehicles. Some people reacted to the news by covering their windshields with floor mats or newspapers; others refused to take their cars from their garages until the mystery was resolved. The mayor of Seattle appealed to the state governor, and then to President Eishenhower, for emergency action against the invisible menace.

Various theories were advanced. Most popular was the notion that radioactive fallout from nuclear testing in the Pacific Ocean was to blame. Some argued that the damage was caused by sand flea eggs hatching in the glass.

The University of Washington's Environmental Research Laboratory concluded, following an investigation, that there was no evidence for a force stalking the cars of Seattle. The pitfall in this case proved to be psychological—after reading the initial stories, which were groundless, people scrutinized their windshields with unusual care. Drivers who had never before noticed the tiny pits that normally occur in all windshields soon detected them and concluded that their vehicles must have encountered the strange force. They encouraged their friends to check their own windshields, who also made the shocking discovery.

The epidemic soon subsided, but for years afterward many people refused to believe that there had not been an increase in windshield damage during the episode. This case graphically illustrates the sort of social process that can generate waves of anomalous experience reports based on a shift in the attentiveness of the population, rather than the presence of anything novel in the environment.

See also GROUP DYNAMICS OF UNUSUAL EXPERIENCES.

For further reading: Medalia and Larsen.

witches' ointment The peasant culture of Europe possessed a rich and ancient lore concerning the properties of plants. Some historians believe that this lore included methods of producing a hallucinogenic ointment or salve. The records of the Great Witch Hunt, which spanned the 15th through 17th centuries, occasionally mention a "witches' ointment." This substance might have produced some of the reports of the WITCHES' SABBATH.

Some of those accused of witchcraft confessed that they rubbed themselves with an ointment prior to flying off to the sabbath. Harner even suggested that the famous broomstick which the witch was supposed to straddle while she flew actually served as an "applicator" for the ointment; the broom handle was anointed and then placed in contact with the vaginal tissues for effective absorption. The difficulty in relying on confessions extracted under torture is that the inquisitors might have expected to hear about the ointment and presented the victims with leading questions. Under the circumstances of the torture chamber, many people eagerly confirm anything they believe their tormentors want to hear.

Another line of evidence consists of accounts of individuals who actually demonstrated the effects of the ointment. Two records, from the 16th and 17th centuries, describe women who believed that they literally traveled through the air to the sabbath. In the presence of witnesses, they smeared the ointment on their naked bodies. They then fell into a convulsive trance state. Upon recovering, they reported the experience of flying and were surprised that the witnesses had not seen their bodies soaring in the sky!

Several recipes for the witches' ointment have been preserved. These contain plants such as DATURA, henbane, mandrake and belladonna, mixed with oil or fat to form a salve. These plants contain atropine, hyoscyamine and scopolamine, all of which are hallucinogens. Atropine can penetrate unbroken skin; the other psychoactive substances could have entered the body through skin lesions, which were possessed by virtually everyone of the time. One of the women who demonstrated the effects of her ointment preceded its application by vigorously massaging herself, which probably increased absorption.

In modern times a few brave souls have attempted to recreate the witches' ointment and have applied it to their own bodies. Kiesewetter (cited by Harner), after rubbing himself with the ointment, fell into a dream in which he was flying in spirals. Peukert (cited by Harner) anointed himself and some colleagues on the forehead and armpits. They reported "a twenty-four hour sleep in which they dreamed of wild rides, frenzied dancing, and other weird adventures of the type connected with medieval orgies." Schrenk (cited by Harner), after inhaling the smoke of henbane seeds, experienced "an intoxicating sensation of flying . . . I soared where my hallucinations—the clouds, the lowering sky, herds of beasts, falling leaves which were quite unlike any ordinary leaves, billowing streamers of steam and rivers of molten metal—were swirling along." These modern reconstructions of the witches' ointment, in combination with the expectations of the experimenters, seem able to produce experiences which could plausibly explain in part the lurid tales of the witches' sabbath.

Some members of the modern witchcraft movement have claimed that witches captured during the "Burning Times" were secretly given drugs by members of the witch cult, desensitizing them to the dreadful pain of being burned at the stake. There is, however, little historical evidence for the existence of an organized witchcraft movement during the persecution period; so this idea remains a speculation.

See also DRUGS.

For further reading: Barnett; Harner (1973a); Robbins.

witches' sabbath During the 15th through 17th centuries, western Europe (and, to a lesser extent, European colonies in North America) was caught up in the Great Witch Hunt. This mass persecution, in which hundreds of thousands were killed, was driven by the belief that an international conspiracy of devil worshippers who possessed magical powers were working to overthrow Christian society. A central theme of this belief was the notion that witches held weird nocturnal gatherings, known as sabbaths. Since the demise of the Witch Hunt, scholars have debated whether the witches' sabbath ever existed outside the paranoid imagination of the inquisitors.

The image of the witches' sabbath is composed of several elements. These include: the flight to and from the meeting (TRANSVECTION), often riding a domestic implement such as a broom; desecration of Christian symbols, such as trampling on a cross or conducting a parody of the Mass; the attendance of Satan, who would demand acts of worship such as being kissed beneath his tail; cannibalistic and orgiastic performances; and transformation into animal form.

The blasphemous and antisocial features of the sabbath closely resemble charges made by orthodox Christians against pagans and heretics since ancient times. Indeed, such accusations were originally made against the Christians themselves by the authorities in the pagan Roman Empire. This propaganda was known to the Renaissance witch hunters, who applied it to their new targets, those they suspected of belonging to the witch cult. By torturing their victims until the accusations, no matter how bizarre, were confirmed, the inquisitors received verification that the evil rites of the sabbath were being performed.

The elements of magical flight and transformation into an animal might have different origins. Ginzburg (1985, 1991) collected evidence for the fragmentary survival, into Renaissance times, of certain pre-Christian practices resembling SHAMANISM. He has suggested that these practices were discovered by the witch hunters and interpreted as features of the witches' sabbath.

As early as the tenth century, church lists of false beliefs to be eliminated refer to:

> certain wicked women who . . . insist that they ride at night on certain beasts together with Diana, goddess of the pagans, and a great multitude of women; that they cover great distances in the silence of the deepest night; that they obey the orders of the goddess as though she were their mistress; that on particular nights they are called to wait on her. (Regino of Prum)

Similar accounts can be found right up to the onset of the Witch Hunt. Ginzburg suspects that a subculture of women preserved an ancient tradition of inducing OUT OF BODY EXPERIENCEs in which they visited the moon goddess. This nocturnal flight could have been incorporated into the idea of the sabbath.

In the 16th century, witch hunters stumbled upon an unusual practice in a remote region of northern Italy. Groups of men periodically induced dreamlike states, in which they would assume the form of animals and fight against sorcerors who threatened the crops. This tradition, interpreted as Satanic by the guardians of Christian orthodoxy, might have been the source of the animal transformation motif in the sabbath image.

Several researchers have also suggested that psychedelic drugs could have played a part in the origin of the sabbath idea. There seems to have been in existence at the time of the persecutions a WITCHES' OINTMENT, capable of producing hallucinations. Perhaps the reports of attendance at the sabbath were sometimes accounts of psychedelic experiences. Many modern historians concur, however, that there never was a conspiracy of Satanists during the Renaissance/Reformation period; the persecution arose from the misplaced fears of the medieval order, as it was gradually undermined and replaced by the modern world view.

For further reading: Cohn; Ginzburg (1985, 1991); Robbins; Russell.

wraith Traditional term for an APPARITION of a person seen at the moment of death. In the classification system of apparitions used by many psychical researchers, wraiths are included in the category of "crisis apparitions."

X

xenoglossy A variant of GLOSSOLALIA, or "speaking in tongues," this term refers to cases in which a person speaks or writes in a language which they allegedly do not know. In Greek, *xeno* means "foreign," and *glossa* means "tongue." The word was coined by the psychical researcher Charles Richet. In 1905 he published a paper in which he reported on a woman who would enter a trancelike state and write passages in Greek, a tongue which she had apparently never learned.

Xenoglossy has been reported in a variety of contexts. Practitioners of Pentecostal tongue speaking sometimes claim that their utterances are ancient languages, or the "tongue of the angels." Spiritualist mediums have allegedly spoken in the languages of the discarnate spirits with whom they are said to be in contact. Contemporary channelers have made similar claims, including reports of speaking in the tongues of beings from other planets. Some people who have undergone a hypnotic PAST LIFE RECALL procedure have spoken in what has been taken to be a language with which they were familiar in a previous incarnation. As in Richet's case, most instances of xenoglossy have in common the entry of the utterer into an extraordinary state of consciousness, whether it be a ritual frenzy or mediumistic trance.

Two subtypes of xenoglossy are often distinguished: recitative xenoglossy, in which the individual produces speech or writing in the foreign language, but is unable to comprehend or interact using it; and responsive xenoglossy, in which the person is able to converse in the language.

One of the best known accounts of recitative xenoglossy was given by Flournoy (1963). In his book *From India to the Planet Mars*, Flournoy investigated the Swiss trance medium Helene Smith, who produced a range of puzzling speech and writing. Smith was able to write words and phrases in Sanskrit, Arabic and even in Martian, although in her ordinary state she could only speak French. The medium herself believed that her abilities were evidence of reincarnation and astral travel. Through careful investigation, Flournoy was able to establish with some likelihood that Smith had been exposed earlier in her life to the Sanskrit and Arabic material she produced. Her father had been fluent in eight languages, and books to which she had access contained foreign phrases and names that appeared in her utterances. In her trance productions, she retrieved the linguistic material from her memory, without recalling the sources of her knowledge—the phenomenon known as CRYPTOMNESIA. Flournoy also demonstrated that her "Martian" script was based on the language structure of French.

Cases of recitative xenoglossy can be very impressive and have often been advanced as evidence for spirit contact, past life memory or ESP. The possibility of cryptomnesia must be ruled out in order to support these more exotic hypotheses. It is almost impossible to establish that a xenoglossic has had no contact with the supposedly unknown tongue at any point in life, unless he or she has lived in extreme isolation.

Instances of responsive xenoglossy are more difficult to explain in terms of unremembered prior exposure to a language. Whereas a few foreign phrases can easily be learned through casual exposure and later parrotted, the level of fluency required to comprehend and converse in a language is not so easily acquired. Unfortunately, well authenticated reports of this phenomenon are extremely rare. Stevenson (1974, 1984) described several cases in which subjects seemed to be able to conduct simple conversations in consciously unknown languages. Stevenson performed exhaustive research into the subjects' backgrounds and found no opportunities for them to have acquired fluency.

Thomason, a linguist, reviewed two of Stevenson's responsive xenoglossy cases and was unimpressed. The conversations tended to be quite simple, if not fragmented. She also noted that the vocabularies of the xenoglossics were very limited and that wildly inappropriate utterances were common—for instance, answering "my wife" to a question about the cost of a supermarket item. Concerning the instances of appropriate responses in the consciously unknown tongue, Thomason observed that "Laymen may be startled to learn that people can guess right, quite often, about the meanings of things said to them in a language they don't know." She concluded that the level of language competency demonstrated in Stevenson's cases could have been learned through casual contacts with the language, augmented by some lucky guessing. Thus, responsive xenoglossy has not yet been convincingly demonstrated to the satisfaction of all.

See also XENOGRAPHY; XENOLALIA.

For further reading: Matlock; Stevenson (1974, 1984); Thomason (1991).

xenography A variant of XENOGLOSSY, xenography is the act of writing in a language that is supposedly unknown to the writer. Xenographic script is sometimes produced by mediums, or in instances of automatic writing. It is usually interpreted as evidence for contact with spirits or memory of previous lives. However, in most cases it is likely that the language was learned earlier in the writer's present life and then retrieved without awareness of its origin.

xenolalia From the Greek *xeno,* "foreign," and *lalia,* "speech," most writers view this term as a synonym of XENOGLOSSY; others define xenolalia as the general phenomenon of speaking or writing in a language unknown to the speaker, reserving the term xenoglossy for xenolalia occurring while the subject is hypnotized.

yaje This large climbing vine, found in the tropical rain forests of the Amazon Basin and adjacent regions, is the source of the most important psychedelic drug used by natives in South America. Lukoff, Zanger and Lu stated that yaje is "probably the most widely used hallucinogen in the world today." Yaje is the term by which the vine is known to the Tukano Indians. Other native words for it are common in anthropological literature, including Caapi, Natema, Mihi, Nixi Pae and Ayahuasca—"vine of the soul," a term suggesting its connection with experiences of the unseen world. Botanists call the vine Banisteriopsis and distinguish several species. When the bark of *Banisteriopsis caapi* or *Banisteriopsis inebrians* is boiled or soaked in cold water, the result is a drink containing the alkaloids harmine and harmaline, powerful hallucinogens.

Yaje has been used for its vision-inducing powers by the peoples of the western Amazon and Orinoco watersheds, as well as by groups on the Pacific coast of Colombia and Ecuador. The vine has served as a "chemical door" to the spirit world, as Harner (1973b) put it; the uses to which this access has been put are tremendously varied.

Reports of traditional yaje users, as well as those of research subjects from modern urban backgrounds who volunteered to ingest harmine, describe a range of typical effects. The onset of the experience can be profoundly unpleasant. The uncomfortable sensations may transform into a sense of freedom and contact with the spirit world. Taussig, an American anthropologist who took yaje during fieldwork in South America, noted:

taking yage is awful: the shaking, the vomiting, the nausea, the shitting, the tension. Yet it is a wonderful thing, awful and unstoppable. . . . In the excretions are vision. The stream of vomit, I had often been told, can become a snake. . . . In the streaming of nasal mucus, in the shitting, in the vomiting, in the laughter as in the tears, there lies a sorcery-centered religious mythology as lived experience, quite opposed to the awesome authority of Christianity in its dominant mode as a state religion of submission.

Foremost among the visual phenomena of yaje are vividly colored FORM CONSTANTs and HALLUCINATIONs. While the hallucinatory content is largely shaped by the culturally established expectations of the users, some themes seem to appear across cultures. Most striking are the common visions of large felines, such as jaguars. Reptiles, especially snakes, are also a widespread theme in yaje visions. The reasons for this pattern are unknown. Harner speculated that the creatures may be manifestations of drug-induced regression to an immature "oral aggressive" state, but why only Banisteriopsis ingestion would produce this condition is not explained. Alternatively, Harner wondered about the possible existence of "genetically based fear cues"— frightening mental images that might have helped forest dwellers avoid danger, and that may therefore have become naturally selected into the human genetic heritage. Yaje might act specifically to disinhibit the brain regions in which the fearful images are stored.

Another phenomenon commonly triggered by higher doses of yaje is OUT OF BODY EXPERIENCEs. They are usually interpreted as departures of the soul from the body. Apparitions of people, as well as a variety of creatures, are taken to indicate encounters with gods, demons, sorcerors and spirits of the dead.

These experiential features are often organized into the form of a journey. Among certain native groups, the yaje experience is literally called a "trip." This psychedelic voyage tends to feature extreme emotions, ranging from euphoria to terror. Typical is the report of a yaje user of the Peruvian Cashinahua people, as conveyed by Kensinger:

> We drank *nixi pae*. . . . Soon I began to shake all over. The earth shook. The wind blew and the trees swayed. . . . the *nixi pae* people began to appear. They had bows and arrows and wanted to shoot me. I was afraid but they told me their arrows would not kill me, only make me more drunk. . . . Snakes, large brightly colored snakes were crawling on the ground. They began to crawl all over me. One large female snake tried to swallow me, but since I was chanting she couldn't succeed. . . . I heard armadillo tail trumpets and then many frogs and toads singing. The world was transformed. Everything became bright. I moved very fast. Not my body but my eye spirit. . . . I saw lots of gardens full of manioc and plantains. The storage sheds were full of corn. The peanut racks were full. . . . I came down the trail to a village. there was much noise, the sound of people laughing. . . . Everybody was laughing. Many of the women were pregnant. I was happy. I knew we would be well and have plenty to eat.

The proximity to spiritual forces engendered by consuming yaje has been thought to grant supernatural knowledge and powers. The belief that one has psychic abilities while in the yaje state, enabling the finding of lost objects and foretelling the future, is widespread; indeed, biochemists Perrot and Raymond-Hamet, who first isolated the psychoactive substance in *Banisteriopsis*, dubbed it *telepathine* in honor of its divinatory reputation.

The vine of the soul has also been thought to grant knowledge of the causes of illness. Specialists with extensive yaje experience reportedly can control the effect of the drug on themselves to some extent; they are believed to acquire healing ability. In some cultures both healer and patient drink yaje; the patient has visions, which the healer interprets diagnostically. In other societies the healer consumes the vine, producing a clairvoyant perception of the patient's body. In a vivid passage, Harner described the contents of a Jivaro healer's vision:

> He had drunk [yaje, or Natema, as the Jivaro name it], and now he softly sang. Gradually, faint lines and forms began to appear in the darkness, and the shrill music of the *tsentsak*, the spirit helpers, arose around him. The power of the drink fed them. He called, and they came. First, *pangi*, the anaconda, coiled about his head, transmuted into a crown of gold. Then *wampang*, the giant butterfly, hovered above his shoulder and sang to him with its wings. Snakes, spiders, birds and bats danced in the air above him. On his arms appeared a thousand eyes as his demon helpers emerged to search the night for enemies.
>
> The sound of rushing water filled his ears, and listening to its roar, he knew he possessed the power of *Tsungi*, the first shaman. Now he could see. Now he could find the truth. He stared at the stomach of the sick man. Slowly, it became transparent like a shallow mountain stream, and he saw within it, coiling and uncoiling, *makanchi*, the poisonous serpent, who had been sent by the enemy shaman. The real cause of the illness had been found.

Hunters have also reportedly harnessed the powers of yaje. Hunters among the Amahuaca studied the movements of the visionary animals they saw in the drugged state, in order to enhance their sensitivity to the animals' habits during actual hunting expeditions. Low doses are sometimes consumed during a hunt; the drug causes dilation of the pupils, enabling hunters to see better in dimly lit conditions. The Tukano say that jaguars have been observed gnawing Banisteriopsis vines, prompting Siegel (1989) to suggest that even non-human predators may have discovered the value of yaje's sense enhancing effects.

For further reading: Dobkin de Rios; Harner (1973b); Kensinger; Lukoff, Zanger and Lu; Schultes and Hofmann; Stafford; Taussig.

yeti Traditional name for a hairy humanoid, featured in Asian folklore and occasionally reported wandering in the Himalayas.

See also CRYPTIC; HUMANOIDS, ANOMALOUS.

yidam In the Buddhist meditation practice called SADHANA, the meditator first visualizes and then merges with the image of a deity. This deity-image is known as a yidam, which literally means "firm mind" in Tibetan. A tremendous range of yidams, embodying aspects of the enlightened personality, are depicted in Tibetan art. There are three major types—peaceful, semi-wrathful and wrathful. These images are also said to occur in the BARDO state following death.

yoga This Sanskrit term is closely related to the English word "yoke" and has a similar meaning. An animal is yoked to a plough in order to accomplish work; a practitioner of yoga takes on a disciplined lifestyle, involving meditation and other exercises, in order to accomplish a profound transformation of consciousness. "Yoga" is a generic term, referring to the spiritual disciplines of Hinduism and Buddhism.

This word also has more specific meanings. Hindu philosophy is divided into six schools, one of which is called "Yoga." This type of yoga is also known as RAJA YOGA, or "royal yoga." Raja Yoga utilizes a range of meditation practices in order to help the yogi become aware of his or her true nature and thus attain liberation from suffering. Various versions of Hindu Yoga understand liberation differently.

Classic Hindu Yoga, as summarized by Patanjali, is dualistic—it divides the universe into two irreducible components. One component consists of the *purusas,* or selves, of each person. The self is pure awareness. The rest of the universe is made of matter. Even thoughts, feelings and mental images are classified as material. Patanjali's Yoga aims to disentangle the individual's self from the mental processes and objects with which it is confused. When we stop identifying ourselves (literally, our selves) with our limited self *concepts,* we attain self-realization and freedom. Classic Yoga is quite similar to another Hindu philosophical school called Sankhya.

Other branches of the Hindu Yoga school are *nondualistic.* Unlike Classic Yoga, they do not view the world as composed of two different kinds of existence. Rather, the diversity of objects and persons that appears in ordinary experience is considered to be an illusion. Awakening from the illusion of diversity into the realization that one's self is not different from the self of the entire universe is the aim of nondualistic Yoga. This version of the yoga philosophy is closely related to another Hindu school, Advaita Vedanta.

In the West, the best known type of yoga is Hatha Yoga, which derives from the Hindu Yoga school. In Hatha ("forceful") Yoga, emphasis is placed on practicing body postures, breath control and various cleansing procedures. Frequently, these exercises are performed merely to promote physical health. Hatha Yoga practices can also be used, in conjunction with meditation, to prepare the body to serve as a foundation for self-realization. When the physical body is relaxed and flexible, and the "psychic" body said to be associated with the breath is in harmony, meditation is said to be more effective in producing liberative insights.

Deliberate alterations in breathing (*pranayama*), used by many yoga schools, should only be practiced under the supervision of an expert in these techniques. Incorrect practice of certain exercises can cause anoxia, or oxygen deprivation. While the anoxic condition can produce some interesting alterations of consciousness, severe anoxia can also lead to brain damage and even death.

For further reading: Feuerstein (1989, 1990).

zazen In Japanese, *za* refers to sitting, and *zen* to a concentrated mind; hence, zazen is literally the meditative practice of sitting with focused attention. The term refers to the range of meditations practiced by Zen Buddhists, from KOAN to SHIKAN-TAZA. However, unlike many other types of meditation, the aim of zazen is not to concentrate the mind on a specific object, but to point the mind toward liberation from all mental habits. Zen master Kapleau noted that:

> The uniqueness of zazen lies in this: that the mind is freed from bondage to *all* thought-forms, visions, objects, and imaginings, however sacred or elevating, and brought to a state of absolute emptiness, from which alone it may one day perceive its own true nature, or the nature of the universe.

Beginners at zazen may indeed concentrate on an object or activity, such as breathing. Novices in koan practice often meditate on the koan as if it was external to them. These activities are only preparatory, however; in true zazen there is no sense of a meditation object distinct from the meditator. Discursive thinking is quieted. The universe is no longer carved into one portion called "I" and another called "not-I." The mind becomes stilled, like a clear pool of water. According to Zen teachings, the meditator then has a chance to perceive the reality that lies beyond the ordinary dualistic awareness. The direct perception of one's true nature which is said to arise from zazen practice is called KENSHO or SATORI.

Advanced zazen meditators do not have to be literally sitting in order to practice. The state of still absorption in the nondual state, first attained during formal meditation practice, eventually becomes continuous. Zazen does not produce paralysis—it is claimed that a master can do zazen while engaged in any activity. It is clear that the "emptiness" experienced in zazen is not merely a blank mind; otherwise, directed actions would be impossible.

In a classic study Kasamatsu and Hirai examined the relationship between EEG (brain wave) activity and zazen. They reported that progress in zazen (as evaluated by a Zen master) was correlated with the presence and amplitude of alpha waves (9–11 Hertz). Advanced practitioners also produced trains of theta waves (6–7 Hertz). The significance of these results is unclear; they might indicate deepened relaxation. The researchers also monitored the effects of a repeated auditory stimulus (a clicking sound) on the meditators. The EEG records of the less experienced practitioners revealed that, after several presentations of the stimulus, they became habituated to it and no longer attended to it. The advanced zazen meditators showed no evidence of habituation—they reacted to each presentation of the click as if it was a novel stimulus. This finding is consistent with the claim that zazen liberates the mind from habitual response patterns, preserving the "fresh" quality of every moment.

See also EMPTINESS.

For further reading Kapleau; Kasamatsu and Hirai; Sekida.

Zeitoun apparitions The sightings of the Blessed Virgin Mary that took place in Zeitoun, Egypt, comprise "the most spectacular and important series of Marian apparitions documented in modern times," according to Rogo. The number of witnesses, conservatively estimated at over 200,000 and perhaps much higher, is indeed impressive. The Zeitoun case raises the question of whether mass consensus can be used to validate the literal reality of an unusual experience report. In other words, if hundreds of thousands claim they saw the Virgin Mary, can they all be wrong?

Zeitoun is a suburb of Cairo. Legend has it that Mary and Joseph visited the place during their stay in Egypt, while fleeing Herod's order to kill all firstborn Jewish children. A church dedicated to Mary is located in Zeitoun. The land on which the building was constructed was donated for that purpose in 1920, following a dream by the landowner in which the Virgin urged him to erect a church. Upon completion of the structure, Mary again came to him in a dream and promised to appear at the church. St. Mary's Church in Zeitoun was the site of the subsequent apparitions.

One evening in 1968, two men who worked across the street from the church noticed something unusual on the church's dome. They thought they saw the figure of a woman, concluded that someone had climbed onto the roof and was going to commit suicide and called the police. A crowd assembled. The police felt that the form was merely the reflection of a streetlight on the dome, but the church custodian suggested that it was the awaited appearance of the Virgin. The crowd, apparently, was inclined to accept the custodian's view. The figure vanished shortly afterward.

Word of the apparition spread quickly. Every evening, throngs would gather to watch the church. A week after the initial sighting, a luminous form was again seen near the dome, plainly visible to everyone present. Over the next three years, mysterious light phenomena continued to appear around or above the church. These occurrences seemed unpredictable; at their peak, they would happen two or three times a week. Their frequency dropped in 1970 and stopped entirely in 1971.

As news of the Marian apparition circulated, the number of witnesses soared. On some eve-nings, there were upwards of 100,000 people clogging the streets around the church, straining for a glimpse of Mary. City officials tore down some nearby buildings to increase the viewing space.

The Virgin would first appear as a bright flash in the vicinity of the dome. Rogo noted that "the apparition would at first appear somewhat amorphous, but would eventually form into a more defined human shape." On many occasions, swirling luminous specks, dubbed "doves of light" by witnesses, could be observed. Sometimes, the dome itself glowed. The color of these effects was white, or bluish-white. The account of Bishop Samuel (quoted by Rogo) is typical of the experiences at Zeitoun:

> At 2:45 in the morning the Blessed Virgin Mary appeared in a complete luminous body as a radiant phosphorescent statue. After a short while the apparition vanished. It reappeared at four o'clock and remained until five o'clock—dawn. The scene was overwhelming and magnificent. The apparition walked toward the west, sometimes moving its hands in blessing, and sometimes bowing repeatedly. A halo of light surrounded its head. I saw some glittering beings around the apparition. They looked like stars, rather blue in color.

The apparitions at Zeitoun were photographed by many witnesses. These photographs typically show a luminous, vertically aligned ellipse of light, with a luminous spherical region at the top; the church dome is visible in the background.

The photographs seem to establish that some sort of visual stimulus was present atop the Church of St. Mary during the sightings. Those inclined toward paranormal explanations might suspect that the stimulus was the Blessed Virgin herself, or, following Rogo, a "pool of psychic energy" created by the anticipation of Zeitoun's citizens. Derr and Persinger reported that the appearances of the apparition were positively correlated with episodes of seismic disturbance in the region. Under certain conditions, such vibrations may be capable of ionizing the air, creating short-lived, luminous PLASMAS.

Even if some natural events produced light phenomena around the dome of the church, the question remains as to why many witnesses saw, in some detail, an image of Mary "blessing" and "bowing" to the crowd. A clue may be found in the account of Cynthia Nelson, a social scientist who visited Zeitoun during the occurrences:

> When I looked to where the crowds were pointing, I too, thought I saw a light . . . as I tried to picture a nunlike figure . . . I could trace the outlines of [this] figure. But as I thought to myself that this is just an illusion . . . the image of the nun would leave my field of vision.

Evidently, Nelson was confronted by an ambiguous stimulus, which changed its appearance in response to suggestions she made to herself. It seems quite likely that if others viewing the stimulus expected or believed that it was Mary, their expectations would shape their perceptions accordingly. After the first evening of sightings in 1968, it is safe to assume that very few people would have gone to see the phenomena in Zeitoun without knowing the commonly assumed identity of the apparition.

There is no reason why this mechanism could not affect hundreds of thousands of people, causing them to see a strange light as a haloed woman. The nature of the stimulus responsible for the events at Zeitoun, however, remains a mystery.

See also GEOPHYSICAL INFLUENCES; MARIAN APPARITION.

For further reading: Bayless (1981); Carroll; C. Nelson; Nickell; Rogo; Zimdars-Swartz.

zembyo This Japanese term literally means "Zen sickness." It has several possible meanings in Zen Buddhism.

If a meditator becomes attached to MAKYO— the illusory sensations that sometimes arise during meditation practice—and devotes oneself to seeking such experiences, this is zembyo. It is a sickness because the meditator has lost sight of the true goal of Zen, the attainment of ENLIGHTENMENT.

Zembyo is sometimes used as a synonym for GOSEKI—the strained, self-conscious behavior that can occur after an ENLIGHTENMENT experience.

Zembyo also refers to certain behaviors that can occur following a spiritual awakening (KENSHO). A more severe kind of Zen sickness is attributed to a disruption of the flow of psychic energies within the body, caused by the shock of awakening to one's buddha-nature. Individuals suffering from Zen sickness find themselves seized by uncontrollable urges to behave in bizarre ways—dancing, waving the arms, humming and shouting. As the spiritual insight is integrated into a person's understanding of life, the symptoms may subside. It is said that the famous seventh century Chinese Ch'an (Zen) master Han Shan, was gripped by zembyo following a spiritual breakthrough. He was able to end his compulsive behaviors only after sitting in unbroken meditation for five days and nights.

For further reading: Kapleau.

zengo Japanese term meaning "gradual enlightenment." The belief that spiritual awakening occurs in a long series of stages, accompanied by much study of Buddhist scriptures, was held by the Zen Buddhist schools that arose in northern China. Most Zen teachers today hold another perspective—that of TONGO, or sudden ENLIGHTENMENT.

zero experience This term was coined by Bharati to refer to a type of MYSTICAL EXPERIENCE. In the zero experience, all thought and sensation temporarily cease. There may be a feeling of joy, or no feeling at all. One is still conscious, but awareness is totally devoid of content. Bharati described his own zero experience:

One night when I was about twelve, it happened for the first time. I was falling asleep, when the whole world turned into one: one entity, one indivisible certainty. No euphoria, no colours, just a deadeningly sure oneness of which I was the center—and everything else was just this, and nothing else. For a fraction of a minute, perhaps, I saw nothing, felt nothing, but was that oneness, empty of content and feeling. Then, for another five minutes or so the wall with the kitschy flowers reappeared, and the fire crackled in the large brick stove. But I knew it was One. . . . Then after some time, no longer than half an hour I would think, things returned to whatever had been normal before.

Although Bharati writes of "oneness" in this passage, he emphasized that this was an interpretation of the experience that he made afterward. During the zero experience itself, he had no thought of oneness, or of anything else. Some scholars have argued that awareness without content is impossible—awareness is always awareness of something. Others, based on experiences such as Bharati's, believe that consciousness is distinct from its contents and can exist independently of them.

See also NIRODHA.

For further reading: Bharati (1976); Spilka, Hood and Gorsuch.

zeteticism A skeptical approach to the study of supranormal experiences. The zetetic examines the evidence with an open mind and questions all viewpoints; at the same time, his or her own biases are kept in check, so as not to distort the process of inquiry. When confronted with a puzzle, the mind struggles to make sense of it in familiar terms; believers or disbelievers in the paranormal tend to interpret anomalies in terms that support their intellectual and emotional commitments. Zeteticism requires that the prejudices of belief *and* disbelief be set aside, so the phenomena can be examined clearly. The zetetic approach is much admired and simulated, but in fact is very difficult to maintain.

The term has been promoted by American sociologist Marcello Truzzi, who borrowed it from an ancient Greek school of SKEPTICISM. He was the editor of the first journal published by the Committee for the Scientific Study of Claims of the Paranormal (CSICOP), called the *Zetetic*. After publishing two issues, Truzzi resigned as editor and quit CSICOP, charging that the committee was more interested in attacking paranormal claims than dispassionately examining them. He went on to edit *Zetetic Scholar*, an irregularly published journal that provides a forum for debate and dialogue concerning anomalous experiences.

See also BELIEF, ANOMALOUS; SCIENTISM.

For further reading: Truzzi.

zoanthropy Greek for "animal-man," this is a variant term for the belief that one has been transformed into an animal, more commonly called LYCANTHROPY.

zombification The origin of the word "zombie" is uncertain. Davis contends that the term derives from *nzambi*, a word in the Kongo language of Africa that means "spirit of the dead." Although the figure of the zombie has become a familiar image in horror fiction, Davis and other researchers believe that zombification—the process of turning someone into a zombie—is a reality, albeit a misunderstood one.

Zombification appears to be a combination of cultural expectations and the effects of psychoactive drugs. The cultural context is the Haitian religion known as Voodoo or Vodoun. In the Voodoo world view, each person is made of five components. These are: the *corps cadavre,* or physical body; the *n'ame,* which holds the body together; the *gros bon ange,* the life force that animates the body; the *ti bon ange,* or individual soul; and the *z'etoile,* one's personal star of destiny. The ti bon ange is rather easily detached from the body—it leaves the body when one is dreaming and even, momentarily, when one is startled. If a sorceror can capture a person's ti bon ange, that person falls under the sorceror's magical control. If someone fears that he or she has been targetted by a sorceror, a *houngan* or Voodoo priest can be asked to protect the ti bon ange by placing it in a jar, which is stored in the temple.

When someone dies, the components are unravelled: the n'ame seeps into the earth; the gros bon ange merges with the universal life force; the ti bon ange hovers near the body for seven days, before departing for the spirit world; the z'etoile remains in the sky, storing the person's destiny for future incarnations; and the corps cadavre, deprived of the form-giving n'ame and the life-sustaining gros bon ange, rots. Followers of Voodoo believe that the process can be disrupted by a sorceror, who can capture the ti bon ange that is rendered vulnerable at this time. The enslaved ti bon ange is called the *zombi astral*—it can materialize as an animal, a swarm of insects or even a human, and carries out the will of the sorceror. Sometimes, it is also possible to create a *zombi cadavre*—the reanimated body, risen from the grave and controlled by the possessor of the ti bon ange.

Those chosen for zombification are usually people who have violated the customs or laws of the community. Thus, the practice can be seen to serve a valuable social function of maintaining community order. In order to become a zombie, the person must die an unnatural death. Frequently, this event is brought about by the administration of "zombie powder," prepared by the sorceror. The powder must make contact with the victim's skin. Various accounts indicate that it can be blown on the victim, deposited in shoes, or sprinkled on the ground where he or she will walk in bare feet.

Many researchers have suggested that the zombie powder contains a poison that can paralyze the victim and mimick the signs of death. The victim could then be buried alive, to be disinterred and enslaved by the sorceror. Davis collected and analyzed several recipes for the zombie powder during his field work in Haiti.

His analyses lend credence to this bizarre possibility.

Davis found that the recipes were mixtures of a variety of substances, many of which are biologically active. From a pharmacological standpoint, the most interesting ingredients are the porcupine fish, the puffer fish and the toad called *Bufo marinus*. The fish contain the highly toxic chemical called tetrodotoxin. This substance is capable of producing complete paralysis persisting for days, as well as the suppression of easily detectable life signs, without loss of consciousness. In Japan, some who have consumed the puffer fish and succumbed to "fugu poisoning" have been pronounced dead, only to recover shortly before burial. The toad contains a poison that gives a bluish tinge to the skin, simulating the pallor of death. It is plausible that someone administered the zombie powder could be mistaken for dead, interred, and survive for some time in the grave.

When the body of the intended zombie is dug up by the sorceror, it is severely beaten. The violence is intended to prevent the ti bon ange from re-entering the body, but it may also serve to rouse the drugged individual who has just spent hours, paralyzed and aware, in a buried coffin. Then, the victim is forced to consume a plant known in Haiti as the "zombi cucumber." Botanists know it as *Datura stramonium,* a member of the genus DATURA, notorious for its powerful psychoactive properties. Ingestion of datura can cause confusion, hallucinations and memory disturbances leading to amnesia.

After surviving the ordeal of being marked for zombification, "dying" from the zombie powder, experiencing one's funeral and burial, being disinterred by the sorceror and plummetted into the hellish whirl of the datura experience, a member of a culture that believes in zombies might well be convinced that he or she has indeed been zombified. As long as the sorceror and the "zombie cadavre" both believe that the ti bon ange is in the sorceror's possession, the victim may feel compelled to obey. Usually, it is said that zombies are put to work in the fields, far from their home village. They are not generally regarded as dangerous—the fear of *becoming* a zombie is great, however.

Zombification has never been demonstrated under controlled conditions (and who would volunteer for such a study?). Researchers have identified and interviewed a few Haitians who are believed to be *zombies savannes,* or former zombies, who somehow escaped from the spell of expectation that compelled them to serve the sorceror. In some cases death certificates and burial records exist for these people. Davis interviewed one such person—Clairvius Narcisse. This informant reported that a sorceror had sprinkled zombie powder in his doorway. After walking on the powder with bare feet, he recounted:

> Before he died he said that his skin had come on fire, with the feeling of insects crawling beneath it. A scar he bore on his right cheek just to the edge of his mouth had been caused by a nail driven through the coffin. Quite incredibly he recalled remaining conscious throughout his ordeal, and although completely immobilised he had heard his sister weeping by his deathbed. He remembered his doctor pronouncing him dead. Both at and after his burial his overall sensation was that of floating above the grave. This was his soul [ti bon ange], he claimed, ready to travel on a journey that would be curtailed by the arrival of the bokor [sorceror] and his assistants... They called his name and the ground opened. He heard drums, a pounding, a vibration and then the bokor singing. He could barely see. They grabbed him, and began to beat him with a sisal whip. They tied him with a rope and wrapped his body in black cloth... Travelling by day and hiding out by night... he reached the sugar plantation that would be his home for two years.

See also POSSESSION; PSYCHOGENIC DEATH.
For further reading: Davis (1986, 1988).

Appendix

*Correlates of Supranormal Phenomena
and Anomalous Beliefs*

Phenomena of the sort described in this book are not experienced only by those with mental or neurological disorders. In fact, they seem to be part of the normal range of life experience for many ordinary people. Within the general population, however, it has become evident that some people are more likely to have such unusual experiences than others. Similarly, belief in paranormal and other anomalous phenomena is not uniform in the population. Research on these puzzles is in its infancy, but certain patterns are beginning to emerge. In the tables that follow, I provide entry points to the burgeoning research literature on the correlates of supranormal phenomena and anomalous beliefs.

I have tried to include all of the major recent studies on these topics. However, the tables should be taken as overviews, rather than exhaustive presentations. New studies are appearing regularly, so the reader who wishes to be up to date should scan reference materials such as *Psychological Abstracts* for relevant material that has entered the literature since the publication of the present volume.

In order to be a sophisticated consumer of scientific research, the reader should bear in mind the following points when studying the tables:

1. Correlation does not prove causation. The research projects noted in the tables all belong to a class of research called the "correlational study." In this type of study, two (or more) phenomena of interest are measured—for instance, belief in the reality of ESP and hypnotizability. The measured phenomena are known as "variables." Statistical analyses are conducted to determine whether there is evidence for a relationship between the variables. When two variables are said to be "correlated," this simply means that there is some relationship between the changes observed in one variable and those in another. In *positive* correlation, there is a tendency for high values of one variable to be associated with high values of the other; in *negative* correlation, increasing values of one variable are associated with decreasing values of the other. For example, studies have noted a positive correlation between psi experiences and hypnotizability—people who report psi experiences are more likely to be highly hypnotizable than those who do not report psi experiences. The existence of a correlation in this example suggests that there is some type of causal relation between psi experiences and hypnotizability; but correlational data alone cannot reveal its nature. Perhaps hypnotizability causes people to be more sensitive to psi; or, perhaps psi experiences cause people to be more responsive to hypnosis; or, maybe a third factor—the level of some brain chemical, say—is influencing both hypnotizability and the tendency to have psi experiences. In order to determine which of these possibilities is correct, *experimental* research has to be done. In an experiment, one variable (designated the *independent variable*) is manipulated by the experimenter, and changes in the other variable (known as the *dependent variable*) are measured. If variations in the independent variable are reflected in the behavior of the dependent variable, this finding supports the idea of a cause-and-effect influence moving from the independent to the dependent variable. Experimental studies have rarely been done with respect to the correlates of unusual experiences and anomalous beliefs. Therefore, we are left with correlations and cannot speak with certainty about the nature of the relations between the variables.

2. *Beware of intercorrelations.* Several of the correlates in the table are themselves correlated. For example, absorption is positively correlated with hypnotizability. Both of these variables are positively correlated with a tendency to report OBEs. Without further statistical analysis, it is impossible to state whether the correlation of absorption and OBEs represents a true relationship between these variables, or

whether it is merely a statistical "shadow" cast by a true relationship that exists between hypnotizability and OBEs. Conversely, the hypnotizability–OBE correlation could be the shadow and the absorption–OBE correlation the true relationship. Statistical tools can be used to disentangle these possibilities, but they have not often been applied in the correlational studies listed below.

3. *Beware of inconsistent definitions and conditions between studies.* The summarized studies used a number of different questionnaires and other instruments to measure the variables. Furthermore, the studies were conducted in various countries, with various types of people as subjects. This variation can complicate the search for patterns in research results. For instance, the variables of absorption, fantasy proneness and hypnotizability have been defined and measured somewhat differently by different researchers and understood differently by subjects in the various countries. Some researchers have virtually equated these three factors; others have viewed them as distinct but related. Similarly, "global belief in the paranormal" and "belief in psi" are sometimes hard to distinguish. For some researchers, "psi" specifically means "ESP and PK"; for others, psi is a general term encompassing ghosts, auras and other oddities. Sometimes, differences in the results of studies may reflect inconsistencies in definition, measurement and culture, instead of telling us something about the correlational variables themselves.

4. *Don't take single studies too seriously.* Scientific research of any kind is a frail enterprise. Errors in the collection and analysis of data occur frequently, and might not be detectable in the published account of the research. Furthermore, significant correlations sometimes are just coincidental. Therefore, any findings reported by only one study must be regarded as very tentative. If several studies find the same correlation between variables, one can be more confident that a relationship exists. So few stud-

ies have been done on the correlates of unusual experiences and beliefs that most of the reported findings cannot yet be accepted with confidence.

The tables that follow include only studies that have reported significant correlations. I have not included in this Appendix studies that failed to find correlations between the measured variables. Negative findings and other important details are discussed in the entries on each correlate and type of unusual experience or belief. The serious student should consult the relevant entries, including "Experiences, Unusual" and "Beliefs, Anomalous," and read the original studies. I urge anyone examining the correlates of anomalous beliefs to study the excellent comprehensive review on this topic by Irwin (1993).

In Table One, the following acronyms are used to designate types of unusual experience:

GLB (global; in these studies, the correlates of unusual experiences in general are noted)
PSI (psi experiences, including ESP and PK)
OBE (out of body experiences)

MEX (mystical experiences)
SPI (experiences customarily regarded as encounters with spirits, such as apparition sightings and seance phenomena)
LUC (lucid dreams)
NDE (near death experiences)
AUR (auras seen around the body; *not* the visual distortions reported prior to epileptic seizures and migraines, also known as auras)
REI (reincarnation memories)
UFO (encounters with UFOs)
DIA (diabolical experiences)

The numbers in the table indicate the study's place in the list of studies following it; citations are given in full in the Bibliography. Unless otherwise indicated, studies found significant positive correlations between the variables (a minus sign indicates a negative correlation; a "u" indicates a U-shaped correlation). Regarding the variable of gender, "m" signifies that the correlation applies to males only; and "f" means the same for females only.

TABLE ONE: CORRELATIONS WITH UNUSUAL EXPERIENCE REPORTS

EXPERIENCE TYPE: CORRELATE	GLB	PSI	OBE	MEX	SPI	LUC	NDE	AUR	REI	UFO	DIA
Biology											
Gender					f1		m2				
Temporal Lobe Abnormality	3	4			5						
History											
Childhood Trauma							6			7	
Childhood Alternate Realities			8				9			10	
Drug Use History	11										
Head Injury		12		13	14						

Experience Type: Correlate	GLB	PSI	OBE	MEX	SPI	LUC	NDE	AUR	REI	UFO	DIA
Traits											
Absorbtion	15	16	17	18	19		20				21
Fantasy-Proneness	22		23		24		25				
Hypnotizability	26	27	28	29		30		31	32		33
Tolerance of Ambiguity				34							
Conformity	u35			−36							
Psychological Adjustment					37						−38
Emotional Arousal	39										
Unlikely Virtues	u40										
Sensation Seeking	41										
Magical Thinking					42						
Anomalistic Beliefs					SEE TABLE TWO						

STUDIES ON CORRELATES OF UNUSUAL EXPERIENCE

1. **SPI X GENDER**
   Pekala, Kumar and Cummings (1992)
2. **NDE X GENDER**
   Pekala, Kumar and Cummings (1992)
3. **GLB X TEMPORAL LOBE ABNORMALITY**
   G.K. Nelson (1970)
   G.K. Nelson and Neppe (1980)
   Neppe (1983a)
   Neppe (1983b)
   Persinger (1984)
   Persinger and Makarec (1987)
   Persinger (1988a)
   Persinger (1988b)
4. **PSI X TEMPORAL LOBE ABNORMALITY**
   Fenwick et. al (1985)
5. **SPI X TEMPORAL LOBE ABNORMALITY**
   Fenwick et. al (1985)

Lavallee and Persinger (1992)
G.K. Nelson (1970)
G.K. Nelson and Neppe (1980)
6. **NDE X CHILDHOOD TRAUMA**
   Ring (1992)
7. **UFO X CHILDHOOD TRAUMA**
   Ring (1992)
8. **OBE X CHILDHOOD ALTERNATE REALITIES**
   Stanford (1987)
9. **NDE X CHILDHOOD ALTERNATE REALITIES**
   Ring (1992)
10. **UFO X CHILDHOOD ALTERNATE REALITIES**
    Ring (1992)

11. **GLB X DRUG USE HISTORY**
Kumar, Pekala and Cummings (in press)
12. **PSI X HEAD INJURY**
Fenwick et. al (1985)
13. **MEX X HEAD INJURY**
Fenwick et. al (1985)
14. **SPI X HEAD INJURY**
Fenwick et. al (1985)
15. **GLB X ABSORPTION**
Nadon and Kihlstrom (1987)
P.L. Nelson (1989)
16. **PSI X ABSORPTION**
Irwin (1985b)
Palmer and van der Velden (1983)
17. **OBE X ABSORPTION**
Irwin (1981)
Irwin (1985a)
Myers et. al (1983)
18. **MEX X ABSORPTION**
Spanos and Moretti (1988)
19. **SPI X ABSORPTION**
Irwin (1985b)
20. **NDE X ABSORPTION**
Twemlow and Gabbard (1984)
21. **DIA X ABSORPTION**
Spanos and Moretti (1988)
22. **GLB X FANTASY PRONENESS**
Council, Greyson, Huff and Swett (1986)
Myers and Austrin (1985)
Wilson and Barber (1983)
23. **OBE X FANTASY PRONENESS**
Myers et. al (1983)
Wilson and Barber (1983)
24. **SPI X FANTASY PRONENESS**
Cameron and Roll (1983)
Myers and Austrin (1985)
Wilson and Barber (1983)
25. **NDE X FANTASY PRONENESS**
Council, Greyson, Huff and Swett
(1986)
26. **GLB X HYPNOTIZABILITY**
Council, Greyson, Huff and Swett (1986)
Nadon and Kihlstrom (1987)
Pekala, Kumar and Cummings (1992)
Richards (1990)
Wagner and Ratzeburg (1987)
Wickramasekera (1989)
Wickramasekera (1991)
Wilson and Barber (1983)

27. **PSI X HYPNOTIZABILITY**
Pekala, Kumar and Cummings (1992)
28. **OBE X HYPNOTIZABILITY**
Palmer and Lieberman (1976)
Spanos and Moretti (1988)
Wilson and Barber (1983)
29. **MEX X HYPNOTIZABILITY**
Hood (1973)
Pekala, Kumar and Cummings (1992)
Spanos and Moretti (1988)
30. **LUC X HYPNOTIZABILITY**
Pekala, Kumar and Cummings (1992)
31. **AUR X HYPNOTIZABILITY**
Pekala, Kumar and Cummings (1992)
32. **REI X HYPNOTIZABILITY**
Spanos (1991)
33. **DIA X HYPNOTIZABILITY**
Spanos and Moretti (1988)
34. **MEX X TOLERANCE OF AMBIGUITY**
Hood, Hall, Watson and Biderman (1979)
Thomas and Cooper (1980)
35. **GLB X CONFORMITY**
P.L. Nelson (1989)
36. **MEX X CONFORMITY**
Hood, Hall, Watson and Biderman (1979)
37. **MEX X PSYCHOLOGICAL ADJUSTMENT**
Hood, Hall, Watson and Biderman (1979)
MacPhillamy (1986)
38. **DIA X PSYCHOLOGICAL ADJUSTMENT**
Spanos and Moretti (1988)
39. **GLB X EMOTIONAL AROUSAL**
Hay and Morisey (1978)
P.L. Nelson (1989)
40. **GLB X UNLIKELY VIRTUES**
P.L. Nelson (1989)
41. **GLB X SENSATION SEEKING**
Kumar, Pekala and Cummings (in press)
42. **MEX X MAGICAL THINKING**
Thalbourne (1991)

Table Two provides an overview of recent research into the relationships between belief in the reality of anomalous events and various factors of biology, personal history and personality. All of these studies are correlational. It is therefore unwarranted to draw any firm conclusions regarding cause-and-effect relationships between the beliefs and their correlates. The cautions concerning the interpretation of correlational research discussed earlier in the Appendix apply to Table Two.

In Table Two the following acronyms are used to designate anomalous beliefs:

GLB (global; in these studies, general belief in anomalous realities were examined)
ESP (belief in extrasensory perception—the ability of the mind to acquire knowledge of events or objects without using known senses)
PSK (belief in psychokinesis—the ability of the mind to influence external events directly)
SPI (belief in encounters with spirits, as in apparitions and seance phenomena)
UFO (belief in UFO encounters; unfortunately, many studies are not clear on what "belief in UFOs" entails—it could mean "belief that people see unidentified things in the sky," or "belief that the unidentified things seen in the sky are alien spacecraft, etc.," two very different propositions)
CRY (belief in the existence of cryptics or "hidden animals," such as the Loch Ness Monster and the Sasquatch)

The numbers in the table indicate the study's place in the list of studies following it; citations are given in full in the Bibliography. Unless otherwise indicated, studies noted found significant positive correlations between the variables (a minus sign indicates a negative correlation; a plus/minus sign indicates that the findings were inconsistent, both positive and negative correlations being reported). Concerning the variable of Gender, "m" signifies that the correlation applies to males only; "f" means the same for females only.

TABLE TWO: CORRELATIONS WITH ANOMALOUS BELIEFS						
BELIEF TYPE: **CORRELATE**	GLB	ESP	PSK	SPI	UFO	CRY
Biology						
Age	−1	−2		−3		−4
Gender	f5	f6		f7	m8	m9
Temporal Lobe Abnormality	10					
History						
Unusual Experience Reports	11					
Childhood Trauma	12					
Drug Use History	13					
Education:						
Academic Achievement	−14	+−15	−16	−17	−18	
Academic Attainment	19	+−20		−21	−22	
Science Education	+−23	−24	25	−26	−27	−28

BELIEF TYPE: CORRELATE	GLB	ESP	PSK	SPI	UFO	CRY
Traits						
Fantasy Proneness	29	30		31		32
Hypnotizability	33	34	35	36	37	
Psychological Adjustment	+–38					
Magical Thinking	39	40		41		42
Narcissism		43		44		
Sensation Seeking	45	46		47		
Reasoning Ability	–48	–49		–50		
Intelligence	+–51					
Creativity		52				
External Locus of Control	53	54		55		56
Control Needs	57	58				
Social Interest	–59	–60		–61		–62
Dogmatism		63				
Religiosity	64	65		–66	–67	
Death Concerns	68	69				70

STUDIES ON CORRELATES OF ANOMALOUS BELIEFS

1. GLB X AGE
Emmons and Sobal (1981)
2. ESP X AGE
Blackmore (1984)
Clarke (1991a)
Emmons and Sobal (1981)
Randall (1990)
Tobacyk, Pritchett and Mitchell (1988)
3. SPI X AGE
Clarke (1991a)
Emmons and Sobal (1981)
Tobacyk, Pritchett and Mitchell (1988)

4. CRY X AGE
Emmons and Sobal (1981)
Tobacyk, Pritchett and Mitchell (1988)
5. GLB X GENDER
Irwin (1985c)
McGarry and Newberry (1981)
Randall (1990)
Randall and Desrosiers (1980)
Tobacyk and Milford (1983)
6. ESP X GENDER
Clarke (1991a)
Emmons and Sobal (1981)

Gray (1990b)
Haraldsson (1981)
Haraldsson (1985a)
Irwin (1985c)
Thalbourne (1981)
Tobacyk and Milford (1983)

7. **SPI X GENDER**
Haraldsson (1985a)

8. **UFO X GENDER**
Clarke (1991a)
Gray (1990)

9. **CRY X GENDER**
Tobacyk and Milford (1983)
Tobacyk and Pirttila-Backman (1992)

10. **GLB X TEMPORAL LOBE ANOMALY**
Lavallee and Persinger (1992)
Skirda and Persinger (1993)

11. **GLB X UNUSUAL EXPERIENCE REPORTS**
Glicksohn (1990)
Haight (1979)
Irwin (1985c)
McLenon (1982)
Murphy and Lester (1976)
Palmer (1971)
Polzella, Popp and Hinsman (1975)
Sheils and Berg (1977)

12. **GLB X CHILDHOOD TRAUMA**
Irwin (1992)

13. **GLB X DRUG USE HISTORY**
Kumar, Pekala and Cummings (in press)
Roney-Dougal (1984)

14. **GLB X ACADEMIC ACHIEVEMENT**
Messer and Griggs (1989)

15. **ESP X ACADEMIC ACHIEVEMENT**
Messer and Griggs (1989)
Tobacyk, Miller and Jones (1984)

16. **PSK X ACADEMIC ACHIEVEMENT**
Clarke (1991b)

17. **SPI X ACADEMIC ACHIEVEMENT**
Tobacyk (1984)

18. **UFO X ACADEMIC ACHIEVEMENT**
Clarke (1991b)

19. **GLB X ACADEMIC ATTAINMENT**
Tobacyk, Miller and Jones (1984)

20. **ESP X ACADEMIC ATTAINMENT**
Emmons and Sobal (1981)
Gray (1987)
Haraldsson (1985a)
Otis and Alcock (1982)

Pasachoff, Cohen and Pasachoff (1970)
Tobacyk, Miller and Jones (1984)

21. **SPI X ACADEMIC ATTAINMENT**
Otis and Alcock (1982)

22. **UFO X ACADEMIC ATTAINMENT**
Salter and Routledge (1971)

23. **GLB X SCIENCE EDUCATION**
Banziger (1983)
Gray (1985)
Irwin (1990b)
McBurney (1976)
Otis and Alcock (1982)
Salter and Routledge (1971)
Tobacyk (1983a)
Jones and Zusne (1981)

24. **ESP X SCIENCE EDUCATION**
Happs (1987)
Padgett, Benassi and Singer (1981)

25. **PSK X SCIENCE EDUCATION**
Irwin (1990b)

26. **SPI X SCIENCE EDUCATION**
Otis and Alcock (1982)

27. **UFO X SCIENCE EDUCATION**
Happs (1987)

28. **CRY X SCIENCE EDUCATION**
Irwin (1990b)

29. **GLB X FANTASY PRONENESS**
Irwin (1990a)
Irwin (1991b)

30. **ESP X FANTASY PRONENESS**
Irwin (1990a)
Irwin (1991b)

31. **SPI X FANTASY PRONENESS**
Irwin (1990a)
Irwin (1991b)

32. **CRY X FANTASY PRONENESS**
Irwin (1990a)
Irwin (1991b)

33. **GLB X HYPNOTIZABILITY**
Haraldsson (1985b)
Nadon, Laurence and Perry (1987)
Pekala, Kumar and Cummings (1992)

34. **ESP X HYPNOTIZABILITY**
Haraldsson (1985b)
Wagner and Ratzeburg (1987)

35. **PSK X HYPNOTIZABILITY**
Pekala, Kumar and Cummings (1992)

36. **SPI X HYPNOTIZABILITY**
Haraldsson (1985b)

37. UFO X HYPNOTIZABILITY
    Pekala, Kumar and Cummings (1992)
38. GLB X PSYCHOLOGICAL ADJUSTMENT
    Irwin (1991b)
    Schumaker (1987)
    Windholz and Diamant (1974)
39. GLB X MAGICAL THINKING
    Thalbourne (1985)
    Thalbourne (in press)
    Tobacyk and Wilkinson (1990)
    Williams (1989), cited in Irwin (1993)
40. ESP X MAGICAL THINKING
    Tobacyk and Wilkinson (1990)
    Williams (1989), cited in Irwin (1993)
41. SPI X MAGICAL THINKING
    Tobacyk and Wilkinson (1990)
    Williams (1989), cited in Irwin (1993)
42. CRY X MAGICAL THINKING
    Williams (1989), cited in Irwin (1993)
43. ESP X NARCISSISM
    Tobacyk and Mitchell (1987)
44. SPI X NARCISSISM
    Tobacyk and Mitchell (1987)
45. GLB X SENSATION SEEKING
    Brown, Ruder, Ruder and Young (1974)
    Davis, Peterson and Farley (1974)
    Kumar, Pekala and Cummings (in press)
    Zuckerman (1979)
46. ESP X SENSATION SEEKING
    Tobacyk and Milford (1983)
47. SPI X SENSATION SEEKING
    Tobacyk and Milford (1983)
48. GLB X REASONING ABILITY
    Alcock and Otis (1980)
    Gray and Mill (1990)
    Wierzbicki (1985)
49. ESP X REASONING ABILITY
    Polzella, Popp and Hinsman (1975)
50. SPI X REASONING ABILITY
    Tobacyk and Milford (1983)
51. GLB X INTELLIGENCE
    Jones, Russell and Nickel (1977)
    Killen, Wildman and Wildman (1974)
52. ESP X CREATIVITY
    Davis, Peterson and Farley (1974)
    Joesting and Joesting (1969)

Moon (1975)
53. GLB X EXTERNAL LOCUS OF CONTROL
    Irwin (1986)
    Jones, Russell and Nickel (1977)
    Randall and Desrosiers (1980)
    Tobacyk and Milford (1983)
    Tobacyk, Nagot and Miller (1988)
54. ESP X EXTERNAL LOCUS OF CONTROL
    Irwin (1986)
    Polzella, Popp and Hinsman (1975)
55. SPI X EXTERNAL LOCUS OF CONTROL
    Davies and Kirkby (1985)
56. CRY X EXTERNAL LOCUS OF CONTROL
    Tobacyk and Milford (1983)
57. GLB X CONTROL NEEDS
    Irwin (1992)
58. ESP X CONTROL NEEDS
    Blackmore and Troscianko (1985)
59. GLB X SOCIAL INTEREST
    Tobacyk (1983b)
60. ESP X SOCIAL INTEREST
    Tobacyk (1983b)
61. SPI X SOCIAL INTEREST
    Tobacyk (1983b)
62. CRY X SOCIAL INTEREST
    Tobacyk (1983b)
63. ESP X DOGMATISM
    Alcock and Otis (1980)
64. GLB X RELIGIOSITY
    Irwin (1985c)
65. ESP X RELIGIOSITY
    Haraldsson (1981)
    Tobacyk and Milford (1983)
66. SPI X RELIGIOSITY
    Tobacyk and Milford (1983)
67. UFO X RELIGIOSITY
    Clarke (1991a)
68. GLB X DEATH CONCERNS
    Tobacyk (1983c)
    Tobacyk and Pirttila-Backman (1992)
69. ESP X DEATH CONCERNS
    Tobacyk (1983c)
    Tobacyk and Pirttila-Backman (1992)
70. CRY X DEATH CONCERNS
    Tobacyk (1983c)
    Tobacyk and Pirttila-Backman (1992)

BIBLIOGRAPHY

Akers, C. "Methodological Criticisms of Parapsychology." In S. Krippner, ed., *Advances in Parapsychological Research, Volume 4.* Jefferson, NC: McFarland & Co., 1984, 112–164.

Alcock, J.E. *Science and Supernature: A Critical Appraisal of Parapsychology.* Buffalo: Prometheus, 1990.

Alcock, J.E., and Otis, L.P. "Critical Thinking and Belief in the Paranormal." *Psychological Reports,* 46(1980), 479–482.

Allegro, J.M. *The Sacred Mushroom and the Cross: A Study of the Nature and Origins of Christianity within the Fertility Cults of the Ancient Near East.* London: Hodder and Stoughton, 1970.

Allison, R.B. "The Possession Syndrome on Trial." In R. Noll Ed., *Vampires, Werewolves, and Demons: Twentieth Century Reports in the Psychiatric Literature.* New York: Brunner/Mazel, 1992, 210–222.

Alvarado, C.S. "ESP During Out-of-Body Experiences: A Review of Experimental Studies." *Journal of Parapsychology,* 46(1982), 209–230.

———"The Psychological Approach to Out-of-Body Experiences: A Review of Early and Modern Developments." *Journal of Psychology,* 126(1992), 237–250.

American Psychiatric Association. *Diagnostic and Statistical Manual, Fourth Edition (DSM-IV).* Washington: American Psychiatric Association, 1994.

American Psychological Association. *The Suggestibility of Children's Recollections.* Washington: American Psychological Association, 1991.

Andritzky, W. "Sociotherapeutic Functions of Ayahuasca Healing in Amazonia." *Journal of Psychoactive Drugs,* 21(1989), 77–89.

Asaad, G. *Hallucinations in Clinical Psychiatry: A Guide for Mental Health Professionals.* New York: Brunner/Mazel, 1990.

Ashcroft, M.H. *Human Memory and Cognition.* Glenview, IL: Scott, Foresman, 1989.

Avalon, A. *The Serpent Power: The Secrets of Tantric and Shaktic Yoga.* New York: Dover, 1974.

Baddeley, A. *Human Memory.* Boston: Allyn and Bacon, 1990.

Baker, R.A. "The Effect of Suggestion on Past Lives Regression." *American Journal of Clinical Hypnosis,* 25(1982), 71–76.

———"The Aliens Among Us: Hypnotic Regression Revisited." In K. Frazier, ed., *The Hundredth Monkey and other Paradigms of the Paranormal.* Buffalo: Prometheus, 1991, 54–69.

———*Hidden Memories: Voices and Visions From Within.* Buffalo: Prometheus, 1992.

Bakhtiar, L. *Sufi: Expressions of the Mystic Quest.* New York: Thames and Hudson, 1987.

Ballester Olmos, V.J. "Alleged Experiences Inside UFOs: An Analysis of Abduction Reports," *Journal of Scientific Exploration,* 8(1994), 91–106.

Bannister, H., and Zangwill, O.L. "Experimentally Induced Visual Paramnesia." *British Journal of Psychology,* 32(1941), 30–51.

Banziger, G. "Normalizing the Paranormal: Short-Term and Long-Term Change in Belief in the Paranormal among Older Learners During a Short Course." *Teaching of Psychology,* 10(1983), 212–214.

Barber, T.X. "Changing 'Unchangeable' Bodily Processes by (Hypnotic) Suggestions: A New Look at Hypnosis, Cognitions, Imagining, and the Mind-Body Problem." In A.A. Sheikh, ed., *Imagination and Healing.* Farmingdale, NY: Baywood, 1984, 51–68.

Barber, T.X., and Calverly, D.S. "An Experimental Study of Hypnotic (Auditory and Visual) Hallucinations." *Journal of Abnormal and Social Psychology,* 63(1964), 13–20.

Barnett, B. "Witchcraft, Psychopathology and Hallucinations." *British Journal of Psychiatry,* 3(1965), 439–445.

Barrett, W. *Death-Bed Visions: The Psychical Experiences of the Dying.* Wellingborough, England: Aquarian Press, 1986.

Bartholomew, R.E. "The Airship Hysteria of 1896–97." *Skeptical Inquirer,* 14(1990), 171–181.

———"Redefining Epidemic Hysteria: An Example From Sweden," *Acta Psychiatrica Scandinavica,* 88(1993), 178–182.

Bartlett, F. *Remembering: A Study in Experimental and Social Psychology.* Cambridge: Cambridge University Press, 1964.

Bayless, R. *The Other Side of Death.* New Hyde Park, NY: University Books, 1971.

———"Marian Apparitions at Zeitun, Cairo." *Journal of the Southern California Society for Psychical Research,* 2(1981), 6–34.

Beck, A.T., Emery, G., and Greenberg, R.L. *Anxiety Disorders and Phobias: A Cognitive Perspective.* New York: Basic Books, 1985.

Begg, I.M., Needham, D.R., and Bookbinder, M. "Do Backward Messages Unconsciously Affect Listeners? No." *Canadian Journal of Experimental Psychology,* 47(1993), 1–14.

Bem, D.J. "Response to Hyman," *Psychological Bulletin, 115(1994), 25–27.*

Bem, D.J., and Honorton, C. "Does Psi Exist? Replicable Evidence for an Anomalous Process of Information Transfer," *Psychological Bulletin,* 115(1994), 4–18.

Bennett, B.M. "Vision and Audition in Biblical Prophecy as Illuminated by Recent Research on Human Consciousness." In B. Shapin and L. Coly, eds., *Psi and States of Awareness.* New York: Parapsychology Foundation, 1978, 101–123.

Benson, H. *Beyond the Relaxation Response.* New York: Berkley, 1985.

Benson, H., et. al. "Body Temperature Changes During the Practice of gTummo Yoga." *Nature,* 295(1982), 234–236.

Berger, A.S., and Berger, J. *The Encyclopedia of Parapsychology and Psychical Research.* New York: Paragon House, 1991.

Berman, M. *Coming to Our Senses: Body and Spirit in the Hidden History of the West.* New York: Bantam, 1990.

Best, J.A., and Suedfeld, P. "Restricted Environmental Stimulation Therapy and Behavioral Self-Management in Smoking Cessation." *Journal of Applied Social Psychology,* 12(1982), 408–419.

Beyerstein, B. "Neuropathology and the Legacy of Spiritual Possession." *Skeptical Inquirer,* 12(1988), 248–262.

Bharati, A. *The Tantric Tradition.* New York: Samuel Weiser, 1975.

———*The Light at the Center: Context and Pretext of Modern Mysticism.* Santa Barbara: 1976.

Blackmore, S. "A Postal Survey of OBEs and Other Experiences." *Journal of the Society for Psychical Research,* 52 (1984), 225–244.

Blackmore, S., and Troscianko, T. "Belief in the Paranormal: Probability Judgements, Illusory Control, and the 'Chance Baseline Shift'." *British Journal of Psychology,* 76(1985), 459–468.

Bliss, E.L. *Multiple Personality, Allied Disorders, and Hypnosis.* New York: Oxford University Press, 1986.

Bloecher, T., Clamar, A., and Hopkins, B. "Summary Report on the Psychological Testing of Nine Individuals Reporting UFO Abduction Experiences." In *Final Report on the Psychological Testing of UFO 'Abductees'.* Mt. Rainier, MD: Fund for UFO Research, 1985.

Blofeld, J. *Mantras: Sacred Words of Power.* New York: Dutton, 1977.

Bourguinon, E., ed. *Religion, Altered States of Consciousness, and Social Change.* Columbus: Ohio State University Press, 1973.

Bove, F.J. *The Story of Ergot.* Basel: S. Karger, 1970.

Boyer, L.B., Boyer, R.M., and Basehart, H.W. "Shamanism and Peyote Use Among the Apaches of the Mescalero Indian Reservation." In M.J. Harner, ed., *Hallucinogens and Shamanism.* New York: Oxford University Press, 1973, 53–66.

Briggs, K. *An Encyclopedia of Fairies.* New York: Pantheon, 1976.

Broughton, R. *Parapsychology: The Controversial Science.* New York: Ballantine, 1991.

Brown, L.T., Ruder, V.G., Ruder, J.H., and Young, S.D. "Stimulation Seeking and the Change Seeker Index." *Journal of Consulting and Clinical Psychology,* 42(1974), 311.

Bucke, R.M. *Cosmic Consciousness: A Study in the Evolution of the Human Mind.* New York: Innes, 1901.

Buddhaghosa, B. *The Path of Purification (Visuddhimagga).* Berkeley: Shambhala, 1976.

Bullard, T.E. *UFO Abductions: The Measure of a Mystery.* Mt. Rainier, MD.: Fund for UFO Research, 1987.

———"Hypnosis and UFO Abductions: A Troubled Relationship." *Journal of UFO Studies,* 1(1989), 3–40.

Bunch, K.J., and White, M.K. "The Riddle of the Colorado Ghost Lights: A Ghostly Mystery Yields to Reflection." *Skeptical Inquirer,* 12(1988), 306–309.

Burkert, W. *Homo Necans: The Anthropology of Ancient Greek Sacrificial Ritual and Myth.* Berkeley, CA: University of California Press, 1983.

Callahan, P.S., and Mankin, R.W. "Insects as Unidentified Flying Objects." *Applied Optics,* 17(1978).

Cameron, T., and Roll, W.G. "An Investigation of Apparitional Experiences." *Theta,* 11(1983), 74–78.

Campbell, J. *The Masks of God: Occidental Mythology.* New York: Penguin, 1976.

———*Historical Atlas of World Mythology, Volume 1—The Way of the Animal Powers, Part 2: Mythologies of the Great Hunt.* New York: Harper and Row, 1988.

Canizares, R. *Walking With the Night: The Afro-Cuban World of Santeria.* Rochester, VT: Destiny Books, 1993.

Cannon, W.B. "Voodoo Death." *American Anthropologist,* 44(1942), 169–181.

Carrington, H. *Death: Its Causes and Phenomena.* New York: Dodd, Mead and Co., 1921.

Carroll, M.P. *The Cult of the Virgin Mary: Psychological Origins.* Princeton: Princeton University Press, 1986.

Cash, T.F., and Pruzinsky, T., eds., *Body Images: Development, Deviance and Change.* New York: Guilford Press, 1990.

Cavendish, R., ed. *Man, Myth and Magic: An Illustrated Encyclopedia of the Supernatural.* New York: Marshall Cavendish Corporation, 1970.

Chang, C. *Creativity and Taoism: A Study of Chinese Philosophy, Art, and Poetry.* New York: Julian Press, 1963.

Chang, G.C.C. *The Buddhist Teaching of Totality: The Philosophy of Hwa Yen Buddhism.* University Park, PA: Pennsylvania State University, 1971.

———*Teachings of Tibetan Yoga.* Secaucus, NJ: Citadel Press, 1974.

Chari, C.T.K. "Reincarnation Research: Method and Interpretation." In M. Ebon, ed., *Signet Handbook of Parapsychology.* New York: New American Library, 1978, 313–324.

Chirban, J. "Developmental Stages in Eastern Orthodox Christianity." In K. Wilber, J. Engler and D.P. Brown, *Transformations of Consciousness: Conventional and Contemplative Perspectives on Development.* Boston: Shambhala, 1986, 285–314.

Christian, W.A. *Apparitions in Late Medieval and Renaissance Spain.* Princeton: Princeton University Press, 1981.

Christie-Murray, D. *Reincarnation: Ancient Beliefs and Modern Evidence.* Bridport, England: Prism Press, 1988.

Christopher, M. *ESP, Seers and Psychics.* New York: Thomas Y. Crowell, 1970.

———*Mediums, Mystics and the Occult.* New York: Thomas Y. Crowell, 1975.

Chyba, C.F., Thomas, P.J., and Zahnle, K.J. "The 1908 Tunguska Explosion: Atmospheric Disruption of a Stony Asteroid." *Nature,* 361(1993), 40–44.

Claflin-Chalton, S., and MacDonald, G.J. *Sound and Light Phenomena—A Study of Historical and Modern Occurrences.* McLean, VA: Mitre Corporation, 1978.

Clarke, D. "Belief in the Paranormal: A New Zealand Survey." *Journal of the Society for Psychical Research,* 57(1991a), 412–425.

———"Students' Beliefs and Academic Performance in an Empathic Course on the Paranormal." *Journal of the Society for Psychical Research,* 58(1991b), 74–83.

Cohn, N. *Europe's Inner Demons: An Enquiry Inspired by the Great Witch-Hunt.* New York: Basic Books, 1975.

Coleman, R. *Wide Awake at 3 A.M.* New York: Freeman, 1987.

Cooper, G.D. "Studies in REST: I. Reduced Environmental Stimulation Therapy (REST) and Reduced Alcohol Consumption." *Journal of Substance Abuse Treatment,* 5(1988), 61–68.

Corbin, H. *Creative Imagination in the Sufism of Ibn 'Arabi.* Princeton: Princeton University Press, 1969.

Corliss, W.R. *Handbook of Unusual Natural Phenomena.* Glen Arm, MD: Sourcebook Project, 1977.

———*Incredible Life: A Handbook of Biological Mysteries.* Glen Arm, MD: Sourcebook Project, 1981.

———*Lightning, Auroras, Nocturnal Lights: A Catalog of Geophysical Anomalies.* Glen Arm, MD: Sourcebook Project, 1982.

———*Earthquakes, Tides, Unidentified Sounds: A Catalog of Geophysical Anomalies.* Glen Arm, MD: Sourcebook Project, 1983a.

——*Tornados, Dark Days, Anomalous Precipitation: A Catalog of Geophysical Anomalies*. Glen Arm, MD: Sourcebook Project, 1983b.

——*Rare Halos, Mirages, Anomalous Rainbows: A Catalog of Geophysical Anomalies*. Glen Arm, MD: Sourcebook Project, 1984.

——*The Sun and Solar System Debris: A Catalog of Astronomical Anomalies*. Glen Arm, MD: Sourcebook Project, 1986.

——*Science Frontiers: Some Anomalies and Curiosities of Nature*. Glen Arm, MD: Sourcebook Project, 1994.

Cornwell, J. *Powers of Darkness, Powers of Light: Travels in Search of the Miraculous and the Demonic*. London: Penguin, 1992.

Couliano, I.P. *Out of This World: Otherworldly Journeys from Gilgamesh to Albert Einstein*. Boston: Shambhala, 1991.

Council, J.R., Greyson, B., Huff, K.D., and Swett, S. *Fantasy-Proneness, Hypnotizability, and Reports of Paranormal Experiences*. Paper presented at the annual meeting of the American Psychological Association: Washington, D.C., 1986.

Cozort, D. *Highest Yoga Tantra: An Introduction to the Esoteric Buddhism of Tibet*. Ithaca, NY: Snow Lion, 1986.

Cytowic, R.E. *Synesthesia: A Union of the Senses*. New York: Springer-Verlag, 1989.

David-Neel, A. *With Mystics and Magicians in Tibet*. London: Penguin, 1937.

Davidson, H.R. *Myths and Symbols in Pagan Europe: Early Scandinavian and Celtic Religions*. Syracuse, NY: Syracuse University Press, 1988.

Davies, M.F., and Kirkby, H.E. "Multidimensionality of the Relationship Between Perceived Control and Belief in the Paranormal: Spheres of Control and Types of Paranormal Phenomena." *Personality and Individual Differences,* 6(1985), 661–663.

Davis, G.A., Peterson, J.M., and Farley, F.H. "Attitudes, Motivation, Sensation Seeking, and Belief in ESP as Predictors of Real Creative Behavior." *Journal of Creative Behavior,* 8(1974), 31–39.

Davis, W. *The Serpent and the Rainbow*. Toronto: Stoddart, 1986.

——*Passage of Darkness: The Ethnobiology of the Haitian Zombie*. Chapel Hill, NC: University of North Carolina Press, 1988.

Deikman, A.J. "De-Automatization and the Mystic Experience." *Psychiatry,* 29(1966), 324–338.

Dement, W.C. *Some Must Watch While Some Must Sleep*. New York: Norton, 1978.

Deren, M. *Divine Horsemen: The Living Gods of Haiti*. London: Thames and Hudson, 1953.

Diener, M.S. Entries in *The Encyclopedia of Eastern Philosophy and Religion*. Boston: Shambhala, 1989.

Dingwall, E.J. *Some Human Oddities*. New York: University Books, 1962.

Dobkin de Rios, M. *Hallucinogens: Cross-Cultural Perspectives*. Bridport, England: Prism Press, 1990.

Dodds, E.R. *The Greeks and the Irrational*. Berkeley, CA: University of California Press, 1951.

Doris, J., ed. *The Suggestibility of Children's Recollections*. Washington: American Psychological Association, 1991.

Druckman, D., and Swets, J.A., eds. *Enhancing Human Performance: Issues, Theories, and Techniques*. Washington: National Academy Press, 1988.

Dupre, L., and Wiseman, J.A., eds. *Light From Light: An Anthology of Christian Mysticism*. New York: Paulist Press, 1988.

Eastwell, H.D. "Voodoo Death and the Mechanism for Dispatch of the Dying in East Arnhem, Australia." *American Anthropologist,* 84(1982), 5–18.

Eberhart, G.M. *Monsters: Including Bigfoot, Many Water Monsters, and Other Irregular Animals*. New York: Garland Publishing, 1983.

Eckblad, M., and Chapman, L.J. "Magical Ideation as an Indicator of Schizotypy." *Journal of Consulting and Clinical Psychology,* 51(1983), 215–225.

Ehrhard, F.-K. Entries in *The Encyclopedia of Eastern Philosophy and Religion*. Boston: Shambhala, 1989.

Eliade, M. *Shamanism: Archaic Techniques of Ecstasy*. Princeton: Princeton University Press, 1964.

——*Yoga: Immortality and Freedom*. Princeton, NJ: Princeton University Press, 1969.

Ellis, B. "The Varieties of Alien Experience." In K. Frazier, ed., *The Hundredth Monkey and Other Paradigms of the Paranormal*. Buffalo: Prometheus, 1991, 70–77.

Emmons, C.F., and Sobal, J. "Paranormal Beliefs: Testing the Marginality Hypothesis." *Sociological Focus,* 14(1981), 49–56.

Engel, G. "Sudden and Rapid Death During Psychological Stress: Folklore or Folk Medicine?." *Annals of Internal Medicine,* 74(1971), 771–782.

Enoch, M.D., and Trethowan, W.H. *Uncommon Psychiatric Syndromes.* Bristol, England: John Wright, 1979.

Epstein, M., and Garlaschelli, L. "Better Blood Through Chemistry: A Laboratory Replication of a Miracle." *Journal of Scientific Exploration,* 6(1992), 233–246.

Erickson, C. *The Medieval Vision: Essays in History and Perception.* New York: Oxford University Press, 1976.

Estep, S.W. *Voices of Eternity.* New York: Fawcett Good Medal, 1988.

Evans, H. *Alternate States of Consciousness: Unself, Otherself, and Superself.* Wellingborough, England: Aquarian Press, 1989.

Evans-Wentz, W.Y. *The Tibetan Book of the Dead; Or, the After-Death Experiences on the Bardo Plane, According to Lama Kazi Dawa-Samdup's English Rendering.* New York: Causeway Books, 1973.

Fabricius, J. *Alchemy: The Medieval Alchemists and Their Royal Art.* Copenhagen: Rosenkilde & Bagger, 1976.

Faraday, A. *Dream Power.* New York: Berkley Books, 1973.

Faraday, M. "Experimental Investigation of Table Turning." *Atheneum,* July (1853), 801–808.

Fenwick, P., Galliano, S, Coate, M.A., Rippere, V., and Brown, D. "'Psychic Sensitivity', Mystical Experience, Head Injury and Brain Pathology." *British Journal of Medical Psychology,* 58(1985), 35–44.

Fernandez, J.W. *Bwiti: An Ethnography of the Religious Imagination in Africa.* Princeton: Princeton University Press, 1982.

Feuerstein, G. *Yoga: The Technology of Ecstasy.* Los Angeles: J.P. Tarcher, 1989.

———*Encyclopedic Dictionary of Yoga.* New York: Paragon House, 1990.

Fischer, R. "On the Remembrance of Things Present: The Flashback." In B.B. Wolman and M. Ullman, eds., *Handbook of States of Consciousness.* New York: Van Nostrand Reinhold, 1986, 395–427.

Fischer-Schreiber, I. Entries in *The Encyclopedia of Eastern Philosophy and Religion.* Boston: Shambhala, 1989.

Flammarion, C. *Haunted Houses.* New York: Appleton, 1924.

Flattery, D., and Schwartz, M. *Haoma and Harmaline.* Berkeley: University of California Press, 1989.

Flint, V.I.J. *The Rise of Magic in Early Medieval Europe.* Princeton: Princeton University Press, 1991.

Flournoy, T. *Spiritism and Psychology.* New York: Harper and Brothers, 1911.

———*From India to the Planet Mars.* New Hyde Park, NY: University Books, 1963.

Fodor, N. *The Haunted Mind: A Psychoanalyst Looks at the Supernatural.* New York: Signet, 1959.

Forer, B.R. "The Fallacy of Personal Validation: A Classroom Demonstration of Gullibility." *Journal of Abnormal and Social Psychology,* 44(1949), 118–123.

Friedhoff, A.J., and T.N. Chase, eds. *Gilles de la Tourette's Syndrome.* New York: Raven Press, 1982.

Friedman, M. *Religions and Psychology: A Dialogical Approach.* New York: Paragon House, 1992.

Friedrichs, K. Entries in *The Encyclopedia of Eastern Philosophy and Religion.* Boston: Shambhala, 1989.

Gaddis, V.H. *Mysterious Fires and Lights.* New York: Dell, 1967.

Gallagher, J.S. "Diffuse Luminous Objects Having Angular Velocities Similar to Meteors." *Strolling Astronomer,* 36(1992), 115.

Gallup, G.H., and Newport, F. "Belief in Paranormal Phenomena among Adult Americans." *Skeptical Inquirer,* 15(1991), 137–146.

Gauld, A. *Mediumship and Survival: A Century of Investigations.* London: William Heinemann, 1982.

Gauld, A., and Cornell, A.D. *Poltergeists.* London: Routledge and Kegan Paul, 1979.

George, L. "Expectancy and Psi: A Critical Review and Reformulation." *Journal of the American Society for Psychical Research,* 78(1984), 193–217.

George, L, and Neufeld, R.W.J. "Cognition and Symptomatology in Schizophrenia." *Schizophrenia Bulletin,* 11(1985), 264–285.

Ginzburg, C. *The Night Battles: Witchcraft and Agrarian Cults in the Sixteenth and Seventeenth Centuries.* New York: Penguin, 1985.

————*Ecstasies: Deciphering the Witches' Sabbath.* New York: Pantheon Books, 1991.

Gissurarson, L.R. "The Psychokinesis Effect: Geomagnetic Influence, Age and Sex Differences." *Journal of Scientific Exploration,* 6(1992), 157–166.

Glasse, C. *The Concise Encyclopedia of Islam.* San Francisco: Harper & Row, 1989.

Glicksohn, J. "Belief in the Paranormal and Subjective Paranormal Experience." *Personality and Individual Differences,* 11(1990), 675–683.

Gloyne, H.F., "Tarantism: Mass Hysterical Reaction to Spider Bite in the Middle Ages," *American Imago,* 7(1950), 29–42.

Goleman, D. *The Meditative Mind: The Varieties of Meditative Experience.* Los Angeles: J.P. Tarcher, 1988.

Goodwin, D.W., Alderson, P., and Rosenthal, R. "Clinical Significance of Hallucinations in Psychiatric Disorders." *Archives of General Psychiatry,* 24(1971), 76–80.

Govinda, L.A. *Foundations of Tibetan Mysticism According to the Esoteric Teachings of the Great Mantra OM MANI PADME HUM.* New York: Samuel Weiser, 1969.

————*The Psychological Attitude of Early Buddhist Philosophy and its Systematic Representation According to Abhidhamma Tradition.* New York: Samuel Weiser, 1974.

Gray, T. "Changing Unsubstantiated Belief: Testing the Ignorance Hypothesis." *Canadian Journal of Behavioural Science,* 17(1985), 263–270.

————"Education Experience and Belief in Paranormal Phenomena." In F.B. Harrold & R.A. Eve, eds., *Cult Archaeology and Creationism: Understanding Pseudoscientific Beliefs about the Past.* Iowa City: University of Iowa Press, 1987, 21–33.

————"Gender Differences in Belief in Scientifically Unsubstantiated Phenomena." *Canadian Journal of Behavioural Science,* 22(1990), 181–190.

Gray, T., and Mill, D. "Critical Abilities, Graduate Education (Biology vs. English), and Belief in Unsubstantiated Phenomena." *Canadian Journal of Behavioural Science,* 22(1990), 162–172.

Green, C. "Waking Dreams and Other Metachoric Experiences," *Psychiatric Journal of the University of Ottawa,* 15(1990), 123–128.

Green, J. "What is the Sasquatch?." In M.M. Halpin & M.M. Ames, eds., *Manlike Monsters on Trial: Early Records and Modern Evidence.* Vancouver: University of British Columbia Press, 1980, 237–244.

Grigor'ev, A.I., Grigor'eva, I.D., and Shiryaeva, S.O. "Ball Lightning Penetration into Closed Rooms: 43 Eyewitness Accounts." *Journal of Scientific Exploration,* 6(1992), 261–280.

Grof, S. *LSD Psychotherapy.* Pomona, CA: Hunter House, 1980.

Grof, S., and Grof, C., eds. *Spiritual Emergency: When Personal Transformation Becomes a Crisis.* Los Angeles: J.P. Tarcher, 1989.

Gross, M.M., Halpert, E., Sabot, L., and Polisoes, P. "Hearing Disturbances and Auditory Hallucinations in the Acute Alcoholic Psychoses: I. Tinnitus: Incidence and Significance." *Journal of Nervous and Mental Disease,* 137(1963), 455–465.

Grunwald, S. *The Renderings of Stefano, Book I: Science and Technology.* Virginia Beach, VA: Donning Company, 1979.

Guenther, H.V. *The Tantric View of Life.* Boulder, CO: Shambhala, 1976.

Guillaume, A. *Prophecy and Divination Among the Hebrews and other Semites.* New York: Harper and Brothers, 1938.

Guirdham, A. *The Cathars and Reincarnation.* London: Neville Spearman, 1970.

Gurney, E., Myers, F.W.H., and Podmore, F. *Phantasms of the Living.* London: Trubner, 1886.

Hacking, I. "The Invention of Split Personalities (An Illustration of Michel Foucault's Doctrine of the Constitution of the Subject)." In A. Donagan, et. al, eds., *Human Nature and Natural Knowledge.* Dordrecht, Netherlands: Reidel, 1986, 63–85.

Haeffner, M. *The Dictionary of Alchemy: From Maria Prophetissa to Isaac Newton.* London: Aquarian Press, 1991.

Haight, J. "Spontaneous Psi Cases: A Survey and Preliminary Study of ESP, Attitude, and Personality Relationships." *Journal of Parapsychology,* 43(1979), 179–204.

Haines, R.F. *Advanced Aerial Devices Reported During the Korean War.* Los Altos, CA: LDA Press, 1990.

Haining, P. *Ghosts: The Illustrated History.* Secaucus, NJ: Chartwell Books, 1987.

Halpin, M.M., and Ames, M.M., eds. *Manlike Monsters on Trial: Early Records and Modern Evi-*

dence. Vancouver: University of British Columbia Press, 1980.

Hansen, G.P. "CSICOP and the Skeptics: An Overview." *Journal of the American Society for Psychical Research,* 86(1992a), 19–63.

———— "Magicians on the Paranormal: An Essay with a Review of Three Books." *Journal of the American Society for Psychical Research,* 86(1992b), 151–185.

Happold, F.C. *Mysticism.* Baltimore: Penguin, 1973.

Happs, J.C. "Conceptual Conflict over Pseudoscience: A Case Study Involving Teacher Trainees and Their Belief in Water Divining." *The Skeptic,* 7(1987), 21–28.

Haraldsson, E. "Some Determinants of Belief in Psychical Phenomena." *Journal of the American Society for Psychical Research,* 75(1981), 297–309.

————"Representative National Surveys of Psychic Phenomena: Iceland, Great Britain, Sweden, USA and Gallup's Multinational Survey." *Journal of the Society for Psychical Research,* 53(1985a), 145–158.

————"Interrogative Suggestibility and its Relationship with Personality, Perceptual Defensiveness and Extraordinary Beliefs." *Personality and Individual Differences,* 6(1985b), 765–767.

Harman, W., and Rheingold, H. *Higher Creativity: Liberating the Unconscious for Breakthrough Insights.* Los Angeles: J.P. Tarcher, 1984.

Harner, M.J. "The Role of Hallucinogenic Plants in European Witchcraft." In M.J. Harner, ed., *Hallucinogens and Shamanism.* New York: Oxford University Press, 1973a, 125–150.

————"The Sound of Rushing Water." In M.J. Harner, ed., *Hallucinogens and Shamanism.* New York: Oxford University Press, 1973b, 15–27.

————*The Way of the Shaman: A Guide to Power and Healing.* New York: Harper and Row, 1980.

Harris, M. *Investigating the Unexplained.* Buffalo: Prometheus, 1986.

Harrison, T. *Fire From Heaven.* London: Pan Books, 1977.

Hartmann, E. *The Nightmare: The Psychology and Biology of Terrifying Dreams.* New York: Basic Books, 1984.

Harvey, A. *A Journey in Ladakh.* Boston: Houghton Mifflin, 1983.

Hastings, A. *With the Tongues of Men and Angels: A Study of Channeling.* Fort Worth, TX: Holt, Rinehart and Winston, 1991.

Hay, D., and Morisey, A. "Reports of Ecstatic, Paranormal or Religious Experience in Great Britain and the United States: A Comparison of Trends." *Journal for the Scientific Study of Religion,* 17(1978), 255–268.

Hebb, D.O. "The Role of Neurological Ideas in Psychology." *Journal of Personality,* 20(1951), 45.

Heery, M.W. "Inner Voice Experiences: An Exploratory Study of Thirty Cases." *Journal of Transpersonal Psychology,* 21(1989), 73–82.

Heim, A. "The Experience of Dying from Falls," (trans. by R. Noyes and R. Kletti). *Omega,* 2(1972), 45–52.

Heinze, R.-I. *Shamans of the Twentieth Century.* New York: Irvington, 1991.

Herring, P.J., and Watson, M. "Milky Seas: A Bioluminescent Puzzle." *Marine Observer,* 63(1993), 22.

Heuvelmans, B. *On the Track of Unknown Animals.* New York: Hill & Wang, 1958.

————*In the Wake of the Sea Serpents.* New York: Hill & Wang, 1968.

————"Annotated Checklist of Apparently Unknown Animals With Which Cryptozoology is Concerned," *Cryptozoology,* 5(1986), 1–26.

Hilgard, E.R. *Divided Consciousness: Multiple Controls in Human Thought and Action.* New York: Wiley, 1986.

Hill, D. "Flagellation." In R. Cavendish, ed., *Man, Myth and Magic.* New York: Marshall Cavendish Corporation, 1970, 988–991.

Hines, T. *Pseudoscience and the Paranormal: A Critical Examination of the Evidence.* Buffalo: Prometheus, 1988.

Hirschfelder, A., and Molin, P. *The Encyclopedia of Native American Religions: An Introduction.* New York: Facts On File, 1992.

Hoffman, E. *The Way of Splendor: Jewish Mysticism and Modern Psychology.* Boulder, CO: Shambhala, 1981.

Holmes, D.S. "Meditation and Somatic Arousal Reduction: A Review of the Experimental Evidence." *American Psychologist,* 39(1984), 1–10.

Honnegger, B. "A Neuropsychological Theory of Automatic Verbal Behavior." *Parapsychology Review,* 11[4](1980), 1–8.

Honorton, C. "Meta-Analysis of Psi Ganzfeld Research: A Response to Hyman." *Journal of Parapsychology,* 49(1985), 51–91.

Hood, R. "Hypnotic Susceptibility and Reported Religious Experience." *Psychological Reports,* 33(1973), 549–550.

Hood, R., Hall, J.R., Watson, P.J., and Biderman, M. "Personality Correlates of the Report of Mystical Experience." *Psychological Reports,* 44(1979), 804–806.

Hopkins, B. *Missing Time.* New York: Berkley Books, 1983.

Hopkins, J. *Meditation on Emptiness.* London: Wisdom, 1983.

———*The Tantric Distinction: An Introduction to Tibetan Buddhism.* London: Wisdom, 1984.

Horowitz, M.J. "Hallucinations: An Information-Processing Approach." In R.K. Siegel and L.J. West, eds., *Hallucinations: Behavior, Experience, and Theory.* New York: Wiley, 1975, 163–193.

Hozeski, B. *Scivias by Hildegard of Bingen.* Santa Fe, NM: Bear and Co., 1986.

Hufford, D.J. *The Terror That Comes in the Night: An Experience-Centered Study of Supernatural Assault Traditions.* Philadelphia: University of Pennsylvania Press, 1982.

Hughes, D. *A Comparison of Trance Channeling and Multiple Personality Disorder.* Paper presented at the American Anthropological Association meeting, New Orleans, 1990.

Hughes, D., and Melville, N.T. "Changes in Brainwave Activity During Trance Channeling: A Pilot Study." *Journal of Transpersonal Psychology,* 22(1990), 175–189.

Hume, D. *Essays and Treatises on Several Subjects.* Edinburgh: Bell and Bradfute, and W. Blackwood, 1825.

Huxley, A. *The Devils of Loudun.* London: Chatto and Windus, 1961.

Hyman, R. "'Cold Reading': How to Convince Strangers That You Know All About Them." *The Zetetic,* 1(1977), 18–37.

———"The Psychic Reading." In T.A. Sebeok & R. Rosenthal, eds., *The Clever Hans Phenomenon.* New York: New York Academy of Sciences, 1981, 169–181.

———"The Ganzfeld Psi Experiment: A Critical Appraisal." *Journal of Parapsychology,* 49 (1985), 3–49.

———*The Elusive Quarry: A Scientific Appraisal of Psychical Research.* Buffalo: Prometheus, 1989.

———"Anomaly or Artifact? Comments on Bem and Honorton," *Psychological Bulletin,* 115(1994), 19–24.

Hyman, R., and Honorton, C. "A Joint Communique: The Psi Ganzfeld Controversy." *Journal of Parapsychology,* 50(1986), 351–364.

Hynek, A.J. *The UFO Experience.* Chicago: Henry Regnery, 1972.

Idel, M. *Kabbalah: New Perspectives.* New Haven, CT: Yale University Press, 1988.

———"Universalization and Integration: Two Conceptions of Mystical Union in Jewish Mysticism." In M. Idel & B. McGinn, eds., *Mystical Union and Monotheistic Faith: An Ecumenical Dialogue.* New York: Macmillan, 1989, 27–58.

Illis, L. "On Porphyria and the Aetiology of Werewolves." In C.F. Otten, ed., *A Lycanthropy Reader: Werewolves in Western Culture.* Syracuse, NY: Syracuse University Press, 1986, 195–199.

Inglis, B. *Natural and Supernatural: A History of the Paranormal from the Earliest Times.* London: Hodder & Stoughton, 1977.

———*The Paranormal: An Encyclopedia of Psychic Phenomena.* London: Grafton Books, 1986.

———*Trance: A Natural History of Altered States of Mind.* London: Grafton Books, 1989.

Irwin, H.J. "The Psychological Function of Out-of-Body Experiences: So Who Needs the Out-of-Body Experience?" *Journal of Nervous and Mental Disease,* 169(1981), 244–248.

———*Flight of Mind: A Psychological Study of the Out-of-Body Experience.* Metuchen, NJ: Scarecrow Press, 1985a.

———"Parapsychological Phenomena and the Absorption Domain." *Journal of the American Society for Psychical Research,* 79(1985b), 1–11.

———"A Study of the Measurement and the Correlates of Paranormal Belief." *Journal of the American Society for Psychical Research,* 79(1985c), 301–326.

———"The Relationship Between Locus of Control and Belief in the Paranormal." *Parapsychological Journal of South Africa,* 7(1986), 1–23.

———*An Introduction to Parapsychology.* Jefferson, NC: McFarland, 1989a.

———"On Paranormal Disbelief: The Psychology of the Sceptic." In G.K. Zollschan, J.F. Schumaker &

G.F. Walsh, eds., *Exploring the Paranormal: Perspectives on Belief and Experience*. Bridport, England: Prism, 1989b, 305–312.

——"Fantasy- Proneness and Paranormal Beliefs." *Psychological Reports,* 66(1990a), 655–658.

——"Parapsychology Courses and Students' Belief in the Paranormal." *Journal of the Society for Psychical Research,* 56(1990b), 266–272.

——"Reasoning Skills of Paranormal Believers." *Journal of Parapsychology,* 55(1991a), 281–300.

——"A Study of Paranormal Belief, Psychological Adjustment, and Fantasy Proneness." *Journal of the American Society for Psychical Research,* 85(1991b), 317–331.

——"Origins and Functions of Paranormal Belief: The Role of Childhood Trauma and Interpersonal Control." *Journal of the American Society for Psychical Research,* 86(1992), 199–208.

——"Belief in the Paranormal: A Review of the Empirical Literature." *Journal of the American Society for Psychical Research,* 87(1993), 1–39.

Isakower, O. "A Contribution to the Psychopathology of Phenomena Associated with Falling Asleep." *International Journal of Psychoanalysis,* 19(1938), 331–345.

Jacobs, D.M. *The UFO Controversy in America.* Bloomington, IN: Indiana University Press, 1975.

——*Secret Life: Firsthand Accounts of UFO Abductions.* New York: Simon & Schuster, 1992.

James, W. *The Principles of Psychology.* New York: Dover, 1950.

——*The Varieties of Religious Experience: A Study in Human Nature.* New York: New American Library, 1958.

Jevning, R., Wallace, R.K., and Beidebach, M. "The Physiology of Meditation: A Review. A Wakeful Hypometabolic Integrated Response." *Neuroscience and Biobehavioral Reviews,* 16(1992), 415–424.

Jilek, W.G. *Indian Healing: Shamanic Ceremonialism in the Pacific Northwest Today.* Surrey, Canada: Hancock House, 1982.

Joesting, J., and Joesting, R. "Torrance's Creative Motivation Inventory and its Relationship to Several Personality Variables." *Psychological Reports,* 24(1969), 30.

Jones, W.H., Russell, D.W., and Nickel, T.W. "Belief in the Paranormal Scale: An Objective Instrument to Measure Belief in Magical Phenomena and Causes." *Journal Supplement Abstract Service, Catalog of Selected Documents in Psychology,* 7(1977), 100 (MS 1577).

Jones, W.H., and Zusne, L. "Teaching Anomalistic Psychology," *Teaching of Psychology,* 8(1981), 78–82.

Jung, C.G. *Memories, Dreams, Reflections.* New York: Vintage Books, 1965.

Kampman, R. "Hypnotically Induced Multiple Personality: An Experimental Study." *International Journal of Clinical and Experimental Hypnosis,* 29(1976), 215–227.

Kapelrud, A.S. "Shamanistic Features in the Old Testament," in Edsman, C. (Ed.). *Studies in Shamanism.* Stockholm: Almqvist and Wiksell, 1967, 90–96.

Kaplan, A. *Meditation and Kabbalah.* York Beach, ME: Samuel Weiser, 1982.

Kapleau, P. *The Three Pillars of Zen: Teaching, Practice, and Enlightenment.* Garden City, NY: Anchor Books, 1980.

Karagulla, S., and van Gelder Kunz, D. *The Chakras and the Human Energy Fields.* Wheaton, IL: Theosophical Publishing House, 1989.

Kasamatsu, A., and Hirai, T. "An Electroencephalographic Study on the Zen Meditation (Zazen)." *Psychologia,* 12(1969), 205–225.

Katz, J., and Melzack, R. "Pain 'Memories' in Phantom Limbs: Review and Clinical Observations." *Pain,* 43(1990), 319–336.

Kavanaugh, K. *John of the Cross: Selected Writings.* New York: Paulist Press, 1987.

Keel, J.A. *The Mothman Prophecies.* New York: Dutton, 1975.

Kellehear, A. "Culture, Biology, and the Near-Death Experience," *Journal of Nervous and Mental Disease,* 181(1993), 148–156.

Kenny, M.G. *The Passion of Ansel Bourne: Multiple Personality in American Culture.* Washington: Smithsonian Institution Press, 1986.

Kensinger, K.M. "Banisteriopsis Usage Among the Peruvian Cashinahua." In M.J. Harner, ed., *Hallucinogens and Shamanism.* New York: Oxford University Press, 1973, 9–14.

Kerckhoff, A.C., and Back, K.W. *The June Bug: A Study in Hysterical Contagion.* New York: Appleton-Century-Crofts, 1968.

Kerr, H. *Mediums, and Spirit-Rappers, and Roaring Radicals: Spiritualism in American Literature,*

1850–1900. Urbana, IL: University of Illinois Press, 1972.

Kieckhefer, R. *Magic in the Middle Ages.* Cambridge: Cambridge University Press, 1990.

Killen, P., Wildman, R.W., and Wildman, R.W.II. "Superstitiousness and Intelligence." *Psychological Reports,* 34(1974), 1158.

Klass, P.J. *UFOs Explained.* New York: Vintage Books, 1974.

———*UFO-Abductions: A Dangerous Game.* Buffalo: Prometheus, 1988.

Klimo, J. *Channeling: Investigations on Receiving Information from Paranormal Sources.* Los Angeles, J.P. Tarcher, 1987.

Kluver, H. *Mescal and the Mechanisms of Hallucinations.* Chicago: University of Chicago Press, 1966.

Knox, R. *Enthusiasm.* New York: Oxford University Press, 1961.

Kothari, L.K., Bordia, A., and Gupta, O.P. "Studies on a Yogi During an Eight-Day Confinement in a Sealed Underground Pit." *Indian Journal of Medical Research,* 61(1973), 1645–1650.

Kraljevic, S. *The Apparitions of Our Lady of Medjugorje.* Chicago: Franciscan-Herald Press, 1984.

Krantz, G.S. *Big Footprints: A Scientific Inquiry into the Reality of Sasquatch.* Boulder, CO: Johnson Books, 1992.

Krishna, G. *Kundalini: The Evolutionary Energy in Man.* Boston: Shambhala, 1970.

Kroll, J., and Bachrach, B. "Visions and Psychopathology in the Middle Ages." *Journal of Nervous and Mental Disease,* 170(1982), 41–49.

Kubie, L.S. "The Use of Induced Hypnagogic Reveries in the Recovery of Repressed Amnesic Data." *Bulletin of the Menninger Clinic,* 7(1943), 172–182.

Kumar, V.K., Pekala, R.J., and Cummings, J. "Sensation Seeking, Drug Use and Reported Paranormal Beliefs and Experiences." *Personality and Individual Differences,* (in press).

Kurtz, P. *A Skeptic's Handbook of Parapsychology.* Buffalo: Prometheus, 1985.

LaBerge, S., and Gackenbach, J. "Lucid Dreaming." In B.B. Wolman and M. Ullman, eds., *Handbook of States of Consciousness.* New York: Van Nostrand Reinhold, 1986, 159–198.

Lajoie, D.H., and Shapiro, S.I. "Definitions of Transpersonal Psychology: The First Twenty-Three Years." *Journal of Transpersonal Psychology,* 24(1992), 79–98.

Larson, G.J., and Bhattacharya, R.S., eds. *Samkhya: A Dualist Tradition in Indian Philosophy.* Princeton: Princeton University Press, 1987.

Lasagna, L. "Let Magic Cast its Spell." *The Sciences,* 24[3] (1984), 10–12.

Laski, M. *Ecstasy in Secular and Religious Experiences.* London: Cresset Press, 1961.

Latourette, K.S. *A History of Christianity, Volume I: to A.D. 1500.* San Francisco: Harper and Row, 1975.

Laurentin, R., and Joyeux, H. *Scientific and Medical Studies on the Apparitions at Medjugorje.* Dublin: Veritas, 1987.

Lavallee, M., and Persinger, M.A. "Left-Ear Suppressions During Dichotic Listening, Ego-Alien Intrusion Experiences and Spiritualistic Beliefs in Normal Women," *Perceptual and Motor Skills,* 75(1992), 547–551.

Lawson, A.H. "Hypnosis of Imaginary Abductees." In C. Fuller, ed., *Proceedings of the First International UFO Congress.* New York: Warner Books, 1980, 195–238.

———"A Touchstone for Fallacious Abductions: Birth Trauma Imagery in CE III Narratives." In M. Hynek, ed., *The Spectrum of UFO Research.* Chicago: J. Allen Hynek Center for UFO Studies, 1988, 71–98.

Lea, H.C. *Materials Toward a History of Witchcraft.* New York: Thomas Yoseloff, 1957.

Levy, D.A., and Nail, P.R. "Contagion: A Theoretical and Empirical Review and Reconceptualization," *Genetic, Social and General Psychology Monographs,* 119(1993), 233–284.

Lewis, I.M. *Ecstatic Religion: An Anthropological Study of Spirit Possession and Shamanism.* Harmondsworth, England: Penguin, 1971.

Lewis-Fernandez, R., "The Proposed DSM-IV Trance and Possession Disorder Category: Potential Benefits and Risks," *Transcultural Psychiatric Research Review,* 29(1992), 301–317.

Lewis-Williams, J.D., and Dowson, T.A. "The Signs of All Times: Entoptic Phenomena in Upper Palaeolithic Art." *Current Anthropology,* 29(1988), 201–245.

Lilly, J.C. *The Deep Self.* New York: Simon and Schuster, 1977.

Lipman, K. "Preface." In N. Norbu, *Dzog Chen and Zen*. Oakland, CA: Zhang Zhung Editions, 1984, 5–11.

Lishman, W.A. *Organic Psychiatry: The Psychological Consequences of Cerebral Disorder*. Oxford: Blackwell, 1987.

Loftus, E.F. *Eyewitness Testimony*. Cambridge, MA: Harvard University Press, 1979.

———"The Reality of Repressed Memories," *American Psychologist*, 48(1993), 518–537.

Loftus, E.F., and Ketcham, K. *Witness for the Defense: The Accused, the Eyewitness, and the Expert who puts Memory on Trial*. New York: St. Martin's Press, 1991.

Loftus, E.F., and Zanni, G. "Eyewitness Testimony: The Influence of the Wording of a Question." *Bulletin of the Psychonomic Society*, 5(1975), 86–88.

Lovecraft, H.P. *Fungi From Yuggoth and other Poems*. New York: Ballantine, 1971.

Luck, G. *Arcana Mundi: Magic and the Occult in the Greek and Roman Worlds*. Baltimore: Johns Hopkins University Press, 1985.

Ludwig, A.M. "Altered States of Consciousness." In R. Prince, ed., *Trance and Possession States*. Montreal: R.M. Bucke Memorial Society, 1968.

Lukoff, D., Zanger, R., and Lu, F. "Transpersonal Psychology Research Review: Psychoactive Substances and Transpersonal States." *Journal of Transpersonal Psychology*, 22(1990), 107–148.

Lynn, S.J., and Rhue, J.W. "Fantasy Proneness: Hypnosis, Developmental Antecedents, and Psychopathology" *American Psychologist,* 43(1988), 35–44.

———eds. *Theories of Hypnosis: current Models and Perspectives*. New York: Guilford Press, 1991.

Lynn, S.J., Rhue, J.W., and Weekes, J.R. "Hypnotic Involuntariness: A Social Cognitive Analysis," *Psychological Review,* 97(1990), 169–184.

Lynn, S.J., Weekes, J.R., and Milano, M.J. "Reality Versus Suggestion: Pseudomemory in Hypnotizable and Simulating Subjects." *Journal of Abnormal Psychology,* 98(1989), 137–144.

M. *The Gospel of Sri Ramakrishna*. New York: Rama Vivekananda Center, 1952.

Mackal, R.P. *The Monsters of Loch Ness*. Chicago: Swallow, 1976.

———*A Living Dinosaur?: In Search of Mokele-Mbembe*. Leiden, Netherlands: E.J. Brill, 1987.

MacKenzie, A. *Hauntings and Apparitions*. London: Society for Psychical Research, 1982.

MacPhillamy, D.J. "Some Personality Effects of Long-Term Zen Monasticism and Religious Training." *Journal for the Scientific Study of Religion*, 25(1986), 304–319.

Maher, M.C., and Hansen, G.P. "Quantitative Investigation of a Reported Haunting Using Several Detection Techniques." *Journal of the American Society for Psychical Research,* 86(1992), 347–374.

Maher, M.C., and Schmeidler, G.R. "Quantitative Investigation of a Recurrent Apparition." *Journal of the American Society for Psychical Research,* 69(1975), 341–352.

Malamud, J.R. "Becoming Lucid in Dreams and Waking Life." In B.B. Wolman and M. Ullman, eds., *Handbook of States of Consciousness*. New York: Van Nostrand Reinhold, 1986, 590–612.

Mandell, A. "Toward a Psychobiology of Transcendence: God in the Brain." In J.M. Davidson and R.J. Davidson, eds., *Psychobiology of Consciousness*. New York: Plenum, 1980, 379–463.

Maple, E. "Aix-en-Provence Nuns." In R. Cavendish, ed., *Man, Myth and Magic*. New York: Marshall Cavendish Corporation, 1970, 42–44.

Marks, D.J., and Kammann, R. *The Psychology of the Psychic*. Buffalo: Prometheus, 1980.

Maslow, A.H. *Toward a Psychology of Being*. New York: Van Nostrand, 1968.

———*Religions, Values, and Peak-Experiences*. New York: Penguin, 1976.

Matlock, J.G. "Past Life Case Studies." In S. Krippner, ed., *Advances in Parapsychological Research, Volume 6*. Jefferson, NC: McFarland, 1990, 184–267.

Matus, T. *Yoga and the Jesus Prayer Tradition: An Experiment in Faith*. Ramsey, NJ: Paulist Press, 1984.

Mauskopf, S.H., and McVaugh, M.R. *The Elusive Science*. Baltimore: Johns Hopkins University Press, 1980.

Mavromatis, A., and Richardson, J.T.E. "Hypnagogic Imagery." In A.A. Sheikh, ed., *International Review of Mental Imagery, Volume 1*. New York: Human Sciences Press, 1984, 159–190.

McBurney, D.H. "ESP in the Psychology Curriculum." *Teaching of Psychology*, 3(1976), 66–69.

McGarry, J.J., and Newberry, B.H. "Beliefs in Paranormal Phenomena and Locus of Control: A Field

Study." *Journal of Personality and Social Psychology*, 41(1981), 725–736.

McGinn, B. "Love, Knowledge and Unio Mystica in the Western Christian Tradition." In M. Idel and B. McGinn, eds., *Mystical Union and Monotheistic Faith: An Ecumenical Dialogue*. New York: Macmillan, 1989, 59–86.

McKellar, P. *Imagination and Thinking*. London: Cohen and West, 1957.

McKenna, T. *Food of the Gods: The Search for the Original Tree of Knowledge*. New York: Bantam, 1992.

McLenon, J. "A Survey of Elite Scientists: Their Attitudes Toward ESP and Parapsychology." *Journal of Parapsychology*, 46(1982), 127–152.

Medalia, N., and Larsen, O. "Diffusion and Belief in a Collective Delusion," *American Sociological Review*, 23(1958), 180–186.

Meheust, B. *Science Fiction et Soucoupes Volantes*. Paris: Mercure de France, 1978.

Meier, S.A. "Theophany," in Metzger, B.M., and Coogan, M.D. eds., *The Oxford Companion to the Bible*. New York: Oxford University Press, 740–741.

Melzack, R. "Phantom Limbs." *Scientific American*, 266(1992), 120–127.

Menzel, D.H., and Boyd, L.G. *The World of Flying Saucers*. Garden City, NY: Doubleday, 1963.

Menzel, D.H., and Taves, E.H. *The UFO Enigma*. Garden City, NY: Doubleday, 1977.

Merkur, D. *Gnosis: An Esoteric Tradition of Mystical Visions and Unions*. Albany, NY: SUNY Press, 1993.

Merskey, H. *The Analysis of Hysteria*. London, Bailliere Tindall, 1979.

Messer, W.S., and Griggs, R.A. "Student Belief and Involvement in the Paranormal and Performance in Introductory Psychology." *Teaching of Psychology*, 16(1989), 187–191.

Meurger, M., and Gagnon, C. *Lake Monster Traditions: A Cross-Cultural Analysis*. London: Fortean Tomes, 1988.

Miller, P.C. "In Praise of Nonsense." In A.H. Armstrong, ed., *Classical Mediterranean Spirituality: Egyptian, Greek, Roman*. New York: Crossroad, 1986, 481–505.

Mishra, R.S. *Yoga Sutras: The Textbook of Yoga Psychology*. Garden City, NY: Anchor Books, 1973.

Moody, R.A. *Life After Life*. Covington, GA: Mockingbird, 1975.

Moody, R.A. "Family Reunions: Visionary Encounters With the Departed in a Modern-Day Psychomanteum," *Journal of Near-Death Studies*, 11(1992), 83–121.

Moon, M.L. "Artists Contrasted with Non-Artists Concerning Belief in ESP: A Poll." *Journal of the American Society for Psychical Research*, 69(1975), 161–166.

Morris, R.L. "Parapsychology." In A. Colman and M.G. Beaumont, eds., *Psychology Survey 7*. Leicester: British Psychological Society, 1989, 232–256.

Morris, R.L., Edge, H., Palmer, J., and Rush, J. *Foundations of Parapsychology: Exploring the Boundaries of Human Capability*. London: Routledge and Kegan Paul, 1986.

Motoyama, H. *The Correlation Between Psi Energy and Ki: Unification of Religion and Science*. Tokyo: Human Science Press, 1991.

Muhl, A. *Automatic Writing: An Approach to the Unconscious*. New York: Helix, 1963.

Mungas, D. "Interictal Behaviour Abnormality in Temporal Lobe Epilepsy: A Specific Syndrome or Non-Specific Psychopathology?" *Archives of General Psychiatry*, 39(1982), 108–111.

Munn, H. "The Mushrooms of Language." In M.J. Harner, ed., *Hallucinogens and Shamanism*. New York: Oxford University Press, 1973, 86–122.

Murphy, K., and Lester, D. "A Search for Correlates of Belief in ESP." *Psychological Reports*, 38(1976), 82.

Murphy, M. *The Future of the Body: Explorations into the Further Evolution of Human Nature*. Los Angeles: J.P. Tarcher, 1992.

Myerhoff, B.G. *Peyote Hunt: The Sacred Journey of the Huichol Indians*. Ithaca, NY: Cornell University Press, 1974.

Myers, S.A., and Austrin, H.R. "Distal Eidetic Technology: Further Characteristics of the Fantasy-Prone Personality." *Journal of Mental Imagery*, 9(1985), 57–66.

Myers, S.A., Austrin, H.R., Grisso, J.T., and Nickeson, R.C. "Personality Characteristics as Related to the Out-of-Body Experience." *Journal of Parapsychology*, 47(1983), 131–144.

Nadon, R., and Kihlstrom, J.F. "Hypnosis, Psi, and the Psychology of Anomalous Experience." *Behavioral and Brain Sciences,* 10(1987), 597–599.

Nadon, R., Laurence, J., and Perry, C. "Multiple Predictors of Hypnotic Susceptibility." *Journal of Personality and Social Psychology,* 53(1987), 948–960.

Namgyal Rinpoche. *The Womb of Form: Pith Instructions in the Six Yogas of Naropa.* Ottawa: Crystal Word, 1981.

Napier, J. *Bigfoot: The Yeti and Sasquatch in Myth and Reality.* London: Jonathan Cape, 1972.

Naranjo, C. "Drug-Induced States" In B.B. Wolman and M. Ullman, eds., *Handbook of States of Consciousness.* New York: Van Nostrand Reinhold, 1986, 365–394.

Neher, A. "Auditory Driving Observed with Scalp Electrodes in Normal Subjects." *Electroencephalography and Clinical Neurophysiology,* 13(1961), 449–451.

———"A Physiological Explanation of Unusual Behavior in Ceremonies Involving Drums." *Human Biology,* 34(1962), 151–160.

———A. *The Psychology of Transcendence.* New York: Dover, 1990.

Nelson, C. "The Virgin of Zeitoun." *Worldview,* 16[Sept](1973), 5–11.

Nelson, G.K. "Preliminary Study of the Electroencephalograms of Mediums," *Parapsychologica,* 4(1970), 30–35.

Nelson, G.K., and Neppe, V.M. "The Neurophysiological Wave Correlates of a Controlled Sample of Subjective Paranormal Experients: A Preliminary Report" *Parapsychological Journal of South Africa,* 1[2](1980), 99–101.

Nelson, P.L. "Personality Factors in the Frequency of Reported Spontaneous Praeternatural Experiences." *Journal of Transpersonal Psychology,* 21(1989), 193–210.

Neppe, V.M. "Anomalies of Smell in the Subjective Paranormal Experient." *Psychoenergetic Systems,* 5(1983a), 11–27.

———"Temporal Lobe Symptomatology in Subjective Paranormal Experients." *Journal of the American Society for Psychical Research,* 77(1983b), 1–30.

———"Anomalistic Experience and the Cerebral Cortex." In S. Krippner, ed., *Advances in Parapsychological Research, Volume 6.* Jefferson, NC: McFarland, 1990, 168–183.

Nickell, J. *Looking for a Miracle: Weeping Icons, Relics, Stigmata, Visions and Healing Cures.* Buffalo: Prometheus, 1993.

Nickell, J., and Fischer, J.F. "Incredible Cremations: Investigating Spontaneous Combustion Deaths." In K. Frazier, ed., *The Hundredth Monkey and Other Paradigms of the Paranormal.* Buffalo: Prometheus, 1991, 194–199.

Noll, R. "Shamanism and Schizophrenia: A State-Specific Approach to the 'Schizophrenia Metaphor' of Shamanic States." *American Ethnologist,* 10(1983), 443–459.

———"Mental Imagery Cultivation as a Cultural Phenomenon: The Role of Visions in Shamanism." *Current Anthropology,* 26(1985), 443–462.

———*Bizarre Diseases of the Mind.* New York: Berkley, 1990.

———*The Encyclopedia of Schizophrenia and the Psychotic Disorders.* New York: Facts On File, 1992a.

———*Vampires, Werewolves and Demons: Twentieth Century Reports in the Psychiatric Literature.* New York: Brunner/Mazel, 1992b.

Oesterreich, T.K. *Possession, Demoniacal and Other, Among Primitive Races, in Antiquity, the Middle Ages, and Modern Times.* Secaucus, NJ: Citadel Press, 1966.

Oltmanns, T.F., and Maher, B.A., eds. *Delusional Beliefs.* New York: Wiley, 1988.

Osis, K., and Haraldsson, E. *At the Hour of Death.* New York: Hastings House, 1986.

Otis, L.P., and Alcock, J.E. "Factors Affecting Extraordinary Belief." *Journal of Social Psychology,* 118(1982), 77–85.

Otten, C.F., ed. *A Lycanthropy Reader: Werewolves in Western Culture.* Syracuse, NY: Syracuse University Press, 1986.

Otto, R. *The Idea of the Holy: An Inquiry into the Nonrational Factor in the Idea of the Divine and Its Relation to the Rational.* Oxford: Oxford University Press, 1923.

Owen, A.R.G. *Can We Explain the Poltergeist?* New York: Garrett, 1964.

———"Stigmata." In R. Cavendish, ed., *Man, Myth and Magic.* New York: Marshall Cavendish Corporation, 1970, 2697–2702.

Owen, I., with Sparrow, M. *Conjuring up Philip*. New York: Harper and Row, 1976.

Padgett, V.R., Benassi, V.A., and Singer, B.F. "Belief in ESP among Psychologists." In K. Frazier, ed., *Paranormal Borderlands of Science*. Buffalo: Prometheus Books, 1981, 66–67.

Pagels, E.H. "Visions, Appearances, and Apostolic Authority: Gnostic and Orthodox Traditions." In B. Aland, ed., *Gnosis: Festschrift fur Hans Jonas*. Gottingen: 1978, 415–430.

Palmer, J. "Scoring in ESP Tests as a Function of Belief in ESP. Part I, The Sheep-Goat Effect." *Journal of the American Society for Psychical Research*, 65(1971), 373–408.

———"Progressive Skepticism: A Critical Approach to the Psi Controversy." *Journal of Parapsychology*, 50(1986), 29–42.

———"From Survival to Transcendence: Reflections on Psi as Anomalous." *Journal of Parapsychology*. 56(1992), 229–254.

Palmer, J., and Lieberman, R. "ESP and Out-of-Body Experiences: A Further Study." In J.D. Morris, W.G. Roll, and R.L. Morris, eds., *Research in Parapsychology 1975*. Metuchen, NJ: Scarecrow Press, 1976, 102–106.

Palmer, J., and van der Velden, I. "ESP and 'Hypnotic Imagination': A Group Free-Response Study." *European Journal of Parapsychology*, 4(1983), 413–434.

Panton, Y., and Fischer, R. "Hallucinogenic Drug-Induced Behavior Under Sensory Attenuation." *Archives of General Psychiatry*, 28(1973), 434–438.

Parnell, J. "Personality Characteristics of Persons Who Claim UFO Experiences." *Journal of UFO Studies*, 2(1990), 45–58.

Pasachoff, J.M., Cohen, R.J., and Pasachoff, N.W. "Belief in the Supernatural among Harvard and West African University Students." *Nature*, 227(1970), 971–972.

Pasricha, S. *Claims of Reincarnation: An Empirical Study of Cases in India*. New Delhi: Harman, 1990.

———"A Systematic Survey of Near-Death Experiences in South India." *Journal of Scientific Exploration*, 7(1993), 161–172.

Pasricha, S., and Stevenson, I. "Near-Death Experiences in India." *Journal of Nervous and Mental Disease*, 174(1986), 165–170.

Pattison, E.M., Kahan, J., and Hurd, G.S. "Trance and Possession States." In B.B. Wolman and M. Ullman, eds., *Handbook of States of Consciousness*. New York: Van Nostrand Reinhold, 1986, 286–310.

Peers, E.A. *Handbook to the Life and Times of St. Teresa and St. John of the Cross*. London: Burns and Oates, 1954.

Pekala, R.J., Kumar, V.K., and Cummings, J. "Types of High Hypnotically Susceptible Individuals and Reported Attitudes and Experiences of the Paranormal and the Anomalous." *Journal of the American Society for Psychical Research*, 86(1992), 135–150.

Pelikan, J. *The Spirit of Eastern Christendom (600–1700)*. Chicago: University of Chicago Press, 1974.

Persinger, M.A. *The Paranormal. Part I. Patterns*. New York: MSS Information Corporation, 1974.

———"Propensity to Report Paranormal Experiences is Correlated with Temporal Lobe Signs." *Perceptual and Motor Skills*, 59(1984), 583–586.

———*The God Consciousness in the Brain*. New York: Springer, 1988a.

———"Increased Geomagnetic Activity and the Occurrence of Bereavement Hallucinations: Evidence for Melatonin-Mediated Microseizuring in the Temporal Lobe?" *Neuroscience Letters*, 88(1988b), 271–274.

———"The 'Visitor' Experience and the Personality: The Temporal Lobe Factor." In D. Stillings, ed., *Cyberbiological Studies of the Imaginal Component in the UFO Contact Experience*. St. Paul: Archaeus Project, 1989, 157–171.

———"Vectorial Cerebral Hemisphericity as Differential Sources for the Sensed Presence, Mystical Experiences and Religious Conversions," *Perceptual and Motor Skills*, 76(1993), 915–930.

Persinger, M.A., and Lafreniere, G. *Space-Time Transients and Unusual Events*. Chicago: Nelson-Hall, 1977.

Persinger, M.A., and Makarec, K. "Temporal Lobe Epileptic Signs and Correlative Behaviors Displayed by Normal Populations." *Journal of General Psychiatry*, 114(1987), 179–195.

Persinger, M.A., and Schaut, G.B. "Geomagnetic Factors in Subjective Telepathic, Precognitive, and Postmortem Experiences." *Journal of the Ameri-*

can Society for Psychical Research, 82(1988), 217–235.

Piaget, J. *Judgment and Reasoning in the Child.* London: Routledge and Kegan Paul, 1969.

Pitman, R.K. "Tourette's Syndrome and Ethology." *American Journal of Psychiatry,* 140(1983), 652.

Plank, R. *The Emotional Significance of Imaginary Beings.* Springfield, IL: Charles Thomas, 1968.

Polzella, D.J., Popp, R.J., and Hinsman, M.C. *ESP?* Paper presented at the annual meeting of the American Psychological Association, Chicago, 1975.

Posey, T.B., and Losch, M.F. "Auditory Hallucinations of Hearing Voices in 375 Normal Subjects." *Imagination, Cognition and Personality,* 2(1983), 99–113.

Prabhavananda, S., and Manchester, F. *The Upanishads: Breath of the Eternal.* New York: New American Library, 1957.

Price, A.F., and Wong, M. *The Diamond Sutra and the Sutra of Hui Neng.* Berkeley, CA: Shambhala, 1969.

Proust, M. *Swann's Way.* New York: Modern Library, 1928.

Randall, T.M. "Belief in the Paranormal Declines: 1977–1987." *Psychological Reports,* 66(1990), 1347–1351.

Randall, T.M., and Desrosiers, M. "Measurement of Supernatural Belief: Sex Differences and Locus of Control." *Journal of Personality Assessment,* 44(1980), 493–498.

Randall, W., and Randall, S. "The Solar Wind and Hallucinations—A Possible Relation Due to Magnetic Disturbances." *Bioelectromagnetics,* 12(1992), 67–70.

Randles, J. *Mind Monsters: Invaders from Inner Space?* Wellingborough, England: Aquarian Press, 1990.

Rao, K.R. "Hume's Fallacy." *Journal of Parapsychology,* 45(1981), 147–152.

Raphael-Staude, J., ed. *Consciousness and Creativity.* Berkeley, CA: Pan/Proteus, 1977.

Raschke, C. "UFOs: Ultraterrestrial Agents of Cultural Deconstruction." *Archaeus,* 5(1989), 21–32.

Ratnoff, O.D. "The Psychogenic Purpuras: A Review of Autoerythrocyte Sensitization, Autosensitization to DNA, 'Hysterical' and Factitial Bleeding, and the Religious Stigmata." *Seminars in Hematology,* 17(1980), 192–212.

Rawcliffe, D.H. *The Psychology of the Occult.* London: Derricke Ridway, 1952.

Reed, G. *Obsessional Experience and Compulsive Behaviour.* Orlando: Academic Press, 1985.

———*The Psychology of Anomalous Experience: A Cognitive Approach.* Buffalo: Prometheus, 1988.

———"The Psychology of Channeling." *Skeptical Inquirer,* 13(1989), 385–390.

Reichel-Dolmatoff, G. *Amazonian Cosmos: The Sexual and Religious Symbolism of the Tukano Indians.* Chicago: University of Chicago Press, 1971.

Reid, F. *Following Darkness.* London: Arnold, 1902.

Rhie, M.M., and Thurman, R.A.F. *Wisdom and Compassion: The Sacred Art of Tibet.* New York: Harry N. Abrams, 1991.

Rhine, L.E. *Hidden Channels of the Mind.* New York: William Morrow, 1965.

———*Mind Over Matter: Psychokinesis.* New York: Macmillan, 1970.

Richards, D.G. "Hypnotic Susceptibility and Subjective Psychic Experiences: A Study of Participants in A.R.E. Conferences." *Journal of Parapsychology,* 54(1990), 35–52.

Ring, K. *The Omega Project: Near-Death Experiences, UFO Encounters, and Mind at Large.* New York: William Morrow, 1992.

Ripinsky-Naxon, M. *The Nature of Shamanism: Substance and Function of a Religious Metaphor.* Albany, NY: SUNY Press, 1993.

Rivers, W.H.R. *Instinct and the Unconscious.* Cambridge: Cambridge University Press, 1920.

Robbins, R.H. *The Encyclopedia of Witchcraft and Demonology.* New York: Bonanza Books, 1981.

Robinson, D. *To Stretch a Plank: A Survey of Psychokinesis.* Chicago: Nelson Hall, 1981.

Rodin, E.A. "The Reality of Death Experiences: A Personal Perspective." *Journal of Nervous and Mental Disease,* 168(1980), 259–263.

Rogo, D.S. *Miracles: A Scientific Exploration of Wondrous Phenomena.* London: Aquarian Press, 1991.

Roll, W.G. *The Poltergeist.* New York: Signet, 1974.

Roney-Dougal, S. "'Occult' Conference Questionnaire." *Journal of the Society for Psychical Research,* 52(1984), 379–382.

Rosenfield, I. *The Invention of Memory.* New York: Basic Books, 1988.

Rosenhan, D.L. "On Being Sane in Insane Places." *Science,* 179(1973), 250–258.

Rosnow, R.L., and Fine, G.A. *Rumor and Gossip: The Social Psychology of Hearsay.* New York: Elsevier, 1976.

Rossi, E.L. "Altered States of Consciousness in Everyday Life: Ultradian Rhythms." In B.B. Wolman and M. Ullman, eds., *Handbook of States of Consciousness.* New York: Van Nostrand Reinhold, 1986, 97–132.

Russell, J.B. *Witchcraft in the Middle Ages.* Ithaca, NY: Cornell University Press, 1972.

Sachs, M. *The UFO Encyclopedia.* New York: Perigee, 1980.

Sacks, O. *Migraine: The Evolution of a Common Disorder.* London: Faber and Faber, 1970.

———*The Man Who Mistook His Wife for a Hat.* New York: Harper and Row, 1985.

Salter, C.A., and Routledge, L.M. "Supernatural Beliefs among Graduate Students at the University of Pennsylvania." *Nature,* 232(1971), 278–279.

Sanderson, I.T. *Abominable Snowmen: Legend Come to Life.* Philadelphia: Chilton, 1961.

———*Investigating the Unexplained: A Compendium of Disquieting Mysteries of the Natural World.* Englewood Cliffs, NJ: Prentice-Hall, 1972.

Sannella, L. *The Kundalini Experience.* Lower Lake, CA: Integral Publishing, 1987.

Sarbin, T.R., and Juhasz, J.B. "The Historical Background of the Concept of Hallucination." *Journal of the History of the Behavioral Sciences,* 3(1967), 339–358.

Sargant, W. *The Mind Possessed: A Physiology of Possession, Mysticism, and Faith Healing.* London: Pan Books, 1973.

Schatzman, M. "Evocations of Unreality," *New Scientist,* 87(1980), 935–937.

Schimmel, A. *Mystical Dimensions of Islam.* Chapel Hill, NC: University of North Carolina Press, 1975.

Schipper, K. *The Taoist Body.* Berkeley: University of California Press, 1993.

Schmeidler, G.R. *Parapsychology and Psychology: Matches and Mismatches.* Jefferson, NC: Mc-Farland, 1988.

———"PK: Recent Publications and an Evaluation of the Quantitative Research." In S. Krippner, ed., *Advances in Parapsychological Research, Volume 6.* Jefferson, NC: McFarland, 1990, 13–53.

Schmidt, M. "Crazy Wisdom: The Shaman as Mediator of Realities." In S. Nicholson, ed., *Shaman-*

ism: An Expanded View of Reality. Wheaton, IL: Theosophical Publishing House, 1987, 62–75.

Scholem, G. *Kabbalah.* New York: New American Library, 1978.

Schultes, R.E., and Hofmann, A. *Plants of the Gods: Their Sacred, Healing and Hallucinogenic Powers.* Rochester, VT: Healing Arts Press, 1992.

Schultz, G., and Melzack, R., "Visual Hallucinations and Mental State: A Study of 14 Charles Bonnet Syndrome Hallucinators," *Journal of Nervous and Mental Disease,* 181(1993), 639–643.

Schumaker, J.F. "Mental Health, Belief Deficit Compensation, and Paranormal Belief." *Journal of Psychology,* 121(1987), 451–457.

———*Wings of Illusion: The Origin, Nature and Future of Paranormal Belief.* Buffalo: Prometheus, 1990.

Sebeok, T.A., and Rosenthal, R., eds. *The Clever Hans Phenomenon.* New York: New York Academy of Sciences, 1981.

Sedman, G. "'Inner Voices': Phenomenological and Clinical Aspects." *British Journal of Psychiatry* 112(1966), 485–490.

Sekida, K. *Zen Training: Methods and Philosophy.* New York: Weatherhill, 1975.

Seligmann, K. *The History of Magic and the Occult.* New York: Harmony Books, 1983.

Sensky, T. "Religiosity, Mystical Experience and Epilepsy." In F.C. Rose, ed, *Research Progress in Epilepsy.* London: Pitman Medical, 1983, 214–220.

Shapiro, D.H. *Meditation: Self-Regulation Strategy and Altered State of Consciousness.* New York: Aldine, 1980.

Shapiro, D.H., and Walsh, R.N., eds. *Meditation: Classic and Contemporary Perspectives.* New York: Aldine, 1984.

Sheaffer, R. *The UFO Verdict: Examining the Evidence.* Buffalo: Prometheus, 1986.

Sherif, M. "A Study of Some Social Factors in Perception." *Archives of Psychology,* 27(1935), #187.

Sherley-Price, L. *The Little Flowers of Saint Francis.* Harmondsworth, England: Penguin, 1959.

Shibayama, Z. *Zen Comments on the Mumonkan.* San Francisco: Harper & Row, 1974.

Shiels, D., and Berg, P. "A Research Note on Sociological Variables Related to Belief in Psychic Phenomena." *Wisconsin Sociologist,* 14(1977), 24–31.

Shorter, E. *From Paralysis to Fatique: A History of Psychosomatic Illness in the Modern Era.* New York: Free Press, 1992.

Siegel, R.K., "Hallucinations." *Scientific American,* 237(1977), 132–140.

———"The Psychology of Life After Death." *American Psychologist,* 35(1980), 911–931.

———*Intoxication: Life in Pursuit of Artificial Paradise.* London: Simon & Schuster, 1989.

Singer, B., and Benassi, V.A. "Occult Beliefs." *American Scientist,* 69(1981), 49–55.

Sirois, F. "Epidemic Hysteria," *Acta Psychiatrica Scandinavica Supplementum,* 252(1974), 7–44.

Skirda, R.J., and Persinger, M.A. "Positive Associations Among Dichotic Listening Errors, Complex Partial Epileptic-Like Signs, and Paranormal Beliefs," *Journal of Nervous and Mental Disease,* 181(1993), 663–667.

Slade, H. *Exploration into Contemplative Prayer.* New York: Paulist Press, 1975.

Slotkin, J.S. *The Peyote Religion.* Glencoe, IL: Free Press, 1956.

Smelser, N.J. *Theory of Collective Behavior.* New York: Free Press, 1962.

Smith, J.C. "Meditation as Psychotherapy: A New Look at the Evidence." In M.A. West, ed. *The Psychology of Meditation.* Oxford: Clarendon Press, 1987, 136–149.

Smith, P., and Irwin, H.J. "Out-of-Body Experiences, Needs, and the Experimental Approach: A Laboratory Study." *Parapsychology Review,* 12(1981), 1–4.

Snelling, J. *The Buddhist Handbook: A Complete Guide to Buddhist Teaching, Practice, History and Schools.* London: Century, 1987.

Sno, H.N., Schalken, H.F.A., De Jonghe, F. and Koeter, M.W.J. "The Inventory for Deja Vu Experiences Assessment," *Journal of Nervous and Mental Disease,* 182(1994), 27–33.

Snyder, C.R., and Shenkel, R.J. "The P.T. Barnum Effect," *Psychology Today,* 8(1975), 52–54.

Sopa, G. "*Samathavipasyanayuganaddha:* The Two Leading Principles of Buddhist Meditation." In M. Kiyota, ed. *Mahayana Buddhist Meditation: Theory and Practice.* Honolulu: University Press of Hawaii, 1978, 46–65.

Sox, D. *Relics and Shrines.* London: George Allen & Unwin, 1985.

Spanos, N.P. "Past-Life Hypnotic Regression: A Critical View." In K. Frazier, ed., *The Hundredth Monkey and Other Paradigms of the Paranormal.* Buffalo: Prometheus, 1991, 78–84.

Spanos, N.P., et. al. "Hypnotic Interview and Age Regression Procedures in the Elicitation of Multiple Personality Symptoms: A Simulation Study." *Psychiatry,* 49(1986), 298–311. New York: Academic Press.

Spanos, N.P., and Chaves, J.F. *Hypnosis: The Cognitive-Behavioral Perspective.* Buffalo: Prometheus, 1989.

Spanos, N.P., Cross, P.A., Dickson, K., and DuBreuil, S.C. "Close Encounters: An Examination of UFO Experiences," *Journal of Abnormal Psychology,* 102(1993), 624–632.

Spanos, N.P., Cross, W.P., Lepage, M., and Coristine, M. "Glossolalia as Learned Behavior: An Experimental Demonstration." *Journal of Abnormal Psychology,* 95(1986), 21–23.

Spanos, N.P., and Moretti, P. "Correlates of Mystical and Diabolical Experiences in a Sample of Female University Students." *Journal for the Scientific Study of Religion,* 27(1988), 105–116.

Spilka, B., Hood, R.W., and Gorsuch, R.L. *The Psychology of Religion: An Empirical Approach.* Englewood Cliffs, NJ: Prentice-Hall, 1985.

Sprinkle, L. "Hypnotic and Psychic Implications in the Investigation of UFO Reports." In C. Lorenzen and J. Lorenzen, eds., *Encounters with UFO Occupants.* New York: Berkley, 1976, 256–329.

Stace, W.T. *The Teachings of the Mystics.* New York: New American Library, 1960.

Stafford, P. *Psychedelics Encyclopedia.* Berkeley: Ronin, 1992.

Stanford, R.G. "The Out-of-Body Experience as an Imaginal Journey: The Developmental Perspective." *Journal of Parapsychology,* 51(1987), 137–156.

———"The Experimental Hypnosis—ESP Literature: A Review from the Hypothesis-Testing Perspective." *Journal of Parapsychology,* 56(1992), 39–56.

Stevenson, I. *Xenoglossy: A Review and Report of a Case.* Charlottesville, VA: University Press of Virginia, 1974.

———*Unlearned Language: New Studies in Xenoglossy.* Charlottesville, VA: University Press of Virginia, 1984.

————*Children Who Remember Previous Lives: A Question of Reincarnation.* Charlottesville, VA: University Press of Virginia, 1987.

Stewart, J.R. "Sasquatch Sightings in North Dakota: An Analysis of an Episode of Collective Delusion." In G.K. Zollschan, J.F. Schumaker, and G.F. Walsh, eds., *Exploring the Paranormal: Perspectives on Belief and Experience.* Bridport, England: Prism, 1989, 287–304.

Storr, A. *Jung: Selected Writings.* Bungay, England: Fontana Press, 1983.

Streng, F.J. *Emptiness: A Study in Religious Meaning.* Nashville: Abingdon Press, 1967.

Strieber, W. *Communion: A True Story.* New York: William Morrow, 1987.

Suzuki, D.T. *On Indian Mahayana Buddhism.* New York: Harper and Row, 1968.

Swords, M.D. "A Guide to UFO Research." *Journal of Scientific Exploration,* 7(1993), 65–88.

Tart, C.T., ed. *Altered States of Consciousness: A Book of Readings.* New York: Wiley, 1969.

————"Concerning the Scientific Study of the Human Aura." *Journal of the Society for Psychical Research,* 46(1972), 1–21.

————*States of Consciousness.* New York: Dutton, 1975.

————"Drug-Induced States of Consciousness." In B.B. Wolman, ed., *Handbook of Parapsychology.* New York: Van Nostrand Reinhold, 1977.

Taussig, M. *Shamanism, Colonialism, and the Wild Man: A Study in Terror and Healing.* Chicago: University of Chicago Press, 1987.

Taylor, S. *Positive Illusion: Creative Self-Deception and the Healthy Mind.* New York: Basic Books, 1989.

Tellegen, A. *Brief Manual for the Differential Personality Questionnaire.* Minneapolis: University of Minnesota, 1982.

Tellegen, A., and Atkinson, G. "Openness to Absorbing and Self-Altering Experiences ('Absorption'), a Trait Related to Hypnotic Susceptibility." *Journal of Abnormal Psychology,* 83(1974), 268–277.

Temkin, O. *The Falling Sickness: A History of Epilepsy from the Greeks to the Beginning of Modern Neurology.* Baltimore: Johns Hopkins University Press, 1971.

Thalbourne, M.A. "Extraversion and the Sheep-Goat Variable: A Conceptual Replication." *Journal of the American Society for Psychical Research,* 75(1981), 105–119.

————"Are Believers in Psi More Prone to Schizophrenia?" In R.A. White and J. Solfvin, eds., *Research in Parapsychology 1984.* Metuchen, NJ: Scarecrow Press, 1985, 85–88.

————*Psychic Experience, Creative Personality and Mystical Experience: Their Interrelationships and Their Relation to Psychotic Experience.* Unpublished paper, University of Adelaide, 1991.

————"Belief in the Paranormal and its Relationship to Schizophrenia-Relevant Measures: A Confirmatory Study." *British Journal of Clinical Psychology,* in press.

Thera, N. *The Heart of Buddhist Meditation: A Handbook of Mental Training Based on the Buddha's Way of Mindfulness.* London: Rider, 1962.

Thomas, L.E., and Cooper, P.E. "Incidence and Psychological Correlates of Intense Spiritual Experiences." *Journal of Transpersonal Psychology,* 12(1980), 75–85.

Thomason, S.G. "'Entities' in the Linguistic Minefield." *Skeptical Inquirer,* 13(1989), 391–396.

————"Past-Tongues Remembered?" In K. Frazier, ed., *The Hundredth Monkey and other Paradigms of the Paranormal.* Buffalo: Prometheus, 1991, 85–94.

Thompson, J.K. *Body Image Disturbance: Assessment and Treatment.* New York: Pergamon Press, 1990.

Thompson, K. *Angels and Aliens: UFOs and the Mythic Imagination.* Reading, MA: Addison-Wesley, 1991.

Thondup Rinpoche. *Hidden Teachings of Tibet: An Explanation of the Terma Tradition of the Nyingma School of Buddhism.* London: Wisdom, 1986.

Thouless, R.H. *From Anecdote to Experiment in Psychical Research.* London: Routledge and Kegan Paul, 1972.

Thurston, H. *The Physical Phenomena of Mysticism.* London: Burns Oates, 1952.

Tobacyk, J. "Reduction in Paranormal Belief among Participants in a College Course." *Skeptical Inquirer,* 8(1983a), 57–61.

————"Paranormal Beliefs, Interpersonal Trust, and Social Interest." *Psychological Reports,* 53(1983b), 229–230.

———"Death Threat, Death Concerns, and Paranormal Belief." *Death Education,* 7(1983c), 115–124.

———"Paranormal Belief and College Grade Point Average." *Psychological Reports,* 54(1984), 217–218.

Tobacyk, J., and Milford, G. "Belief in Paranormal Phenomena: Assessment Instrument Development and Implications for Personality Functioning." *Journal of Personality and Social Psychology,* 44(1983), 1029–1037.

Tobacyk, J., Miller, M.J., and Jones, G. "Paranormal Beliefs of High School Students." *Psychological Reports,* 55(1984), 255–261.

Tobacyk, J., and Mitchell, T.E. "Out-of-Body Experience Status as a Moderator of Effects of Narcissism on Paranormal Beliefs." *Psychological Reports,* 60(1987), 440–442.

Tobacyk, J., Nagot, E., and Miller, M. "Paranormal Beliefs and Locus of Control: A Multidimensional Examination." *Journal of Personality Assessment,* 52(1988), 241–246.

Tobacyk, J., and Pirttila-Backman, A. "Paranormal Beliefs and Their Implications in University Students From Finland and the United States." *Journal of Cross-Cultural Psychology,* 23(1992), 59–71.

Tobacyk, J., Pritchett, G., and Mitchell, T. "Paranormal Beliefs in Late-Adulthood." *Psychological Reports,* 62(1988), 965–966.

Tobacyk, J., and Wilkinson, L.V. "Magical Thinking and Paranormal Beliefs." *Journal of Social Behavior and Personality,* 5(1990), 255–264.

Tributsch, H. *When the Snakes Awake.* Cambridge, MA: MIT Press, 1982.

Trismegistus, R. *Into Thy Beak I Commend My Spirit: Strange Happenings in High Places.* Mt. Seymour, B.C.: Black Feather Press, 1989.

Truzzi, M. "Skeptics and Pseudo-Skeptics." In T. Schultz, ed., *The Fringes of Reason.* New York: Harmony Books, 1989, 204.

Tucci, G. *The Theory and Practice of the Mandala, With Special Reference to the Modern Psychology of the Subconscious.* London: Rider, 1969.

Twemlow, S.W., and Gabbard, G.O. "The Influence of Demographic/Psychological Factors and Preexisting Conditions on the Near-Death Experience." *Omega,* 15(1984), 223–235.

Tyrrell, G.N.M. *Apparitions.* New York: Collier, 1963.

Underhill, E. *Mysticism: A Study in the Nature and Development of Man's Spiritual Consciousness.* New York: Meridian, 1955.

Vallee, J. *Dimensions: A Casebook of Alien Contact.* New York: Ballantine, 1988.

Van Eeden, F. "A Study of Dreams." *Proceedings of the Society for Psychical Research,* 26(1913), 431–461.

Van Gennep, A. *The Rites of Passage.* London: Routledge & Kegan Paul, 1960.

Wade, N. "A Pyrrhonian Sledgehammer." *Science,* 197(1977), 646.

Wagner, M.W., and Ratzeburg, F.H. "Hypnotic Suggestibility and Paranormal Belief." *Psychological Reports,* 60(1987), 1069–1070.

Waite, A.E. *The Book of Ceremonial Magic: The Secret Tradition in Goetia, Including the Rites and Mysteries of Goetic Theurgy, Sorcery and Infernal Necromancy.* Secaucus, NJ: Citadel Press, 1961.

Walsh, W.T. *Our Lady of Fatima.* New York: Doubleday, 1954.

Walter, V.J., and Walter, W.G. "The Central Effects of Rhythmic Sensory Stimulation." *Electroencephalography and Clinical Neurophysiology,* 1(1949), 57–86.

Waltzer, H. "A Psychotic Family—Folie a Douze." *Journal of Nervous and Mental Disease,* 137(1963), 67–75.

Wambach, H. *Reliving Past Lives: The Evidence of Over 1,000 Hypnosis-Induced Past-Life Recalls.* New York: Barnes and Noble, 1978.

Wasson, R.G. *Soma: Divine Mushroom of Immortality.* New York: Harcourt, Brace & World, 1968.

Wasson, R.G., Hofmann, A., and Ruck, C.A.P. *The Road to Eleusis: Unveiling the Secrets of the Mysteries.* New York: Harcourt, Brace Jovanovich, 1978.

Watkins, A.J., and Bickel, W.S. "A Study of the Kirlian Effect." *Skeptical Inquirer,* 10(1986), 244–257.

Watkins, M. *Waking Dreams.* Dallas: Spring Publications, 1992.

Weil, A. "The New Nutrition for the Whole Person." *Magical Blend,* 27(1990), 67–70, 89–91.

West, L.J. *Hallucinations.* New York: Grune & Stratton, 1962.

West, M.A., ed. *The Psychology of Meditation.* Oxford: Clarendon Press, 1987.

White, K.E. *A Guide to the Saints.* New York: Ivy Books, 1991.

Wickramasekera, I. "A Model of People at High Risk to Develop Chronic Stress-Related Symptoms: Some Predictions." *Professional Psychology: Research and Practice,* 17(1986), 437–447.

———"Risk Factors for Parapsychological Verbal Reports, Hypnotizability and Somatic Complaints." In B. Shapin and L. Coly, eds. *Parapsychology and Human Nature.* New York: Parapsychology Foundation, 1989, 19–35.

———"Model of the Relationship Between Hypnotic Ability, Psi, and Sexuality." *Journal of Parapsychology,* 55(1991), 159–174.

Wierzbicki, M. "Reasoning Errors and Belief in the Paranormal." *Journal of Social Psychology,* 125(1985), 489–494.

Wilson, I. *The Bleeding Mind: An Investigation into the Mysterious Phenomenon of Stigmata.* London: Paladin, 1991.

Wilson, S.C., and Barber, T.X. "The Fantasy-Prone Personality: Implications for Understanding Imagery, Hypnosis, and Parapsychological Phenomena." In A.A. Sheik, ed., *Imagery: Current Theory, Research, and Application.* New York: Wiley, 1983, 340–387.

Windholz, G., and Diamant, L. "Some Personality Traits of Believers in Extraordinary Phenomena." *Bulletin of the Psychonomic Society,* 3(1974), 125–126.

Witkin, H., and Lewis, H. "The Relation of Experimentally Induced Pre-Sleep Experiences to Dreams: A Report on Method and Preliminary Finding." *Journal of the American Psychoanalytical Association,* 13(1963), 819–849.

Yeshe, L. *Introduction to Tantra: A Vision of Totality.* Boston: Wisdom, 1987.

Zaehner, R.C. *Mysticism, Sacred and Profane: An Inquiry into some Varieties of Praeternatural Experience.* New York: Galaxy, 1961.

Zaleski, C. *Otherworld Journeys: Accounts of Near-Death Experience in Medieval and Modern Times.* New York: Oxford University Press, 1987.

Zimdars-Swartz, S.L. *Encountering Mary: From La Salette to Medjugorje.* Princeton: Princeton University Press, 1991.

Zimmer, C. "Great Balls of Steam." *Discover,* 14[7](1993), 20–21.

Zuckerman, M. *Sensation Seeking: Beyond the Optimal Level of Arousal.* Hillsdale, NJ: Lawrence Erlbaum, 1979.

Zum Brunn, E., and Epiney-Burgard, G. *Women Mystics in Medieval Europe.* New York: Paragon House, 1989.

Zusne, L., and Jones, W.H. *Anomalistic Psychology: A study of Magical Thinking.* Hillsdale, NJ: Lawrence Erlbaum, 1989.

INDEX

Boldface page numbers indicate main essays.